This is a work of fact and truth. All names, places and incidents are products of the author's real life happenings or incidents throughout his incarceration and are to be construed as real. All events, locals, organizations or persons living or dead are entirely factual.

Based on a true story.

Published in the United States of America, via Create Space
ISBN:9781456320638

Michael L. Brown, Author/Investigative Journalist and Paralegal/Legal Consultant
Email: justiceandassociatesllc@hotmail.com

Any letter or questions can be directed to
Michael L. Brown, Reg. # 04909-090
P.O. Box 24550
Tucson, Arizona 85734-4550

To Order this book, Type the following in your search bar www.amazon.com Michael L. Brown

Proceeds' from this book go to the Michael L. Brown Defense Fund

“INJUSTICE ANYWHERE IS INJUSTICE EVERYWHERE”

This is based on the true-life story of Michael Lynn Brown. This story is about injustice in our world, and how that injustice was dealt to one man. This is a story about how injustice can have long-lasting effect on all of us.

DISCLAIMER:
If there are any errors in this book, they are not the fault of the author. In late September 2011, final draft copies of this book were sent by the publisher for review and correction.
The copies of the last proof were intercepted and "Banned" by USP-Tucson's ISM Supervisor Ms. Serrato.

TABLE OF CONTENTS

ACKNOWLEDGEMENTS

My Grandparents; Rufus and Mary Moore, who raised me. My biological father, Walter Michael Brown. My children; Jazzman, T'keyah & Michael Jr. My step/Godson, Marcus. My children's mothers; Angie Payne, Ingo Reynolds & Kim Fitzgibbons. My children's Grandparents; Dorothy & Louis Payne, Lydia & Thirl Reynolds, Donna & David Cocums. My siblings; Matthew, Linda, Bruce, Tricia, Sasha. My siblings' children – my nieces and nephews; Tiffany, Darnel, Preston, Earthen, Bruce, Brandon, Amia, Briana, etc. Too many to count. My Step/foster Brother Aaron. My pops & my kids' Grand pops Charles. My role model Thirl Reynolds, RIP 01/08/2005. My biological uncle the Browns, Elebys, Gaston's, Moore's, and Orr's – there is too many to count. My cousins all of the Barksdales, Brights, Browns, Caldwell's, Elebys, Gaston's, Massys, Moore's, again, too many to count. My mother, who was my mother, sister, aunt and cousin, and friend to everyone – Linda Evelyn Brown, who left us and went to Heaven on July 22, 2005. I know you are up there watching and having fun. I love and miss you very much. You know I am still fighting. I am in no hurry & I will see you when I get there. Richardson and R. Harper are always helpful to me with issues. And special thanks to the Wilson's. My new niece Makayla.

Love, Joy & Peace,

Michael L. (Justice) Brown

P.S. To all my old friends. I am not sure where you are, or what you have been doing. Probably the same with most of my family. I keep all of you in my prayers. My new friends; most of you are mention in the book. To those I haven't written about; Like Lenny Picard & Marquette (Big Q) Applewhite A. Henderson, R. Harper, A. Richardson, V. Zuniga, H. Joseph, Q. Jackson, J. Walker, C. Nguyen, Thanks! Very special thanks to D. Fabricant~

CONGRATULATIONS

To my daughter, Jazzman Brown, who's grown into a beautiful woman.

To my daughter, T'keyah Reynolds, who graduated from High School, June 6, 2011 and is already on her way to college.

To my son, Michael L Brown Jr., who is staring High School this year. Work hard at school and football camp. University of Wisconsin is a good goal for you.

TO BE AWARE AND ALIVE

There are thousands of innocent people in prisons across America today. In the last 15 years, 328 individuals wrongly convicted and imprisoned have been exonerated. Almost all of them are murder and rape cases, and are probably because they were high profile or capital cases. The implementation of DNA identification is regularly used to clear innocent people of crimes they did not commit. Many false convictions come from overzealous police, federal agents, prosecutors and judges who seem to be more concerned with politics, economics, publicity and racism rather than with pursuing a criminal case based on facts.

Then there are the defense attorneys, who are court appointed (excuse me, public defenders, a.k.a. "public pretenders") who are appointed by the courts and paid by the district attorney's office. Like the judge, they are only concerned with drawing as much money out of the government as possible and lining their pockets. They have no vested interest in obtaining justice for the guilty or the innocent. And we can't forget the Grand jury, which by the way, if you aren't in a major city like Chicago, Los Angeles or New York, practically ensures that your minority peers will not have any say-so in determining your fate, even though the constitution promises to provide a jury of your peers. Even if you do, you probably do not want or need them deciding your fate anyway, because they are out of touch with the reality of urban life anyway. The jury is making a decision based on a feeling based on their being manipulated by the government actors in the courtroom, and not on any consideration of any real evidence.

The jury will usually believe all the courtroom antics presented by the government. The general mindset usually is that the government would not charge you if you were not guilty, so you must be guilty, right. The jurors do not understand all the tricks of the prosecution, nor the performance they present to create a case. The prosecution is highly trained to lie and make the witness liars as well. They will overwhelm you with pre-approved motions to sways things in their favor. The judges are all pro-prosecution. And why shouldn't they be? Every one of them was a prosecutor before being appointed to their judgeship and they graduated to leading this wonderful fictitious production of lies and deceit.

When it comes time for sentencing, it's no holds barred. Sentencing more and more people to prison who may possibly be guilty, but with unfair and unjust sentences- especially for minorities- just is not just right. The judge enhances the sentence, lacking any preponderance of evidence, and violating the United States Constitution. Ninety percent of people on death row are minorities. Thirty-five percent of all adult black males are in prison. A minority will always receive a much harsher prison sentence and a black man is much more likely to receive the death penalty than a rich white man or woman. Keep in mind that a life sentence is no different than death sentence, and actually, a death sentence is actually more humane.

Thank God for DNA evidence, which has played a key role in freeing many innocent individuals, but biological evidence is far less likely to be available or provide definitive proof in the majority of cases.

Ninety percent of false convictions involve misidentification by supposed eyewitness, which is the most unreliable kind of evidence. A large part of those witnesses has been given a deal by the government for their testimony. They are paid to witness with their lies.

Other studies show the leading cause of wrongful conviction on murder cases is a false confession and perjury by co-defendants, informants, police officers or special agents of FBI such as forensic scientists.

Officers also know, based on many years of experience, that there are groups of people who are more likely to confession under and pressure intimidated by the law and the police.

There may be more murder exoneration because such cases attract more attention especially when a death sentence is imposed, but what about other types of cases? They are forgotten, lost or just gone. America seems to be turning into a place of selfishness where no one cares anymore. This means that more people are often wrongfully convicted for run of the mill crimes such as drug cases. Then a judge can increase a defendant's sentence by his own findings based on a preponderance of evidence, and nothing more for proof. They can find someone guilty of conspiracy based solely on the word of a convicted drug dealer who is making a deal for a lesser sentence and nothing more.

The facts are and have been shown in many studies. If we were to review prison sentence using even a small level of care and scrutiny, for below what would be acceptable when a death sentence is involved there would surely be thousands of falsely convicted persons exonerated.

The problem remains that nobody cares. There is not enough help available someone who is falsely convicted. Their voice is just another scream, echoing in the halls of a federal or state penitentiary and mingling with the scream of those that are truly insane. Michael L. Brown, a.k.a. Justice, wants to ask you, "Can you hear our screams? Please listen to our screams!"

INNOCENT AND UNJUSTLY SENTENCED

No excuses. This book is full of experiences. My words are written with hopes of helping as well to make people aware of what is going on inside and outside of themselves. My story purpose is not to glorify crime or glamorize drugs and illicit sex, but to help people understand what may lie before they make wrong choices. "What happened to me can happen to any one of you or even your loved ones." It is my hope that in writing this book I can make a difference in the lives and thoughts of the people who read it.

I am a person who likes to put things and people into perspective. I am an author, poet, entertainer, artist, promoter and a builder. I am very physically and mentally fit as well as a very spiritual person.

I tell my story in a "third person" for easier understanding and also in order to get some help for myself and lend help to others. It is through the grace of God and His love that I write this book. With His Sanctifying and actual Grace, I am determined to give hope to other innocent prisoners and to encourage all jailhouse lawyers to truly and honestly keep assisting those who need help.

I would also like to express my gratitude to the many jailhouse lawyers that have helped me. I express the same gratitude to many God-fearing brothers and sisters that have befriended and encouraged me throughout the years.

In prison or on the streets, life can be a struggle, but take Jesus Christ as your Lord and Savior first and keep the faith. Remember, through it all, love is everything.

I want to thank the many people that loved and shared chapters of my life with me, especially the people who have supported me throughout my life. In this book I scream, "Help us!" There is certainly never enough help.

Most programs like the Innocence Project and school like Northwestern College of Chicago are overwhelmed by requests for assistance. But due to limited resources, they only take high profile cases, or cases that involved D. N. A.

It only takes one person. A friend, family member or stranger, because one person in prison cannot do it alone. All he will be finding himself doing is screaming in the halls of the insane, echoing screams of nothing. Many people agree that it is better for ten guilty men to go free than one innocent person to be convicted. Is it better for 10,000 guilty people to walk free rather than have one innocent man convicted? The cost benefit policy answer is, of course. "No."

Every time an innocent person is convicted, it means guilty people remain free to commit crimes.

We all know of at least one wrongly convicted and punished for a crime he did not commit and that being our Lord Jesus Christ.

Knowing is just half the battle. Seeking more knowledge and applying what you know is the other!

This is not to discourage you rather, it is to encourage you. It is always best to know what is happening, as knowledge is always the key.

How does one get out of a situation? If you ask me, it is based on knowledge, determination and willpower.

Of course, help from the high power of God, and maybe some outside help from someone, is a bonus. Your help does not have to come from attorney, a politician or even a private investigator, but it should be someone who is willing to do some of the things needed to be done that an imprisoned individual cannot accomplish on their own.

One must learn the law, the system, and anything and everything they can about it.

Currently in the United States, more than two million individuals are incarcerated, more than all other countries combined. About 10% of these are completely innocent. That is roughly about 200, 00 people in prison for offenses they did not commit. This, of course, didn't and couldn't have happened by accident, right? This was done to tear gut outs of the lower middle class, the blacks, and other minorities, and poor, but yet at same time creating jobs for the white world of prison officials! Citizens beware.

Chapter 1

FREE AND TRAPPED

It was autumn, September 16, 1993, a twenty-four-year-old black man, won't soon forget his release from prison, (Michael Brown) just having completed almost three years of his four year sentence for possession of drugs, guns, and stolen property. It was his first conviction, but some would say he had an act for staying in trouble. When Michael did something, whether it was good or bad, it did not matter, he did it to saturation and completion. There was a drug war going on in Wisconsin and Midwest, and the entire Heartland was infected in one way or another as a result. It was all over the country and Michael Brown got himself caught up in it by trying to defend his family and friends. Looking out for his click near cost him a life bit.

Before all the trouble, Michael was doing pretty well. He graduated from high school and was working his way through college. Things turned to be harder than he expected for both him and his family.

Being the first one in the family to go to college was a big responsibility, and a part of him doubted that he could do it, but he stuck to his studies. That is until he got himself tangled up in the drug scene. He knew the insanity of it all, but his addiction to the game was comparable to actual addition to the drugs. Michael hated that about himself, but the luxuries made it easy to overlook the self-loathing and disgust of the whole ordered. The power and control fulfilled his personal ego needs, and the money afforded him the college education he was after as well as financial support for his family. Getting involved in the drug game at an early age was a powerful entrapment because a turned into much more than a game- it became part of life. Although it was not their intention, most of Michael's family, including his mother, unconsciously conditional Michael into the drug lifestyle.

Both of Michael's parents were drug addicts. His mother served time in federal prison because of her addictions. Such would counsel her son about the pitfalls of the drug game. She would advise him not to join in a gang & not to be mixed up in crime and drugs. Then, as times got bad and the family was in desperation due to his mother's setbacks, Michael finally resorted to criminal behavior and the drug scene just to put some food on the table. Michael was well aware of his wrongs and when he was finally caught, he took full responsibility for his crimes & did not try to rationalize his actions. He accepted his punishment and did his time. He naively thought he could pay back his debt to society and that would be the end of that. Obviously, as it turned out, it was not going to be that easy.

Michael's mother did not approve of her son's involvement with the drug world, but Michael did not see any other possibility available that could provide for their family.

Michael had just been released from prison. This was his chance for a new start of life. He had no intention of getting involved with drugs and gangs, with the end result of being in prison again. The last three years had been enough of that for a lifetime. He was sick and tired of being sick and tired. He watched friends and family going back and forth, in and out of prison, sometimes for very serious crimes, such as robbery, murder, and prostitution. While in prison, Michael gave a lot of thought to what he could do to live a normal lifestyle. He called upon God to show him the way to a better, non-criminal life.

After spending almost three years living, learning and praying to God, God did in fact come through.

Michael's first move was to invite an old homie named Jessie Clark, who went by the nickname of Old School, to pick him up at the prison gate. Old School took Michael to another home's place that of Derick Evans aka, "Paid in Full." Michael knew that Paid in Full would help him out. They had done business in the past-Michael would deal for Paid in Full when he needed cash. This dude Paid in Full was no joke. He was known as one of the biggest and baddest drugs connects in Madison Wisconsin. Originally, from Chicago, Paid in Full was also called "D", and D was definitely known as "The Man." D was the type of guy you either absolutely loved, or undoubtedly hated him. Most of the sisters loved him for his money and power. He was seen as the biggest "trick" in the Midwest. Anybody that was somebody knew who "D" was. There was a rumor that "D" was a big snitch and set up artist, but Michael did not want to believe the rumors about "D". Nonetheless, even though they were friends, Michael still was not about to give "D" and information that could be used against him, or so he thought. His only concern in going to see "D" directly from prison was cash. He did not believe the snitch jacket that was put on "D" anyway.

Michael's next objective was to strengthen his four-year relationship with his girlfriend, Ingo Reynolds. He really loved Ingo. She had long brown hair, and was 5'5" tall, 120 lbs. She had beautiful brown skin, a "Red Bone" like no other.

Any man could do a double take at this woman, especially a Brother man. Ingo was known as a rowdy black girl from the South side. She was very intelligent and she had money. Michael was introduced to Ingo through his brother Tuttie while they we walking up the street, seeing Ingo throwing fisticuffs with another woman. Tuttie played the hero by breaking them up and throwing the other gal into the lake. Michael came to realize how much he really loved Ingo. He was unwilling to give up on her, even after she virtually abandoned him while he was in prison.

Michael only wanted a little love and support while serving time. Both Ingo and her family did at least give him that much. Michael would call Ingo and her family time to time & his calls were always welcomed if he needed someone to talk to. The Reynolds was a successful businessman who retired after working twenty years with the City Sanitation Department. He later went into real estate business, followed by running a Bar called County Keg. You could say he was also a winner. Thirl was a healthy 200-pound black man who stood six feet tall. He was considered a businessman who was extremely devoted to, and who would do anything for, his family. He was also quite the ladies man and certainly a charmer. He has an uncanny expertise about the ladies. Michael considered Thirl his personal mentor in many things. Thirl lived in a million dollar home with his wife Lydia, daughters Ingo and her older sister Layla, and his son Nate. Layla was very pretty and smart. She had gone to college to study becoming a lawyer. Michael learned that Nate was a white man; When Nate, who was two years older than Michael, came home on leave from the military.

Thirl was a black man who was originally from Arkansas. His wife Lydia was a Ukrainian born Jew and a beautiful woman both inside and out. She grew up in Milwaukee, Wisconsin. Nationalities never concerned Michael. Being from the ghetto in Chicago himself, all Michael wanted was fine looking red one and a high yellow girl, who was sassy and smart. That was Ingo! She did not always act like it, but one would think she was from the ghetto as well. Some of what came out of her mouth was even worse than things Michael was known to say.

Ingo went to West High School and Michael went to East High. She was sixteen years old; he was a senior and seventeen. She lived in Arbor Hills, which is one of the Madison's upscale, wealthy neighborhoods on the West side.

Ingo, like many black girls, acted as if she had something to prove, but not to Michael, because he already knew.

After about an hour or two, Michael and Jesse left Eric's house. From there they went to see the parole officer. Michael was given a strict set of rules and regulations describing whom he could or could not see and what he could or could not go, where he could or could not go. The first place he visited after left prison was Eric's place, which was included as one the places he visited after he was forbidden to go.

Michael was treated with respect at Eric's place because he was known to have kept his mouth shut and had not ratted on Eric. He also stood up to the Crips, Bloods, G.D.'s, and Vice Lords, whom he encountered in the Drug Wars. Michael took no crap from anyone. Looking back at how crazy that really was its obvious how easily he could have been killed.

"D" used to tell everyone how brave Michael was and that he was "D"'s main man while the whole time trying to get Michael back into the drug game.

"D" looked out the window and, seeing Jesse's I-Roc, Z-28 Camaro, asked Michael. "So, what do I have to do to get you to come back into the game with me?" Michael replied, "I want to run my own business, raise my family. And stay out of prison." "How do you plan to finance that?" "D" challenged. Michael assured him, "I'm not sure of that just yet, but I know I'll find a way." "Are you sure what you really want to do?" D asked. "How would you like one of these?" "D" tempted as he pulled out a kilo of cocaine. Further tempting Michael, he asked, "So, what else do you need? Do you want one of these nice rides, like Jesse's I-Roc? I got one of those for you too, if you want it." "D" boasted as he pointed out the window at a brand-new I-Roc sitting across the street. It took a lot of will power for Michael to say "No", "I'm cool…" "D" insisted interrupted him, insisting "At least take this, man," as he handed Michael a roll of cash. "I owe you that, at the very least." "D" urged.

Michael would later live to regret taking that wad of cash from "D". After leaving "D" house, which is near Ingo house where Michael paroled to, Jesse drove Michael to his mother's house. When they pulled into the driveway, he was pleased to see the old house freshly painted green. The house was about fifty years old, but it was still very nice. Flowers were everywhere and were very beautiful at that time of year. Michael used to regularly care for the property and the lawn. There was always someone running in or out, as it was also quite the party house. The home was filled with love and fun, but too often, Michael and his friends were into things that were wild and dangerous. The new Mercury Cougar Michael previously had given his mother been there, and the place seemed different-something was amiss.

He was about to tell Jesse to drive off when he saw his two baby sisters come out of the house. As he got out of the car, he told Jesse to wait than went to the house before the girls could go too far away. “Where are you two going?” He asked the girls. Michael smiled, and their face beamed with delight. “We are going to the grocery store,” answered the older of the young girls, repeated by the younger one.

Of Michael’s two young sisters, Sasha was seven years old, short, thick dark and mean. Then there is Tricia who was nine years old, tall and skinny with a high yellow complexion. They looked like the little ghetto Bay-Bay kids that he had hoped they would not windup looking like. They were not raised that way, but Michael and his other siblings, Tammy, Tuttie and Bruce, were. He playfully inquired of the girls, “Did you miss me?” To which they both replied, “Of course we did, silly.” Then the older of the girls asked him, “Are you here to move us out, because Mom is acting crazy and always getting drunk.” They continued, “We can’t stand her boyfriend either we want to leave like Tammy did. Michael did not know yet about Tammy. “Tammy moved out?” he asked. He was surprised. “Yes, she did,” said Tricia, “And we’re getting kicked out too!” “Kick out?” exclaimed Michael. “When?” he asked. “Tomorrow,” said Tricia and Sasha simultaneously.

He did not know what could have happened. His mother was renting and trying to purchase the house. The land was contracted from one of her friends, Oscar was his name. He was an “Old School” Gangster and a businessman from New Orleans. He made it big in real estate and renting properties worth millions. Michael had done some favors for Oscar and his family back when he was still in the dope game.

After talking to his baby, sisters Michael went into the house to see his mother. At first, she did not recognize her son because she was intimately entwined with her boyfriend. This was so out of character for her she was always more reserved than this. The boyfriend noticed Michael at first. Michael instantly sized him up as an old light-skinned country boy about six feet tall, medium build with gold teeth. Obviously, he was a drinker and possibly a drug user. Quite startled, he asked Michael, “What are you doing here? What do you want with my women?” Michael wanted to smash him instantly. Once she recognized Michael’s voice, she excitedly squealed, “Oh my god, my baby’s home!” She saw the scowl on her son’s face and asked him, “What’s the matter baby?” Michael later learned that her mom’s boyfriend name was Old Country. He never took his eyes off him. His mother noticed the look and said, “Mike, now don’t even start tripping.” She came over and gave him a big hug. Michael told her he wanted to talk to her. He could smell alcohol on her breath. He grabbed her by the arm and started leading her out of the room. Then exclaimed, “I want to talk to you, alone!” When they got to the other room, he asked her, “Who is that dude?” pointing toward the other room.

They talked for a while and Michael wanted to know why Tammy left in such a hurry and he wanted to know why his mother’s boyfriend was not helping with the bills. “Mike, don’t start tripping. Tammy went to stay with Kaniza. She cannot seem to get along with anybody and she probably will not be there long anyway. She tried to act like my mother, and nobody is going to tell me how to live my life and we have to move because there was nobody helping with the bills.” After she explained the situation with Tammy moving, and the house & the bill, and how nobody was helping make payments. Michael asked her, “Why doesn’t he help with the bills?” referring to Old Country. She did not have an answer. He asked her, “What’s up with Oscar? I cannot believe he is throwing you out! How much money you owe him?” he asked. “Thousands, maybe,” she answered.

"Thousands?" asked Michael. "Yes, thousands, maybe tens of thousands" she exclaimed. "Damn it!" protested Michael.

"What have you been doing since I've been gone?" Michael asked. "Trying to provide a life for these kids," she explained. Michael yelled, "I can see you found the money to get drunk, to get high and find a boyfriend!" After a minute or two, Michael calmed down and said, "I'll talk to Oscar." "You can't talk to Oscar, he's about to jail himself," she told him. Michael glared at his mother, shaking his head. "We have to be out of here tomorrow," his mother explained. Michael wanted to explode in rage, but managed to keep his cool. After they talked a while, he had to tell his mother, "Look mom, you've really in bad shape, and you need to get some help with your addictions." This upset her, and she responded by smacking him in the face. She screamed and commanded, "Get out, if all you're going to do is talk about me, and not help with your younger brother and your sisters, then leave!" she cried.

Michael was the oldest of the kids. His kid brother Bruce was ten years old. "Hi, Mike. So, your home?" he heard a youngster ask from the doorway. He turned and saw his little brother Bruce. "Hey, little man. Yea, I'm home, but I have to go and handle some business, but I'll be back soon." He explained. Michael gave the three kids a little spending money before he left. When he got back to the car. He knew that Jesse could tell that Michael was distraught. "What's up man, are you okay?" Jesse concerned asked him. "I'm all right man, it's nothing." He avoided. "Let's go." They drove off. Michael wanted to talk to Jesse about what was going on with his mother, but he was embarrassed and, besides, he did not think Jesse would understand. Jesse had been a dope user too and had recently gotten out of prison, as well. Michael could not be certain if Jesse was clean and sober. "Take me to Ingo's house," he told Jesse. Michael was thinking he would be free of his troubles at Ingo's, but he could not have been more wrong. Jesse asked Michael, "When are you going to come over to my place and kick it with my step daughter?" He continued, "She's been waiting and expecting you." "I know, but Ingo's also waiting and expecting me and I'm already late." Michael explained. "The last time I saw Ingo, it wasn't a very good visit about three months ago, and truthfully, it wasn't pleasant visit," he said.

We can be physically free. However, bound by so many aspects of the world, i.e. wealth, goods, material things, drugs, sex, and sin. Our attachment to all these, and not ever realizing just how bounded we can truly be by these vises.

CHAPTER 2

LOVE, LUST SEXUAL IMMORALITY; BIRTHS

In had been several months since Michael has last seen Ingo. During his incarceration, Michael was lucky if he saw Ingo twice a year. Even as he was approaching release, she would not come to visit. Whenever he called, she was never home.

Ingo has turned into a different person. He did not know her anymore. He tried to make himself stop loving her, but he really could not. He loved Ingo and her family. They had taken him in clothed and feed him, cared for him and treated him as part of their family. No one had ever treated him that way before. Ingo's family had even bailed him out of jail & helped him hire an attorney. When he was in his "Crime Prime." Michael did not want to let the Reynolds's family down, because they believed in him, he could not let them down.

Michael wanted things to be how they once were with the Reynolds's, minus the drinking that would get bad at times. Ingo and Michael both hated the fact that Ingo's parents drank booze, which is why Michael was surprised to see how Ingo was turning out. Michael practically blamed himself even though he knew he should not, and Ingo seemed to thrive on that self-blame.

Ingo visited Michael when he was at Oregon prison work farm. He thought she only came because she knew he would be coming home soon. Michael's Parole Officer went to visit Ingo's mom for verification of Michael's plan to live with them. Then, a few days later, Michael received a surprise visit from Ingo. It was bad timing because Michael was already entertaining another visitor when Ingo arrived for the surprise visit. He was sitting with his home girl lover, Kim. Michael and Kim met ten years prior, when he first moved to Wisconsin, to live with his Aunt Ida. Aunt Ida took Michael in after his mother went to prison and his Grandmother died. His grandmother was Ida's Aunt and she helped to raise Ida in West Memphis, Tennessee, where they had been born. They later moved to Chicago, Illinois, and then in 1973 Aunt Ida moved to Wisconsin to get away from Chicago's West Side Projects.

Ida and Michael's mother grew-up in Chicago neighborhood near West Roosevelt and Washburn where she lived with her husband and eight kids. Her husband Sunny and Michael's Uncle Darnell who was his mother's eldest brother. Ida's son, Al, had almost been killed after being shot nine times in a gang shooting, that is when Ida decided to move the family to Wisconsin to get away from the gangs, drugs and violence.

She was employed at the University of Wisconsin Laboratories and this is how Michael wound up meeting Kim, not knowing that she would later become such a major part of his life.

Three months before Michael was to be released from prison, Kim came to visit him again. About to be paroled, a half way house was out of the question. Not knowing why, but learning later, his Parole Officer would not let him Parole to his Mother's house.

So, one day, he was visiting with Kim without Ingo's knowledge. Kim was good to Michael and baby Jazzman whom Angie gave birth to while Michael was in prison. Michael was only with Angie a couple of times while hanging out at Summer Set Circle. This was one of the worst ghettos and low-income housing projects in Madison,

Wisconsin. At that time, it was actually the worst part of the city with shootings, murders, gang, and plenty of drugs.

Michael had met Angela through his Auntie Too Short, while he was hustling and slinging dope at the projects. Auntie Too Short was not a blood relative, but her sister Blackie and his mother were like sisters. Auntie Too Short and Blackie moved to Wisconsin 1979-80, around the time Michael's mother went to prison. They use to hustle and do just about everything together. Blackie had five kids and Michael's mother had four kids.

Auntie Too Short was a hustler, pimp, player and a whore. She liked both sex and money. Angie was living with her cousin Genies close to where Michael lived. Genies took a fondness to Michael, even before Angie came into the picture. Her brother and Michael were close, and so were their mothers.

Angie and Michael were very young. She was visiting her cousin for the summer. Michael was nineteen-year-old and always a hustler. Angie was a very pretty and wild black girl from the dirty South, Little Rock, Arkansas. Michael had never been with a country girl before and sure did not know what he was in for. Angie tired to take over his life but Michael was "looking for the next flight." As his mother would tell it, "looking for the next flight" was what he was thinking about while he was getting it on with her. At least he was grateful that Angie gave birth to his first child, the most beautiful darling girl, Jazzman, whom he adored with his entire being.

Angie and Michael would fight like mad most of the time, especially after she became pregnant. Him being the wild pimp, player and hustler that he did not consider himself any of he just wanted to make something of himself so that he could have a good life. When Angie told him about her pregnancy, he did not want to believe that it was true much less hear anything of it as he felt he was not ready for that. It was the end of the freshman year for most students and Michael wanted to return to college.

Auntie Too Short and Genies persuaded Angie to hook up with Michael because he had money. He was ghetto rich and it didn't take Angie long to figure that out, especially with Regina and Genies in her way all the time. Angie came onto Michael with a heated fury trying to trap him in a corner. By her persistence, she ended up scaring him away, but unfortunately not before seducing him to sleep with her on several occasions.

Ingo was Michael's woman, but he had slept with a few other girls before her. While in college, both Michael and Ingo slept around on each other but they were best of friends and partners, so there was no big deal. As families can be, they started messing around together.

They left it alone that way for a while. They were okay with going to separate schools. He messed around with some of her friends and she messed around with some of his friends, like one of Michael's good friends John-John and his homie Maurice. Ingo and Maurice had gone to grade school together, so it is not as if they were not familiar with each other. When Maurice hooked up with Ingo, he was one of Michael's best friends at the time. There was also Aaron, who was like a brother to Michael, and John-John. Ingo messed around with John because he was older; two years older than Michael. Originally, from New York, John had his own apartment downtown on campus and a lot of high school and college students went there to party.

One day Michael saw Ingo at a friend's party. She was with a bunch of her girlfriends and drinking heavily dirty dancing and acting very nasty. When Michael had first met Ingo, he had been seeing a girl by the name of Corey Conklin. She was a rich white girl from the West side and the third white girl Michael had been involved with. Corey had a body and a tan better than most mulatto or black women. Corey's family had money like it grew on trees and they lived in a million dollar mansion.

One day, Michael's friend John-John informed him that she had a crush on Michael. John-John was always into rich white girls, but there was some kind of falling out between him and Corey. Corey was originally from New England. From a mile away, one could tell she carried the background of an Italian girl. She had an accent and her father was an attorney who was always working and traveling all over the world.

Her father was also the president of a large corporation that was located right across the street from their house. Her grandfather was an attorney and Judge and her beautiful mother looked just like Sophia Loren. Some people thought that maybe she could have been a model back in the day.

It did not bother Ingo one bit that Michael had another girlfriend. In fact, it actually made her long for him even more. But sisters like Ingo did not like seeing a brother with a white girl. Even though there was real teenage love between Corey & Michael, it unfortunately did not last long as their background and their parent's history was just way too different.

Michael and Corey did have a wonderful sex life as they once ran away to Miami together for a little "get away." But for Michael, it was more like running from home and him being a grown man. Seeing that he often came home with large sums of money his mother somewhat wanted him to go out on his own anyway. At times he would surprisingly bring home as much as ten thousand dollars, a large amount of money in those days.

Michael began seeing Ingo but had been with Kim on the side in 1983 and this continued for about ten years. Most of the time they only considered themselves as friends but eventually they became more intimate and eventually became sexual partners. It was obvious that Michael was attracted to Kim from the very first time they met. Michael's cousin Herman had wanted to hook up with Kim's older sister Kelly. The plan was for Michael to tag along with Herman to keep Kim distracted so that Herman could get to Kelly. At that time, Michael would not mess around with white girls, but when he met Kim, things certainly changed.

Kim was one of the finest looking girls Michael had ever seen. She had pretty long blonde hair that was almost down to her ass. Her hair was not the first thing Michael took notice of. Kim hourglass figure with those forty-eight "Double D" cup breasts on a fourteen year old that captured the attention of one fifteen year old in particular.

It was not just her marvelous body. Kim had a pretty smile and good attitude. She was quiet for the most part, but if anyone was to try and pull something over on her or take her for granted, she would put them in their place in a heartbeat. Fortunately, for Michael, she let him get away with just about anything. But after time has passed, that all changed and Michael eventually saw less of her as the years went by.

Michael admired the fact that Kim was such a strong, hearted woman, but he did not like the fact she smoked heavily. On her first date, Michael tried to make an advance on Kim, but she told him to back off, which made him respect her even more.

They would spend endless nights together talking life and just about anything, that came to mind. Prior to Kim Michael's grandmother was the most important woman in his life, but being that she has passed-on, there was now a longer anyone for him to talk to. Then Kim came into his life, and she was like a blessing from God himself. Michael knew there was something special about Kim, but he did not know exactly how special.

When Ingo came to visit Michael just days prior to his release from prison, Kim cut all communication with him. Ingo was not happy that during the visit Kim had asked Michael to tell Ingo to leave. Michael did not ask Ingo to leave and he informed Kim that he needed to talk to Ingo. "I've always been there for you, and I have even brought your daughter to visit you," she complained. Michael replied, "That's true, and I am truly grateful, and I love you for all of your support."

Kim told him that if she has to leave that she would never come back again. "Fine then, don't come back," he shot back at her, "I don't take kindly to threats." "So you're not going to make Ingo leave?" she asked again. "No," he retorted, like I said, I need to talk to her, and I haven't seen her in a long time."

Ingo was someone Michael could talk to and he could tell her anything. Ingo had an uncanny way of understanding and always gave Michael positive feedback and advice.

Michael was surprised that Kim did in fact storm out of the visiting room. He actually wanted her to leave because he did not want there to be a scene between either of them, but when she said she would never come back that was highly unexpected.

Kim was indeed always there for Michael and Ingo was not. Ingo was too busied running and messing with dope. Reliable sources on the street kept Michael abreast of all of Ingo's doings. He learned she was messing around with his brother Matt again, among others. That did not really bother him it much and luckily, for her, he was still willing to take her back regardless of what she was doing. Feeling deserted and without a place to go, he did not want to go to a halfway house, which is part of the reason Kim and Michael had a falling out.

Michael could not seem to let go of his feelings for Ingo as they had too many good memories together. He has never before had a Sister quite like Ingo and he never thought he ever would. Michael was especially close to her son Marcus, whom he treated just like his own, even though he was Ingo's son from a previous relationship. Michael was blessed to be there when Marcus was born. Its funny something happens inside of a man when he is fortunate to see childbirth for the very first time.

Michael explained to Kim that he had nowhere to go upon his release from prison except to Ingo's house. Kim wanted Michael to come to her house but she did not think her parents would approve, even though she had her own car and own place. Michael's known gang association as a convicted drug dealer along with a history of violence led Kim to believe that if she brought Michael to live with her, her parents would disown her. Michael wondered, "Could Kim have been living with another man?"

With the wonderful memories Michael had of Kim and Ingo, they would always be a part of his life. He prayed to God that they could really understand his situation as a convicted prisoner. He knew he would always love both of these women.

"We may be physically free and at the same time, trapped by our money, trapped by the drug abuse, and trapped in bad relationships. These are never good things but with God, we can overcome all these imprisonments."

Sex and pro-creation outside of the divinely ordained institution of marriage, can be a most binding pleasure. Sex without love, without the commitment, especially outside of marriage, is wrong pure and simple. God intended for a mature man and woman to commit to one another for a lifetime. Commitment is a marriage that is ordained of God, and not by State with their Licensing or Certification.

CHAPTER 3

MONEY, DRUGS, SEX & SIN

"Come on Michael," insisted Jesse: "Are you sure you don't want to stay at my place? I got plenty of room, and I already promised Melissa that I would bring you." Jesse continued, with persistence, "Melissa has been waiting to see you." "Quit stalling man, make up your mind, it's just ahead at the next exit, if you're going to." What harm could it be?" Michael thought. "It couldn't do any harm to at least go see her." Then Jesse threw in "She's got money too!" "Sure man, why not," Michael agreed. Michael allowed himself to be coerced by the idea that Melissa had plenty of money. She also had some powerful connections in the business and underworld. Melissa was a fine-looking girl, but her mom was all that and a whole lot more. She was not the little girl Michael knew in the recent past.

When Jesse was released from prison, he had hooked-up with Melissa's mother. Michael was still in prison, but Jesse corresponded with him regularly. Jesse had previously told Michael about Melissa. Jesse showed Melissa some older photos of Michael and she wanted to meet him.

Michael knew her a little from high school, but the Melissa he remembered was rather plump, to say the least.

As Jesse and Michael walked into the house, Michael could see Melissa from the back, as she was getting ready for work. He knew she worked at a massage parlor, but that was the extent of what he knew of her work. He watched her for several moments and thought she has a body of Paula Abdul. As a matter of fact, as far as he was concerned, Melissa and Paula Abdul could have been twins. Then again Michael thought, "Paula Abdul has got nothing on this girl!" Melissa was five-foot-one and weighed about 110 pounds. She was wonderfully thick with long brown hair beautiful light brown bedroom eyes. She was so dazzling that she could have made a sad man stop crying or a monk leave the monastery.

Melissa caught Michael as he was checking her out from behind. She turned and they stared into each other's eyes for what seemed like an eternity. She finally spoke and said, "What's happening here?" Still in awe and dumfounded, Michael thought to himself "Wow, what a beautiful girl!" "Damn Michael," Melissa injected. "What they been feeding you in there?" Then she said, "In the pictures I saw of you, you were skinny as a rail." "You looked like you jumped right out of a Muscle Fitness magazine." She eyed Michael and appeared pleased with what she saw. "I didn't know you were going to visit me, especially on your first day as a free man." As she spoke, her natural beauty mesmerized Michael and all she was wearing was a little black shirt and a black bra. (She was still in the process of getting dressed.) Michael was stuttering to find words to say, but he could not get any out. So he stood here, staring in awe. Melissa reached over and grabbed Michael by the ass pulled him into the bedroom and closed the door. She wrapped her arms around his neck and pressed close against him and kissed him on the mouth. Their tongues met, explored and departed. She seductively whispered, "Welcome home, Michael!"

Then asked, "What are you doing later on? Will you pick me up from work?" Michael let out a little gasp and finally replied, "I'm not sure that is a good idea," he admitted. "I got a girlfriend and a kid." He continued, "I really miss them and I need to see them too," he declared. Melissa asked Michael what his girlfriend's name was, because she wanted to know if she knew the girl. "Are you happy? Do you love her?" Melissa interrogated. "Hey listen," said Michael, "I'm not so sure about all the questions, but her name isn't important right now," Michael interjected. Melissa asked him, "Well, do you need anything?" More seductively, she said, "I can make you feel good right now, if you want!" she softly rubbed her hand across Michael's face. Then she slid her hand down to his chest and onto his stomach. She reached down and into his pants. She gripped a hold of his manhood and ever so slowly started squeezing and rubbing him to firmness. Beads of sweat began to build on his brow. It felt so good that he allowed it to happen. She reached around his backside and gave his ass cheek a good squeeze. Her other hand strayed away and he felt her stuff something into his back pocket. Melissa stood up then said, "Don't be a stranger Michael; I would like to see you later." It was almost a command. "Maybe we can get to second base then," she whispered seductively into his ear. Michael noticed she had put a good-sized roll of cash into his pocket. "I won't make any promises I can't keep in my mind," he tried to say with authority. Seeing what Melissa was working with and a little of her capabilities, his wheels were churning.

"What if," he thought? "What if"

Michael really needed to get to the Reynolds house. Ingo's parents were planning something special for his homecoming and he was not about to disappoint them.

When they pulled up to the house, Michael noticed someone peeking out the window. It had to be either Ingo or Marcus. Michael told Jesse to pull over on the street and he would walk to the house. "Thanks for chauffeuring me around today Jesse," thanked Michael. "Hey, it aint nothing but a thing," assured Jesse. "You just keep in touch and are sure to call if you need anything." "I'll remember that," Michael replied.

As Michael got to the door, Marcus jumped up and gave him a big bear hug. "Welcome home Mike!" Marcus said with glee. "Thanks buddy," said Michael. "It's really good to see you to."

"Are you doing okay?" he asked Marcus. "Yes, I'm fine," came the reply. Michael told Marcus he wanted to see his mother. "I'll see you in a little but later." He promised. Michael went down the stairs to Ingo's bedroom. Ingo gave him a hug, but it did not seem like a 'welcome home' kind of hug.

She told Michael they would be eating dinner with her parents followed by going home to her apartment. They then went upstairs to see her parents whom were warm and friendly as always and asked why it took Michael so long to get there. He told them he had to stop at his family's house to see them prompting Ingo's parents to ask if everything was okay for now, but Thirl and Ingo seemed to indicate that Michael wasn't forthcoming about his family's situation.

As usual, Mrs. Reynolds cooked a wonderful filling dinner. After dinner, they talked about Michael's plans for the future. They wanted to know about his living arrangement and how serious his and Ingo's relationship was. Thirl even offered Michael a job with one of his businesses.

"Michael, what do you know about septic tanks?" asked Mr. Reynolds. "Well, I know they hold a lot of shit," chuckled Michael. Mr. Reynolds laughed too. "Not much, really," admitted Michael. "Are you at least willing to learn?" Mr. Reynolds asked. Michael really wanted to impress Mr. Reynolds so he said, "Yes, I am willing to learn."

Dinner could not get over fast enough. Michael was dead tired and wanting to feel how good a real mattress felt on his back. He also wanted to make sweet love to Ingo. Somehow, he knew she was different. He could not quite put his finger on it, but either spiritually or emotionally there was something that had changed about her.

Michael thanked Mr. & Mrs. Reynolds for the wonderful welcome home dinner and for the job offer. Knowing that Michael and Ingo needed to be alone, they offered to keep Marcus for a couple of nights. Grandparents are wonderful blessing in so many ways.

When they arrived at the apartment, they both had only one thing in mind, and that was the sweet loving they had been starved for from each other. In route to the bedroom, they undressed one another. At first, they were a little shy because it had been so long since they had been together, but they made love like they never had before. Once into the rhythm of each other, it was beautiful eternity. Oh so very natural and sweet they were together.

As good as it was Michael knew that something was different with Ingo. He wanted some answers too. Why wasn't Ingo keeping touch with him in prison? No letters at all. He wanted to know. "Do we have to go through that right now?" she asked. That would later become her standard answer to any question Michael would ask.

She wouldn't even answer when Michael asked why she had slept with his brother, "D" and Moe. She avoided his questions, so he stopped asking her. He didn't feel like fighting with her anyway. Inside, Michael knew he still needed answers for the questions he harbored in the back of his mind. He wanted to get rid of the flashes and images of Ingo, hanging-out with the various boyfriends she had had at his house.

Their sex wasn't the same. They used to make love for hours and sometimes all night long. There was more than just sex between them. Back in high school days they us to ride bicycles across town together. If they weren't together, they were on the phone, talking for hours sometimes all until the sun came up.

Now things had changed. Michael knew deep inside that they had grown apart, but he thought that at least their sex must have been the result of true love.

There was at least one thing special that Michael always kept in his mind and that was the result of their memorable past. Ingo gave birth to his daughter T'keyah who was absolutely the most beautiful and special person in his life. T'keyah was the sprouting of their love for one another. God's blessing to Michael was that it would make him cry every time hearing his little girl laugh.

After making love that first night out of prison, Michael fell asleep. When he woke, Ingo was gone. "Where could she have gone this early?" He thought. She never left like this before. After not coming back right away he got to worrying.

The phone rang and Michael answered it. It was a fellow gang associate from back in the day. Michael asked him how he knew where he was. He said he got the number from Ingo. "Have you seen Ingo?" Michael asked him. He said he saw her going into a bar just a little while ago and that she was on her way to the dope spot where everyone goes to cope their dope.

Now he knew where Ingo was. He had heard about her getting involved with the dope scene but he didn't want to believe it. It was like a blow to the face. Inside, Michael felt responsible, as before he went to prison he was the one who brought the stuff around in the first place.

With cocaine on Michael's list of "radical behaviors" which always made him hyped out making wrong decisions, he was really worried about Ingo. He didn't like the idea or thought of seeing Ingo turned out the same way he once was.

While serving time in prison, Michael committed himself to stay away from drugs. He didn't want to windup like other family members who were always in trouble. Michael decided not to use or deal drugs in any way and he surely didn't want someone he really loved involved with drugs either.

Michael was worried sick while waiting all day for Ingo to come home. It was early the next morning when she finally walked in the door. He told her he didn't want a junkie for a woman and that he would help her get help she needed to get clean, but she threw it back in his face, saying "You used to get high all the time Michael!" She told him that she liked getting high and she had no intention quitting any time soon.

Michael wanted to share his prison experience with her so perhaps she would consider the possible consequences of drug use, but before he could say much, she fell out on the couch. He let her sleep, which is what she needed most right then.

The next day, Michael went to his parole-ordered drug treatment program. He didn't believe he really needed treatment he was already determined not to use anymore, but treatment was a mandatory condition of parole for a convicted drug dealer.

Michael called Jesse and asked if he could give him a ride to his treatment. Jesse agreed with no hesitation, as he also had to do a treatment program when he was released from prison. Funny thing is he didn't look like an ordinary chef. Originally, from Texas, Jesse looked as if he had been through World War II. His body was covered with scares from knife and gunshot wounds, and he had to speak from the side of his mouth due to one gunshot wound and he had lumps the size of golf balls on his head. Jesse was also one hell of athlete. He was six-foot-four and muscled like a side of beef. At forty years of age, he could shame many of the youngest in most any sports.

Jesse finally arrived to pick up Michael. Ingo woke up as they were leaving. She slept in, as she didn't have to work until later in the evening. Ingo worked at the hospital kitchen. "Where are going this morning?" she asked. "The same place you should be considering going too," said Michael.

Michael came to realize that he would be doing the program for the entire day, it turned out that the drug treatment program was also a criminal-thinking program. Michael was told that if a parole hasn't used in years, even if they didn't have the desire to use, they are still required to complete the entire program. It made for a long day that couldn't end soon enough as he longed to see his daughter and needed to do some checking around to find out where she was at. He also needed to see his sister Tammy who was a freshman at Madison Area Technical College and worked at the "Merry-Go-Round" at the mall.

Michael finally went to see Tammy. She had been staying with Kaniza (across the street from the college.) It was really nice, neatly kept apartment.

Tammy met him at the door and gave Michael a big hug. She started right in about moving out from their mother's house and how she and their mother couldn't get along because of her mother's drug use was getting worse. She told Michael how their mother would leave, expecting Tammy to always take care of the kids while she went out to party, and that their mother wanted Tammy to pay for both her and her boyfriend's bad habits. Michael understood and could relate to what Tammy was telling him as their mother did the same thing to him when he was younger.

Michael wasn't disinterested in discussing Tammy and his mom's situation, but what he really wanted was to know about his little brother and sister's situations. To Michael, it was as if Tammy abandoned them when she left like she did. Tammy's excuse to Michael was that the kids were old enough to look after themselves and that she had her own issues to worry about, such as her college studies. Tammy had graduated high school a few months before Michael was released from prison.

She was really looking forward to college, and Michael was very proud of his sister as she took the better path in her life. He believed it was her destiny to go to college, and she would make for herself many opportunities for a wonderful future. Michael asked Tammy where he could see his daughter Jazzman, who was born 4-29-90 while Michael was in state prison. Michael cherished Jazzman and knew that she was his! Tammy really didn't know the exact address, but gave him directions on how to get there.

Based on what Michael remembered from last time Angie was living in the Northport Apartments but he wasn't too sure as she had moved from her last known address and wasn't writing Michael in prison, although he regularly wrote to her.

When Michael and Jesse got to Northport, there were several police officers milling about. History dictated that this was not a good prospect for them, so Michael had Jesse drop him off a block away so he could walk to the apartment. He had a weird feeling about the place, as if something was happening there. He didn't want to be seen in that neighborhood, as he didn't want it turning into a parole violation. He wanted to somehow sneak into Angie's apartment so he could see his daughter. As he was walking up to the building, a police officer popped-up out of nowhere and called his name, "Michael, you just stay back and let the police handle this situation," he commanded. Michael didn't know what the cop was talking about. He didn't even know the cop obviously knew who he was. The officer told him that someone had taken Angie and her kid's hostage. "Angie who?" Michael asked. "Angie Payne?" The officer answered in the affirmative.

Michael yelled, "Let them go, I need to get my daughter out of there!" Michael wanted to take matters into his own hands. Michael would put whoever was messing with his daughter six feet under, but the cops kept Michael back and brought in more police for back up. They finally got Angie and the kids out safely and the guy who held them hostage was taken into custody. Michael thanked God that Angie and Jazzman were okay.

After about an hour of interrogation, they finally let Angie come out of the apartment with the kids. Angie told Michael that the police wanted her and the kids to go to the police station for more questioning. "I'll talk to you later, don't start tripping." She said blowing him off and driving away. Michael was about ready to snap!

There was nothing more that Michael could do, so he decided to go to his mother's house where there were some people helping her move. The landlord was arguing with his mother and was only give her twenty minutes to get out of the house. Michael pleaded with the guy to give her a little time and said she would soon be moved out. Michael asked his mother's boyfriend if he could help them get moved and he was more than pleased to do so. Michael called Jesse to get a moving van or U-haul for an even quicker move. Thankfully, they were able to get all his mothers things into storage with no issues arising.

Back at Ingo's apartment, things were not getting any better. Ingo was always leaving Marcus with Michael while she went out to get high. Marcus wasn't his biological child but Michael took care of him like he was one of his own. He thought maybe she needed a little break, but she only got worse and began taking Michael for granted.

He started to see less and less of her, and on top of all that he and his mother's addiction and his own treatment to contend with. Michael was hearing rumors from his old friends about Ingo messing around, but didn't want to believe them because he still had a great deal of love for her.

He heard Ingo was out getting high chasing other men. He was told he should watch out for Eric, who Ingo had been seen with on several different occasions. Michael wondered what was up with Eric and why he wasn't acting like a friend anymore. He knew Eric was a Man-ho and he didn't trip on what went on with them while he was in prison, although Eric was supposed to been his close friend. Come to find out, Ingo was actually doing all this before he even went to prison

Once when Michael called home, Ingo must have been messing-around with Mo because he answered the phone and hung it up in a hurry. And here she was, messing with dope. Michael tried to get her help like he did with everyone else. He would hunt her down from dope house to dope house and club-to-club. He would finally find her, asking her if she was ready to come home. "I'll be there when I feel like it," she would blurt back at him.

Michael respected the fact that Ingo had somehow managed to keep her job at the hospital. She would even come home from work and fix dinner for Michael and Marcus, but that only lasted for a while. They seemed like a normal family and actually did pretty well for the first couple of weeks.

Michael's friend "D" was still trying to get him back into the dope game. "D" would come by the house and leave dope and money, and figured it was only a matter of time before he could get Michael back into it with him. Ingo wasn't any help, she would be gone again, leaving Michael to pay the bills. Enough was enough, and Michael finally had all he could take.

Ingo ended-up in jail for a catfight she got herself into at a bar. The bar was next to a liquor store where everybody hung around, so it was a very easy place to buy and sell dope. "Badger Road" was known for the dope market.

Michael and Ingo continued getting into arguments over her being gone all the time. She would get mad and storm out, slamming doors behind her. Michael watched her leave through the window and noticed she didn't take her car, so he figured she most likely had headed for the bar located just around the corner. Michael kindly asked the neighbor to look after Marcus while he stepped-out to go after Ingo.

Ingo was already drinking doubles. When Michael walked into the bar. "Come on Ingo," he said to her. "You've already had enough." "I'm not going anywhere until I'm good and ready!" she spurted at him. "Are you trying to kill yourself or what?" he asked her. "I don't want any part of the crap. This is not good for my recovery," he admitted.

"Please, you got to stop this insanity," he pleaded. Another girl who was sitting at the bar overheard Michael pleading with Ingo and interjected, "Yeah, come on girl go on home to your man." Ingo turned and screamed, "Bitch, mind your own damn business and stay out of mine!" The other girl tried reasoning with her, "At least you have an old man who cares about you and probably doesn't get high either."

Ingo screamed at her again. "I'm not gonna tell you again, you best stay out of my business!" Michael told Ingo, "If that's how it's gonna be, I'm leaving." And he meant it. The other girl interjected again. "Go on home with your man, girl." Ingo screamed. "I told you to mind your business!" Then she jumped-up and smacked the other girl in the face.

The girls started fighting like a couple of wild cats. Michael and the bartender were still trying to break it up, when the police arrived. "Break it up, break it up!" yelled a couple of the cops.

One of the cops accidentally pushed Ingo and she turned and started hitting the cop. Michael got between them, trying to clam Ingo down, but she was out of control and wouldn't listen. After a few minutes, they were finally able to get the situation under control, and both of the girls were taken to jail. Michael was fortunate that he wasn't arrested, because being on parole; he wasn't supposed to be anywhere nears a bar.

Michael went back to the apartment and waited, but Ingo never called. The girl Ingo got into a fight with called and explained that Ingo was in the hole. Michael being the kind man that he was, apologized to the girl for Ingo's behavior. She owned-up and apologized for butting her nose where it didn't belong. After they talked a little bit about the pitfalls of drugs and drinking, Michael asked her if she had ever given any thought about quitting and getting into treatment. She admitted, "I've given it some thought, but I'm not ready, yet." She asked Michael, "Do you think you could do me a favor?" He answered, "I don't know, what it is?" "Do you think I could come over as soon as I get booked out of here?" She asked. "I don't think it's a good idea," he told her. "It's really important," she insisted.

She said she would make it worth his while if she could stop by. Michael sensed something really strange about it. "No don't stop by, he said. "I don't even know you." She told him, "I'll be there, soon as they book me out." Then she hung-up the phone before he could object again.

A little bit later, the phone rang again. Michael thought it was the strange chick again, but it wasn't. "Mike?" said a female voice on the other end. "Yea? Who is this?" he inquired. "You know who this is," the girl's voice said. Michael hung up the phone. He knew the voice, it was Kim, and he was still pissed off at her for walking out on him the way she had. He was thinking, "Some beat friend she turned out to be."

Within a few seconds, the phone rang again. It was Kim again; he was surprised she called back. "I'm sorry Mike," she immediately said. "I know you're mad and I shouldn't have left you like that," she admitted. He interrupted, "What are doing calling here and how did you get the number? If Ingo finds out you called there's going to be trouble, ya know?" Kim told him, "I talked to Kaniza, and so can we talk now?" "Sure, we can talk." Michael said. "Let's talk about how you took off and changed your number so I couldn't get a hold of you. I haven't heard from you in months." "Mike," she interrupted, "I really am sorry and I knows what's happening there. I felt really bad and I want you to know that you can come and stay with me." Michael asked her, "Now, why would you want me to do that?" "Because I need you," she admitted, "and you need me."

"What about Marcus?" asked Michael, "You know I would have to bring him with me?" "That's fine, it's not a problem," she said. After giving it some thought he said, "Okay then, come and pick us up."

Michael would end up moving into Kim's loft apartment, which was nice but rather small. Her apartment was just down the street from Angie's place, so Michael and Kim would bring Jazzman to visit once in a while. Michael didn't really want to stay with Kim as he was still holding a grudge and was disappointed with her, but he still loved her. He also felt like he couldn't trust her either, because he thought she had her heart and mind set on someone else. Nevertheless, Kim's place would have to do until he found something better.

He really liked the neighborhood, which was up the street from where his family lived on East Bluff. Michael didn't like to be tied down, especially after dealing with Ingo who he still loved and didn't want to give-up on. Michael thought he might have let her down when she needed him the most.

Michael felt tied-down by Kim and it made him angry. They talked about Ingo and Michael thought that even Kim was kind of looking out for her. That was important to him because he still cared a lot for Ingo. He just didn't want to be used as a crutch by her, but both Michael and Kim continued to look out for Marcus.

The first night that Kim and Michael were together was incredible for both of them, and Michael thought it definitely for real. Kim told Michael, "The entire three years you were locked up. I wasn't with another man." "You expect me to believe that?" he asked. "Yes, I do." she insisted, "Because it's true. I have never wanted anyone else." The way she said it made him want to believe her, but he didn't know how to tell her. No other woman could do that to him before her. This was as good as it gets. They would sometimes make love all night.

But the sex wasn't all that mattered to him. Kim has a way of making him feel appreciated and loved in a special way.

When Michael was with Kim, he forgot about his troubles with Ingo and his mother. It was a relief that Kim didn't use drugs anymore. Before Michael was sent to prison, he and Kim would snort a little cocaine every once in a while, but they had both given it up.

Their days were routine. Kim worked a morning shift at Oscar Meyer. She had a brand new crib, a brand new car and everything was going great. What could have possible gone wrong? Michael would think of her beauty and he knew she had love for him. They made love daily. They went to a movie every weekend at East Gate Cinema to catch all the new releases. Kim also used to play dress-up just to make things exciting for Michael. Sometimes he could talk her into wearing certain outfits just to look funny. They would have a lot of laughs together and hit the clubs or sometimes go dancing all night long. They liked the frequent a Mexican Restaurant called Chi's Chi's and another one just East of Washington's called Pedro's. Michael had a fondness for seafood, so they would alternate. Almost every weekend they would go out and have a wonderful time together.

Things were going too well, so Murphy's Law would seemingly have to assure that something would go wrong. Sure enough, it did. Ingo happened to find out where Kim lived and began stalking Michael. She was telling various folks that she wanted her man back. From bad, it went to worse. Michael felt terrible for the hassles he brought to Kim, but he had no intention of going anywhere with Ingo. He also felt really bad for how this affected Marcus.

Good things were happening for Kim and Michael, and he was grateful he didn't have to be around a drug user. Michael wanted to do everything possible to help Marcus and be there for him any way he could, and he had to reassure him that he wasn't going to go back to Ingo. Even while out of prison Michael felt trapped. So much was on his mind with the drug treatment alone and on top of that all the drama with Ingo.

Not long after Michael moved in with Kim, Ingo told him she was pregnant with his child and she started acting real crazy towards them. She had already been stalking Michael while at Kim's place, and how she began stalking him at his treatment program in Tellurium.

Michael had to spend eight hours every day in that program and he would get furious when Ingo would go to his mother's house and act as if she wasn't bothering him and Kim.

Michael told Kim he didn't think it was his child she was pregnant with because she had been messing around with other men while he was away. They only had sexual intercourse a couple of times after he had been released from prison, so it was a very reasonable assumption that Michael didn't think he was the father.

If Ingo thought lying would bring Michael, back to her she was delusional. Ingo only made things between her and Michael even worse when she jumped Kim at Michael's mother's Thanksgiving dinner. Michael was getting use to the idea of being with only one woman, and if this were to be a reality, it would have to be Kim. Michael's original plan was to eventually get his own apartment, but Kim treated him like a king. She spoiled him rotten and gave him whatever he wanted.

Kim was familiar with Michael expensive taste in clothes and she brought him lots of nice things. It wasn't that Michael wasn't his own man. He was on the employment hunt daily trying to find that perfect job, since he had no intention of getting back into the dope game.

Unfortunately, Michael, although he was free, found himself once again trapped and into it again. He needed fast money and he knew how to get it. Of course, he was getting his product from "D". Ingo would steal the dope from him and sell it herself. She even stole a new scale that "D" gave to Michael.

Ingo was strung out in a real bad way and it was doubtful she would ever quit using. When Michael first started dealing, he sold some dope to the girl that Ingo got in the bar fight with. That was the favor she wanted to see Michael about that night she was released from jail. The reason Michael didn't want the girl to come over that night was because he didn't want this girl to know his past involvement in the dope game. One day, though, she just showed-up with a wad of cash and a stack of credit cards. Temptation was getting thick for Michael.

When the girl showed up at his door, she told him she heard he had product from Ingo. "How do I know you aren't the police or an informant?" Michael asked her. Putting her hands on her hips she said, "Do I look like the police?" She was sporting the black eye Ingo had given her in the bar fight. Then she asked, "Would a cop do this?" as she pulled her pants to her knees. She was a very attractive girl, standing their exposed. She said she was a doctor and also that she had been there earlier but got ripped off and she wanted Michael's help so she could get back home. Michael took her to D's house and introduced her and made two g's profit for making the deal go down.

Michael eventually started to hang out at D's more often. He was getting deeper and deeper into the drug scene once again. It had only taken three weeks, not the three months Michael wanted folks to believe, to get into the drug scene.

The doctor girl was the first customer and there would be another for several more months. Michael hung-out neat the street by Angie's place, mainly because she was still getting high and struggling with life. Michael really wanted to be close to his daughter, Jazzman. Angie eventually released Jazzman to Kim and Michael, so she began living with them as well, which was the very best place for her to be. Michael wanted Jazzman with him and Kim as a family.

The guys who sold dope for Michael were Angie's cousin Zac and an old homeboy named Cutter. Zac was trustworthy but a little gullible, which would eventually prove to be his downfall. Whenever Michael asked, Zac would always pay back money he owed. Zac had the bad practice of fronting dope to his friends and his girlfriends. He did it so often, that it convinced Michael to only deal with Zac on cash, up front basis.

Cutter was a dope fiend and, unlike Zac, he knew all the friends and all the addicts. Cutter mother also sold for Michael and she was good to be in business with because she didn't use. She was a real nice lady and a real good cook. Whenever Michael needed advice on any certain recipes, she would give it to him.

Michael loved his cousin Fossil like a brother. Fossil lived in the Northport Apartments with his girlfriend. He was a dope fiend and he knew a lot of dope fiends as well. Fossil wanted in for his piece of the pie, so Michael started him off slow.

Fossil got high too often and whenever Michael gave him anything, it didn't last long. Whenever Michael needed a driver or security services, he would pay Fossil for them.

Michael was helping Angie out a little, but mostly for the sake of his daughter, Jazzman. She wound-up turning her apartment into a dope house and she was close to being on her way to eviction. Michael had high hopes for Angie and he thought maybe she would somehow make more positive changes, but things weren't looking too good. Angie would often look after Kim when Michael was out of town.

Michael had a trip to Miami coming up and he just couldn't put it off as it was a very important trip and it was something he needed to do immediately, so he left Jazzman and Marcus with Kim. Fortunately, it was only temporary setback as Michael didn't want to be away too long from his family. Michael himself would find occasional opportunities to fly back home just to spend time with Kim and the kids, but he would turn right around and fly back to Miami the next day.

Ingo once tried to follow Kim home, but Kim would lead her to Angie's place because Angie would stop Ingo from jumping Kim. They eventually wound up fighting anyway even while Ingo was pregnant, so it didn't change anything.

Sometimes Michael would give Angie money or weed and dope to sell so that his daughter and the other kids could be better provided for. As luck would have it, Michael would lose out on a club while he was out on his trips, so he started to spend more and more weekends at home.

Money was getting harder to come by and he had to find some way of making fast money to get the bills paid, so he started hustling more and more. He was often out at nights and being away from his family was beginning to take a toll on him.

Michael's street life became a day and night thing. The whole scene and the money were engraved in his blood now and he couldn't live without it. He had to have dope product to sell and the money was coming in quickly.

With all this dope and money, females were next on his list. Whether he liked it out not he was now "fresh meat" with big money.

Michael was getting involved with different women almost every night and Kim didn't like it. She had caught him once and it slowed down a bit, but making fast money was part of his life now. Michael did feel bad for hurting Kim with his promiscuity, but he also knew that he had to take care of things.

Michael wanted so much to get custody of his daughter, Jazzman. He had also wanted to complete his treatment, get a job, and do the right thing for only himself but for his family, but his heart it wasn't right. But what was he to do? He was hanging around "D", making money and the word on the street was spreading and getting louder on him.

Michael couldn't go anywhere without the ladies sweating him, so it was obvious to figure out that he was getting his freak on. After being locked up for three years, he quickly became a sex addict. He was having sex multiple episodes daily.

Michael began to neglect his commitment towards Kim. He used Kim's abandonment while he was in prison as an excuse for his wild behavior. In his heart, he wanted a relationship with Kim, but he was his own man, and he couldn't have restrictions of a relationship put on him. He wanted to have his cake and eat it too.

Michael's actions didn't show Kim that he didn't love her. But he would try to compensate for insincerity by buy nice things for her.

He asked the doctor chick for some advice, because he was going to buy Kim a nice ring and diamond necklace to replace the half-karat diamond necklace Kim lost during the fight with Ingo. He would give Kim gifts of jewelry at least three times a year, on Christmas, birthdays and their anniversary. He would give her necklaces, rings, and bracelets… Michael thought that as long as he brought her nice things, she wouldn't trip on him for his emotional neglect. In his mind, he was only buying time until he could get his own place, and custody of his daughter.

Michael should have noticed something was amiss, as Kim didn't seem to be rushing him. Every once in a while, on Saturday evenings, Michael would take Kim and the kids out to movie and dinner. Whenever Michael wasn't too busy with his work in the Clubs, he would make it a night with the kids. Michael would show Kim off at the Clubs. He really didn't like taking her very often because the girls would want to hit on him and hate on Kim. It didn't matter so much because Michael and Kim always had a good time when they were out together.

After Kim finally left Michael, he began messing around with a woman named Melissa. He learned she was a masseuse at the Rising Sun Massage Parlor, which was down the street from the courthouse. Melissa was another one of those girls who would give Michael anything he wanted. She wound up buying him a cell phone and a pager and even a little hoop-tee Chevy. The only thing she wanted in return from Michael was sex, good sex, and more sex. As they say, "You can't rape the willing." Melissa was tired of the fat old men at the massage parlor and both of them had wonderful sex together.

Melissa gave more than good love to Michael; she started a chain reaction with him. Michael was messing with quite a few women at a time that things weren't as clear as they used to be and how he thought they would.

One early morning the health department came knocking at the door to see Michael and Kim. One would've thought it was the cops or something as they were really banging on the door. Michael had already been feeling a little sick, as he and Kim hadn't had sex for several days and his underwear were sticking inside his pants.

The people from the Public Health service informed them they both had nonspecific urithitis, which is commonly known as Chlamydia. Scared and worried they were both given a shot of a powerful antibiotic and a prescription. Both were relieved that it wasn't HIV. Michael knew for sure that God had to be on his side. He was still feeling very ill and he felt like dying when the health officials want to know who his eleven sexual partners were because all needed to be tested.

One night Ingo caught Michael at the Club at a time when he was a little drunk. She wanted to attempt Michael into one last roll in the hay. She actually threatened to blackmail him towards Kim and Michael had been "hooking up" with a lot of girls, but these were women that meant nothing to him. He still went home to Kim, but he would brag about how many women he been with prior to coming home to her, which was obvious, thoughtless, insensitive and emotional abuse which she really didn't deserve. Michael just looked at it as if he was being cool not realizing his pride hindered him from seeing reality.

Being with so many different women, Michael couldn't keep track of all of them. A few of them later stand out in his memory.

Like this mulatto girl with light skin named Yvette. She was a little older than Michael but that didn't matter to him as he remembered her from his high school days. Back then, she didn't pay attention to him, but he soon found out that she turned out to be a real freak.

Then there was this really square girl named Tuckie. Michael ran into her while hanging out in the hood where she lived. Everyone thought Michael was going crazy as he had a beautiful woman at home as well as all the other beautiful women that had been sweating him, but there was something about Tuckie that really appealed to Michael.

She turned out to be a wild one and by all accounts, she was absolutely down for him. While Michael was hustling for fast money in her neighborhood, she was a great help for him. Her kid's father was a good friend of Michael's and they were dependable customers. At least it started off that way, but then it later became sexual.

Another blast from the past was a girl named Shayla. She was a security officer in the ghetto and was still looking mighty fine. Her father was an attorney and Michael believed she could do much better for herself then being a simple security officer. He used to think she was too good for him, but time would show that he thought wrong.

One day Michael almost got busted when Shayla's wannabe cop boyfriend named Chris, the owner of a security service tried to arrest Michael. Luckily, they had nothing on him so they had to let him go. Tuckie also lived over there and was a great customer. She was a good hustler and she would always come back looking for more dope.

The real kicker would be several days later, when Kim and Michael went for dinner and then to Kaniza's apartment. Kim and Michael bought the movies and wine coolers and, as they were entering the apartment, someone was speaking from behind the door. It was one of Kaniza's friends. When she came out, Michael thought, "Oh, my God she beautiful." "You must be Michael?" she asked, and then said, "I'm Jenny Bush. I've heard a lot about you." Michael acknowledged, "So, you're Jenny. I've heard a lot about you too." Michael was being really friendly and if sexual thoughts were a crime, he would have found himself in a noose. Michael sat, as he couldn't take his eyes off of her.

He was holding the movies that he and Kim had just purchased, with everyone else already waiting for Michael to start. Kaniza kicked Michael for the left side and smiled at while Kim kicked him from the other side and asked him to hurry up and start the movie already.

Michael went to the kitchen to get a fresh wine cooler and brought one for Jenny as he was there anyway. As he handed the wine cooler to Jenny, he touched her hand and dropped the wine cooler. Everyone just looked. They ended up cleaning up the mess Michael created and he then realized he needed to focus more on the movie then Jenny.

After watching the movie for a while, he went into the baby's room to see his newborn niece, Tiffany. Jenny said she wanted to hold the baby before she left, but Michael knew she was hinting to hook up with him. He could see the look in her eyes. Soon after Jenny left, Michael thought he heard some noise from outside. He went out to investigate and found Jenny sitting in her car. When she saw him come out she rolled down the window and said, "I was wondering when you were gonna come out." "How did you know I would?" "I'm not sure of that," she admitted, "I just knew you would." Michael sat with Jenny in her car until he figured out he better get back inside before someone begins wondering where he had gone. He told Jenny he thought she was beautiful and that he wanted to hook up with her. Jenny said, "You look better in person than you do in pictures I've seen. It's too bad you're married," Michael agreed with her. "I consider Kim as my friend," she said. "I think you know my husband too." All Michael could think of was that even so thin line that he was about to cross.

Michael was only thinking about how beautiful Jenny was. Tall, light skinned and a body likes Jasmine Guy on "A Different World." But with a much prettier face. And she was a God-fearing Jehovah Witness woman. Michael wanted to know this girl, even if she did happen to be his girlfriend's new friend. She had grown-up with Kaniza in the hall, and Michael really liked Kaniza.

Michael told Jenny goodbye. "I'll see you later," he said. She replied, "I'm sure you will." Michael walked away thinking he couldn't wait until the next time he would get to see her.

When Michael moved to Middletown, he was rolling hard. Any normalcy he had in life had now turned completely to hustling. Michael and Kim moved out of the loft for many reason.

One of those was because Kim lease was up and it was getting hot anyway, but the heat wasn't the weather, it was the drugs. Michael was coming up fast in the ranks of the dope scene, and within a year of his release from prison, he rented an apartment on Sherman Road that was near and old abandoned schoolhouse. It was soon to be his spot to conduct drug deals.

Michael told Kim that heeded the apartment to get his parole office off his back, so he had to have an address. The parole agent already knew that Michael wasn't living with Ingo anymore.

Ingo would spitefully call Michael's parole agent trying to get him violated and sent back to prison. Ingo was thinking that if she couldn't have Michael, no one could have him. Another reason they wanted to move was because Ingo was stalking Kim, but it wasn't just Ingo, there were other women stalking her too.

Business was good and the cash was rolling in. Michael brought a sky blue, short body 225 Buick. It was two years old and had low mileage. The car would change color in the dark and he got it at a bargain. Unfortunately, Michael had to borrow a couple grand to buy the car from a friend named Tathy who worked for both him and D.

D was spending most of his time in New York, traveling back and forth to make large dope buys. Michael and Tammy were being vendors for D in the Midwest to make his big profits. Since D was in New York making these connections, Michael kept busy doing his own thing where he was. When D would come back into town, both of them would get together and split their profits. Michael's cash flow was nowhere compared to the minimum wage standard that he would most likely earn at a nine-to-five job.

When Michael and Kim argued or fought, he would get himself a girl or two and take them to his apartment. He kept no money or dope at his own apartment as he knew better than to leave dirty laundry lying around for possible of parole officer nosing around. However, every now and then the parole officer would come around to rattle Michael's cage a little. Tammy asked Michael if she could stay at his apartment because she had a falling out with Kaniza. She would take it the wrong way and get angry whenever Michael would tell her that "D" would need the apartment whenever he came to town.

Time passed and in less than a year, Michael was already wanting out of the drug scene. Something just didn't feel quite right to him and he wanted something good in his life-something that didn't involve fast and easy drug money. So he secured a job with a large Marketing firm called Vector Marketing and within a few weeks he became their top sales representative. He only made a fraction of the money he had made in the drug scene, but at least he wasn't selling dope and he could actually feel good about what he was doing.

Unfortunately, it didn't last long and Michael returned to hustling. Before he did, he was determined to try his hand at his own business, so he went into business with someone he had met in prison. It wasn't another convict, but a Wisconsin State Correctional Officer by the name of Robin. He was a good Christian man which Michael would discuss the blessing and saving grace of Jesus Christ. Robin was originally from Detroit, Michigan before he was saved he had connections in Michael's hometown. He and his brother, who worked at Oregon Prison camp found Jesus, got saved and continued to live a straight life. Michael longed for that salvation himself. He wanted a relationship with God, so he decided to move to Allied Drive, his old neighborhood, which was close to where Ingo had recently moved. The plan was to sell clothes, so both Michael and Rubin (Robin?) started their own version of a flea market and they were trying to build a storefront of their own.

Rubin had recently lost his job as a temporary employee as a Correctional Officer. He was trying to support himself and his three kids, so thing had to be legitimate for Rubin. But for Michael, things just weren't happening fast enough.

They were having trouble getting a storefront, so Michael tired borrowing a little cash from Eric just to get the store off the ground, but Eric turned him down. He didn't like the idea of Michael starting his own business. Michael wanted to travel to New York with "D" to purchase clothing direct from the garment district, but "D" wanted him to buy dope instead of clothes. Eric wouldn't lend Michael any money for the storefront, but he did give him plenty of dope. Michael really wants out but Eric insisted he stay in. Unfortunately, Michael wound up giving in and giving up on the store idea, giving the entire clothing inventory to Rubin.

It was a big mistake doing this and, not only this; it broke Kim's heart knowing Michael spent some time with Tuckie at his apartment. He was keeping his daughter Jazzman everyday and Tuckie was helping him out. Wanting full custody of Jazzman, he planned to get a bigger apartment, so one day he packed up and moved near the lake.

The apartment was nice and it had a country club on the other side of the lake. Michael now lived in an upper scale type of neighborhood, something he longed for a long while.

Michael kept things cool and wanted to stay out of sight because his name was too well known around the other areas and that was one thing he surely didn't need at the time. Thanks to Kim who came through for him once again, she helped him with his credit to get things rolling. Unfortunately, Michael had to buy another car due to his engine blowing up. He paid a large amount for a down payment on a Porsche 911. The maintenance fees were something he could tolerate, but getting the Porsche, he knew inside was a bad idea.

While Michael was in New York, he met up with some local girls and he would fool around with then whenever he went there on business. Eventually he would get tired of them when he would come to realize that they were nothing but "Gold Diggers," not to mention his fear of contracting another sexually transmitted disease.

One of the girls in New York was related to "The Great White Hope," and she had a lot of money to spend. She didn't mind sharing what she had a long as she could be with a black man from the streets who represented the "Tales from the Hood," and Michael was all that.

Another time in Madison, Wisconsin, Michael met a girl named Muffin. One day he was at a Car Wash when he caught her showing an interest in his Porsche. Muffin herself drove in a really nice custom drop top Grand National. At that time, that type of vehicle happened to be the fastest American-made production car on the road, so Michael knew it was "top stuff."

Muffin was a very smart, and a very beautiful woman. Michael was a little leery of woman like her, but he was very curious of what she was all about. He though they had similar minds, but he knew that she had to be up to no good. He would later learn that Muffin was just another "Gold Diggers."

During that same year, Michael was doing his thing in the dope scene and letting nothing get in his way. That one girl in particular who was hanging around came straight from the devil's den. A sexy sweetheart on the outside with a fantastic body, on the inside she was as mean as a she-wolf. At just five-feet-six, jet-black, with a body like singer Monica, Michael found an interest in her for the dope scene.

She had an attitude like Aretha Franklin and game that would take a whole army to tame.

Muffin herself was originally from Chicago and could sell just about anything. There were many more who wanted to get Muffin in their game, but she joined and stayed with Michael's team knowing he was glad to have her onboard. He gave her the freedom to run her own show and, in turn, she helped him make a lot of money.

More than compelled to keep this girl; he did so for several years to come. Michael himself was rolling faster than everyone and partying even harder. He hung out in the city almost all the time and with his friends Eric's connections, Michael would go party at nightclubs such as The Click, The Upper Room, All Jokes Aside, Club Ultimate, and many other clubs within the city. While in Madison, Wisconsin, they hung out at Perlies, P's and a new joint owned by the homes called The Underground.

One day Eric introduced Michael to his friend Darren who happened to be originally from the South Side of the city and lived between 87th and 98th streets. Eric wanted Michael to serve Darren and within a short time, they really got the ball rolling because there was only one thing they wanted and that was to make more and more money. Eric would frequently introduce Michael to a lot of his customers for better business, knowing quite will they would do good selling. Little did Michael know that Darren was the neighbor of some of his own family off 87th and 98th street. His uncle Bubbie used to date Darren's sister and Michael himself served Darren a few times, but mostly quarter, halves and ounces of product.

Darren was a DJ at Perlie's on the South Side off of Park Street and they all used to hang out at a little joint there in town. Another guy that was around about that time was Michael's cousin Derrick Eleby. At that time Derrick happened to be around Madison, Wisconsin and Chicago, Illinois while Derrick had been hustling a lot of weed during to him losing his job from a shoe store.

Derrick would stay at an apartment that Michael him get in Madison whenever he wasn't in Chicago, but the city was just too much competition for Derrick, so he came to Wisconsin. He was determined to make some cash for his new family, but his girl didn't want him to leave her side.

Whenever Michael went out of town, he would always look out for him and sometime hook him up too. For some reason Derrick couldn't stay on top of his game. Michael looked out for his cousin Kerman the same way. He also helped him out with money, dope and a crib so that he could have someplace to do his thing as well. They would use the crib to entertain customers as well as a place to keep their dope.

Unfortunately, things got cut short, as Michael's sick uncle had passed away, so he had to make a quick flight to Miami. He gave his pager to Derrick and Kerman to hang on to and to keep business going. Later, Michael's cousin Kerman would receive a page from Darren who was looking to finally score.

Kerman went ahead and served him with product as Darren introduced Kerman to an unknown person. This particular person was too determined to learn about their business operation.

Michael told Kerman that he wasn't interested in meeting anybody right there and then as he was out of town and didn't have the time. He did look familiar, though.

Michael knew he hadn't even done any business with this guy, but he did let him witness a transaction between Darren and himself and this would be the biggest mistake he had ever made. Michael told Kerman to continue using the pager for business until he returned from Miami. Kerman would wind up selling this guy more of a cut than dope for even more than double the price and Michael had a feeling something was up, wasn't right and that he might he having some trouble. He just didn't like the feeling that was coming up.

On another note, Michael's daughter Keya, the "love child" was born. It was late and he almost missed her birth at Madison General on Park St. due to all the business he was doing. She was beautiful and came headfirst screaming loudly just as Michael arrived. Ingo showed her emotion that she was upset Michael was late. She kept asking, "When are you coming home?" as well as "She's our love child, Michael."

Ingo was right about Keya being their love child, as she was born out of love at the time. But Michael had no intentions of coming back as he was in too deep to turn around and go to a normal life.

Two weeks had gone by before Michael would see Ingo and Keya again. He was traveling all over the Midwest as well as New York City making money and selling dope. He would hang out in clubs whenever he was in town relaxing and spending time with his dope family as well as fronting dope, of course. He would pick up on girls now and then and once in a while, he would let them pick up on him.

Most all the girls Michael would pick up were the finest girls in town as Michael knew he didn't need their cash, but he surely wasn't about to be kissing any female ass regardless of how fine she was.

One time he picked up this not-so-attractive girl. She was pretty in a way, but she really wasn't Michael type. She was hanging around with her friend and those friends were buying him drinks.

Michael's intention was to go to the bar to meet someone for a dope deal, but instead, he wound up in bed with her and her friends. The guy he was supposed to meet never showed, so after a long night of partying, Michael passed out and the girl snorted all of his dope.

When he woke up, he was lucky that they offered to pay for the dope they had just snored. They said they had been looking for some good dope all night but couldn't find any until they met up with Michael. One of the girls, Caroline was a big girl, about 6'1 inches tall and about 200 lbs. Michael asked her, "How did I get here?" "You were drunk and we didn't want you taking a risk in driving," she informed him. As wasted as Michael was, he just hated drunks and, believe it or not, he wasn't a big drinker either. He just happened to have too much that particular night that he passed out. Michael himself believed alcohol had to be one of the devil's tools and he had no idea of what was yet to come down the road.

There were two other girls there with Caroline. They were pretty too, but none of them were his type. Caroline spoke with a German accent and she said, "I hope you're not mad, Michael." He told her not to worry about it. "Where's my clothes?" he asked. "They're right over there," she said and pointed next to chair with his folded, laundered clothes.

"You had a little accident so I washed them," she told him. "Since you looked so fine without your clothes, we had a little fun of our own," she admitted.

Michael remembered he was supposed to have met up with Eric in the city, so he told the girl's thanks for the night of partying, but he had to get going." The girls asked him, "Where are you going?" He told them, I'm late for an appointment with a friend in Chicago." "Is it okay if we take you?" asked Caroline. Thinking about it for a moment, Michael said sure.

With all the partying he did, Michael had a hangover and, being that the girls would be taking him at their own expense; he was more than willing to let them take him.

Michael later met up with "D," picked up the product and returned to Madison. About a week later, Michael was at The Underground Club. Trouble came again, but this time it wasn't his fault. Ingo showed up completely inebriated again. "When are you coming to see out baby?" she asked him. "Are you going to be a deadbeat dad or what?" Michael told her to be cool and that he would talk to her later, but Ingo kept at him causing him to do his thing, which was partying with other women around the club.

Michael continued to avoid her and went on to more dancing and drinking and doing his own thing. Ingo, however wouldn't get out of his face. It bothered Michael so much that he got irate with her and had to go outside for some fresh air, Michael was showing off his Porsche to a couple of women out there, but before he could pull away to take them for a ride, Ingo came out of nowhere and jumped into the car.

Michael told Ingo to get out but she stayed, so in turn he gave her the ride of her life. Ingo got so sick and dizzy to the point where he thought she was about to throw-up in the car. Michael then promised her that he would make time to come see the baby if she went back into the club, so she did.

Back in the club, Ingo in all her drunkenness got into a fight with Michael's cousin, Ann Eleby. They were fist-to-cuff when the police finally arrived and eventually broke them up. After everything was over and people stopped circling around the area of the fight everyone just started to leave and go their own way.

Some time passed and Kerm accompanied Michael when he went to see the baby at Ingo's. The babysitter brought Keya out and set her on Michael's lap. She was a beautiful child only about a week old. Michael instantly fell in love. It was more than appropriate for Michael's sister to be the one to give the baby the right name Keya.

Isn't she beautiful? She's our love child, Michael," Ingo said. "How could you even dare say that she's not your child?" she asked. Michael had to agree that Keya was a beautiful child. He asked, "Are you sure she is my daughter?" Ingo was angry at the fact of Michael even asked that and said, "Of course she's your child, Michael!" He asked, "Where did she get that nose from?" Avoiding the question Ingo interjected, "When are you going to leave that bitch Kim and come home to us?" Michael injected, "Don't call her a bitch, Ingo." He made it very clear that her apartment was not his home.

Ingo hit Michael in the head like he had never been hit before. He was dazed for a few seconds and then he reacted without thinking and hit Ingo back.

Ingo went flying across the room and Keya fell through the glass coffee table.

Ingo grabbed the phone and screamed, "You're going back to prison!" Michael snatched the phone from her and she started swinging on him again, but he defended himself. "I'm calling the police," she screamed, and then she ran out the door. He tired to follow her and catch her outside, but she got away. Kerm stayed there with the baby and Michael left for home. "Thank God the baby didn't get hurt in all of this," he thought to himself.

After a while, the police showed up at Kim's checking the car, they could tell it was hot from running. "Mr. Brown, since your car is still hot, we are taking you in for obstruction of justice and assault on your child's mother," ordered the police man. Michael went to jail until Ingo came and told her version of the story. This time around, she told them the true version of what had happened. Later Michael would find both them going to court.

Michael was out on bail for the moment, and waiting for a court hearing. In the meantime, he was so angry at Ingo from all the trouble she caused him that he wanted to get to the bottom of the entire ordeal with a blood test to determine if he really was the father of Keya. If she were indeed Michael's daughter, he would have to do the right thing and be her father and look after her.

Until then, it would have to business as usual. It could have had something to do with his own experience with Keya, but something within made Michael long to meet his own biological father. Michael called his mother on the phone and asked her what his father's address was.

Michael's father lived in South Chicago behind the Jay's Potato Chip Factory, near the 90/94 Interstate just off of the Chicago Expressway. Michael got out of the car and walked up to the walkway. He wanted to at least see his father's face, and let his father see his. Michael wanted to say his peace and gets things off of his chest. He knocked on the door and an old white lady answered the door. Michael asked, "Is Michael Brown here?" "Who shall I say is asking?" she asked him. "His son, Michael Brown," Michael, said.

In a few seconds, she came back and opened the door again. "Come on in," she said. As Michael went inside, he saw this guy coming down the stairs. "I was wondering when this day would come," he said to Michael. "How are you son?" his father asked him. The old white lady who answered the door was Michael's grandmother. She didn't say much. Michael Brown, Sr. told Michael that it wasn't his fault he didn't keep in touch, as he just didn't know where he could find them. He said he know his mother had taken them to Wisconsin and that she had gone to prison, but that was when Michael's father went to live with his grandmother.

His story didn't make sense to Michael. He asked "Would you like to see your grandchildren?" he responded and said that he would love to. "When can I see them?" his father asked. Michael told him, "Whenever you want to," "How about in a couple of weeks, I come and see them then?" he responded.

Mr. Brown Sr. asked his son, "Are you the one they talked about on the radio all the time?" Michael said, "Probably! I have a lot of friends and business here in Chicago." They talked and walked out to Michael's car as they said their good-byes for the evening.

A couple of weeks later, Michael got into a really bad accident in his Porsche while he was returning from a visit with his parole officer. He had been driving over railroad tracks over a hill when he was hit square on the blind side by a station wagon full of kids. Michael could smell booze and weed emanating from the station wagon before he passed out. Luckily, Michael wasn't hurt too bad and the hospital he was taken, released him that same night, but ordered him to rest.

Michael couldn't let this accident hinder him from hustling, so without a vehicle for the time being he walked toward his house as it was nearby the hospital Michael had been taken. Prior to stopping-by the house, he made a phone call to his mother and asked if she would like to come to dinner with him, Tammy, and Kim as well as his father. Her response was that she wasn't sure, so Michael left it alone and told her that he would just be in touch with her at a later time. As he came up toward the house, he could see his father through the window talking to Michael grandmother. Michael knocked on the door. He could see his father heading towards the peephole. He opened up the door and asked if he'd like to be invited to dinner with him, Tammy and Kim. Michael informed his father that he his mother Linda if she had wanted to come, but she said she wasn't sure, so he left it alone for the moment. Linda was more inclined to know where Michael was at and he wanted to talk about other things, but Michael just wasn't in the mood at the time.

Michael's father agreed to go with them; so all three went to the Prime Quarter Steakhouse. This steakhouse had a reputation for excellent steaks and drinks so overall it was a wonderful, relaxing evening, despite what had happened earlier in the day.

Michael wished that his brother Matt, Tuttie, could've joined them as well, but unfortunately, he was in county jail, so there was nothing he could do about that. The only means of communication Michael had with him at the time was talking over the phone. Regardless of that, though, they enjoyed the evening and ordered more than two hundred dollars worth of food and drinks. Michael Senior started telling Tammy and Kim the same stories he always told and being that they were always inclined to hear them, they weren't falling for them. Michael really didn't care about why or what had happened between his father and mother, all he wanted was an apology for the years they had missed. Unfortunately, this was something he would never get.

When Tammy and Kim went to the bathroom, Michael Senior told Michael that his sister Tammy wasn't his biological daughter. "You're lying," Michael said. "I don't think my mother would've ever lied to me as she tells me everything." "I don't think I want to hear any more and please don't say anything more about this to me or my sister." Michael's mood changed dramatically and he became angry from all that he had heard or didn't want to hear.

Kim returned from the restroom and Michael got up and went to the restroom. This was really bothering him and he felt he couldn't keep the secret his father had just shared with him inside any longer. It was only right that he mention this to his sister Tammy, as he loved all his brothers and sisters very much. However, both he and Tammy were the closet and pretty much told each other everything. Michael sad to Tammy, "You know what my father just told me?" "What?" she said. "He said that he's not your biological father and I think he's lying." Said Michael. "Don't say anything to him because I don't want anything to do with him after this evening." "Mom didn't and wouldn't lie to me about this, nor did she mention anything like this to me before, so she certainly wouldn't have a reason to lie to me now."

Michael and Tammy headed back to the table. The bill soon came, both Tammy and Kim kicked Michael underneath the table as they wanted Michael Brown, Sr. to at least pay half of the bill, but Michael insisted on paying the entire bill himself. He just wanted the day to end so he could start fresh the following day. One thing was for sure, and that was the Michael was very grateful that he could at least be sure he had Kim and Tammy as part of his family.

Dinner ended and everyone, including his father, went to Michael and Kim's apartment for a little while. After dropping Tammy off at her place, Kim went to bed while Michael and his father had a couple of drinks and talked for a while. He wanted Michael to invest with a friend of his in a lingerie business or another plan of start-up a trucking company. His father was a truck driver without a truck. Michael just wasn't up to discussing all of that at the moment, so he declined all of his offers but told him that he would give it some thought.

Michael was trying to figure this man out. When Michael came to bed, Kim woke up for a moment and said, "I don't really care for your or his excuses, Michael. I was hoping he would hurry up and leave, to be honest with you." "Don't worry," he told her. "He's leaving tomorrow. His money, sex and drugs are a deadly combination, and he knows it."

CHAPTER 4

DRUGS, RAIDED, BARELY ESCAPE

It wasn't long after the visit with Michael's father that he was surprised with a police raid. It was around New Years Eve 1994. The police tried really hard to get Michael to give them information about some of his friends.

It happened to be one of those multi-jurisdictional drug busts. Michael saw it coming as Kerm was dealing with someone unknown person who would come around with Barren at times, and it just so happened that this man turned was working with the police. He even called Michael himself on the phone once. Michael had asked him where he got the number and he said that he had gotten it straight from Kerman and Darren, but Michael knew he was lying. He had talked to Kerman about the guy once before and mentioned that he really didn't feel comfortable about this dude, but Kerman kept selling to him.

He told Kerman he had thought that the guy was somehow involved with the police or even that he possible could be a Federal agent or something, but it was too late. Michael immediately called his attorney and told him what was going on with this guy calling him at home and all. His lawyer learned that there were some feds in town and that they had something on Michael.

Michael's lawyer told him that he should come see him when he had a chance, so Michael went that same day. Michael's lawyer Mark showed him photos of some new informants, and one of the photos was of the guy who happened to be with Darren. Michael couldn't believe he was seeing, so he ended up calling Kerman and Darren and arranged a meeting at Kim's to give them the news of what he had just learned.

During the meeting, Kerm received a page from the undercover agent. Michael told Kerman and Darren to see where this guy was going to lead them, but not to sell him anything. They agreed. Time passed and they were gone for a long while, but sooner than Michael realized they returned. When they came back to Kim's, they said they followed him to some unknown place they had never been, which turned out to be an undercover police station, Michael received a phone call from a neighbor who told him that someone was sneaking around outside their apartment trying to listen in at the front door. No sooner than he hung up, and another call came in. It was someone posing as a realtor trying to sell Michael some property. Michael knew what was going on.

He left the man to continue knocking until finally he gave up the ruse. It was five o'clock the next morning when Michael and Kim tiredly woke up to a knock at the door. Still in her panties and bra, Kim went to see whom it could be knocking at their door at such an early hour. She peeked through the peephole; before she knew, it was the police kicking in the door and screaming. "Freeze, you're under arrest!" They immediately separated and Michael and Kim into different rooms and began questioning them. They found over twenty thousand dollar in case in the apartment.

Later on, they would learn that the police also raided Kerman girlfriend's house and the safe house where Derrick had been staying. They informed Michael they had found drugs and were considering charging all four of them. Kim stayed strong through the whole thing and Michael was surprised that they took him to a hotel instead of jail. They were insisted that Michael; work with them or he would face going back to prison and likely stay there for the rest of his life.

Michael demanded that he police permit him to talk to his attorney. "You might want to listen first," they told him. They told him who had what they wanted from him. They were after Eric and his connections, but Michael made it very clear that he wouldn't be any help to them.

When Michael's attorney finally arrived, they ran it all down to him. The attorney told Michael, "You may want to consider cooperating with them as they probably don't have much on you, but they will make it up if they have to," he said "D and your friends are trying to frame you as the kingpin, so what are you going to do?" he said.

"You're the attorney," Michael said. "What you think I should do?" he asked. His attorney told him, "You really need to think about it, but you're going to have to tell them something if you want to leave here today."

Michael and his attorney played their game. Thanks to Michael, everyone got off their charges or got off light. Michael wasn't dumb and he knew how to play the game so he used the oldest trick in the book, the old double cross, but they got their man anyway, after Michael getting away with the money and the dope. He gave the interrogators some bogus information about a hot house, so when they busted in they would find nothing. People always wondered how Kerman got out of the charges for sales he made to the agent, but wasn't hard to figure out.

"D" and Tathy ended you getting caught and turning on each other. Michael was gone before the cops even arrived. The cop caught "D" and Tathy with dope money and guns, Michael certainly would have told them if he knew the cops were coming. They followed Michael when he left "D" and Tathy, so he had to discard the dope.

Some friends were throwing a party at Perlie's for Michael. Before stopping there, he stopped by his mother's and switched cars while thing cooled off. Once the heat finally cooled off, he went back to Perlie's to see if "D" and Tathy had made it out.

As he arrived, he saw Ingo going into the bar. He went to get the he had thrown out the night before. The money was hidden in some fake soda cans. Michael lay low and hid with Ingo until it was time for him to see his agent. Upon arriving to see the agent, there was someone already waiting for him. It was the officer who was working on the case and threatening Michael.

Later Michael would learn that he beat the case, but unfortunately, he would be forced to leave the city, the state and the entire Midwest for that matter. He was told, "If we find any little thing on you, we are going to bury you or you could be buried by someone else." Michael had no choice but to move along with his problems.

"Geography won't change people, but God can. When money is involved, that only creates more problems. When you cheat and commit adultery, you hurt not only yourself, but everyone who loves and cares for you."

CHAPTER 5

FORCED TO MOVE TO MIAMI TO LIVE

Michael didn't need to be told twice. He heeded the advice he was given and moved to Miami where he had family. He wanted to be as far away from his trouble in the Midwest as he could and the sooner the better, so within a couple of days he was on his way.

Miami was all it was said to be. However, for Michael he missed his kids and his siblings, Michael's family was from Pensacola and he had moved to Miami when they were young. Michael did visit them several time when he was younger, but that was such a long time ago. He would go there to get away from trouble, but he would learn that geography doesn't change things, and no matter where you go, you're going to take your problems with you.

Michael was determined to make things work out this time around, and so was his family. Michael fortunately had an Aunt in Miami, so stayed with her for a while.

He arrived in Miami with a U-haul full of furniture. Kim was going to come down and move in with him, but she decided to come down at a later date as so much had gone on the last time they saw each other. Michael couldn't help but feel that she had abandoned him once again.

Michael's plan was to get everything ready for Kim. His family dream was slipping away and Michael's Aunt was a 75-year old widowed Jesus fanatic who started preached to him from the jump.

When Michael's Uncle, who was his Grandfather's brother, died, he left his Aunt financially supported with two pensions from the military and the other from the school district he had worked for.

Living with his Aunt was a fun filled spiritual adventure that reminded Michael of the Cosby show, only without Bill. Michael's Uncle wasn't gone quite a year yet and they were all still grieving his loss.

Michael soon knew he had to find a job for whatever money he could get. He soon landed a job at the local Winn Dixie. Winn Dixie was one of the largest grocery store chains in Miami, but unfortunately, it just wasn't for Michael and he didn't stay long. His sister and her girlfriend Angie as well as Michael's friend Rob Sutton all helped make the move to Miami. Rob's mom grew up with Michael's mom so they had known each other since they were kids.

Michael's cousin Derrick was actually closer to Rob than Michael was to Rob. Rob had recently returned from serving in Desert Storm having helped to liberate Kuwait from Iraq. He offered to drive Michael with all belonging to Miami.

After the grocery store job didn't work out, Michael landed a job working construction. This was something he had done before from time to time ever since he was kid. He also decided to move from his Aunt's house in Coconut Grove to an apartment in North Miami Beach.

Kim finally came clean and told Michael she wasn't going to move to Miami. She had spent a lot of time trying to convince herself that it was the right thing to do. It really upset Michael, as he wasn't about to go back to the Midwest to most likely end up dead or at the very least, back in prison. Michael did feel a little bothered by her decision, buy while there was nothing he could do at the moment; he did miss his family very much.

Some time would pass before Kim would decide to come down to Miami to visit. Kim coming down didn't really help matters any as it only made him miss her even more. The entire time she was there, he wanted to keep her in the house where they could make sweet passionate love, all day all night, but he couldn't force her to stay, as he knew she had her life as well. Once in a while, they would go and visit some family and the South Beach, for Michael had to be really careful with his actions.

He had only been in Miami a few months and already had a reputation with the girls. There were hot beach bunnies, inspiring models, actresses and runaways. He was friendly to everyone, and if they needed anything, he would often get it for them. Michael would give up the shirt off his back if somebody really needed it. Sharing little food and clothing meant nothing to Michael. He could never turn someone away if they needed someplace to stay or something to eat. The girls were just his friends and nothing more.

Some of them had fallen for him and they knew this story. He asked them not to come around while Kim was in town, but some of them just couldn't resist. They wanted to see Kim and see what she looked like.

Just like anywhere else, girls of color wanted to know what was up with a brother seeing a white girl. Someone would come to the door and Kim would ask him, "Who was that?" "No one." He would tell her. Michael had discussed it with some of the girls before Kim got there but they would explain that they were jealous but out of respect for Kim. Michael was calling Kim three or four times every day from Miami and his phone bill was enormous. He just couldn't believe that he was not only homesick, but love sick.

To take his mind off of thing for a minute, he got a side job as a substitute teacher and another one as a bouncer for local security company. He was mainly working the clubs along South Beach but was mostly attracted to the music and the people.

Michael decided that this is what he wanted to be doing, and that he would leave Miami because he was missing his wife, his kids and his family. Once a month Michael would return to Madison for family court. He would come back every chance he could to see his kids, Kim and his family. Rather than flying, he would usually drive back in his sky blue Cadillac STS Seville, which was the car he brought after his accident and the lawsuit settlement money before he left for Miami. The rest of the left over money was used up to his attorney.

The phone bill Michael run up in Miami had become a financial burden on him, as he was paying more for the telephone bill than most people had to pay for rent.

Kim insisted that Michael call her every day. He would even call her even if he had supermodels in his house, but out of respect for Kim, he called from another room.

Michael missed his girls, Kim, Jazz and Keya, who was a newborn, as well as the rest of his family, consisting of Marcus, Ingo and his brothers and sisters, but nothing or no one could replace Kim.

A couple of times Muffin would call Michael and come to visit, but she had more guys coming around to see her than Michael had girlfriends and he had a lot of them. This was making Michael very homesick.

Finally, Michael made up his mind that he was going to bring Kermit and Herman, so they could drive him back and forth. He would stop by various family members' homes along the way. The music conventions and freak neaks had Michael thinking that all of this was costing him too much, as every paycheck went to bills. Most funds went to the telephone and the maintenance of his car.

Things were light, and Michael wound up having to sell his 14-karat gold chain that he had for years, for fifty pounds of weed and some cash. Surprisingly, Michael had been crime and drug free for years, but this could be a major relapse for Michael and a sudden u-turn back to the street, in Miami, most weed was virtually worthless. In Chicago and Madison, Michael could make real money. He made the trip every other month. Michael seemed to change after his move, but it wasn't the move that changed him, it was something else.

CHAPTER 6

RETURN TO HIS FAMILY, THE MIDWEST & HIS DAUGHTER'S

Michael returned to Madison, Wisconsin, to be with his family. Shortly thereafter, he applied for a job doing construction. He hooked with Arthur Fuqua, aka Butter, in his old neighborhood. Butter turned out to be Michael's only friend there. He also met some new friends, Carrie, Sunset, and Onyx.

For a single man, Michael's life in Miami would have been very cool, but Michael missed his family too much. Now that he had returned, he had to get back into the groove of things without crime and drugs. Michael didn't want anything to do with, if he could help it. He was steadfast for a while, with the exception for the weed deals. Michael couldn't see anything wrong with a little weed selling to jump-start something positive, which he found out to be a big mistake later.

As they say in therapy, "If you hang around the barber shop for long enough, you're bound to get a haircut."

While Michael was visiting on his bi-weekly visits, he was at a stop light near where some fellows were installing a pipeline incorrectly. They were likely to cause a major explosion, but Michael stopped them and gave them some unsolicited advice. The boss thanked him, and kindly offered Michael a job on the spot, which he had no choice but to take.

Michael agreed to start with the company, Vogel Construction, the following week. The foreman was an older white dude, cool and well built. Kim was ecstatic that Michael was in town and made a trip back to Miami to get hid things for him.

With his car jam-packed, a State Trooper pulled him over and said, "You must be crazy to scratch up this nice car." Michael told him, "I'm just trying to get back to my new job, my wife and my kids." "Well they must be very important to you?" agreed the trooper. "Absolutely!" declared Michael. "They're everything." The trooper let Michael go without a ticket. He told Michael, "Be careful and God Bless!" Michael felt that the Trooper meant it too.

When Michael got back, he helped Kim move to their new apartment. Kim, Michael and Jazzman would get to bring Keya home every weekend. Being a member of the Laborers Local Union, Michael had a great job with great benefits and worked with great bunch of guys. He was back in the rhythm of things and began working at the agriculture building off of Odana Road. From there he went to work on some of the biggest buildings, including some of the largest projects in the state.

The next major project he worked on was a drain pipeline that extended under highway 51 and I-90. During the winter Michael worked one way or another on the gas mains for the entire city if Cottage Gove. His blood, sweat, and hard work and tears where literally everywhere.

Michael's first job happened to be on the West Side of downtown Madison, where he saw his old friend Butter. Michael met Butter when he used to work for Ray-O-VAC with his cousins Herman and Kerman, back in the eighties. He had only known him for a couple of months when he made his first dope purchase from him. Butter was a well-seasoned dealer, but his legal problems, coupled with a cocaine habit, convinced him to get out of the business and stay out.

Michael admired Butter and, in spite of his drug habit, saw him as an older and wiser man with big money. He ran into Butter again in the old neighborhood on Williamson and Dickinson. “What’s up, Man?” Butter asked him. It wasn’t long before Michael and Butter became good friends.

Butter gave Michael an old car that he could drive to work so that Michael wouldn’t destroy his Cadillac at the job sites. Michael would stop by Butter’s house regularly, where he would meet Melissa Quamme, Butter’s girlfriend and his friends Angie Cramer and Stacey Pete. It was also there that Michael met Carrie, aka Dog Pound. Dog Pound was a feisty longhaired skinny little white girl. Butter called her Dog Pound because she was “Gansta,” and her mother raised and sold dogs. As small as she was, Dog Pound had the nerve to flirt with Michael whenever he was speaking to Butter. He also met a pretty red head that had thick and wipe hips, about 5’5” tall and big mouth name Sonnet, aka Sin. Sin would try to give Michael her number even though he was clearly not interested. It was obvious that these girls were game for just about anything, but Michael was trying to keep both feet on the ground.

Sonnet was working for J.C. Penny’s in the sales department. Michael later bumped into her in a café downtown and sooner than later, they began messing around.

“Loving, missing your family and doing the right thing have all got to coincide. You have to take care of yourself and your family with God on your primary concern. Family is a blessing from God. Lonesomeness is a self perpetuating curse.”

CHAPTER 7

THE SEX INDUSTRY

ONYX (who was originally from Tampa, Florida) was a bigger girl whom Michael had met around the same time as Sin and Carrie who were friends of Butter and his roommate Marlin. Onyx had moved to the Midwest for school and run her own escort service and stripper agency. Onyx kept trying to seduce Michael; Michael wasn't interested for some reason.

Marlin, who was also one of Michael's guys, was from the neighborhood in Chicago. Michael noticed that Marlin and Butter were having trouble getting along. Marlin claimed Butter was messing with his girls, while strung out on dope. Michael saw this as nothing but unnecessary drama and so did the girls.

Michael worked a lot but felt he still had too much idle time; Michael was still looking for a way to improve his life and his income. Michael picked up some of the ideas from Onyx and started his own upper class escort business.

Michael placed ads in all the papers for contractors and clients. Michael soon acquired plenty of clients and working girls. Things went smooth and rapidly for Michael.

From newspapers, word of mouth, pagers and telephone appointments, Michael would send clients to girls and girls to clients. The Agency expressed to clients and the girls in person and in contract. Both parties had to be over eighteen and there would be no sex solicited the service was for entertainment purposes only. Business and the agency was providing seductive dancing, giving messages or going to dinner. It was a very good business that earned Michael some great extra cash, or so he thought until Butter came down talking about his drama with his roommate.

It turns out Butter and his roommate had gotten into a big fight and had no choice but to move with one of his girlfriends for a while as he gotten thrown out, Michael, being the man that he was, came through and helped them out with a little rent, but it turn took use of that he was helping them with. In one of the bedrooms of Butter's girlfriend's apartment, Michael quickly set up an office to run his Escort Service, where he thought he would make a boatload of money for himself and the contractors.

As Michael had been back home for several months, the bills had been getting neck high and were will climbing. Yes, he had some prospects, but Carrie and Sonnet were sweating him. He had some prior experience about the business because of his past stripping days while he was in college and living in Miami.

Michael was familiar with the business as he had grown up around drugs, whores and pimps most of his life, but he really didn't know the full extent of how demanding the Escort Service was as it was more complicated than Michael realized when he had decided to get into it. He hated the trouble that lurked with a sinister grin in the business, as all he wanted was a little fast and easy money, nothing else.

Michael in the meantime had been working construction since returning back home and running the Escort business as a second income. It was in the summer when he started working construction and it was fall when he started the Escort service. When tax time came around, Michael felt he was doing really well, but yet something still seemed to be missing and he just didn't know quite what it was yet. He was making good money, over two thousand dollars an hour, which was good money in the mid nineties. Being the over achiever that he was, he wanted more of his family and himself. He had to have a second job or hustle to being in even more fund to bank. He knew that he wasn't about to give up his job in construction, as he loved his work.

Wanting nice things for his family, he didn't think the flowers and small gifts he brought home for his girls, Kim, Jazzman and Keya, were enough. Short of selling dope, Michael didn't mind doing what he had to do to take better care of his family. After, a while, he rationalized that small drug sales every now and then wouldn't hurt anything.

Acting on advises from Butter and his cousins, Michael; started to pick up a little dope every time he went to Chicago on Holidays and weekends. He would go their shopping or visiting and pick up an ounce or two, break it down into bags and sell to Butter and his cousins. At the time it would profit Michael a few hundred and other times even a couple of thousand dollars each month, even though he was only selling to family and friends, it still worked out well with his other business on the side. Other's had began selling for him as well as getting high on the side. Getting his product from family or people that he knew from his youth, as well as only dealing with those he wasn't in position to get in any trouble, but he couldn't have been any more wrong. Something was about to go down.

Michael worked construction through the summer, fall and winter. He loved the work, but the weather sometimes got bitter and unbearable. He loved his family and wanted to do the right thing, so he kept at it and endured it, even through the inclement weather.

Michael really loved being a father; he especially loved when Jazzman and Keya got the chance to sit at his house every other weekend. That was always a joy with him! He was still looking after Marcus as well. Michael had made it clear to Ingo that he would not be coming back to her, but that he really loved Marcus as his own son and he couldn't let him go.

The escort service was taking off and business was booming. Michael had to spend a lot of time at the office set up at Butter's place. At first he had more clients then contractors, and then he would work recruiting at nightclubs, which was keeping him away from a lot. As much as Kim liked the money that was flowing in, she was concerned Michael had started drinking a little and became worried that this would all just suddenly come to an end someday. But what could she do? Since she never knew when that "someday" would come, she just went with the flow soon, they were out of debt, which was a good thing for both of them, as that was one thing they didn't have time to worry about. Michael continued showering Kim with nice gifts, and as time passed they would find themselves moving out of their little business partner, Butter, would drive Michael around in at times.

Michael, on the other hand, was recruiting girls for the escort service. His girls, Sonnet and Carrie were recruiting men for sex. "Fringe benefits," they would call it. Michael was establishing himself as a good businessman as he now had as many contractors as clients and the money just rolled in hand over fists.

One night Butter crashed the car, so they graduated from driving a Seville, to driving a two toned gray Fleetwood Cadillac. It took Michael several months to pick that Cadillac, as he wanted to be sure what type of ride he wanted to get. Before the Cadillac came around, he drove around in a red drop top 1966 Chevrolet, and before that a Monte Carlo.

It didn't take folks long to learn that Michael was back in town and pushing dope again. He was only pushing the dope every once in a while, and only with those people he knew he could trust. Or so he thought!

They paid him, so he was down for it whenever it came along. He also kept a little dope for Butter and some of his employees as a little bonus gift or perk of the job. They would get through Aaron, who was like a brother to Michael as his cousin were always into something or up to no good.

Construction work was good and legitimate money for Michael. He had insurance and benefits for his family. They lived in a two-bedroom apartment and he knew they needed a place, so they had plans for the upcoming tax return check.

Michael was back in Madison for almost a year now. Like any other good American, he was working hard. For the most part, he keeps himself drug and crime free. Then one day he began smoking weed again. Michael thought he would just do a little, but business picked up, it would never happen.

Michael had never been displeased with running an escort service. The money was great and he loved the entertainment aspect of it, but for Michael, it was an opportunity to help people. He was never into the power trips, much less the sexual aspect of it. Plus, there was an old debt from a girl named Jennifer (one of Kim's friends) that he had. It was from a past investment for a drug buy that he wanted to pay off once and for all, but he didn't want to cause his family any problems.

Jennifer wanted the money back that Michael had lost in bad dope deal. He didn't want any problems to come back on Kim, but it was too late as Jennifer somehow found out where they lived and came to their place and caused a big scene until the police arrived.

Michael was fed up with it and didn't want to give Kim a reason to leave or abandon him, so he gave Jennifer a little something. He started to party with her at the clubs, at Butter's and he was treating her like a Queen. Michael was friendly with her and she quickly fell dangerously in love with him. He had some feelings for Jennifer, but not so much as loving her. As far as he knew, they were just friends and nothing more.

He learned that this was a fatal attraction that he would soon shrug off. Michael was wondering why they called "The Pipe Layer!" He knew how stupid he was. They were both cheating and there was little love between them. The problem was the money that was involved.

"Relationships cannot be built on money," "Sex for sale is idolatry and adultery."

CHAPTER 8

ENTERTAINMENT AND MUSIC BUSINESS, MICHAEL'S SON'S

Michael opened his first club at a recording studio. Many of his friends came over to watch, listen and mess around with the music equipment. Even the kids had a blast watching and recording the audio and video. He had all the equipment including turntables, microphones, mixers, effects and recorders, it was all there. He needed extra cash, so he decided to start charging at the door. He also let the strippers and escorts dance there for money.

It was about time for the income tax check to arrive. It would be the most legitimate money Michael could have ever received. He had a couple of bill and he still owed Kim's ex-friend Jennifer, who had now become their enemy. They also needed to get into a bigger place and they were spending a lot of money for Jazzman's daycare.

Kim and Michael both worked a lot of hours, but their credit was a problem, as they really didn't have any. They also had to pay Michael's Fleetwood and Kim's Hyundai, which ate up a lot of their cash. They knew they should have paid off the cars in the first place. They both searched for a bank that would give them a loan, but the interest was too high. Not only could they not agree on a bank, but also they couldn't agree on a house either.

After a while, Michael was willing to take anything available but Kim wasn't so willing. Something was wrong and Michael would soon figure out what it was. It was Michael unfaithfulness to Kim. His spirit wasn't quite right, and Kim could clearly see that God wasn't finished with him yet. Things were actually much better, but he hadn't even turned the corner yet. Michael didn't intend any disrespect and felt Kim should trust him a bit more as he believed it was something he would grow out of. Little did he know that things were about to get much worse?

Since they didn't purchase a house with the tax money, Michael decided to use to get his business off the ground. He was tired of using the room at Butter's place as his office.

By using the Quick Filing method, he was able to pick up his tax return check right away. He had a good reputation with the tax preparer who told him to follow his dreams. He noticed a sign that said, "For Lease," in the window. Like a brick hitting his head, Michael realized he could lease this place and have his own office. With the office equipment he had, he would be more than able to open up a recording studio and run his escort service at the same time.

He presented his idea to the tax guy. To his surprise, the same guy told him to follow his dream was now saying, "It's not a good, idea Michael." Needless to say, Michael was a little upset at him telling him that and said, "Its white guys like you that make a brother feel like he can't achieve anything." "Wait," said the tax dude, but Michael had already snatched the tax return from his hand. "All right then" said the tax manager, disbelieving, and "Let's see what you got. Bring me your business proposal." To prove his wrong, Michael did just that. So several days later, after making some zoning ordinance changes to his paperwork, the proposal was agreeable.

Michael held his first concert within a few weeks. From then on, he was hooked. Butter soon became Michael's main man. He managed the club and the girls for Michael. What started out to be a recording studio and office soon got really crazy. Michael's first piece of equipment was a house stereo, but every week he would by additional equipment that was needed.

Needless to say, it got very expensive after a while. Being a D.J and quite a proficient rapper, vocalist and dancer, Michael needed a break, which he was soon going to be getting when coming back from his cousins in Miami after licking up a little dope with them.

He stopped in "Jew town" (at 18th and Halston) to pick up an outfit or two and then he went on to Madison Avenue. While at Madison Avenue, Michael ran into a group of guys. At first, he didn't know them but, as it turned out, it was crew from the West Side "Do or Die", who had just released their first signal "Crucial Conflict and J.D." who at the time was the Chicago top selling solo rap artist.

Another group there was "Psycho Drama." They were there to promote their demos ad talent. Michael immediately zoomed in on "Tongue Twista," and they got on topic fast. He invited them to Madison, Wisconsin to do some recording at his studio and possibly a show.

At first, he didn't seem to be to interest, but then Michael proposed that they come to Madison to do a concert promoting their singles. Luckily, they were down for that and as Michael spoke with J.D., he told him he may be able to help him with some things. Michael told him, "I'll scratch your back if you scratch mine." J.D. told Michael that he just wanted to get his grind on, which meant he wanted to hustle. Michael told him he could easily help him with that.

So J.D. ended up in Madison. Michael and he sooner became new friends and partners. Before long, however, Michael would learn that this was a dangerous merging especially when more money began coming into picture.

J.D. helped Michael design his entire studio. He also helped him pick out various pieces of equipment. Michael was surprised with the amount of money it really took to get the business off the ground. Just the studio alone took up every last dime he had, but Michael wasn't too worried as he was using J.D. as a feature artist when they started recording with him. J.D. had a few videos out already and his sales were like gold on the streets.

Michael being the business guru that he was, got offers from free publicity at local radio stations as well as at Discount Records, a downtown music store on State streets. The record store invited them to be a part of a huge upcoming State Street Block Party.

This huge event drew in more than a quarter million people. Discount Records asked Michael to provide entertainment, which would bring attention to their store, so did.

Michael hosted the talent contest to dig up additional entertainment adding to the acts he would surely utilize. It was a good was to discover new artist as well as to promote his own business. The events were a blast. J.D. put on an excellent performance. A long with D.J and Cohen, came with his partner who brought their family group Fat-4-ever from Milwaukee, who also performed and did a wonderful job.

Michael was constantly meeting and making new friends, but he also made some enemies in the business right away. Having to sign certain people and cut other caused him to both make and lose friends quickly. Forming groups and singing artists for his company wasn't easy, but Michael loved it, second only to his family. Sometimes Michael made the mistake of putting the one above the other, which wasn't good for business he had well.

Some of the people that Michael signed with his company were family and friends, but business had to remain and unfortunately, he couldn't keep everyone happy all the time. His partner Butter, being his main help, and everyone else, who was working for Michael, knew that he was really coming up in the business and they wanted in. There were certain few other friends of Michael's who helped simply out of kindness and friendship. They would haul & help set up shows. While it was mainly Butter and Michael who did most of the work there was also his cousins Buddy, Maurice, Herman, Kerman and Fossil who later came with so many girls you wouldn't believe it possible.

Michael pops also help him build stage, along with some other friends and family. Ron, from his high school days, and a new country white friend, H.B. aka Hillbilly or Lorenzo Thomas, became Michael advisor. They met at a construction job working for a good company called Findorff, while building the Frank Lloyd Wright Madison Convention Center. Michael first started working as a laborer and excavator. H.B. was very intelligent and had graduated as a law student, but for some reason he chose not to practice law. Like a lot of people that Michael knew, H.B. had a drug habit and he like to drink, which everyone with experience knows is a deadly combination. Michael didn't pick his friends like how many people pick a book, by its cover, but H.B. was an older country white guy from Tennessee. Michael picked his friends by their character and their content.

Michael wasn't open long before he started putting on concerts. The first were done at a whim with last minutes preparations. With fifteen hundred dollars, Michael made fifteen thousand within a couple of weeks, and all legitimate money. Michael was definitely hooked now. He would stick with his business of music and make it his life from then on. The key was in sales. A person had to be in the right place at the right time and they had to have the right product. Michael was a provider of the right product.

Thanks to the assistance of J.D. and Cousin Maurice, Michael was going to promote and work with the group, "Do or Die." Michael was born for this type of work. He had been promoting parties for years prior to this gig and music promotions were only a step up from that. Thanks to a parade of flyer, free radio advertisement from WART radio, Z104 radio promotions from Discount Record Shops, the concerts were off the chain. Michael's first concert sold more than 500 tickets at $12.00 dollars each. His second big concert was the promotion from the group called "Crucial Conflict."

Michael picked up his first limo after that show and quit his construction job. He didn't realize at the time how foolish that was, but he was already in and there would be no turning back. He wasn't in the race for nothing, and nobody was going to stop him from being a winner. Michael did very well and got better and better with each production he put on, even if it meant breaking all the rules. Kim would bring the kids to watch the first few shows and the Kids always supported Daddy. The kids would sing all the songs in the car and fall asleep on the way home. Business was a success and it was time for celebration because the show was about to go on the road. There was more work then Michael could handle and at the time, he was getting evicted from his first building, which was in a strip mall off Broadway and Monona Drive. There were those that were counting on Michael. At the same time, he was breaking all the rules. It began with capacity violations. The facility was more than double capacity each week, and he only had one bathroom completed for over one hundred people. Michael was living dangerously, and remained in debt to the city officials and other authorities for giving him this opportunity.

Michael had more people with the neighborhood businesses that weren't happy with Michael's accomplishments. There was an old hotel across the street, and a music equipment store next door, a convenience store on the corner and both an AA & NA meeting place just adjacent. Sometimes things were loud and crazy as something was always turning up missing or stolen. Michael winged it as best as he could, but security was completely out of control.

Michael permitted the stripper and escort to put on their show to bring in even more money. He thought it would be good for business, but it wasn't long before he was forced out of the building due to all that was going on. Michael needed to find a new facility.

While in the process of looking for a new place and under the extreme pressure of his large and ever growing following, he decided to put on a concert. The headliner would be the group Crucial Conflict, the hottest group in the city at the time. They were up coming and so was Michael. He was thinking along the right lines and selling a little dope at the time. He wasn't robbing or killing anyone and his girls were blowing up his escort service. Business was so good that he had to hire a couple of men. Michael was the only man for a while, but not every woman was looking for a big handsome black man, they wanted white guys or even others.

Michael was in need of help and needing it as soon as possible. He hired a few dudes, hard-bodied white dude; with one being Michael's main man Eric. Eric was a healthy, hard-bodied white dude. He was a law student and the escort service was his hustle. Eric was from Boston, Massachusetts complete with accent and best of all; he was Brady Bunch handsome but built like the Incredible Hulk.

Eric started getting so much money and attention that Michael was getting a little jealous and that just wasn't like him. This only made Michael get into his job all the more. He would refrain from renting himself out, except for very high profile customers.

Michael loved the money and attention that came with the job. He was so busy that he wasn't staying in physical shape like he should have. His mind was on business most of the time.

His first job as a dancer was at the party for a group of law school graduates. He left with a couple of grand and had a great time doing what he did. Michael remembers that there were a lot of women, but there was one thing that he didn't like, and that was being treated like a dildo with legs. It also troubled him the way the gays looked at him, which he later had to learn came with the territory. The gay guys would try and dance with him, but couldn't feel right about it, so it was something he always avoided. Michael's last job was a double he pulled with Eric at a bachelorette party at which they both had a blast.

Most of the jobs were held at someone's house or hotel and security would need to be sent to get the contracts signed and to make their presence known, then they would wait outside the door during the performance. Unfortunately, this wouldn't necessarily stop someone from harm. There were assaults and rapes and even catching AIDS in some gigs, they worked at. Unfortunately, even one of Michael's escorts was murdered from all the hype going on. One girl who had worked for Michael was moonlighting for another service and she was killed while doing a show at a hotel.

The service unfortunately didn't provide security for the girls and the last incident was the one that motivated Michael to hire security for all of his promos. But there had been times even security wasn't as secure as he had hoped would be. Michael had been interviewed by a couple of television stations, defending escort services and explaining how they worked. This brought in business, but as the same time legal investigation, enemies and anger from his attorney as well.

//Entertainment, fame, money and power can be deadly when you're not prepared to handle such as these. If there were to be used for positive, they had to always include God as the primary focus. //

CHAPTER 9

MICHAEL'S SONS BIRTH & MEETING

(ALLEGED CO-CONSPIRATOR)

A true friend can be as close, or even closer, than one's own family, and would never bear false witness, cheat, steal, or hurt their friends. A friend such as this is far and few between and they likely only appear once or twice in a lifetime. Michael was one such friend as this, but those he befriended, lied and sold him out for a price...their life.

Michael was introduced to Stacey Pete and Angie Cramer through Melissa Quamme a tall, slim, pretty girl who was a friend of Butter's girls. Butter worked with them at the Holiday Inn, formerly the Ramada Inn on East Washington.

Michael met another girl, named Mary, whose family owned a bakery across the street on Williamson. She was well built like Zsa Zsa Gabor, and like Zsa Zsa, she was spicy and had money.

Mary came to Butter's to see Michael all the time she would just pull up in front of Butter's house whenever she would come to visit.

One day she pulled up in the middle of the street and Michael asked her, "Have you got a problem and are you looking for someone?" "No, I don't, and no, I'm not," she told him. Later she would admit she lied. From the first time they met, it was on. Michael and Mary had some of the funniest freakiest time you could imagine, but those times wouldn't last. He would later learn that Mary was trying to sleep her way up the ladder in Madison and he was high as she could go. She went all the way down to Chicago with Michael and got infatuated with rappers, money and men.

Mary finally went on with a guy named Krash man, but not before Michael literally worked the crap out of her. She wanted out of the street life and wanted to catch Michael as a husband, but he made it clear that he was already a husband. It was around this tame that Michael met Reanna & Breanna.

They told Michael they are sisters. They also lied about their ages. Michael believed them at first because Butter backed-up their story, saying he knew them and that he had dated their mother a year after they began working for Michael. Michael thought he was giving them their 18th birthday party, which he hosted at his club.

Michael soon got his second club on East Washington, which was a good club. He would put on small shows, mostly with groups coming up every weekend from Chicago. Things really picked up and got rolling after his third big concert with Crucial Conflict.

It was quite a big production to put the whole thing together. Michael spent as much as twenty thousand dollars just get it started, and when he was finished, he paid everyone off. Michael broke just about even and was grateful for that. A total of more than fifty grand went through Michael's hand just that one night alone, but it was all legitimate. Out of everything, Michael lost out on his vending t-shirts and pictures. He put a list of money in all of things and made a little money back because he was worried about all the big stuff. He was glad however, for the concert was such a hit and went off without a hitch and with no accidents.

It became a Chicago and Midwest thing. Everybody wanted to help put the show together. Michael's customers from the escort service and the guys he did business with in Chicago helped him the most. There was Old Man Jim, a dope customer and retired General Motor's worker who wanted to see Michael get his dream off the ground. He, out of everyone, gave and invested the most time. These guys may have only wanted Michael so keep them in fresh girls and dope, but remain legitimate. Carl Higgins, aka Lil C., wanted to film his first video in Michael's facility. He wanted to bring all the groups from Chicago and he was great help as well. Michael's friend J.D. wanted headliners, money and props that were already going to his cousin's Cory's group, Crucial Conflict.

The G.D.'s began claiming it was their concert, as were the V.L.'s. It was Michael's event thrown by H.E.A. Production. (Honest Entertainment Anonymous) and, being honest, they truly were. It was a big production all the way around.

There were a lot of groups performing, with talent contests, catered foods, limo's, clothes, the whole works. Then there would be after-concerts parties. The groups that would show there were Crucial Conflict, Do or Die, Chaotic Intentions, Cash Man, Down 4 life, J.D. Walker, the Career Criminals and Twista.

Twista was present when Michael's second club was shot up for gang banging and someone throwing gang signs. Michael insisted that everyone respect the rival gangs, but someone must have said something someone didn't like. When the cops would show up, almost everyone would leave the scene. It was amazing to see how quickly people could run out of a furnace.

They packed the house though, which was an old 1920 theater called The Barrymore. It was well cared for and still in good shape. The Barrymore was in Michael's and people in that neighborhood esteemed the place very highly, as did Michael.

He couldn't have been more pleased with the support he received from that particular community. His involvement aided just about everyone to make a little money. Unfortunately, just before the concert, they lost an idol and the show was opened with a little unwanted news, but out of respect for that idol. Michael announced a tribute to a performer named 2Pac, who had passed just minutes before the concert owned Michael started with a prayer and a moment of silence to acknowledge 2Pac's, contributions to life. Then they started the ball rolling in this prime location that Butter found, which happened to be the best spot yet. Being across the street from "Little Africa," the minority projects on Darbo Street was a bit of a problem.

People came around to gang bang and sell drugs; they were rowdy bunch to say the least.

Michael thought he had a good security team, but they proved to be questionable. There were some folks at odds with each other and there were young girls and guys permitted entry for a little dope, which wound up being more valuable than the normal entry fee of five to ten dollars. The problems that came with the dope were definitely not worth it as on concert nights the cover charge was usually twenty or thirty dollars for the bigger venue.

Some events were standing room only. There were also engagements such as birthday parties. They would often bring in groups from Milwaukee, Chicago, Los Angeles, and even New York. Every weekend it seemed that there was something happening.

It was on East Washington that H, B, encouraged Michael to purchase his first limo. Owning a limo actually cut costs he would have normally had to pay to transport groups coming from out of town, and Michael could use it whenever he wished. Owning a limo prove to be less expensive than paying two thousand dollars to rent a limo for a night.

It was around this time that Stacey was trying to catch Michael's attention. Michael saw Stacey as a little young, but she was very pretty. It was after about a year or so when she really started to come onto him strong and she was very serious in her endeavor.

Stacey acted like she was interested in what Michael did in the entertainment and music business. She made it quite obvious that she wasn't going to quit until she hooked up with Michael.

He didn't pay her any attention until around Thanksgiving or Christmas. By then Michael was thinking he needed to move from the present building into a larger one. Thanks to Kim, Michael came to realize that everyone working for him had his or her own agenda and motives. He thought it was none of his concern, though, as long as it didn't interfere with his business endeavors. He just wanted to work hard at staying legitimate, period, nothing else.

Michael had a personal concern about Stacey, which was that she was claiming to be in love with him. She would jump on every opportunity to help Michael. Because he needed security, he would put anyone he could on his staff that needed a job.

Doug Cooper, later to become head of security, met Michael through one of Aaron's girlfriends named Jacquie, James Fleming, aka Skin met Michael in 1993 while serving time in Oregon Prison camp in Oregon, Wisconsin State Prison farm.

Michael had previously seen Skin at a McDonald's on Northport Drive, which is when Skin asked Michael for a job after hearing about Michael's club business booming. So Michael decided to give him a chance. Then there was Robert Sutton, who Michael saw again, when he went home to Chicago, who also needed a job once he learned that Michael was coming up again.

Michael's club on East Washington was closed after about a year, so he rushed to get a facility on Stoughton Road, which made it his third club now. He was determined not to lose another club like he had the last one.

Michael was now not only over one hundred thousand dollars in debt due to municipal fines, rent capacity violations, underage drinking, drug being sold on premises and selling alcohol without a license. As started earlier, Michael was breaking all the rules. He almost wanted to quit, but the reminded himself that he had never quit anything and he was determined to be a success.

The City was slick. Instead of closing Michael down, they issued him citations one at a time. They left the fines stack up with the hope that he wouldn't be able to pay them, and when that happened they got a legal injunction for the police to close him down within 72 hours. Michael didn't care, and he opened the doors anyways. He reacted with a petition signed by a few hundred loyal customers, but the last minute something inspired him to back down. There was talk through local community that they were going to do whatever it took to close Michael down, and they swore to it.

The family, friends and parents of some the local patrons, who were mostly young girl's moms, would come down every once in a while to the entertainment. Still, they couldn't get past all the underage drinking and weed smoking. Before that, Michael thought they had come to an understanding that anyone who was caught doing anything unacceptable would not be permitted inside any longer. He would clean them up and send them home.

At this point, it was all about the music for Michael. He really was leaving the club one East Washington due to another offer presented to him. The job allowed him to in town around his family and still run his business, while working for a major music company.

He had job offers in promotions, productions, and even an A&R job with one company, and Michael he had the skills to do all three. Here he was with more than he could handle and making more money. He was doing all he could and know he needed to slow down. Eventually, he lost the club and wasn't thinking very clearly.

It was around this time that Michael gave up the job something later wished he never had done. The last construction project he worked on was the University of Wisconsin, Kohl Center, where worked as a laborer and excavator.

Michael was closed down and he was very hurt, and so were many others. People had come to his place to practice their craft and stay out of trouble, but now they had nowhere to go. The best thing that happened to Michael at the club on East Washington was his son Michael Lynn Brown, Jr., his first and only son. Michael Sr. was out of town a lot of the time.

He first found out from Kim when she called him at the club. She said, "I have something to tell you." "What" asked Michael? She started to cry on the telephone and she told him not to get mad. He promised he wouldn't, but he told her to hurry and tell him because it was making him mad by her taking so long to tell him what needed to be said. Michael had been thinking she crashed the car or something, but then she said, "I'm pregnant!" "Why in the world would I be mad about that?" he consoled. "I'll be right there as soon as I can get someone to fill in for me," he told Kim. "Don't come home now," she ordered. "Why not?" he asked. "I need you to work because we need the money," she instructed. "Besides, I'm going to Dawn's." Michael told he would meet her at home, and while she was still on the phone, he announced, "Drinks for everyone, we're going to have a baby!"

Then he asked her, "It is a boy?" "I don't know, silly." She laughed. "Okay baby, I'll see you at home," he told before hanging up. Michael passed out blunts to all who were at the club.

Nine months later, on April 13, 1997, they were still in business on East Washington when Michael, Jr. was born. He would be the only child Michael would have with Kim. Michael spoiled Kim during the entire pregnancy, while she would do her best to pick on him and try to get under his skin but that never worked. Michael loved Kim and the baby within her womb. They arrived as the hospital via limo, and just in the nick of time. The room at St. Mary's Birthing Center had already been prearranged, Michael having filled the room with balloons and flowers. Michael would be certain to give Kim and the baby the same treatment every month from then on. He held Kim hand all was through the birth. Michael noticed that the doctor was more or less around their age as well as a fan of the Chicago Bulls. "Great team!" Michael thought for a brief moment.

Kim went through labor like a pro. It was the most beautiful moment Michael has ever experienced, but he almost missed the outcome of it because he and the doctor were engrossed in the TV showing the Bulls game and Michael Jordan as he was taking them into the playoffs. Michael, Jr. Finally broke into the world with Michael, Sr. cutting the umbilical cord.

Thankfully the labor was uneventful and Kim could finally get some well-earned rest, Michael used that opportunity go to the club to check on his money and celebrate with his friend and employees, drinking until the next morning.

Michael's forth club, which was much smaller than the first three, was on Stoughton Road. It was really quite a dump, and he only had the joint for about a month. Most of him time was spent fixing up the place which included adding another bathroom and office. They painted the place and got all the necessary paperwork that was needed to open the club.

The first weekend they opened would turn out to be the last as hardly anyone showed. There wouldn't be any sneaking on Stoughton Road that night. Fortunately, for them though they had a huge following and received some free plugs on the radio. A flood people came that and there was a line all the way around the block. The club was already mobbed and they stuffed in like it was the last train to heaven.

When one person left, two more would come in. It was only filled and Michael wasn't surprised when the police came to shut it down because of exceeding the club's occupancy limit needless to say Michael was furious and did something he would later regret. He opened up the garage door and let the people inside while some were exiting the other end. The police obviously couldn't handle all the people, as there were just too many. But Michael ended up making more trouble that night and new the City would certainly refuse to issue a permit for Michael to open the club.

Spring 2007 turned into summer and Michael was out of a job and a club. He still had some money left, so he slid it back into the drug scene to keep his head above water. He felt like a dope fiend, not having a club. An owner with nothing to own, a music man without his instrument. He was floored. Michael was looking for a facility where he could reopen the club, but that wasn't going to be an easy task after what had happened at Stoughton Road. There were actually death threats and public officials told him that they were going to get him if he opened another club.

The search for another facility took time, and Michael didn't have the drive he once possessed due to all the closures he had already experienced. He was feeling lost without a club and it hurt all his other business senses. There was nothing he could do at the moment but jump back into the drug scene. There was no question, Michael had to provide for his family and he thought that a little weed couldn't hurt. The thought, "There's the problem and this is how it starts. New life, game over with sin and death."

CHAPTER 10

BUSINESS & FRIENDS, HOW MANY OF US HAVE THEM?

Jim was an old friend that Michael met through Aaron who had come back into town to hang with them. Jim and Aaron were pitching in with Michael to get the club going as well as hustling. They were working and buying a little something every so often. All the dudes who had worked for Michael were tired of doing nothing and they were ready to get back to work. Mostly because it was such a cool job and the money was good, not to mention the perks. Michael wanted to get another club opened.

Jim was waiting to receive a big settlement from a lawsuit, and he wanted to go into business with Michael.

He pleaded with Michael for a business venture, knowing Michael needed the money. Not only was Jim willing to put in the money, but also he was willing to sign his name on the dotted line at the bottom of contracts. Michael wanted Jim and others in business with him. "We could all be very successful, wealthy, and legitimate if we all worked together," Michael thought.

Jim, however needed to find a place to stay, plus he didn't have money, food or clothes because he had just returned from Colorado so he didn't have anything with him at the moment. Michael knew exactly what to do. He needed a place of business and Jim needed a place to stay and he was getting all this money from a lawsuit. So Michael was willing to help Jim out. He figured he would get his money back plus some good interest on the return.

Michael helped Jim get into a sublet apartment down the street from his house off east Washington. Michael had just recently moved into a three-bedroom condo. There was one room for Michael and Kim, one for Michael, Jr. One for Jazzman and Keya, who stayed with them every other weekend, things came to mine. They had moved there right around the time of Michael, Jr.'s birth. They lived at 4650 Morningside Road where they would stay while taking care of Michael's sisters, Sasha and Tricia. They also took care of Bruce for a while then they all moved in with Michael's sister Tammy, who at the time was staying at Wexford Ridge.

While living on Hayes Road some pretty significant things happened. Besides the fact that they moved into a much nicer place, they also had to take in Michael's brothers and sister because they had been left alone several times. Their mother was consumed by her drug addiction, and she would leave them alone for days at times. They lived in a really bad neighborhood at the time. It was where Michael's brother Matt had been shot and a couple of their friends had been killed there as well. His mother was evicted and the Sheriff moved the family's belonging into storage. All of the family photos, which happened to be in a collection in the safety of his mother and siblings. Michael's sister Tammy was in college and his brother Matt was in jail, so Michael again was left to do everything and take care of everyone.

The winter turned out to be very special. Kim and Michael took a long needed vacation to New York for New Year's Pennsylvania. Now they were close to downtown Manhattan, just minutes from Time Square and next door to one of Kim's favorite restaurants, "Popeye's Chicken." Reservations were all cancelled due to the snowstorm. No one was allowed inside, so they slept most of the next days and it was very romantic for Michael to make love to Kim most of the night.

They finally awoke after a short nap and a long night of beautiful lovemaking. It was around 12:00 a.m. and the countdown to the New Year. They walked to Time Square and ate at a big sports restaurant. They took pictures and then went to a club. They laughed so much with each other and had really good fun. They danced all night until they couldn't dance any more. It was just so nice doing these things with Kim and, truthfully, Michael realized his missed doing these things with her.

They walked around Time Square and took pictures before calling a cab back to the hotel where they stayed for the next couple of days. Things were very romantic, as they would light candles, drink wine and listen to the radio while enjoying each other company throughout the night. Unfortunately, all good things come to an end, and do after a couple of days of lovemaking and romanticizing, they went back home. Kim drove most of the way home saying it was the safest and best vacation she ever had in her life.

It was right after they returned home that Michael ran into some old friends. The first was Ron Wilson, who had helped Michael construct his first stage at his first club. He then ran into Ollie, aka John Morkin, who came to visit Michael from Minnesota. Ron and Michael went to visit Ollie when he was still a newlywed. Ollie was a family man, and also a businessman who was very successful at whatever he did. Ron was in his second marriage with his first child, while Ollie was a multi-millionaire who was looking for his next good investment, and at the time, Michael seemed like an excellent investment. Ollie and his father owned "Spring Grove Livestock," which was the biggest and best in the country. Michael and Ollie were old high school buddies and enjoyed reminiscing with each other. Ron and Michael would spend the summer at Ollie ranch and the three of them hung out like the Three Amigos.

Michael and Kim eventually moved around the corner where Kim found the most beautiful place on Morningside Road, which happened to be where God had blessed Michael with his son Michael Jr.

Jim and Michael had a spot where they hustled. Allegedly, Jim had tried to rape Angie, who was a friend of Andrea, aka Alayha. She was a little wild even though she played the shy role. Michael met Alayha one day going over to Herman friend's house to serve some product and she was there with two other girls. They acted older but come to find out there were only teenagers. Michael was only there to see Herman.

The teenagers wanted to come with Michael, and he later learned they were stalking him for some time, as they knew all about him. Alayha also claimed that she wanted to get in the music business, so Michael took her to a music convention in Chicago that was sponsored by WGCI Radio. This was the big break for guys who wanted to break into the music industry. While they were there, Alayha slept with some of Michael's guys who she really didn't know. Michael was disgusted because he had been there and done that before and this wasn't the time or the place. He thought, "You live and you learn."

At the music convention, Michael wanted to pick up new knowledge as well as new talent. He also ended up giving a little speech to those that were there who wanted to listen to him.

Afterward Corey and Crucial Conflict along with Heavy D invited him. They introduced Michael as an overnight success with multi talents as well as someone who they knew worked hard for his money.

They were invited backstage to the tables where they had been eating. Michael went along as well as to take care of some business that he needed to take care of and even hollered at Twista for a minute. He was sitting all alone and quiet, shining brighter than the biggest star.

Twista and Michael agreed to hook up again real soon. Michael assured him that the shooting incident at his club wasn't Twista's fault and that it could have happened to anyone. Some true legends were there and they kicked it with some of the best and brightest starts like R. Kelly, Franky Beverly, Shante Moore, Shante Savage, and Ron Isley and there was s special tribute to Curtis Mayfield that evening.

Michael then hooked up with Jim again soon after that night. He soon became Jim's friend, loan shark and dope connection. Once more, Jim got his money and new business partner status once again.

They got serious and down to business. Jim did all he could to prove himself to Michael, even though he knew it wasn't necessary to do so. Jim found a place they could open up on the West Side in one of the wealthiest parts of Middleton, Wisconsin.

Michael through it would be good to bring in a different type of crowd so they decided to open the new club on Seybold Road, which is a nice area. Michael was going to stay in the background as a silent partner this time around, as they had to consider the warning and notice from before. This included a new warning from the realty company who didn't necessarily agree with the city's policy or that they were blackballing Michael.

It was in everyone's best interest to let Jim handle everything. Jim came up with the name "Starlight Productions" for the business. Michael thought that the name sounded gay, but at least it wouldn't bring any attention back to Michael.

Michael wanted to make the business legitimate and successful so that at the right time would smear dog filth in the faces of those who were trying to pull him down. Michael was determined to make this club the best successful venture yet.

It was the largest place that they had ever opened some 44,000 square feet. It had two large bathrooms and a lot of different adjacent rooms. This club had two smaller offices and one bigger office for Michael. Instantaneously, the place became a hit.

They were right back to throwing concerts and everything else. One of their first concerts was with a group called "Big Vanilla," a local artist from Chicago alone with L.S.G. They would later hold talent contest.

Sunday night was always ladies night with free food and drinks, and it was always a hit. They had amateur dance tryouts and Rob brought Michael out of retirement by getting him to dance for all the ladies/ Michael began drinking like crazy sometimes all day, at times he would have some kind of drink in his hand while mixing it up with the crowd.

Jim had his own office and was not hooking up with all the girls. Michael found Jim's hidden skills and determination. He used to be a longtime supervisor at the grocery store, which is where he and Aaron met and worked together in the past. Michael was introduced to him ten year prior.

Jim wasn't ready to deal with the responsibilities of running a recording studio, artist, and nightclub with strippers, employees, customers and the escort service and the female subcontractors. They were turning tricks on him and walking all over him.

Even Butter had to come out of retirement to help. It was Fossil, Doug, Rob, Skin, and Michael once again. At times even Vic would help out when he wasn't robbing someone or gangbanging. H.B. would also come and help every once in a while. They were hired but they were quickly relieved of the duties for fear of any added trouble.

Michael's sister Tammy was working for them also. She was in charge when she was around, which was good except for her feisty mouth. The club was always packed with new crowds as well as the regular clientele. After a while, it became just like the other clubs, bad but good at the same time. Michael had more security and, among other things, some new equipment, and the planned to officially get liquor license this time around as well.

They learned they were not in the jurisdiction of Madison, but instead in the city of Middleton, which gave, them better options and different authorities to deal with. The city's Mayor was a farmer whose office was on his farm. He seemed fairly cool until someone convinced him that Michael and crew were bad news.

The local police were every bit the country boys. The escort service was booming and Michael was in and out of town like never before. He would only travel out of town mainly for the companies he worked as well as for his own music productions.

The crowds continued to get bigger, and the day finally came when there was just too much to take care of. Michael was making more money, which meant more problems. For Michael to keep focus on just one of two things was damn near impossible. He started to really dig Stacey, and she started digging Michael even more.

Now that she had graduated from high school she was always around to talk to, it was easy for them to hook up. Although Michael didn't think that she really understood that, she was only for a good ear and sounding board. Her answer to every problem was to tell Michael to chill out, spend time with her and have another drink. At the time, it seemed to work and it all started when they had a long talk one night.

Stacey was fighting with her parents. Michael instructed her to listen to, honor and respect her parents. He tried to explain to her that life was too short and too important. Stacey expressed her desire to go to college and make something of her life, but said she also enjoyed hanging out. This happened around the time of the clubs at Stoughton and Seybold Roads. It was on Stacey 18th birthday that she and Michael messed around for the first time.

It was in a hotel after one of Michael's infamous hotel parties. Stacey and Michael were the last ones to leave. They got down real fast, deep and hard with both of them uncertain of how it even started. They had sex and felt something, which were probably the effects of the alcohol. Michael and Stacey were building some sort of a special bond between them, but Michael would never fully understand what or why.

Michael wanted Stacey to be better and different than all the rest of the girls up to that point. At one point, he thought he wanted her to be his girl. They started hanging out at "Starlight Production" together. Michael was "blowing up" and he was getting high no matter what. The club was way better than before. As with the rest of the clubs, Kim and the kids would come by to visit, but usually in the daytime or whenever Michael hadn't been home in a while.

He would tell the girls to become scarce as they couldn't have them coming around and smothering him with their dance costumes on while his kids were playing on the stage and singing with the microphones. Michael would record and film the kids and even joining in and singing with them. They had a lot of fun doing that.

They were also gambling for the big money all the time and the cops were over there all the time looking for something or someone.

There were nights of fighting and sometimes a couple of shootings. Only by the grace of God, no one was killed or seriously hurt in any of Michael's businesses. Michael wasn't involved in anything illegal at this point, other than the fact he smoked a little weed. He was trying to keep it as legal as possible and he believed he had accomplished that. Vic, on the other hand, was in trouble. His own people were trying to kill him for robbing them. They had dudes on their own women and Michael was drinking more alcohol then he did water. For some reason, he always felt as if something was missing, but just couldn't pinpoint it.

Then, one day it happened. They got raided, arrested and booked, but luckily released on bail. Michael unfortunately was rearrested two days later on other charges. Stacey, on the other hand got her apartment soon after that, less than a mile from Michael and Kim's house. It was behind Embers Restaurant, which was across the street from Michael's old club at 3824 East Washington.

After that, Michael stayed home and out of the streets more and more. He was trying to make it again and had to figure things out. He was in a deep rut and he couldn't get out of it. God was calling his name so loud and clear then, but he just couldn't hear his call as that time. Be it known that now Michael can hear God and his voice is coming through loud and clear.

The rest is History. It was the "Beginning of the end" of life with "Sin and Satan" August 21, 1997.

CHAPTER 11

ROBBERIES 1-3 OF 5 INDICTED FEDERALLY

July 31, 1997. First, there was the Wendy's robbery. Michael confirmed that he had nothing to do with that. But he does remember someone joking about how Alphonso Dean, aka Fossil had a hard time getting his 300 pound body through the drive through window.

August 14, 1997. Secondly, there was the Kohl's Grocery Store robbery. Michael only knew that James Fleming, aka Skin, who always was talking about robbing people and places like Kohl's, committed this robbery. Skin was obsessed with robbery and he bragged about his robberies all the time. Especially, with anybody who would listen. Michael would tell him he didn't want to hear it and that he needs to keep his business to himself. The reason Michael knew that Skin had done it was because he asked Michael to bring Brandy McClanan, his girlfriend and some cocaine. After they arrived, that is when he first heard anything about the robbery.

Michael called Skin to ask for directions to his place. In fact, Michael called him a couple of times because he had never been to that town before. He had only been through Ederton, Wisconsin and he surely wasn't familiar with it.

Surprisingly, once he arrived to meet Skin. He knocked on the door and Stacey opened the door. Michael was a little jealous but mostly disappointed with her for being there.

Of course, Michael didn't tell Kim about his feeling for Stacey, he just told her about the situation. It was then that Michael knew Skin was having sex with Stacey, and she surely had to have been involved with the robberies.

Michael didn't say anything and walked to the back of the house where Skin was. He noticed a large sum of money lying on the bed as well as some food stamps as well. That was when he noticed his Cousin Victor Caldwell sitting in the corner.

"Did you bring the stuff?" asked Skin. "Yeah, it's right here," Michael, said removing the cocaine from his pocket. Michael wanted to talk to Skin alone.

Other than weed, Michael never knew nor would allow Stacey to see any drugs. But he knew that if she was here with Skin, there is a reasonable probability that she was getting high.

Skin paid Michael for the drugs and gave him a few bucks for gas for bringing Brandy out there. Michael left with a nagging feeling about Stacey and her possible involvement in Vic and Skins' madness.

Thirdly, there was the robbery of the Great Midwestern Bank on August 20, 1997. Michael knew only after the fact that Skin had committed this robbery.

Michael had just come home from a long night at the club, drinking, doing drugs. Skin called him no sooner as he walked into the door. Skin asked Michael "Can you come out here and pick me up. I'm in Milwaukee?" Michael knew that Skin's wife was at home waiting on him. Michael told him that he just walked in the door and he was tired and the he would send him a bus ticket.

Skin told Michael "I don't want to come back to Madison, I want you to come out here because it might be the last time you see me." Michael asked, "What's wrong?" "Just meet me at my dad's house," Skin told him. Michael agreed and told Skin he would be there in about an hour to meet up with him.

Michael was just about to open the door to leave for Milwaukee. "Where are you going, you just walked in?" Kim asked. "I have to go and meet Skin, I think he's in trouble again," Michael said. "Can I go with you?" Kim asked. "No, I'll be right back," he replied. Kim got upset. "Then you need to take your daughter with you, because I got an appointment to go to." Kim never liked the fact that just about every night she would have to sleep by herself in a lonely cold bed. Michael reluctantly got Keya ready to ride with him to Milwaukee.

Michael knew Skin had to have done something serious by the way, he sounded over the phone. Skin never involved Michael in any of the gun battles or anything serious so, Michael thought it wasn't a problem if he brought Keya along with him.

They arrived in Milwaukee about an hour later. Michael called Skin for directions. Skin gave him the direction to a strip mall on the North side of town. Skin, Rob and Jill were there when he arrived. They were all happy to see Michael. Skin and Rob told Michael that they had a gift for him for all he had done for them. "Were going to take you and Keya on a shopping spree." They purchase gifts for him and Keya. Something Michael had done for them and their kids.

Michael found it a little strange that they never had any money, and never did they offer any explanation, not that Michael was going to ask for one. They shopped for about an hour and then went out to eat at one of Michael's favorite places, Speed Queen Bar-B-Q. They all sat and ate a wonderful meal, then headed back to Skin's father house.

Once inside the house, Skin took Michael aside and threw a wad of money to him, "This is for being a friend and always looking out for everyone." Michael accepted the money and didn't question where it came from. "What's the matter? You look like you just seen a ghost or something? It isn't enough, do you want more?" That is when it dawned on Michael, considering the large sum of money that was spent on the shopping spree; Michael calculated every bit by a couple thousand.

Michael was always willing to help a friend. He had sponsored many shopping sprees. But he told Skin, "Nah, I appreciated it. My rent and club bills are overdue and this will surely help," Michael said putting the wad of money in his pocket. Skin interjected "We may need you to something for us anyways, that we can all profit from before leaving Madison." "Where are you going?" Michael asked he knew something was up. "Honestly, don't ask any questions so I won't have to lie to you. But I was thinking on going down south. Rob was thinking about visiting his grandparents." Skin said. Michael didn't push the issue any further. Skin said, "Go ahead and take your daughter home. While you there, do mind picking up my girl Brandy?" Skin's asked Michael. "I got you," Michael said. As Michael began to leave, Rob asked, "Why don't you leave your car and let Jill give you a ride back to Madison. She had to go there anyway. Oh yeah, don't forget to bring your limo so we can really party." Rob asked. "Sure," agreed Michael. Just before they were ready to go Skin called Jill into the back room. Michael was curiosity was killing him. He peered around the corner and saw Skin get a show box and remove some money from it and gave it to Jill. Then he gave her a hug.

Michael, Keya and Jill were on their way back to Madison in Jill's car. This would be only Michael's third time hanging around Jill. He wanted to feel her out and find out what was going on. Michael made light conversation. Jill was willing to tell him everything. So he just sat there listening. She explained that Skin and Rob had over fifty thousand dollars in that house. "It ridiculous, to have all that money," Jill said. He was initially shocked, but he didn't want to lead on as if he didn't know what was going on. To keep her talking Michael just answered with "For real."

They talked for the entire ride. The conversation was so interesting Michael didn't realized that they were already in Madison. By the end of their conversation, Michael was worried.

He was concerned for their safety. Michael just looked at Jill and said as he was getting out of her car, "I enjoyed out conversation. Just keep yourself safe, and don't get yourself into any trouble.

He felt sorry for Jill because neither of them really knew what she had gotten herself into, by merely associating with Rob and Skin. At this point, Michael only had a piece of the picture. He was still trying to piece it all together.

Michael had taken his limo to the paint shop for a new paint job. He used his limo mostly for the transportation of the groups of acts coming to perform at his club or for recording sessions and the escort services. Michael had been seriously considering starting a limo car service.

Michael picked up the limo and headed home. When he arrived, Kim was still a little mad about his late evenings then jumping up first thing in the morning and heading for Milwaukee without her made her even madder. Handing her a wad of money and the packages of clothes that Skin's and Rob brought for the kids changed her attitude. Then Michael told her he was leaving again to return to Milwaukee. She was a little easy about Michael's statement. He knew in her head her wheels were spinning. Thinking on how to spend this money. Michael drove back to Milwaukee.

Michael called Skin again to get directions. Skin told Michael to meet him at Grand Avenue Mall, which was the largest mill downtown Milwaukee.

By this time, the entire crew got there. Rob, Skin, Stacey, Angie, Victor Caldwell (aka Slick Vic), Brandy and Michael and a few girls he really didn't know all went out to party.

Michael was driving his limo and Stacey was driving with Cali and some other girl she grew up with. Cali was a real hot chick, half-black and half-white. They all went to the mall and went shopping with Rob and Skin. There wasn't one person that didn't get something new to wear for that day.

They were all at the mall for about an hour. Fortunately, for Michael, while there he had heard that NBA legend Latrelle Sprewell was supposed to be at the mall, and sure enough, he was. Michael and Mr. Sprewell met and talked for a minute while shopping for some Hilfiger. Michael went into the store on the first floor while Stacey was already at the counter to pay for her purchases. Latrelle Sprewell, was a forward for the New York Knicks's and is well known for grabbing rebounds, blocking shots, scoring points and the fight he had with his head coach prior to being traded to the Knicks's. He was heading for the counter just as Stacey was. Stacey was also a fan and Latrelle was hollering at Stacey.

Michael was tripping because Stacey was one of many to Latrelle, who had all these girls around him. Latrelle looked up and noticed the look on Michael's face. "What's up?" said Latrelle. 'Nothing man, just chilling," Michael said. "Oh my gosh, does she belong to you?" he said pointing to Stacey. "Something like that," was all Michael could come back with. "But it's all good." Michael said handing Latrelle his business card and said, "If you're ever in the need for a limo service, recording studio or club for partying, give me a call." "That's what's up. I may just do that." Latrelle said looking at the card and putting it in his pocket.

Michael went to his limo. He didn't know where everybody else was but he knew they knew where the car is parked. As Michael began walking across the street, he noticed Stacey touching Laetrile's hand.

Soon there was a brunch of girls around him, including Cali. She was a fine red bone with Carmel complexion and funny colored eyes. There was no doubt in Michael's mind that Cali is a traffic stopper.

Michael waited for the others to come back to the limo, as he was ready to leave. He noticed a Cadillac parked next to his limo with a 'for sale' sign in the window. It was sky blue with true spoke and blue leather interior. Michael was checking the car out when everybody appeared from nowhere.

After they left the mall, they drove to a hotel on 27th street. There was a Hispanic girl working the front desk. She gave Michael the sex me look. He knew she was interested. Michael flirted with her and he convinced her to rent five rooms at a discounted rate under the table. The normal cost for these five rooms would have been a lot more than they paid. The Hispanic girl told him that she wouldn't be inputting this transaction in there system. So they would have to be out before the manager came in at 11 o'clock.

Each of them had their own rooms including Cali. This was just another party for them, which they did quite well and often, which was at least two or three times a week, but this time it wasn't Michael who was footing the bill.

They all went out and picked up party supplies, which consisted of junk food and alcohol. They all knew that Michael doesn't leave home without some weed and nose candy.

These guys of course, had more on mind their minds. This was right up Michael's alley. He made a call to a few local guys to add some flavor to their mix. Michael requested one woman from each race.

Sometime late, there was a knock at the door. Since Michael was waiting for the girls to arrive. He peeked through the peephole. When he opened, the door standing before him was five absolutely stunning women. The Black girl and the first one through the door was red head with long hair & high cheekbones. She looked like Nia Long, but she was lighter. She was about 5'5" with a fat ass. The Hispanic girl, second through the door was a cross between Angie Martinez and J-Lo. She definitely had the body. The third through the door was European girl. She was tall maybe 5'8" with some nice mouth full of breast. She had a supermodel body and nice lips. Last through the door was the Asian girl. She was about 5'3" with a compact body. Nice ass tits and body. "Now, let's party," was all Michael said after the girls entered the room. These four women shut the whole party down. Every man in the room stopped what they were doing just to admire the four different flavors.

That was a night surely to be remembered and the source of several wet nights for Michael. One of the things Michael was glad for was he wasn't footing the bill for this party for a change.

They had all the booze they could want, weed and junk food and some cocaine. They also had plenty of women. Stacey started acting crazy and possessive, one of the girls arrived. Michael told Stacey, "You shouldn't have anything to say, stay cool." She simply brushed Michael off and walked away. Later that night Michael had saw Stacey going into Skin's room. Normally he would have tripped, but not tonight. There were just so many girls half-naked running around.

Michael first took the Asian girl into a room the one at the end of the hall. He name was Spicy. She undressed and Michael's mouth just opened like "Damn she is beautiful nude too." The room at the end of the hall has mirrors on the ceiling, mirrors on the wall so Michael could see it all. They had sex everywhere, on the floor, on the sink, on the bed, on the coffee table, even with him back up against the wall. Michael knew that he needed to save some energy for the other girls.

Next Michael took the Spanish girl. Her name was Desire. She undressed and her body was perfect. They had sex on the bed and the floor. Michael learned a new word that night. She kept repeating "aye pappy, aye pappy." It wasn't long before someone was knocking on the door. Michael kept going as if he didn't hear it. They were engrossed and neither wanted to break their rhythm. She didn't stay long.

Then the Black girl was escorted to the room at the end of the hall. Her name was Delight. It wasn't long after he learned her name that they were getting it on. She was like flexible and she could put her body in some unusual position.

Lastly, there was the European girl. Her name was Passion. Michael wanted her to be the last, because he wanted to take his time and put it down. He would watch her facial expressions while he was fucking her. The looks alone would be worth a price in itself.

There were those damn knocks again. Michael ignored them. This time Stacey let her presence be known. Michael just exploded like a time bomb and the knocks continued.

"Bitch, get away from my man and get your ass out here!!" Stacey was yelling from the other side of the door. Stacey was obviously mad because Michael was doing his thing. She embarked on another crazy trip, yelling and screaming like a mad women. Michael finally told the Asian girl to get dressed.

Stacey finally went away, but not before, she kicked the door a couple of times. Rob and Skin got Stacey away from the door. Michael decided he would just get fucked up.

Stacey's glares at Michael were the looks of a mad woman, the music was playing, and the guys were finished with the girls and started shooting dice. Eventually Stacey got all crazy, so Michael took her into the room. When they got there, it was on like "Donkey Kong." Michael fucked her brains out on the bed, on the floor, in the bathtub. Stacey was screaming "Do it to me baby, do me!!! Let's go half on a baby." Michael knew at that very moment he was in love with Stacey.

Michael awoke the next morning and everyone was gone. He was all alone in the room

With quite a bad hangover and couldn't remember much about the night before. The phone rang. Michael answered it, a voice said, "My manager is here and you better get out of that room. He's about to call the police." The phone disconnected. Michael knew he hadn't done anything illegal or at least he didn't remember if he did anything illegal. He just remembered the deal he made with the desk clerk last night. Michael grabbed his clothes and went downstairs. Once he got to the front desk the manager came from his office in the back and started screaming, "You people get out of here; you didn't pay for your rooms. I'm calling the police if you don't leave right now," he accused. Michael didn't want any problems with the police. So they all left.

Once Michael got outside, he noticed a van parked next to Stacey's car. "Where did you'll get that?" asked Michael. Skin told Michael that they just purchased the van. "Whose name is it in?" asked Michael. "It's in Stacey's name," answered Skins. Michael just looked over at Stacey thinking to himself "Dumb bitch." In her defense, she said "I didn't know it was in my name until they had already done it." "Yeah, right," was all Michael could say.

The hotel manager came out into the parking lot and started screaming, "The police are coming, so you guys better get out of here!!" "I'm out of here," said Michael as he jumped into his limo. "Where are you going?" asked Stacey. Michael told them that he was going to the city. They knew Michael was talking about Chicago.

Rob and Skin had asked Michael to purchase a large amount of cocaine for them the night before. He already had the money in his limo. Michael was on a mission.

They were in the City in no time. While he was there, he checked on the club situation. Michael had become a custom to being in the City again. He frequently came to Chicago; to go shopping, take care of some music related business and of course getting the product. There was always work to be done. He figured he would get a room and turn it into his laboratory to cut, mix and cook the cocaine.

As usual, Michael calls his connection and told him what he needed. His connect was an old childhood friend named Yogi or Yog for short and the one rule they have is to call in your order before coming to pick it up. Yog was one of the best dealers in Chicago. The rumor was Yog was worth a couple of million. Michael couldn't figure out why Yog was still in the game if he was worth a couple of million. After getting all this money, Michael finally concluded that it was plain old greed.

Yog's mother was a schoolteacher, but his father was a stone cold hustler. Michael didn't even know if Yog's father was still alive. Yog's uncle, who worked for the Chicago Police Department, always had things ready by the time Michael got there. If things weren't ready, it only took a minute to get things ready. But for some reason Yog told Michael it was going to be a minute and that he would give him a holla when it was ready.

To burn time Michael went to his cousin's house to wait for Yog's call. They lived on 15th in Harvey Illinois. Michael's Uncle Charles his long time girlfriend Marcel, his three daughters Marty, Markets, Marashalon, and two sons who also lived there. Michael would go there to talk business, because he felt safer there then on a phone. If anyone asked about his conversations, he would simply tell them it's about the music business.

One time in that area, Michael experienced an evening that could have turned deadly. He was robbed and stripped of for his chain, money and clothes. He was left but naked for dead in sub zero weather. The culprit also stole all the Christmas present and his 1989 Oldsmobile 225.

Uncle Charles wasn't a blood relative, but he had known Michael since he was born. Michael remembered well all the parties at his house back in the 70's. Uncle Charles had kids from a couple of different friends of Michael's mother. Aunt Nita, who is Michael's mother closest friends, and Marcel, the three of them grew up together. They used to say that Marcel stole Nita's man once upon a time. Michael's mother would say that Uncle Charles was just a man whore anyway. Uncle Charles used to be quite the basketball player and could have gone pro, Michael heard. But he settled for the life of a family man. He worked more than 30 years in the steel mill and did what he had to do to take care of his kids.

Yog's finally called back a couple hours later and told Michael to meet him in downtown Chicago. It was there that Michael made the largest purchase of cocaine from Yog. He was buying a kilo. You never knew it wasn't all his, but Yog didn't need to know everything. He was going to split it with Rob and Skin, who actually paid for the whole kilo, they were only getting half. With this purchase, Michael was planning to get out the game once he's done selling it.

Michael's legitimate business was suffering and his rent needed to be made current. It was already the middle of the month. And his club, studio, escort service and limo service weren't making enough moony collectively to pay all his bills. At times, he didn't know which business to focus all his attention on. He wasn't an accountant, but overall his projects were successful and he always brought in a lot of money. But at the end of the day, what he was making kept him afloat.

Michael meets up with Yog and got the cocaine. They made small talk. Michael had to figure how to get out of downtown without being pulled over by the cops. Michael hid the cocaine in his secret compartment. Michael knew that dirty cops might pull him over and find the kilo. He's going to jail or he could possibly end up dead somewhere.

Michael was able to make it back to his hotel room without incident. The hotel was on 116, right along Interest 94 close to the Indiana border. Michael made a quick stop at the local grocery store and purchased items he knew he would need to mix and cut the kilo. Michael retrieved the cocaine from the theft proof compartment. As soon as he got to his room, he immediately got down to business. This cocaine looks like diamond sparkling, but most people call it fish-scales. He got his purity tester, and he put in a small amount of the cocaine. He let the cocaine go to the bottom, after 3 minutes he knew the purity of cocaine. He finished cutting and mixing the kilo, into two. He bagged up eight ounces, which was called a "Big Eights." Once he delivered the cocaine to Rob and Skin, he was out of here.

He had four fake deodorant and hair spray cans that he got from town. They had screw off lids and the bottom allowed him to hide items inside.

Michael kept the half-uncut key for himself, and took the other half that he had made an entire key and took it to Rob and Skin. They were so excited when he showed them the kilo. Michael thought to himself it's time to get paid.

He called Do or Die's manager so that they could meet. Michael had to put down a deposit for them to perform at his club in a couple of days. This time the party was going to have a different theme. A pajama jam. He took care of his business with Do or Die and securing their services. Their people knew that the party at the club they were going to have a ball out of control. Michael has had Do or Die to his studio and club before.

Other groups have came out before, groups they all took to a liking to Michael Crucial Conflict, Synpas, Dub, J.D. Walker, Psycho Drama, C.O.G., Twista and many other groups. Michael had even been in talks with the Brats and Jesse Powell to have them perform at his club.

Michael was very busy with his businesses and trying to figure out where to put his money. He got calls from fans and groupies who hung out at the club. Usually, on a good day. He would get 20 to 30 calls from the ladies wanting to know what was going to be happening this weekend, especially when they hear advertisement over the radio and on TV informing the public that this week there was going to be a special guest. He knew this performance would be spectacular. Sometimes even when things would be put together at the last minute, he would still make more money than ever.

To indict Michael for crimes that does not meet the definition of a federal crime. The Hobbs Act and felon in possession of a firearm were the charges that made his case federal. Michael later learned that the government could indict a ham sandwich and get a conviction.

The grand jury in any jurisdiction in America has a vested interest in indicting someone. Most have worked in Prison Industrial Complex or have worked for a company that relies on governmental contracts for support of the Prison Industrial Complex. There is no justice, when the prisons are filled with just-us. The prisons in America are the modern day plantations.

“Innocent until proven guilty?” “No, the reality is you’re guilty until proven guilty.”

CHAPTER 12

STATE CHARGES, PROSTITUTION, SKIN AND ROB AS FUGITIVES

Michael received a page from his attorney. He used to call him and it seemed every time he did call he wanted money. It seemed as if the attorney somehow always knew when Michael had cash on hand. Michael thought it had something to do with the groups he lined up for any particular evening. If that wasn't the case, he knew it had to do with some criminal activity since Michael's attorney would always fill him in on what was happening around him.

Even if Michael wasn't involved, his attorney thought he should know certain information. It could also have been about some contract negotiations or some other such thing. He would sometimes help Michael out with this aspect of the business. Although his attorney didn't necessarily specialize in this area.

Michael then received a page from his mother. It was a 911 page; he knew that it was something important and seriously wrong. Michael went back to his hotel and the first call he made was to Kim. She answered before he could get a word in, "Where you and what are are you doing?" "I'm in Chicago, taken care of some business," he explained to her, he went on "I had to get some packages and I had to get the group paid so they'll show up for tonight's show." Kim asked him, "Have you seen tonight's news on the television? Your club was raided last night, haven't you heard, and they busted some girls for prostitution and they're looking for you for questioning." "Questioning for what?" Michael asked. "I wasn't even there last night. I had nothing to do with what ever happened there last night." He continued.

Without thinking, Michael said out loud, "I got money, I got work, and I'm not coming back." Kim asked him, "So, you would just up and leave me and then kids?" "Of course not, but I'm tired of the police messing with my businesses and me when I'm doing everything in my power to stay legitimate," he said.

Kim told him that his mother and his attorney have been trying to get in contact with him. Michael told her that he was going to have to call her back after he called his mother and attorney. "I'll see what I can find out. But stay where you're at for right now." Kim said. They ended their call and Michael called his mother. "Hey baby, where you at?" she asked him. "I'm in the City taking care of some business." She knew exactly what that meant. She said, "You know they raided your club last night and arrested Jim and some girls? It's all over the news." Michael turned on the TV and the news first story was about him. News announcer: "Music producer and Promoter Michael L. Brown, is wanted for questioning in connection with running a prostitution ring." Michael sat at the edge of the bed listening to the news. Michael told his mother, "They're overstating what they claimed I'm involved in. Let me go so I can call my lawyer. I'm tired of these people always trying to give me a bogus rap." She said, "Whatever you do, don't run. Come back. I know you didn't do anything wrong and you weren't even there, but you must come back to prove it." Michael told his mother, "All right, mom, I won't take off." He wasn't surprised that she knew exactly what he was thinking, mothers know their children.

Michael called his attorney and the first thing he was asked, "Where are you." His attorney asked. "I'm in Chicago taken care of some business." He informed his attorney.

"Well they raided your club last night and they're looking for you for questioning," he old Michael. "Yeah, I'm aware of that." He replied. "There is no warrant for your arrest as of yet," he said. Michael asked, "What should I do?" His attorney told him, "come back and let's fight it, but don't do anything until you hear from Me." his attorney told him and ended their call.

Michael left the hotel room after talking to everyone over the phone. He went to Skin's and Rob's room and he told them what happened. At same time, Skin and Rob had told Michael that the girls who drove them to their robbery had called and told them that the police knew she was involved with the robbery because someone seen her car or something like that. Neither skin nor did anyone believe her story. But either way Michael wasn't concerned because he had nothing to do with it.

Of course, Michael didn't want his friends to get caught either. Skin, Shecka, Rob's girlfriend, and Brandy were arguing that Skin and Rob were giving Angie and Stacey too much money. Brandy and Shecka didn't like it, but Brandy seemed more upset then Shecka.

It was obviously out of jealousy and they were stressing that Skin and Rob should not trust Angie, Stacey or Jill their getaway drivers. Skin was under the impression that the two of them were connected and that is why he called Jill on the phone. It wasn't long before he hung up without saying much. He told her he would call her right back and then he went on a rampage, smoking crack. Rob, on the other hand, was cool and collective. He told Skin, "Pack you stuff we're leaving as soon as I get back from shopping for my kids." Skin said, "I agree, I've been waiting to take a trip down south. Maybe I'll get a chance to hook up with Master P."

Michael left and went to his room to think. On the way, he stopped for something to drink at an outside vending machine because he wanted a chaser for his Hennessey.

While out there, he heard a loud voice like someone was fighting. Once he hit the corner, he had seen two girls in their early twenties fighting with this older white guy in a new SUV. They were screaming, "Help! Help! He's raping me!" Michael ran over to the SUV and asked, "What the hell is going on?" one of the girls asked him, "Please help us." Michael asked the guy, "Who are you and what the hell is going on?" the guy said, "There just a couple of whores." Michael asked the girls, "Do you want to be in there with him?" "Hello no!" they both responded. "Well then give me my money and wallet back." The guy order, then he said, "Then you can go." Michael asked the girls, "Do you have his wallet? If so, give it back and let's go," he said, one of the girls gave the man his wallet back and they got out of the SUV. Michael told the guy to "Get out of here." The guy put the truck onto drive and drove off. When the truck was inches past Michael he looked at the license plate, which was from Indiana with one of those doctor tags on it. Once the SUV was gone Michael turned around and he had not noticed how fine these girl where until he got a full view of them both.

One of them was a tall slender, white girl who looked like a supermodel, and the other looked like she was half-Spanish, medium build, with a big butt and nice size breasts. Spicy and sexy who spoke with an accent, "Thank you, that guy was a real jerk." "No problem." Michael offered. Michael asked, "Where are you two going?" the other girl jumped in, "No were, definitely not home." The Spanish girl said, "We going home." Michael asked, "Where is that?" the other girl said, "That jerk just drove off with everything we owned in the world." Michael offered them to come up to his and he'd call a cab for them to get home. He knew he was breaking rule number one and it wasn't time to play "Captain save a Ho," he could help himself, plus they both barely had any clothes on.

They all went up to Michael's room. As soon as they got in the room, the girls went into the bathroom together. Vic asked Michael "What you going to do now?" Michael answered, "I'm going to wait until Kim and my lawyer call me back, and then I'll probably do what they say." Vic went over to the bar and fixed drinks while Michael rolled some weed in a Swisher Sweet.

One of the girls came out of the bathroom wearing nothing but a towel. "Close the door," screamed the other girl in the bathroom. They had just taken a shower. The other girl came out a couple minutes after. Vic asked them what kind of drinks they wanted. Vic began asking a thousand questions.

Michael's mind was somewhere else. All he could think about is his current situation. Vic asked Michael again, "What are you going to do?" Michael thought to himself, that's a good question."

Vic pulled out some cocaine that Michael had given him earlier; both Vic and Skin were smoking it in the room. He gave some to one of the girls, the other didn't want any. She got up sat next to Michael on the bed. "What's wrong, are you scared of women or something?" she asked. She continued, "You don't find me attractive?"

Michael sat there for a minute, lost in his thoughts. But he snapped out of his thoughts once he felt her hands touching him. Out of habit, his body began to respond to her touches. She was on top of him. Before he realized it, he was inside of her and she was kissing him. The other lady found her way over to the bed where Michael and her friends were, to help take care of Michael. Vic returned to snorting cocaine. Vic thought Michael wouldn't notice that he was stealing from Michael. Michael had so much on his mind that he ignored Vic. Michael was deep into this Spanish chic and her friend but his mind wasn't far from his legal problems. Suddenly, there was a knock on the door. "Get them whores out of your room, before I tear a hole in their asses," Stacey warned. Michael didn't feel like having to deal with Stacey and the cops as well. Stacey had proven herself many times that she could act a fool, especially when she thought she had the right to.

Outside of Kim, Stacey had the rights to Michael or so that's what she thought. She banged on the door again screaming, "You need to be trying to figure out what you are going to do, but that's okay, I'm leaving."

Michael told the two girls to get dressed. He did the same. He wanted to see Stacey before she left. For some reason, he was a little concerned where Stacey, Angie and Brandy would be going with Rob and Skin. That could cause all of them trouble especially the girls.

The two girls were hugging Michael all the way to the door. They didn't want to let him leave, but he had to find out what was going on.

He went to Rob and Skin's room and he saw that they were partying beyond the limit. Both of them were really drunk and high. Skin had received another page from his getaway driver. She told him someone had gotten her license plates and the cops had identified her car. The police questioned her about her car and they wanted to know if she was involved with the robberies. She said she didn't tell them anything. But Michael could hear her crying on the phone throughout the conversation.

Skin said something to her and hung up, then Skin and Rob went into the bathroom to talk. After they finished talking, they came out and said, "We have to go." Rob was doing most of the talking. Skin came out and went right back to getting high, smoking crack and drinking.

Rob called out to Skin, "We have to go, we need to get ready and we have to get something together, so come on." Rob seemed to be getting irritated with Skin. Eventually Skin jumped up and left with Rob. He yelled to Brandy to stay there and to not go anywhere. Brandy was concerned with who Skin would be leaving with. Was it Stacey or Angie? And what they are doing following Skin. Brandy thought she knew what they were going to do, but she wasn't quite sure.

By the time, they got to the car. Skin could be heard screaming. "Brandy, what the hell is wrong with you? You left the room with all the money and dope in it and I don't have any keys!" Skin was heated and reached out like he was going to smack her. Angie and Stacey sat there smiling. They were only riding with Skin for the money. He would give anything to anybody, all the stuff in the room or that Brandy was crowding him as he had more of a thing for Angie than Brandy, but he surely had a thing for Stacey.

Rob yelled, "Come on man, we don't need to make a scene and you need to be the one looking after the money." Skin responded, "All right man, you go and get what we need and I'll be right here when you get back." Skin went straight back to the room, which was locked. He began yelling at Brandy again. Michael told him to chill out and that they would just have to go get another key from the front desk. Michael went to get the key and on the way, he stopped by his own room. When he got back to his room Vic was still there getting high, since he didn't know where Michael put his money and dope. At first, he didn't think the girls would still be there, but they were. Michael wasn't any further than a few feet away from the room anyway and he left the blinds wide open, so that he could see what they were up to. It didn't take long for Michael to grab his money, clothes and dope and take them down to his car. He hides the dope in his secret container and put them in the hidden compartment in the car.

Skin walked out when Michael grabbed his money, clothes and dope and took them down to his car, to get another room key. Leaving the two girls behind in the room. When they reached the hotel lobby, there were two strange looking guys in front of them. Two white guys who were asking the hotel manager a lot of questions. Skin and Michael grabbed their money, clothes and dope and took them down to his car. They could see her shaking her head no. These guys were obviously the police. Skin and Michael ducked behind some tall plants as they left. Michael went up to the front desk. He asked the manager whether he could have another key, but that she said she could come and unlock the door for them. That was fine, but Michael pondered, "This must be the first hotel that would give a second key?"

Nevertheless, Michael just wanted to help Skin get their stuff together. Then the hotel manager asked, "Which one of you is Mr. Brown?" "I am," said Michael. "Good, because I couldn't let anyone in without your consent." said the manager.

"The room is in your name and that is the hotel policy," she explained. She gave a little grin and Skin was looking at her as if he wanted her to hurry up but he didn't say a word. Then the manager asked, "Who are you boys and what did you do?" "Why do you ask that?" Michael asked. "Oh, I don't know," she answered. She looked into Skin's eye, which seemed to be saying hurry up and caught hold of the fear in them. Skin had a look that would scare anyone. She asked. "Did you kill someone or something?" Skin answered, "No, ma'am, I just robbed a bank and he had nothing to do with it," pointing to Michael.

Michael looked at Skin like he was crazy, "Why would you say that to a stranger?" Michael couldn't believe what just came out of Skin's mouth. The manager asked, "Did you'll hurt someone?" "No ma'am," Skin quickly replied. "That's good," she said. She opened the door for them. Skin asked her to wait just for a quick moment. He went under the mattress to get some money out; he came back and gave her a hundred dollar bill. She looked at him as if he she was afraid to take the money. She looked at Skin, then Michael and then Skin again. She tucked the bill in her bra and turned around and left.

Skin started to put his things together. As he was just about finished, Michael looked down at the parking lot from the room window. Kim had just arrived. Michael almost forgot that she was on her way with the kids. It seemed like little Michael was pointing directly up at Michael like he knew where his daddy was. Michael could have sworn that he heard him say, "That's my daddy!" Michael couldn't hear him, but he knew what he would say. Kim jumped out of the car and took Michael out of his baby seat. The girls, Jazz and Keya got out of the car right after Kim got out. They must have seen Michael because they came straight to Skin's room.

They Trooped up to the room like an army. Kim and the trop came straight to Skin's room, and when she got to the door. Michael opens it. Immediately, Kim told Michael, "Get your stuff; you're coming home with us!" It seemed as if Kim just knew what to do. Kim didn't always say what she thought or how she felt about certain things; she would just let Michael do what he had to do. Michael told Kim, "I'm not coming back to Wisconsin so they can railroad me." Kim told him, "You need to come back so you can prove to them that you didn't have anything to do with these crimes." Michael told her, "Not now!" "What are you saying; you're not going to leave me and these kids?" Kim asked.

Kim made Michael think about that one. She knew Michael would never do that. But he wasn't thinking rationally. He was tired of being harassed by the cops, especially with this thing that he had absolutely nothing to do with. They had no reason for putting Michael in jail, and that is what he told her.

Kim explained, "This is exactly why you have to turn yourself in and get this shit over with." She looked Michael in his eyes as if to penetrate his soul. Michael simply said "Come on, let's go to my room." Kim headed out the door with Michael toward his room. Michael wondered, "How in the hell does she know which room is his?" Michael was right behind her and his little army was behind him.

Vic and the two girls were still there. "Vic, I'm going back to Wisconsin to turn myself in," Michael said as soon as he walked into the room. Kim took one look at the two girls as well as Vic like they were all naked and snorting cocaine.

“Come on Michael, let’s go,” she demanded. Kim just shook her head. Michael couldn’t fool Kim as she probably figured out what was happening in his room. Michael got the rest of his things and they left.

Michael drove his limo and Kim followed him in her car. They left Chicago and went straight home to Madison. Michael knew he had to go back and face the music and his responsibilities. He knew, he didn’t tell anyone to solicited sex. He was a silent partner; he had no involvement with how the business was run.

His family is all that mattered to him. He didn’t want to be away from them for any long period.

CHAPTER 13

ARREST, BROKEN PROMISES & STACEY'S APARTMENT

When they got back to Madison both Michael and Kim went straight to the house and stayed there because they wanted to decide what they should do and how they were going to do it. They were waiting for the lawyer to call back to learn what he heard about the matter. Michael was wondering if there had been a warrant issued for his arrest yet.

In the meantime, Kim cooked dinner and then put the kids to bed. They tried to put their minds at ease for the moment, went to bed and made love all night. They didn't have any company over, nor did they want to answer their phones. They were exhausted from all the hype going on, not to mention all the lovemaking. Before they knew it the sun was up, and Michael woke up full of energy and ready to go. He was thinking about the state of his club and the arrest of Jim and the girls. He was also thinking about Rob, Brandy, Shecka, and Skin. He didn't want to think too much about them. Though he knew, they were all adults and could take care of themselves. It wasn't that he didn't care about them but he was more concerned about the dope. He just got and ho, he would turn it into cash. Michael's mind was on business as usual.

There was a knock on the front door. It was Fossil and Spanky, and it made Michael want to leave to handle his business. They both wanted to know where he had been, & if he had some free weed to smoke and something to drink. They also wanted to know about the raid on the club and what he was going to do about Jim and the girls. Spanky was Michael's next-door neighbor and the Shecka's brother, who was also Rob's girlfriend. He wanted to know what was up with his sister. Michael told him he didn't know anything about them nor had he talked to them. He told them the last he heard they were on their way to hook up with Master P.

Rob thought he would get a job from him so he could keep working in the music industry. He didn't exactly tell Michael that but that is what he was lead to believe. Michael told Spanky he wasn't sure what was going on.

Fossil asked Michael just about the same questions Fossil was like Michael's third cousin. Michael's family is related to Vic. Michael's mother's first cousin is Ida Caldwell his grandmother's niece. Ida took Michael's family to Wisconsin when they didn't know their father or their mother was in prison. Vic is her nephew through marriage and thus her husband's nephew.

Michael asked Fossil "Why do you want to know where Vic is at anyway?" "He's nothing but trouble." Fossil answered "You're right, but he's still family." Michael looked at him and shook his head. Michael told Fossil and Spanky that it's going to be one from here on out and as soon as he can he's going to get his lawyer on phone and find out what's going on. Michael tired calling his lawyer several times but he wasn't able to get through. He left several message from him to call Michael back. Michael did however ask the secretary if she had heard anything knew concerning his situation. She had not which must mean as far as Michael was concerned; he wasn't really in any legal trouble yet.

It was after that Fossil and Spanky asked Michael "what are you going to do, sit around the house all day long?" Michael thought about it for a moment and told them, "Let's get out of here. I have my cell phone; if he wants to talk to me he can call me on the road." Michael had to let his people know he had money and that the show must go on.

Michael's work was the strippers and the musical performances. He loved it and that's what he lived for to put on performances. He also had to let the people know he had plenty of work, dope, cocaine, girls and he was ready to let it go for the right price. Michael told himself "I'll stay in a safe spot until I know things are cool."

He left the house that morning and went out to his limo once out there he started his limo and began to clean it out. He rolled down the windows and for some reason it wouldn't go back up. He showed the guys his new rims and tires some real pimp wear and was anxious to have them put on the car. Fossil and Spanky were anxious to see them on the car as well. They wanted to drive around in class. Michael was at first a little hesitate to go anywhere especially in an eye catching limo. He remembered he had dope in the hiding space in the car and now he had to go and get the rims put on and the window fixed.

They went to the car repair shop. As they were leaving, Kim came running out the front door. She was screaming something but Michael was already gone. He hollered out the window "I'll be right back." Figuring if it was important, she could page him or call him on his cell phone.

As soon as they left, Michael noticed some undercover cops following him. First, it was one car about a block from home, but then there was another one. Michael was driving the limo and Fossil and Spanky were driving the van right behind him. Behind them was a blue undercover cop car followed by a second grey one. The shop where they were headed was only about a mile or two from the apartment.

They were about three signal lights or a half a block away from the repair shop when Michael says the patrol car. He knew they were about to stop him, so he turned left on A Street. The shop B. F. Goodrich was E. Washington. As he turned the corner three-cop cars put their lights on him, they began screaming, "Don't move! Let me see your hands! And slowly get out of the car."

Michael should have been shocked that they were harassing him but he wasn't. He was anxious to get out of the car and while he was doing that he noticed all the people witnessing him being arrested, some of whom he knew. Like Stacey and her girlfriends.

It was a long drawn out process and it seemed like it took forever. The first thing Michael though was "I had nothing to do with any of this." His next thought was "the dope hidden in the stash spot in the limo." They couldn't possibly know about that. Because he was the only one who knew about it. As soon as he stepped out of the car, his cell phone rang. Being the big head dude, that Michael was he answered it. It was Breanne and Reanna calling from jail letting Michael know that they had been arrested. It was then that Michael knew what he was getting arrested for. He was about to tell her what happened when she said, "I was busted for prostitution. We got called to service and Jim took me there and as it turned out it was an undercover agent and I tried to sell sex to him."

By this time, Michael had gotten back into the car and could hear the cops screaming "Get out of the car with your hands up." Michael was about to ask Breanne a question but decided not to. By this time, the police were really getting angry and were at the side of the limo. Michael carefully got out of the car with his hands behind his head. One of the cops was threatening him and screaming pretty loudly. "What the hell are you doing? Out, with your hands behind your head."

The cop got a little rough when he was cuffing Michael. He roughed Michael up and twisted his arms and kicked his legs apart while he screamed at him. Michael wasn't accustomed to this kind of abuse and it had been a while since his last arrest. The cop threw Michael in the back seat of his unmarked police car and told the other cop to move the limousine because it was illegally parked.

Michael was pretty angry and was telling the cop he hadn't done anything wrong. The cop told Michael he was under arrest and read him his Miranda Rights. He asked Michael if he knew Breanne and Reanna and Michael told him that he did. He asked Michael if he knew Jim Mass and Michael told him that he did.

"They were arrested for prostitution last night," said the cop. "You are under arrest for part of that solicitation for prostitution," the cop informed Michael. He told Michael that the girls were called out from his club to go to a hotel where they solicited an undercover agent in a sting operation.

Michael tried to inform the cop by saying, "I don't own the club anymore so why am I being arrested?" The cop told him, "They all said they worked for you." Michael asked, "You believed them?" the asked Michael "Where are your friends, Robert Sutton and James Flemming?" Michael told him "I don't know I'm not their baby sitter."

The one cop told the other to search Michael's limo. Michael was sure what they were looking for but he wasn't about to say anything that would lead them to Rob or Skin. He was more concerned with them finding the dope. "You don't have my consent nor do you have a search warrant," Michael said. He tried to sound cool and not alarmed in anyway. The cop probably thought Michael was just another smart-ass as they took Michael to jail. They also took the limo.

Michael was concerned that they didn't just leave the car there. When he got to jail and called his lawyer, he told Michael he would be there to see him, but there was nothing he could do until after he was arraigned. Michael sat back in jail and went to sleep. This was long overdue and he needed rest. Most of the dude's in there already knew Michael and they all wanted to talk and ask him for some advice and his opinion. Questions from the dope game to the music business. But Michael's only question was "how did I get here?"

Michael sat there in jail and did a lot of thinking. He had to ask himself some difficult questions. He told himself that he was thru with this criminal lifestyle and he wanted to work hard on his career in the music business. He knew his only crime was buying and selling a little dope now and then but that was it.

He didn't think that running an escort service was illegal. He knew for sure that it was morally wrong but in the big business and other businesses he was in there was no room for morals. Another question that caught Michael by surprise was the police had asked him "Why'd you choose young girls to work and sell sex for him." "First off," he told them, "They're not supposed to be selling sex. And second, these girls are not under age." The cop told Michael that they are underage. Michael said, "That's not what they lead me to believe." Michael informed the cop "I catered their eighteenth birthdays and they showed me identification." Just at the moment, Michael realized that he never really examined their ids because he trusted them. Besides, they certainly looked their age.

That night in jail, Michael prayed instantly for God to help him. He asked God to bless him and he promised to get rid of the sin in his life and never allow it back. Michael could not understand how he had gotten so far off track. Another empty promise that never really knew he wanted to keep anyway although he did know he wanted to get out of jail and he wanted to see his business prosper what he didn't want was to do crime anymore. Michael woke up that next morning and called Kim to tell her about his relationship with God. Who had always blessed him and that he should start reading the bible again. Kim agreed.

He also called Stacey. He had a few reasons for calling her. He wanted to tell her that the cops asked about Rob and Skin, plus he wanted to see how she was doing. He wanted to see if she was worried about him as he had been doing some thinking and a part of him did not want to continue his relationship with her. Michael really didn't want to hurt Kim anymore and neither did he want to hurt Stacey. As it started out Stacey was just a way for him to release sexual tension. He would have to talk to her some more at a later time. More than anything he could go to her and not have to worry about anything because with her is relax, relate and release. However, that he had changed slowly and unexpectedly. When he called her to his surprise, she seemed more concerned about him than anyone else.

The first thing she asked, "What's happening? What are they arresting you for? When are you getting out of there?" It had only been a day and he had called her partly to break up with her and to tell her that he did not want to continue with their relationship anymore. He was not sure why but he just could not tell her. He answered most of her questions with the standard. "I do not know" and "Everything is going to be alright." It had only been one night that she missed him. Michael realized that they barely spent a night without seeing each other. Even if it had been just as friends.

Michael did do what he felt was half of the job he told Stacey he wanted to stop all the drinking, drugging and crime. He told her that he was tired of that lifestyle. And he told her something he wasn't sure he'd ever told her, that he wanted to turn his life around and give it to God. He expected her to respond in some crazy way, but she did not. There was a moment of silence and then she said, "If that's how you feel. Then that's what you need to do." He told her that means I'll have to stop seeing you and she told him. "I'll do whatever I can to help you if you want."

Michael was curious about what she was thinking and what she had just said. Stacey's response made it even more difficult for him. Michael thought he needed to get some money and he had to continue with his business. His dream was to be a businessman and to make money. That of course would take money to do. But where was he going to get the money. What was he going to do with the dope and the money he already had? Then a thought came to his mind he did not care what happened to the money and the dope as long as he didn't get charged for it. He thought about all this time on the phone with Stacey. He knew Stacey was getting to know him very well. Because there was a big pause in their conversation. She said, "I'm with you, but you know it's not going to be easy." He went to sleep thinking about their conversation. "I know I have to go in front of the judge and make bail the next day. That's first and foremost."

He slept all night. The next day he went before the judge and made bail. Kim and the kids picked him up, as always, she would say, "I told you that you needed to quit running around on these streets. And be home with me and the kids." Of course he did for the first couple of days, but little did he know that things were about to get a whole lot worse.

Michael was about to lose his mind when the devil came on with a vengeance. It was not on purpose and it was really not his fault but he was just not ready for the things that were about to happen to him. He was by no means going to slow down yet. As soon as Michael was released on bail, his attorney was sweating him for money. He did not know it then but the pressure to pay the attorney along with the other people he was responsible for was about to drive him crazy. Michael thought he could handle the pressure but soon his entire world would be turned upside down.

Kim thought he was busy and never at home before, but she had not seen anything yet. Michael's attorney came to court and interviewed him just months before he would have permitted the court appointed public pretender to represented him.

Michael was glad to see his own attorney, but really all he wanted was to get out of there. Michael's private attorney Mark Leisenberg was well respected and feared in his area of expertise. His brother and many of his relatives were also attorneys. Mark also had a so-called relative that was a judge before he was forced to retire for some illegal activities he was supposedly into. There were allegations that he ran an illegal gambling operation and whorehouse, because of him another judge killed himself rather than go to prison. That's the rumor.

Mark and his brother were brilliant attorneys as long as you had their fee. Some of their brilliance was their connections to the right people. Although sometimes they had to deal with people whose character was questionable at best. Mark followed Michael home. He wanted his retainer fee immediately. He also wanted to see the employment applications of the girls who said they were of age. And also wanted the affidavits and contracts that prohibited them from soliciting sex while working thru his agency. Michael knew it was a smart move to have his attorney draw up the contracts.

Michael gave him his retainer fee and an extra five thousand dollars. He also gave him the applications and the contracts. They went to the restaurant because Mark wanted to talk in detail about Michael's case. Michael assured Mark that he didn't keep dope at his house, but when he did, it was only enough for personal use. Michael believed his attorney also wanted to check out how he was living, so he could determine what to charge him for the case. Mark wanted more than most American's earn in an entire year. And this was just the fee for Michael's prostitution case as that was all he was accused of at this point.

Michael badly wanted to tell him about the half kilo of cocaine he had in the hidden compartment in his limousine but he did not say anything about it and he did not need to. Michael asked mark if he could help him get his limousine back and whether he could help him get his club back. Michael explained to Mark that he had his recording equipment there, which he would need to be able to pay for his services. Mark told him that he may be able to but he'll have to check about the club. Mark then said, "You need to clean up your house because it smells like dirty diapers. And I'm only telling you that because I consider us friends." Michael thought to himself. "The nerve of this guy". But he was only being honest and keeping it real. Because Michael realized once he walked through the door, it did smell like dirty diapers. Michael told Kim what Mark said and she apologized because she forgot to throw away the trash before he came home.

Michael enjoyed hanging out with the kids they had a ball. Michael realized how much he had missed them. He rationalized his not being there because he had to be the breadwinner. That meant hitting the block and getting that paper. He knew that the time he spent with the kids was very uplifting for him. It made him completely forget about his legal problems.

Michael decided he would just stay home for the most part. Everyone was calling him, trying to figure out what was going on. A few days later Jim got out of jail and went to see Michael. And he told him the entire story. It was pretty much, what the police said and what Breanna and Reanna had told Michael. Michael asked, “Why didn’t you go with the girls and screen the guy with the contract like you should have in the first place? The reason I expected you to screen the guy before you sent them out was to determine whether he was a cop. A cop will not sign that contract.” Jim responded, “The girls didn’t want me to go with them.” Michael frowned, “Jim tells me this? Who’s the boss? You or them?” Jim basically didn’t have a response for that question. Michael went on “if you would’ve done as you were supposed to it would have limited the agency’s liability. Furthermore, what two consenting adults do is there business. And we would not be in this jam.” Jim stated, “I know man, I know I messed up.” Michael intended to let him have it, but he knew it would not help their situation.”

CHAPTER 14

GANGBANGING, FAMILY, FRIENDS AND BUSINESS

They told on Michael's mother (60-70s), they told where his mother was located when she was on the run (70's). They killed The King, Uncle David (70's). They shot several times and almost killed Cousin Al and many other family members (70s-80s). Michael was shot at and almost killed several times by them (80s). In self-defense and retaliation Michael fought, shot, and almost killed several people for them and himself (80s). They testified against Michael in the '80s. Michael went to prison for them in '89. Michael was set up by them upon his release in '92. They tried to take over Michael's clubs in the mid '90s. They fought and shot and caused Michaels business problems in the late '90s. They lied and testified against Michael in his federal case in 2001.

Michael has had too many experiences. Michael believed in the positive and productive. Why would Michael or anyone else join and remain a gang member. Michael did not know. Michael knows it is not for him anymore. Michael knows that being responsible for himself is difficult enough. Michael cannot afford to be responsible for anyone else.

Gangster Disciples (G.D.'s), Black Disciples (B.D.'s), Vice Lords (V.L. or Lords), Black Pea Stones (Stones), The New Breed (Breeds), Black Souls (Souls), Latin Cobras (Cobras), Latin Gangsters (Latin Folks) and many others- all of these gangs except the Latin Kings originated in Chicago, in the sixties. As did Michael. Now, these gangs are all over America and the world with thousands of members. To most gang members it is more than a gang its family, a way of life. The only one they have or know. It was the same for Michael twenty years ago, when he was a teenager. His mother was in prison; he did not know his father. His grandmother was old and ill and his grandfather was working and (on the hustle), and Michael's uncles were too busy living their lives and did not know how to raise children. Michael turned to the streets and his (street family). Which were already banging and a part of the movement and struggle? Back then, it was different you were a member if you were from a certain area or neighborhood. Or if your friends or family were. You had to fight, live or even die for it. It was what you lived, loved, wanted, needed, believed in, knew and breathed. There was a lot more loyalty back then. There was a lot more unity, also. There were reasons and causes. Most of the people were people who needed help but there was nowhere else to go. Some people rebelled against their friends, family or neighborhood and did not join at all. While some people rebelled by joining the rivals of their friends family and neighborhood. That is not the smartest thing to do then or now. Most of us believed it all starts out with good intentions. Helping to provide protection from the cops and racists, helping with food, clothing, shelter, jobs and money for those that had none. Some or most of the founder and original members of these gangs wanted or needed these things and turned to each other. Later, as things started to advance, people started to turn on each other, within their same gang or on other gangs who had the same problems and were looking for the same solutions. Most of them were just as needy and poor.

Michael had a lot of family who were members of all the different gangs in Chicago. Michael's grandmother had a dozen different foster and adopted kids. Who were his aunts and uncles? Not including his mother's friends and associates who he had known since he was born. Before Michael was a teenager when the city was still relatively safe, he would travel the city to hang out with different aunts and uncles. From State way Gardens to

Argile Gardens, Inglewood to Roseland, Robert Taylor's to High Park to Humble Park, from Ida B. Wells to the Icky's, from north Chicago to the south side. The wild hundreds, Westside to the west suburbs.

Michael had family members in all these gangs in all these areas. One of Michael's favorites, Aunt Blacky (AKA Veda Brown) is Bubbie Dog's (AKA Matthew Brown) sister the mother to one of Michaels favorite cousin's Larry Brown (Blacky's Son). Bubbie Dog is brothers with one of the Barksdales, a brother from a different mother who is one of the founders of the (B.D.'s). Both of them have kids by the same woman. Their kids the Wilson Sister (Wilson's and Barksdales) are more of Michael's cousins. Michael's mom and Aunt Blacky moved to Wisconsin after David was killed. And his cousin Al was shot several times and almost killed. Soon after that, the gang problems got so bad that many of Michael's family members left Chicago to go to Madison Wisconsin and many other areas. Eventually the gangs and their problems followed. When Michael started his clubs and other businesses, many years later some of the issues he had were directly related to the gang problems. Every club was in a different neighborhood and different gangs attempted to claim his club. Some of Michael's relatives worked and hung at the club. And they claimed different gangs also. Jimmy a Breed; Fossil a B.D.'S; Vic a Stone, Larry a V.L.'S; Red was a Soul. Michael was not in any gang and had not been in years. He was a businessman. And becoming successful and legitimate was his goal. After the first two or three clubs were closed down Michael turned to a cousin who offered his help lil Jimmy, who was in 1997, in his late teens or early twenties, and all grown up. Michael watched Jimmy grow up and would always look out for him and give him food and money when he would come over to his house. Or when he caught him out and about. When Jimmy started coming to the club Michael used to let him in for free though he didn't have to as Jimmy was doing fine on his own by hustling. Michael looked out for him then noticed that he didn't need to do that either. Jimmy had a lot of influence with a lot of people at the club, especially the youngsters. Jimmy could really hold his own.

Michael and Jimmy were related through Michael's uncle Bubbie Dog who was Jimmy's stepfather and the father to a few of Jimmy's younger sisters and brothers.

Jimmy was not looking out for Michael and his girl Stacey who had just gotten an apartment around the corner from where Jimmy's girlfriend had an apartment not far from one of Michael's former clubs. Right after Michael was released from jail for his prostitution arrest and the closing of one of his former clubs Michael called on Jimmy. The police had taken everything from Michael whom now had to start all over. Jimmy was one of Michael's resources he had used when he had financial and legal problems as well as the gang problems he was having. Fighting, shootings, gambling and drugs. Jimmy also helped Michael get back on his hustle, which he needed more than ever after, his arrest and Stacey had just gotten her first apartment. Michael needed a place to hustle from and had to help Stacey get the minimal amount of furniture that way he could use it for a point of operation.

Stacey had always helped Michael with his business, cleaning, marketing and advertising for the clubs and concerts and transporting the girls for shows and much more. Stacey had always given Michael her full support. Michael never asked her to get involved with anything illegal especially not any robberies with Rob, Skin or Vic. Michael really liked and protected her and her friends. In addition, Skin had told Michael to look out for Stacey and he did. Skin had done plenty of favors for Michael and Michael trusted him for the most part. So he didn't ask why or what the money was for that Michael was giving to him. That was their business; Michael wanted no part of it. Michael started hanging out at Stacey's and it became his base of operation. Stacey and Michael started messing around more and more.

Michael started to notice all the gangs of the city were leaving Chicago. Flocking to places all over the Midwest. These were some of the notorious street gangs in America. And some of the most organized criminals since Al Capone. Michael himself was raised in this element and was also dying to get out. Not everyone was happy about Michael and little Jimmy getting together in business. Michael particularly as well as other cousins, rival gangs and former business partners.

Michael believed in and followed the original concept at the beginning when he thought it was for the good. Now he knew it was every man for himself. Michael hung out with his sometimes business partners, family and friends but some of them were plugged (in a gang). It took everything Michael could muster to get out. What he didn't realize was that just hanging around them was bad enough. It was actually one of Michael's mother's cousins Teressa who told the cops where they could find Michaels mother when she went on the run to Wisconsin. Teressa was the eldest daughter of Ida Caldwell, Michael's favorite aunt. Teressa was also the sister of Michael's favorite cousin, Al Caldwell, the father of Alphonso Jr. (AKA Fossil). Michael admired Al that was another reason he looked out for and hired his son, Fossil at his businesses and clubs. Fossil was a B.D. from the project in Chicago, where he left because or trouble. Fossil was about twenty-one years old when he came back to Wisconsin from Chicago. Michael gave Fossil a job as a doorman since he was 6' 3" and 330lbs.

Michael probably hung out with fossil the most since they worked together and were related. After Rob and Skin went on the run. It wasn't like they had anything in common, as Fossil used drugs and Michael did not. Michael brought Vic around as Vic used to help Michael when Michael's mother was in prison. Michael and Vic are not really related but Michael is related to Fossil and Fossil and Vic are first cousins. They started attempting to muscle in on Michael's businesses.

Nobody else seemed to give Skin a break especially after he had spent seventeen years in prison for robbery, violence and a whole slew of other charges.

Michael met Skin after he had saved his cousin Larry from getting jumped when they were all in prison. Rob and Michael hooked up the second time around in 1993-1994, while Michael was on his way home when he was living in Miami. Rob came home from the war and needed a job. Michael talked to Rob about his dream to get off the streets and into the music business. Rob had similar dreams and interests as Michael and this is how he wound up in Madison with Michael and his family. Rob also hung out with Michael's cousins the Eleby's and got hooked up with a job. Later Rob a got a job at Michaels club when it got off the ground and then he got his own apartment.

Now that Rob and Skin were both gone Michael started hanging out with Stacey who was his chick on the side.

Jim had a conflict with both Fossil and Vic. Jim was a tall slim dude with a cut up build. And stood about 6'1" with light brown skin and a big afro. After his prostitution arrest in 1997 weeks passed before Michael's attorney finally called and told him that he could get his music equipment back. Michael really needed his equipment and it was better than selling dope in the streets and getting caught from something dumb. But, ever though Michael knew it was dumb, he was still doing that on the side and working with his girls as strippers and escorts. As much as he didn't want to do it, he really had no choice as he has just gotten out of jail and this business was booming.

For a while, Michael was concerned that some of his customers would be undercover cops, plus he had to consider what had happened when he turned things over to Jim and how he got a hooked into trouble without his being involved.

Michael's lawyer didn't want Michael involved anymore. Michael's attorney really didn't care about him, as all they ever cared about was his money.

It wasn't long until business started to slow down, which may have been because all of Michael's call being forwarded to Stacey's or because his customers thought that things were too hot at the time.

Things got really slow after the club closed down. Michael had no club to play music, collect money at the door, or to promote concerts.

Without a good place for concert promotion, he was washed up. When authorities don't want someone in business, that person is finished for good - - they know how to do it.

After several weeks, Michael got his equipment back. There was no word about getting the limousine back or about the dope that was stashed inside. Michael was still hustling with his cousins Lil' Jimmy, but it wasn't his thing to work for somebody else and he didn't like stealing full-time.

He had at least fifty thousand dollars' worth of equipment, including portable mixer boards, effects machines, recording machines, reel-to-reel tape desks, two-way turntables, CD burners, beat machines, and microphones and speakers galore, but no place to work a studio or club or place to perform.

All that Michael could think about was where he would work and where people could come to see him, listen, dance and record. This was the primary benefit of having his own club. If the music was good, the clientele would love it and ask who the artist was. If it was bad, the crown could be ruthless at times with their views, but business was business and Michael had to learn to take criticism and move on.

Michael also had thousands of recordings that he hadn't even put out, yet, and didn't want to sell, as he didn't think he'd get their worth. Some recordings were from some of the biggest and best stars in the business, most from the Midwest. Most of these guys claimed to be a part of something or some group or gang. Anybody that ever made music in the Midwest was at Michael's studio and he recorded there. Over the years, Michael had collected quite an assortment of recording that many people had given him to listen to and he knew that these recording could be worth millions - - and the gangs and groups were trying to put claims on them.

Without a place to produce music, Michael was like a junkie with dope, but without a syringe. He just had to have it and it was most of what he thought about. After being out all day and night hustling, he would come home and suffer with thoughts of not having a club. Kim would continuously tell Michael that he had to get a job, but a job was not part

Michael's plans. There would be no way for Michael to catch up with his bills by working a 9-to-5 job, he thought. Plus, he had to pay the lawyer if he was to stay out of jail.

Michael love the music business and most of what came with it when he first started the business, but now the business was like a gang war. He had worked at a job as a laborer with the Laborers Union. Twenty to twenty-five dollars an hour wasn't a bad wage and Michael really liked being a part of the building trades and was strongly considering going back.

It got too much for Michael after a while and he was putting in a lot of overtime with the music business, raising his three brothers and sisters, his own two daughters, and his son Michael. Things were becoming overwhelming.

Michael didn't think he had the time to go back to work and there wasn't a job that could provide him with the type of money he needed, so he stuck to his plan of opening another recording studio and a club. This was also Michael's reason for getting back into the dope scene, but it would only be a temporary fixture until another club and his big break. Once Michael promoted another concert and made a purchase of one more needed piece of equipment, he would be back out of the dope business.

This was the primary reason Michael borrowed money from Rob and Skin, as he needed the additional equipment and a better place to open another club. Michael had around fifty thousand dollars in cash plus he had some dope. (It was not money he received from the robbery that he had nothing to do with and had no prior knowledge of.) That still wasn't enough money, so he bought some more dope to sell, and then he could finally get out of the dope scene, once and for all.

An entire month had already gone by. The lawyer told Michael that the police could keep him limousine for thirty days before they would release it to him. He could have made more money with it or he could have sold it.

During this time, Stacey began doing things that Michael hadn't noticed before. She was suddenly concerned about Rob and Skin and, every time they would call, she would jump up. It was obvious that something was going on, but Michael wasn't sure what. He first noticed it when he was in the "Third Club" on Stoughton Road near highway 51. He was so busy then that it escaped him as only a passing thought, but it was the first time he actually got jealous. He was doing the best he could to look out for her, but with a full plate, he didn't treat her the way she deserved to be treated.

Finally, Michael opened his fourth club with Stacey's help and ended up spending more time with Stacey. Michael would treat her special by giving her gifts of jewelry, dresses, clothes, and flowers every once in a while. They spent time in nice hotels every time they went out of town and also traveled the country, east to west coast.

Michael started beefing with his cousins, who were doing their crew thing with their gang members – except Vic, who was robbing. Looking back, Michael could see it was no wonder that Kim was mad at him. Stacey deserved it, though, even if she was just a friend, because she had done so much for Michael and the cause.

It was then that Michael started to notice that Stacey would jump for Rob or Skin, though, and he didn't know why. He certainly didn't like it, but he never tried to control Stacey. Little did he know Stacey was hanging out with his friends and family who were hanging out with their gangs and homeboys? Anyone from gangs, friends and even family can turn on you. One could get implicated in something that one had absolutely nothing to do with. One can get indicted by the Grand Jury or even killed just for being a member.

CHAPTER 15

LETTING GO AND LETTING GOD

On the day after Halloween 1997, Michael was to throw a big party at his ex-girlfriend Ingo's house. She had a two-story crib with a basement on the South Side of Madison. It was a real convenient place to have a party, as it was right off the highway. Michael needed to throw this party because it would help him reestablish his reputation and keep his following of customers. His business was growing again and he had a few extra dollars in his pocket, at least a few hundred. So he put this party together, which gave him a chance to use his equipment that had been collecting dust for month.

The party was a great success except for a couple of things, it was packed and rocking as the guys and Michael were free styling and playing some of the music that some of his artists had previously recorded. It was never before heard music but the crowd really loved it.

Stacey and her girlfriends helped promote the show and one of Michael's nemeses Eric a.k.a. "Paid in Full" showed up. He and Michael had been partners before his first prison sentence and they had separated not Seeing Eye to eye. It was rumored that Eric tried to set Michael up but it didn't work out. They hadn't seen one another in years, so neither one of them knew what would happen now. Eric had been gone for a while, but not as long as everyone had expected. It was said that he only did two or three years of a twenty-year bit.

Michael was out doing his thing for a while and here he was with the power, the money and a following of some security. It was Ingo that let Eric in knowing full well that he and Michael had past differences. Ingo went to the D.J booth to tell Michael that Eric was there and that he wanted to see him.

Michael went over to see Eric. They talked for a minute even though Michael had too much work to do to be talking to him and didn't want to waste any time, but he went ahead into the other room to talk with Eric. What could have been really ugly and even deadly, they agreed to squash. After they talked for a couple of minutes, Michael's boys came to see if everything was okay with him. Eric was only there to hook up with the ladies and Michael did for him what he believed Eric would have done for Michael.

Michael went to supervise the party for a moment. He made his rounds to see how things were going and so far the night was going fairly well, but it was about to turn disastrous. The police were at the door.

It was no mystery that Michael was there. He just got his limousine back after his attorney told him he could come to his office and pick it up. Kim had driven Michael there earlier that evening to pick up the limo. The first thing Michael did was check the stash compartment. To Michael's surprise, the dope was still there. He got up and took a look around to see if he was being watched and he wasn't. The inside of the limo had been completely torn apart. They took apart the color television and radio. The sound system was one of the baddest around, being loud and ghetto, but its' wires were strung all over the place and the privacy glass was half down. He left the limo there, gave Kim the "it's cool" look, and went in to see the lawyer.

Michael went to thank the attorney. He told him that he would be getting a chunk of money real soon. "What's so important about the limo anyway?" asked the lawyer. "It's old and raggedy," he said. "Well it's a classic and there aren't many like it left in the country," explained Michael. It was a 1989 Cadillac Fleetwood stretched and custom-fitted, Michael invested more into it with some fresh blue candy paint, pimping rims and tires, just like a true "gangsta pimp" would have done.

This could be why Michael didn't get many straight-laced customers leasing his limousine; although he did get a lot of cool people and hip-hop junkies who enjoyed the pimp smell, as well as the smell of new leather inside. If you wanted to impress a hip woman, this was the ride to do it in.

Michael could leave without the lawyer telling him to be careful and to watch his back. He also told Michael that the police were overly interested in his limo. So he asked Michael if there was something inside of it. This was the same limo that Michael parked in front of his club, drove his girls around in and would use his white Lincoln for big concerts and classic events. That's what he would use if he ever had dinner with the President himself.

"One last thing," said the lawyer. "Don't be surprised if they put a tracer in your ride." Michael left that evening leaving Kim holding some dope while he went out to sell some. The Halloween party was all scheduled and the show had to go on.

The limo was sitting right out front of Ingo's house and Michael remembered what his lawyer had told him about the police possibly installing a tracer on his car. He figured that's how they knew where he was. Then again, there had to have been over a thousand flyers given out advertising the party, and also all kinds of radio promotions, none of which should have mattered as they were on private property and they had every right to do as they wanted on private property.

This was a big house and you really couldn't hear any noise outside. Michael figured that Doug, the doorman and security guard, would handle it as he always did. He was a wannabe cop, who stood 6'4", and weighed 300 lbs and was solid as a rock.

Michael went to the door and Ingo was outside talking to the police. They knew how Ingo felt about cops and hating them as well. Prior to this, the only criminal case Ingo ever had was a battery against a police officer when she beat up a policeman and gave another policewoman a black eye.

She was more like arguing than talking to them when Michael stepped outside and right away, the police officer said, "Mr. Brown, this party has to end right now!" "What for, did we break any laws?" asked Michael. The officer said, "There are just too many people and the noise is way too loud." Ingo blurted out, "You show me one person who has complained, and let me talk to them. Besides, this is my house, why are you talking to Mike, when it should be me that you're talking to!" "Excuse me ma'am but we are talking to Mr. Brown because we know this is his party," said the officer. Ingo blurted out, "This is bull shit and police harassment against my baby's daddy." While Ingo was up in the police officer's face, the officer asked Ingo to step back and pushed her. She went smooth off on him.

The first thing Ingo did was hit the male officer then she hit the female officer. The female officer hit the ground. Then Ingo hit the male officer again. You could see his jaw loosen and fall. Both officers took a minute to get up and Ingo was in her fighting stance.

"That's what you get for putting your hands on me and all your bull shit harassment," Ingo instructed them.

As soon as the officer regained their composure, they went straight for Ingo and took her down to the ground and Michael stepped between them and ended up in a wrestling match. The next thing anyone knew, they were hauling Ingo off to jail.

Both police officers were pretty badly beaten up. Eventually all the money they had made that night was used to make Ingo's bail and hire her a lawyer. Now Ingo had her second case, the same as the previous one, fighting with the police, which is a felony charge.

"You can't dig yourself out of the hole the Devil has helped you dig yourself into without the help of God," Michael told her.

CHAPTER 16

FRAMED, MILWAUKEE ROBBERIES, GOD SPEAKS THROUGH MULE

Michael went home the next morning after the Halloween party. He took the kids to school and went to Stacey's apartment. When he arrived at the parking lot, he saw an undercover agent in an unmarked car. He then saw Angie's car and wondered what was going on.

Michael went up to the apartment anyways. He knew he hadn't done anything wrong so he had nothing to worry about. Once up the stair, Michael could see that something was going on, so he asked Stacey what was wrong. "Nothing," she told him. "Just stay right here," she said. Stacey walked down the stairs as Angie came up the stairs. Michael asked Angie, "What's going on?" Behind him he heard, "You are not on the lease and you shouldn't be using a key Mr. Brown and you have been warned about this before," said the woman. First Michael wondered how the woman knew his name, and then he told her, "You must be mistaken, because I have never been warned. In fact, I've never spoken to you before." Then he told her, "There's no law that says that I can't check up on my friends, and furthermore, Miss, how do you know my name?" he asked the woman as he left Stacey's.

Michael went to his cousin Little Jimmy's girlfriend's apartment, which was around the corner. Little Jimmy used to come to Michael's house before he went to prison. His cousin wasn't so little anymore as he was over eighteen and pushing plenty of dope in the neighborhood, but the hood was already getting too hot for him. He was well known by all of Madison especially the folks and the police on the East Side. He needed to find a new spot to sell dope, hang out and rest while working off his pager.

Little did Michael know, but Little Jimmy was going to be helping him out in more ways than he could help himself. Little Jimmy wasn't Michael's cousin by blood, but to Michael they were as close as it gets. They cared about each other and Michael would look out for him and give him money when he used to look out for Michael when he was a shorty as well. The only difference was that Jimmy didn't have to hustle for Michael back then.

Jimmy was Michael's Uncle Bubbie, a.k.a. Dog's, stepson with whom he had three kids with Jimmy's mother. Michael used to hustle out of her spot when he first got into the game. Bubbie really wasn't Michael's blood Uncle, but his sister and Michael's mother were best friends from the South Side of Chicago, and they all had the same last name.

Michael did some genealogy research and learned that they were distant relations. He didn't tell anyone except his Aunt Blackie's son, Larry, who was the oldest of the five kids. Two of the kids were twins but they had been adopted.

When Michael got there, Angie wouldn't tell him anything. "Nothing," she told him. "You will just have to ask Stacey," she told him. "I already asked Stacey and she said nothing," he told her. Angie told him, "It's nothing you want to know about or get yourself involved in." "What is that supposed to mean?" Michael asked her. "We just got into a little trouble last night," she admitted to him. "But it's all straightened out now," she excused. "How can I not worry about it when it involves you and Stacey? Both of you are important to me," he told her. Stacey came in and said, "Please, just let me handle it Michael. She handed something to Michael. It was a new Versace silk shirt. It was very nice and must have cost a fortune, so he asked her, "Where did you get this?" "Don't ask questions," she said, "do you like it or not?" "Yes, of course," he admitted. She then handed Michael some money, totaling about two hundred dollars.

Michael folded the cash and placed in his pocket like there was nothing to it. He was somewhat concerned about where she had been all night and into the morning, but once he was given the clothes and money he forgot all about his line of questioning. Michael decided to leave the apartment for the moment since they weren't going to tell him anything anyway, so he quit asking questions.

As soon as he got to the door to leave, the landlord was standing there. She asked Michael, "What are you doing here? Your name isn't on the lease." "I'm just here to check on my friends," he informed her. Just then, a man came around the corner and introduced himself as a police officer. He asked Michael, "Are you Michael Brown?" "Yes, I am," admitted Michael. "Do you have some identification?" ask the officer. "Yes I do," he said.

"What's this all about," said Michael as he reached for his ID. The officer said, "You are under arrest, Mr. Brown." "For what?' asked Michael. "A robbery that occurred in Milwaukee," the officer informed. "Are you sure you have the right Michael Brown?" Michael asked surprised. "I have never been involved with any robbery in Milwaukee," insisted Michael. The police officer took out his handcuffs and said; "You can explain that to the detective's downtown."

Michael didn't know for the life of him what this was all about, as he didn't have anything to do with any robbery, especially the robbery in Milwaukee. As soon as he go to the police station, Michael called his attorney. He couldn't get through to him so he left a message on his machine.

Michael sat there in the police station very confused about the whole ordeal. After a while passed, they transferred him to Glendale Police station in a suburb of Milwaukee.

Michael noticed a cop who looked like a priest. He told the officer that they had the wrong man. The officer told Michael they he had nothing to do with it. He said, "Don't worry man. If you had nothing to do with it, then you don't have anything to worry about."

On the way to Glendale, they told him that he would be going to Milwaukee County Jail because Glendale didn't have a jail. Just a couple of minutes into the trip at the third stop light on E. Washington Avenue they came across Kim who was trying to flag them down. At first, the cop driving wouldn't stop, but Michael asked if he could give his wife his jewelry because it was very expensive. "Could you also tell her what is going on," he asked. "That's against policy," said the cop. "Look man, she's my wife and she has two little kids at home and I couldn't call her to tell her anything," Michael pleaded with him. So the officer pulled over and told Kim that Michael was under arrest for robbery in the city of Glendale, Milwaukee County. He said, "I'm taking him there so he can be booked and processed. You can come and see him then." Kim asked, "Can I get his jewelry and money so it doesn't get stolen or misplace?" Then she told him, "Look, you have the wrong man. Mike wouldn't do such a thing. He had a family and he's a local businessman." The cop told Kim, "Ma'am, I'm sure it will all be straightened out when we get to the station." He handed Kim the jewelry and the cash. Michael had at least a couple of grand in small bills, and the jewelry was worth a few grand as well Kim looked as if she was about to cry, but she didn't. She was always strong when it came to situations like this.

They arrived at the Glendale Police station that evening. Michael was booked and questioned and then taken to a holding cell until he could be transferred to the Milwaukee County Jail. He was tired and he slept all through the first night. Michael was emotionally exhausted from all that was going on and he desperately needed sleep but before going to sleep in his cell that night, he prayed to God.

Michael needed to talk to someone who would understand-someone who cared and would see him through this ordeal. Michael wasn't sure whom else he could turn to, so he naturally went to the Creator. He was taught by his grandmother that when he really needed someone, he could always turn to the Creator.

The next day Michael was transferred. He went through a long day of processing at the Milwaukee County Jail. It was no breeze and it took twelve hours to get booked in. Michael waited on benches, concrete floors and was fed cold brown lunches. When he finally got to the cell house on the fifth floor of Pod D, he was ready for so overdue sleep.

Milwaukee County Jail is a place where you had to make yourself known. A person really has to stand their ground and try to look mean and Michael could fit the part, as he was a big tall man. For Michael, this was the first jail he was ever in where they were really serious about gangs, but probably not as serious as where he came from, but that is where most of the gangs originated.

Milwaukee was less organized, than Chicago but they were doing what is considered "block banging". There were still guys there who were willing to die for what they believed in. although they were more into the numbers, the number of their gang members and the number of street blocks where they came from meant a whole lot more. All that night Michael could hear Brown Street echoing throughout the pod.

Michael was placed in a cell with a dude from the North Side, which is predominately Spanish. The guy wasn't accepted by most of the Brothers in the jail.

Spanish guys aren't supposed to be in a cell that isn't your race you are supposed to act like a fool and refuse to enter the cell until they put you with your own race. Michael didn't do any of that as it was way too late and he was too tired for that game. He wanted to rest and he wanted to talk to God. Michael asked God what he did to deserve what he was going through.

Here he was in this crazy place for something he had absolutely nothing to do with. Michael learned from the interview with the Glendale Police detective that some woman supposedly picked him out of a photo lineup. She said she saw him leaving the scene of a robbery in Glendale. They said out of all of the hundreds of photographs they showed this lady, she picked out Stacey's license plate number, and the cops received information that Stacey was affiliated with Michael.

Michael told the Glendale Detective the same thing he told the officer that picked him up at Stacey's apartment. "I didn't have anything to do with any robbery in Glendale or anywhere else for that matter," he insisted. Just like the first officers, the Glendale detective informed Michael that is he didn't have anything to do with the robbery, he would have a chance to prove it and would be out in a couple of days. "We just want you to go through a line up," said the detective.

Michael introduced himself to his cellmate named Juan. Juan overheard Michael praying and asked if he really believed? Michael SAID HE DID. "What about you Juan, do you believe?" asked Michael.

Juan said that he did. "But believing in God won't make things any easier." Said Juan. "I know that's right," admitted Michael.

The next day Michael woke up and called Stacey. She asked him how things were going. He told her that he was okay and things were fine. "I'm really sorry about what happened," she apologized to him. She also told Michael, "I already told them that you had nothing to do with it and that we did it." For the first time Michael asked Stacey, "What is it you guys did?" "We robbed s store or a restaurant in Milwaukee suburb Glendale," she told him. "Who do you mean 'we' robbed," asked Michael. "I could be facing a life sentence for this crap," he instructed her. "Don't say that," she said. "You didn't have anything to do with it and you'll get out," Stacey said. Michael replied, "That's not for you or me to determine at this point. It's completely up to these people who are holding me. "Supposedly some lady had picked me out of a photo lineup and that is not good for me," he told her. "The truth will come out Michael, I know it will," insisted Stacey.

Michael said, "Only God can help me and everyone else who believes, but I need you to tell me what happened and you have to tell me now!" demanded Michael. Stacey told him, "I drove the car and Angie waited in the car with me while Rob and Skin went in and did the robbery." "Why do you keep hanging out with those guys and doing crazy things?" Michael asked, Stacey was silent and wouldn't answer at first. "Stacey answers me," insisted Michael. "I don't know why," she admitted.

"You guys are going to wind up getting me a life sentence for something I had absolutely nothing to do with!" accused Michael. He continued, "You know that the cops don't like me and they'll put whatever they can on me! They would love to see me out of business and locked up for good." Stacey agreed, "I know," she said. Michael was heated and just hung up on her. He could imagine her saying she loved him on the other end of the phone.

Not long after Michael hung up the phone, he was called to the officer's station by one of the deputies. "Brown, report to the officer's station." Michael walked in a room and asked, "Did you want to see Brown?" The deputy said "Come with me, you have some visitors." Michael followed the deputy to where there were a couple of agents awaiting. "Mr. Brown, have a seat," said one of the agents. "We are here to talk to you about a robbery in Glendale and the whereabouts of some of your friends," he reported. "You must have heard the conversation I just had on the phone with one of my friends. So you must know that I didn't have anything to do with a robbery and you know damn well who did," demanded Michael.

"We can see that you are not going to be very cooperative with us, but I can guarantee you, Mr. Brown, that one day you'll wish you would have been more cooperative," the agent promised. "Like hell," insulted Michael, as he got up and pounded on the door, yelling, "Deputy, get me out of here" the deputy came and took Michael back to his cellblock.

Once he got back to the cellblock, Michael telephoned Kim to tell her what had just happened. Kim assured Michael "I don't think I told them anything." "What do you mean you don't think you told them anything."? Michael asked. Kim spoke up, "Well, I don't know. I know how you feel about anyone telling anything to the police, but it may help in the long run. Nothing else has. If you don't tell them something you are in big trouble. If you know where Rob and Skin are at, you should say something. All I am saying is to think about it. You need to think about your family and yourself. I don't want you doing anything you don't want to and I really don't agree with telling the police anything either, especially when it involves your friends, but what do you do? You are the only one that has to tell them and try to straighten things out. Michael just thinks about what I'm saying."

Michael went back to his cell that night and couldn't sleep a wink. He tossed and turned all night long. It wasn't just because of what Kim had said to him, but it was all the thoughts about how he had gotten into this situation in the first place that were running through his head.

Michael was placing most of the blame on the police, but some of it he put on the lady who picked him out in the photo lineup. Michael knew he was innocent and the lady should have known that as well. He had to acknowledge to himself that he shouldn't have been associating with those guys in the first place-those guys he considered to be his friends.

Before going to sleep, he was talking to his cellmate, Juan. Juan asked him what he was in for. Michael told him that he was there for a robbery he didn't do. "Yeah right," replied Juan. "That's what they all say," he retorted. Michael explained what happened and a little about his friends and what they had allegedly done. He couldn't see any reason in violating a convict's most sacred rule about something that Stacey had already admitted to. Besides, Juan was only there for a parole violation. It was a chance that Michael shouldn't have taken, and luckily, for him it didn't backfire on him. He also told Juan about the conversation he had with Kim as it was still troubling him and he was surprised when his cellmate told him, "Hey man, maybe you should think about what she told you." Because of that comment, Michael thought Juan shouldn't be trusted, and then he thought about something else he had said, "If you didn't do it and you want to clear the record, and then tell them all you know and be done with it. Be careful though, because it still won't mean that they will believe you and set you free."

Just as he was about to fall asleep, Michael got down on his knees and asked God to please help him. Not just with this case he was up against, but also the other case he was facing for soliciting prostitution in Madison. Michael knew he wasn't guilty of that case either.

Michael knew it was time to go because he was scared. It would only be a matter of time before they may try to come after him for something else. Plus he thought the longer he stayed in jail, the more likely it would be that they would convict him on this bogus robbery charge. He knew he needed to make some kind of move.

He was calling Kim and Stacey every day and he began to reevaluate every aspect of his life. He wanted to be out of anything and everything that had to do with crime. The people he really needed to explain this to were his kids. On the phone, they were beginning to ask questions that were hard to answer. He would tell them that daddy would be home soon and that daddy had to straighten something out. The kids acted as if they understood and believed everything he said to them-his word was like gospel to them. Marcus only had one question, "Daddy when are you coming home! You are coming to pick me up, aren't you?" Michael would simply tell Marcus, "Yes!"

The days started to slow down drastically. Michael hated this place and he came to realize how ridiculous the gang banging nonsense really was. All the block banging didn't make any sense and it was getting on his nerves. That nonsensical mentality has done nothing but kill people over some cheap material goods, money and property that weren't theirs to begin with.

Sitting in jail, these different neighborhood folks wanted to kill each other over absolutely nothing. They wouldn't even be concerned about their criminal cases. The ones that were there were there for allegedly killing their baddest killers in the city, state and country and nobody mess with them.

Milwaukee was known for the highest murder rate per capita in the country at the time. A guy they called the Mule was in jail for not just one or two murders, he was there for six murders, and they say he was getting high with five women, who were supposed to be dope fiends or at least users. He killed them for some crazy reason and just left them where they lay.

Then there were a couple of others guys who were also supposedly dope fiends and he threw that in for good measure. They say Mule killed his friends and relatives. Some of the guys were talking about taking Mule out, but nobody dared to say a word to him. Michael took it as a compliment that he was the only one Mule talked to. He told Michael, "Kid, if you didn't do what they said you did, then don't worry about it. Do what you have to do and pray that God will help you out." Michael knew what Mule meant by the second part of his comment. In the Bible it is said that God talks even through a Mule/Ass, (see Numbers 22:28). And this guy was called Mule, so Michael figured he definitely had the right name. Mule was built like Lee Haney, and he could knock out a bull with his bare hands.

Mule had recently finished doing time down south at Parsham Prison in Mississippi. He also did (twenty years) at Angola Prison in Louisiana (for murder). His past history was remarked on the news report after he was arrested for his current murder allegations.

Mule didn't do much but sit around and play chess. Mule was on the news again and so was Michael's buddy, Skin. One of the other dudes pointed it out to Michael, "There goes your friend for another bank robbery." Michael got on the phone and called Stacey to tell her he just saw Skin on the news report for a robbery. Stacey told Michael she had just talked to Skin about him. She told Michael that he was supposed to tell the detectives everything he knew, because Skin was going to contact the police and tell them the truth, that Michael had nothing to do with any of his robberies. Stacey told Michael she was going to do the same.

Michael didn't know how he could tell the detectives much of anything because he didn't know where Rob and Skin were. He didn't even know what, how or when they did what they did or were said to have done, not to mention that Michael was firmly against talking to police. "Don't worry about it Michael," said Stacey. "I'll tell them everything."

Michael asked Stacey to go to the bar where he had been on the night of the robbery he was accused of. He needed her to find a witness who would confirm he was there at the bar that night. He also called Kim and asked her to do the same thing just to make sure one of them would come through for him. Kim said she would follow through for him but Michael wondered how the bar owner would help but remember him being there that night.

They knew who Michael was and so did many of the bars regular customers. How many black customers actually frequented that bar wearing lots of expensive jewelry and carrying bags of money? And he always arrived driving a limousine surrounded by an entourage of young women and brought drinks for everybody. Both Stacey and Kim agreed that someone would have to remember Michael.

He went to sleep that night thinking in general about his life. He told himself that he didn't want to continue living the kind of life he had been living. Thinking back long ago to when he was serving his state prison sentence; he remembered making a promise to himself and to God. Michael wanted God to help him travel another path and do something different with his life, something positive. Michael had already promised that he would never get involved with drugs or crime again. "How did I get off track? What happened?" he thought to himself. This is also, what Mule had said to him. He told Michael that if he didn't do it, not to worry about it. "Whatever it is that they know let God handle the rest." Here is this guy facing life in prison for several murders and he's telling Michael about cooperating with God the Father. It may have been the look on his face, but Michael won't soon forget the look on Mule's face. It was Mule doing the talking to Michael, but the voice seemed to be coming from somewhere else.

It could have been from the preoccupation of Michael's thoughts, but the next day seemed to be zipping by. He was pondering, where he went wrong and how he wound up back in jail. He was also thinking about how he was going to get out of there. He wanted to ensure he would make his life better and he wouldn't make the same mistakes to end up back in the same predicament. After praying again to God, he tossed and turned all night. He busted out in a cold sweat every night he was there. Michael thought it was because he was coming down off the drugs and alcohol, but it wasn't. Plus Michael was having visions and hearing voices. They were telling him "Come to me and I will set you free spiritually." The upper left corner of the cell lit up and there was a man standing, or more like hovering, over him. He was surrounded by light, pointing his finger and glaring directly at Michael. It was as if he was inviting Michael to follow him. Michael felt inviting warmth from the light that was around the man. He had the friendliest smile Michael had even seen and Michael wanted to go with him in such a bad way. Michael knew he had to be dreaming or having a nightmare, but this was like no nightmare he ever had before. He climbed down from his bunk and washed his face and told himself that it was just a dream. Eventually he climbed back into his bunk and went to sleep.

When Michael awoke the next day, he finally got the call he was waiting for. It was the detectives to take him for the line-up that he was sure would set him free. Michael didn't have any qualms about it because he knew he was innocent. Standing in the elevators with the officers, he was beginning to feel like something wasn't quite right. He wasn't sure what it was, but he thought of the message from Mule saying, "nothing was for sure."

There was this older Brother on the elevator who asked, “Who is this line-up for?” “Are any of you other Brothers going to the line-up?” He asked. “It’s for me,” said Michael.

“But I didn’t do what they said I did,” Michael said. The Brother asked Michael, “What are they saying you did?” “Robbery, but that’s not my thing and I surely don’t need the money,” Michael said realizing. He was giving way too much information. Then the Brother asked him, “What is it that you do little brother?” Michael didn’t want to say, because he thought his last comment might offend the older Brother. He didn’t want to make enemies or create any problems either, but he told him, “I own some clubs in Madison and I work in the music industry.” “What is your name, little brother?” asked the older Brother. “They call me many names, but I am Mike Brown.

“You mean like pimp Ice Mice or just-Ice?” He asked. “Man, I heard all about you on the streets and on the radio,” he retorted. “Whatever you heard, it probably isn’t half true. I’m not famous and I am definitely not rich,” confessed Michael. “Man I heard you own an escort service and some clubs in Madison and that you threw a lot of concerts and stuff, but you started out as a dope dealer and a pimp,” informed the older Brother. Michael admitted that much of what said was the truth, but he never considered himself a pimp. He said that’s just what he was called and that there is much more to him than that. He admitted that he was in the music industry and that he threw parties and concerts. The older brother told him, “I also know one of your brothers named Skin. He was in prison with me and let me tell you that, that brother is one loose cannon.”

Michael was shocked at first. He thought that anyone who had been to Wisconsin State Prison system had to have seen all the fights that happened. Skin attempted to escape from medium and maximum security joints, just like Waupun and (KM) Kettle Moraine and they would have had known him, so to Michael it wasn’t a shock to hear the talk.

The older Brother asked Michael, “How did you get hooked up with a guy like Skin anyway?” Michael answered, “In State Prison, when I was a kid.” “Did you know Skin was supposed to have told on his rap partner the same guy he escaped with back when he was a kid,” he informed Michael. “I didn’t know that,” admitted Michael. “I met him when he saved my cousin Larry from being jumped by some G.D.’s from Milwaukee. They say he might have set the whole thing up,” said Michael. The older brother said, “And now was getting off this elevator to go to a line-up.” Michael had nothing else to say to the guy.

He figured the other Brother was trying to engage him in small talk, but then walked into the room with Michael. There were two Glendale police officers as well as two officers from Milwaukee. One of the officers from Milwaukee handed Michael a tag with a number on it. He was number one-the first one who would go through the door. Michael was ready to get this over with. The last guy through the door was the old school Homie-He was going to be number seven. “Here little Homie, give me your number and take mine. You know when going through a line-up you don’t have to keep the number they gave you. It could actually be a set up,” said the older Homie.

Michael exchanged numbers with him prior to entering the line-up. Each participant was asked to step forward, and then step back. They were asked to face to the left and then to the right. “Number one, step back in line,” came the voice over the intercom. “Okay, you can all leave,” squawked the intercom.

Within twenty-four hours, all participants would receive something. Old School asked the officer, "What happened, did they pick me?" "As a matter of fact, they did." Admitted the officer, "So you mean I am getting arrested? What am I being charged with?" "Nothing, unless you were able to commit this robbery while serving life in prison," said the officer.

Old School commented, "Of course I didn't commit a robbery, plus I would never go out to that racist town of Glendale. They're almost as bad as Madison if not worse." "You hear me, Young Blood?" he asked Michael. "Yea, I hear ya," said Michael. "I hope you know you owe me one, cause that was obviously a set up that was meant for you," he attested. "Thanks Old School, I mean that brother, thank you," said Michael. "You really want to thank me Young Blood, you could leave me some of that big money on my account," he said. Michael said, "You got that coming brother, don't worry about that."

Old School was probably in his fifties and down on his luck, if there was such a thing. He was in jail for a parole violation from his life sentence and had only been out of prison for a few days.

As soon as Michael was about to get off the elevator to go back to the cellblock, an officer said, "Brown, you have a visit." Michael went into the visiting booth fine attorney Mark waiting to see him.

'How are you doing?" he asked. "I'm fine." Said Michael, "but I'll be better when I am out of here," he proclaimed. Mark told him, "I have some good news and I have some bad news. Which do you want first?" Michael said, "It doesn't matter." "The lady didn't pick you out of the line-up, but you probably know that already," Mark said, "Yea I already know," said Michael. "The bad news is that I'm not going to be able to get you out today," he affirmed. "Why the hell not?" asked Michael. "I didn't do anything to deserve to be in here," injected Michael. "That's not exactly what the lady said," said the lawyer. And what we have here is a case of mistaken identity, which is what they're going to say. The truth is the cops really want to make you for this. Even knowing full well, you're innocent. They tried to pin this rap on you and they tried to set you up for the line-up."

Michael said, "I figured that was the case. All of this is bad news so far, so what is the good news?" The lawyer said "The good news is it seems your wife Kim and you young friend Stacey went out and found some folks who can ID you as not being at the scene of the crime, but bar-hopping in Madison that night."

Michael said, "That's because it's true. I told you I didn't do it. So now what? When are you going to get me out of here?" "It's as easy as that," said Mark. "You should have a court date in a day or so and hopefully I can get this thrown out at that time," he said. "Indeed hopefully. Robbery isn't my M.O. and neither is rap or murder," declared Michael. "I need you to believe that and I need you to fight for me like you know that," said Michael. "I do believe you Michael and I will fight for you too," said Mark.

Michael went back to his cellblock and called Ingo. His attorney told him that Ingo and her parents had called him and came by with the retainer money. Ingo already felt that Michael dogged her, but she always came through when he needed her.

She tried to get Michael one of the lawyer friends from Milwaukee, but that would have cost her too much. Mark was willing to do it for what she was willing to pay. Kim also pitched in with a little of the money.

Michael though this would be easier than it was because he was actually and factually innocent. He didn't want to involve Kim or his Attorney Mark, not to mention Kim preaching to him as well. Ingo told Michael, "Well, you are going to hear it from me anyway. I told you that your friends and those young white girlfriends were going to get you into trouble. The next thing you know, they are going to get you a life sentence in prison."

"Ingo, don't be saying that, you know I didn't do this robbery. It's not my thing, unless it was somebody I knew with a whole bunch of money or dope," said Michael. "You see what I'm saying?" asked Ingo. "But Ingo I think I'm done with all that after this," assured Michael. "Yeah, sure you are Michael," accused Ingo. "You best watch yourself, because I and my mom or Kim won't be there someday. Haven't you see that the police want you really bad?" she asked "Yeah," said Michael. "But they're supposed to get me for something I actually did, not for something I didn't do," Michael retorted. "Also, I know you will always be there for me. I know that because you love me and I know I'll be there for you no matter what," Michael assured her. Then Ingo said "Whatever, Michael!"

Michael knew when she said that, that she was either fed up with him or very angry with him. He went to sleep that night praying to God that this would be over soon so that he could get out and be with his kids and family, He hadn't seen them since Halloween and now it was just days from Thanksgiving. This would be the longest Michael had been in jail since being released in the early nineties, which was over five years at least, and he had to admit that he was scared. He was learning how easily a person could actually get locked up for a crime they didn't do and had nothing to do with.

Michael swore to God that if, He would get him out of this, and he would stay out for good, stay out of the streets and stay home with his family. He would stick to the Word of God once and for all. He wanted to see what God was trying to say through Michael Brown because now God definitely had Michael's attention and he was listening.

The next morning after Michael woke up he called Kim and told her his thoughts on following the Word of God.

She told him, "It sounds to me like I heard this all before and I hope this time you mean it more than ever," he promised. "I do believe you Michael and not just because I want to. I know you," she informed him. "Thanks for not just believing in me but also for going out and getting the evidence that shows my whereabouts that night as well," he said graciously. "You are welcome. Now you need to get yourself home to me and the kids, we need you." She said.

Michael told her, "Just as soon as they permit me to. I will be home." After Michael hung up with Kim, he called Stacey. For some reason he felt he needed to talk to her. He told Stacey about the same thing he told Kim and how he wanted things to be different and how God was obviously trying to tell him something. Michael was determined to learn what that was about himself. He told Stacey that he didn't want to live his life as a common criminal.

He had dreams and goals and he had kids too. He told her that he wanted to be rich and famous at first, and he still did but it wasn't quite the same. Now he wanted to help people and make a difference. He didn't want to do that from some jail cell or prison. He also told Stacey that this might mean the end of their relationship.

He needed to straighten out and get away from all the bullshit. He didn't like the idea of going to jail for something he didn't do, let alone for something that his friends did. He told her that he would understand if she was mad at him, but he had to do what he had to do. He sat there for a minute and waited for an angry response from her, but instead she said. "I understand Michael. I want the same thing too." She never called him Michael before.

Her reply floored him and made him wonder how he could let her go when she was there to go to bat for him. She certainly more or less seemed to understand Michael and the street life that Kim and Ingo didn't understand Michael wasn't sure if he needed to or really wanted to stop because he still needed to make money. He just had to learn how to make it the right way and not the wrong way. His old way was hurting the people he loved the most. He was thinking he could get what he needed and quit and Stacey was sure to help with that. Michael knew he was stinking thinking again, so he told himself to snap out of it.

The next day Michael has a court appearance about midday. His lawyer Mark was present to argue his case for Michael. The prosecutor began by saying that this couldn't be a mistake and that Michael was picked out in a photo lineup. He also brought up that someone identified Stacey's license plate number with information from Madison, which put Michael under the suspicion that got him arrested.

The District Attorney went on to declare that Michael knew whom the real perpetrators were, but wouldn't cooperate with the police. Then Michael's lawyer cut in and said, "That's not my client's job. He knows nothing and doesn't know where they are." The judge was silent. "Michael did cooperate and told the truth. He went into the line-up and that was to frame my client," retorted Mark, "Not only that, but my client has several witnessed that put him in a bar in Madison at the time of the crime," insisted the lawyer.

The judge took a minute and they came back with his decision. "I base my decision on the facts that I believe the affidavits that were presented to me claim they didn't know this man personally. That he was not with them at the time this crime was supposed to be committed. It would have taken too long for the defendant to travel to Milwaukee, commit a robbery and return to Madison at a bar. My decision takes into consideration all the other facts that don't make an actionable charge, thus I dismiss this charge."

"God speaks to us all the time. He never quits talking to us; we just quit listening to his small, still voice within us. To listen and obey is the best thing we can do. God speaks to us through his Word the Bible. We must talk to God as a regular person, pray and He will respond to us and get our attention. Even if He has to take you through something that will find you alone first, He will get your attention."

CHAPTER 17

COOK COUNTY JAIL, CHICAGO;

GOD KEEPS SPEAKING

Kim was in the courtroom and luckily, Michael was able to leave the courtroom with Kim that day. The kids, Jazzman and Michael Jr, were asleep in the car. They went straight home and Michael took a long bath while Kim fixed him something to eat. They went immediately to the bedroom to make up for some long overdue lovemaking. Before they fell off to sleep, Michael told Kim how much he loved and cared for her and how much he appreciated all she did for him and the kids. He went to sleep with some peace of mind, not knowing what the next day would bring.

Michael stayed home for a day or two after he was released from jail. Time flew by fast and when he finally left the house, it was already Thanksgiving 1997. He went to his mother's for Thanksgiving just like he did every year. Kim and the kids went to her parent's house. Michael was never allowed to spend any time with her and her family because they never offered and never invited him. However, Kim was always welcome at Michael's family house and she always had a good time there.

Michael's mom was living with her new boyfriend Tom, so this year things were a little different. Tom was a big white man, about 350 lbs and 6'3" tall. He was an old dope fiend who worked most of his adult life at the Post Office. He was in his early forties and Michael's mom was about to turn fifty. Truthfully, Michael respected Tom. He didn't have anything personal against him and Tom himself respected Michael, at least to his face. Michael didn't like the fact that Tom was a doper. He never actually saw him use but he heard that he did and he didn't like it. Michael heard that Tom had said some mean things to his sisters, but he never acted like that around Michael.

The only person Michael ever considered being a father to him and the family was his Pops, because he did the most to help raise them. He would come around to see them and check on them and he was always welcome there.

Michael spent some time with his mom, his brother Bruce and his sisters Tricia and Sasha. Tammy came over a lot as well. His brother Pat, a.k.a. Ruttie, was in jail at Kettle Moraine State Prison in Wisconsin and called on the phone. Michael talked to him and promised to send him some money and visit him.

Michael and his mother smoked some weed and had a drink together. Her favorite drink was Hennessey. It wasn't long until Kim came over from her parent's. Michael was always glad to see Kim and hear that she had a good time, even though Michael wasn't invited to go with her. He didn't like it, but he didn't hate them for it either. He had been black all his life, and he knew what it was like to be discriminated against because of his skin color, criminal record or both. Whatever it was, either way it wasn't right, because he had always been good to their daughter.

He never put hands on Kim and he never even called her names. She used to say, "I know I am a mean bitch, so just go ahead and say it, because you help to make me that way."

Every time they would fight or have differences, Michael would just leave. That is how he dealt with things.

He always gave Kim anything she wanted and took her anywhere she wanted to go. He used to say; "No one can push your buttons but you if you allow them to." Whenever they argued, it was never a big deal. It was usually over Michael ignoring Kim's woman intuition or because e wasn't paying attention to her.

Michael's beef with Kim was usually over needing money, because that would fix everything. Whenever they had disagreements. Michael would act as if he agreed with her, then he would end-up doing his own thing. Once in a while, he would put on his mean facemask and say, "I hear what you're saying." If that didn't work to manipulate her in the way, he hoped he would just leave. Michael's major issues were drinking and smoking weed. He didn't see it as a problem and he kept doing it for days now and he wanted to see Stacey.

When he got to Stacey's they were waiting for him and having a party. "It's about time you got here," said Stacey. "Where have you been?" she asked. "I've been around and had some things to do with my family," Michael told her. "I've been doing some thinking." Michael said. Stacey told him, "That's cool, so have I." she took him by the hand and guided him to a table. "Here you go," she told him, nodding at the table.

There were some of his favorites: weed, booze and food. Stacey couldn't cook all that well, but it was way better than jail food. She also had the latest 2Pac CD"Still on the Rise," the second CD released following his death. Michael was definitely a 2Pac fan. He could relate to him and he knew he was fighting a battle of the spirits and good versus evil.

Michael played the CD and it was all that and more. Unfortunately, 2Pac died on the night of Michael concert at the Barrymore Theatre on September 16, 1996. During the show, they gave a moment of silent prayer after announcing it on stage.

Michael still had some problems and most of them centered on money and rent, which was late the last few months since his arrested. He also still had a case pending in New York for possession of a firearm.

Michael just wanted to forget all about that for a day. He could have tried to hide the gun in a better place, but he forgot he had it and he only kept it for "just in case and protection" purposes.

He had been fighting this case for about a year already and his lawyer told him that his chances of beating it were slim. He would have likely had accept a plea for a little time. His lawyer said that if he could come up with enough money, he could either get him probation or even get the case thrown out.

Michael caught the case while working in New York with Dajoint Promotions. It was there that he got work with some major labels doing promotions and production Michael was basically doing whatever he had to so he could get a foot in the door. His job was looking for new artists and giving them the chance to set up concert dates or the label company would more likely to drop him, them and their contracts.

It was a difficult job, but Michael loved it. He thought it was what he needed to stay in touch with some of the big heads. He also figured that they would help him pay bail and also get him one of their high-dollar attorneys-someone like Michael Wright who recently had done work for Busta Rhymes.

Michael decided to take Kim's advice because she was right. She told him not to show up because they wouldn't spend money to come and get him. It would cost too much, but he was still too busy trying to beat it out. Since he caught the gun case, he had to quit going to New York unless he had to go to court. He had given up his job there before they offered him a position as an A&R, four days a week, which allowed him to come home on weekends. Of course, that's what they were saying, but what would really happen could possibly turn out to be totally different thing.

Michael would get so involved in his work at times that it would take him at least seven or more days to get it right. As he had it now in the Tri-State area, he had to be out for big parties and meetings. After all, he was the Midwest Regional Promoter. He would come home as much as he wanted to still make it to his hearts content. More than that, he was addicted to street hustling, which usually involved dealing dope, cocaine and weed. He didn't consider himself as that kind of a person. His perception was clouded by his own pride. He saw himself as a street businessman with a master's degree at being a player and a hustler who played women. He would gamble on anything for a buck, but he would never rape, steal or kill for any reason or for any price. That was Michael. Well, at least that's how he saw himself.

If Michael thought things were tough before, they were about to get a lot tougher. He had been out of jail for a while and was making plenty of money at the club. He recently had caught the prostitution case in Madison and he hoped and prayed to God that everything was going to turn out good on that, but he wasn't sure if he was going to get out of that. It was really bugging him and he just wanted to get out of everything. Michael's first court date, "the preliminary hearing," was to decide if enough evidence existed to go to trial. The alleged victims, Breanna and Reanna, came to testify that it was unknown to Michael and unplanned, that they were not commanded, controlled or encouraged by Michael in the acts of prostitution. In fact, he discouraged prostitution and that was the truth. It was more like he turned his back on it. He told them not to do it, and if they did, it should be done on their own time, not on his and not with his consent. If they were going to do it, they should surely get what they thought it was worth.

Even the alleged victims said Michael didn't perpetrate a crime against them, but the judge still bonded Michael over for trial because he had said that there was no way Michael couldn't have known what was going on or had knowledge of it because of the money that was involved.

Michael's attorney said the judge was "nostalgic" and said that nowadays girls dance for a lot more than five dollars. That comment surely didn't gain Michael any favor with the judge. It was only a few months later that, that particular judge was forced off the bench for some of his own misbehavior.

Michael was contemplating these issues when he was at Stacey's apartment. He was under a lot of pressure, not to mention that he was still struggling with not having a regular income or a place to go because of not having a club.

He was there at Stacey's getting drunk and venting his frustrations, hollering, screaming and singing to some of 2Pac's old songs that were playing on the CD "Hail Mary, come with me, Hail Mary can't you see, do you want to ride or die?" Then played another of his favorites, "I wonder if Heaven's got a ghetto?"

Michael's lil cousin Jimmy came over with a couple of his Homies and he brought a bong just for Michael. Stacey also had a couple of her girlfriends over as well, including Melissa, Angie, Cali, and Nicole, Jim's younger girlfriend whom he met through Angie and Stacey.

It was a packed house that included Jim, Fossil, Shelly and her man Manny. Michael didn't like Manny at first because of all the fights he had with Shelly. He used to argue with her and jump on her. Later, Michael would find out that it wasn't at all like the rumors had indicated. Michael didn't agree with beating-up on a girl or woman, but Shelly and her girls were really out there as far as girls were concerned.

It was evident that Shelly wasn't hitting on everybody, but acted as if she was all sexy. She was a big flirt, but she also liked to argue and fight. They were actually a funny couple when you got to know them. They partied all night and Michael got completely wasted. For several hours, Stacey got Michael to dance, which he only did when he was lit up. After a while, the party started to slow down but before it did, Stacey and Michael went into her bedroom for a showdown. They started off slow and then the next thing you know, she was going downtown and Michael was coming up. They went from the back to the front and from the side to upside down and then ended up in the closet. Yeah, it was one of those nights again. Michael was already going against his promise he made. He was only supposed to go to Stacey's to check up on her as well as to collect some money she had collected for him after he went to jail. He had also left her some weed and some of his pimp cloths. Michael was breaking his solemn promise to God and was really felling like a lowlife.

Michael though, "If it wasn't for her wild ass, I wouldn't be in this mess in the first place." He knew it wasn't fully her fault. Michael just wasn't seeing the signs clearly, because God was trying to tell him something. It wouldn't be long before things would be back to as normal as they could be, considering his situation. Michael's main man was calling him and asking information about the rap game and the dope scene. He was wondering if Michael was still down.

Without thinking, Michael said, "No doubt man." A week or two had gone by and Michael was already feeling restless. He missed not having a club and people from Madison to Chicago were asking about him and wanted to know what was going on with the concerts. Michael would tell them, "Soon man, soon!"

Kim wasn't sweating Michael, but she would make subtle suggestions like, "Baby, you should call the union and try to get a job from them." But to Michael, her suggestions were sounding like demands rather than requests. The fact of the matter was that Michael didn't think he could get back on top fast enough. He had too many bills already.

The last union job Michael had was at Kohl's Center; named after (Herb Kohl) the United States Senator from Wisconsin, Mr. Kohl also happened to own the Milwaukee Bucks NBA Team. Michael walked off the job a few months after his co-worker asked him, "Man what you are doing here? You're still too young and you have plenty of talents and opportunities. You should go and get your goals straight and follow your dreams."

After hearing, that Michael left that very same day. That Kohl's job had almost killed him while he was digging in a trench. Not only that one day was he almost electrocuted to death when a live line fell into the ditch. As the years passed, he looked back and sometimes wished he would have stayed on that job, but another part of him made him want to follow his dreams.

Michael stayed in touch with some of the guys, like Hillbilly and his pal Big Jesse-Two big fat and intelligent white guys who were always giving Michael advice. They tried to keep Michael out of trouble. Hillbilly would tell Michael that his friends were nothing but trouble. He would say, "You need to follow your own dreams and be your own leader."

Finally, after all the urging and asking Michael for dope and with all the bills stacking up on the night stand, Michael wanted to get his club open again. He decided to go to Chicago and pick up some drugs to sell and make some fast money.

One of the individuals that were urging Michael to sell him some dope was Cricket A.K.A. Jim Maas. Michael told Jim if he would get him some dope that he would be the one selling it for him. Jim said, "Yeah man." Michael didn't know why he was going to trust him as they were already having problems with the prostitution case. Jim was even considering taking a deal to testify against Michael. The lawyer had warned Michael about it and asked Michael, "Do you think you can trust him?" Michael said he wasn't sure and then the lawyer said, "Then don't."

Michael has always been a forgiving person and some people would say that, that was his weakness, but Michael wanted to help Jim get on his feet so that he could get out of Stacey's apartment Jim needed to get his own place and get rid of his legal troubles.

So, Jim and Michael left on their way to the city to get the dope. They were riding in Michael's Cadillac limousine. Michael had new rims with him and now he didn't like them. His plan was to sell his rims and his limo or trade it in for something a little less conspicuous. A lot of people had offered to buy it but he was never in the need of cash at the time.

Michael called everyone he knew but couldn't find anybody interested in buying it. He also called his pal Yogi to see if he could get a front and go like usual, but he was in the gambling house and he would be a while, so Michael went to visit his family in the meantime.

Michael also went to visit a car dealership to see if they would be interested in the limo. Unfortunately, he couldn't find an offer he was willing to take and after spending the entire day in the city, he was ready to go home. He gave Yogi a call back again to see if he was available, and he was told to come right over. Finally, after waiting all day and most of the late afternoon and evening, Yogi hit him with a kilo. He told Michael to give it back to him when he got back on his feet.

Michael left Yogi at the gambling house on 63rd Street. He couldn't help but notice the half million dollars in cash that was sitting on the table. They were shooting craps, playing poker and black Jack. Had Michael not been from the city and Yogi not been his pal, he certainly would have been thinking of ways to get that cash. Here he was already thinking about it and having to force himself to refuse. "Oh well," Michael thought to himself. Besides, his boy had just hooked him up with a kilo of cocaine anyway.

They left the gambling house because there were lots of police officers there. Michael was concerned at first, but then he knew his man Yogi must have hired some security and paid them off. Locals knew what the house was for and you could plainly see all the players pull up. These people drove cars worth hundreds of thousands of dollars and up to almost a million. These dudes had millions of dollars worth of jewels on them.

The Chicago Police Department could go in there and rob everybody blind and not care who any of them were, but of course they were some of Chicago's elite and the cops couldn't be so rash and hasty with that kind of move.

They were undoubtedly paid off or told to leave them alone by their own bosses. Everyone knew the game and how it worked.

They took 63rd Street right to the Dan Ryan Expressway, which is also called "Highway 90," that took folks back to 159 mile and straight to Madison.

Michael decided to get off and violate his own golden rule, "Stopping at a hot spot known to police." He wasted no time to stop in Jew town to get him some of the world's best Polish sausage. Michael was hungry, but that wasn't the worst of it. He pulled in front of the Polish stand that sat at the end of 18th Street, which was right next door to the liquor store. He was going to go in and get something to drink. Michael usually had someone else drive him while he was in the city, but this time he drove because he knew his way around and Jim didn't.

When Michael entered the liquor store, he saw someone he knew. He mentioned that he was selling his limousine as well as the rims. The guy asked Michael if he could see the rims and followed him outside to see them. When he got outside Michael saw t hat Jim had moved the car to the other side of the street so that no one would think they were selling drugs.

The guy that wanted to see the rims was an old school homie in his late 70's or early 80's-a true businessman who owned the liquor store and managed it himself.

He couldn't pass up a good deal to make some quick money. The old timer used to be a police officer and he remembered when Michael's grandfather used to have a spot down there. He used to always call Michael "little Mr. Moore" after his grandfather.

Michael opened the trunk to show the old timer the rims. As soon as he did, two old white dudes pulled up and Michael knew from the start that they were undercover police.

They yelled, "Freeze, it's the police!" Then they asked for some ID. Michael walked around to the other side of the car to get his insurance papers out of the glove compartment, actually, he was just going to tell Jim to be cool and keep the dope out of sight. Michael came back to where the police were and showed them his ID and insurance papers. Them they asked him, "What are you doing in this part of the city?" Michael answered, "I'm just showing this man here some wheels I have for sale." "Where did you get them?" asked the police officer. "Are they stolen and do you have a receipt?" "Yes, I have a receipt, but I don't think I have it with me," admitted Michael. "Do you realize that you have to have a permit to sell stuff down here?" the officer asked. "No, I didn't know that, but I was just showing them to him right now," retorted Michael.

One of the cops told Michael, "This happened to be a high crime area and you could get into trouble down here. "I didn't know that sir," said Michael. The other cop asked Michael, "What did you say to the guy in the car?" Both of the officers looked to be over fifty years old, but one of them seemed older and should have been retired.

The first thing Michael did when they asked to search the car was look in the direction to high tail it out of there. The older cop must have sensed it and said, "Don't even think about it." Michael said, "No, I don't mind if you search the car." "Bring in this high crime area, we don't need to have a search warrant to search a vehicle," insisted the cop and then he began to search the car.

They asked Jim to step out of the car and looked him over with curiosity Jim sat in the car for a good five minutes before they searched the car. The cop searching the car came out and said, "I found it." Michael looked at Jim as if to say, "Didn't you put it in the secret stash spot?" Then he realized that he had never shown the secret compartment to Jim. Michael's next thought was Jim could have cuffed it, but then it was obvious that Jim was only thinking of himself.

The cop came back with the dope in his hand. "Whose is this?" he asked. Michael just looked at Jim. "If you tell me where you got this or tell me where I could find a pistol, I may be able to make this disappear," Michael and Jim said nothing. "Okay the, Mr. Brown. You are going to jail," said the officer.

Jail will get the attention of most anyone. The same with a lot of great men of the Bible in their day as well as in the world today.

"God does not want any of us to be in jail. God wants us all to be free. Free of sin, free to make choices and free of ignorance. God loved us so much that he sent His only begotten Son out of Love. John 3:16 There is a reaction for every action Galatians 6:7 everything works for the good of those who love God. God is good and all that is good comes from God, James 1:1

CHAPTER 18

COOK COUNTY JAIL, WITNESS

Michael spent the first 18 hours in the 16th Precinct waiting for his fingerprint check to come back. Then he was put on a bus for Cook County Jail. Cook County Jail happened to be the biggest and wildest maximum-security prison in the United States and quite possibly the entire world. It's as big as three football fields long and two football fields wide. It holds more than nineteen thousand people on a bad day and more than twenty to twenty five thousand people on a good day. This jail is absolutely crazy. It takes more than three days just to get processed in.

You go from one line to the next. Fingerprint, mug shots, the works. They even have a penis doctor to run a metal test strip up your penis to check you for sexually transmitted diseases. Then you are herded from one big holding pen to the next. Hundreds of inmates sitting, sleeping and lying anywhere they can find space. Then you're taken in for x-rays and a physical examination. After they have given you the once over, you face several lines for bombardment of questioning. Where are you from? Where did you last live? Just to mention a few. Before they finally take you upstairs to a cellblock, they start all over again with the strip search. "Line up, face the wall and strip buck naked," they demand. "If you are holding anything, now would be the time to get rid of it or face additional charges." The dogs are ready and if you don't get rid of it on your own believe me, they will.

This jail has some of the biggest, meanest jailers, ready to butt heads with any challenger and these dudes play for keeps.

When Michael was there, a young boy had disappeared after his family saw him get arrested. It was later found out that the boy had made a fatal mistake of getting smart with one of the officers. He wouldn't do as he was ordered and they beat him to death and buried his body in the prison graveyard. The officers told the family that the boy had gone home on house arrest. The young boy's body would have never been found, but a rookie female officer who witnessed the beating blew the whistle on the rest of the abusive jailers.

That is only a minor example of Cook County Jail. If a person isn't strong and blessed with a little grace, they would have to be quite lucky not to be assaulted by some abusive jailer. If an abusive jailer doesn't get you, an inmate will get you if you're not tipped up with a gang.

The Cook County Jail is the prime example of the rest of Chicago. It is one of the most segregated places on earth as well as one of the most corrupt. The city of Chicago is probably most known for its organized crime, but that has shifted to the street gangs.

The Vice Lords and the Gangster Disciples are the two major black street gangs in Chicago. They don't appreciate being referred to as street gangs. They consider themselves to be organized mobs. There are also the Spanish gangs-the Latin Kings and the Spanish Cobras.

They run the streets way different from the old days of the twenties. In the past, it was mainly the Irish and Italians who were the most powerful with the money.

The city also was known for its segregation. The Whites lived mainly downtown on the North Side and close to their jobs, while the blacks lived on the West and The South Side of downtown. No Blacks or Spanish people live near the Whites. In the eighties and nineties, the Blacks and Spanish folks didn't like each other because of the power struggle between gangs and territory wars fueled by drug money.

Inside Cook County Jail, there is no difference. In fact, it's worse. It's controlled by black gangs but Spanish gangs aren't punks either. Whites in the jail are like an endangered species, as they almost don't exist, comprising about one thousand of the twenty thousand inmates there. There are more dope fiends in Cook County Jail than there are white people. About twenty-five percent of the jail population is dope sick and kicking heroin. Many of them in the processing lines would get kicked in the ass by jailers to keep them moving. They were all over the place-puking while in route to the hospital for treatment. The hospital would prescribed methadone to help them kick their habit and one would see a lot of the white men there.

Michael was placed in division six, the G.D. gang unit. It had two tiers and a main dayroom with three of four tables, a row of showers, sinks and toilets in the north side of the pod.

The tables and showers were used in order of esteem. First, the G.D.'s then any of the other gang members, and lastly guys who weren't in any gang.

Michael sat there not wanting to call his family or contact anyone. He was sick and tired. He didn't want to burden them with his problems. Michael was placed in a cell with two other guys-one named Tim who was charged with murder. The other was named Jim who had a very lengthy record, and was in for petty robbery. Michael introduced himself and told both of them where he was from. They both thought that Michael looked familiar. "What do you represent?" asked Jim. "Well I was G.D. and affiliated back in the day, but now I'm against gang violence because it took the lives of my family and friends from both side of the fence-the G.D.'s and EL Rukens. It took innocent bystanders. My mother was down with some of them who actually testified against her, but there was a lot of conviction for me," Michael retorted. "I know where you're coming from," said Tim. Then Jim asked, "So what is it you do up there in Wisconsin?" "I am a music promoter and producer," Michael told him. "Have you worked with anybody we may have heard?" asked Jim. "Only with just everyone who came out of Chicago," Michael boasted. "That's where I know you from," injected Tim. "I heard you name on the radio and some of my boys have been trying to get to your studio in Madison to do a show at your club," Tim said. "Aren't you some of King David's people from out of South 98th Street?" Tim asked. "And don't you have some cousins that are Big Black Peastones on 89th Street?" Michael asked. "How do you know all of that?" Tim said. "Man, this is the city, and anybody who is somebody is known by everybody." Michael said, "Yeah, but I ain't nobody." Tim said, "But you are, and you got a little money." "What are you in for?" he asked Michael. "Drug Possession. I had a kilo of cocaine," admitted Michael didn't want to tell them it was given to him on a front then he asked them how much time they thought he would get. Jim told me, "It depends on who your lawyer is and who caught you with it. If worst comes to worst you'll probably get a year in jail or house arrest with some probation."

Michael was thinking to himself, "For a kilo, that's impossible" Tim and Jim could see the surprised look no Michael's face. Tim said, "As long as it wasn't bagged up. Was it?" he asked. "No, it wasn't" said Michael.

Michael remembered Yogi, Tweet and plenty of guys in the hood who were caught with more dope than he and some of that was bagged up. Almost a hundred g's worth of and none of them ever went to the joint for it, so Michael thought these guys could be right.

Then Tim said, "I know you and your family have money to get a lawyer." "Maybe" said Michael. "But I don't talk to them like that and for that I do my own thing," he affirmed. "All right then, we'll see how you feel after doing a couple of days in here," chuckled Tim. "This isn't anything to fool around with," Jim inserted.

Michael was completely worn out and didn't feel like talking any longer. He told them he just wanted to do some thinking and get some sleep. "That's straight," said Tim. Michael didn't notice that Jim had left the room. Some other guys came back asking to talk to Tim as Michael laid back. "Just relax for a minute Lil Barksdale," Tim said, "Please don't call me that," Michael asked. "All right then, Mike." Tim said.

After Michael had a little nap, he got up and decided to call somebody to let them know what was going on. When Michael got up to use the phone, which was upstairs, he noticed Tim sitting next to some dudes who were getting tattooed. Michael wanted to call his sister Tammy, who he always felt he could talk to, but he couldn't remember phone number. She had recently moved back to the city with their cousins in Gardens and Michael was unsure about calling anyone else. Michael felt like he was letting his family down and he didn't want to hear the complaints. He remembered he had made some promises and hadn't been living up to them. Michael was going to call Ingo, but he knew better that to ask anything from her or he would have to hear it from her as well. After giving it some thought, he finally called Stacey. She wouldn't be able to give him much help, but he wanted to let someone out there know what had happened and what he was going through, plus Michael knew that Stacey wasn't going to preach to him as that would have only put him in a bad mood, but all the same time he was really sick and tired of living like he was. Maybe he needed to call for help and hear all the conflict. It may be what he needed to make him see more clearly.

The truth was one thing that Michael really needed to hear. Whatever they may say or had to say, he had to hear it to motivate him, keep him out of jail and any other life threatening situations.

Michael called but he couldn't get through to anybody. The next best thing he could do was talk to God. He needed to ask God what he should do now, so he went back to his cell and got down on his knees and prayed, "God, please help me. I am sick of what I have been doing with this life. I don't want to spend the rest of my days in a prison and I don't want to die before I really had a chance to live. Please show me the way to get through this situation and I will do whatever you say." He continued, "I want to spend the rest of my life doing what is best for my family and my kids. I want to help them not make the wrong choices that I did. I am sick and tired of the error of my ways. God, help me quit and I swear I will never do it again. Amen!"

Michael didn't realize that both of his cellmates were standing there watching him. One of them asked him. "Man you really believe in that mess?" "Yes, of course I do. There has to be a God, man. There is a God and he has to help me because I have no one else." Then Jim who was younger then Tim but older then Michael said, "I used to believe until I lost my brothers in a drive-by shooting and they believed in Jesus too," said Jim.

After Jim said that, they received a call to the infirmary and sat there for hours. He unfortunately had to stay there through mealtime and eat a sack lunch. They called his name again and this time it was for an interview for a home confinement program. Michael asked the officer in charge, "What do you want me for?" The officer told him, "For the home confinement program." "Can you call them back?" Michael asked. "You can't go anyplace until you see the doctor," The officer instructed. "Besides, just because they call you don't mean they will accept you. Although, they probably will because they think you are eligible."

"You need a place to go to with a phone here in the city of Chicago," he was told. "I do have that," Michael admitted. He thought about where he would go and realized that he didn't have anybody in the city he could stay with. His sister and cousins lived in the Gardens, but he didn't have their phone number.

Michael finally got to see the doctor. He wasn't sure what to expect or what it was for. They told him it was because he had requested to see the doctor, because he was complaining about not being able to urinate properly. Through previous test Michael found out, he had an infection. They gave him medication he was supposed to take for three days with plenty of water. The doctor told Michael he would do well if he would stop drinking and sleeping around and that that was the only way he could have caught the infection he had, the doctor told him that if there was a next time he may not be lucky.

Michael could only say, "Thank you sir." He didn't ask what he had and the doctor hadn't explained it to him, but Michael knew something was wrong with him, as his body would be going crazy sometimes. Kim and his mother used to tell him he was a hypochondriac. Michael though it was from not working out anymore and drinking alcohol a lot, but he was beginning to understand now why they would say that to him.

Once the doctor was finished with him, they began dividing the men into groups of their being treating and those waiting to be treated and they still had a long line of guys left. The rest of the guys were trying to see a Chicago Bulls game on a television set. There had to have been at least a couple of hundred guys waiting and watching the game at the same time.

After some time, they finally started walking down the hall and they took Michael right past division six, which was his cellblock.

He asked, "Where are we going? I'm in division six." "Not anymore," said the guard. "I was told to move you," "Why and where to?" asked Michael. "You're going to division two which is for non-trouble makers, upper class businessmen and family types who have never been in trouble before. We've even had Bulls and Bears playing up there recently/" "So what does this have to do with me," asked Michael. "I'm not sure, but someone will be down to see you about it," the officer informed him.

A large officer who looked familiar to Michael came to see him. He was a big man, about 6'6", 350 pounds and rock solid. He had a baldhead and he was as black as Michael. It wasn't long before he remembered the guy as he had worked security at one of Michael's homies events.

Headlining was George Clinton and it was sponsored by one of Michael's guys Motown, Lil C, and Krash. They kicked it all night, smoked, drank and ate together at the after-party in Oprah's studio. They even sold him some work, swapped some girls and got high with his security officers, some of which were off-duty Cook County Sheriff's Deputies. Michael could never forget that night or the people who were there. It was almost a year to be the day when they had shared business tips; George was one of the best. "Man, you are definitely going to make it in the business," President P. Funk himself told Michael.

The big officer told Michael, "There may have been some sort of threat on your life because you have some O.G.'s in your family or in the music business, so they moved you for your own protection." Michael could not imagine who would want to hurt or even kill him or for what reason. He knew nothing and he was no better or worse than the next guy.

Michael was the only one in the cellblock when he got there. It wasn't long after when about a hundred people crowded in. Most of them were older family men and businessmen who had probably never been in jail before and more than likely had petty misdemeanor cases like traffic violations, no driver's license or jaywalking. Then came a couple of local celebrities, musicians, actors and even a local weatherman from the local television station. One of the richest men in there was an older black man who owned a big semi trucking company.

He was there for shooting two gang bangers who had been stealing off his property. He may have killed one kid and seriously wounded the other. The guy was treated as a hero by some of the prisoners, but others wanted revenge.

Michael stayed in that cellblock for another day or two before they called him again. This time they said, "Brown, pack your things, you're leaving." "Where am I going?" he asked. "Home, you're been bail out." Michael wondered who paid his bail. He didn't even know how much it was. They came to get him and took him downstairs to property where he retrieved his personal belongings. Michael found out many things from the staff and inmates. Some V.L.'s were supposed to have had a hit out on him because of his affiliation with some of the V.L.'s but it was eventually squashed.

There were other guys who rode under the five stars that were Michael's homies whom he had worked on the Westside, like Crucial and Do or Die. They were two of the biggest rap groups to ever come out of the city of Chicago. He had worked with him a lot more. There was even talk that some of his own were coming after him for some money on some kind of hustle or scam.

There were some B.D.'s or G.D.'s that Michael almost couldn't believe. He asked the dudes if there were really others checking him out and they said that it was true. Michael looked back at the police and they confirmed it by shaking their heads. Then one of the police walked up to him and said, "Big Timmy said to be cool."

Michael knew he had something to do with it, weather it was good or bad, he told the cop, the big black dude that he knew it was either a BD or G.D. as he was carrying colors under his uniform. Then when he turner and flexed his arms Michael could plainly see his tattoo, it was a six pointed star-the star of King David.

Most of the officers who work for Cook County Jail are plugged-in one way or another to gangs-Black, White or Spanish. Some get hooked up once they become officers, and those dudes usually come from the suburb or far away. Some get plugged in just to stay and live there; whole some come there wanting connections or to be a part of something big and powerful in the city. A lot of them are from the city and claim to be ex-bangers, but all they really come in for is to get a rank.

Some work the inside communications, connections and supplies, while other go directly to the big boys who run the gangs and the mobs or who come back from penitentiaries on writs just to run the streets from the joints. Most make money by risking their lives for middle class pay for simple things like passing messages, bringing in drugs and other supplies for money and power.

It can take up to three days to get booked in the Cook County Jail and it can take almost half that time to get out once bail is paid and then another whole day to a day and half to get released from there.

Getting out can be dangerous especially at night and if you're not in one of the Spanish gangs-the Latin Kings, the Spanish Hood, and they want to keep all rival gangs out. They don't want outsiders to be messing with their money and they especially don't want outsiders to be messing with their money and they especially don't want blacks messing with their women, so every night they stand outside jail looking for people who don't belong there so they can rob or kill them. It's so bad that they have undercover police work the area to look for these guys who still rarely get caught.

There is a big parking lot with a fence around it where police are always watching. Most people still get arrested of killed when they get out of jail and it's usually at the bus or walking to catch a train. Unfortunately, some are even contract hits. If you want to find a guy you have a beef with or someone you have really been looking for, you can usually find them either coming in or getting out of the county jail. Sometimes the police are the ones who sell the information for money, just to make a name for themselves.

Finally, after waiting for hours, Michael made it to the last door at the sign-out desk. He found out that Kim had posted his bond. She had come through for him again. He was 1st out the front door, which was actually the back of the building, opposite the courthouse that had a gated parking lot. Once he got outside the door and walked for a while, he saw Kim's car. Michael was so happy to get out. At the time, he really didn't want to hear her mouth, but even that couldn't dampen his spirits, as all he wanted was get out.

This would only be a small taste of what Michael was to face in the future. He was deaf to his own cries and he could have changed his way before it was too late, but that's just what it was, too late. "It is so important to listen to your inner self, and learn from your past experience. Learn from your mistakes."

CHAPTER 19

HARASSMENT BY THE COPS

Michael got to the car and sat next to Kim in the front seat. Fossil sat in the back seat with his three hundred pounds of big self. He was the first to break the silence and told Kim to fire up the blunt. Kim handed Fossil the bag of weed and told him to roll it up. "I know you didn't like it in there," Fossil said to Michael. "No way man," Michael admitted. "That joint is not a fun place and I never want to return." Kim said. "I brought Fossil so he could give me directions to fine this place. K Michael already had an idea of that. "I had to sell some stuff and get some money from Ingo and her mom as they put up most of the money," Kim said.

The ride home was pretty quite with Kim not having much to say. At the time, that was a blessing in itself from Michael's perspective, as he knew the silence wasn't going to last with her.

Kim was only being polite at the time and didn't want to say what she was really thinking with Fossil present in the car. However, it wasn't like that with Fossil, as he put Michael on a few things and let him know what he was thinking.

"Jim was full of it for letting you go out like that," said Fossil. "I go to tell you, I found a new spot for the club and they want to give it to us right now." Michael felt the same way Fossil did about Jim. He was pleased that Fossil found a facility for the club, however, he knew it would take some work, time and money to get it up and running. At the same time Michael was feeling blessed. He had to wonder if this was God's answer to what he had been praying for. He desired something other than the dope scene, prostitution and hustling. Michael could see Kim looking as if she was dying to say something, but she didn't say much during the entire trip home.

They got to Madison pretty quick as they always did when Kim was driving, unless it was during rush hour. This was probably the first time Kim drove Michael from Chicago and he didn't fall asleep on the way home. The reason Kim quit going with Michael to Chicago was because he would make her drive and then he would fall asleep. But it was usually for business and she didn't have any problems with doing that for him. Finally, they arrived and Kim said, "Mike, this is getting to be a little ridiculous. You have been going in and out of jail lately. Maybe you need to think about doing something different." "You are right Kim, I am. I just need to be given one more chance," Michael pleaded. "I feel as if my calling is in the music business, but the powers that be won't give me a chance. I just need to get me another club up and running so I can get into my music career. But before I can do that, I must give up my payments to my attorney and get that case out of the way."

"What about the case in New York?" asked Kim? "You have to do something with that one too," she demanded. "You're right I will, but I need money for that case and for the lawyer too," retorted Michael. "Maybe you should just not show up there, get a job back in construction and focus on the case here," said Kim. Michael couldn't believe his ears as Kim was never one to avoid responsibility, but she was always trying to get Michael to go back to work in construction. He told her he would think about it, but until then, he would get down to business. She just looked at him like she didn't know what else to say about it.

Michael was thinking quietly as they pulled into their parking lot. They went into the house and he asked her, "Where are the kids?" She told him, "They are at Dawn's for the evening." "Go and get them. I want to see my kids," he told her. "Why don't we just leave them for the night? I could use some time off and we aren't through talking yet." "We aren't, huh?" asked Michael. He knew she had something to say or do, but he wasn't sure what that was. "I need to take a shower," he told her.

When Michael got out of the shower, Kim was standing there and it seemed like a dream. However, he realized that he wasn't dreaming, nor was he sleeping. This was for real. Something spiritual was happening. Not only did Michael hear the voice of God, but also there was something different in the way he felt inside. He looked up at Kim and she was standing there watching him. At first he thought that maybe she heard it too, but whatever had happened there it wasn't normal, and what he was feeling wasn't normal either.

Michael told Kim, "I must give it up to God and I must read his word. You have to read it too and you have to help me. I have to hear it. That's what God is telling me, I have to do it." "Mike, I'll help you and read it with you, but if you feel that this is something you have to do on your own, then you have to do whatever it is you feel you have to do."

Michael quit talking and sat there thinking to himself for a while. He was trying to figure out what he was going through. He didn't know it then, but he had received instructions on what to do and to turn his life over to God and Jesus.

He sat there thinking until Kim came to him and put her hands on him. She gave him a hug, which he really needed just then, and said, "Baby, come to bed now, everything is going to be alright."

That was really out of character for Kim because she was rarely emotional and touchy. It's just the way she was-the total exact opposite of Michael, as Michael was more emotional and explosive than Kim, but not as a woman would be emotional.

Michael grabbed a hold of Kim and kissed her. "Come on, everything is going to be all right," he said, as he pulled her down onto his lap. They sat there holding each other for a while. "Come on baby, let's go to bed." They got up and Michael led Kim into the bedroom. They sat on the bed together and kissed passionately, like they never had before. That night they made sweet and wild passionate love all night long.

Both Kim and Michael had never felt anything like they did that night. It had been some of the wildest sex they ever had. Michael couldn't compare Kim to any other women he had ever known. It had made him realize more than anything that Kim and he had a true love.

Michael thought he was dreaming again, but he knew he wasn't. He could barely get up in the morning, and he really didn't want to feel like it, although He did get up when Kim brought him breakfast in bed. The kids came in hollering, "Daddy, daddy! Get up daddy, what are you doing still in bed? Daddy where have you been?"

It was one of those times when the kids could have asked for anything and he would have given it to them. Michael was so happy to see his kids that it brought tears to his eyes.

He told them that he had to go away for a while, but that he was back now. "Let's play," he said. "I missed you guys so much." Michael didn't notice when they got home, but he was aware that it was a school day and both of his girls, Jazzman and Keya, were home

Keya lived with her mother Ingo, but she still lived with Michael and Kim pretty much every holiday and weekends.

Then Michael Jr. came crawling into the room. He couldn't talk yet-his only words were "daddy "and "mamma." He was only nine months old and obviously going to a mamma's boy. He would call out "daddy" whenever he heard the girls say it; otherwise he would look for his mama. Which was to be expected, as daddy wasn't there much?

Kim would sometimes act a little jealous whenever little Michael would come crawling to Michael when he came in the door. He would say, "Daddy, Daddy," and come to his daddy like he owed him something. He would reach his little arms up for Michael to pick him up. Of course, Michael would lovingly pick him up and give him a big bear hug and Michael Jr. would giggle excitedly.

Michael stayed home all day with Kim and the kids. He wasn't going anywhere. He didn't even want any visitors, but it wasn't long before he got one. It was the same old Fossil and Michael already knew what he wanted. Yes, he claimed he came just to see how Michael was doing, but what he really came for was to bum a free high as usual.

Fossil was on his way to his new job at a video store just around the corner from Kim's house, but he would go wherever Michael happened to be just to get a free high. Fossil was so desperate at times, he'd come to Stacey's house or he would have even gone to the Devil's house if Michael were there. He knew Michael had a grand size weed habit and that he also had some smoke for sale. Fossil would rather run errands for Michael than work, if he did have weed. Not only that but he knew he could get some on credit if need be, because Michael knew Fossil always had some more coming in from somewhere.

Fossil, much like Jim, always had some sort of idea or scam to get some money. Usually it was something stupid that Michael wasn't interested in "Some dumb dope fiend move" as they would call it in the streets. While Fossil worked in the club, he would get all the weed he wanted. Michael thought he knew Fossil had a family, a girlfriend and some kids to take care of so Michael felt obligated to pay him a wage of at least ten dollars an hour. With that type of pay, Fossil would buy a little cocaine and weed almost every night.

Jim on the other hand, was expecting some return, because Michael had invested in him and another one of his worthless projects. Some ecstasy and PCP is what Michael was supposed to produce besides the little stuff that Michael was able to sell himself.

People were saying it wasn't any good at all but Michael was such a good salesman that he could convince people he had sold it to others and they would think that it was the best they ever had. He himself tried it as well, but it didn't get him high. He had to put a lot of effort into selling just to get his money back. Michael was so good at his sales that he was getting high just from his own sales pitch.

Michael told Fossil that he would get with them real soon, but he had no interest in getting out there anytime soon, "Man, I have a way to make some money and get on our feet again," Fossil said. Michael told Fossil he wasn't interested. Fossil was a slow thinker, as he was always getting high and drunk. One night he even pissed on himself and actually mentioned the word robbery! Michael wasn't down with that. Finally, Fossil left and went to work. Michael spent time with Kim and the kids just playing around with them and watching television, just listening to them talking and playing. For once, he was even paying attention to Kim. They had fun that day, but the fun was soon about to come to an end.

Michael was never a homebody and that was something he was looking for because he always had a lot of fun when he stayed home. This particular day he had fun like never before. Michael knew it would only be a matter of time before he had to go make a living as he was only living because of how he achieved it.

The next day Michael got up and it was time to get busy. Christmas was only a few days away and his kids needed presents, there were bills to pay and he wasn't going to be taking care of them by lying around the house having fun. He got up and went out to get something going. He stopped by Stacey's house as soon as he dropped the kids off at school.

She was just about to leave for work and Jim and Nicole were lying around taking it easy. As soon as Michael walked in, Jim said, "I'm glad to see you Mike, and believe me bro, I'm sorry I couldn't look out." Michael told Jim to forget it and that it wasn't his fault.

Michael walked into the bedroom where Stacey was and she just smiled, happy to see him. "I've got something for you that I think you'll be glad to have," she proclaimed. Michael couldn't imagine what she could have, but then she handed him a wad of cash and said, "That's all I have." "Where did you get this from?" asked Michael. "Don't worry about that, because you don't want to know. You would just get mad if I told you anyway," she told him. Michael asked her, "Have you been hanging out with Rob and Skin since you've been back from Milwaukee? And which one of them are you sleeping with now?" "Are you serious? I can't believe you just said that to me," said Stacey. For some reason Michael told her, "I do have some concern for you, and if this is going to get me or even you into any trouble, you can have this money back right now." Michael vowed against anything that was going to land him back in jail and the last thing he wanted was anything that he had no part of.

Stacey looked at Michael as he expressed his anger. He told her that he meant what he said. Although he really needed the money. Jim came and knocked on the door and said "Mike, when you get done, I need to talk to you. I have something for you/" Michael said, "I'll be right there in a minute." Stacey gave him a kiss and asked him, "Will I see you later?" He didn't say anything for a minute as he looked at her, then he said "Yeah, I'll see you later," and Stacey left for work.

Michael went out to talk to Jim. He told Michael that he had some people from this real-estate company holding the club and those they were just waiting for some more money. They could open the new club if he was ready to. Then Jim handed Michael some money and said, "That's from the dope I sold." Michael didn't think it was any good, so he had given up on making anything on it. Jim and Michael left to meet with the real estate agent.

Michael brought along a blank check he had received from Kim earlier. He always did business like this and usually the check cleared, even if he didn't have all the money on hand. This was going to be one check that Michael would hope later wouldn't have cleared.

They got all the keys from the real estate agent and began moving all the equipment into the building within the next couple of days. He gave them a check for the first and last month's rent, plus a security deposit.

He had to get right to work in order to make the money he needed and the show had to go on. Michael had to get the club opened and he needed the money and the business to get going to secure him.

One of his promise to take care of his family and pay his bills, Michael went right back to hustling without a second thought. A few days later, he got some dope from his cousin Jimmy. Jimmy told Michael that Stacey had done something for him, which turned out pretty lucrative. She helped him sell all the cocaine and weed while Michael was gone as she wasn't trying to leave him totally without money and didn't want all of the money coming from Skin and Rob's robberies.

Michael was avoiding Stacey and her crib as he didn't want to get into any trouble with her games again, but the fact remained that he still maintained strong feelings for her. He needed to remember that he had a woman and kids at home. He wanted to do the right thing, but he just didn't know how to be a faithful and committed man as he had never been that before.

Michael had strong feeling for Stacey that he couldn't seem to let go of, no matter what he tried. He could talk to her and she seemed to listen without being critical of what he had to say. Stacey was up with his behavior, smoking, hustling and chasing other women, which came with being a pimp, player and a hustler. She never said anything of it, even though Michael didn't set out to be all that. It's just the way things turned out.

Stacey insisted on helping Michael and investing in his ventures and didn't mind the reputation that came along with it. Michael believed that was part of the reason why she still hung around. Of course, it didn't help his moral standings as Stacey was a part-time drunk like Michael was at times, probably even worse than he was. Stacey was a freak that could truly throw down in the sack. Michael would visit her to have sex with her anytime to get his frustrations out.

In fact, no matter who else or what else she was doing, she enjoyed it and would get mad when he wouldn't come by to get some.

At this particular time in Michael's life, he felt as if he wanted and needed Stacey to help him be that man he believed he was supposed to be. He was nine years older than she was, but he had to admit that in some ways she was emotionally older than he was.

Stacey had also become a big part of Michael's legitimate business plan. He had just put this last club in Stacey and her sister's name with their consent.

They had had several meeting on what was supposed to go on and it was all supposed to be as professional and legit as it could possibly be and they were determined to make this club the best one yet. It was definitely the biggest one by far, with more than four thousand square feet.

The plan was for Stacey and Tammy to be well involved in the management and fill in any shortcomings that Michael had in the business. Michael felt he owed it to them for the help they lent to Kim and himself. He felt it was his job to dream, but anything they wanted to do was always the best for the club. The business was there for Stacey to do but as usual, she acted as if she didn't want it. That was until she saw how badly Michael needed her help. Anyone else would have messed it up and Michael knew that Stacey wanted him to succeed. It was more than just a job or a business; it was his goal and his dream- dream for him and a lot of others who were involved.

It was also an outlet for entertainment for a lot of people in Madison and the Midwest, Michael finally opened the club one weekend after getting the place all dressed up and ready. He had all his equipment there and his office supplies. He was getting plenty of requests to open as well as lot of free advertising from local press. They were all supportive of him because it was more than just a club. They knew it was a music entertainment company as well. For many different reasons, there were a lot of folks who wanted to see Michael succeed.

Like a lot of women he knew, Stacey wanted to be the boss of Michael's business, but he didn't feel he needed that from her. But what he did need was some advice and some assistance. Michael decided to go without her that first weekend because he had made it on his own one way or another for many years already.

They opened and people came. Like many times before, he opened without all the paperwork and permits. He figured he would get all the proper paperwork after a couple of weeks or when he could better afford it. Just as he had several times in the past, Michael never had much heat on him and thankfully, the police were not watching every move he made. He later learned that most of their information came from informants. Michael had more than one informant in his cabinet that swore they needed the business and opportunity just as much as Michael did.

The news was all over town that Michael's club was open. The cars kept coming and he could always draw a big crowd. Michael knew he needed it now more than ever-he needed both the money as well as the business if he was going to be a success.

Michael looked outside and saw the endless stream of cars arriving before he knew it, he had more than a couple of hundred customers, including some he never seen before that night. Some of them were talented musicians and performers while some were the finest women he had ever seen. There were also those who he had been ordered by the courts to stay away from.

Michael had only seen Breanna and Reanna on one time before at a gas station in Monona. He asked them how they were doing out of concern as he didn't want them to think that he wasn't thinking about them. Michael also missed spending time with them and talking to them because they were a lot of fun.

That's when they stood up in court and told the court he had nothing to do with soliciting prostitution. Now Michael was getting a message from his girl, Carrie, who was having some big legal problems of her own. Michael's doorman, Doug, was insisting that he let them in a talk to them in spite of the court order. Michael didn't like it when Doug didn't do as he was told, but he had to admit that this time Doug was probably right.

Doug went back to the office to see Michael. "Hey Bro, those girls are here and they need to see you, so you need to let them in the door," demanded Doug. Then he put in Michael's face, "So when did you start following some bullshit court order? Look Mike, it's in your best interest, and they are insisting on coming in>"

Carrie happened to be standing there next to Michael. "I'm not sure I would do that, if I were you. Do you think you can trust them two?" she asked. Michael looked her in the eye and he could see she was dead serious. "I wouldn't trust them Mike, they are no good."

Carrie was speaking out of selfishness plus experience. She knew Breanna and Reanna, but so did Michael. "Shut your mouth Carrie, I got this," he commanded. Michael told Doug to send them in. Michael knew that Carrie never liked them in the first place because she thought they took business from her, plus she knew that Michael was messing around with both of them instead of messing around with her. She wasn't off by much.

Carrie also knew about the court order. She was out on bail for a murder case and wasn't supposed to be out on the town. She was on protective custody but insisted on seeing Michael. He had advised her not to at first, but then he recanted because of her insistence, and he knew she would be safe with him. She had a contract hit on her head for her cooperation with the police in the murder case. She had taken a plea deal to testify against the guys who were involved with a robbery and a murder. She confided in Michael that she didn't want to testify, and she was looking for a way out of it.

Michael advised her to be careful and sure, of what she was doing, but that there may be a way out of it. He promised that he would support her no matter what she decided to do. Michael was praying that she wouldn't actually go through with testimony against those guys. It certainly wouldn't bring back the dead, but it would put someone away for life in prison.

Michael didn't have to say much to Carrie. She already knew how he felt. They had first met years ago in front of Butter's house and they were close ever since. She was one of the girls Michael hired at his club and escort service. She was just a young girl posing as an older one.

While Michael was talking to Carrie, Breanna and Reanna came walking up. He stood up, "Hi, nice to see you two," he smiled and gave them both a hug. "Listen I'm not mad at you two and I hope you're not mad at me. What's done is done. All we can do is learn from it, and make the best of the situation," he said. Both of them said, "You're right," as they hugged and kissed him with gratitude. Michael said, "Come on. I'm buying you a drink and lets some a number, go dancing and have some fun."

Michael was feeling much better about thing after that, but his problems that evening hadn't even began yet. It wasn't long after when he noticed there were some new people in the club. He could see four new brothers who were from the city. They were obviously up to no good. They had a couple of fine looking sisters with them whom Michael had never seen before and they were looking at him. A few minutes after Michael noticed them they walked up to him and said, "Aren't you Ice Mike?" One of them asked him. "That's not me or my name anymore." Michael informed them, "but who's asking?" he asked. One of the dudes said, "We're B.D.'s. Friends of some of your friends from the city."

That got Michael to thinking. He didn't know these guys and they didn't know him, but they did know his old street name. He had friends and enemies from the city, from B.D., V.L.'S and Black Pea stones. It's usually not cool when someone knows the old you and when you don't know for sure who they might be. When you are living the street life, you can never remember all the things you have been involved with-not if you've lived like Michael has.

A different one of these guys said, "We're here to talk to you and possibly ask for help." "What sort of help are we talking about?" Michael asked. The guy answered, "We want to solve a problem out guys are having with a friend of yours." Michael asked. "Who is this friend of mine you're talking about?" "We know who you are plugged in with." they said. "We know you are friends and family with the Barksdales and the Wilson's, which makes you royalty."

Michael agreed that they were his friends and they were like family, "But what does that have to do with my friends and my family?" he asked. It's about one of the girls who used to work for you. And she is about to testify on one of ours," the guy told Michael. Michael had an idea, but he asked anyways, "Whom are you talking about?" The guy said, "Her name is Carrie. The little white girl you were talking to a while ago."

Michael saw Carrie from the corner of his eye. She was walking towards him but then she turned and stated going back. She must have known what was going on. "Carrie is a friend of mine, and I knew her very well," said Michael. "There's nothing to worry about. She is no threat to your guy and she doesn't want to testify and she's trying to back out of it. To hurt her would only bring heat on your guy. This isn't Chicago and there's only one way out."

Michael really didn't want to get involved, but he had to say something to help Carrie. He didn't want to see her get hurt or killed. One of them asked, "Can you give me your word on this? I'm giving you all I can," Michael said. "There's nothing to worry about I promise. So just take it easy, have a couple of drinks, and a good time, on me."

They walked away from Michael. Two of them were about the same height and weight as Michael, with some cold-blooded eyes. These were young guys younger than Michael. A third seemed a little leery. He was taller light skinned, muscular and looked to be on the wild side. This guy was the last one to walk away without taking his eyes off Michael. Michael looked him in the eyes as if to say don't sweat it man."

From there Michael went to look for Carrie. He wanted to warn her to get the heck out of there, but Carrie was nowhere to be found. In the mist of the altercation, Michael noticed some cops sitting in their police cars outside. Michael went back into his business.

People were coming in flocks and droves it began top snow outside. Michael went to the DJs booth to tell him "pump it up and let it ride." The place was packed and the party was jumping, until Doug came to see Michael. Doug told Michael he was needed at the front door by the police. Michael thought. "What now?"

The police had no reason to be there now other than for harassment. Doug said, "they want to see some paperwork stating this is private property and something saying we have a right to assemble this private party for our company and employees. Michael assured them of this but the officers didn't want to hear it.

Michael looked angry with Doug. His thought was that Doug was getting soft and this is what he always did. It always worked before, even when they had an incident around the corner at Michael's third club. That time they had to say that the police were attacked and there was some damage to their cars and they tried to stop the party. That was over a year ago, but Michael thought this was probably the same cop. He was considering how to handle this situation. Doug said, "They are trying to force their way in to search, or get a search warrant to shut the place down." Michael looked at Doug with frustration. "Okay man, give me a minute," Michael said. Doug went back to the front door as Michael took a moment to pull himself together. Michael was thinking a Brother can't even have a little party to help some brothers and sisters get some money in the music business without this cop's harassment. Michael went toward the front door, and as he walked through the club, he told people who were smoking weed to put it out. Not that he really cared, because he smoked weed too, but the police were outside.

Knowing they were out there, he was more conscious and prepared for them. In the earlier days, Michael would blow smoke in their faces, but that was when he could get away with it. He went from that to hiring what he called the spray guys. Their job was to spray incense whenever people were smoking weed and pick up paraphernalia that was lying around the place but, He didn't have any of those guys on staff for this first party at this club.

Michael went to see the police who were now standing near his office, which was full of unpacked boxes. There were two cops standing in the doorway who were holding up traffic that was trying to get in. One of the officers said, "Good evening Mr. Ice Mike, or should I say just Ice." "That's not my name," retorted Michael. "Can I call you Mr. Brown?" asked the officer. "Yes sir, that's my name," Michael told the officer. "We had a call from the area about a disturbance. May we come in and take a look around?" Michael told the officer, "No, you may not." The officer asked him, "Do you have a business license to operate as a business, theater or night club?" The officer obviously knew something about how Michael operated, because he could always find a way to make something up. Michael would make excuses to but time until they could find some sort of way to stop him or slow him down. He gave them his normal routine statements. "It's a music and promotion company. This is a private party, and we have every right to assemble," Michael told the officers.

The black cop said, "We don't see any club or theatre permits and that's what you need to charge money." "We're not charging for anything, we accept donations," Michael insisted. Michael could see a group of girls behind the cops. They had money in their hands, saying, "Come on Mr. Policeman, move out of the way and let us in." Michael was looking for his briefcase in his crowed office. That is where he could find his copy of the city, federal, and state laws that allow him to operate, along with his business and tax licenses.

After looking for a while, Michael finally found what he was looking for. He usually kept them close at hand, but he hadn't needed the documents for some time he also hadn't taken the time to unpack everything. He just wanted to do his thing and give people a place to get down. Michael gave the documents to the police officer and they both looked a little surprised. One of the officers said, "Okay then," but the other one said, "We better double check this stuff," "Come on man," said the first cop, "they aren't doing anything wrong," so they both left.

At least that's what Michael thought at first when they walked away. But then they came back they said, "We have orders from out boss to shut this place down," said the officer. Michael noticed out the door that more squad cars were arriving. "Are you sure you want to do this?" Michael asked. And then said, "You could be facing some serious repercussions once my lawyer hears about this. You have infiltrated private property, don't you know?" Michael informed them. One of the officers said, "An alarm went off in the building next door," said the officer. "That's not what you told me before," Michael asserted. "Yes we did and that is what this is about." Said the officer. "Was it that you seen a perpetrator run over here or something?" Michael asked them. They both looked at each other and said. "No." By now, Michael was steaming mad and there was an entire army of police cars outside. One of the officers, the Black one, said, "Look man!" Michael interrupted, "No you look man. This is straight up harassment!" the officer said, "No man this isn't on us. We're just following orders. We were willing to let it go, but I don't think the other cops are willing to do that."

Michael knew their excuse for coming was straight up B.S. he could see the cops in the background were waiting to run in and do them all in, so he said "Alright man, just give me a chance to break it to them." for the first time ever Michael was giving in.

Michael went over to the D.J and had him announce to shut it down. He fought it as best he could without getting stupid enough to get himself arrested. He held the cops at bay for about an hour. At the last tally, they made a couple thousands buck. They could have doubled that by now. Michael needed that money, and really couldn't afford to give it back, nor could he do anything to hurt his business reputation in the hood.

Michael decided that he would keep the money and the next party he would give frees weed and drinks. He announced over the intercom, "The party is over, thanks to the cops! Please everyone, stay cool and calm. The next one will be on me. I'm really sorry folks, but we have to wrap it up."

Instantly there were people screaming, "We want our money back!" Michael was trying to leave so he wouldn't have to deal with that. He snuck out the back door without anyone seeing him, but he could surely hear the complaints for refunds and the police breaking it up Michael strolled through the back and thought about the cop's story. They told different stories. One was a complaint about an alarm. Michael looked through the window of the next-door building and saw workers inside. They were partying, dancing and singing with the radio blasting and Michael could tell that this wasn't any sort of disturbance. It just further proved that the cops were lying and were out to get Michael and shut him down.

Michael stood there thinking for a minute. He was tired of all these conflicts. Then his pager went off, followed by his cell phone, which he answered. It was Carrie and she told Michael that she was sorry that she left. "Don't worry about it, I understand. Make sure you know what you're doing when you take the stand against those dudes." "If you have any more a part in it than what is being said, remember you have to what's best and righteous. Do you understand?" She said she did. "All right then I have to go. I just don't feel like talking anymore," said Michael. Carrie said, "Those dudes that came to talk to you were some of Po's people weren't they?" "They were, and I'm glad you left," Michael admitted. "But you don't have to worry, it was taken care of. I got your back Carrie. I'm in your corner, whatever you choose to do. Just do what is right. Just pray on it, and don't worry about it anymore." Michael could finally hang up the phone after what seemed like an hour. Carrie was hard for a girl, but with Michael, she was known to let down her guard. Before she hung up, she asked him" "What's wrong Michael?" He said, "Nothing!" She said, "I heard the cops just shut down the party?" "Yeah, it's true," he admitted. "Where are you at?" "I'm out back." "Why are you there?" "I'm sick and tired of the whole thing," he told her, "especially the police harassment."

"I don't want to give the people their money back." Carrie told him. "Boy you are crazy." "I don't really like the idea of doing my customers this way, especially my loyal ones.

This is the second time I did something like this. The first time was years ago at my first club in Monona." Carrie said "You've been doing this thing for a while now, maybe you should consider retirement." "Then what would I do?" Michael asked her. "I can't live without it, ya know! And neither could some of my people." She told him, "It doesn't have to be forever. Maybe just till things cool down and I'm sure you'll find something else to make some money anyway." "Well, maybe I better get going," said Michael. "I already got guys handling the police and people." "It's about time they did their jobs," Carrie inserted. She asked him. "So why don't you meet up with me for a drink. We can smoke some weed and hang out a while." "Thanks Carrie. Sounds good, but I'll have to give you a rain check on that. I have my car and my limo here and I have to take care of business right now," Michael told her. Carrie said, "Mike, thanks man. I really appreciate you." "You're welcome, and don't worry about it," he told her. Rarely did Carrie get like that with Michael or anybody else. Carrie is a little, skinny feisty white chick and she could make herself up to be pretty when she wants to, but most of the time she was a tough chick. "Will God hear us in spite of our wrong?"

CHAPTER 20

REMEMBERING HIS BLESSINGS

Michael, Doug, Fossil, Jim D.J, Trend, Lil Jimmy, Stacey, Angie, Tammy, Sara and a few others all met at Stacey's house to have a little meeting. Michael showed his disappointment in them and the entire situation. He was actually just venting his anger and after he went off, he apologized to everyone. He then left and went home for the first time in a long time, but before leaving, he looked at everyone to see if he could tell who had betrayed him. Then he had to realize that it wasn't anyone else but his own fault, and he had to accept his own responsibility for whatever was happening. Michael called to talk to Kim. She just listened to what he had to say, which is what he really needed then. Sometimes she could be really good at that. He told her he loved her and loved that they had made wonderful love that morning. Michael took his kids to school as he always did. He stayed home for a couple of days talking to Kim and playing with the kids, but after a few days, he would get restless again.

Kim was back to trying to convince Michael that he should go back to work in construction. Like he told her before, he told her again what the family needed and how they were going to get it. They needed money to pay the bills, including attorney fees, which could be provided through the music business. Kim just looked at him and shook her head. She knew Michael wasn't hearing where she was coming from.

A couple of days later Kim told him one of his favorite statements, You go to get up, get out and get something going. Can't be sitting around looking sad all the time. If it's going to kill you to be here, then go ahead and do you thing, and so that's what he did.

It had been only a week since his last club scene and he was anxious and raring to go inching with excitement, he had to be on the move.

Michael went Stacey's apartment to find her mad that morning because she hadn't seen him in a week. The last time he had been there, he took off and left without an explanation. The apology to the staff was all he had said before taking off that day.

It wasn't that Stacey deserved an explanation as she was just Michael chick on the side, and he hardly gave Kim explanations, and she was his wife. Stacey was so mad that she wanted to fight him. You could see it in her eyes. "So you're back." she spurts at him. "How nice to know you care to come around." Michael said, "Yeah whatever."

"I needed to spend some time with my family and so some thinking about all this." All of what," she injected. "All this," he said as a matter of fact. Then she said, "When you decide what you want to do, you let me know." Then she left the bedroom and headed for the front door. "Get back here," Michael commanded. "Didn't you forget something?" he asked "Oh yeah," she spurted. She handed him a handful of money. Michael wasn't sure where it came from and at that moment, he didn't really care. He was in need of some extra case anyway because it was only a few days until Christmas and Michael was a big fan of the holidays. With the kids wanting presents, you sort of had to be.

Michael stayed at Stacey's and began to set up shop again, selling mainly weed and doing a few shows with exotic dancers and strippers, regardless of things really beginning to thin in that area. He also pushed a little cocaine. Michael always had some trick or scam to fall back on to earn money and it usually never resulted in any violence.

Around this time, he met a woman by the name of Myjanta, who claimed to be a friend of Alayha. Michael wasn't hanging around Alayha anymore because of the prostitution case. Myjanta claimed to have met Michael a couple of times at his club and she had been flirting with him in a hard way. She also claimed to have some tight connections with some people who had the best price for weed, even better than what Michael could get it for. The word from her was that it was cheapest in the Southwest, in Albuquerque, New Mexico.

Myjanta used to say, "This weed you're selling is dirt compared to the weed I can get and a lot cheaper too!" She been telling Michael that for months, but every time she would want to buy weed from Michael, he would always tell her she was B-Sing him and trying to pull his leg. He would also tell her that it would bite her on the ass one day, if he were to pull her up on it and call her bluff. "Then try me," she challenged. They were both talking business, but Myjanta was flirting with him at the same time. Stacey, on the other hand didn't have time to play games. She would fight for what she believed was hers especially if she felt she was being disrespected. Of course, so would Michael, but Stacey didn't play at all when it came to Michael, unless of course he was drinking.

Christmas came and went without a hitch. He was glad to have made it through without a problem. Michael was able to buy his kids and everyone else some nice presents. He wouldn't have felt right if he hadn't. This included his whole family, which usually meant new clothes for Michael and Kim. Then there were the kids, who would always get what they wanted and needed. They would also get presents from Michael and Kim's parents, even though Michael was never invited to her parents, as he wasn't raised to be prejudiced like that.

For years, it didn't bother Michael, but inside him, it did have an effect. Ingo and her parents had always bought presents for the kids and Kim bought presents for Michael's other kids.

Really and truthfully, that wasn't his department; it was Kim's job to do that each year Michael bought Kim some nice jewelry, as that was all he could think of to buy for her. Every year she would get bigger and better pieces. Whatever she wanted, she would get.

If it made her feel good, it made him feel good. He loved to see the look on her face when he gave her jewelry. She always looked like a happy kid at Christmas, with all smiles. It allowed Michael to have more of his way without a complaint from her for at least a few days. He always dreamed of being able to buy anything for his family like big diamond rings, and now Kim had one for every finger.

Michael usually stayed at his mother's house for Christmas. He was waiting for Kim to be done at her parents so that she could come to his mom's place for a little while. He gave her an "A" for that, because Kim is and Michael's moms didn't get along. Kim would always put forth an effort to come and try to get along any time she could. At Christmas, dinner Michael's mother would fix something special for Kim because she was a vegetarian. They would all have a great time. Listening to music and dancing. Sometimes they would even have competitions to see who had all the new and latest dance trend down.

It was funny sometimes because the family would find out that Kim and Michael were dancing way out of fashion. This year was different though, because now Michael had a son. Michael Jr., his namesake, was his first boy and hopefully not the only son to go with his two girls. Michael loved them all very much and proved it by spoiling them. Keya was like a little con artist, but they all knew how to get whatever they wanted from their daddy.

During this time, Michael's mother was supposed to have been in treatment for cocaine use. At least that's what she would tell Michael, but she couldn't fool him as they had been through this before. Thankfully, she really had put her life back together and was happy again.

Michael thought it was different because Tom wasn't Pops and they hadn't spent Christmas without him in many years. They were a dysfunctional family, without question, but Pops was the best and closest thing they had to as a father. If his mother was happy, then he was happy. That was Michael's main concern; at least this is what he would tell himself.

Michael never really liked his mom being with any man, not even with his Pops at first, but after he came into the picture, he was the only man for her.

Michael had a child's protection over his mother. Here he was almost 28 years old and still acting like a little boy around his mother. Michael knew he was always going to be her little boy. All things aside, they parted and were happy as could be, considering his situation, as Michael was facing a great deal of difficulties.

Soon enough, Michael's pops arrived after Kim got there. He came to bring presents for Michael's younger siblings and to take them out. It gladdened Michael to see him come for them for once. Pops stayed for a little while, while mom fixed him a plate and took pictures.

Michael hoped Tom wouldn't say anything to offend his Pops, because if he did, Michael would have to defend his Pops. Michael would have certainly left immediately if they hadn't respected his Pops. Surprisingly, happily and thankfully it all went well.

Michael and Kim ate dinner and then smoked some weed while drinking Pepsi, Kim's favorite drink. She wasn't much of an alcohol drinker. Michael and his mother, on the other hand, drank Hennessey straight up and smoked some weed he had gotten from his cousin Jason, Uncle Darnell's son. Jason would get some fireweed from his boy, a Jamaican dude named Jim. He stayed on Northport Drive, which was up the hill in a really nice area. This weed was the fire. One would think it was laced with something, but it wasn't. You would get blown away with just a few hits and it really had a kick. It cost an arm and a leg to get, at maybe a hundred dollars an ounce.

But it was a business with less of a risk of prison time. It was getting late, so Kim, the kids and Michael went home way after dark. But before leaving, Michael had a few more drinks and wanted to play with the kids and take some more pictures, but the kids were worn out and just too tired so off to bed they went.

Once the kids were in bed, Kim and Michael stayed up to talk for a while. Michael had no idea it would be the last time they would be a family at Christmas. He had a strange feeling that night and wasn't sure what it was. He remembers kissing his children and putting them to bed, as Michael loved all his children equally, and this night he was feeling a deep love for them. Little Michael was thinking he was his little man after his heart he was being and looking so cool with his little Green Bay Packers outfit all snuggled in bed.

Michael sat there contemplating how really blessed he was. Kim and Michael went into their room where they talked and then made sweet passionate love with each other. Michael thought they were going to pro-create another baby that night. At least, that's how he was feeling and that's how much he loved her.

After Kim fell asleep, Michael stayed awake. For some reason, he just couldn't sleep. For a moment he watched Kim as she lay sleeping, looking so lovely and at peace. He then began to think about all the junk he had on his mind: the criminal cases, the time he was facing in prison, his brother Pat, a.k.a. Ruttie, who was in jail and had been there for years, his brother Bruce who was in foster care because of Michael. It wasn't exactly his idea, but he had gone along with it. Because he let Kim convince him, it was the best for him at the time.

Bruce had begun stealing from them and Michael tired to manhandle him to calm him down and make him realize that what he was doing was wrong, but he still wouldn't stop stealing from them.

Kim convinced Michael to call the police just to scare him, but that was only a temporary thing. It actually turned into something more permanent when Child Services kept him and placed him in a foster home. Michael was mad at the time and he was to bust with his own life and business, so he felt he couldn't really spend any more time with Bruce. He was doing all he could for his brothers and sisters, whom he had temporary custody of at the time. Bruce, on the other hand, was Michael's partner for a while, and he was real helpful most of the time, but then he begun stealing from them and giving them all sorts of troubles. One time he stole Kim's diamond earrings, which Michael knew were worth thousands of dollars.

They thought that teaching I'm a lesson would help Jim out, but it only made Michael sick to his stomach and every time someone asked him about it, he would get sicker about his brother's habit.

However, in the end it worked out, as to this day, Bruce has stayed out of trouble and out of jail. If Michael could do it all over again, he would take the time to talk to him and do a lot of things differently.

Michael missed his brothers and sisters, as this was the first time that any of them were around since they were born. Bruce had called and was supposed to come by. Pat had also called to wish everyone a Merry Christmas and to ask for some money. Michael told him he would send him some funds, which he did the following day. He also promised he would visit soon. Michael wasn't so good about sending money or visiting, but he did get around to it once in a while. He would send money when he thought about Pat or had a little extra cash, Michael didn't always have extra cash on hand like everyone thought he did as it cost money to run a business-much more than people realized.

Another thing that made Christmas different was Stacey. Having a chick on the side made things really different. Michael thought he really cared for Stacey and she cared for him. Most of the time she seemed to care for him, but other times he just wasn't so sure.

As Kim slept, Michael started to think about Stacey and missed her. He needed to see her. The only way to cure that longing was to actually go and see her, so he did.

“We need to keep focus on the positive things in our lives if we are to let go of the negative things that bind us. It's too easy to remember the bad that happens to us.”

CHAPTER 21

TEMPTATION OF MONEY & SEX ROBBERY 4 OF 5 FEDERALLY

Michael got up early, about 5 am to leave the house the next morning. Stacey was supposed to have spent Christmas with her parent s and then go home to wait for Michael so she could give him a present. She told Michael she would be there as soon as she just wanted to spend some time with him.

Michael got there and walked upstairs and opened the door with his key. To his surprise, almost everyone was asleep-at least they were until Michael got there. From the looks of the place, they had been partying pretty hard. Bottles, blunts, roaches and trash where everywhere.

Underneath the little bitty Christmas tree, there was a little unopened box. Stacey's girlfriend Nicole was sleeping on the floor with her arms wrapped around her boyfriend Jim, Michael's new co-defendant.

Michael stepped around them and went into Stacey's bedroom. He opened the door and stood there looking at her all sexy, sweet and innocent. There was a part of her most people didn't see and she didn't display. It was mostly her tough side she showed to everyone else. Michael was about the only one who would see her true side.

Here she was lying there naked as if she had been waiting for Michael. She knew that Michael would want her to be this way. She was so tall and lanky, blond and sexy, but there was more to her than all that. She was very pretty, with nice wide hips, nice size butt and, those breasts were just as pretty as the rest of her. Stacey was a hit, just like all the models on the circuit.

Michael would tell her all the time that she was beauty as he had been around a lot of entertainers with talent including models, escorts, actresses, singers and dancers. Stacey was born with all of it. She just didn't want to spend her time hanging out with her friends partying all the time. Michael really wanted to help her change. He looked at her and asked himself, "Why do I keep messing with her?" he had a good wife and children at home. He knew he loved his wife very much as she always had his best interest at heart.

Michael thought his interest in Stacey was because she was fun, young and exciting. She came without any strings attached and she was down with whatever he did. He didn't have to say much or ask questions and that's the way he liked it.

Michael was worried about Stacey though because of whom she was hanging out with, most of who were Michael's friends. These were the people Michael had introduced her to, but he personally didn't hang with these people because he knew what they were like.

Stacey adored Michael and she had many skills and talents. She was wild like an untamed mustang and was not about to allow herself to be tamed. As hard as Michael tried, he knew he had to let her go, but after he had told her, he just couldn't do it. So here he stood thinking of all this as he watched her lying there naked and asleep. The rising sunshine reflecting on her smooth and sexy skin. Michael told himself, "Just leave man. Get it over with. You are both hindering one another from growing."

Finally, Michael was taking his own advice. He took the present he had for her out of his pocket, set it on the dresser and turned around to leave. Just then, he heard her soft, voice, "What are you doing? Where are you going?" he turned around to look at her. He thought he must be dreaming, because she was lying there sleeping and snoring just moments ago now. Stacey was lying on her back showing her smooth and sexy stomach, with the sunlight glistening on her naked body.

Michael said, "Are you talking to me?" "Whom else would I be talking to?" she asked. "You're the only one here and you're my man aren't you?" Michael wasn't sure about all that just then. Sometimes he wasn't sure what he was doing or why and sometimes he would realize he needed to be home with his family and kids-they certainly needed him-but other times he believed he was born to be in the show business and in the streets and, if that was the case, Michael wanted Stacey there with him.

Stacey said, "I like you as you are Michael. No, matter what you are doing or whatever you want to be. Now get over here and be with me." Michael looked at her and "Maybe I shouldn't, I need to do some thinking." He told her he had a lot of stuff on his plate and he wasn't sure what he wanted to eat. She answered, "Well, okay then, just be careful and don't worry about a thing, I got your back Michael." She turned away so he couldn't see her sexy body. "How was your day? Was everything okay?" she asked him. Michael replied, "I wasn't sure you really wanted to know." Stacey replied, "I'll be all right," which was one of her favorite statements. Then she said, "You'll be all right in the morning." "Yeah," said Michael "I will indeed and I'll see you then." With obvious sadness she said, "All right then." Michael gathered up all his self-respect, turned and left. They talked for much longer then Michael realized; because when he got outside there were a lot of people milling about.

He stayed at home for most of the day and fought it as best as he could, but people were calling him about work. There were a few people he needed to see and it was at Stacey's where he kept his office. He was selling mostly weed, but he would pitch some dope if he could get it for free or really cheap, which he usually would through Lil Jimmy and Yogi. Michael was always scamming, mixing, cutting and playing the middleman.

He was kicking it with many of Stacey's friends, Angie, Shelly and Shelly's boyfriend, Manny. Michael met Manny before through a few situations he had with Shelly. Manny went to Michael's club to see him after he thought Shelly was cheating on him with Michael. She may have been cheating on Manny, but it surely wasn't Michael. Michael knew nothing about it, but the majority of the time he usually knew everything that was going around his club or more importantly around him. With the girls around him, it wasn't hard to stay away from with especially all their gossip.

Shelly was a very pretty girl, but she was a little dingy and wild. She was pretty quiet when Michael first met her, but she got well acquainted with the girls who likewise got well acquainted with her. If the girls really wanted to, they could certainly keep a secret. However some of the guys thought they knew their girls, like Manny thought he knew his. He jumped in Shelly's face a couple of times at Michael's clubs. If anything, Michael wouldn't and couldn't stand for anybody jumping on the girls, unless of course, it was in self-defense, but in this case, he didn't believe it was.

Michael broke it up and told them he didn't want or need any of their problems on his property. He already had too much heat as it was. He figured the cops were close by and he couldn't be sure if they were watching or not.

Michael would assure Manny that there was nothing going on and wanted to learn whom a certain kid was that Shelly and her friends were making a fuss about. This kid was also known to be a tough kid in their age group. The word was that he could get a lot of dope and would also take some. It wouldn't be long before Michael and Manny became close and started to hang together. First as friends of their girlfriends, then as customers and clients. After Michael made all the deals he could there at Stacey's House, things began slowing down and he would notice that Stacey sat there all quiet with a crazy look on her face. She wasn't acting all normal. Michael noticed that Stacey still hadn't opened the Christmas present he had given her Christmas morning. After all his deals, he put all his tools of the trade away, including his scales and dope, then went to her and asked, "Why haven't you opened your present yet?" "Because you didn't open yours" she relied "I didn't know you had one for me," Michael admitted. Stacey handed a present to Michael. "You open yours first," he told her. "No, you go first," she said "No you first," he said. "Let's do it together, at the same time," she suggested. "All right," said Michael. She counted, "One, two, and three."

She opened her box and Michael could plainly see her eyes light up when he saw the nice little diamond ring he bought for her. It wasn't very big, but it was very nice. Michael had explained his situation to the sales lady, and she didn't like the idea of a guy with a mistress. He had told her that he wasn't so sure he wanted to be in the situation. But Michael knew if had to choose, he would definitely choose Kim as they had been together for so many years and she had taken care of him and his kids.

However, Stacey wasn't so easy to simply walk away from. She would do stuff that Kim wouldn't do. Non-responsible street stuff. The lady at the jewelry store became a counselor. Then Michael told her about his mother and she helped him choose the right ring, which was similar to Kim's ring, one each for the adult ladies in his life, not forgetting his daughters.

Michael stayed there with Stacey and partied for a while. Plus he had plenty of business to take care of and people wanted to do something with all their holiday money. Michael had plenty of dope for them to spend it on. Many people came over and kicked it with them. They were smoking, drinking and joking and when the crowd finally dwindled down, it was just Michael and Stacey. Even Jim a.k.a. Cricket, had disappeared somewhere with his little girlfriend, Nicole. Michael and Stacey listened to music as they drank themselves to a hunger to sober up on.

Stacey put on two of her favorite songs, "It's a Thin Line Between Love and Hate" and "I'm Not Going to Cry," both by Mary J. Blige who sings about true love. Michael thought that something was up, but he was too drunk to care. Not that he needed to be aroused by Stacey as he was keeping true to one of his commitments and keeping it strictly business. He wanted to go out and get something to eat but Stacey insisted that he let her fix him something.

Stacey had almost every good quality that a young lady should have, but cooking wasn't one of them. What she would end up making didn't cure Michael's hunger. He tried to fake it as long as he could, but when he couldn't any longer, he finally convinced her to let him take her out for dinner.

Michael knew that Kim or Ingo could surely cook circles around Stacey. Ingo was a great cook when she wanted to be; at least she was for sure a microwave queen. She cooked for Michael only if she knew he was going to be home. Not knowing when Michael would be home wound up being her excuse for not cooking.

Then the entire family would end up eating at McDonald's or some other fast food joint. Ingo got tired of cooking for Michael and he hardly ever showed up for dinner anymore anyway. If and when he did show up late, she'd leave it in the oven so he would eat and turn right around and go back out the door.

Ingo cooked all the time when they were first together as she loved to eat good food. When they were last together, she had been running a lot of errands and Michael wouldn't get many good meals at all, especially a cooked meal from her when she had something else on her mind.

That night Stacey and Michael went to a sports bar that Michael used to frequent. It was the Oak crest Tavern. A lot of folks that Michael knew were there as well that night. Mostly young pretty women and the staff who worked there. They were always nice and would serve him free drinks. The staff really didn't need to because he always spent plenty of money there with sometimes buying drinks for the entire bar, especially the pretty ladies. Stacey, like Kim, didn't like when Michael would buy drinks for the entire bar while they were with him. He was always recruiting workers and trying to make partners, plus he is a natural flirt and was always picking up women for pleasure and business. Michael always had his motives. He did it because he was simply a nice guy with a good personality who had plenty of cash.

They ate some good food and both of them were getting loaded. Michael had bought the bar a couple of rounds of drinks. A few ladies went over to thank Michael. Stacey gave him the evil eye as if to say, "They had better stay away from me." She may have even said some threatening comment to one of them while he was in the restroom. When Michael came back, they were acting different and one of them said something to him that he couldn't exactly make out.

She was saying something about someone. Michael tried to explain his motives to Stacey, but it got worse rather than better, so right there and then, Michael decided it was time to leave.

Michael would tell Stacey that her jealousy needed to stop and that she hadn't been that way in the beginning. It was one of the reasons why Michael liked her so much. The quality with Stacey that let him do his thing was starting to hurt her. Michael went to her and told her it was time to leave. He could see that the girls were about to get into a fight. Stacey would've more than likely been the one to throw the first punch as that was the way that she was, especially when she got drunk. She would fight with almost anyone if she felt she was in the right.

Michael had to take her home and he was angry. Whenever she got that way she could easily get out of control, and he knew it. When they finally got to the apartment, Michael told her what he was thinking about the way she was acting. At first she looked at him as if he was in the wrong, then she said, "Forget the witch!" Michael let her cool off and fixed them a drink from a giant size of Hennessey, which was the Christmas present she had bought him.

Stacey always had some drinks for Michael, but never a bottle this large and he intended to drink every bit of it, but this time around, only sharing it with Stacey and not all the other freeloaders they used to hang out with.

Sometimes Michael got really tired of them, but rarely would he ever say a word about it. Michael would bring Stacey something to drink almost every day and, in turn, she would always get Butter to go to the liquor store for her and her girlfriends, one of which was Butter's girlfriend Melissa. Eventually, they got Michael to go for them. Another reason why they left Oak crest bar that night was because Stacey wasn't twenty-one years old yet. Michael would get her into a few bars at her request, along with a couple of her friends, but back then if a girl was pretty enough she could get into most bars in town. Some girls, of course, couldn't get in, but Michael would use his influence, money and charm to get them in at times.

They were at the apartment getting tore up, drinking Hennessey. A few of their so-called friends came over and Stacey and Michael had now broken the ice and were talking again. She went over and gave Michael a kiss and pulled him towards herself, as if to say, "Come into the bedroom." Usually she would be very seductive and get Michael to lead into it, but that wasn't working as Michael had so much on his mind.

Stacey would pick a fight with him to get him angry and use sex to apologize. He would gladly give her some make up sex, and then they would get into it like never before. Sometimes they were very aggressive with each other.

She would begin with oral sex, knowing it was Michael's greatest weakness. At home, that was out of the question, because Kim didn't like it and also didn't like it done to her. She always had an excuse to get out of it. Michael didn't see anything wrong with it back then. There was no excuse for her not supplying his needs, although she did sometimes. It just wasn't enough and she complained about it. So Michael felt as if she wouldn't, he would go to Stacey who would satisfy him without complaint. A couple of times Kim had told Michael "Go get one of your whores to do it, because I'm not going to." And she meant what she said. Of course, Michael did just as she suggested. Today he knows he was wrong for doing just that.

Stacey was doing her best to be super, super sexy and super seductive. She was really putting on her best show of it, but Michael's mind was still racing. He went into the bedroom with her. As soon as he got in there, she went down on him immediately. She blew him like a real champion. His pants were still around his ankles when she dropped to her knees.

When Michael dropped to his knees, his stomach started turning inside out. He didn't want to let that break his groove, but his stomach was coming up. He got up from the floor and ran to the bathroom almost tripping over his pants. When he got to the bathroom, his head was face first in the toilet and his guts came up. The liquor had got him like never before. The worst sickness during the best oral sex ever.

Michael didn't know what could have made him sick this way. He threw up and 'ralphed' all over the floor. After it was over, he laid down for a little while Stacey began to clean him up and take care of him. When he was at home, it was Kim who took care of him.

Since it was Stacey who was the one trying to get him drunk all the time, this time it was on her. She liked to get him drunk because he was so much fun to be around. When Michael was drunk, he was less business-like. He would always be telling jokes, singing and dancing.

He would let his guard down and get into some freaky fun. Michael never thought he would turn out to be like that, because he hated drunks when he was young. His Uncles Darnell and Willie were a riot when they were drinking, but after a while, they would get all stupid and start acting serious.

Before Michael knew it, he was in bed and he wasn't sure how he got there, but he knew it was time to get up. He used to leave Stacey's place in the early morning to make it in time to take his kids to school, just like any family man would, because they were a family. Once the kids were in school, he would spend some time with Kim. That would usually mean he was sleeping and Kim was busy cleaning the house and playing with Michael Jr.

Michael would get up after a couple of hours. His pager and phone would be going off. Kim wouldn't answer his phone because she that it was for Michael. When the phone rang, usually she would say Michael wasn't there. She would tell those who Michael respected that he was asleep and not to be bothered. It was about the only way they could have any time together. After Stacey got her apartment, Michael would never be at home. He would usually be at Stacey's for a couple of hours after the club closed. Back in the day when Michael had the clubs in Los Angeles, New York and Chicago.

There was one time he was hanging out with Butter and some girl when he was too drunk to drive. That time he stayed home the whole days for some peace and quiet, but Fossil kept calling. He knew like all the other times it wouldn't be long before he would come over. At times, he kept calling like that when something was up. He would have customers who wanted to spend some real money, so Michael would have to get up. Other than that, Fossil would just be looking for a free ride and a lot of times Michael just didn't want to deal with him.

Michael had been suffering from a really bad hangover and there was nothing worse than doing business with a hangover. He finally got up to deal with the customers that had been calling. He had to get to his dope spot where he chopped it up, which was at Stacey's house. She had been blowing up his pager with calls and it was time to take care of business.

He didn't leave until he cleaned himself up and ate some good food. Kim cooked for him and he took a long, hot shower. He picked up his kids from school and took them to the store for some junk food. Finally, it was time to get over to Stacey's and take care of business. He had people that were going to meet him there. Who had been waiting on all four corners of her block for him? Michael, needed a drink, had to get the hangover off and having a drink was the best way to do that.

He finally arrived at Stacey's about mid-day, early evening. When he arrived, Stacey and some other people were waiting on him, as her friends had wanted some of what Michael had. Sometimes Michael would allow Stacey to deal some weed for him as she had been doing that anyway before he met her. However, he didn't permit her to see him with any cocaine, much less dealing any.

Michael did his best to keep very little around her house as soon as he got some, he would get rid of it. He only kept her out of that part of the business because, at times, he didn't even want to be in it himself.

As soon as he walked in the door, Stacey told him he had a phone call and he asked who it was. She told him it was Fossil and he said it was important, so Michael took the call as he was serving some of Stacey's friends and getting his customers stuff together.

Fossil was talking some crazy mess when he got on the phone. Michael though he had some people who wanted to buy something, but he was talking about robbing someone. Michael though he heard him say something about a place he used to work at.

Thinking back on it, it all made perfect sense to Michael now. Fossil was always talking about scamming or robbing someone. Michael was barely listening to him until he heard him say 'robbery.' Once he heard that word, it was time to hang up.

Michael already had enough troubles due to other people's stupidity. The cops were sweating him every day now with looking for Skin and Rob. They would come and see him at the strangest places and times just to rattle his cage. Twice they went to see him at his house when he was entertaining out-of-town guest. The cops thought he was entertaining Rob and Skin, but they were wrong. Another time they came when Michael had just returned from a big business meeting with one of his friends in the recording industry.

Michael drove him back to Madison from Chicago where they were working and taking care of business. He had promised his friend a long time ago that if he ever came to Madison he would show him a good time. Michael was supposed to hook him up with a nice woman so he could get away from it all but instead of that, the first thing they got when they pulled into the driveway was police harassment. These detectives claimed they were looking for Rob and Skin and they thought Michael's friend was one of them. To those white detectives, all blacks look the same.

Michael was trying to get back on his feet and was only trying to take care of business. It obviously wasn't over between him and the cops. Eventually the cops brought in more detectives for harassment before he was to leave town. The cops went to his hotel room just to harass him.

Michael told Fossil that he wasn't down with any of that, and he should've known that. "I know, I know, so don't trip," apologized Fossil.

Michael knew he would trip and right at that moment he was about to hang up. Fossil asked Michael if he could talk to Jim, who he had been talking to before. Michael went back to taking care of business because he had plenty of people to serve. A couple of them were in the apartment and then a few more were outside at all the corners of the block waiting. Michael was taking care of this while getting on his high as well. He would take a drink every chance he could and take a hit of the blunt that was being passed around. Usually he wouldn't take care of business this way, but he had this drunken monkey on his back.

Business was booming for the next several hours and Michael began to feel a lot better between the money, the drinking and the blunt. They had music playing and some of the guys were playing video games in the corner of the room. Michael looked over at Stacey and saw her looking back at him like he was a pork sandwich or something. She was starving for him and he knew he owed her something from the night before, a good pimping. She got him too drunk and he couldn't finish what they started. When Michael thought how sexy looking she was, it wasn't long before they were reading each other's minds. They walked into the bedroom simultaneously.

She was more seductively than ever before. There were hardly ever words said between them when they were intimate. They were both lying on the bed and both put their drinks down when Stacey jumped on top of him and asked, "Is that mine?" Michael answered, "Sometimes it is." "That isn't good enough," she proclaimed. "Show me why and how it could be any different," said Michael. Stacey unbuckled his belt and took his pants down. Michael grabbed her and turned her over on her back.

He had to pay her back. They went at it deep, smooth and hard. They went from the bed, to the floor, to the closet and back to the side of the bed. He had her hanging off the side of the bed as she was calling him big pimp daddy.

Pimp was one of the names Stacey used to call him. After awhile, they took a break to get some drinks and catch their breath. Michael heard a knock at the door, it was Jim. He wanted to borrow one of the cars. Michael told him no, but Stacey let him borrow one of her cars as long as he quit knocking at the door.

Michael cracked the door and gave him the keys. "Can I borrow a twenty," asked Jim. "I will give it back tonight when I get back." Michael gave it to him and told him to keep it. "Just leave us alone so we can finish."

Michael and Stacey got right back to where they left off. She got up on top and rode him like a pony or a wild bull. She started screaming like he had never heard her scream before. They were sweating bullets. In fact, she even started to get him tired until it was time for him to hit it from the back. She was in the doggie position and on all fours. He had seen nothing like it before, and then they were lying there on the floor. Michael heard a sound. He thought it came from the kitchen. Since he was already thirsty and needed a drink, he told himself he had better get up and check it out. Last, he heard, he didn't think anyone else was there, as they weren't expecting anyone.

As he was about to get up there was a knock on the door. Someone said, "Mike, I need to talk to you." The both of them were really quiet and Michael was so tired he wasn't sure if he was hearing what he thought he heard. By now, he had to take a piss and as he got up, he heard someone say, "It's about time; you are going to make a baby." It was Fossil and Jim. "What took you so long? We've been knocking on the door forever." "Man, we've been trying to buy something from you because everyone else has garbage," Jim declared.

"What are you talking about," asked Michael. After he came out of the bathroom, he noticed they had some money and a little dope sitting on the table along with some bottles of liquor. Michael started to ask them where the money came from but then he thought about it and realized that he really didn't want to know or care. "It's none of my business," he told himself. He was trying to take care of his business and while doing so they began smoking cocaine in a steady flow. Michael had told them before that he didn't like them doing that in the house and they usually didn't when he was around but as soon as he was out of sight, the pipe was fired up and in their mouth.

They talked about how they had robbed this movie gallery where Fossil worked. Michael didn't want them to think he was scared or some punk, so he told Fossil, "You best be careful and you shouldn't be doing that stupid stuff and then going around and telling other people your business. Why would they come over here bringing the heat on Me." that was the last Michael heard about it and he never asked another question.

He sold them a couple pieces of dope that day and they did their thing. Stacey and Michael were at it again for almost twelve hours. That was one of the longest and best times they had ever shared in the sack. At least that's what Michael was thinking and what he told him at the time.

"Fornication is deterioration of the soul and our sinful nature is never satisfied."

CHAPTER 22

MICHAEL'S COURT CASE FOR POSSESSION

A couple of days later, Michael had to go to court in the City for his dope case. He wasn't sure what was going to happen. He was very much concerned about it and even a bit worried as he thought there was a possibility that he would go to jail that day, so he prepared for that possibility. He left his house that morning unsure of what could possibly happen, although he was sure of one thing and that was he did not want to be doing his time in Illinois or especially in Cook County.

That case probably concerned him more than anything right then. Kim didn't seem to have any worries about it though. His thought was maybe she had wanted him to go to jail. Maybe she was tired of him not being home all the time and not spending time with her and the kids, or maybe she just didn't care anymore. Michael didn't know what to think. He knew in the back of him mind that she loved him and he loved her, but was their love a figment of his imagination? His mind was racing. If that were the case, was their love true or was it a lost cause?

Before leaving town, Michael stopped at Stacey's. She was getting ready for work and she asked where he was going. He told her he was going to court and she asked him who was going to go with him. He told her nobody. She asked, "Can I go with you?" Michael asked, "Don't you have to go to work?" "I'm supposed to but I would rather go with you," she said. "Okay, come on then." He welcomed her. "At least then, if they put me in jail, you can drive my car back."

They both left not knowing what to expect and they had a two-hour drive in front of them Michael couldn't think, as his head was somewhere else.

He gave some serious thought of just leaving everything and not even coming back as he felt comfortable driving and he didn't want to look back.

He told himself that if they let him walk out of the courthouse he would never come back and that was that. Stacey was trying to talk to him but he was daydreaming. She was doing all she could to strike up a conversation and Michael was just agreeing with her but he really wasn't listening.

Then she started laughing. Michael asked her what was so funny and she said that he was funny and had a weird look on his face. "You've not been listening to a word I've been saying since you began driving and then you always wonder how you slip and miss things," she told him. "And right now it's because you're really deep into your thinking. What are you thinking about anyway? Your case?" she asked him. He told, "Yeah, it's mainly my case I'm thinking about. That and where we're going. How did you know that?" he asked her. "Because I know you," she admitted. Michael thought to himself, "That's dangerous, because I don't like it when people get to know me."

By the time Michael looked up, they were already in the city and just one exit away from the Cook County Courthouse, According to the clock he was already late, so he parked the car and ran upstairs. It took them a minute to find the courtroom, and when they did, he found out that court hadn't started yet.

The building was huge and people were just about everywhere. It turned out to be one of those times hurry up and wait. "Things" The clerk came around and started calling names. He called Michael's. "Here," said Michael. The clerk told Michael to sit still and pay attention because he would be next. It took a while but not long, to where Michael would be up to bat. “Mr. Brown,” is all he heard. He told Stacey, “If they don’t let me go, it's been a good ride. You have been a good riding partner.” She said, “Man, ain’t nothing going to happen to you.” Michael said a silent prayer and asked God for help. He said, “God I have no right to ask you, but could you help me on this?”

“Come on man, you don’t want to keep the judge waiting,” Michael heard someone saying. He walked into the courtroom. It was a big place the bailiff hollered out, “All rise, the honorable judge is residing.” With all that was going through his head at the time, Michael couldn’t remember the judge’s name they called out, but then he heard, “State of Illinois verse Michael L. Brown.” The judge asked Michael, “How do you plead?” Michael answered, “Not guilty, your honor.” The judge spoke up, “Hold on a minute. Are you represented by an attorney, Mr. Brown?” “No sir, I am not, your honor.” The judge said, “Well, were you allegedly caught with a substantial amount of dope or not?” The judge looked at the paper. It stated two different amounts. Michael had copy of the paperwork the clerk had given him and it listed two different drug amounts. One said it was an ounce and the other said it was a kilo. Michael was wondering which one they were going to use. The judge was a mean looking dude who was known as a hanging judge.” He had no facial expression, but Michael could tell he was curious.

Then he said, “I see there is something wrong here, maybe a mistake. I also see you can pay for an attorney, so I suggest you do that because this is an important matter.”

Michael said, “But your honor, I don’t have an attorney and the money isn’t mine or in my name.” “Don’t worry about that, you do have a choice,” the judge said either you can hire a private attorney with a percentage of the bail money, or you can hire one of the student attorneys we have here or you can go with a public defender, which would cost you some of the bail money. It’s your choice and you’ll have to be quick about it. My advice is to use the money to get the best attorney you can afford. I’ll give you a couple of minutes while we take a recess.”

In the back of the room, Michael could see several so-called lawyers looking like witch doctors and ambulance chasers. They all looked at him hoping to be picked. Michael walked past all of them but one of them said to him, “Let me see your sheet please.” Michael handed it to him. Within a few seconds after reading it he said I think I can get you off of this.” “Oh yeah?” Michael inquired. “Yeah,” Said the lawyer.

“They shouldn’t have been stopping you in the first place as it looks as though all the paperwork was in order. Your license, registrations, insurance and you didn’t have any warrants for you arrest. It looks like someone messed up the evidence. They don’t know exactly how much you had.”

“Which was it, the ounce or the kilo?” the lawyer looked at Michael as he asked the question. “I’m waiting for the answer,” he said. “Never mind that question,” said the lawyer. Michael told him anyway. “It was the kilo,” “Not anymore,” said the lawyer. “From here on out it was an ounce.” He told Michael to sit there and wait for a minute that he would be right back Michael looked at Stacey and they looked impressed.

Another couple that was there were pointing at them and laughing. Michael could barely hear what they were saying. “That one there, he’s the one,” said the stranger. Just then, the arresting officer walked up to him and said, “Hello Mr. Brown, how are you doing?”

Michael answered, "I'm alright, I guess. I just wish I didn't have to go through this mess." The officer said, "I think it will be alright," and then the officer walked away. Michael wasn't sure what he meant. The lawyer came back and said, "I got this one. I can get you off." Michael asked, "Are you sure?" "Nothing is sure in life, but this case is as close as you can get. Even with this hanging judge, but first you have to sign this as it appoints me as your attorney." Michael asked how much it was going to cost him. The attorney said "25% of your bail money." They walked back into the courtroom and the court was called back into session.

"Mr. Brown," the judge asked, "Did you find yourself an attorney?" The attorney answered, "Your honor, Mr. Brown is now being represented by counsel." And then he stated his name. The judge said, "Well, let's begin." The prosecutor yelled out, "The charges are possession with intent to deliver one kilo and then one ounce." The judge asked, "Which one is it?" Michael's lawyer hollered, "Objection! The D.A. said, I think it's a kilo, your honor." Michael's lawyer objected again and the judge said, "The court takes notice of your objection counselor." The D. A. presented his case and told the story, Mr. Brown was pulled over for an illegal U-turn in a high crime and drug neighborhood and during the stop he was asked for a driver's license, insurance papers and registration, which was presented. After that, the officer asked Mr. Brown what he was doing hanging out late at night in a bad neighborhood with his trunk open. Mr. Brown stated that he was showing one of the store owners some merchandise, which turned out to be some tires and rims that he had on sale."

"The officer then asked Mr. Brown is he had a receipt for the tires and rim. Mr. Brown stated he had one, but that he wasn't sure where it was at the moment. The officer then asked Mr. Brown if he would consent to a search of his vehicle and Mr. Brown said no. The officer then took it upon himself to search the vehicle, because he had observed Mr. Brown fidgeting and looking nervous. In this search the officer found some cocaine in the back of Mr. Brown's vehicle, a Cadillac limousine and at that point Mr. Brown said it was his."

The judge asked, "Is that all counselor?" The D. A. said, "Yes sir." Michael's new attorney began his big opening with "What was my client being stopped for and then searched for your honor? Seems he had all the proper paperwork. There were no warrants for his arrest, he cooperated with the police officer and he was in his limo, which takes a little more to search that, a regular vehicle." The judge sat there saying nothing and looking like a mean Ben Franklin. Then he asked, "Is the arresting officer in the courtroom?" The officer stood and said, "Yes, your honor."

The judge asked him, "Step up here officer." He asked the officers, "If this is all true, why did you stop this man?" The officer said, "It's all true. I stopped him because he was looking suspicious." The judge sat there a minute and said nothing. The courtroom was totally silent, and then the Judge spoke, "I find that Mr. Brown presented all the proper paperwork. He answered all your questions satisfactory and there was no reason why you should have been searching this man's vehicle. This case is dismissed." The gavel was slammed down onto the stand and Michael almost jumped out into the audience. Michael heard some of the other cops say, "Way to go Fred. You really cracked this one the day before your retirement." Then another cop said, "Yeah, you got caught by the oldest cop on the force. You should have ran, it would have ran, it would have cost you a whole lot less.

Michael did in fact think about running at the time, but knowing how Chicago police were, he didn't like the idea of getting shot in the back. One of the cops said that Officer Fred couldn't see the side of a barn.

The judge ordered silence and said, "Mr. Brown, you are free to leave. This is your lucky day. Take yourself back to Wisconsin and don't let me see you in my courtroom again."

Michael left the courtroom as fast as he could. The cop that had arrested him then came out along with his attorney. They were hollering, "Hold on Mr. Brown. Wait a minute." The cops said, "Here's the receipt to get your car and here's the parts to your rims." He had the parts in a bag. The attorney said, "You can get the rest of the money that's left in about thirty days." He told Michael that only after he asked about his bail money.

Stacey and Michael left as quickly as they could. They were more than ready to go from that courtroom. Michael thanked his attorney and they were out of there.

On the way down the stairs, Michael stopped for a minute and gave thanks to God. Stacey asked Michael, "What did you say?" He told her, "I gave thanks to God." Stacey said "Amen!" this was the third time that she acknowledged that there was a Jesus. Michael knew the fact of the Lord, he just wasn't living it as he intended.

The next day things were back to normal. Michael had to go pick up his cousin Vic from the hood and some other family members, including Vic's mother, who wanted him to go with Michael because Vic had robbed a couple of dudes who they used to cop dope from. Vic would always use Michael as an excuse for copping something. He mentioned to these guys that Michael was coming over to bring something for them. Michael himself didn't know what was going on and was dumbfounded. In his mind, Michael knew that Vic hadn't changed a bit, in fact he involved, but something inside made him. They threatened to kill Vic and they were pretty angry as well and told Michael not to be in the car or around him when they caught up with him. These guys were so angry that they even threatened Vic's mother.

After talking to Michael, they went into her house. They had to, as Michael needed to settle things down for a minute. Vic and Michael were always doing something crazy like that, but not quite as bad. Once before, Vic had robbed some of his own fellow gang bangers in Madison. They tried to beat him up and shoot him in Michael's club, but Vic had run into Michael's office where they wouldn't or couldn't go. Vic was working that night when he saw one of the guys he had robbed earlier. They circled him with a well-known gang move, but Vic saw it coming and went to Michael for a gun, something Michael didn't have at the time.

Michael wouldn't give Vic a gun because he knew that Vic would have killed one of them and then, of course, it would be his fault and Michael wasn't about to get involved with any of that.

They did manage to get a few punches in on Vic before Michael could break-up the fight. Both Doug and Michael, in fact, broke it up and Michael unfortunately wound up promising to pay them off sometime later down the road, which was something he didn't want to do, much less even offer to do, but he kept his promise and did exactly that.

The day after court Michael picked up some dope and Vic a few blocks from his mother's house. Michael really didn't approve of what he did, but he also didn't want them to kill him either. Michael always thought of Vic as family and he loved him as such, but later on down the road, he would come to think of him differently.

In any case, Vic came with Michael back to Wisconsin. Needless to say, he didn't get any better and things only got worse so much worse that it got to the point where Michael couldn't take him anywhere anymore. It was true that he was still safer in Madison, but that only lasted for a little while.

From the very first day they arrived in Madison, Vic started to rob people. There was no way Michael could stop him and it got to the point that Michael finally had to ask him to leave. He knew that Vic was either going to get busted or killed. Michael was concerned that he might get caught in the middle of Vic's random robberies and that's something Michael certainly did not need.

Michael himself had been using a little dope, but not as hard as Vic. Vic was a violent user and Michael just wasn't down for or like that. Vic would use the threat of violence and it was sad to see that he was robbing good and worthy people, people that Michael actually considered friends.

It was around this time that Michael was called by some big time music executives. They wanted Michael to take his promotion game on the road from the Midwest to the Southeast. The timing couldn't have been better for Michael, or so he thought. He wanted to take the job and leave the same day, but it was more complicated than that, because he had two criminal cases pending against him. There was the one in New York and the other one in Madison and he wasn't sure what was going to happen with either one.

Michael told the executives who offered the job to him about his case. From their perspective, they thought that it shouldn't come out too bad on his behalf.

There was one thing that Michael had in his favor and that was some good attorneys and it showed that they had been doing their homework. Michael had told the music executives that he could surely use and needed the money. In turn, they informed him they would work around his schedule, as they were interested in Michael booking concerts for mostly Midwestern artists. They knew of some artists who hadn't been doing well with their labels on the circuit, so it would have been to be a combination of major record companies. They were thinking of maybe having one from the West Coast, one from the East Coast and even one from the Midwest.

The music executives wanted to know if Michael could do for them what he had doing for himself for years. He confidently assured them that he could and that they should get back to him. What they didn't know was that most of Michael's bookings had been in his own clubs.

Michael was waiting for their response, but he wasn't just sitting and doing nothing. He couldn't and wouldn't just do anything. He still planned on doing his hustling in the meantime until he heard a response from the music executives and, luckily for Michael, he knew how to do that very well.

It was right after that when this girl Carrie paged him one day and asked him for some weed. She wanted to meet him at Stacey's apartment. She also wanted to give him something, but she wouldn't tell him what it was. Well, she went over all right, and she was packing a gun. It was a ten-millimeter nickel-plated automatic with hollow point bullets. Michael asked her, "Where'd you get that?"

Then he quickly said, "Never mind, I don't want to know." He also asked her, "Does it have any bodies on it?" That was all that was important to him. She told him "Not that I am aware of." Michael then asked her, "What's the catch? What do you have a gun for?" She knew Michael didn't play that way, plus she owed him one anyway. "I just need a little weed and some cash," she told him. "How much do you need?" Michael asked her. "A half ounce and a hundred dollars," she told him. Michael told her it wasn't a problem. He went into Stacey's bedroom and gave her the gun. Michael never kept any weapons around the place, much less anywhere else. What guns he did have were from way before and he kept those at the club plus they were legitimate and belong to Doug. They were only kept for security and safety purposes and not to threaten anyone with.

A could of days later Michael received a call from the execs in the music business. The plan was for Michael to leave in a couple of days for a meeting in New Mexico and from there they would go to Arizona and then finally to California. Michael's responsibility was to stop in every town along the way to set up gigs.

Michael received the call while he was at Stacey's apartment. He told her the good news and asked her to go with him, but she said she couldn't go because of her job. That was all right with him as he completely understood, plus he knew she had to work anyway. Regardless of that, later on that evening, they began celebrating. They had a bunch of people come over, including a guy Manny and Myjanta brought over to buy some weed. Michael's friends asked what all the commotion was about.

Michael explained to Myjanta what the celebration was for and she expressed to Michael that the weed he was getting was too expensive for the garbage that it was. Myjanta said she could get way better weed from Albuquerque where Michael was going to be in a few days from then. She also said she was going home for the holidays, but in her mind, she was thinking way more than just talking to him. She made sure to tell Michael all of this while getting high and flirting with him in a hard way.

Michael told her to sell her ticket and that she could ride with them. He told her that she had better not be messing with him about the weed hook-up either. She said, "I ain't playing with you man! Are you playing with me?" and Michael said, "I don't play games." Here he was again kicking against "God's Gold."

Chapter 23

BUSINESS TRIP TO THE WEST COAST

Michael took a couple of his guys with him and they left the next day. Surprisingly, Michael felt that he should take Vic with him. He had to do something to help him keep from getting himself killed because of all his robberies.

They drove in Michael's van as he had a few pre-arranged meeting already with CEO's from the promotion company. On the way, they also stopped at various bars and a few college campuses, so Michael could hand out promotional goods.

Master P was hitting the circuit at the time and it had slowed some for him. Soon enough, Michael hit Albuquerque, which was about 1500 miles and a 24-hour drive from where they had started. In total, it took them about 36 hours because of all the stops and the added miles.

By this time, they had run out of weed due to the fact that Michael brought the smoking hogs with him. He obviously hadn't been thinking at the time because, if he had, he would still have some left to smoke on his own, that would've been fine with him as he would've let them roll their own even if he had to pay for it himself. He didn't want to wait to get high, but then on the other hand, he didn't know where the guy's mouths had been. Sometimes he couldn't even be sure of his own mouth.

Michael knew some of the girls he had been with had done some real nasty things that he actually liked, but he also knew that if they did it with him; they had likely done it with someone else. And these guys would do anything with anybody, especially if the girl was fine.

The finer looking the girl, the worse the odds of catching something. He couldn't understand what some fine-looking girl would want with one of these guys anyway. They weren't good looking and they certainly didn't have anything to offer. All they wanted was to get high, which only increased their odds of catching something. Some of the girls may have thought the guys had money because they were with Michael, but they did not. They were not in business with him, only riding partners and most certainly not business partners.

Michael handled his business at times with some of these guys on the road, but mainly because most times Michael as well as these guys were all straight up horny. It was a blessing from God the Michael never caught anything serious, because he never did like using a condom. Especially while on the road, he would never wear them, even though he knew deep in his head that he should because that was the smart thing to do. As he looks back today, he realized how foolish and hardheaded he was then, and he knows of many people who were not so lucky or blessed.

When they finally got to Albuquerque, they were out of weed and Michael had a couple of hours before he was to meet with his business associates so naturally, Michael went to find some weed. He was fortunate to pick up a few pounds from one of friends and who also happened to be my janta's ex-boyfriend. Michael purchased it about three-hundred-dollars a pound. The weed was decent and it would have cost him about twice as much back in the city.

When Michael met with his business associates, he was high as a kite. They asked Michael if he was all right. Michael said, "Yeah man, I just needed to relax and ease my mind." He said, "As long as you aren't like that all the time and it doesn't affect your business."

Later that evening they met at a nice restaurant across the street from a club called The Underground. Michael had heard about it and wanted to set up a gig there, especially if it was as good as it sounded.

He was fortunate to get them a gig right away now that he had told the club owner who he was working with and who he was representing. It turned out that this club owner had heard about the groups from the Midwest, groups such as Crucial Conflict, Twista, Do or Die Common and Keya. They had not yet heard about Psycho Drama, Saw Buck, L.S. and a few other guys that were on the rooster. They heard of Snow and really liked him. That was good news to Michael and he knew then that they were going to do this place right and there was not going to be any problems with the artists Michael had lined up.

That night it was strictly business. Some pleasure was to find guys later at their motel. It was just a little party as Michael left his guys at the hotel with some weed and drinks-nothing major. Myjanta and her friends stayed and kept them company. Michael of course, had company too. Some local girls they had picked up at the club that evening-a couple of Native and Spanish Girls. Unfortunately, for Michael, he could not remember the whole scene as he had a lot of good weed and some good Spanish liquor that night. Truthfully, he was completely out of it.

The next day they drove to Flagstaff, Arizona. Things were already set up there and Michael had people waiting to see him from a local promotion company called Magis Entertainment. They were really inspired with Michael as he had presented them, but in all actuality, they were rookies. It was a simple deal there in Flagstaff. The deal was that Michael would bring the groups to a couple of clubs around town to get them noticed and get the word out. It was simple enough and easily done. Things were really going smooth for the time being.

After that meeting, Michael headed out west for California. He had an appointment to meet with a local radio show host. As it turned out, the lady who was hosting the show was someone he had already met. She first started in this field as a promoter, but ended up hosting radio shows.

It took them half the day to reach California. While at the radio station, they were waiting to talk to Chocolate, who was in charge of promotions. They were told to wait until they went to a commercial break and then they would be taken into the booth.

They could see three ladies in the glass booth, including Sonya and two men. Sonya is Chocolate's real name. In any case, the commercial finally came on and they went into the booth. They politely introduced themselves. There was one lady in particular who looked like a ten-year younger version of Chocolate. She introduced herself as Sonya Green, Vice President of Promotions.

Michael's eyes bucked and his head just about jumped off his shoulders. His partner looked at him as if to ask, "All you all right man?" Michael said, "I'm cool." He had to choke up a little because he was stunned.

When they came back on the air, Michael was asked to introduce himself. He introduced himself as a friend of a major record executive and owner of a successful entertainment company who specialized in music promotions and productions.

Sonya asked, "What are you guys in town for?" Michael explained that they were looking for talent. "However, today they were in town to promote acts on their roster." "New up and coming hot stuff." Michael said. He continued, "Most of which is from the Midwest. Groups that I've been working with for years and who are now on the market." Then Sonya asked, "Is it true Mr. Brown, before you were in the music business, you were working construction for a few years, while running a night club which had strippers?" Michael had to admit, "Yes, that is true Ms. Green. I did those things and worked in many fields. I was good at it until I found out that I really loved this field." Then she asked, "Would you say that anyone could make it in this business if they really wanted to?" "Yes if they want it bad enough, one can do just about anything. But in order to be really good in production, you have to had a little more than talent," he proclaimed. "Like what?" she asked. "Well, you have to have some supervisory skills and be able to put things together." Michael continued, "And you have to have a good ear."

"The same for productions," Michael said. "You have to have good people skills to work with and they have to want to work with you." "I'm not sure what you're trying to get at Ms. Green, but I'm sure it has something to do with the entire fine artists that will be coming your way." He said. "For example we have Do or Die, Crucial Conflict, Twista, Common, Ant Dub, L.S. and many others. I have many tapes and cd's to leave with you, if you'd like me to." Michael said.

She responded and said, "I have only one more question for you Mr. Brown. Do you have any family back home in the Midwest? Maybe a wife and some kids?" Michael said, "Well yes, there is a misses and I have a couple of kids. Two girls and a boy and for my name sake, it can be tough sometimes being on the road, but its part of the job and the misses respects what I do. I love it!" Michael continued, "If I could, I would like to give a shout out to my family, Kim and my kids, Jazzman, Keya and Michael. And let me finish by saying that when these guys come to town make sure you get out and see the awesome shows they will be bringing to you."

Just then Michael's partner jumped in and said, "Make sure you go out and buy their albums at your local store, folks. You won't be disappointed."

Then they went to a commercial. Michael partner asked him, "What was that?" "I don't know, you tell me," said Michael. He asked Michael, "Do you know Sonya?" "Well no and yes, I sort of know her," said Michael. "Never mind," he said. "That was a little personal if you asked me, but it was still a good interview." "Well I didn't…," said Michael. The interview was starting to get him pissed off.

Sonya came out of the booth and Michael had to ask her. "What was that?" Sonya said, "Please forgive me, I don't know where that came from. I guess it was from what happened when I last saw you. The way you left, and then you never called me. When I tried calling you, you were always too busy and never called back." He thought to himself and said, "You never called me." She looked at him as if he was lying. He thought about it and had to realize that she did in fact call him last winter. "Oh yeah, I remember." She called him to say hi and ask for some advice of how to get into the music business. He then gave her the quick version, as he had to take care of his own right there and then.

There was another time she had called asking personal questions when he was in the middle of taking care of some business. Michael did not really appreciate that at the time when he took care of business that is exactly what it was, taking care of business with no interruptions.

He was on his way back to the hotel room with the guys to have some good and relaxing fun. He had remembered more than about her calling back because one of the guys that worked for Michael had talked to her and told her that Michael had and would promise to call her back, but he never did.

Michael told her, "Listen, I really apologize about being brief with you and never getting back to you back then, as you may know by now, this is a very hectic business and there are and will be times that I won't be able to call people back, so my apologies to you again." She said, "its cool Michael, I was just looking for some more of your good advice and opinions again. I thought you were different and special or maybe I thought I was different and special to you, but you just treated me like another one of your ho's."

Again, Michael said, "I'm really sorry. Can I take you to dinner?" She said, "No" "Come on, let me make it up to you," Michael asked her. "You're only asking because you want something." "What?' asked Michael. She said, "You need some promotional work, and I'm the one you can count on."

He did not have to think about it to know that she was right. She was thinking ahead of him and this could be just right. Michael asked her again, "Let me buy you dinner?" Just as he asked her, his partner came around the corner with Sonya's co-worker. They were arm in arms. They asked, "Would you two like to join us for dinner?" She looked at Michael with a half grin and said, "Okay, why not." "Let's go then."

They went to some fancy restaurant on the ocean shore. It was a fine and relaxing dinner. Afterwards Sonya really was not into talking too much, so Michael pulled her aside and told her, "Listen, I don't know what you're mad about, but I meant everything I said back then. I always speak what I mean and I mean what I say about what I feel. It seemed to work because I see you are doing something different and you took my advice and followed your dreams. I see you like what you're doing." She said, "Yes, I do like it." Michael said, "Now, I need something from you." "And what might that be," she asked him, while looking at him somewhat angry and sexy too. She had really changed for the better, and if Michael had not known, better he would have thought she had a face-lift. Maybe he did not notice it before, but she did do something. He did not want to offend her so he kept quiet about it. If he had offended her, he would not have gotten what he wanted from her.

She said, "Okay, what is it?" Michael said, "It's not what you think. I need you to give some of my guys some big airplay. I need for you to hook me up in some places with nice venues, as well as any groups that could open for them who are known locally and are good." She looked at him considering what he said without saying anything for a minute.

Then she said, "That's what you want? This is all about business?" Michael didn't know what to think and he always said or told himself, "Never mix business with pleasure," What was it she wanted? What did she expect?"

Michael had been very professional and very respectful with her and was sure he didn't want to do what she wanted to put him out there for. He looked into her hazel eyes, which now seemed sad and different; he knew it had to be him, so he asked her, "What do you think?" She said I don't know.

He said "Well then, if there's nothing else how about a night cap?" She looked at him and said "What?" "Wait a minute," he said. Then he kissed her. She didn't stop him and then she said, “Some good loving for good old time’s sake?” “You mean sex?” asked Michael. “Whatever you want to call it,” Sonya said.

She grabbed his hand and as he grabbed hers, they kissed again. Michael wasn’t really a big kisser, but he could break his own rules to get what he wanted from Sonya, especially if it meant to make it in the business. Michael liked what he was feeling and she was looking good in a business suit shirt. She was flashing those sexy legs like Ms. Jackson when she was being nasty. Once again, Michael said what he thought. “Let’s go, my guy has some rooms. He’s staying there before we go back to L.A. and I’m not sure if I'm staying, but I have to take care of this and lock the deal in.”

Once at the hotel, Michael went to the desk and informed them, “I’m Mr. Brown. I have reservations and I'm checking in.” They went to the room and they were at it from the front door to the bed. They had some wonderful sex and she rode Michael better than a semi rides a trucker.

Then she told Michael, “You make me feel bad, because I took what you said to heart. I thought you really cared.” “I do care,” assured Michael. “I’m just who I am.” Then he asked Sonya, “Are you going to take care of that little business I asked of you?” “Of course I am.” She assured him.

Later when Michael saw his partner, he told him it was a done deal. They had all the free promos they needed in that area, as well as access to all the hot clubs and local groups they needed to open up for their headliner. He asked Michael, “How did you do it?” “Just a little persuasion,” Michael said with a smile. Then he asked Michael, “Do you know that girl from somewhere? Do ya’ll have a past? Why didn’t you tell me?” Michael told him, “I wasn’t sure what to expect.” “She told her friend everything and boy that woman is in love with you,” he told Michael. Michael admitted that he was in love with only one woman and he had been for many years, and that was Kim. He also mentioned the feelings he had for another woman, but I’m glad to have helped or influenced her to get off the streets and into something like she did.” Michael continued, “I have to go now as I have other important things that need to be taken care of back home. I don’t know what it is man, but I get the strange feeling that I won’t be around for too much longer.”

Michael left that night without saying good-bye to Sonya. He felt he needed to or he may not have left, plus he had to get back to Albuquerque to pick up the crew and get back on the road. He was already violating the golden rule and had his van packed for two days, not riding around dirty.

They arrived in Albuquerque in the early morning. The weed was strapped in plastic bags with coffee beans and then packed with dryer sheets in the kicker box.

They had a twenty-four hour drive ahead of them, and of course, like always, Michael did all the driving, as he was the safest and the fastest. He wouldn’t trust anyone else to do the driving unless he had to. It was either him or Kim that did any or most of the driving.

In the midst of driving, Michael thought to himself, “The road to God is bumpy, understanding none.”

CHAPTER 24

POLICE HARASSMENT

They arrived back in Madison the next day and the guys had smoked most of the weed that Sonya had given Michael. There was still about an ounce that Michael had taken out of the ten pounds. In doing so, he noticed the difference in the quality of the product and the result of the different prices.

Once back and settled, Michael then got into his hustling groove. He was selling weed for one-thousand-dollars a pound, which was a three hundred percent profit. He would get a few at seven-fifty or eight hundred, but Kim told him it was foolish. Michael knew what he was doing. People thought he was selling if for fifteen hundred to two thousand a pound, but they were selling it in ounce bags. He was still selling cocaine whenever he could get it on a front, which he did every once in awhile for his cousin Lil Jimmy or the guys in the city.

Michael would come up with a good hustle or scam whenever he had a chance, but never within the threat of violence.

To his surprise, he sold out that first week and was ready to head back to Albuquerque. However, he didn't leave until he could afford to, plus he had other things wrapped up in all other ways. He still had the legal issues pending in New York, which was scheduled for Court in February.

When he could get some dope to sell, he would share it with Vic, Fossil and Jim. Jim and Fossil would come up with something every now and then, but Jim was another story. He would never give Michael anything, but he would always talk Michael into another deal. Michael at the same time was also buying some merchandise every now and then from Vic. Once he even acquired a large screen television in a dope trade.

Vic and Jim were now staying in Madison, with most of the time spent at Stacey's house. They were only supposed to be staying there temporarily until they could get on their feet, which wasn't by choice.

It was Stacey's idea and Michael didn't put up any resistance, but he did warn her about those guys. She thought she knew what she was doing and the guys probably promised her something, but Stacey was too nice of a girl and they wouldn't have had to offer her much.

Vic spent most of his time on the streets ripping people off and Michael would take him home once in a while to clean up and take a shower. They would feed and take good care of him while he was there. Michael felt sorry for Vic a lot of times.

When Michael's mom was in prison, Michael stayed with Ida, which was Vic's Aunt. Michael and his brother would go to Ida's house for the summer to have fun and they would feed them well there too. Vic had lots of connections in the dope scene as well as in the music business and, fortunately for Michael, he was able to meet a lot of people through him.

Kim wouldn't mind Vic staying for a day or two, but then she would tell Michael it was time for him to go. At first Michael would get mad about it because she knew how Vic's mother and Aunt looked out for Michael and his family when they needed it, but Kim made Michael realize it was Ida who looked out for them not Vic.

Michael told Kim that he could always use Vic's place to do deals from the streets and have a place to return his calls. There was one thing that Michael had realized and that was, if nothing else, he did in fact pay Vic back many years prior. None of the old dudes would ever go near Vic, not even to deal with Michael because they hated Vic and wanted his head for all the bad stuff he had done to them or robbed from them.

Nevertheless, Kim didn't want Vic around because it wasn't good for her and the kids. He always smelled of alcohol and drugs and that was something that Kim never wanted around the kids. Kim also admitted to Michael that she was afraid of Vic and she thought he was liable to do something to her or Michael.

That was that, and Vic was no longer welcome at their home. Michael believed that when Kim felt something it would usually come true. From then on Vic could only stay at Stacey's place.

Michael told Stacey his concerns regarding Vic, but she acted as if she didn't care. Michael thought that Stacey just wanted to prove Kim wrong, so she permitted Vic to stay. Michael didn't say a thing about it anymore until one day some of his dope turned up missing from Stacey's underwear drawer. Stacey didn't even know it was there because it was only a temporary hiding spot for small amounts.

Michael had other hiding place that he did tell Stacey about, but she didn't think anything of it. She thought Michael was crazy and that he probably misplaced it. Stacey and her friend Angie, who she had hooked Vic up with, went to the store. One that particular day only Vic and Michael had been in the house, so it didn't take long to determine what happened or who done what.

It wasn't long after that when a little necklace that Michael wore turned up missing as well. No one else had been in the house when that turned up missing. Michael didn't realize it was missing for a while, but before Vic came around things didn't disappear as they had now begun to. Even with a lot of people coming over to party, things still didn't disappear like they had been lately. Michael never did dare accuse Vic, but if he was to place his bets, he was sure he would win.

Michael's big screen television also turned up missing. The TV was under a blanket in Michael's van, which was parked in front of Stacey's apartment. Besides Michael, Vic was the only other person who knew where it was. Enough was enough!

Vic soon returned after being gone to three days and Michael had just hooked him up with a nice bag of product so that he could sell it. He came in the door with a dumb sob story that he had been robbed and was broke. Michael was doing his best to keep his cool and luckily, for Vic, he turned his back on him for a moment. He didn't realize yet that some dope had been stolen off of Stacey's dresser.

Michael told Vic that they needed to talk. Michael told him he would have to get some help and quit getting high while he was in Madison. He also told him that there were plenty of good treatment centers that would give him the treatment he needed for free. It made Michael fell like a hypocrite because he was thinking he may be in need of some help himself, but Michael believed thing were different for him.

Sure, he drank and he smoked some weed, but he could still work and manage a business. Vic smoked crack for more than twenty years and the funny thing was that he was a pretty good guy when he wasn't screwed up on crack, but he was still worthless and didn't do any good when he was hanging around Michael. As time went on Vic got worse and worse and was using more and more.

Vic begged Michael to give him another chance, and Michael had to give it some thought, that was until Stacey learned of the dope missing from her dresser. Michael asked Vic about the dope and Vic said, "Yeah, I took it, but I promise I will pay you back." Michael took it really personal and knew it wouldn't stop there. They confronted Vic about the television and the necklace. It wasn't long after that Vic tried to run out on them and take off, which was a straight dope fiend move, as he must've known that Michael was done with him.

Michael grabbed him to pull him back in the house and he tried reaching into his coat pocket to get his dope, but Vic took a punch at him to try to get free of Michael's grasp. Michael really lit into him by hitting him with a combination of rights and lefts. Needless to say, Vic fell to the floor, but as he was going down, he pulled down the shower curtain and hit the side of the bathtub. Stacey came running in to see what was going on. "What's going on?" she asked. "Vic went running out the door." Michael looked in the mirror to see if he had any marks and then he noticed the necklace he always wore was missing. It was a 14k gold necklace with a gold cross that Michael just got for Christmas that was worth about fifteen hundred dollar. It wasn't on the floor, so he figured Vic must have taken it.

Michael told Stacey that Vic must have just stolen from him again. "What did you do Mike?" she asked. "I tried to get my stuff back from that idiot," Michael said. Stacey looked at him as if he was doing something wrong. She was taking Vic's side. Michael was still looking for his necklace on the floor, but he knew Vic probably left with it out the front door. Michael couldn't understand why Stacey was so absorbed with Vic.

After a few drinks, Michael was able to calm down and pull himself together. He chalked it up as a loss and he had to keep moving forward. He had too many other things to worry about. He had to think about his family, his legal issues which were his freedom and then there was his work to keep the money coming in. he also had to pay his lawyer to keep him free on the streets with his family while the legal issues was still pending.

So Michael kept doing what he had always done. It wasn't east, though, as now he always had something on his mind. Not only that, he also had the police following him and chasing him. There were two detectives, Hietzky and Druanduran, who worked for the local Madison Police Department. They were always keeping a close eye on Michael. Every chance they got they would come to him and ask, "Where are your friends Rob and Skin?" Michael would insist that he didn't know where they were at "You know more than I do," he would tell them and that was the truth. Michael hadn't seen Skin since they left on the run.

Although he did see Rob once when he came to see him after he was arrested and beat the case in Milwaukee, however he had given a different story to Angie and Stacey. The detectives were relentless and wouldn't believe that Michael didn't have anything to do with the robbery. They were doing all they could to hurt Michael's business and cramp his style, which took its toll after a while, because he couldn't even cheat on his wife without the detectives knowing about it.

They would follow Michael to every bar, club, hotel, restaurant or residence he visited. A lot of times, he would see them tailing him everywhere he went. Pretty soon, it got to the point where if he didn't see them, he knew that either something was wrong or something was up. He really hated it.

As bad as the detective's harassment was, it was really nothing yet because it was about to get worse. He just didn't know it at the time.

A few days went by and Michael hadn't heard from Vic. Part of him thought that this was a good thing but then another part of him was really concerned.

Michael was leaving Stacey's house on his way home. It was late in the evening and he was in the habit of looking across the street into the parking lot to see if the police were watching him. A neighbor had also stopped him across the street. Michael could see in the neighbor's bedroom across the way and she could see through theirs.

She stopped Michael at the gas station up the street one-day. The neighbor was a very attractive, dark skinned woman and a little older and taller than Michael. "Excuse me sir," she said. "Is your name Michael Brown? And don't you drive a red limousine, a burgundy car and a blue limousine?" she asked. Michael though it odd that this lady knew all this about him. He didn't even know her name, so he asked her, "Who wants to know?" "I think you're always getting followed by the police for something," she said.

Michael asked, "How do you know that?" "Well for one, I see them sitting in the parking lot across the street watching you all the time. Now they're staying in my building in the morning, noon and night. Whatever it is that you're doing or what they think you're doing, maybe you should stop it now."

Michael thanked the lady. "I'm not doing anything and it's a clear case of police harassment," he assured her. She told him, "I know who you are as I've seen you on TV and the news before," she said. Michael wasn't sure what to think about that. He had indeed been on the news for both good and bad reasons. One thing was for certain; she surely didn't like the fact that the police were in her building watching Michael.

It was the same day that Michael was coming home late and he was stopped in the parking lot by some sort of police. He wasn't sure who they were as he thought it was the state investigators or maybe the feds, but. One thing for sure was that they weren't the regular city cops that had been following him around. They used their cars to block him in so that he couldn't get into the parking lot. They shined their bright headlights into his face so he couldn't see into their cars. "Mr. Brown, we need to talk to you," someone said. "Who are you?" asked Michael. "You know who we are. We need to know where Robert Sutton and James Fleming are at." Michael said, "Like I already told the other cops, I don't know where they are at. I haven't seen them since they left town. Don't you guys talk to one another or what?"

They told him. "You had better be telling the truth, or you will wish you had." Then they showed Michael pictures of Rob and Skin together and another photograph of Rob and Skin with a bunch of girls. Some of the photographs were old and some of them were pretty recent.

Before they left, Michael was asked, "What does that mean to you?" "It means nothing to me," Michael retorted. "Now you can get out of my way so I can park my car and quit harassing me! I told you I don't know anything about where they are!"

Michael got back in his car and started to move it. One of the guys came over to his car and said, "No, I won't. It's my job. It's your job!" then another cop came up and injected, "You'll wish you came aboard with us before this is all over, Mr. Brown." Michael asked the cop, "Is that a threat? Because if it is stop. I already told you. I don't know and don't have anything to do with whatever they did. I have nothing to do with their problems or with you guys, so please stop harassing me!"

One of the cops grabbed Michael's arm and said, "Don't be stupid Mr. Brown." Michael snatched his arm back and said, "Don't touch me!" as Michael pulled away, he thought about how badly these guys really wanted to find Rob and Skin.

There was yet another incident when Michael and Kim were out to dinner at Applebee's. Kim had just gone to the bathroom and two officers from some department came to the table and sat down. "Hello, Mr. Brown, what's going on with you?" asked the officer. "Who are you, and what do you want?" Michael asked. "We're the authorities who are looking for your friends, Rob and Skin," announced the officer. "We believe you know where they are. In fact, we believe that you may be harboring them." Michael said, "You're wrong, and I'll tell you as I told the rest of the police who have been harassing me, I don't know where they are and I have nothing to do with whatever they are doing." The officer told Michael, "Okay Mr. Brown, believe me, you will regret that you had." "Yeah, whatever man," injected Michael. They left just as Kim was coming back to the table.

Kim saw them leaving the table. "Are you all right?" she asked Michael. She could see that Michael was really upset. She knew him well enough to know how he was feeling. Michael knew better than to avoid her, but he said, "Nothing is wrong." She asked, "Who were those men you were just talking to?" "Just some cops harassing me about the whereabouts of Skin and Rob again." "Was it Hietzky and Druanduran?" asked Kim. "No, it wasn't them. I'm not sure who they were or what department they are from." admitted Michael. "Are you ready to go?" asked Michael. "But we haven't had our desert," she informed. "Let's go, they ruined my appetite," said Michael. "I'll get you something at Perkins." Kim looked at Michael in disgust and disappointment. Michael cracked a joke to break the tension, "Or if you would rather, I can be the desert." "Come on, let's go then," she agreed.

Michael didn't know which incidents were first or which departments they were from. They all sort of blended together, but all four were different. Michael came in drunk and told Kim about the parking lot incident. She was totally without surprise Michael wanted her to have, she was glad he was home early and at least earlier than usual. She began rubbing him and then gave him a kiss, which was very rare behavior for Kim. Michael was usually the one to start things of that nature. It had been only the third time in three decades that she was initiator.

Michael was definitely sick and tired of the harassment. So much so that he missed Kim's advancements and then he passed out. He woke up the next morning and thought it was all a dream or some kind of a nightmare. He noticed a scratch the cops gave him on his arm. He thought about it for a while and came to realize it was for real. At that time, he was remembering something that Kim had said right before they went to bed. She said, "Maybe you ought to consider on what they're asking." "What do you mean?" he asked. "I'm no snitch and I'm not going to do it." Kim said, "So ask yourself what Skin and Rob would do? Would they do it for you? You have a family to think about and your own legal issues too."

Michael pulled the covers over his head. He was mad about what he was saying. Michael had told Kim it was against his rules, but he didn't know where they were anyway. Just as he had told the police all along, he really didn't know anything about those dudes. He knew the police didn't believe him, but he thought Kim would.

"Bad company corrupts good people." Michael thought to himself.

CHAPTER 25

JIM AND VIC'S BANK ROBBERY. 5 OF 5

CHARGE TO MICHAEL

A day or two after the Applebee's dinner, Michael was back to hustling in the streets. He got home just in time to take the kids to school. Kim woke up because the phone kept ringing.

It was Jim on the phone and he told her it was an emergency. Michael got up to take the call, "What's wrong?" asked Michael. "Hey man, I need you to come and get me a room," said Jim. "Why can't you get your own room?" Michael asked. "It's an emergency, and I don't have anyone else to call," he proclaimed. "Okay man, where are you at?" "I'm at the Holiday Inn West.' "I'll be there as soon as I can." "Thanks man, I appreciate it."

Michael got up and started to get dressed. The television was turned on and there was breaking news report that someone had just robbed an M&I bank in the East Town Mall. The suspect had come into the bank, threatened to use a bomb and escaped on foot, running through the mall.

Michael was dumbfounded, it sounded like Jim, but he couldn't have been that stupid, could he? Michael had a funny feeling about it, but he wasn't sure.

As he left out the door, Kim stopped him and told him to be careful. He swore he would be careful. Michael drove straight to the Holiday Inn West. When he got there, he went right into the lobby. As he entered, he heard someone calling his name. It was Jim standing in the phone booth.

"What's up?" asked Michael. Jim said, "I need you to get me a room." Michael asked, "Why can't you get your own room?" Jim said, "Because I lost my I.D." Jim pulled out a big wad of cash. Just then, Michael saw Angie walking over from the entrance. Jim gave Michael the money and he got the room he needed. He didn't even think to ask Jim where he got the cash, but Michael figured it wasn't his business and if he really had wanted to find out all he would've had to do is hang around long enough and they would tell him.

When they got to the room, Jim handed Michael some money and said, "Thanks, and this is for your help." The he said, "Let's party tonight." He asked Michael if he wanted a room too. Michael said, "Yeah, if we're going to party, I'll get a room too."

Michael went down to the front desk to get another room. The next thing Jim did was bring out a wad of money. He asked Michael if he had brought any dope Michael admitted to him that he always had a little in his stash place. He then pulled out his stash and gave it to Jim.

Michael rolled some blunts and had a couple of drinks and then went to his house to get some more weed. After leaving his house, he then went to Stacey's place to get some cocaine. When he walked into Stacey's house, there was Vic standing there talking to Stacey and her friends. Michael was furious. "What the hell is he doing here?" they knew how Michael would react. The last time he had seen Vic was when he stole from him and tried to start a fight.

Vic said, "Listen Mike, I'm sorry. Man, I was stoned and broke at the time." Michael wanted to smash him. Vic said "Man, if you just take this, in the next day or two I'll give you the rest." He handed Michael a wad of cash.

Michael's mother always said his greatest weakness was his heart and that it would cost him dearly in the future. She couldn't have been more correct. Things his mother and grandmother said were and still are haunting Michael to this day. His grandmother would tell him, "Forgiveness is the key to growth and happiness. We must do it or die," which was contrary to what his mother would say.

Nevertheless, Michael did forgive Vic and then told him that all was well, but he needed to pay him back as soon as he could afford it. Michael then told them that they were all invited to a party at the Holiday Inn, so they all left together to go there.

It was a cool party. They smoked, and drank, and gambled from the time they arrived until early that next morning.

This was a party just for their hangout crew. A little later Michael had some business to take care of, so he left to go around the corner.

By the time Michael returned, more people had arrived. There was Fossil, Manny and his girlfriend Shelly. They were all getting high while Shelly was snorting coke in the bathroom and Michael began slamming booze harder than most.

They bought all the dope that Michael had. They also had fronted some from him, but Manny was selling his own. Michael didn't resent him for it because it would take time for Michael to get his re-cop, plus Manny bought from Michael when he had it-not because they had to, but out of respect. They knew if they needed it that Michael had it for them. He couldn't stay there and watch them get high and kill themselves with that dope. It wasn't as if Michael thought he was any better, because he was also killing himself with his own heavy drinking and smoking.

After all their money in the dope deals, the crap games and at the card table, Michael went down to the bar. He took Stacey and Fossil for no particular reason. Michael drank a lot at the bar that night and he bought drinks for every fine woman in the place.

Stacey was obviously unhappy about that but Michael really didn't know what he was doing or how much he was spending because he was drunk as heck. Michael continued with a bottle of Hennessey for himself. He got so drunk that he couldn't even dance, although he usually danced very well when he wanted to and when he wasn't really drunk, but this time around, he would fall down and get back up to dance again until he couldn't stand any more.

He went back to sit at the bar. The bartender didn't want to serve him any more liquor because he could tell that Michael had more than enough to drink already but Michael was flashing a big wad of money. The bartender's eyes got big, but realizing how much Michael had to drink that night he still didn't have the heart to serve Michael any more liquor.

Stacey then walked Michael back upstairs towards the room. As she walked in, those that were still there continued partying in the room. Michael sat down to take a rest for a few minutes, but wound up in the bathroom throwing up. Eventually he got himself put back together to rejoin the party for some more drinking and smoking. Michael overheard Vic and the other talking about pulling a sting that night or the next morning. That entire night was a bit hazy for Michael as he had way too much of drinking and smoking.

When Michael woke up the next morning everyone was gone, there were two rooms the guys had paid for. One of them was for Jim and Nicole and the other for Stacey and Michael. Michael was wondering where everyone had gone and what happened throughout the night, as he couldn't remember being so drunk and all. He had walked up nursing one serious hangover when he began to remember what had happened the previous night.

When he woke up earlier, Stacey was still in bed with him. He didn't think they had done anything since they still had all their clothes on. Michael got up to find Vic was passed out on the floor. It concerned him a bit but while he was out, he decided to check and make sure he still had all his money as he still had questions about Vic from previous times of him stealing from both him and Stacey.

Michael was getting frustrated because now he couldn't find his keys, so he went over to ask Jim if he knew anything about it. He was also thinking that he could finally catch Stacey and Vic in the act, as he knew that she was sleeping with one of those boys with Vic being the worse and wildest of them all, but that was what Stacey likes to have.

As he was leaving, he was also thinking of getting something to eat and his stomach was growling. There was no answer when he knocked on Jim's door so he went downstairs for some breakfast. Before he even got to a table, they all showed up. First Stacey and Vic then Jim and Nicole. Michael asked them what was happening and where they had been? Stacey greeted Michael with a smile and a kiss and then said, "I just had to take care of something." Michael didn't pry and then asked, "Where are my keys?" "They're upstairs," she said. "You would have lost your head if it was attached to your neck as drunk as you were last night," she said.

They ate breakfast and while the waiter brought the check, Vic offered to pay the bill. Michael asked Vic, "Where did you get money?"

Michael remembered taking everybody's money from selling all them dope and then the gambling. Vic was sitting across from Michael. "Man, I took care of some business this morning." He told Michael. "What kind of business?" Michael asked him. "Just something I took care of by myself." He said. Michael sat there thinking to himself for a minute. They finished eating and went back to the rooms. Michael found his keys with Stacey's help and got ready to leave, on his way back to Chicago to buy more dope. Vic wanted to know where he was going and Michael told him he had to the city to buy some more work. Vic gave Michael some money and said, "Count this towards what I owe you."

Michael didn't think the money had anything to do with a crime. He was just glad that Vic was finally paying back some of what he owed, but Michael also knew that it was about time for Vic to be moving.

Vic had gotten too wild robbing dope dealers, stores and banks and that was another reason that Michael didn't want any part of that around him at all.

Michael got ready and left for Chicago. He had some business to take care of and had a plan. As much as he thought about it and didn't want to, he asked Vic to come along with him. Michael wasn't planning on telling him anything, but he was ready for him to go back home. Michael started to recall some things from the night before. Like Jim, for example who had robbed the bank across the street from the East Town Mall and threatened that he had a bomb. Jim's girlfriend Nicole was just a juvenile and she had taken off on him. And then he had Vic, who robbed a bank.

As they drove down the highway, Vic threw his jacket out the window. He said that someone might recognize him from wearing it around town or during the robbery, because Vic had gotten lost trying to exit the back so a lady had to show him the way out.

Michael thought that it was too much, getting lost in the bank he had robbed, a lady having to show him the way out, possibly getting recognized with his jacket on and everything, it was just too much to handle. But he didn't say anything to Vic because he didn't want Vic to think he was nervous. Although Michael was concerned and it was, time to take care of his business. He had to pay his bills. He thought if he could get away from all the idiots for a while, everything would be okay.

He went to the city and picked up some work and he left Vic at his mothers' house once he was done with his business. When he left him, he harbored no hard feelings, but he still thought that Vic needed some serious help with his drug addiction. Michael already knew that he probably wouldn't get the help he needed, but that wasn't for Michael to worry about nor did he have time to be worrying about Vic either.

No sooner than Michael was leaving Vic's mother's house that Vic asked Michael if he would come and get him if and when he needed some help down the road, especially after Michael got himself into a new club and whatnot. Michael said he would, however he knew he couldn't forget about what happened at his club back in Madison the last couple of days they had been open. Some of Vic's own fellow gang members tried to kill Vic in Michael's club. The weird thing was that some of these guys Michael actually considered being old friends and now he heard they were looking for Vic again. Vic just never learned from past experiences. Vic just kept robbing his own crews over and over again. The obvious had been stated a long time ago, he really had a serious problem and these guys weren't about to let it go. Not all of these guys were punks but, even if they were, they had taken way too much crap from Vic already.

Vic was acting crazy the last time Michael took him on the road. He had been trying to rob everybody on the tour and some of the big crews had big guns. Michael's crew was out-numbered by them, but Vic didn't care as he just got crazier every day.

The cops were on Michael twice as hard now and he was tired of it. It was bothering him in hard way. He had trouble sleeping and he couldn't go anywhere without seeing the cops just about everywhere. All this heat and it wasn't even his own-it was all because Rob, Skin, Vic and Jim.

It was really taking its toll on Michael's mind and his business. He began hearing voices at night telling him to do the right thing. "Help us and tell us what you know and where they are."

It was probably only a couple days after Vic had robbed the bank, then Stacey received an eviction notice from her landlord. Michael was sick and tired of it all. It was way too much harassment...

"Money, sex and the police were not the problem, the problem was themselves."

CHAPTER 26

THE TRUTH SHALL (NOT) SET YOU FREE

To tell the truth. To different Police Officers and Federal Agents, on different occasions, in different places. Twice not in custody, twice at a jail and/or prisons in Milwaukee, Madison, Waupan, WI, & Whiteville, TN., between 1998-2000.

Michael was tired of himself and his family being followed, chased, threatened, harassed, tortured, and eventually framed for another one of these robberies in Milwaukee. Michael knew, after the first time, how easily they could frame him for something he didn't do, or even know about. Michael wanted to prevent being framed again, for crimes he knew nothing about and had nothing to do with. Michael had the talks with the authorities in person, by themselves, once with a former attorney.

Every person I've talked to in every single jail/prison I've been in who's ever spoken to any sort of Arresting of Investigating Officer/Agent said, "I wished I'd never talked to them."

More than half of the people on Death Rows across the Country, and in every jail/prison everywhere, would not have been convicted if they hadn't thought they could talk their way out of the situation, by agreeing to speak with the Arresting or Investigating Officer/Agents. Each of them were 'Read their Miranda Right,' but didn't heed the advice.

Even if you are completely innocent, the cops think you're guilty. That's why they arrested you. They WILL get you to say something and they WILL use it against you.

Cops are cops 24/7. They take classes on how to get people to tell on themselves. There are many methods, besides the old 'Good Cop, Bad Cop' routine, which everybody knows.

With the new, 2010 Supreme Court Ruling [Berghuis v. Thompkins, (2010) 130 S. Ct. 2250] that just came out, you can no longer 'just be silent.' You now have to tell them "I don't want to talk to you, I want a lawyer." And keep saying that, because they will try to ignore you for another 5 to 10 minutes, like they are deaf.

The Number One piece of evidence used in both wrongful, and legitimate Convictions, is what the person said to the cops, after they were arrested, and advised of their right to remain silent.

JUST SHUT UP. The Policeman IS NOT YOUR FRIEND. DO NOT talk to them. They will lie and say things you didn't say, if, for some reason, the recording magically got erased (or 'lost'). They WILL edit recordings of what you actually did say.

The two times Michael believed the truth would set him free, it didn't.

"Honesty comes hard to the government." United States v. Wilson, 298 F. Supp 2d 801, 809 (SD Texas 2003).

John 8:32 ("and ye shall know the truth, and the truth shall set you free"). NOT IN THIS COUNTRY.

CHAPTER 27

BY ANY MEANS NECESSARY, GOD STOPS BULLETS AND TRAFFICKING

Now back in Madison, Michael was making money to pay his attorneys. He was due back in court and he would be hearing the same old song about having to pay more money. He was beginning to believe that he had more stress and problems than anyone he knew.

Things kept him really busy now and he especially needed to get back to New Mexico for another weed purchase. He needed some better weed and he needed it fast. He was regularly raising his prices, which was good for profits and was continuing to bring it back from Albuquerque.

After about the third trip the dudes Myjanta was dealing with wanted to meet Michael. It was definitely in his best interest to meet with them too, so Myjanta took Michael and his crew to their house. It was a big ranch style house out in the woods with a lot of cars in the front and back yards.

They pulled up in front and got out. They were watched through riflescopes as they approached the house. Once at the front door, they were all searched and then led inside. The house was chock full of youngsters with beer and whiskey bottles all over the place. They had all sorts of animals, dogs, birds, big fish tanks and even an alligator. Outside on the rear porch they had a boxing ring and a swimming pool. They even had a cock-fighting pit next to a pit for pit-bull dogfights.

Michael was introduced to the guy who was supposedly in charge. There was a great deal of security, but Michael was already looking for a quick way out of there and to find a weak spot if needed-especially after seeing at least a thousand pounds of weed and several kilos of cocaine on the pool table.

Michael was thinking that this would be a lick to make some real money. A guy named Diablo said, "I like to meet who my guys do business with." He looked over at Michael with resistant speculation in his eyes. Michael told him that he agreed. "I like to meet whom I do business with too," Michael told him.

When Diablo got close, Michael got a good look at him. He was about Michael's age but everyone else was a lot younger. They were all teenagers and in their early twenties. Diablo was about Michael's size, which was about 5'9" and around 210 pounds, although he was bigger cut and with a lot of muscle. "Nice to meet you Michael, or should I call you Iceman or Just Ice?" he asked Michael. "You can call me whatever you like, but don't call me if it's not about business," Michael said, cracking a joke.

They left for Madison and it wasn't long before Michael went back to New Mexico on his sixth trip. He traced the weed from the guys he was dealing with to the other side of the Mexican border. Michael had been in Mexico on music business and on vacation many times before, so he was familiar with his surroundings over there. He was always listening and trying to pick up a little something as that's pretty much how he did business.

Michael was dealing through some girls who had introduced him to these guys. It was becoming less and less that he needed the girls, but they somehow always heard when he was in town. He was climbing the ladder and dealing with some of New Mexico's biggest guys. Needless to say, they were part of a very dangerous group, which was the Mexican mob. He had taken their advice and put a secret drug box in his van and car. Both of these were in the doors, which could hold up to a hundred pounds of pot, even though he hadn't received that much from them yet.

Michael was about to be making one of his biggest scores ever. It would be either 50 or 70 pounds; depending on how much fun he had with these guys. As usual, they arrived within twenty-four hours and started partying. They got a few rooms in a nice hotel and called a bunch of girls who, in turn, invited some of their friends. Every time they went, they met more girls because everyone had a friend or two. And with each visit, Michael would add another ten pounds of weed to his purchase.

He was up to about fifty pounds already. Michael also did a lot of shopping for his family and also for Stacey, while he was in Mexico. He bought a bunch of outfits for the kids and a Spanish style lamp for Kim. He figured it would get him out of the doghouse for not being home on Valentine's Day. He also bought some things for his crews' girls as well.

While he was at it, he also bought another diamond necklace for Kim and a little less expensive Spanish style necklace with sort of a flower on it for Stacey. Michael liked both necklaces and looked forward to seeing the girls wearing them.

This was an important trip because it was going to get Michael out of his immediate debt, plus enable him to purchase more weed. This one trip would make him at least sixty thousand dollars and he would have thirty thousand dollars left for his next trip.

Once they got the weed loaded up, they went back to the hotel and packed up to leave. It was really late and they were all so tired from the long day, so they wanted to sleep a few hours before taking off. They had already checked out of the hotel, so they went to visit a lady friend of theirs to get some rest. There were several ladies there of course, so they kicked it with them for a while flirting, drinking and smoking weed.

They went to Lisa's apartment, which was next door to her parents. Lisa was in one room with Manny and Michael was in a room over the garage with Julie. Fossil knocked on the door. He wanted to talk to Michael. "Mike man, we don't have any weed for our road trip home. Can I have some out of the stash spot?" he asked. Michael was only halfway thinking when he told Fossil it go ahead. They needed a little party on that night as well, and like a fool, he permitted Fossil to get some out.

The weed was hidden in a speaker box in Michael's van. He had two fifteen inch speakers with secret compartments that looked like the box that was smaller than usual. It gave 12x36x2 inches to hide stuff inside and Michael had placed the pot in bags lined with coffee beans and dryer sheets so dope-sniffing dogs couldn't smell it. It couldn't be seen either.

Giving Fossil the go ahead to get some weed meant he would be cutting the package with a knife and then taping up the hole. Michael wanted to check on him, but never had the chance.

Fossil came back and called Michael out to roll a few blunts. They smoked weed and drank booze with a woman on each arm. Fossil was sitting in a loveseat with a girl beside him when Vic popped up out of nowhere. "Mike, why don't you buy some more cocaine so that we can party?" Vic asked. "Don't you have any left?" Michael asked him. "Not really," Vic said. "What do you mean, not really?" Michael spurted. "You need to chill and so do the girls," Michael insisted. Vic looked at Michael with disappointment and didn't say anything else. He went back to snorting up what cocaine he had left and wasn't seen anymore.

Michael suspected that Vic was going to go and smoke more cocaine on his own and probably in a closet or some such place, but Michael didn't really care about Vic and his nonsense as he had girls who kept pulling him into one room or another. Every time he was about to get it on he would get interrupted by someone else calling him into another room for something.

This time it was Fossil and Vic. Fossil had more blunts rolled for them to smoke and Vic had a crazy plan to pull something off. He was after a smooth hit against the dudes they were buying from without any violence. Michael insisted that now would not be a good time, as he knew that they played dirty and were strapped to the dime with every weapon. Vic said, "No man, they aren't."

Michael asked Vic, "How do you know that?" Vic said, "Me and Manny checked the place over already."

Michael asked Manny who he thought was in the room. Manny was with two girls and one of them was Lisa. He said, "There's only two guys and they are sleeping. One of them is in the living room and the other in the kitchen weighing dope at the table and counting money with a money machine." Michael had to admit, his mind started clicking and spinning once, he mentioned the money machine.

Michael thought a minute and asked, "What about the dog?" "They're sleeping." Manny said. He said they were so knocked out that they were able to go all the way to the window. Vic and Manny would take chances that Michael wouldn't dare dream of. Michael felt as if something wasn't right and then Vic said, "Come on Mike, damn man."

Michael told them "I don't believe this is the time." And as he was speaking, he looked at Fossil's face as Michael could read his face very well. Michael wanted to for some reason, and then asked him, "What are you thinking Fossil?" "Mike, maybe we should try it," Fossil said. "Like I said, I don't think so," insisted Michael. "How about we just have a drink and smoke a blunt for now?" They all sat down and said nothing.

Both Vic and Manny both disappeared into the bedroom, while Michael went back to the front room as someone had called him for some business. He could see Vic sitting in a chair while Michael sat down with two girls on the couch.

"Come on man, let's so do this thing," Vic pleaded with Michael. "I'm not going anywhere but back home when we're ready." Vic pulled a gun on Michael. It was the ten-millimeter Carrie had given Michael that was now staring him square in the face. "What the hell are you doing Vic?" Michael asked. "Put down the gun!" he demanded. Vic blurted, "I'm tired of working for you for ten-dollars an hour! I want to do my own thing now." Just then, Vic was distracted. As he turned away, he flinched with just enough time for Michael to hit him with all he had.

Vic flew across the room and Michael jumped on top of him and hit him several times. He couldn't get up off the floor. Michael was mad as hell that Vic pulled a gun on him. He was also scared that Vic couldn't get up, but Vic had pulled the trigger with the gun pointed right between his eyes.

Michael simply reacted and hit Vic with a strong punch and pulled the trigger again. The gun wouldn't go off. Then all a sudden, it began working out of nowhere. "Bam! Bam! Bam!" Vic fired off at least three more shots.

A girl named Julie pushed Michael down and yelled, "Come on!" As she ran out of the way of Vic's firing, Michael heard the bullets flying past him. At first Michael thought, he was hit, but he kept swinging on Vic. He was bleeding everywhere. It wasn't long before he was out of bullets or because of a gun jam.

In the midst of all that, Vic had the audacity to asked Michael why he hit him. "You pulled a gun on me and started firing! That's why!" Michael said. Just then, an old guy came running up the stairs carrying a shotgun, and a lady behind him had a pistol in her hand. He screamed, "What is going on up here?" "Who's doing all the shooting?" Michael didn't stick around to answer any questions and neither did Vic or Fossil. They all ran out the door and jumped over the balcony. Michael saw big fat Fossil come over the railing right behind him thinking the ground would sink when he hit. They all ran to the van.

Once they got in, Michael couldn't find his keys and realized Vic had them. Just then, Vic jumped into the van, handed Michael the keys and yelled, "Drive man, drive!" They took off. Michael didn't want to be going anywhere with Vic, but he didn't have much of a choice at the moment. They could hear the cops coming and they could see the flashing lights in the distance. As they were backing out, Vic put the gun to Michael's head again. Michael asked him to put the gun down. 'No I won't. Why did you hit me?" he asked Michael. Michael told Vic, "Because you pulled that gun on me like you're doing right now, you fool!" The road was real bad and Michael lost control of the van, went off the road and hit a tree. Michael jumped out of the van and took off running.

He went straight down Central Avenue until he got to a restaurant. When he got inside, the place was crawling with police. Two officers were standing at the front door, which quickly alarmed Michael. He had to calm down and act really cool.

Michael got in line to order some carry out and he figured that wouldn't attract them to him. It worked and it gave him some time to think. Before he got his food, he saw Fossil. They were surprised to see each other inline. He obviously jumped out of the van and followed Michael.

Michael went to the line where Fossil was. "Hey man, nice to see you," he said. "Let me buy you something to eat," Michael offered. They got their food and walked down Central Avenue acting real cool so as not to alert the police. They could hear the police radios requesting back up and to be on the lookout for three black men who were involved in a shooting. They walked to the nearest hotel to check in and rest for a while.

Michael called Kim, who not as responsive as he had expected her to be. She told him something he did expect, and he didn't want to hear it. He should have known it was coming when she said, "I told you so." She was referring to Vic and the rest of his so-called friends. "You just wouldn't listen to me. Like I said, you should have stayed home with us on Valentine's Day," she injected. What she didn't know was that Michael had spent most of his money buying her presents that she would never get to see. Michael felt bad about being out of town on Valentine's Day. As far as he was concerned, he had to feel for his family, which justified his being away, but he simply apologized, "You're right Kim."

Kim told Michael to report the van stolen. Michael hung up the phone. He realized he hadn't told her that he loved her, and he felt bad about that. The next person Michael called was Stacey. He told her the story of what happened. She didn't seem to care much more than Kim did and it was probably because she was having a party. She did tell Michael "Happy Valentine's Day" and Michael told her thanks. Stacey told Michael that she didn't want him to leave, but he said, "Whatever," and then hung up the phone.

Michael called the police. There was no telling what Vic would do as he had the gun that he pulled on Michael. "He may get into a shoot-out with the police before letting them arrest him," Michael thought to himself, but what was he to do? There was nothing he really could do about Vic.

The police arrived at the hotel and Fossil was there to greet them. He had told the officers that Vic had taken the keys off the table and the gun had dropped to the floor and fired and it was all an accident. Michael and Fossil weren't trying to rat on Vic as they were trying to protect themselves and their family. The cops bought the story and left and said it would be treated as a joy ride.

Michael and Fossil went to sleep that night without having any company. Of course, they didn't sleep well as Michael was still worried about Vic and hoping he was okay.

When Michael got up the next day, he called his sister Tammy. He told her the whole story with not really wanting to hear what she would say about it.

Tammy also said, "I told you so!" and continued with, "I don't like your friends Michael! Face it, all you have now is me!" Michael had to learn the hard way that Tammy may be right.

Michael needed money to get him and the guys' home. He still wanted to cop something too and he more-or-less had to in order to catch up. Tammy told him, "I will give you whatever you need, but I won't give you money for drugs or for your friends. You can leave their asses down there as far as I'm concerned." But Michael knew he couldn't just leave them down there, as Fossil and Manny didn't really do anything to hurt Michael. Plus, who was going to help Michael bring back the weed? He needed to cop the weed so he could play catch up, so he hired Myjanta and she was glad to help Michael cop a few pounds of weed.

Michael didn't tell Tammy what he was up to, but she was no dummy. He wrapped up most of the weed in some dryer sheets and coffee beans to prevent the dogs from detecting it he also tapped some to Myjanta and the rest in the duffel bag. Myjanta and Michael were on their way to Chicago leaving Albuquerque that afternoon.

They arrived in Chicago the next day. The train for some reason took about five hours longer than driving did, but they weren't worried about it. Michael was just glad to be back in town.

Once they got to Union Station in Chicago, Michael called his mother and Kim to come get them. It would take a couple of hours to get there and Michael called Vic's house during the wait. Vic had been living with his mother while he had been hustling out in the streets.

Vic's mother answered the phone and asked Michael where was he. He told her that he was in Chicago and then he told her he didn't know where Vic was. He told her the whole story, including the gun and van incident. "Well, he is here," she told Michael.

Michael was surprised Vic made to back with the police looking for them. It was strange because Vic had only been there a couple of times from what Michael knew and he didn't know his way back.

The phone was handed to Vic and Michael talked to him and said, "Where is my stuff?" Vic told him, "The police got it and they took me to jail for no license." Michael didn't believe him. "Yeah right Vic," he said. "If you went to jail for weed you would still be there."

Vic's mother was on the other phone listening. "Michael, I thought you went there for the music business?" she questioned. "I thought you weren't a drug dealer Michael," she injected. Embarrassingly, Michael had to admit to her that he did a little hustling but that was only every now and then.

Then Michael asked Vic, "Where is my van?" "its right outside Michael," Vic said. "I'm on my way to pick it up." Michael told Vic he was coming to get his van. He was there within an hour and Vic's mother came to the door.

"Where's Vic?" he asked, "He's not here anymore, he left," she informed him. Michael was thinking, "She lied and I thought you were a Christian." Then she said, "Here's your key." She asked, "What's going on with you and Vic? You guys used to be so close." Michael said, "He started to steal from me and if you don't believe me then ask all these guys." Fossil then said, "Yeah, he almost killed us too."

Michael drove back to Madison in his van, which was now hard to steer because of them hitting a tree. But Michael didn't care as he got back to business as usual. He knew he needed to get back on his grind and so he did just that. He knew it would be a long, hard road to catch up, but with a little hustling here and there, he knew he could do it. Michael also found out that the cops had captured Rob in Milwaukee. The word was that he was going to trial for the robbery of Great Midwestern Bank in Madison. It was unfortunate, but that was something Michael couldn't worry about at the time, given the circumstances.

To take his mind off of thing for a minute, Michael began hanging around his childhood friend Aaron. They just simply hung out and partied for a bit. Michael was doing a lot of that so as not to stress out and worry about other things, but Michael couldn't keep him mind clear and think straight.

Aaron enjoyed having Michael around because he loved to party and one thing he did have was all the party supplies. Michael always had plenty of dope to party with; after all he still had some of the best ever grown. One would swear that something had to be laced with the weed because it was that good. Michael was also hanging out with Manny, Angie, Stacey, Spanky, and his neighbors David and Lonnie.

There was one girl in particular who was all up on Michael in a nice way. She always had a reason for her friends to call Michael and have him come over to hang out. She was a pretty smart girl who seemed to know a lot about Michael.

She told Michael how he got started in the business and she knew all about the business Michael had ever been involved with. She been to several of Michael's concerts and had saved all his flyers and advertisements. She also knew about Michael's wife Kim, and even knew a couple of his little girlfriends. He would later learn that she went to school with a couple of them, but she wasn't that close to them. In fact, she was a friend with Aaron's chick on the side, who was a young babysitter at the time named Lil Kim.

Michael liked the girl a lot, but he didn't like the fact that she was so young. She was only seventeen but very sexy. She was also the daughter of a very powerful and popular man who was a big time lawyer.

Michael told her that if they were ever to do anything, he was not afraid of anyone. He also informed her that he wasn't stupid enough to bring about unwanted problems.

She said that neither did her, but that she wanted him and asked if that was all right. "Nothing or anybody should be able to stop us from being friends," she protested.

They had this conversation only after the second time they were ever alone. She called Michael over to buy some weed and that wasn't all of it, as Michael wanted to see her as well anyway. The temptation was more that he could endure because she was so beautiful, but very young. Michael thought that maybe it was a set up at first as they very next day he had to go testify at Rob's trail.

He didn't want to go to the trial, as he was afraid of the outcome. Plus, he also wanted to stay with her. She said all nice and sweet, "Okay, I'll let you go." He thought that they must teach this stuff to girls very early in life. It took every bit of energy he had to say no to this young girl.

Kim just about had to make him go to the trial as well. She made him realize that if he didn't go they would have a warrant out for him and he would have a third case against him.

So reluctantly, Michael went to court not knowing what to expect. He told Kim and the kids as well. It was Kim who insisted on going with him, not Michael after all, because he just wasn't up to going in the first place. When they arrived, they had to sit upstairs in the prosecutor's office with the rest of the witnesses.

Michael didn't like that, but he did it anyway. What else could he do other than go to jail for contempt of court?

Michael sat next to Angie and Stacey. They were both on the stand for less than two minutes each. Michael was called out next. He was asked about the statements he had given to the officer in Milwaukee when he was arrested. He did some things that maybe he shouldn't have done.

Michael told them the name of the person in charge of the crime and it was Skin that actually told on Michael to them anyway. Stacey had told on herself, but all of this had come from a statement Michael made before. He also told them he didn't have anything to do with it and he didn't witness anything. All he knew was what he had been told. The only reason he told the authorities was because they were trying to convict him of a crime that he had nothing to do with.

The prosecutor tried to stop Michael and wanted him to quit talking, but he told them what he thought. He told them that he thought the system was racist and prejudiced and that he was forced and tricked to say what he had to say. Michael went on to say how the authorities had twisted his words around. Then the prosecutor jumped and said, "I have no more questions for this witness your honor."

The prosecutor was the very same one that sent Michael to prison and Michael didn't tell them anything but the truth. Next Rob's attorney came up to question Michael. He got right to the point and said, "So, they forced you to make that statement, did they?" he asked. "Yes, they did," said Michael. He continued and said, "Skin told you he did it and he also told you to tell them he did it didn't he?" "Yes, he did," Michael, admitted. Rob's lawyer went to say something in the way of how Skin was doing the right thing and also elaborated on how Michael had already testified that he didn't have anything to do with the crimes. "Is it true that the police had arrested you for the crime that was completely incidental to this crime Mr. Brown?" asked the attorney.

"Were you not already exonerated of any part of these criminal charges?" he asked Michael. Michael answered, "Yes" to the questions. He then asked Michael "Is it true you believe the judicial system to be prejudicial and racist because of that arrest?" Michael testified, "For that and for a lot of other reasons." "Objection, your honor," blurted the Prosecutor as he jumped up from his chair. The Judge ordered the jury to disregard the last statement. Rob's lawyer walked back to the defense table stating, "I have no further questions, your honor." "You may step down Mr. Brown," said the Judge. As Michael was leaving the stand, he looked at Rob and his attorney, who gave Michael thumbs up.

Michael though he was only being righteous and truthful. Here he was feeling as if he was the only one on his side with his butt on the line. Michael had a legitimate love for Rob and he would help him anyway he could.

Finally, the trial ended and Michael was happy to take Kim and the kids out of the courtroom and high tail it out of there.

On the way out of the courtroom, Michael was thinking, "Courtroom verdicts don't change people. Each of us had to find God ourselves and ask for His guidance to find change in ourselves."

CHAPTER 28

NEW COMPANIONS

As they went home from the courthouse, Michael didn't want to be thinking about Rob. Michael hoped Rob would win his trial, but if Michael could help it, he didn't want to have to be in any more courtrooms for a while.

It was back to business as normal, as if there was a normal. Michael was in dire need of finances for his own up-and-coming courtroom drama. Michael's court date was scheduled on the East Coast, in only a couple of days, but he didn't plan on being there. He had already decided that this would be the day he was going to go on the run. He was only buying time to earn as much money as he could until then.

He rented a storage unit for his personal belongings. Michael plan was to go to Canada where his Pop's brother, who was also an attorney, lived. One can never know when he is going to need an attorney.

Michael would have liked to go to a place that didn't have an extradition treaty with the United States so he could just lay cool until he felt ready to turn himself in and straighten out this whole mess.

Michael talked to his mother and his Pops about his plan, but they didn't like it and told him so. They thought it was a bad idea. Michael was their son, and they understood him well enough, but they also knew that the judicial system wasn't fair and it was trying to hang Michael. Michael's mom and his Pops had different perceptions of the system.

His mother had served a prison term and Pops was a life-long civil servant. They tried to talk Michael out of going on the run and he played along with their request. They didn't believe that Michael would wind-up leaving them, as that was the last thing they wanted from him.

When Michael mentioned Mexico Pops told him how dangerous Mexico could be for him and his family. "I know you will be able to prove your innocence," he assured Michael, but Michael told his mother and Pops that he was going to leave and soon.

The day Rob was released from jail for winning his case, Michael moved all of his personal belongings into the storage and he was hanging out partying in his motor home, making money and saying his good-byes. Kim, Michael and the kids were spending a lot of time at their friend's house with Dawn and Tracey, who were cousins.

Tracey was a real slickster who used to go out with Rob, but not now. She was seeing a couple of other guys, one of them being an Iranian sugar daddy that gave her money whenever she needed it.

Tracey wasn't the prettiest girl in the world-in fact; she had a face that most brothers would say was real thick. She was the opposite of her cousin Dawn who was more attractive and was in better shape. Michael thought of them as country girls. They were free-spirited ad they really looked out for Michael and Kim. Kim was always reluctant to go to her parents for any help, which Michael completely understood. Michael was spreading his wings and trying to make some money for their trip. He was tired of all the responsibilities on his shoulders and he didn't want to worry about anything, as he was getting ready to disappear for a while.

Michael was also working on letting Stacey go. There was also a part of him that realized she was trying to shake him. They both realized that they weren't good for each other anymore, but there was still a part of him that did not want to let her go and he truly believed that she felt the same way. Still, whenever Michael needed anything, Stacey would come through for him. Their sex was wonderful, but maybe it was only drunken sex because mostly all they did was drink and have sex. Michael didn't love Stacey more than Kim, it was just different, but it was turning out to be nothing but trouble. He never received any good advice from her, which is what he needed most. Kim always gave good advice even though Michael never listened to her. He knew he never wanted to hurt Kim, as she was heart and his best friend. She was closer to Michael than anyone else could ever be.

Michael flew back to New York by himself. He had given his attorney most of the money he owed him. Michael could have paid it all to him, but he wanted to wait and see how good of a job he would do for him. In total, the attorney wanted twenty grand.

When Michael arrived, the attorney told him the he didn't believe they could beat the case. This was the first time he had ever told Michael this. Michael thought at first it was about money, but it wasn't. The lawyer told Michael he could get him three years minimum and mandatory parole in about a year with at least half of that on house arrest. Michael thought this would be a good plea deal, but he didn't want to do any time away from his family and he didn't have any relatives in New York. The attorney told Michael he could possibly be allowed to do some time in Wisconsin that may run concurrent with his New York time.

Michael told the attorney that because he was innocent he was still hoping to beat the case and the lawyer said, "I hope we do too, but just in case, we have to be prepared for a loss." Michael didn't like what he was hearing from his attorney, but he knew it was the truth.

As if things weren't already bad enough, when Michael was leaving the courtroom, he received a call from his other lawyer in Madison. "Where are you at?" he asked. Michael told him he was on the East Coast and he would be back in a day or two after the music convention was over. "You need to come and see me as soon as you get back," he informed Michael. Michael promised he would, but now the entire conference was messed up because he couldn't concentrate. All he could think about was his family, freedom, life and court.

Michael was attending the conference for a few different reasons. One was to speak about entering the music business and the other was to scout new talent. Michael was hob-knobbing with big time connections and these parties are where most of the big deals were done.

Then of course, there were all the girls. They weren't Michael's priority, but it was definitely a plus. Michael kicked it with a lot of people that day. There was Puffy's Mase, who had now found God. There was Heavy D, of course, and even Lil Kim. They gave Michael some good business advice and they all had a good time and made some new connections. Business was booming and everyone was able to achieve what they came for. Michael caught the next plane home because his attorney had told him it was important to see him right away. Some of these business associates he was leaving were absolute legends in the music industry.

Michael was hanging out with Aaron because he didn't worry about anything but getting high and having a good time. Michael spent more and more time with Aaron because he felt he could easily talk to him even though Michael believed Aaron was only pretending to care. Aaron helped Michael acquire fake I.D. in his own name but he wasn't able to use it around town because everyone knew who Aaron was including the cops.

Aaron was willing to help Michael any way he could and he knew Michael would never put him in a switch.

On one occasion when Michael went to Aaron's house to pick up Aaron's birth certificate, Aaron was having a going-away party for him.

Michael had planned to leave a few days after the party as he thought his new friend was there at the party with her girlfriends. She told Michael that she was going to wait around for him, but then she went to Michael's motor home. They both ended up talking for a while and they had a little smoke and a drink at the same time. She asked Michael, "What's wrong? You look worried." She wanted to know if there was something, she could do to help and Michael told her he didn't think so, but he told her his problem anyway.

Most of Michael's stress was stemming from his pending court cases. He told her he felt he was being singled-out because of his status and who he was. He also told her he never intended for his life to turn out the way it was and that he was only trying to make something of himself. Michael also just wanted to make some money and take care of his family without hurting anyone, which he never did. Michael went on to tell his friend that he felt he had no control over himself and had let himself down. He spoke of his love for his family and for his wife and how he felt he should've stayed away from Stacey. She knew who Stacey was because they had gone to school together. She also claimed she knew a couple of other girls that Michael had messed around with. Some of her spill was truthful and some of it wasn't. Michael was supposed to have met with another girl that evening, but it wasn't looking like he was going to make it.

They sat there talking and Michael told her all of his problems without even really thinking about her. She told him "I understand, because truthfully no-one understands me either." He asked her, "What do you mean?" she explained how she was the daughter of a popular and prominent lawyer and politician. She also told of her father's strict rules and how her father really wasn't much different that a poor, young black man with a criminal record.

She told Michael how she felt about having to live in the shadow of her older sister, who was Ms. Right and Perfect to her daddy. She told Michael how she felt that nothing she did was ever right. She claimed she was a child of this generation and she wanted to be free, free to listen to rap, R&B and just to have fun. She didn't want to have to worry what anybody else thought of her and just wanted to focus on college and career.

Michael got a good ear of her past, present and future. The she told him about her boyfriend. She mentioned that he was a jerk and that he was only interested in what he could gain out of her, like money, popularity and sex. She was happy to have someone listen and talk to her, and she used Michael to vent.

She was so beautiful that she could have made a gay man straight. She was about 5'7" tall with blond hair, grayish blue eyes and the most beautiful smile. She had a body that would have made Pamela Anderson want to get it on with her and even somewhat resembled Anderson in an innocent way.

She told Michael she was interested in this other guy, but her father had his henchmen work him over and make it look like a car accident. A friend of the family set her up with her present boyfriend and she said she was mad at the last boyfriend for not standing up and coming back.

Michael tried to sit and listen to her without being consumed with his own situation, but he was captivated by her eyes and she wouldn't let him go. She had him really feeling her emotions.

She got quiet for a second and asked, "Am I boring you?" Michael told her, "No, please continue." She said. "I love what you're doing with the club and helping people with their music careers. I see what you do and you have a lot of love for it." "I do love it," admitted Michael. "Then don't quit," she told him, "You have to keep going." Michael told her he was tired and frustrated, but he really didn't want to talk about it anymore right then.

Then he asked her, "Can you keep a secret?" "Sure!" she said. "I'm leaving the country and I hope to never come back," Michael admitted. "Never?" she asked "Maybe not ever, but at least not for a while, until I get myself together, and all these people off my back." He continued. "I am innocent and tired of getting harassed by the police all the time."

She said, "I hope I can see you again and if I don't, this was the best night I have ever had." Michael agreed with her and said, "I wish it never had to end." She said, "I will never forget you and you always stay in my dreams." Every man likes to be admired and Michael was probably just an older guy she felt she needed to lie to and kick it with. Even to this day, Michael wonders what she may be up to. Hopefully she isn't with a dude like Michael used to be. Every man wants a girl to talk to and who will listen to him. By choice, Michael never saw the girl again because he knew he would never be seeing New Mexico again? And it was his plan to make it his last trip. He was tired of going to jail and he certainly didn't want to end up in prison.

"Alcohol, drugs, materialism, money, idolatry, adultery, all these things along with sex without love isn't for Kings and Queens, it is for people who create problems to forget about their problems. It's a human's sinful nature that makes them hunger for more and more of this. We need to seek Spiritual fruits, and quit our running around. True companionship comes from Jesus."

CHAPTER 29

MICHAEL'S BIG SCORE

Back at their house, Michael, Kim and the kids pulled into the parking lot. They could see two undercover policemen in a car that had pulled in right behind then. "Take Michael Jr. and go into the house," Michael told Kim. "Leave the diaper bag here." As soon as he stepped out of the car, the cop said, "Mr. Ice Mike," referring to his old street name. "I wish you wouldn't call me that," injected Michael. He hadn't missed his court date, so he knew he hadn't done anything wrong. He thought they didn't know of his plan to take off and leave. "What were you doing over here in the projects?" asked the officer. "Visiting my mother," Michael told him. "What do you have in the bag you put back in the car?" the officer asked. "None of your business," Michael blurted. "It happens to be for my kids." The officer asked if he could search the car and Michael said, "Of course you cannot search my car."

Just then, Michael's mother came out. "Is everything alright?" she asked. "Why are you harassing my son?" she asked the officers. One of the officers stepped forward and said, "I knew Michael when he was Ice Mike and I thought I'd stop for a chat," the officer said. "I don't have time for a chat and I am not Ice Mike anymore," Michael assured. "Now can I go?" Michael asked. "I guess so," allowed the officer.

The other officer stepped forward and said "He has an outstanding warrant for his arrest" Kim interjected, "What does Michael have a warrant out for?" "I believe it is for child support," said the officer. The officer searched Michael and then placed handcuff on him. "Can my mother and my wife take my things?" Michael asked. "Sure, no problem." As they were looking through his things, they saw the fake identification. "Who is this?" asked the officer. "This certainly isn't you and I know Aaron. Isn't this your brother?" he asked Michael. "So, what are you doing with his I.D. and why does it have your name on it?" Michael admitted, "I used it to fake out the media and the police and to keep them off my ass and so that I could have a little privacy as your boys won't stop following and harassing me all the time."

After giving Michael the third degree, they took him off to jail and booked him. He couldn't answer their questions, but he played their little game. Michael didn't want to get himself or Aaron into any trouble; Aaron didn't deserve any problems because he was only trying to help Michael. Michael told them he got the I.D. from someone else.

The next day Michael was told he had a bond for child support payments. If he paid a few grand then he could go free. He also learned that day that he had some type of infection or virus and he was scared that it might be some type of sexually transmitted disease.

Michael thought because of the way he had been living and having sex with all kinds of different women, it had to be something like that. He half called it right when he learned that the infection was in a gland within his penis. It painfully affected his urination. The doctors told him there might be something wrong with his prostrate, liver and bladder, which would've been the result of too much drinking and fast living.

Michael was in a work release program in minimum custody, so he scheduled an appointment with an outside hospital clinic, which the Sheriff approved. He had called Kim and was waiting for her to come and pay his bail bond. He instructed Kim to get the money he had at home and in the bank, and to meet him at the doctor's office. After the doctor's visit, they planned on going back to the jailhouse and paying his bail so he could be released.

When she finally showed up, Michael jumped into the car and said, "What took you so long?" "We need to take all the money with us," she instructed. "It's crazy to give them all that money when we are going to need it." "Can't you just sit it out for thirty days?" she asked him. Michael looked at her and expressed his anger.

"How would you like to sit in jail?" he challenged. "Pull the car over." Kim wouldn't pull over, but when she had to slow down for a traffic signal, Michael jumped out of the car. "Michael," she screamed, "Are you crazy?" Michael screamed back, "No, but you are if you think money in more important than me!"

Back when Ingo didn't want Keya to stay with him at the time and both Kim and Ingo were not getting along, but by now Ingo was calling Kim all the time and Keya was calling Michael and Kim to come and pick her up. This resulted in the cancellation of Michael's support payments and the dropping of the warrant.

Michael gave up arguing with Kim because he didn't feel like walking back home so he got back into the car. Kim was beginning to make sense to him and he was also suffering from withdrawals by not having any alcohol in his system.

Michael looked over at Kim and she was crying. They never really fought very much and this was probably one of the worst fights they had ever had. They got to the jail and paid the bail so Michael could be released. He totally forgot about his medical treatment and Michael never went back to the doctor. Making money was his only priority. He knew he had to make more money and fast. It was only a few days after that Michael would make his last trip to Mexico.

Michael quickly got back on his grind to get more products. He decided it was time for a big score, which he thought was the only way to get back on top of his game. Manny was more down for the big score than Michael was and was pushing Michael into it.

They left for the southwest to mess with those Mexicans. Michael had enough money to cop a few pounds and he was able to triple his money off of what he already had. All of his bills were due and his lawyers were sweating him for money, so he knew he had to do something.

Manny brought his friend David who had gone with them once before. David had done a few things to prove that he was trustworthy, such as helping to sell most of the weed for a high price. David had heart and he did little hits around town. He had been in some altercations with a few guys wanting their money back, but nothing major. David fought these guys off single-handedly smashing them and leaving them with fear in their eyes. One thing was for sure that Manny was down whenever he was needed and Michael thought they might need him for this job.

Michael, Manny and David were on their way to cop some product. Both Manny and David were Latino and ran with a couple of different gangs, but they were now hanging around with Michael. Manny came prepared with handcuffs and a tazor gun.

They arrived in New Mexico twenty-four hours later in the early afternoon and they went straight to the hotel. They knew they had a couple different options: they could both go straight across the border and buy fifty pounds at a hundred a pound, or they could have someone bring it to them for about two-hundred a pound. They chose the second option because Michael didn't like the idea of crossing the border. He thought it made everything so much easier when he could deal with one person instead of many, at the Mexican border. It was too great a risk for the money. Manny called the connection and he agreed to meet them later after Michael took care of some music business. They agreed to meet at the hotel room.

Later on, when the Spanish dude pulled up in his Lincoln, he was dressed to impress as usual and had a drink in one hand and a twelve pack in the other. The Spanish boys loved to party. This guy was about ten years younger than Michael and a hundred pounds bigger.

Manny and David were anxious to get the Spanish dude. It was unusual that he was by himself because he usually brought along a couple of fine ass women and a couple of his boys for security. Sometimes he would try to get Michael to swap women with him. He said he liked northern women and Michael had to admit that he liked the southern women.

Manny wanted to rob the guy, but Michael told him to be patient. Michael was to stay out of the way and back up Manny and David. Because the Spanish dude had a drink in one hand and a twelve pack in the other hand, they figured the drugs must be in his car. It would have been unusual for him to leave it in the car. He had dealt with them twice before and he had finally started to get comfortable with them.

In the past, Michael had to go through Julie and Myjanta to deal with these guys that hadn't bothered Michael much except for the fact that he didn't trust them anymore. Julie and Myjanta were making too much off of Michael and he always had to wait on them. Things didn't always pan out and there were times when they couldn't even find them. So, for a time, Michael had Manny do the transactions after that, mainly because Manny was Mexican. Michael was a dark-skinned nigger who was not to be trusted. Michael didn't really like the racial crap they would say, but he also never did anything about it.

Michael spoke Spanish better than Manny did, and it was his money. That's how you're supposed to do business, and this is what he told them.

The Mexicans finally came around to trust Michael but he never forgot their racial crap. The plan was to get into the hotel and stall them. Michael was supposed to be at a business meeting and they were to call him from the room with all the information, such as where the weed was and how they were supposed to get it. Manny and David were getting anxious and just wanted to go right in and rob the man at gunpoint, but Michael wouldn't do it that way. He preferred to use his brain and then his hands if he had to. Violence was to be used only as a last resort.

Manny and David had all sorts of plans and lots of weapons but Michael was set against that. Both Manny and David went in and began drinking with the Mexican guy. After a while, they called Michael and asked him what the hold-up was and they told him that the dude wanted to take care of business. The dude watched them talk and he was hollering in the background, "What's the holdup man?" Michael was thinking, "The holdup is that you need to get drunker."

Michael told him that he had to take care of some business and he hoped to get it done real soon. Michael was outside looking in and he could hear they were getting drunker. He told Manny, "Keep on drinking." Manny said, "Bet!" Michael asked where the weed was and the Mexican dude told him it was in the trunk of his Lincoln. They were smoking a lot of weed. Just having come from the other side of the border meant that he had a lot of fresh weed. Michael called a couple of different times to get him to stay there, but by the last time Michael called, they were pretty drunk and high. By now, they wanted to get some liquor and Michael told them to go ahead and get some.

Michael also told them that he would be there right after he picked up some girls to bring with him. The Spanish dude was cool with that, but he told Michael to hurry. Michael knew he wasn't going to go anywhere if he hadn't already. The dude loved Michael's game and the women he brought over as well, but his best love was his money.

As he put Manny back on the phone, Michael heard him going into the bathroom in the background. He was in there for a while. Michael could hear the dude trying to talk to Manny. Manny said, "Man just let me get him and take his car and we could be out of here! His keys are right here anyway! What are you waiting for man?" asked Manny.

Manny got to the point but almost too late. He threw David the keys and said, "Go and get it out of the car and take it to Mike." About two minutes later Michael saw David coming towards him with a big green garbage bag over his shoulder. David looked like a big Mexican Santa Clause. When he got to Michael's car, the trunk was popped. "David there's the bag inside," and then said, "There's more where that came from."

Michael asked, "Why didn't you grab it all?" "I couldn't carry it," he answered. Michael told him, "You're supposed to make a way." As David and Michael were talking, Manny was listening on the other end of the phone and Michael could see and hear everything that was going on in the hotel room. Manny said, "He's on his way out." Michael could hear the toilet flush. "David, you have to go back to Manny and get the rest of the weed, because if we're going to risk our lives for it, we better get everything he's got."

David walked into the room and just as the dude was coming out of the bathroom. Michael heard the Mexican ask. "Is that him you're talking to on the phone?" Manny said, "Yeah, and he just picked up some girls, so maybe we should go and get some liquor and be ready." "Alright then," said the Mexican, "Let's go."

They walked out to the car and headed for the liquor store down the street. Michael wasn't sure what they had planned, but he hoped they would come up with something to stall the guy. There are many liquor stores that have drive-ups, but instead they parked and went inside. David stayed in the car and as soon as they went inside, then went to the trunk and got the rest of the weed. It was another bag just as big as the first one, and he threw it in the Dumpster. Michael flashed his lights to indicate that he saw him, and at first he wasn't sure if David got the message or not, but David reassured him that he had seen him with a wave of his hand.

The guys came out of the liquor store with two bags and luckily, David had just barely made it back into the car before they came out. As they drove away, Michael went to get the package out of the dumpster. It was a big package and it had some weight to it and as there was at least a hundred pounds between the two packages.

That little transaction in itself took less than five minutes to complete totally unnoticed and with no violence whatsoever. To Michael that really meant everything was all-good to go. All he had to do now was figure out how he was going to get his guys out of there.

Michael was thinking that these were the kind of guys he needed on his team and he certainly wasn't going to leave them.

Michael sat back and prepared a contingency plan while he waited for them to call. He waited patiently as it was a while before they called his cell phone.

This time it was the Mexican dude. He was sounding upset. "I'm taking off, you're on some bull shit time," he accused. "Look dude, I will call you as soon as I'm ready. Something has come up." Not even one minute later, the Mexican dude left. Michael watched him walk to his car half drunk. Right after he hung up with him, Michael called Manny and David as the Mexican dude was pulling out of the parking lot. "Come on," he told them. "I'm outside where I dropped you guys off. Let's get out of here."

As soon as they jumped into the car, they headed out of town. Once they were a little way out of town, they stopped and properly wrapped up the dope, hit the road and drove home.

Their trip back was uneventful until them his St. Louis. Michael had reluctantly let Manny drive even thought he didn't have a driver's license. This was one decision that Michael should've never made because Manny caused a three-car accident and Michael was really worried as they had a hundred pounds of weed in the trunk of the car.

Manny rear-ended a lady's car that in turn bumped into the car in front of her, which unfortunately happened to be a patrol car. To their surprise, no one was hurt, and fortunately, no one even had a scratch on their car.

The police still wanted to see everyone's license, registration and insurance. Manny didn't have a license, and a drug smugglers rule number three is, "No on without a driver's license will drive.

The highway traffic in downtown St. Louis was really bad and luckily, for them, the cop that was involved in the chain of hits in their accident was suddenly called off to an emergency. "We're saved," they all said to one another. They once again jumped in the car and left with Michael driving from there, as he was the only one who had a driver's license.

They made it back home in a few more short hours of driving. Once at home, Michael walked into the house and Kim said, "That guy from New Mexico had been calling for you." Michael told Kim that if she see the area code from New Mexico not to pick it up and said he would explain it later. Kim knew exactly what that meant and she usually did what she was told.

Michael then gave her about a pound or so of weed and told her a little bit of the story. A little later, he told her that he had to go out for a little while. They had so much weed that they simply used the bathroom scale, which usually put them off five pounds or so and everyone bought from them was very pleased.

Michael knew he had blown one of the best connections he had ever had. This was one that took him all the way across the border to meet with some real big boys, some of whom wouldn't take this lying down. Even if they money wasn't a big concern for them, it was all a matter of principle.

Michael was selling the weed for a thousand dollars a pound. It was really good weed and it was selling quickly. Initially, it was an even three-way split between Manny, David and

Michael, but Michael had almost sold out, so he decided he needed it more than the others to pay his lawyer and his bills, plus he needed the money to keep him on the run.

Manny, David and Michael all got their third of their split. Manny wanted Michael to stay and party with him because they couldn't find Stacey and Shelly and he still had some weed he needed to sell.

Manny offered to keep it at his place, like he had done so many times before, but Michael said he wanted to check on Stacey, even though he knew he should be home with his wife and kids instead.

Michael had fallen for Stacey in a bad way but just didn't realize it yet. It was more than what he thought, as it was more than good sex. He was surprised that Manny wasn't mad or concerned and thought maybe he knew something Michael didn't. Michael used that as an excuse because he wanted to get his money and dope from her. Michael knew that he could've easily gotten it from her the next day, but he really wanted to see if she was being faithful to him as well as to see if she was being respectful.

Michael left Manny and went to Stacey's mom's house. Her parents were on vacation and he thought maybe she could be partying at their house. Stacey loved to party as much as she loved sex.

When Michael got there, the place was packed with cars lined-up a block away and he could hear the music bumping, thinking for a moment, Michael entered through the back door versus using the front door, figuring he would surprise Stacey to say hello, pick up some money and jet.

When Michael got to the back door, he could see and hear some dude trying to rap. Then, out of nowhere, Michael saw that Stacey was fighting and wrestling with some guy. He was all over her. Michael watched for a minute to see what this was all about and wanted to see who was interested in whom, and whether it was serious. Stacey liked to pick fights and mess around, but she would only go so far with someone who was close to her, and this was starting to look that way to Michael.

Eventually they stopped and went upstairs. Michael watched them as they went into her bedroom and, He began to get mad, but at least now, he thought he knew what kind of game she was playing. He watched another dude go into the bedroom and they were both flirting with her.

One of the dudes left and Stacey went to her dresser drawer to pull out some weed. Michael began thinking that this was simply a weed deal that was until they sat on the bed. He noticed that one of the dudes grabbed her and kissed her Michael was Livid and didn't know what to think, so he left and went to Dawn's house, where He had been keeping his weed as well. He hung out for a moment and left with the thoughts of what he just witnessed at Stacey's house.

Michael needed to snap out of it, so he headed back home to his wife and made love to her all night long.

Waking up the next morning, Michael was still upset about Stacey and what he had seen her doing with those two dudes. Why didn't he know anything about it? Why hadn't he seen this coming? He guessed it was just a matter of principle and he decided to investigate what was up with her.

Kim asked him, “Where are you going?” He said, “To take care of some business/ I’ll be back.” He had plenty of people calling for weed. Some of them want huge quantities, but others only wanted a little which was best to get from Stacey bit for some strange reason she wasn’t home yet.

Michael went back to Stacey’s mother’s house, but no one was there. The door was open and the house was trashed. He looked for his weed but it wasn’t there. He came out of the bedroom and began to leave when he ran into Angie. “Where the hell is your friend?” He asked her. She looked surprised. “I don’t know,” she told him. Michael knew she was lying to him. “You know I care a lot about her. I have risked a lot for her, and I don’t like to be played like no sucker. If she doesn’t want me then I don’t want her. I don’t want to have to lose my wife over her.” Angie and Michael used to be real close and they used to talk a lot. Her nickname was Lil Al and Michael’s was big Al, which was short for alcoholic Al Capone. She said, “I know it’s not what you think Michael.” Michael said, “Yes, it is.”

Angie told him she had nothing to do with it and Michael said, “I know that Stacey is your Girlfriend, and you have loyalties to each other, but I wouldn’t let you lose everything and get hurt without saying something.” She replied, “I know Michael, you talk to me and tell me things already and I understand.” “Alright then,” he said and started to leave. When he got to the stop sign at the corner, he heard music playing from an approaching car. It was Stacey with three guys, two of which were the ones who had been with her in the bedroom the night before. They drove by and she tried to hide, but Michael pulled a u-turn and got right behind them. They ended up stopping in front of her house blocking the driveway. Michael could only back up and they couldn’t go anywhere.

The guys jumped out and said, “What? You got a problem of something? Stacey got out of the car looking scared. She yelled at them, “Come on, let’s get going.” Michael wasn’t sure what else she said, but it seemed to him that she was defending them. “What’s up?” asked Michael. “Is this what you want? Is this your man or something?” He asked her. She didn’t answer. Then she said, “Why are you tripping, you got your wife!” Michael said, “Oh, so that’s what this is about? Just give me my dope, my money and my scale.” She didn’t say a word. One of the dudes interrupted, like Michael wasn’t determined to get his stuff. Michael took it because he wasn’t going to give them anything. They Stacey walked up to Michael with the dude standing next to her.

The guy was bigger and taller than Michael and immediately Michael went into a defensive stance. Stacey and the dude got too close for comfort and he felt threatened, so Michael pushed her out of the way and hit the dude. One of his boys rushed in and Michael knocked the hell out of him as well. The other one came up and Michael got him with a combination. Stacey jumped into the middle of it and got hit with all the swinging and punches Michael was throwing and now all of them were on the ground.

One of the dudes jumped and went for his car. It looked to Michael as if was going for a weapon. Michael said, “If you do that pal, you might get killed.” Michael already knew that the dude had a gun and Stacey got up to ask, “What is wrong with you Michael?” Michael answered her, “Messing with you is my problem! But it's over now!” Then someone said, “Don’t worry, the cops are coming.” Michael jumped in his car and told them they better move their car, as he didn’t think they wanted any more of him.

Stacey jumped into Michael's car and said, "What's wrong with you? Where are you going?" Michael told her, "Don't worry about me, just go on and go with your little boyfriends. They're more your age anyway." "I don't want to go with them," she told him. "I want to go with you."

Michael noticed her face was swollen where she had been accidentally hit in the jaw. He said, "I can't make myself tell you that I don't want anything to do with you anymore. I was a fool and I almost lost my wife and kids all over you! They are all that I have." Stacey said, "They are not all you have, what about me?" She asked him. "Give me all my stuff," Michael demanded. Stacey handed him all of the jewelry he had bought for her. "And don't forget the bracelets and the pager," he said.

"Why are you doing this, Michael?" She asked him. "Because of what you did and because I also saw what you were doing last night," he informed her. "What, I can't act stupid?" Then one of the neighbors yelled out, "The police are coming!" "I'm out of here," said Michael. He looked at Stacey and said, "I'm sorry, just let me go." She wouldn't get out of his car. "I'm not going anywhere without you," she told him. "Get out, you got to go!" he demanded. "The police are coming!" "I'm going with you!" she demanded. Michael drove away with her in the car because she wouldn't get out. They drove down the old highway that ran parallel to her street.

They got far away and Michael could still hear the police sirens. At this point he was mad with her, but. He didn't mean to do it and he was sorry. "I'm sorry," he told her. Then he parked the car and told her, "I'm under a lot of stress right now and it's mainly because of my situation with the courts. I feel as it's so unfair and unjust with everything that had been going on and it's just too much to handle right now," he told her, "I really do care about you." "Is that all?" she asked. "No," he admitted, "I love you, but I have a family and I don't want to hurt them. We should really just break it off." She said, "No, I will not!" "I don't really want to either, but we have to." Michael apologized again about her jaw and Stacey said, "It's okay, it's nothing." "You better take me back home before someone thinks you kidnapped me otherwise there will be another hook up later okay?" She asked, "Do you promise?" but Michael didn't respond to the question.

He dropped her off around the corner so as not to be seen by her family or the police. Michael took off and went to his house and told Kim what had happened but not about what he was feeling. He told her that the police may be coming and she sat back to express her sadness, but then she smiled and aridly laughed and Michael said, "What's so funny?" "That's what she gets for trying to be all tough," Kim said, "For trying to steal my man." Michael said, "Yeah, that may be true but that don't make it right." Kim agreed, "You may be right, but she was still after my man."

Michael couldn't say anything, because he was just as guilty and he felt really bad about what just happened.

He quickly hid when someone came to the door, thinking it was the cops, He went to Manny's place and Manny told him he had heard what happened. He didn't think the police were looking for him, but said it was better to be safe than sorry.

They left to get a hotel room. Michael kept dialing Stacey's pager, but there was no response. Finally, Manny heard from his girl Shelly that Stacey had gone to the doctor. Shelly was one of Stacey's closet friends and now they were on their way back home.

Michael took a risk and went over to Stacey's mom's house, but not until first getting some flowers and balloons for her. When he got there, her mom answered the door. She asked, "Can I help you?" Michael answered very politely, "Hello, Mrs. Pete, I'm here to see Stacey. I brought these for her."

"Oh you must be Michael Brown." She said. She either knew of Michael's reputation or Stacey had told her what had happened. "Yes, I am," admitted Michael. "What happened?" she asked him. "I'm not sure," he told her. "Then why the balloons?" she asked. "Well, I was supposed to protect your daughter and I should have stopped her from getting hurt." She said, "Oh," as if surprised.

Stacey must have heard them talking because she came right out of her room. "Come on baby, let's go," she said. They left and went to one of the nicest hotels in town. It wasn't until they were in the car that Michael noticed that Stacey's jaw was all wired up. He felt really bad about what had happened to her. And he probably apologized about a thousand times that night. Once they got to the hotel, she accepted. She grabbed Michael and ripped his clothes off as he tore at hers. She said she was sorry and from then on, it was on.

He hadn't been drinking or smoking much weed, but he was higher than before. It was some of the sweetest make up sex they ever had. They did everything they could imagine and they did it all night long. At times, they ended up in a cold sweat, and then went right at it again and again.

The next day Michael replaced Stacey's pager with a newer and better one as well as replaced all her jewelry. Fortunately, for her, she only had the wires on her jaw for a couple of days before Michael had to leave on the run. This wasn't Michael and Stacey's last time together.

It got to be as if nothing had happened and Stacey wouldn't leave him alone, and for some strange reason, Michael cared even more for her.

"We must have the faith in order to believe and achieve with Jesus. We only need the faith of a mustard seed, and we can move mountains. We will be taken through trials and tribulations that will test our faith and our love. But with Jesus, we cannot lose."

CHAPTER 30

RUNNING AND GETTING CAPTURED

Michael sold all the weed he had and was planning to make another trip to Mexico before he took off. He was staying in his motor home in an R.V. park in town, but he was hanging out with Kim and the kids during the daytime-playing basketball and having water balloon fights and pillow fights like they always did, but now they could really get wild.

Rob was out of jail and back to doing his thing. He brought back one of Michael's old workers, a woman named Chada. She was a really down lady and Rob had a crush on her. They had been staying at Michael's old house and Rob had also been messing around with Kim's friend, Tracy, and their neighbor Shecka, who had testified for him and helped him get off his charges. She was his alibi witness and the key to the defense at his trial. Everyone said she lied, but Michael thought that either way what she did was honorable.

Michael received some extra money from Dawn who was another one of Kim's friends. In the past, Kim and Dawn had been close, but Michael felt he might be responsible for their separation. He believed that true friendship was important but Kim told him that there were two reasons why they weren't close anymore and neither of those reasons included him-as it was only girl stuff. There was a trust issue and Michael didn't want Dawn to know what their plans were or where they were going. Kim had already thought that Dawn would be a weak link anyway, not so much out of force but out of her attitude of wanting to do the right thing. She was liable to tell the cops where they were and there was also the fact that Dawn was acting a little different because he had received some money from a lawsuit. Dawn wasn't trying to offer any help to Kim when she needed it, but Michael didn't care about that even though it did hurt Kim.

What Kim didn't know was that Dawn had lent money to Michael for what was supposed to be his final trip to Mexico. It was a bad idea and Michael wished he hadn't involved her, but it was something that was already done. He told Kim about Dawn lending him money and reminded Kim that Dawn hadn't helped her when she needed it. Needless to say, Kim was pretty heated about it and felt unappreciated by him doing that without first telling her, but Michael just blew it off because it wasn't really her problem.

Michael went to get the money early the next morning and Dawn was purposely scantily dressed when he got there. She gave Michael a look that could make a gay man straight. He didn't really pay her any attention, as he was there for only one thing, and that was the money.

It was the day before Michael was supposed to be leaving for Mexico. He had been spending a lot of time away from friends and family and partying in his motor home. They were ready to leave in the morning, but he was still in town because he was still determined to drive his kids to school. While doing so, he kept a low profile so as not to attract any attention. Most of their stuff was in storage so that wasn't a concern or a worry to him.

They had a Chevrolet Suburban that Kim had bought with her income tax return check. Rob was in town to say his good-byes and to thank Michael for helping him get off at his trial. He also wanted to say he was sorry. He showed how much he really cared and Michael didn't take it as just an act, he knew Rob was being sincere when he said things like that. Rob told Michael that he felt responsible for him having to leave the way that he was. He also felt the same regarding Skin and Vic. None of them forced Michael to be their friend, but he could have chosen not to hang around them. He was only trying to make something of himself for his family, but he thought he could help them at the same time.

Michael still felt it was wrong to run and hide, but he couldn't face everything right then. His parents and grandparents told Michael that he was running at a time when he shouldn't be. Michael's grandfather told him, "You got to stop running and take care of your family." This came from the same man who ran from the South to the North, post-slavery.

Regardless of all the "sorry's and don't runs," they partied hard that night, at a trailer park which was a five minute drive from home. (Right outside Madison.) Stacey, Angie and a few other girls were there as well. Manny, Rob and David also went over to say their good-byes. Everyone was totally wasted and before Michael knew it, they went from playing games and music to Stacey in the back room under the sheets. He couldn't be certain how he wound up there, but they went at it for hours.

He remembers waking up in the morning, naked and in a cold sweat. He heard a car pull up and then heard the knock on the door, then the window. "Boom! Boom! Boom!" he heard the female voice saying "I know you're in there I can see your naked body!" Michael was thinking that she sounded familiar. It was Kim. She said, "Open up and let me in! Is this how you're going to do me? We're supposed to be leaving remember? What's up!" she kept banging and banging. Stacey said something to the effect of, "Forget that stupid witch." "Shut the hell up," Michael told Stacey. He thought he was having a nightmare, but no such luck. Kim kept pounding on the door. This was the first time in years that Kim came looking for him. She knew what sort of dude Michael was and what he was up to. Michael thought that Kim wasn't insecure in their relationship in any that he could tell.

Michael grabbed his clothes and quickly got dressed. In the process, he absentmindedly grabbed the gun and he noticed that Rob and his buddy from Milwaukee were already gone. He started to look for his money and the dope he had with him, which wasn't much.

He opened the door. "What's up?" he asked Kim. She pulled the door wide open and stepped inside the room. Luckily, Stacey had just put her clothes on, but Kim wasn't a dummy. "Nothing's wrong," she told him. "What's going on here, Michael?" she asked. He played dumb and answered, "Nothing is wrong," he excused. "You promised me you were coming home last night and that you would take Jazzman to school this morning," she reminded him. "When you didn't come home, I thought something was wrong. You're due in court today. Remember, you have to go on the run?"

Michael said, "Shut up!" He didn't want Stacey to know, but obviously, everyone else already knew. But at least they didn't know where he was going or whom he was going with. Stacey pleaded to go with him for a long time and she actually gave him the idea. Then Kim looked at Michael and asked him, "Why are you so upset with me, and why do you have that gun?" she had noticed the gun sticking out of his waistband. "Why do I feel like I interrupted something here?" Kim asked. "Come on," Michael said as he grabbed Kim's arm and led her outside. "Why did you come looking for me and why all the questions? I told you I was going." He blurted at her. "But you didn't," she responded.

"I am tired of all this crap! It's either me or her Michael!" she warned "How did you know I was with her?" he asked her. "It's a woman thing," she confessed "What do you mean?" he asked her. "Rob came to Tracey's without you, but with his friend." Michael asked, "So Rob told you where I was at?" She told him that Rob didn't but his friend did. Michael was thinking, "That snitch." She said, "Don't tell him I tricked him."

Michael didn't know the dude, but that was against the rules and any man knows that. "Come on," she said. "Are you coming with me, or what?" Kim asked. "Just leave the bitch here and let's go!" Michael said, "I can't leave them here." Kim said, "If you're not there in half an hour to pack the U-haul, then I'm not going with you." Michael said, "You know I don't like to be pressured. If you don't want to go, you don't have to go." Kim left and Michael took Stacey and Angie home and they he went to Tracy's to pick up Kim. They went to the storage unit and packed all their stuff and Tracy went over to help them. They had a U-haul truck and one car.

The plan was to go to Chicago and pick up some money that was owed to Michael. He had connections there and in just a couple of days, he was expecting a nice royalty check for his work in the music business and he didn't want to leave without it.

They landed at a R.V. park in Evanston, which was just minutes outside of Chicago. The place itself was a riverboat town and they stayed there for a couple of days. Trace also stayed with them for a little while and Michael wanted to do all he could as fast as possible.

He spent time in the streets a couple of days after they arrived collecting all that he could on the favors that were owed to him. Things were tough for him for a few days. At night, he went back to the motor home to be with Kim and the kids, which included Jazzman, as they had to bring her at the last minute. They had been planning on leaving her with her mother, but they just didn't have the heart to leave her.

They relaxed and took it easy, watching TV, swimming and fishing at night. They would sit outside, talking and kicking back. He had Kim, Jazz, Michael Jr. and Keya with him with Michael all the while thinking about how he was going to make this whole thing right.

In the daytime, he would visit his cousins in the City to say good-bye. He left Kim and the kids at the R.V., park while he took care of business. Kim had Tracy at her side to help out, but she was really just waiting for Rob, he was spending time in Milwaukee with one of his girlfriends and then he would be in Madison with Shecka, totally ignoring Tracy.

After a few days went by, Tracy left. She already knew what was up with Rob and his little games. Kim felt even more alone after Tracy left, as Michael got more involved with taking care of his business and trying to collect his debt. His family in Chicago was trying to convince him to stay in the City and look for a job and an apartment. Well, sure enough, he started to do just that at first. He got a job with a temp service because he wanted Kim and the kids to feel safe and secure. He wanted to stay positive.

When Tracy left, Kim didn't want Michael to go anywhere, as he was never the stay-at-home sort of guy. Michael on the other hand didn't trust Tracy and thought it was probably for the best to move to another R.V. park. He didn't want to get caught or take any chances having someone find-out where he was.

Things started to get frustrating and harder then he thought they would be, but he wasn't about to give up, nor was he going to resort to crime, as it just wasn't his thing anymore. He did have some weed and cocaine with him and sold a little bit of it while it was rather slow, because he didn't have a spot.

Michael went to his cousin's house and his Uncle Charles already knew what was up with him. Michael didn't have to tell him, as he was no dummy. He seemed to know everything, but he stayed quiet and he listened to Michael's conversations. One day he asked Michael, "Boy, why do you have your family on the run?" Michael admitted, "I don't agree with what they are offering me and I didn't want to do it, but the cops are always harassing me about everything else, so I had to go and believe me, I didn't do it or anything wrong!"

His Uncle asked, "What makes you think they won't look for you around here?" Michael was silent. Then Uncle Charlie said, "You are always bringing everyone here." He wasn't angry, but he was concerned about his nephew. Then he told Michael, "I don't want any dope around here."

Uncle Charlie was very clear about that. Michael wanted to ask if it was okay if they stayed for a short while so they wouldn't have to pay rent and also so Kim could have someone else to talk to while Michael did what he had to. Uncle Charlie told him, "Do what you have to, but don't bring any dope around here."

Michael's Uncle had a vacant upstairs with two empty bedrooms. This was Michael's old hood and a lot of people around knew who he was, even the police, but they weren't tripping on him for the time being. Once he was pulled over by a cop who said, "Just-Ice, you have a warrant for your arrest in Wisconsin, for a prostitution charge and also for questioning. I'm not tripping though as we have plenty of criminals to keep us busy around here."

Kim and Michael were staying at Uncle Charlie's house. Michael was stressing big time and calling Stacey who was paging him repeatedly. She needed someone to talk to who wasn't going to just complain about things and try to get him to turn himself in.

They started off talking once a week and then it went to two or three times a day. Stacey made Michael feel like he wasn't the only one making phone calls to someone. He wasn't supposed to call or talk to anyone, as that's what both he and Kim agreed to. Kim on the other hand was calling her friend Tracy and her mother who were trying to convince her to get Michael to turn himself in. They told Kim that the police were going to catch Michael and were likely to shoot him.

One time after being out all day, Michael came back to the motor home and Kim was acting really crazy. He thought it was that time of the month for her. Kim happened to have public authority officials in her family and Michael assured her that everything was going to be all right and not to worry about that stuff.

After discussing it, they went to sleep. Michael awoke in the middle of the night to call Stacey. Michael and Kim hadn't made love in a few days and he was getting anxious about it. However, it didn't mean anything, but it did create a little stir, as Michael wanted to be close to Kim all the time, which was the main reason they took off together. Stacey, however, had a little jealousy inside of her and said something in the way of he should've taken her instead of Kim.

The next morning when Michael woke up Kim was crying and he asked her what was wrong. She told him that she wanted to go back home and she missed her mother. “My mother said the cops were going to shoot you when they catch you,” she admitted. She continued, “I want you to turn yourself in before anything happens.”

Michael stood and gave her a hug and said, “I thought you really wanted to do this with me, but now I see that you don’t. Kim, I thought you really wanted to be with me. Was I wrong?” Michael asked. She didn’t have a response for him. In turn, Michael told her to pack her stuff and he would take her back home. “I can't have you with me and you calling your mother all the time as it would only lead the police to me and my location,” he told her. It was a big weight off Kim’s shoulders, as she knew in her heart she really wasn’t up to this whole idea of running. Michael told her to take the car and he would drive the U-haul.

They drove straight home. When they got to the city limits, Michael told her, “Go to my Pop’s house, the cops would never expect him to drop her off there.” Pop’s is a civil servant and has nothing to do with Michael, but he was concerned about their welfare.

Michael had told Kim not to call her mother, but she would do it anyway against his wishes. Once they got close to Michael’s Pop’s house, he told Kim to call Tracy and tell her to meet them there.

Pop’s stayed in a house outside Madison suburbs and Tracy met them there. Michael asked her to look after Kim and the kids. “Kim please take care of my babies,” he pleaded with her. “That’s all I ask. I will get back to get you and I really love you, but just so that you know, I’m just not ready to go to jail and I have to be able to prove my innocence, so until then, I’m not going to turn myself in.”

Kim said, “I want you to do just do me one favor. Take care of yourself and don’t go with that bitch, Stacey.” Michael said, “I won’t go get her.” She asked him, “When are you leaving for Chicago?” Michael told her, “Soon, at the most in a couple of hours.”

Michael left to try and collect on some old debts, so he went to Manny. He just couldn’t leave town without seeing him, as they were good friends. He then stopped to see Rob. After seeing Rob, it didn’t take long before he had to see Stacey.

She acted as if she already knew he was coming to see her. She met him at the park behind her house. She came with Angie right away and gave him a big kiss and a hug. “I love you,” Michael told her, and then, “I missed you.”

Michael told her, “I just wanted to see you again since I’m in town for the moment. I plan on leaving within the next twenty-four hours.” Stacey told Michael that whenever he came back, she wanted to leave with him. He then told her, “Yeah whatever.” He thought she was only playing, as she needed to go back to work at Pizza Hut or something like that.

No sooner than meeting Stacey, Michael had to leave to go to his brother’s Aaron’s place. His brother told him that cops and Feds had come to his house looking for him. He understood, and for that reason, didn’t stay there very long.

As he was leaving, he saw a young female friend-The politician’s daughter. She pleaded with Michael to stop and talk with her. He did, and as he came closer to her, she ran up to him and gave him a big hug and a kiss. She told him that she had to see him today, but

Michael excused that he couldn't and wouldn't be able to. "What about tonight?" she asked him. "Maybe, but I have to go right now," he said and left.

Just down the street, Michael saw yet another young friend his sister had gone to high school with. She was now a doctor living in New York and was married to a doctor. She made Michael promise to come see her after work that night. She begged him, "I have to see you and I something to tell you. It's important," she pleaded. "Okay," Michael told her, just so she would let him go.

He was running late to pick her up, so he was rushing down First Street as he thought it was parallel to E. Washington. The only reason he was going was because she pleaded that it was so important. For some reason that phrase kept sticking in his mind and he guessed it really did have to be something serious.

As he pulled into the shopping center on E. Washington, lights were put on him and sirens were blaring. He thought of running but for some reason he didn't. He looked back and there were three police cars. Michael was in a car that Manny had bought and fully paid off for him and that Michael had picked up from his little cousin Jimmy. This car would later become a conflict between Manny and Michael, but they would scathe through it and become best friends again.

Michael sat there in a sweat. He knew he had outstanding warrants in Madison and in New York. The cop knew who he was when he got to the car. "Well Mr. Brown, how are you doing? Can I see your driver's license and registration?" asked the officer. Michael handed it over and the cop walked back to his patrol car taking what seemed like forever. Michael was seriously thinking about running as he watched the cop through the rear view mirror. Sitting in Manny's car, he thought he should run, but who knew what Manny may have had in the car, maybe even a gun.

Michael was thinking, "All of this, just to see this girl who had something to tell him and he just had to know what it was." The last time they had gotten together, she was trying to get in his pants to talk.

Michael watched the cop coming back to the car. He already knew that he was under arrest but the cop said, "I have to issue a ticket for speeding." Michael could hardly believe what he was hearing. "You also have a warrant." Michael asked, "A warrant?" The officer continued, "Yes a warrant out of New York, but it's not a pick up warrant. They don't seem to be interested in pursuing it at this time so that means they won't be coming to get you, but if you should happen to show up in New York, then they will be more than happy to take you in."

The officer let Michael go with only a ticket for speeding. That night he didn't get to see the girl, instead he went straight to Stacey's to tell her that he had to go. She told him, "Hold on, I'm going with you, but can't we wait until the morning or tomorrow?" at first Michael said, "No." he told her about the traffic stop for speeding and about the warrant from Madison that hadn't come out yet, but that it was time for him to go.

Stacey somehow talked him into seeing it her way regardless of that being a close call. Naturally, they went to their regular spot where they knew the light would be left for them, the Motel 6. They had some of Michael's guys come over for a little party. There was Rob, Manny, Angie and Shelly, along with some of their friends. Michael was reminded that hooking up with old friends could lead to trouble, but he didn't see it coming.

They were in the parking lot waiting for some people to show up. Michael was in his old Suburban and it had a .380 pistol inside of it. Intelligently, he took it out and threw it under the car. To his surprise, a cop saw him doing something and asked if he could search the vehicle. "No, you may not," Michael told him. The cop asked who was driving and Stacey told him that she was. The officer wrote them up for a noise violation after getting everyone's I.D.'s and then they left.

Michael didn't sleep at all that night, but he got totally drunk. Early the next afternoon he was determined to leave and he didn't wait on Rob because he knew he wasn't coming.

Angie and Stacey went with him; He told Tracy that Rob wasn't sure if he and Stacey were ever going to come back. Just then, Tracy said she wanted to see Rob.

They got to the city and Michael was trying to collect some money and was also looking for a place to stay. Michael moved his little motor home to an R.V. park in Crystal Lake, Illinois, which is a huge vacation resort. It is said to be owned by Al Capone. It was a beautiful place to stay for the evening. They ended up staying one night and went to the city the following day. It was close to Michael's birthday and he had a plan to find a good hiding spot until he left for Mexico.

Some of Michael's friends in the city and in the hood were planning a party for him, but what he really wanted was for them to give him the money they owed him as he still had a royalty check coming.

Michael spent all his time hustling for his money and looking for a job at the Union hall.

After some time, Rob finally came to town with Shecka but he was trying to avoid Angie. Rob had been trying to convince Michael to hideout in Milwaukee, and to show him, he took Michael to a place he knew. They left Stacey and Angie at his cousin's house. Angie knew Michael's family, so it was cool for them to stay there, but Angie was angry with Rob. Michael felt for her, but he really didn't want to hear her crying as he had his own problems to worry about.

Later on in the day, Michael ran into some of his boys and some celebrities. They told Michael they were going to hook him up with something and it turned out to be dope. In all honesty, all he wanted was his money, because that was what he needed most.

They kicked it with friends for a minute and then Michael went back to his Uncle's house. "You don't look like yourself," he told Michael. Michael was feeling strange too, but he said, "I'm alright." That night Stacey and Michael's lil cousin borrowed Michael's car to go to the store, and were gone for over an hour. Finally, they came back with a bunch of liquor and they were all smiles. Michael asked her what she was up to, but he couldn't get a straight answer. It wasn't long after they returned that Stacey decided to get a hotel room. She wanted to leave while Angie was still sleeping. The hotel was far from Michael's motor home, which was somewhere up north.

Little did he know but this was to be the last hotel he'd be staying in. Stacey checked them in as Michael was completely out of it until he got inside. She literally had to carry him inside and take his clothes off him, as he was tired mentally, physically and emotionally. Stacey massaged him, as she was wet from a shower. She then began kissing him all over his body. Michael instantly got a new charge of energy, and they got down until the early morning. This would be Michael's last night with Stacey.

They got up and took a shower the next morning as they were going to head back to Uncle Charlie's house. As they arrived, Angie was angry with Stacey. More than likely, she was angrier with Rob than she was at Stacey, because he never showed up.

They began to smoke joints and drink booze. They told jokes and Angie finally started to loosen-up and laugh a little. They sat down and partied for a few hours. Stacey then went to Michael and told him they needed to talk. "Okay, but give me a minute," Michael told her. "I got some homies upstairs and they want to talk to me. More than likely they've got some birthday presents for me," he told her. They also happened to have three fine ass strippers with a home girl named chocolate thunder and another girl named Too Sweet-they were all local strippers. Hot off the press and the market was one of the girls having a radio commercial. They were all up there as Michael's birthday present. They also wanted to buy some weed from him. Michael informed them that he had his girlfriend with him and they would have to wait until his birthday, which was tomorrow night. Chocolate Thunder told him that she was supposed to be going out of town to do a show in Atlanta and she had to leave, so Michael walker her to her car. She said she'd be down the street at her mother's and for him to catch her there later. Then the other girls left in a drop top 5.0 while Michael went back inside to talk to Stacey. She was pissed off. She asked, "Can I talk to you, Michael?" Michael said, "Yes." She said some really mean things out of anger that Michael excused. Then she calmly said, "I have to go home and see my mother." Michael thought his was like déjà vu as Kim had said almost the same thing. Then she added, "I also need to get some clothes and take Angie home."

Michael said, "That's why I wanted to bring your clothes and not Angie. How do I know you're going to come back and how long will you be gone?" he asked her. "I'm immediately coming back, I promise I will, Michael," she assured him. "I will take you then," he offered. "I don't think that is a good idea as they're looking real hard for you." Stacey told him. In turn, Michael said, "I don't want you to leave because they may follow you back." Stacey said, "No, they won't." Michael asked her, "How do you know? Ah, forget it. Do whatever you want." He permitted. Stacey went back downstairs. Michael blurted out, "Just leave me alone for a minute." Stacey was beginning to get mad. Michael said, "Don't be getting an attitude with me. You can go or you can stay-do whatever you want to," he barked at her. "I don't want to stay away, I just want to get my things," she pleaded with him.

Then she said, "Why won't you introduce me to your friends?" This was the first time she had ever acted jealous with him. Michael then said, "Whatever you do, don't start tripping, especially around these black girls." Stacey got up and walked downstairs to the bar, as Michael knew she was furious.

Michael's Auntie Hummer walked in and said, "Just let her go Michael, you don't need that." Michael sat there for a while. He could see the strippers sitting on the porch down the road and looking his way. He thought they probably wondered what was up with him. He finally went downstairs and handed Stacey the keys. "I'll see you when you see me," he told her. "Not coming to take me?" she asked him.

Michael couldn't figure out if she was trying to use some reverse psychology on him or not, but then she got up and started to leave. When she got to the front door, Michael was feeling abandoned again, almost as bad as he felt when Kim wanted to leave and go home. "Wait a minute," Michael said, "I'm coming with you." Stacey asked him, "Are you sure?" "Yeah," said Michael. "Let's go!" Michael's Aunt Marcel looked at him, as it was the last time she would ever see him.

They took Highway 90/94 all the way to Dan Ryan Expressway on the toll on O'Hara. It was a smooth drive all the way to Belvedere Illinois. When Michael saw a Highway Patrol car in the median of the highway, he played it cool as he wasn't really going but about five miles over the speed limit, but just in case, he slowed down a little.

Later they were going down the road, smoking a little weed and drinking. Michael didn't see any cops, but then out of nowhere a cop came up on them really fast. It was almost as if he was trying to pass them up but. He got right behind and turned his lights on, and then his siren, Michael took a minute to slow down and come to a stop. The officer came up to their car and Michael rolled down the window saying, "Is there a problem officer? I know I wasn't speeding." The officer asked, "Can I see some identification and your registration please?" "For what? What's the problem?" Michael asked again. "Your tail pipe is hanging down, and you were speeding," said the cop. "No I was not speeding," Michael argued. "Would you like to come back to my car and see the radar?" he offered. "No, I'll believe you," allowed Michael.

Michael handed over the credentials. The officer said, "Just wait right here and I'll be right back." As the officer went to his car, Michael said to Stacey, "I'm going to jail." "Didn't you give him your fake I.D.?" she asked him. "Yeah, but I have a bad feeling about this one."

The cop came back to Michael's car and asked, "What is your full name, birth date and social security number, sir?" Michael gave it to him "That is not correct sir, can you repeat it for me?" the officer asked. "That doesn't match with what I have. Sir, would you please step out of the car?" "Yeah, sure," Michael said as he stepped out. The state Trooper said, "I'm going to ask you one more time, if things don't match up, I am going to have to place you under arrest." "What is your real name?" he asked. Michael said. "Michael L. Brown, DOB is May 30, 1969." The officer told Michael to wait right there and walked back to his car. Just then, a second and younger State Trooper pulled up and got out of his car. "Mr. Brown, you're under arrest as you have an outstanding warrant in New York and a warrant in Wisconsin and agents also want you for questioning."

He read Michael his Miranda rights and made sure he understood them. He took Michael to his patrol car and then said, "You are a dope dealer and a pimp. Are those girls' whores or what?" He asked, "Do you have any drugs or guns in the vehicle?" Michael said he did not. "I bet," said the Trooper.

He went to the car, got the girls out and started searching. Michael could see Stacey lipping, "I told you not to come. I told you not to drive." Michael didn't say anything. Then he saw the officer pull out Stacey's purse and pour out some dope and money. Michael wondered where she got all of the dope and money. She told Michael all she had was her check. Then the Trooper read Stacey her rights and put her under arrest as well, and put her in a separate cop car.

They took Michael and Stacey to a little holding station by the local toll both in Belvedere, Illinois. After that, they were transferred to a local police station.

"The Kingdom of God is among you. The Kingdom of God is as close to you as your tongue is to your heart. You must confess with your mouth and believe with your heart. Our God will save us. Even when it seems our God doesn't save us from our earthly problems, He will save us in Heaven. He is still God, and God knows what is best for us."

Chapter 31

ALMOST SAVED BY THE BELL

They got to the county jail located somewhere between Loves Park and Belvedere, Illinois, it was a small jail in the middle of town. The only thing Michael could say to Stacey was, "I'm sorry. This is your fault." She said, "Shut Up, it's not my fault and do not say that! You'll get out Michael"; she hoped and spoke aloud. Michael told her, "You just need to go with your life." She said, "I will not. Not without you." Michael had to ask her, "Where did you get all that dope and money from? You told me you were broke", he accused. "I got it from your friends in Chicago," she said. "For your information, I was going to make us some money, Mr. Need to know it all," she told him.

It took the booking deputies hours to book them. Finally, Michael made it to the cellblock. He just sat there feeling numb and not saying anything to anyone. He was not even planning to call anyone, as he thought that no one could help him now. Somehow, he was going to have to work through this problem by himself. As he sat there, he heard someone say, "You are wrong!" He ended up calling Kim on a three way on her cell phone. He told her she had better sell the motor home and that there was some dope and money inside of it. He also told her that he did not think he was coming home anytime soon. "Do not say that," she told him. "Where do they have you?" she asked, and he told her was in a jail somewhere in Belvedere, Illinois.

Michael told Kim to go about her business and find someone else. "Make your first priority you and the kids. You have to be strong and smart. Take care of yourself so that you can take care of the kids", he said. She asked, "What am I to do about the kids? What am I going to do about Jazzman?" Michael told her, "You know what to do and you know what's best. Just do me one favor," he said. She responded, "What's that?" "Never give her up," said Michael. "You are the best for her, and you are probably all she has. I do not want her to end up like me or her mother," he said. His emotions crept up on him and. He could not say much else; he told her he loved her more than he ever loved any woman. "I know it probably doesn't mean anything to you now as I know you are more than likely going to leave me," he confided. "No, I'm not", she said. "Yes, you are", he replied. "I can feel it. Just please go on with your life and do something with it, because I may never get out" He said. She interrupted, "Yes you will, you did not do anything". Michael said, "I know I did not but the system doesn't care about the truth. Justice has become a matter of what the courts decide is the truth."

Michael told Kim, "I am an ex con, a black man, and I'm a target. You do not understand anything about that." She said, "It's not like that Michael," He just gave a little laugh and said", you are unaware of how the system works in reality. The whole reality of living a black life is completely different from that of a white person. Well hope and pray that little Michael learns fast, because his mamma does not know what is really happening out there. Then he said, "I got to go." "Wait," she said. "I have one more question and if you answer me honestly, I'll never leave you."

She continued with an angry tone in her voice, "Why did you drop me off and pick up Stacey when I asked you not to?" "Do you really want me to answer that?" he asked her. "Yes, I do." She said. "Listen," he said, "You are staying, or leaving shouldn't be based on that. I think you are going to leave anyway and in all reality, you probably should." Kim got very mad and said, "I just want you to answer my question!" Michael said, "I just want you to go. Get the stuff and the money." She said, "Mike, answer the question or I will leave all that stuff for whoever wants it. Were you with Stacey?" " Yes, Kim". "Why?" "I do not know for sure, maybe because I am a man and I love sex."

She then asked him, "Is that all? Do you really love her Michael?" " I do not know maybe," he admitted. "Maybe", she accused. "Yes," he added. "Why Mike?" "I do not know why really. There is just something about her; sorry was wrong about all of this. I guess I did not want to be alone, and I could not help it." Michael asked, "Are you happy now? Did you find out what you needed to know? If it matters, I want you to know that it was never my intention to hurt you", he pleaded.

Michael told her he loved her again and all he could say was that he was out of control. If she decided to stay with him, he would leave Stacey for the last time. Then he hung up the phone.

He sat on the bunk, which was next to the table on the floor and some older black dude from Chicago came up and said, "You should never tell on yourself, young blood. Especially if you need some help and you want them to stay." Michael said, "Thanks for your advice, but I really do not need it now. Please just let me be." Michael then stared at him with a look of disgust.

He sat there about to cry not so much for losing his freedom but for losing his family. The next thing he knew, he was crying. He got up and washed his face before any other inmates could see his face.

Than all of a sudden, he saw a light. The Bible in the cell seemed to be glowing and calling him. He could literally feel it calling out to him. Michael picked it up and began reading it and once he did, he immediately started to feel better. Once he started, there was no stopping.

Tired and exhausted from the long day and reading this wonderful book that called out to him, Michael ended up reading himself to sleep, but it was not long before he was awakened to someone calling his name. "Michael, Michael, wake up. Wake up and come unto me", the voice said. Michael could not be sure, if these were actual words or if they were just feelings. He thought he was having a dream, but he was not. He opened his eyes and brilliant light filled the room. Then he was heard the voice again and it said, "Come with me". "Me?" Michael asked. "It's your time, my son. You have to let it all go and come home now, as there is no life without the Lord Jesus. There is no where you can run to anymore." Michael began to visualize the faces of all the people he loved. Those who would talk to him and especially those who knew Michael loved the Lord. He saw the face of his grandmother, his grandfather, and his Aunt.

He saw a little boy and girl standing near an old woman. They looked like Angels to him and they had a glowing radiance about them. Michael really was not sure what was happening around him. He was afraid, but then, at the same time, another part of him felt safe and loved.

Michael then awakened and looked about the room. He thought it had just been a dream yet everything had seemed so real. He was dumbstruck and confused so he prayed to God for help and understanding. Then he looked down and saw the Bible in front of him.

Michael opened it by putting his finger down and looking at where it pointed. It was St. Luke 19:10; "For the Son of Man has come to seek and to save that which was lost,"

Michael turned back a few pages and looked down to see St. Luke 7:21, "And in the same hour cured many of their infirmities and plagues, and of evil spirits; and unto many that were blind he gave sight." Then Michael turned to Chapter 15 of St. Luke and read the parable of the lost sheep.

These scriptures spoke to him in the most profound way. He was lost, but now he was found, and saved through the blood of Jesus Christ.

Right away, he got up to call Kim and tell her about his dream as well as how the scriptures reached out and spoke to him. Kim was not trying to hear Mike. "Yeah Michael," she placated. Michael then called Stacey to share his dream and his inspiration with her. Stacey seemed a little more interested in what he was saying than Kim did. "So, how are you doing?" she asked him. Michael thought to him, "She isn't even listening to what I told her". God is with me now, and you must pray with me that he will be with you as well," he insisted. "Okay, I will", she placated. "We should probably not see each other anymore, Stacey," he instructed. He told her, "I do not think I will be getting out of here any time soon and you should go on with your life." She interrupted, "I can't, and I won't without you," she said. Michael responded back and said, "That's what you say until things get too hot. I do not want to be doing the same thing and being with the same people anymore." She accusingly asked him, "So you never really loved me?" "Of course I did or at least I thought I did", he defended. "I loved something, but maybe it had more to do with the sex part, rather than a real relationship."

Look, you know I am facing prison time right now and I do not know if I am going to get out. I am about to be sentenced with some long prison time and I will not be able to deal with any drama right now, much less later, and besides, you are going to take off on me anyway. Right now, I need to be thinking about my kids and myself. What I need is help and I can only get from Jesus." She asked, "What do you mean? Do you want help anymore? What about me, Michael?" Michael said, "I do not need any of your help anymore and the reality of this is, is that there's nothing I can do for you now or anyone else." He hung up the phone.

As time passed, Kim and Michael's mother came to visit Michael and left him some money. He was glad to see both of them and they were glad to see him. Michael did not seem like the same person they were expecting to see. The only things that he had in mind were his experience with his Lord and Savior, Jesus Christ. That was all he wanted to talk about, but Kim still wanted to bring up the issues with Stacey and him. As far as Michael was concerned, that was a part of his old life, he wanted nothing to do with. He was moving on to new and better things, but there was something she wanted to tell him.

Federal agents had been constantly calling her and wanted to meet with her. "I do not think you should talk to them," he advised. "They know where to find me and other than that just leave it alone and concern yourself with you and the kids," he advised her.

The Dane County Sheriff's Department from Madison, Wisconsin came to get him on the tenth day. It was a few hours late from his being released, as they had only so many days for a legal extradition, or they would have to let him go. The cops were saying they would have to let him go in another twenty minutes if Dane County did not show up. As fate would have it, they showed up in less than twenty minutes. Just as Michael was about to leave the building, they turned up and arrested him.

Michael's transition into his new life with Jesus Christ was different and difficult at the Dane County Jail. He was locked up with some of the street brothers and it was hard to shake the influence of the brothers at first. Michael knew he had to shake the influence as he had a lot of old friends, foes and even some enemies in the jail.

Michael did not hate anyone, but there were some who hated the old Michael. With so much hate, Michael was never scared nor a punk or anything. He just was not sure where he was going in a new life of his. He did not want to be in jail. At the same time, he did not want to be the old Michael either. He just did not know at that time how to let go and let God take over. It was something that was going to take a daily effort as well as a constant vigilance to maintain, especially for a man as hardheaded as Michael did, but his determination was going to assure his success, and deep down inside, he knew it would happen.

Michael was housed in cell block 628 the oldest part of the jail, where they put the men who were facing a lot of time, for serious crimes.

Michael did not think he was in either of those categories that cellblock had a mix of characters and criminals. There was Terry Crawford aka T.C. who had a beef with Michael in the streets. T.C. had shot at Michael and his friends. Then there was Michael's homier Bo Walker who was one crazy dude and was going to jail for busting someone up. He was in jail, this time, for busting up his own wife. Bo just been released from prison and now he was on his way back. There were also three so-called relatives-Michael's Crazy cousins, Dino, Nicky and Jason, and Tracey's Cousin, Jacob Jenkins. His was the most serious case out of all them, - facing first degree murder and was seconds away from slipping and tripping. He spent most of his time studying his case and gambling. A few white guys came in and out. Michael's girl Sonnet had a brother there who was half Jamaican and half-Romanian, which was one Crazy mix.

From the very first moment that Michael stepped into the cellblock, he made it known that he was standing with God. This was all he wanted anybody to know. He wanted to be left alone so he could pray, read and study the Word of God. A Bible was sitting on his bunk waiting for him, as if it was calling his name. Everyone knew how serious he was about it.

Michael has to see his lawyer right away, but unfortunately, they got off to a bad start because Michael was supposed to see him before he went on the run. The lawyer came at Michael with an attitude and acted as if he was ready to send him up the river. Michael was facing charges of two counts of solicitation of prostitution, one count of minor forgery of an identification card, and one count of bail jumping. The time totaled twenty years for each of the two prostitution charges, equaling forty years, five years for felony bail jumping and another five years for forging an I'D... This was the I.D. that was given to Michael by Aaron, but, he could tell the courts that himself. Michael's lawyer told him the charges and the time he was facing totaled fifty years. He conveyed how serious it was and suggested that Michael should try to get the best deal he could. Michael told his attorney that he was not about to plead to something he did not do.

After talking to his attorney, Michael called Kim to let her know what was happening. She did not act surprised and she said that she thought he could get himself out of it. He was not as optimistic as she was. Kim mentioned that she wanted to come and visit him right away, but Michael had a lot to deal with at the moment and he was not ready to get himself all worked up wondering if she was going to stay with him or not.

There was also the idea of the Feds calling her, which he did not like very much. Nonetheless, he already told her that he would take care of it and she should tell the Feds not to call her anymore. He told her to tell them to go see him, because he did not have anything to hide.

Michael was there a few days before he called Stacey. He was not sure if he was going to keep it up with her and he told her he just wanted to be friends and help her with what he could. Michael just was not serious about their relationship anymore, as he had too much to deal with, but she was still adamant on staying in a relationship with him. He told her that the Feds wanted to talk to him and he was not sure what for. He figured it had to be something regarding Skin and Rob. Stacey told him she was not worried about anything and he told her that he was not either.

A couple of days later, Michael started to get a real weird "Health Wellness" feeling. A feeling made worse when Sonnet's brother told him that she had H.I.V. and that she just moved to Las Vegas, with her girlfriend. Michael immediately put in a request to see the jail nurse and had some blood test done. He had had sex with Sonnet a few times and wanted to make sure things were all good with his health. Michael met Sonnet in Wisconsin after he moved back from Miami. Sonnet worked at his first club and the Escort service, she became one of his "Main Girls," as an Old School Pimp would say.

During Michael's first six months in county jail, he was busy getting himself saved and recommitted to his Lord and Savior, Jesus Christ. He finally found himself at a Sunday service. The preacher asked if anyone wanted to give his or her life to Jesus, but nobody responded.

The preacher asked again, and this time Michael stood and raised his hand. The preacher told him to come down and he did. Immediately, he accepted Jesus Christ into his life. He immediately felt the weight of the entire world lifted off his shoulders. When he returned to his seat, he was experiencing something he had never felt before. He was praying, sweating and crying for no apparent reason. He felt like his old self was now dead and gone. Indeed, he felt reborn.

He went back to the cellblock after the service and cried for the rest of the evening. He just was not sure what was happening to him, but it did not matter, because all he knew for sure was that now he had a wonderful calming feeling about him.

The next morning he called Kim, which had become a daily thing with him now. She was hysterical because the Feds would not stop calling, asking questions and harassing her. Michael asked, "What kind of questions are they asking you?" "Questions about Rob and Skin," she said. "The next time they call you, tell them I want them to come see me. Let me take care of it," he told her.

It was not long after this that the Feds came to see Michael. They asked him about some of the same things they had been asking Kim, all of which Michael told them he had nothing to do with. He explained that he had already told them everything he knew the last time they harassed him. He also warned the Feds to leave his family out of it, or else. All that did was piss them off and they told him, "You never give the Federal Government an ultimatum". The last thing they told him was, "You better be telling us the truth. If not, we'll be back."

Michael's lawyer brought him a memo indicating a date and a time the Feds were going to see him again. It was not a laughing matter, so he went down on his knees in prayer to ask for God's help.

All that night and the next day, Michael waited and prayed. The time came around and the Sheriff Deputies took him to the interview room. After sitting there for an hour, the deputy came back. "I think you just got lucky Mr. Brown because they did not show up," said the Deputy. "There's no such thing as luck and everything is controlled by God," Michael responded. The Deputy looked confused. "What did you say Mr. Brown?" He asked. "Do you believe in God?" Michael inquired. The cop in turn told him that they have already heard it all.

Stacey would be going to court in Illinois in just a few days, for possession of a controlled substance; Michael called her out of concern. Stacey had come and visited Him that weekend, he tried to talk her out of it, and because he had made a commitment to Kim that, he would not see Stacey or any other woman again. Kim also made a like commitment to Michael. Stacey convinced Michael that she loved him and needed him. She told him that they would be together from the beginning to the end and He felt trapped. Stacey also told Michael that the feds were going to see her as well and that they wanted her to put it all on him. She told Michael that she would never do that. "What should I do?" Stacey asked him. "You have to tell the truth. Tell them everything and leave out nothing." He continued, "That's what I did and if that doesn't work, at least you know you did the right thing. In addition, it will be easy to live with. "Do you understand?" he asked her. "Yes, I do Michael," she assured him. "I can handle myself now."

Michael never expected to hear from the Feds again. If he did, it could only help him. He knew he had told them the truth and according to the new life he was living, "The Truth Shall Set You Free."

The next bit of news he received was good news. His H.I.V. and STD tests came back negative. He told himself that he would never live in fear like that again. There would be no more promiscuity and he would never forget the moment the nurse came with the news.

He had been getting ready to shower when she came in and said, "Mr. Brown I have the results of your blood test," she asked him, "Would you like for me to come back later?" He jumped up. "No, please give me the news," he demanded. He was too anxious. "Good or bad, just give me the news." "Right here and now?" she asked. "Yes!" he pleaded. "The test says you are non-reactive." 'God Bless, God Bless!' He knew he had been with a couple of girls who were questionable

Michael was there about two weeks when he found out Rob was arrested again. He had just been released from jail for a robbery and now he was involved in another one, with his brother and Angie. Stacey told Michael about it the same day the Milwaukee police came to see him. He was not quite sure why they came, but he

Learned that Rob apparently robbed a place using the Suburban Michael had loan him, the same vehicle Kim purchased for Michael with her tax return money.

Michael told the officers he had nothing to do with it and he would not help them. He told them to leave him alone and they did. The next news he received was from his lawyer, who said it was nothing to talk about over the phone. The lawyer told Michael that the Feds targeted him. The attorney did not know why, but he told Michael they had had made appointment to meet with the attorney. Michael got mad and said, "I do not want to talk to them, even if they do not believe me!" "You do not have to act that way with me," said his lawyer. Michael said, "I am sick and tired of the way these people operate in this system."

Michael was seeing both Stacey and Kim once a week for visits. Both of them wanted to be able to see him at least twice a week, but he was only permitted two visits per week. Here he was trapped again, stuck between two women and he did not want to give up either one of them. Michael honestly believed he loved them both. He tried to decide which of them had his best interest at heart. Which one could he count on to be there forever? His love for Kim was genuine, pure and long lasting. He was lonely and he wanted out of that jail. It is rough when you first are locked up. He was still suffering detox, cold sweats and his pores reeking of weed and alcohol. The toxins were seeping out of his pores, so was that type of lifestyle. It does not stop simply because he found God. No, it does not work like that. At least it did not for Michael, because he was struggling. He was still clinging to the old way and the old lifestyle clung to him like Velcro.

Eventually Kim and Stacey found out what was going on. They both asked Michael to stop seeing the other one, but he refused. He told Stacey he would stop seeing Kim and his children, but what he did not tell her was that he would always be in love with Kim. Kim, on the other hand, was told, "I won't stop seeing Stacey. She needs my advice among other things," he told her that Stacey was helping him with his case and vice-versa. He told her Stacey had told the truth and he loved her for that. Kim acted as if she was giving Michael an ultimatum. Michael loved and respected Stacey, but he was not ready to let her go just yet. He knew it would happen one day, but a part of him did not want it to be so.

Not long after this, Michael had his visit from the Feds. He prayed it would not happen, but it did. Things were not over yet. They came around with the Federal Prosecutor, who acted like a real jerk. He began by asking Michael about some stuff that he knew absolutely nothing about. Then he asked him the same questions the Federal Agents had already asked him before. Michael gave him the same answers he gave the Agents. He asked about things that did not have anything to do with any robberies,

He should not have been talking to these people, but he had nothing to hide. Michael did not do anything wrong or illegal was relative to any robberies. All Michael ever did was sell a little dope and deal with the women.

The Feds finally had enough and quit questioning him. At one point in the interrogation, Michael asked, "Why are you dudes harassing me? I had nothing to do with it!" The lawyer told Michael he would let know if he got out of line by kicking the chair under the table, and he was bruising Michael's leg. Michael was getting fed up and the interview was over as far as he was concerned.

After the interrogation the lawyer said, "I was not sure if you were a target or not, but now you really have made them mad." Michael said, "All I did was told the truth".

Not long after this, the State came with a plea bargain and the lawyer told Michael he should consider taking the deal. Michael did not agree. He could not accept going to prison for something he did not do. He knew he did not make anybody become a prostitute even telling the women not to solicit sex. Yes, Michael had turned his back on a few things, and told the girls to cover their own ass, but any prostitution was on their own time and never on his property.

The court ordered a Presentence Investigation Report (P.S.I.), before they would consider any plea deal. They offered Michael a five-year sentence on all charges and he almost took it, as five years would be the maximum and they agreed not to arguer anything less with the sentencing judge.

The sooner the better, Michael thought because he was tired of sitting in that stinking jail. He decided that he had to accept some responsibility for what those girls did; after all, he did own the business.

By that time, Michael was feeling that Stacey was beginning to drift away. She started to miss the weekly visits, where she had always asked for more time before. She wanted Michael to call her regularly, sometimes up to three times a day. Before Stacey began missing their visits, Michael told her they would have to be together forever. They would have to get married or stop seeing each other. "I'm not going to stop seeing you," she surprised him by saying. So Michael decided to call her bluff and set it up. It was around that time that she stopped showing up for their visits. But even before that, they would talk everyday on the phone as if nothing was amiss and Michael would write to her almost daily. He would send cards and she would never miss a visit with him. He would tell her about God and they would laugh, joke, talk and even pray together. Stacey knew of Michael's revelation and that he was a different man. Michael knew that he wanted to change for the better and he was never going back to his old ways. He was a new creation with Christ and had new positive thinking with God. He wanted nothing but God's blessing and his own freedom. He also did not did not want to be by himself. Michael knew that if Kim found out about Stacey, she would be hurt and may take off. He certainly did not did not want Stacey to get hurt or stay God-less. More importantly, he always wanted her to remain truthful about everything.

Michael got up because he could not sleep and he began drawing something to calm, his nerves. Until he saw the finished product, He thought and believed that he was going crazy, but there was something familiar in his drawing. It was like a dream he never had before. He put the drawing in a big envelope and sent it to Stacey to tell her about the vision he had. He called a couple of days later after she received his letter. "Wow!" said Stacey. "That picture was amazing Michael! I did not know you were an artist" Michael felt strange when it came to him. "There are a lot of things you do not know about me," he offered. "I just haven't found all my skills yet," he said. The two of them got to talking and Stacey said, "I have something I need to tell you Michael," "What is it?" he asked. It got quiet for a moment and Michael thought of the worst-case scenario like being pregnant or something. Is she H.I.V. positive? Is she leaving? Michael thought to himself. "Tell me!" he demanded. It must be important he thought, Michael was building a huge phone bill with all the collect calls and Stacey's mother was complaining. He had told her that they should not be talking so much, but Stacey would trip if Michael did not call her on a regular basis. When her mother got to tripping, they would do a three-way call through Angie and few other people. Stacey would always set something up through Angie. It did not matter much because they were growing apart now. Kim, on the other hand, seemed to be growing steadily closer to Michael now. "Alright Stacey, I guess it's important. You know I hate for anyone to start something and not finish it."

She came out and finally said it, "They're trying to make me say something." Michael said, "Wait a minute!" Then he asked, "Who is trying to make you say something?" "The Feds are trying to make me say that you were involved with us and that you went with us or that you told us to do it," she confided. "But that is a downright lie," blurted Michael. "I know. They tried to make me take handwriting and a polygraph test," she said. "What for?" he asked. "You do not have to do that!" he said. "I know, but they said they could get a court order to make me," she told him. "Then tell them to get the court order," said Michael. "If you do not want to do the test, they can't force you." Michael had never heard Stacey sound so scared before. "Maybe you should just take the test," he advised.

She said nothing for a while, then Michael said, "Stacey is there any reason you do not want to take those tests?" She responded, "Well!" Michael thought Stacey had told him the truth about her involvement with Rob and Skin. He thought all she ever did was drive. "Did you write the note?" Michael asked her. She was hesitant to answer him at first, but then she offered, "I do not know." Michael was hurt because he already knew she was lying to him. Michael said, "I know I did not do it and I know you did not tell them I did." Stacey said, "Of course I did not." Michael said, "Look Stacey. If you feel there is no way out for yourself, you can blame me if you want to. I am sure everyone else will. All I know is that I had nothing to do with it, so just tell me the truth or do with what you can live with. Just remember, we all have to face God with it in the end."

"Listen, I love you and I never meant to hurt you or for it to turn out like this," pleaded Michael. "I know," Stacey assured him. "I hate that you met those guys and ever got involved with them," Michael said. "I feel as if it is my fault." Stacey interrupted, "It's not your fault Michael." Michael continued, "You will always be in my heart and in my prayers."

That was the last time Michael talked to Stacey from the county jail. Previously he did have the opportunity to apologize for breaking her jaw and running up her credit. He also conveyed his sorrow for how their relationship had turned out and all Stacey would say is, "It's not your fault Michael and you are still innocent."

Not long after that, Michael was sentenced and sent to prison, but not before one more tragedy that would be a very valuable lesson as well as another message from God.

Michael never said anything to Kim about what happened between him and Stacey, as it was an answer to his prayers, but not at first. He was really missing her and he asked God to help the two women and to help Him get rid of whichever one he needed to. God heard his plea and helped him answer his prayers.

Michael was due to be sentenced in a couple of days and he was seeing Kim and the kids during both visiting days, every week Also had been to a couple of court appearances in the meantime. Thankfully, his Pops was always there for support, which was expected. His mom was also doing her best at showing up and lending support. Something was coming over Michael's mother. He believed that it had to be the hand of God, because she hated anything to do with jails or courts and she never was there for Michael before, even when he was a kid. Pops would bring his brothers and sisters to visit him as well. Michael would preach to them and they were used to it by then, but his brothers and sisters would now always listen to what he had to say.

Michael went to sentencing, hoping and praying and expecting it to go smooth. While in the court holding cell, another relative of Michael's, Jerry was there for child support. He was in a cast and he had his head down. Michael regretted not saying anything about Jesus to him then. He knew that eventually he had to make him aware of God.

Michael prayed right there and then and Jerry could hear him praying. Michael did not know about what his cousin had done until sometime later. His cousin would later shoot his young teenage daughter, paralyzing her and then killed himself. Years before this happened; his cousin was one of Madison's biggest players, after winning a multi-million dollar lawsuit.

Michael was feeling very sad that day, as he was not happy about signing a plea to surrender his freedom for a maximum of five years. While making the plea, he quickly learned that it was actually for seven years and not five, made them quickly stop proceedings and informed them that it was not what he had agreed to. They called a recess so Michael could talk it over with his lawyer and his family.

He did not want to go to jail but he knew he had to and wanted to get it over. After receiving some advice from his Pops and Kim, Michael decided to take their plea deal for the five to nine years. He was sentenced to seven years.

He went back to his cell and was soon moved to another cellblock that housed people waiting to be transported to prison.

In that cell block there was a brother named Chris, from Beloit, Wisconsin. He was the biggest dope dealer busted in that area. Chris had multi-millions and was a killer since his early teens. He was a Federal prisoner and he came back to testify against 50 guys to reduce his life sentence. Chris claimed to be a Christian with a message from God. He did not know who Michael was at first until they called Michael's name for a visit. Chris then asked Michael, "Mike Brown, do not you know me?" Michael told him, 'I do not think so.' Chris insisted he did and explained that they had the some customers. Thankfully, Michael's deals had been through someone else as Chris was testifying against everyone he knew.

"I have a message from God for you Brother," he told Michael. He went on to tell Michael what God had said, "You must turn to God or forever be cursed. God knows you will do the right thing, but not before things get much worse."

Michael thought to himself, 'How can it get any worse? I have already lost everything I've worked so hard for.' Chris also told Michael that he had been to some of his clubs as well as to some of his concerts. He reminded Michael that they had worked together on a Crucial Conflict concert in Rockford.

Chris looked different now. He weighed well over four hundred pounds and had lost most of his hair. Michael thought he still had a glow about him that could have very well been the result of his relationship with God.

They talked a lot and studied the scriptures. They discussed their old lives and the potentialities of their new lives and talked about how they would have to do almost everything differently than they used to. Chris and Michael were in the same cellblock for about two weeks before Michael left for prison, but before Michael left, he noticed something strange. The jail was seriously overcrowded but in the cellblock that Michael and Chris were in, for some reason there was only the two of them. Michael also noticed that while visiting his family, Chris was visiting with a Federal Agent. Of course, he had no clue what they were talking about but there was a guy in the cell before Michael was sentenced who was meeting with the same agent.

The guys moved out of the block because Michael told him to stay out of his business. Michael learned that every time he went for a visit, the guy was asking questions about him and his case. He would ask questions about Michael's girlfriend Stacey. He later found out the guy used to go out with Stacey.

Chris told Michael it was part of his agreement with the Feds to testify against some guys. He told Michael, "If that guy is meeting the Feds; he's also doing the same thing." He told Michael that the person had said something to him about testifying against somebody, but the person had told everybody else in the cell black that he was back on an appeal. His name was Richard Wallace and he was very jealous about Michael's relationship with Stacey.

Michael told Chris everything about the indictment. He told him that he had absolutely nothing to do with any of it. Chris told Michael that he already knew and he had heard about it from Richard Wallace. He also told Michael that the Feds had Richard Wallace in there to get information on him. Michael was dumbfounded that the Feds would go to such extremes to nail Him

"Now that I walk through the valley of the shadow of death, I will fear no evil; I walk with the Lord Jesus Christ… I Surrender." "Now I am free from the sin of death and from the things of the world. I am freer than any bird on the wing. I am freer that many who have never been a prisoner." "I am free as free can be with the Lord," said Michael L. Brown. We haven't a clue to the real measure of His Power and His Glory, it's is immeasurable."

CHAPTER 32

SPIRITUAL TEMPTATION AND THE FEDS LAST ATTEMPT

A couple of days later Michael was taken to a reception center for prisoners called the Dodge Correctional Institution in Waupun, Wisconsin. He was able to visit Kim and the kids before he left the jail. They talked, cried, and even got to laugh a little. Kim told Michael that she would never leave him and that she could not wait until the nightmare was over so they could be together forever.

After Michael arrived at Dodge, he was blessed to be housed in a cell with another Christian and believer in Jesus. Michael had been at Dodge, about 10 years prior. He knew the whole booking procedure, but had a feeling that he had never felt before.

Michael's cellie was a good, older dude who was a registered nurse from Philly, and this was his first time in jail. He had also given his life to Jesus and was deeply committed. His cellie was also an ex-dope dealer and he knew many people, including Michael's mother. He happened to be married to the sister of Michael's mother's old friend, Jim Stewart. His brother, Big John was an ex-dope fiend who cleaned up, turned businessperson, and managed a summer camp program.

At the reception, center inmates spend the first three days in complete isolation. The intake guards spray inmates for lice and then it is off to the basement for fourteen days of quarantine. They called it the dungeon. This place was not a joke, it permanently Ed Geins from Plainfield, Wisconsin, who had murdered some people and dug up dead bodies to skin them. He made things like lampshades from their skin and used the skulls for soup bowls.

Michael and his cellie studied the Word of God daily. The Bible was probably their major source of conversation other than talking about their families. They would talk for hours about both their old lives and their new lives in the Lord.

The Feds wanted to see Michael and they made an appointment a week in advance. He told his cellie about his situation, and how he did not do what he was been accused of. His cellie's advice to his was, "Do not talk to the Feds or anyone else. If they have a problem with that, just tell them that you do not recall any of your old life and do not want to," which is just what Michael did when the Feds came to see him.

The Feds told Michael that they caught Skin. Some dude from Milwaukee told Michael that Skin was already trying to escape. The Feds told Michael about some plot Skin had to kill a police officer. Michael just though they were playing him, and making it up just to get back at somebody.

While he was talking to them, he realized that Jim was always talking about that sort of thing and a lot of other crazy crap. Michael told the Feds that he did not did not remember much of his past. "I have a new life with God now I do not think of anything else," he told them. Then he smiled and felt good for saying it.

The federal agent asked Michael, "Are you sure you do not have anything else to say?" "No," Michael assured. "This is your last chance," offered the agent. "No, thank you!" said Michael. "You will regret not giving us the information we're after," threatened the agents before leaving. They were like vultures, who wanted anything they could sink their claws into. They did not even seem to care if it was make believe, just so it sounded good, but Michael did not want any part of that game.

Sadly, there came a time when Michael's cellie transferred out and his new cellie was an old burned-out white dude who was in for child molestation. This dude had molested his stepdaughter. Thankfully, for Michael, he was also a born again, Christian and it was evident that he was sorry for what he had done and really wanted to change. It was not was not going to be easy for him in prison because he would have to be on the alert for other inmates who prey on sex offenders. These guys could be ugly to people who have done these sorts of things, to children.

Soon Michael was taken to another part of the prison called the barracks, where there were rows of double bunks in giant rooms. He was going to CCA, a Correction Corporation of America facility. This was an out-of-state private prison set up to make money off the state and Feds because of America's prison overcrowding. Michael was soon to be on his way to Tennessee.

He was looking forward to it and felt he was meant to do God's work, but again, he just did not like the idea of being so far away from Kin and the kids. Michael thought so much about it that he even began to have nightmares about being so far away, but at the same time, Michael could not think about anything else besides God and trying to stay focused. He would wake up in cold sweats and find himself wiping away tears. "If there is anything else I could do, please let me do it, but let me do it here." Michael prayed.

He feared that bad things would befall Kim and his kids, and not only that; policy stated visits were allowed ninety days after arrival.

Kim and Michael did not have a marriage license either and with the ninety days almost up, Kim was anxious to come and visit. Then the worst thing happened, they packed Michael out and told him he would be leaving within seventy-two hours for the Whiteville CCA. Things became so hard for him that he could not eat, could not sleep and could not even think.

Michael just did not want to leave and be so far away from his wife and kids. The devil sure knows our fears and was using Michael's against him. To make matters worse, theca had been on lock-down for six months and had already had two major riots. Prisoners and staff were beaten to death and questions were arising everywhere on what exactly happened. Private prisons are overcrowded, which was and still is a major problem across the country. Michael was not happy to have to deal with it, but he knew with God's blessing he would be able to get through it.

When the bus arrived, Michael was so tired from the night before that he did not think he had the strength to make this long trip. The full bus started out on a nine-hour trip, which ended up being the ride from hell, as it took almost twenty-four hours. It wound up being a circus ride and they could have been killed because of foul weather. Even the redneck racist officers were as scared as the inmate passengers were. Everyone during that long trip learned a new respect for the fury of Mother Nature.

Things were just as strange when they arrived at the CCA facility as it had already gained its own reputation Michael could feel the anxiety in the air.

After praying, Michael finally went to bed and slept for a few hours. He awoke to the danger of tornados. The prison facility was situated in one of worst tornado belts in

Tennessee, Whiteville County. This area of Tennessee was known to get more than thirty hits year.

The prison was located on some old farmland that was formerly a plantation. Michael asked questions because he was a real history buff. In today's human cattle industry try, prisons especially private prisons were the new job market in the area

The first time the inmates were permitted to leave their cells to go to the chow, Michael gave the place a good once over. It was mostly a black population run by some real rednecks guards.

It had not yet been an entire week and Michael was already witnessing a sexact. A brother was all over a gay white counselor and they were about to do it right there "Johnny on the spot."By the time Michael made it into the chow hall, he also saw several drug deals going down.

The food was better than what one would expect, but the name of "Whiteville" was somewhat unsettling. For a black man, it was not cool to know the place was run by racist redneck country boys. The last riot there was caused by some redneck Correctional Officer.

The joint had three hundred staff members. Most were black female officers, but white people had the administrative positions.

The sisters there were crazy and wild. Most were just street girls, but others were small town family girls just wanting a job. Most of them had come from furniture factories and farm jobs before being hired as Correctional Officers.

Whiteville County is located an hour east of Nashville and an hour west of Memphis. The officers treated the inmates with respect by killing them with kindness. This had to do partly with the whole "Southern Hospitality" thing, unless of course you done pissed someone off. Then one could expect the K.K.K. or Uncle Toms or some other power to be on you.

Michael really liked the chapel there. Almost every day there was some form of religious function going on. Next to that the really liked the library. If they did not have a particular book or study material, they would eventually get for you. They had a lawyer who would come two or three times a week to assist the inmates with legal aid free of charge.

Michael was advised about a legal issue, regarding his punishment being too severe and he was determined to fix it. At least he got some legal action to reduce it.

Michael had his fair share of temptation and issues with himself and he was doing all he could to change. He found out the hard way that change was not easy or quick. His first issue was with his cellie, a dude he was transferred with from Wisconsin.

Michael got into a fight with a big bully rapist from Milwaukee named Green. He must have thought Michael was a punk, but he learned the hard way that Michael was for damn sure no punk. None of the inmates there or any officers dared break up the fight-they just stood by and watched. Afterwards they told Green, "That's what you get!"The whole thing started because Green had grabbed Michael after Michael had already told the guy he did not want any trouble, much less did not want to play. At first, Michael was not sure that the guy was serious when he looked at Michael and said accusingly, "What are you looking at?" Green was in the process of taking some other inmates commissary so he could buy himself some weed. They were in a no smoking cellblock and Michael did not want to smell like smoke or be involved in anything.

Michael took right into the dude because he thought the dude was going to take right into him. When it ended, Michael had a scratch on his head from hitting the concrete. Green had grabbed him and slammed him up against the wall, but Michael got him back with a combination. Green was already bloody, could not see and Michael did not want to hurt him, but thereafter nobody messed with him.

Michael was moved into another cell with a guy originally from Milwaukee nickname Green Eyes. He lived in Madison where he caught his case, but his people were from Chicago.

Michael came to find out that Green Eyes had been to his house when he used to throw parties back in the day. To his surprise, he had even gone out with Michael's cousin Ann and had partied with Michael's mother.

Michael started to get himself together in Tennessee, but he had to face some distractions. His homie Green Eyes was light skinned with short wavy hair. Many inmates called him pretty boy, but he was actually very tough. He scored with the women as well as with dope. Unfortunately, that was his downfall and he paid for it. He had twenty-five years for the attempted murder of one of the Henderson boys, who were a well-known black Madison family.

Green Eyes was not Michael's cellie for long until before he was locked up in the hole for messing with the female guards. For some reason he just could not seem to leave the women alone. A white female officer told her black girlfriends she had been messing with Green Eyes. Once the Lieutenant found out, Green Eyes was thrown in the hole for it.

Green Eyes and a few other inmates were screwing women guards like crazy. They were even selling them to other inmates. They were getting the women to bring drugs into the facility. Some of the women even got pregnant and then married those inmates.

Green Eyes put the word out about who Michael was. He let the brothers know who Michael was on the streets with all the girls and the dope, and how he was in the music business.

Michael also had a relative in Tennessee called Big Paul, a.k.a. Stage Coach, who was a high-ranking Vice Lord from the city. He caught his case in Madison for robbery and kidnapping. He had admitted that he took dope but never took anything from any girl, especially sex. Michael believed him because he knew Big Paul's style. They called him Stage Coach because he had robbed the entire Chicago Transit Authority and everybody on it. For that, he got twenty years. Big Paul's wife was related to Michael by marriage to Commesel's sister-in-law. Sometimes when Michael could not find dope, he would use her to help him find it. She seemed to know everyone in the hood and could get just about anything.

Years before, Michael looked out for Paul when he got out. Paul was 6'5" with light skin and the girls would say he was a very handsome man. He had Indian blood and wore his hair in a long ponytail. Michael would look out for him when he moved to Madison, even though back then he never did anything for Michael, but now he called himself on it to return the favor. Paul wanted to give Michael some dope and get him back in the game, but Michael let him know where he stood with Jesus.

Big Paul respected Michael for his decisions and determination, but he tried as a lot of others did to get Michael back in the game but it was not even a concern for Michael as he was obviously making a change in his life.

Michael stayed on the weight pile and did his daily routine, which helped him to stay out of the mix. Michael was doing all he could, but he did not have a lot of time like most of the guys did. Most of them had twenty-years to life. Michael also had a friend there named Pinion who was a professional thief from Milwaukee. He and Pinion would kick it and eat like kings with their officer friends. Then there was Snapshot a.k.a. Roger, a photographer, pilot and wild game hunter. He was in because of pornographic photos he had taken of young girls and their mothers.

Michael's greatest work was in his love of the Lord and he walked with Jesus more and more as time went by. He would pray several times a day and read the Word of God even more. He would attend church services everyday and everyday he sat down to talk to the Lord. Ever since Michael was saved, he had been feeling this great pull. The pull showed him that he was being led by the Spirit and to stay in the Lord's way. Michael ate, drank, slept and talked about the Word. He did not know where it was coming from, but it was there and it was most powerful. It was finally time for Michael to make up his mind to find out whether he was going to forever serve the Lord or not.

Michael thought his job was going to be a preacher like his grandmother, and he began acting as his grandmother did. He watched the Word on Television and he listened to the Word on the radio, as down South they know how to bring it on strong.

Michael slipped a few times and had to learn, that no matter how sincere a person believes they are, the devil won't stop working against them. He works all the harder against those that are blessed by God. The devil brought it doubly hard against Michael as he had given a few female officers the man speech about quitting their relationships with loser inmates. He advised them to find someone who would really care for them and would spend money on them and take care of them the way a man is supposed to. If they were going to mess with inmates, they should go for the rich dudes. A couple of officers hit Michael with a pound or two of weed expecting him to do his part, but Michael just gave it away because he did not want to start dealing dope again. He was done with that life and he did not want to be known for that anymore. Michael only wanted to be known for his work in the Lord and his commitment to Jesus Christ.

Big Paul was not the only family Michael had in prison. He found out that his second cousin worked there as well. The police accused Michael of having his cousin bring him dope, but that was not true. They tried to accuse him of being the main supplier of drugs inside the prison, but later found out that someone else was bringing in kilos of powder cocaine on a weekly basis.

They asked Michael about Tony and Joan, which were his Uncle Darnell's ex-wife and daughter, who had been working there. Tony was supposedly scared because once before she had halfway said her boyfriend was going to stick Michael up at his club on E. Washington, but Tammy had forewarned him of it.

The cops already knew all about this but acted dumb about it. Michael told them the only work he did now as for Jesus. The funny thing is that Michael had heard about a chick named Joan who worked in the kitchen but he never figured that she would turn out to be his Aunt. Knowing that, Michael made sure that he stayed out of any kind of trouble. In general, Michael was not known for causing trouble anyway, so he was comfortable after finding out about his relatives working there.

Some of the other brothers were as serious about their walk with God as Michael was. They talked to the Administration about possibly having an opportunity to do Bible studies and prayer meetings before going to their jobs every day, and it was granted.

They had these meetings once a week and would get together and pray separately whenever they could find the time and the place.

On one particular occasion, Michael and about fifty other guys were on their knees praying with eyes closed and their faces in the chairs when the next thing Michael knew, he felt as if he was not there anymore. His body stayed put but the rest of him lifted up to Heaven. He could see what the entire world was doing, most of which he wanted no part. He could see the past as well as the future. Michael saw himself in the free world doing God's work. He was definitely feeling god's blessings around him.

When he opened his eyes again, unfortunately, he was still in prison, and he surely did not want to be. He had been with God, Jesus and all of his burdens were lifted again. He felt as if he had a new beginning.

After completing a year in Tennessee, he got a special visit with Kim. She had come to see him and it was the most wonderful thing for him. It had been a long while since he had seen her and it was just nice to see someone else other than the prisoners around him. When Kim came to visit, his fans were not in the visiting room, nor were they happy that she was there. When some of the female officers came in and saw Michael with a female, they gave him mean stares and when he got back to his cell that evening, they really let him have it.

Michael wished them well, but they were stuck on that non-interracial dating stuff. Michael let them know that love is about love and it supports no particular skin color.

Michael had gotten himself into some trouble that weekend, even after Kim had pleaded with him not to get into any kind of trouble. No matter, it was just something that happened and, more than likely, it had to do with Kim visiting him that weekend.

In any case, the day that Kim did come to visit Michael she brought his jewelry along as well. Altogether, she brought his watch, a couple of rings, and his engagement ring. She also brought a one quarter karat diamond ring which was a family heirloom and very expensive.

Michael would always ask about it and she would ask him, "What do you think, I sold it or something?" Then she would ask, "Do you love that stuff more than me and the kids or what?" It was not true of course, but Michael did have affection to material things.

God was testing Michael because he had stuff sneaked in from a visit and then got caught wearing it back from a visit the next day. Kim was so right and she wound up having to take the stuff back. It certainly was not worth having that jewelry in prison. All it would do is get other inmates jealous or they would try to steal it and end up getting Michael in trouble or someone else killed over it.

It was just another temptation leading Michael back to his old behaviors. Another one of so much of what Michael had wanted to stay away from. All the jewelry went back with

Kim except for a 14k gold chain and pendant with diamonds that Michael decided to keep. In the end, the cops wound up taking that from him as well and in return, they gave him an incident report for smuggling contraband. This incident report would definitely have an effect on his upcoming parole hearing.

Michael was concerned about it and put in a great deal of prayer over it. “All that over a necklace that was connected to my old life and some kind of false status,” he said to himself. He would never see that necklace again. Michael could almost be certain that one of the jealous female officers got hold of it just for spiteful purposes. God must have answered his prayers about that whole jewelry incident, as he never heard anything about it and for some reason it seemed to disappear. Thankfully, his parole was not going to be affected and Michael’s parole was obviously most important, as he wanted to go home to be with his family. However, Michael was still having some issues with the person he used to be. There are people who spend a lifetime on the streets building a reputation, but when they get a little older, they have to work twice as hard to change the entire negative image they have created and remove all the material nonsense.

Michael eventually went to his parole hearing and received a twelve-month deferment. It was not what he wanted but it was better than what he could have received, like for example, a twenty-four or thirty-six month deferment. That would have brought him back home to Wisconsin, but unfortunately, it did not happen that way. God just was not finished with Michael yet.

At first, Michael started it the wrong way. He was doing everything he could, like taking all the programs that were offered. He was doing all he could to help himself and others. Michael even took a “Discipleship Training Program” so he could get out of prison and help everyone he could to find his or her salvation. He wanted to be a missionary.

Michael was still an infant in Christ and he was barely being saved himself, but his intentions were more than noble. He just was not fully prepared yet. Michael received another special visit, but this time it was not a good one.

He was called to the mailroom after regular hours, and he knew something had to be wrong. Once arriving at the mailroom, there were some officers waiting for him. They immediately took him to the Warden’s officer. Michael knew it could not be a good thing. “Sit down here,” he was instructed “There is someone here who wants to see you.”

Michael sat there for a while, and then two Federal agents came in. They presented Michael with a subpoena for a handwriting test. “Do you know what this is about?” the agent asked. “Yes,” Michael admitted. “I heard this is because you think I did something.”

Michael sat down and took the test. When he was finished they asked, “Do you have anything else to say?” “No, of course not.” Michael proclaimed. “Are you sure Mr. Brown? This is your last chance.” Michael said, “That sounds like a threat to me!” “Take it however you want,” snorted the Agent.

After they were done with him, he went back to the block and called Kim. She said, “I’m glad that’s over with,” as they, both thought the same about that test. Kim also told Michael that they had been trying to prosecute Rob, Skin, Angie, Stacey, Fossil and Jim and that they had already gone to court for it. That was a real surprise to Michael. After Michael talked to Kim, he called Stacey.

Michael felt the need to make amends with everybody he had hurt and he felt he had offended Stacey. She really thought nothing of it and told Michael to forget about it. She told him that her brother was getting married and she was going to sing at the wedding. Michael wrote a wedding song and mailed it to her.

It was around Christmas time when he called her again. He wanted to know what was going on with her and this whole situation with the Feds. He called her via three ways through his cousin Marketa, as Marketa was friends with Stacey. Stacey did not have much to say, which really was not like her. She told Michael that she was sorry, that none of it was Michael's fault, and that she would try to talk to the Feds. Michael agreed but told that it was just too late for all that now.

He also told her that he loved her and he never meant to hurt her. He let her know that he was trying to fill a void in his heart. She told him that she understood. Michael said that he would keep her in his prayers and he apologized for everything that he had done in his old life that may have put her in any kind of bad situation.

He also talked to her about her salvation and turning to God. "Maybe you are right," she admitted. "I know I am," assured Michael. "I hope that you are right and I wish you all the best," said Stacey

Stacey was even more quiet and different. Something was going on and Michael could not get her to talk about it. All that was left for him to do was to pray for her and everyone else, so that is exactly what he did.

Michael was always spreading the Word and sending God's message to anyone, he thought would listen. He knew Carrie was listening and they began to get closer. She had touched his heart and he had touched hers. It was not anything sexual and it had stayed that way for a long time as Michael and Carrie were like sister and brother. He had her on his visiting list and she was planning to come and visit, but for various reasons it never happened.

Some time passed and Michael received some good news regarding his court motion. He found out that soon he was going to be transferred out of there, but not before more trials and tribulations came along.

A second riot was supposed to be a peaceful protest about food and other prison living conditions. This riot ended up getting worse, when the Assistant Warden's Fiancée was raped and some officers and staff was almost beaten to death. Then Goon Squad was called in and quite a few innocent people were beat up bad. They tear gassed the place and brought in the dogs. Quite a few people were shipped out of the Colorado, Wisconsin Super Max joints, many inmates received new charges, and the entire facility was put on lock-down for months.

"Be a living witness and testify to the world." "Let your walk be your testimony." "Your talents are gifts of God you are given to help God's people and God's purpose."

CHAPTER 33

OLD & NEW FRIENDS, CARRIE'S MURDER, KIM'S MOM MAKES UP

Michael was transferred back to Wisconsin on a writ for his appeal. It was the beginning of spring and the ride back was much smoother than the ride to Tennessee.

Michael's appeal claim was ineffective assistance of counsel. He had to prove he had told his lawyer to do something and it was not done. He was relying on Kim and his mother as witnesses. However, Michael's mother went to a hospital for a medical emergency and Kim did not show up at the evidentiary hearing

He was sad that they were not there; Michael had no choice but to represent himself in a legal sense for the first time. He presented everything correctly and almost won. His lawyer told him a big lie by saying he had never received Michael's motion or messages because his answering machine was broken Thanksgiving which was his reason for not getting Michael's messages. Michael's "stand-by" lawyer told him he would have won if he could have proven it by witnesses. Michael was frustrated and mad as hell that Kim did not show up to help him prove his case. This would have proved to him where she was really coming from. Later on down the road, she tried to fix it with a subsequent affidavit but it was too late.

Once back in Wisconsin, Carrie came to visit Michael and he was glad for her love and support. Not a week would go by that Michael would not hear from Carrie. She wrote to him often and at times, they would talk on the phone for hours. Michael would preach to her as he did with everyone else. He talked about God and His Love with the hope she would be saved. He felt that she was changing for the better because of his preaching and he was glad for that.

Michael was taken to D.C.I. to await his transfer back to the CCA. He wanted to be close to his family so he was doing everything he could to be moved back. Michael was filing motions in court, praying to God and hoping He would listen. Eventually, God did prove that He heard Michael and he got his way. He was able to stay in Wisconsin and Michael knew it was because of the hand of God.

He ended up being assigned to a lower custody and was designated to a joint with work release in Black River Falls, Wisconsin. What a blessing it was to go to a work camp! Michael had to wait in D.C.I. for thirty days before his transfer to Black River Falls. While he was, there he ran into an old family friend named George, who used to be close to Michael's parents back when they lived in the Dardo area during Michael's childhood. Michael always wondered what happened to him, so they talked and reminisced about the old times. He was one of Michael's old friends who taught him about being a man and about hunting, fishing and how to shoot a gun. Michael was glad to see him and thanked him for all he had taught him. Michael also had the opportunity to tell his parents that he seen George and that he was doing okay and so far, so good physically.

His court had given him a sentence of one hundred and twenty-five years for raping his granddaughter. Michael believed that George was innocent, as did George's wife and his younger three kids.

George himself had ten kids in all and a few of them said to tell Michael 'hello' because they remembered him from the old days. Michael talked to George about Jesus, and they had the opportunity to pray together before Michael had to leave for Black River Falls.

Michael arrived at the Black River Falls Correctional Center after stopping in another new joint in Fox Lake. He was now starting to run into a few of his homies whom he knew from the streets. They were all surprised to see him in his new life with God. Many of them originally thought Michael had gone back east or overseas with his music career. They had always wanted to talk about the girls and the money, but Michael did not want to talk about any of that. He now talked about his wife and kids, but more than anything, he talked about Jesus, He shared how he was saved and about what Jesus had done for him. He talked about what he was doing with his life and what he planned on doing for Jesus.

Michael wanted to open a recreation center and a church and get into gospel music, possibly even some form of gospel rap. Michael felt that this is what the Lord was leading him into and he was serious about it.

Most of the dudes just looked at Michael as if he was crazy, but some of them were supportive and told him to go for it. He had his heart set on this and he was not letting anything get in his way.

Kim came to see Michael within two weeks of his arrival in Black River Falls. It was only a two-hour drive from her home. It was still summer and it was a beautiful place. There were picnic tables outside and Michael could not could not wait to play with the kids in the sand box.

As soon as they arrived, Michael could not stop the kids from talking too much. They wanted to play with their dad while Kim cooked up some food on the grill outside, then they ate and held hands. Michael started to think about him and Kim, but it would have been stupid to sneak in the woods to have sex. It was not worth the charge for an attempted escape and being locked up in Super Max with extra years added to his sentence.

Michael would have to admit that he did think about it, but Kim was good at cutting him off with, "We can wait," and "You'll be home soon anyway, and we've already waited this long." Michael did not think it was strange for Kim to want to hold out as she was always patient, but not near as passionate as Michael was.

Kim was looking better than ever to Michael. Neither Michael not Kim had been with anyone for a least a couple of years, but there was something about Kim. She had been talking about other people's relationships about how they were doing and who they were doing it with, but this just was not like Kim. She was not like most girls who were materialistic and she did not tend to discuss other people's business. For that matter, neither did Michael. All Kim ever really wanted before were the necessities of life, but now she was talking about Cadillac trucks and platinum jewelry. She also talked about working with some fine guy who was a firefighter, but Michael thought nothing of it and was never jealous. He loved Kim more than any of that, and did not need to be jealous of her.

Kim also told Michael what she would do if he ever got out and then went back to jail again. He certainly did not like this type of ultimatum, but she would not have to worry about that anyway, so Michael kept quiet about it.

Michael's stay at Black River Falls was not long but he had a ball while he was there. He led by his example and was telling all what God told him. God wanted him to get folks involved with anything that was positive which he did.

From the very first day, there was trouble for him because of the woman who had checked him in. Unfortunately, he knew her from the streets and she knew who he was.

Michael and the woman who checked him into the joint agreed to keep it between themselves and not to mention it to anybody. They both took the risk of being transferred and they did not want that. The place was too sweet for both of them to risk a transfer but it sure did not stop the temptation of flirting, mostly on her part.

She was pretty, but not Michael's type. This girl had to be part Russian or German. One could not really tell by her name, but her size said it all. She was about 6'4" weighed over two hundred pounds, and was not afraid to fight with the biggest men around.

After she got the hint that nothing was happening between her and Michael, she started to flirt with a couple of other guys. Michael made it clear to her that he was a Christian and was trying to live a Christian lifestyle. She was still cool, but she kept her distance from him. Overall, they remained friendly and got along well.

One of Michael's little homies was also there. They called him K.J., but his name was little Fred. He was Michael's brother cellie at a joint in Kettle, Maine. He was very wild and he and Michael kicked it a lot. One of K.J.'s little brothers used to be a manager of one of Michael's rap productions. To Michael, K.J. was no one nice with the ball on the courts. He should have been playing college ball somewhere, but instead he was doing time in prison. He wanted to get out and do the same old thing. That was disconcerting to Michael who was always trying to preach to K.J. and convey to him that if he did the same old thing, he would get the same old results, K.J. of course, was not was not trying to hear any of that from Michael. One day Michael heard him say that he did not did not believe in God and that there was no such thing as Jesus. That was something Michael did not did not want to hear.

The place was cool as far as prison could be, but Michael still did not did not want to be there. Most of the guys there were young and would be fighting all the time with rival gangs. Michael wanted to get out of there in a bad way but they were not about to give him work release. He was trying to move somewhere closer to home.

Soon winter blew in and Michael joined the basketball team as the team captain and with the city league as an assistant coach. The Warden's team played for a city bar and they were the best in the league.

They were undefeated the entire time Michael was there. Michael knew the Warden from the boot camp prison, where he had tried to ride Michael to death but could not. Still Michael admired him for his strength and courage. The Warden had once told Michael years prior that he had built a monster, because Michael was so cut up physically and body builder perfect.

Michael would work out with weights most of his time and went to church twice a week. He had a Bible study class, which he led every night. Occasionally a few people would show up, but mostly it was just Michael, 2 white guys and a preacher's son from Racine Wisconsin.

Michael remembers well the revelation the preacher's son had while he was there. It was heartbreaking and not very positive. While Michael was out working in the wooded area, he heard a voice tell him to read the paper. He only read the paper every once in a while, but this time it was different. He read that her baby's father had murdered his friend Carrie. He shot her in the head and the chest and she bled to death right in front of her child. Michael had plenty of photos of Carrie and he had just heard from her the day before she was murdered.

Michael was really saddened by this. He immediately called Kim. She may not have understood it, but she put up with it mostly because Carrie was respectful towards Kim.

Carrie was not was not the finest, but they were good together. She was pretty, but it was in the core of her heart where her true beauty resided. Michael was glad for their last conversation. Even more than that, he was glad that they had talked about God. He believes he helped her be saved, as they would talk about God all the time and Michael knew that she believed in Jesus as her Lord and Savior. He felt it in his heart that Carrie was in heaven and just knowing that always made Michael feel so much better. He knows that when he gets there himself, he will see her again as Carrie was so much more than just another pretty face, she was Michael's friend.

Kim went to Carrie's funeral and paid their respects. She also donated some money for her child's college fund. Michael wrote a letter to Carrie's mother. He promised to donate a little more money to Carrie's child college fund after he got out of prison.

Carrie was the first girl who worked for Michael in his clubs and escort service. She was also one of the first girls Michael met when he moved from Miami back to Madison.

Butter and Michael nicknamed Carrie; "Dog Pound" because her mother raised grey hounds in their house. She was little, but tough. Quiet as could be, but she had her head together and was gentle.

After Carrie died, Michael decided to move closer to Madison. He started sending his resume to different prisons for higher qualifying jobs, such as a cook or a driver. That got him approved to go to Winnebago Correctional Center (W.C.C.), which was just one hour north of Madison.

Before he left for W.C.C., he was offered work release if he would stay, but he wanted to get closer to his family. In Black River Falls the only place a person could secure a job was with the local wood factory.

Michael thought he stood a better chance of landing a better job in another place, so he left Black River Falls in gratitude of the hard work that helped make him bigger and stronger physically. Just prior to leaving, he had a strange experience. It came in a box. Michael's favorite officer called him to the office after inspecting the present. "There is more to this than what it says," he was told. Michael had received two thermal work shirts that were obviously really nice and expensive. He thought the gift was from Kim at first, but it was not was not. It came with a card from Kim's mother, and written in the card was, "Merry Christmas," and it said, "Hope this finds you in good health and hope you get out soon, so that you can be with your family and kids. Your kids are such jewels and a pleasure to be with." It really touched Michael's heart. It was not was not what the card said, but that Kim's mother had sent it. Michael saved that card and still has it to this day.

Michael and Kim's mother never really got along or even talked. He had thought that she hated his guts because he was black, but now he had to consider that maybe he had been wrong. Michael had known Kim for almost twenty years, in that time they had been homies, lovers and best friends. Michael never did anything purposely to hurt Kim. One thing for sure was that he had never put his hands on her, he never called her a name and they never had any serious arguments. He would rather just walk away and leave the situation if it got bad, which would really get Kim in fury, and he knew that, but he loved her more than anything.

Kim and Michael shared a very special love. She could not really comprehend how much he loved her and Michael wanted Kim's parents to accept the fact because he sure was not was not going to give up on her. This time Michael was completely serious about changing and just maybe Kim's mother believed him. It could have been something she heard Kim say as the only time Michael and Kim's mother ever spoke at length, was while Kim was pregnant.

Fifteen years into their relationship, Kim and her mother were going to buy some baby clothes for Michael Jr. They did that a lot when Kim was pregnant, but her mother would always call before coming over and then she would wait in the parking lot. Once she went over and saw that Michael was leaving did she say "Hi?" She acted as if Michael had a tail and he would bite or that he stunk as some people believed about the black race.

Michael was very nice and respectful to anyone who was nice and respectful to him, and even to some who were not Michael always thought it was Kim's mother who would call and hang up when he answered the phone. Then she would call back and talk to Kim when she answered. Maybe it was all in Michael's head, but Kim would never say anything about it to him.

Michael did not did not usually out of his own house. If he did, he had enough sense and respect to do it when Kim was not was not around Michael knew Kim's position and respected Kim's mother. He also did not did not smoke weed around his Pops out of respect for the way he thought.

Kim used to say, it was not was not true that he mom hung up when he answered, but Michael felt that it was.

Almost twenty years had gone by since the time her mother came back from an out of town trip and caught Michael and Kim in bed together after a late night party. She was really tripping and said, "Get that 'nigga' out of my house!" Michael had to admit, he might have had the same reaction if it had been his daughter, but Michael is not and was not was not a racist. Michael now thought he may have been wrong about Kim's mother, but he still never forgot when she caught them both in bed. Back then, Michael was living the life of a crook and both of Kim's parents worked in law enforcement, so they were protective of her. Her mother was a welfare fraud inspector and her stepfather had been a County Sheriff his entire life.

Michael would not want someone like himself for his own daughters and all Kim's parents really knew about Michael was what they heard through rumors, and various police reports they read. To know Michael is to love him or at least that is what he thought.

The only thing Michael wanted from Kim's parents was to be respected and he would give them the same. He also wanted them to know that he loved their daughter and that she was happy and had nothing to worry about. Michael really did want to get along with them and would have liked to go wherever his wife and kids went for family gatherings such as Christmas and other holiday outings, but it just never happened that way. It was Michael's hard-earned money that bought their gifts; he should have been permitted to see them receive them. No such luck.

He was happy when he received Kim's mother card. He politely wrote back to express his thanks and he told her that he was coming out of prison a new man. Michael wrote that he was now crime and drug free and he walked with Jesus. In order to stay positive and productive, Michael hoped they could at least get along, because he loved their daughter so much and would never give up on her. He prayed to show this even more to Kim.

"Be faithful with the little gifts God gives to you, and he will give you more." "As we get closer to God, He gets closer to us, but we must make the first move. God forces Himself on nobody, but the devil will try us repeatedly. After each time comes a bigger blessing from God."

CHAPTER 34

ARRESTED, CHARGED AND A FEDERAL INDICTMENT

Michael left for Winnebago, Wisconsin in January. The place was nice and situated between two State Prisons. The prison had a D.A.T.C., (Drug and Alcohol Treatment Center) which was a low security treatment facility. Behind that was a block of buildings connected to the State hospital. There was an O.S.C.I., which was a State Medium Security prison in front of them about a half mile away. This was the biggest joint in the state and it was filled with sexual offenders.

W.C.C. was situated on Lake Winnebago with a beautiful view of the lake. This lake was known around the world for its Sturgeon, where caviar comes from. There were not were not fences like at most minimum-security prisons. It was built like an apartment complex, right in the city of Winnebago, a small town next to Oshkosh, which was a slightly bigger town that had a major University. Twenty minutes from there was North Green Bay.

This facility had work and school release programs for about one hundred prisoners. A few of them served as maintenance men for the joint. Michael was designated to be a driver and maintenance man, and got paid for both jobs.

Inmates on work release had regular jobs. Some of those dudes had thousands of dollars in their accounts, but most of them had to pay restitution. Michael worked as a trainee and learned the routes. He drove more than one hundred people to work on a daily basis. There were probably about ten different stops.

Michael was also a vehicle maintenance man. He was paid a few hundred dollars a month for each job and he did not did not have to pay rent. Only the work release program guys had to pay rent. Michael had a lot of freedom, if there was such a thing while serving time in prison.

Michael drove all around Appleton, Oshkosh and the surrounding cities. He went to Waupun a few times picking up some washers and dryers at a bunkhouse that had been converted into a women's prison. He would also go to Madison a few times during the week to move equipment for officers to the new W.D.O.C. building.

While driving, the desire to see Kim and the kids was always there and many times in a bad way. He told Kim about his trip, but she told him, "Do not do it Michael," she had warned. "You could get caught and get in a lot of trouble, you do not want that right? Plus, you do not want to lose your job either."

Michael was there for months and always just an hour away from home, but Kim still had not come to visit him. He thought that maybe it was the weather or perhaps she was just too busy, but for some reason something always came up and she could not make it.

Michael knew that something was not was not right. He chalked it up to the devil's workings so that he would not believe anything was wrong concerning Kim. He began getting weird feelings about all the reasons why she never came to see him, but he tried to ignore those feelings because he thought it was not was not worth worrying too much about it as he would be going home soon and nothing else mattered.

Michael was working out at the weight pile everyday, which was a good way to vent uneasy feelings. The institution permitted the inmates to buy and use bodybuilding supplements, which Michael did to continue his health and top physical condition. He had access to the kitchen, and since Michael was a great cook, he took full advantages of that as well.

He was also taking some correspondence courses for college credits and paying for them himself. He figured his classes were going to be a big help some day and he wanted to go into a legitimate business once he was released.

Michael had been at W.C.C. a few months, just doing his thing on a daily basis and he had his schedule down. His first priority was God's work and telling it to the world.

Michael had a choice to do some other things offered to him there. He did volunteer work at the old folk's home. They would go out and clean up storm damage as well as painting and moving at the V.F.W. hall

Michael wanted so badly to get into town to familiarize himself back into public life. This prison camp was all about transitioning back into the community and it gave him plenty of practice. Michael quite often went into town to buy stuff for the prison, get things serviced and wash vehicles.

One day he was working like crazy and had just come back from making a run but instead of relaxing and kicking back, Michael went into the library to get some current news from the newspaper. For some reason he felt drawn to the library.

He picked up the paper that some older guy had just set down. The guy used to be a lawyer and accountant. He even looked and acted the part.

Michael looked at the Milwaukee paper, beginning with the front page. In it was a story that mentioned his name or someone with the same names as him and his friends. Michael continued to read that this individual had been indicted with Rob Sutton and James Fleming. The rest of the people were Victor Caldwell, Stacey Pete, Alphonso Dean, Nicole Wampole and Angie Cramer. It seems that they all had pleaded guilty and took a deal to testify against Michael Brown and Rob for a string of armed robberies in the Madison area.

Michael could not believe was he was reading and even more he could not imagine what it meant. He had to read it over repeatedly to fully understand it. When he had finished an older white guy who had read the paper before him said, "Is that you Mr. Brown? Or is it someone who has the same name as you?" Then he asked, "Are you alright? Is there something wrong?" Michael could hardly hear or understand what the guy was saying, but it was obvious from the look on his face. It was as if he had been hit right between the eyes.

Michael did not did not even know how the old white guy knew his name and he could not remember ever talking to him before. "No it's not me," Michael told him. "It's intended to be, but I have nothing to do with this or these people that are involved."

Michael snatched up the paper and asked him not to tell anyone else about the story. He said okay, but Michael had no way of knowing whether the guy would keep his word. The next thing Michael did was give Kim a call and she began crying.

Kim was trying to hide it, but it was obvious he telling her about what he had just read upset her. This gave Michael more reason for concern. "Kim, they got me in the papers and I've been indicted for some stuff with Rob and Skin," he told her. "I know," she said. "People have been calling me about it all day long and it's also on the news," she informed him. “What did it say on the news?” he asked without thinking. “They are saying that you will be going to prison for a very long time.” Michael asked, “Prison, for what?” and adding, “I haven’t done anything. I did not have anything to do with Skin and Rob’s craziness!”

Kim said, “I know baby, just calm down, okay.” Michael said, “Yeah, but I need to see the police reports, because I do not even know what the indictment says.” Kim said, “I’ll call my people and see if we can get a copy of it.” Michael told Kim that if she was not able to get a copy of the charges, they would try something else. “Mike,” Kim advised. “Whatever you do, do not talk to anyone. Do not say anything okay? Not one word, do you understand me?” He told her not to worry. Then she said, “And whatever you do, do not run. I’ll be here for you baby.”

He was upset for doing the right thing but was even more upset for associating with his so-called friend. There was no excuse for the others to place blame on him for something he never did. Michael was disgusted and left the building and went back to work with all the terrible thoughts on his mind.

Michael called Kim again to tell her about the feelings he did not did not like. “You know that I do not have anything to do with this, do not you?” Michael asked. “I do not know why they are coming after me as I do not deserve any of this.” Michael asked himself aloud, “Why me Lord? I have changed, and you know that I am not the same person I used to be. I have given my life to you for years now!”

Kim said, “Baby, you are going to have to trust Him now and leave it in His hands.” Michael said, “I told those people the truth every time they came to question me and if it was not for me they would not even have a case!” Kim said again, “You did not do anything and you have to trust in what you believe, which is God!”

Kim was hardly a believer, but she was making sense this time. Michael admitted, “You are right.” He did not did not even have to ask and it was as if she could read his mind. “Do not worry baby, I’ll be here,” Kim promised. “I’m not going anywhere, and do not you go anywhere either,” she commanded. “Do not you run off or do anything stupid, please promise me that baby.” Michael went back to work and back to the business of driving and fixing things around the prison, but things stayed on his mind. It was the following weekend that Kim finally came to visit him and see how he was doing.

Throughout that time, Michael called several lawyers to no avail-not a single lawyer would take his calls. He did not did not have any more money and they probably knew that. They could smell blood and they knew that Michael was not was not worth their time. Michael was adamant and wrote them letters, but he got no response. Therefore, he did the next best thing and that was to speak to an accountant who was in prison, and who had already been through law school. He was a great jailhouse lawyer and he told Michael, “Well, it can't be too serious, not about you anyway, because it’s already been a week and they haven’t been here yet, and they knew where you are.” Michael thought he was right about that part.

Michael wanted to know what was happening and why, He continued to read his Bible regularly as he always did sometimes until he could not keep his eyes open any longer.

Michael talked to another jailhouse lawyer whom had also been to law. This guy pretty much told Michael the same thing the first jailhouse lawyer had told him, saying: “Until you get the full discover and the story, we won't know what is really happening." He also showed Michael some statues on things pertaining to conspiracy. The arraignment was scheduled on March 16. It was in the paper the same day.

Kim came to see Michael and she had a list of the charges against him. This really put Michael in a zone of sorts, as he could not believe what he was reading. He did not did not know that his friends had done all these crimes. Michael was charged in the last five of their twenty-one charges.

The first was a robbery at Wendy's. Michael did not did not know anything about that before it happened and had heard about it after the fact. He only remembered part of it because it was either Stacey or Vic who told him a joke about it. It had something to do with Fossil not being able to fit through the drive-thru window because he was too large of a man. Even with hearing that about Fossil, Michael was not was not sure, if it was true or not because he thought, it was just a joke about being fat.

The second was a robbery at Kohl's. Michael had heard Skin planning and talking about that for months. He did not did not think Skin would actually go through with it. The first time Michael heard about it, he was at home. Skin called Jim to ask Michael to bring his girlfriend Brandy out to where he was and to bring him some dope.

He said he had money with him at the time, so Michael took Brandy, and some dope to Skin. That was the first time Michael learned they had been doing things with Stacey. Upon arriving, Stacey answered the door and Michael's first thought was that they were screwing around. That made Michael a little jealous and disappointed, but Stacey had told Michael that she loved him and he felt stupid.

He did not did not know that it was Kohl's until they told him about it. He also saw food stamps and banded moneybags with Kohl's name on them.

Michael had been at his house the entire night when the Kohl's robbery went down. Rob had come by to wash some of his clothes at Michael's house, and brought rolls of quarters and gave them to Michael and Kim for using their washer and dryer.

The next was a robbery at the Great Northwest Bank. They had to have been crazy for robbing that bank.

Kim was always nagging Michael to go out and get a regular job. She also nagged him about where he had been all night and for hanging out with those dudes.

Skin had called asking Michael to come out to Milwaukee, making it sound like it was an emergency or something and that he was not was not planning to come back. Michael thought he was joking about that and did not did not believe him until he said he was serious. He had said all that same type of stuff before and Michael told him that is he needed to get back home to Madison, just as he had said many times before, that he would send him a bus ticket as soon as he got up. Skin, on the other hand, said it was not was not like that. He told Michael that he had plenty of money and that, if anything, Skin owed him.

Michael knew he was serious then, so he went up to Milwaukee. When Michael arrived, he learned where the money had come from but still accepted it.

The fourth count was a robbery at the Movie Gallery. This was a dope fiend move by Fossil and Jim. Michael had to tell Kim where he was the night that happened. It seems that night he had been hanging with Stacey at her place. Michael could see the look in her eyes and he did not did not know whether she wanted to hit him or what as she was pissed off. It hurt Michael more than anything to open up an old wound, but he wanted her to know the whole truth. Michael had noted to Stacey that Fossil and Jim were trying to be like Skin and Rob, which was not, was not a good thing.

Before they left, he gave them all a hug and a kiss. Michael could feel something was wrong when he kissed Kim. He did not did not know what it was, but something just was not was not the same. It was not was not a bad feeling, but it was not was not right either. If he could have known things were going to happen as they did, he would have taken off at that moment.

He discussed this with Kim but she told him not to do it. "Do not forget about me and the kids Michael, if you did that, you would be leaving us forever," she reminded. "I could send for you and we could live free, until I prove my innocence," Michael told her. Kim told Michael not to do it or even consider it anymore. She begged him not to leave them, and most of all, not to run.

A few days later, Michael was called to the counselor's office. He thought that maybe this was it, but when he got there, he was asked to sign some papers for his upcoming parole hearing. The counselor said they were going to let him go home.

Michael's parole hearing was not was not until June, which was about two months away. He had already completed most of his time in prison as well as all of his programs, so it seemed more than likely he would be paroled. Michael had been in the camp for more than a year. Overall, it had been almost three years without incident.

A few days later, Michael was back from work after dropping off some of the guys when he was called to the front office. He thought it was strange, as he had just left there. The officer who usually talked to him was being very quiet.

It was for the nurse, and she had some refills for him. Michael was thinking he was going crazy. It had been only two weeks since his indictment, but at the same time, he was not was not feeling right. He decided to call Kim about what had just happened. Out of nowhere, after being quiet for a moment, she said, "I'm going to have to raise these kids without a father!" Michael had no clue where that came from.

"Why are you tripping?" he asked. "If you remember, I did not do anything. I'm innocent, remember?" Kim started to cry. "I do not know Michael, I am really scared," she sobbed. Kim never used to call him Michael she always called him Mike or Baby.

Michael tried to calm her down by saying. "Just remember Kim I am innocent, and I will be able to prove it." She said she knew that.

Michael thought for a moment about what the government had done to Timothy McVeigh. He was about to be executed that very day at the Terra Haute Prison in Indiana. He had won his appeal because of government misconduct. Some dirty cops withheld important information that could have helped him, but he had decided he did not did not want to appeal of fight, as he just wanted to go out as a man, plus he had already confessed. Michael told himself, "I hate this government which is racist, and will do anything to make a bogus case just to assure they win."

Michael told Kim, "everything would be alright", and she calmed down a little bit. Then he said, "I got to go."

Michael got off the phone and went to his room. He immediately got down on his knees and prayed to God with great intensity. So much so, that he did not even hear himself being called back down to the office. In a moment of clarity, Michael heard his name being called and got up to head down to the office.

As he did, he looked out the window and saw the lock-up van parked out front. It was the only one with a cage in the back. Michael thought someone was being locked up and thought that this was it. He went down to see what they wanted. First, he stopped at the nurse's office and asked her if she wanted him. She said she did not and pointed to the office. "They came and got your medical charts for some reason," she told him.

Then Michael knew. He could feel it. It was like April fool's day, but this was no joking matter. He stepped into the office and they said, "Come in Mr. Brown." Then they closed the door and Michael was told to sit down. "We hate to inform you of this, but we have to take you to lock-up. The Feds have a warrant for your arrest."

Michael was dumbfounded. "Wow," he said, "What for?" he asked with no real surprise in his voice of facial expression. "Did you know about this before?" they asked him. "Somewhat," Michael admitted. They all looked at each other as if they did not did not believe him and then someone said, "I hope you are right, because the Feds do not play and you seem like a good kid." He put the cuffs onto Michael's wrists. "Would you like to call somebody?" he asked Michael. He responded with, "Yes please." Michael called Kim and said, "Baby, they came to get me. They have a Federal warrant out for my arrest and they're taking me to the Oshkosh Medium Institution." Kim advised Michael not to tell them anything. "I'll be there for you baby," she promised. Kim sounded better than she did earlier, but still Michael could tell something was wrong. He just did not did not know what it was.

"Going to Church. It is better for you not to know the truth than to know the truth and do nothing. Religion is nothing but a political word. A relationship with God is what we must have. We must return to our first love, with the Lord and Creator of love. Cry out to the Lord for help and he will help. He will answer; he is the only one, and He is our Holy Father."

CHAPTER 35

THE INDICTMENT & DISCOVERY FROM THE FEDS THE WITNESSES,

On March 15, 2001, a 21-count indictment was filed in U.S. District Court, Western District of Wisconsin against Michael L. Brown, James Fleming, and Robert Sutton. Brown was named in 9 of the 21 firearm and robbery counts. Fleming was named in 19 and Sutton was named in 7 counts. The offenses occurred between January 29, 1997 and January 24, 1998.

They took Michael to Oshkosh and put him in the hole for a couple of days. He had a cellie, but he did not did not really talk to him or anybody else.

All Michael did was pray. He was crying on the inside because everything was just so overwhelming for him. To take his mind off things, Michael would read his Bible and write letters to Kim every day. He was scared now and was probably scaring her as well. Kim did not did not reply to any of his letters and he could not reach her on the phone either.

While he was in the hole, Michael saw a guy that he had met in prison a few years prior. His name was Tyron and he was from California.

After some time passed Michael finally got out of the hole and was put in the barracks. Michael had been to Oshkosh several years before during his first prison term. The barracks were open dorms with about two hundred bunks in each.

The day Michael got to the yard, he ran into another old school homie he had known from the hood when they were kids. It was Maurice Weathers a.k.a. Lil Mo whom Michael had not seen since his college days. It was funny how they called him Lil Mo because if anything, he was not was not little at all. He was about six feet tall and all of two hundred sixty pounds of solid muscle. This dude was nothing to play with. The last time he had talked to Mo was when he was at the State Boot Camp ten years prior.

He called home to his girlfriend Ingo and Mo got on the phone to tell Michael not to call there anymore because she was his woman now. Michael had not called there in a while and he had not seen her for a while.

The last thing Michael had heard from Mo had come in the form of a threat. Mo told Michael that he was going to kill him because he had whipped his kid, Marcus. Michael knew and had raised Marcus. To see Lil Mo after all that, he just was not was not sure what to expect. No matter, as Michael did not did not have a problem with fighting anyone only if that was what was needed. Mo asked, “What did you do?” Michael told Mo how the Feds had indicted him. Mo’s eyes got bigger and said, “Damn man,” which did not make Michael feel any better, but Michael told him right away, “I’m going to beat it, because I did not do it.”

Michael told, “Man I’m not the same person I used to be. I’m with God now, but I do not have a problem fixing any problems.” Mo said, “I do not have any problems with you either and if you are talking about that thing with Marcus, that’s old and I should be thanking you from saving him from his mother and all that other stuff.”

Michael was shocked to hear what Mo was saying because it just was not was not like him. He was a wannabe killer and bully, but he had never pulled any of his talk on Michael. Mo started to ask about Michael’s music business and the clubs, and Michael told him that was not was not his life anymore. "Maybe some other time because I have to go and pray." "Okay dude," Mo allowed. "I'll catch you later then."

Michael was there for about a week before they finally came to get him to face the federal charges. Before they did Michael spoke with Tyron. Michael told him what happened and Tyron just shook his head and said, "Dude, I told you about those dirty Feds and those white girls," which was what he was in for. Then Tyron started telling jokes, because he saw that what he was saying was upsetting Michael. Michael was also introduced to many other guys, most of who acted as if he was some sort of celebrity.

Michael was taken to face the federal charges. In route, one of the officers was talking about Tim McVeigh and how people think just like him. The officer said he thought that those who did should be killed with him. Michael got to thinking they may have heard him over the phone. He really did not did not feel that way; he just said crazy things when he was mad like most people do.

It was not was not until later that he learned there were a lot of innocent men, women and children in that building. Many of them were black people. Michael was a Christian now, and he loved and cared for everyone, it was just that he was mad that day and spouting off at the mouth.

Michael was taken to the county jail that served as a Federal holding facility. He knew most everyone there and noticed a jail employee that he knew. It was Ingo's cousin, Sara, who was a black girl.

They put Michael into a cell with another homie he used to do business with, who was the Prince of the Black Pea Stones, Stacey Miller.

He said, "What's up man?" Then he asked Michael what they had him in for? Michael knew that he already knew what he was there for, but Michael told him anyway and said that the Feds indicted him.

Stacey told Michael about his career and how it had taken off since he had last seen him. Michael was the one who had brought him into the music business, the promotions and production end of it. Now he was facing federal charges and being indicted for drug conspiracy. Like Michael, he also thought he could beat it and only get a couple of years at the worst.

Michael took him in and made a big investment of cash with him. Michael was glad he could help him out, but it had caused a whole bunch of other problems and created new enemies. It also got Michael labeled as a gang member, particularly as a Vice Lord and because of that, Michael began to go downhill and it caused them to part ways.

Michael told Stacey Miller exactly what he told everyone else, that he was a new man with God. Michael was looking to get out and preach the Word of God and do God's work. He also told Stacey that he had no hard feelings about the past and that he was keeping his focus on his case as well as keeping his mind on the Lord.

After a couple of days, Michael went to court. It was his first appearance and he was appointed an attorney. This was also the first time he saw Rob and Skin in quite a while. When he got to the courtroom-holding cell, Skin was already there. Skin could not really see where Michael was, but Michael could hear him loud and clear echoing through the holding area. His voice was like no other, and it would come out at the trial against Michael.

Skin either heard Michael talking or when they called his name out, “Mike is that you? What are you doing here?” Skin yelled out. Michael thought for a moment and then yelled back. “I do not know, you tell me. I had nothing to do with this and whatever it was you did, you have done to yourself.” Skin said, “You sure did not do anything and I do not know what the hell you are doing here.”

There was not was not much talking between them after that. Then Rob came in as always he was laughing and smiling. He acted as if he was having a good time, but then Michael could not see him either. Michael just knew his laughter, but he could not see what there was to laugh about.

Rob yelled, “What’s happening?” Michael said, “I do not know. You tell me.” Rob said that he did not did not know either. “You are the last person I would have expected to see here, Mike.” Michael said, “Yeah me too!” Rob asked, “Where are all the others, like Stacey, Angie, Vic and I'm?” Michael told him that he did not did not know and that he did not did not know anything about the whole thing.

“I was at a camp and about to go home in a few weeks,” Michael told him. “I’ve been out of state doing most of my time in Tennessee,” Michael said. Skin said, “I’ve been in Portage Max doing life for my other robberies.” “Life?” Michael asked in surprise. “It may as well be 500 years, I’ve been on lock down for drug dealing in prison,” said Skin. “That’s crazy man; you haven’t learned a thing, have you?” Michael asked him.

They went into the courtroom and Michael’s lawyer came in late. He introduced himself, “You must be Michael Brown, and I’m Joe Summers. I’m glad I was assigned to you as you are the least involved according to the indictment.” Michael responded, “I did not do any of this!” “Then you should be glad you got me to defend you.” said the lawyer. “I am the best there is.” Already the lawyer had been late to court, and he had not been to see Michael yet, whereas Rob and Skin had met their lawyers weeks and months prior to this court date. They had come to them earlier that day to talk to them as well. Michael should have known something was up.

They were told all the charges against them and the sentence they faced. All Michael remembered was that he was facing life in prison without the possibility of parole for something he did not did not even do.

After the court hearing, Joe the lawyer came to see Michael and told him not to worry. “I really think you can get off.” Michael tried to tell him something, but he did not did not want to hear it. He told Michael to tell him later, because he had to go. “We’ll be getting the discovery within 30 days and then we’ll talk more okay? If you have anything before then, there, here is my card. Call me and I’ll talk to you,” said the lawyer.

Michael was taken back to his cell and told to pack his things because they were going to move him to a more secure cell. He moved to cellblock 619 in the newer part of the jail, and everyone in there was facing some real serious time or a parole violation.

There was this one dude named Eric Moral, whose brother was the lightweight boxing champion of the world, as well as another Lil homie from Milwaukee, who claimed to know Michael. Michael did not did not know the dude. Michael was there a couple of days before he considered calling Kim.

Michael was hoping that nothing much was happening with her, as he had not heard from her in a while, but just knowing that got him to worrying about what was going on. One morning while he was in the shower, his name was called for mail. Being that he was busy taking his shower; he asked if one of the brothers would get it for him. Michael was kind of hoping it would be some money or good news from Kim because she had not gone to court as he had expected her to. Michael could only hope everything was okay with her and the kids.

When he finished his shower, he found the letter on his bunk. Surprisingly, it was from Skin. As Michael read it, he thought it might be some sort of trap as he used to trust Skin, but not anymore. As he read, he was surprised that it was something good. It read, "Mike I'm sorry about all this, because you had nothing to do with any of this. All you ever did was tried to help us." Skin also wrote that he would do whatever he could to help Michael prove he was innocent and get him out of it. In the meantime, he told Michael to talk to his lawyer and get back to a prison that has enough legal materials where he could gather more information to prove his innocence. Skin also said that others had been asking him questions about Michael. He explained that he told them all; that Michael did not did not have anything to do with any of his crimes. Skin continued to say that he told them it was all his idea and his plan.

With the letter fresh in his mind, Michael immediately called his lawyer because he believed this letter would be helpful as favorable evidence in his case. The entire plan for the robberies was Skin's idea and his name was on almost every count of the indictment.

Michael's lawyer did eventually come to see Michael and told him, "Yes, this is good stuff and yes we can and will use it as evidence in your case." He also told Michael to bring anything else that he thought would be of help. He advised Michael not to write either one of his co-defendants or anyone else about the case. Michael told him that he understood and then went back to his cell too exhausted to even call Kim. It already had been a few weeks and still he had not heard from her. He was beginning to wonder what was going on. He eventually caught up with her but she was not was not saying much. "What's going on Kim?" he asked her. He knew it was a lie when she said "Nothing!" Needing some funds, he asked her if she could please bring him a couple of dollars. She responded by saying that she would, but also acted as if she did not did not want to talk to Michael and she hurried to get off the phone. "I love you," Michael said to her. Kim barely said it back to him and was really quiet as if she did not did not want to say it. "I love you too," she said quietly. She did not did not say anything else and then Michael said, "Everything's going to be alright Kim. You watch," Michael assured her. "I'll prove my innocence and get out of here," and he hung up the phone. Little did he know that months would pass before he spoke to Kim again.

Michael had been in the jail for about a month. He was supposed to have been taken back to the state prison after a couple of days. He certainly wanted to return there to have access to the legal library. He knew that the best thing he could do at the moment by learning the law as well as studying his case.

He called his lawyer to try to get him a court order to return to the prison and it was soon granted. After finally returning back to the prison, he found that he had a bunch of fan mail from both people he knew as well as many that he did not did not know. The majority of the mail was from women but none from who he wanted to hear from the most, Kim.

It took almost a month before Michael received his discovery documents. As he had waited, he studied the Federal statutes that he was indicted under, plus the Federal Rules of Criminal Procedure and the Rules of Evidence. The lawyer was not was not lying when he said it was like a foreign language.

It took all of Michael's intelligence to make heads or tails of what he was studying. Upon finally receiving, the documents his lawyer made an appointment to see him. Michael thoroughly studied his law books until he knew every word, where it was, and how to find it.

Every person who is indicted for a criminal offense should study the law and their case very thoroughly, as a lawyer does not have the vested interest that the accused person does. A lawyer is likely to miss important defense issues. What surprised Michael the most was how many lies were told and how his name came up as being involved in things he was not even close to being involved with.

In the beginning, no one had stated that Michael was involved in anything. Then after his name came up, not one of the co-defendants stories fit together until after they made statements, which were obviously coached. Michael's lawyer noticed this as well and said he could tell they were obviously lying. Now he had to prove that they had been coached and were lying. He had to get the jury to see it too.

The lawyer said he could do it, but he would need Michael's help. He told Michael if he could think of anything or anyone who could help, to please let him know and he would get on top of it. "Is that fair enough?" the lawyer asked. "Fair enough," Michael agreed. Michael thought it sounded good and then wondered if the lawyer was only placating him. He would soon find out.

Michael told Joe that his greatest fear was of the jury, because there was a great deal of racism in the Madison area. Common white folks would not understand how Michael lived and did not did not like black guys like him. Joe said that he would not go to trial with prejudiced people on the jury and that it was going to be a tough road ahead. Joe also told Michael that it would be best if he was to go to the Dane County Jail, so they would not have any more mix-ups. This was probably why it supposedly took so long for the discovery to get back to Michael as it had been sent to the Oxford Federal Prison because it was thought Michael was there.

That should have been a warning to Michael, but he chalked it up to as an accident. Joe convinced Michael that it would be best for him to move and he promised he would come see him at least once a week; just to be sure, things were okay. Michael agreed to the transfer and it was arranged at the next court date, which was only a month away.

As the days went by, Michael got deep into his case. He could remember things and was learning new things. He remembered quite well, who had been around him and other details that were very important… Everything that he remembered and learned, he sent to his lawyer.

After a time, the lawyer sent him a letter telling him that he had more than enough information for his case. He told Michael that he wrote too much and had too many questions. So many questions that the lawyer said it would be better if he just came to visit him to answer all the questions he asked.

Michael was really wired and he thought it was all good, important information. After all, it was his life that was on the line. The lawyer told him the last guy who had a case similar to Michael's went crazy with all the thinking and questions and it appeared to the lawyer that Michael seemed like that kind of guy. On the other hand, Michael did not did not really appreciate his tone of comparing him as such, so he wrote and told him that he was out of line talking like that and that he did not did not have time for nonsense like that.

Michael gathered all of his paperwork together for the motions the lawyer was going to file for more discoveries and for a severance to get a separate trial. Michael told the lawyer that Skin was willing to give them a statement for Michael's benefit and that he would tell the truth. The truth being that Michael was not involved in any part of the robberies. Skin was willing to help Michael get the severance and the lawyer said that he would use that during the trial to help him, but for some reason he never brought it up during the trial.

They went to court a few weeks later for several motions. Unfortunately, Michael did not did not win a single motion. After learning about all that, Michael realized that this was going to be one very heavy case.

Michael stayed in the county jail while he fought for an extension of time and he was fortunately granted that one motion but had to push his lawyer to do that. Time was quickly passing by and they were only a month or so from trial. The lawyer had still not spoken to any of Michael's witnesses. Needless to say, he was getting very frustrated with how things were proceeding.

When Michael went back to court the second time they stopped and picked up Rob from Fox Lake State Prison. They rode to court together without saying much of anything. Michael was really angry because he knew that were it not for Rob and Skin, he would not be where he was.

Rob broke the ice by asking Michael how his mom, Kim and the kids were holding up. "I guess they're okay." Michael said. "I haven't talked to them in a while, but to my surprise my mom did come to see me while I was back at the prison." Michael had cried like a baby because he was so glad to have seen her.

They talked mostly about old times and Michael's brothers and sisters. Michael felt there was something his mother was not was not telling him but he could not be sure. His mother was supportive and Michael told her just like he told everyone else, that he had nothing to do with the crimes they are trying him for. "I am totally innocent!" he told her. He also admitted that he was scared, especially of having to have his fate determined by an all white jury and of dying in prison with no family around. "I know Michael, but please do not worry because that's not going to happen," his mother assured him, which was exactly what Michael needed to heat at the time.

Rob said he knew and that he had talked to Kim. Now Michael was really mad as he thought, "How in the heck would he know something like that?" "You talked to Kim? What's up with that?" Michael asked. Rob said, "I'm in the same cell as your brother and I wanted to talk to Tracy." Michael knew there was more to it than that, but he told himself to just forget it. He did not did not say anything more about Kim or the situation.

When they got to the jail, Michael saw someone who had been very close to him but that he had not seen in many years. It was his brother. He was back in jail for some petty theft charge. He had come back to court and was in the bullpen waiting to go to prison, so the officers let them visit together for a little while.

Michael let the officers know that they had not seen each other in years and thanked them for allowing such time. They first hugged and then talked for a minute. Michael told his brother that he better stay out of jail. He told him that he should surrender his life to Jesus and asked him to look out for his kids. He said he would look out for Michael's kids, but he did not did not know about the Jesus thing, as he did not did not believe in all of that. "Why not?" Michael asked his brother, "It's the truth we were taught by our grandmother," he affirmed. "It's the best thing we can do with our lives," he said.

Michael's brother gave him his girlfriend's phone number and told him to call her if he needed anything. "I'm serious Mike," he added. Michael said that he would and said, "You have way too much time on your hands in jail. You are almost twenty years in and out of here man, you have to learn to do something different, and Jesus is truly the only way," he preached to him.

He looked at Michael and he knew Michael was not was not playing and said, "Okay bro." Then Michael was taken back to cellblock 619, the pre-trial cellblock.

Michael entered the door and saw a couple of guys there that he knew. Lil' Danny Williams and this little dude from Milwaukee, who was in the cell block next door to Michael when he was brought from his court hearings. Besides Danny, Michael was the second oldest and second biggest person. Danny was shorter than Michael, but he was a legend. He was always muscular, but he was not was not right then. All the drinking and partying had caught up with him and his body. Danny was there for a drunk driving accident and was about to go back to prison. It was not was not anything new to him as he had been there several before. One of those times for armed robbery. After they got to talking, Michael told him that he could have a chance on getting his health back and getting in shape again, by being right with Jesus.

He did not did not like what Michael said at first, but after he thought about it, he knew Michael was right. He knew he was going to prison. He was caught red-handed and had confessed to the crimes. He was hoping he would only get county jail time rather than prison time, but things did not did not look too good for Danny.

Like Michael, he knew what it was like to go back in when a person feels they are better than that. Danny and Michael had not talked for a couple of different reasons, even though they were about the same age and they had known each other since they were kids. Danny was really close friends with Skin and his cousin. So close that they even called each other cousins. Danny knew why Michael was there because he had seen it on the news. Since Danny was so close with Skin, he thought that Michael would be mad at him too, but that was not was not the case at all. Michael told him that he was a man and a born again Christian and that it was not was not in him to be that way. Danny also knew Michael was innocent and he told him that he thought so.

Danny knew how Skin was. They had been close for a while and when Skin was on the run, Danny had been the only guy Skin had come back to see.

Skin told Danny everything, as they had been robbery partners before. Surprisingly, Danny ended up telling Michael all about his case as well as about some of the other robberies. It took Michael a minute to absorb what he was saying and then he said, "Danny, I know you know the truth and that Skin's your boy, but I'm innocent and I'm asking you to help me out." Danny said, "Why do you think I am telling you all of this? I want to help you, but I am not lying for anybody," he told Michael. "I'm not asking you to lie," Michael assured him. "I'm talking about the Feds. I won't lie for them as that won't make me a witness." "You see Michael," he said. "The only problem I have is that I have a criminal record," said Danny. "That's cool," Michael assured him, "We'll take a chance and see what happens." Danny proceeded to write out and sign an affidavit.

Michael wrote to his lawyer and told him all about Danny and everything he had to say, and included a copy of Danny's affidavit.

A guy named Jerry Cole, who was in the same cell block also made an affidavit stating that he did robberies with Skin and Skin's neighbor, who happened to be Skin's girl Jill Phillips. She had driven for Skin during the robberies.

When the lawyer came to see Michael, he did not did not say a word about it. When Michael finally brought it up, he said he would have to get to it the next time he came around to see him. There was something about the lawyer that was really bothering Michael. When the lawyer and Michael first started out, the lawyer had mentioned that he would be there to see Michael every week. It had been only once a month and he sometimes would not respond to Michael's letter or answer his phone when Michael called. He was obviously avoiding Michael for some reason, but Michael could not really figure out why.

Danny was not was not the only person to help Michael-there would be two more coming his way. The next one happened while Michael was talking with a preacher. Michael studied the law most of the time if he was not busy studying the Bible, but when he was not doing that, he was either listening to God or watching God's Word in action on TV

Everyone there knew who Michael was and what he used to be about, but now Michael was all about working for the Lord and fighting for his freedom.

Michael was caring about his family, and he was out there in the open with it all. He would go to the television first thing when they cracked the door in the morning and he would watch the pastors preach the Bible for a couple of hours. That's all Michael wanted to do other than a little recreational time or watching Jeopardy whenever it came on at four o'clock, but it was not like that was not a mandatory thing like the televangelists were. Michael just enjoyed watching them. He would also watch Unsolved Mysteries, but again, that was not was not mandatory like the televangelists were.

The only other mandatory thing for Michael was peace and quiet whenever the door locked which was around eleven o'clock each night. It was then that Michael could quietly read his Bible do his Bible studies and pray.

Michael would sometime lead them in prayer. He was almost sure they would want him to lead in prayer as his prayer always made them feel so fulfilled and satisfied and they highly respected that. Michael, being the man that he is, never tried to be in any type of control and have others learn by his fear. He could have done that at any time but he just was not was not that type of person. He was the biggest and wisest but like God; Michael did not did not operate that way. The guys there knew that they could come to Michael and get whatever he had and while he did not have much, he did have more than most. Like any God fearing man, he was always willing to share his wisdom, knowledge and God's Laws.

Michael even had a couple of girls that the guys could call and talk to by using three way if they needed to. If anything, it made the guys feel some degree of self-fulfillment by having a female to talk to every once in a while. There were so many people that Michael inspired while he was there. At times, it seemed that everybody was into reading and studying the Bible with him. He explained things, as he understood them, as if he did not did not know he would find an answer for them.

Michael spent so much time reading the Bible, at times he did not did not even think about coming up for air much less eat. After studying his Bible Michael would study his case and brainstorm ideas with whomever he could find that knew something about the Federal System or the law.

Michael's brother's girlfriend Janelle was helping him as well. He would dictate stuff to her and she would graph all the government's and potential witnesses' statements. He was very grateful for her help and he told her that when he got out she would always be welcome to call him if she needed anything.

Sometime Michael would find himself calling her almost every day. They would talk about God, his case and his brother. At one time or another they were supposed to get married, but he never really knew the outcome or what really happened between them.

Michael would pray with Janelle for his case and for his brother. Surprisingly, Michael also got closer to Angie, his oldest daughter's mother. He would preach to her about getting her life together and surrendering it to God so that she could stop drinking, doing drugs & stealing. Unfortunately, Angie had more time in jail than Michael had in prison. She listened to Michael but did not really pay any attention. Being the good-hearted man that he is, he still had to do what God wanted him to do, and that would be just to tell them about God and pray that they would one day listen to what he had to say. There were times that Michael had to admit that he struggled, suffered and doubted himself because he did not did not know what was going to happen to him.

Whenever he would feel down like that, Michael would call and talk to his mother, but he did not did not do that very often because he really did not did not like talking to her very much. Every time he would call, he would find something out about her that he did not did not like hearing. Instead, he would call his cousin Lolita, as she had been leaving messages and begging Michael to call her all the time. He just was not was not up for any negativity talk, so he would not stay on the phone very long with her either. All he could do was give them his love and blessings with a few words of wisdom-any other gossip stuff was irrelevant to him.

Things were getting hard for Michael, as he had already been where he was for months and he had not heard one word from Kim. Lolita mentioned to him that Kim had a new man. The dude she was supposedly seeing, her ex, Michael Davis, obviously put Michael over the top in disappointment and disgust.

He could not talk to Lolita much after hearing the news about Kim. Lolita had also told Michael that she knew his co-defendants were lying to get their deals from the Feds, just like the local cops had done. She told him that Vic was in Oxford planning to come back to testify, and that she talked to him all the time.

Vic told Lolita how it was all a lie against Michael and she wanted to help him prove his innocence. She also said that Fossil and Vic said, "To hell with Mike," Michael asked Lolita if she would be willing to testify, and she said she would. He told her that his lawyer would be in touch with her soon to talk about what they had discussed. "Have him give me a call," Lolita with great assurance told Michael.

Michael gave all of Lolita's information to the lawyer, but he never contacted her. Michael tried to call Lolita after that, but she was never there as she was always working. A couple of times when he did catch her, she explained that she had not heard a word from any of Michael's legal teams.

Needless to say, Michael was very upset and he talked to his lawyer about it, who informed Michael that all of his witnesses had some sort of credibility problem or that they were too close to him. He also said that he believed they would only sell Michael out on the stand.

Michael was at his wit's end so he decided to call his mom. He told her that he wanted her to talk to the lawyer. His mom replied that she tried several times but she could never get through to him. Michael told his mom about what he had heard Fossil, Vic and Kim were doing and saying about him. Unfortunately, she already knew about this but did not did not want to tell Michael, as she knew it would upset him even more.

His mother also told him that Kim had put a "For Sale" sign on Michael's cars and that she wanted someone to come and get all of his clothes. He had heard that Kim would be moving next month, but he did not did not know where and neither did his mother. Michael was livid and of course, he had to hear all this from everyone else, which only made matters worse.

He decided to try reaching Kim again and this time she finally answered. Michael asked her if everything that he was hearing was all-true and she said, "You never cared about me when you were running the streets Michael, plus you were screwing all those other women without a care in the world."

"That was years ago, and you forgave me for that," Michael excused. "We have been together for years and I've changed my life," he attested to her. "I'm a different man and I know that any excuse will do if you are looking for one, but you should never use an excuse to do whatever you want to," he said. "We both have changed Michael." She said.

Then Michael asked her, "So, does this mean we're through?" She said, "I do not know, I'm not sure Michael." He asked her, "Do you love him? Whoever he is? Does he love you?" She answered him, "I do not know Mike." She wanted to hang up the phone before he said, "One last question Kim. Are you coming to my court hearing to tell these people what happened?" he asked. "I do not know Mike," she replied.

"You have to tell the truth Kim. You need to talk to my lawyer. Has my lawyer even talked to you yet?" he asked. "No, he hasn't," she exclaimed. Michael told her "Well you take care of yourself and the kids. Have you even told the kids about what is happening?" Again, all Kim could say was. "I do not know," Kim, told Michael she was sending Jazzman to Tammy's for the weekend and maybe to stay for the rest of the summer. "Keya had been really sick and I think maybe you should call her," Kim told Michael. "I will," he said. "What's wrong with her?" he asked. "She has some sort of illness of the pancreas and they're not sure what's wrong with her," said Kim.

Immediately, Michael hung up the phone and called Kenya's mother Ingo. Ingo told him that it was true and they did not did not know what was happening to her, other than she was really sick. "It has something to do with her pancreas, and there is only one other little girl in the whole country who has it, because of their age that they can't do anything about it right now," Ingo told Michael.

Ingo started to cry and told Michael that Keya was in the hospital in a coma and was not was not responding to anybody, Michael told Ingo, "We have to give it to God right now and pray that she gets better." Ingo got all upset and told Michael, "Forget all that God stuff! He isn't doing a thing for us right now!" Michael interrupted, "Do not say that Ingo." Kim had told Michael the same thing about Keya and the situation with himself. Likewise, Michael told her to pray as well. He also told Kim as he told Ingo that they should not worry and everything was going to be alright. "We just need to give it to God, talk to Him and ask Him for his help."

Michael got off the phone and was feeling very weak. He thought he was just thirsty or he needed something to eat, so he told the guys, "Let us fix something to eat and have a spread on me, okay." They all knew what that meant. A "hook up" as it is called in jail. A jailhouse burrito made out of Ramen noodles and beef sticks, stuck together with potato chips. Manny said, "Do not worry, I've got this, it's on me. Right now you need to sit down and relax as you do not look too well bro." Manny was one of Michael's old running partners on the street and, if anything, he knew when Michael was tired and needed a break from things.

It was beyond Michael's understanding how they wound up back together at the "Chuck Hole" as it was called. They also called it listening and talking to the preacher about Jesus Christ, their Lord and Savior.

At the time, Michael was doing his best not to complain about his case, but it was difficult because of the burden it put on him. He told the preacher that he did not did not do the crimes and that he had absolutely nothing to do with them. Michael then explained how he had given his life to Jesus years prior, and that he had done nothing but learn, listen and work with Him. The preacher said, "Sometimes God allows us to be tested."

Michael thought that maybe this is what this whole thing was about. He knew that nothing in this world happened by chance or accident. "There is action for every reaction and that's what God gives us," the preacher said.

It was right as the preacher said this that Michael heard the officer say, "Just calm down Mr. Occassio, we'll take care of everything." Michael thought for a moment, "Occassio, well that's Manny's name." Then Michael heard Manny say, "You better!" then another cop said, "What are you going to do Manny?" Manny said, "My name is Emmanuel Occassio. Only friends call me Manny and you are not one of them!"

Michael knew that was Manny. Then the preacher said, "I can see you are preoccupied with something. You should just focus on God and he will take care of everything else. Keep God first, have no far, worry or doubt and God will bring your through it."

He then told Michael he had to go to the missionary field, and that he would try to get back before Michael's trial so that he could support him in his time of need. He said if he could not, that he would be praying for him. "Let me know if you need anything." Michael told him that he would, and then they prayed together. When they were done, Michael went and prayed in his cell. He wanted to talk to God one-on-one and separate himself from what he thought could be a set up by the cops.

Manny's name was mentioned several times in Michael's discovery.

Michael knew he was with Rob and Skin on several occasions during the crimes but he was not was not indicted. Not that Michael wanted him to be indicted, but Manny was far more involved than Michael was. Michael thought that maybe Manny's presence was actually as a plant. Michael did not did not know how to take it so he would go without seeing him for as long as he could. When they were called for count time, there was not was not any way that Michael could avoid Manny-they were to stand face-to-face to be counted. And when they did, Michael did not did not say very much to him. The last time they had talked it was not pleasant, it was a big misunderstanding over a dumb car deal, but even then, Michael thought it was more his own fault than Manny's.

What happened was that Manny had promised to pay Michael $1200 for a 1998 Oldsmobile, but only paid him $600. That was before Michael was busted. He got $200 afterwards from him, but he never ended up paying the rest. In turn, Michael had the car repossessed by Kim as he had heard this car may have been used in some of the robberies by Manny and Fossil around the time Michael's truck was with Rob and Angie. Unfortunately, the police impounded the truck even though it was still in Michael's name.

Needless to say, Michael had Kim sell it in order to get his money back. Of course, Manny was upset about it. Michael had warned him not to do anything stupid while it was in his name, and he needed to get it out of his name as soon as possible. When that did not did not happen, it gave Michael a lot of concern. He finally had no choice Michael wanted his money back right then and there.

That was three years prior, when Michael first started doing time for the prostitution case. It all happened while he was in county jail before he ever went to prison, but now that it was three years later, Michael could not be sure what to expect from Manny, and so he said nothing and went back to his cell.

All Michael could think was that Manny was still a plant, as the Feds did not did not allow Michael to be in the same cellblock as Rob and Skin, which was a major clue.

After an entire day of not talking to each other, Michael heard a knocking at his door. It was Manny. He said, "Mike is that you man? What's up man?" "Nothing, what's up with you?" asked Michael. "I was wondering why you were not talking to me," said Manny. To Michael he seemed to be straight. The statement he gave for the most part was accurate and true, as far as Michael could tell anyway, but he said he had been on missions with all of Michael's co-defendants. Michael had never been involved with Manny or any of the others, so Michael thought what he was telling him was good and helpful.

About the only thing that Michael did not did not like was Manny telling the Feds that they sold drugs all over the country and would rob rich drug dealers. Manny told Michael that he knew what he was going through and would do anything he could do to help him out.

Michael asked him why he told the Feds all the stuff about robbing the drug dealers and Manny explained it was the truth about he was not was not going to lie. He also said that he thought it was something Michael himself would do. Sure enough, Michael thought that Manny had him there by saying that.

"Man, I'm sorry about the car, but I told you," Michael said. "Man, I do not even care about that anymore as it was a long time ago," said Manny. "Besides, I got cars and so do my girls." He asked Michael why he did not did not speak to him when he came in. "I do not know man. I thought it was a trap or something," Michael said and then asked, "Why did not you speak to me?" Manny said and then asked, "Why did not you speak to me?" Manny said, "Because I was not sure how you were going to react. Plus we were beefing the last time we talked, but I'm hoping that we're both bigger men than all that now."

"Now you have all this and you need to stay focused on it. I know it must be disappointing with all of those people you took care of, giving them jobs and now they put you in a switch like this. You did none of this Michael and you must be sick about all this crap that happened to you." Michael had to admit, "I am sick and I'll only make it through with the grace of God. I am not the same person I was back then. I am a new man. I am a Christian and we all should be. I'm riding with Jesus now and no one else." "That's a good thing Michael," Manny said.

Michael told Manny that his lawyer had supposedly been looking for him. "He has a few questions and hopefully you can help me out some," Manny said. Michael would if he could but he would not lie for him. Manny also knew he would not need to lie for Michael because Michael did not did not have anything to do with any of the robberies committed by his co-defendants. "I hope you are right," Michael told him. "Do not worry Mike, you'll be straight," Manny offered. "It's easy for you to say. You are not facing the rest of your life in prison and your wife did not run off on you and your daughter isn't dying," Michael vented, Manny's smile turned to a frown as Michael spoke. "You are right man, but you just said that you had God, so keep your focus on that man," said Manny. As long as Michael had known Manny, he had never heard him speak with such feeling, and it was encouraging to hear, especially coming from him.

Manny went on to tell Michael helpful things about his co-defendants and what everyone was up to since Michael had left. He was still close to Fossil but he did not did not like what Fossil was doing. Manny said that he had told Fossil what he thought of it, but Fossil ignored him and would change the subject any time it was brought up. Since they were neighbors, Fossil would always be there for free drinks, free things and to smoke some weed.

It was only a few days after Michael's conversation with his mother, Ingo and Kim when Manny would go to Michael's cell where they would get to be real close friends, even closer than they were before. When Michael first met Manny, he threatened to do something violent to him if Michael did not did not stop jumping Shelly, especially at his clubs. She used to hang out all the time with her girls and she would never invite him in. He never understood why and never knew what was up with her doing that to him. Michael would invite him in so that he would not think that they were hiding anything from him. After doing that, they would become close. Especially after Rob and Skin left town, he needed someone he could trust and that someone was Manny. Michael also needed someone who wanted and needed to make some money hustling in the streets, and Manny fit the job.

Michael was just days from going to trial and he fell out. It seemed that nothing was going his way, but he would not give up. All Michael kept doing was studying the case and praying to Jesus. Manny took one look at Michael and had to ask, "Are you alright?" Michael in turn said he was. "Just a little tired, is all." He took the food Manny had made for him and stood up to take a bite, then fell to the floor. Michael could feel pain in his chest and he saw flashing lights in his head.

The next thing he remembered was that he was on his way to the hospital. The nurse told him she was concerned about his heart rate and blood pressure. All that night Michael stayed in the hospital and then was taken back to jail early the next morning. He was put in a special cell, because health officials said they were concerned about his overall well being physically.

Once they realized that Michael would not be hurting himself, they let him out later that day. Michael knew these health officials had to be crazy since he would never hurt himself. All Michael wanted to do was get back to his cell to study his case and pray to God. He had to promise to remember to eat and that he would not hurt himself so that they would allow him to return to his cell.

Manny and everybody else were very happy to see Michael return to the block. The following day another doctor came to see Michael but it was not was not your ordinary "health doctor," as this one was a shrink. Michael talked to her for a moment, but he could not remember what he said. Regardless, he accepted some medication that would help him to get to sleep, as he was not was not sleeping at all.

Michael's nightmares consisted of people who were trying to kill him or put him in prison. For some reason all, the people that were trying to put him in prison were white folks. Some of them had the devil in them. Some were on his jury and screaming, "Get him! Hang him!" At first, he thought it was just the devil trying to get him, or was it his mind playing tricks on his again? He was not was not sure.

Michael told his lawyer about the meetings with the shrinks, the nightmares and the medicine, but he said nothing about it. He was too busy, did not did not have time to hear what Michael had to say and would rush out of the visiting room. The lawyer would only ask Michael what he wanted to get out of him and what he wanted to hear and, of course, Michael would answer all his questions.

Michael asked his lawyer questions, but never got a straight answer from him. He would simply say, "You need to keep and stay focused and need to concentrate on your case Michael." In turn, Michael would give him more names of witnesses to interview to which the lawyer would say that he could not find them, they were too close to him, and that most of them had criminal records. Michael would tell him, "Well, I can tell you one thing and this is for certain, they are more credible than the government's witnesses who are also close to me."

The lawyer would never take the time to listen to Michael and he would make him feel worse than he already did every time they visited. He would look at Michael all crazy-like and in turn, Michael would feel the need to call for the guard to allow him to go back to the block.

The lawyer told Michael, "If you want to win this case, then we're going to have to do it my way. I'm the lawyer and you are not." He also informed Michael, "I think you are going crazy man." Michael responded, "I'm not crazy!" and asked, "Why do you say things like that?" The attorney said it was because of the way Michael acted and all the letters that he wrote to him.

Michael tried to explain, "Look, I'm fighting for my life here, and you are supposed to be helping me. I do not have anybody else to help me right now and I have lost everything I have owned and only through the grace of God will I be able to prove that I am innocent of these charges!"

"Do not you understand that?" Sometimes Michael felt like he should just kill himself before the system ended up killing him, but he could not and would not do such a thing. "Just send me to die a slow death in prison," he would think to himself this way all the way through his trial. He was feeling funny the whole time, but this time around, it was no laughing matter.

Michael and his attorney, Joe Summers, did not did not have many meetings after that, but whenever they did, all they did was argue and fight. They never agreed with each other regarding Michael's defense.

Time was flying by and soon it was time to go to trial. Mr. Summers had not called any of the witnesses that Michael had asked him to. At this point Michael still had a little faith in his lawyer because deep inside himself, he knew that he was innocent. Michael just wanted to get it over with, but this time around, Michael knew that the Lord was with him and he would really put his faith to the test.

Michael had just a few more visits with the shrinks before going to trial. They were concerned that he was not was not taking the medication prescribed to him and felt he was trying to avoid them. Michael just simply did not did not trust the shrinks or the health officials, and after he told them how he felt, they brought in a different shrink to see him.

The new shrink was a beautiful German born Jewish girl who could not have been more than twenty-five years old. She was pleasant and nice and acted as if she really understood Michael at least this woman seemed really interested in what he was saying and was not was not trying to get him to take unnecessary medications. Michael was willing to see her more often, but he still was not was not to the point of completely trusting her. He wanted to tell her about the dreams and nightmares he had been having lately as well as the voices and visions he had been experiencing, but Michael simply attributed them to the devil. He wanted to ask her about it but he thought better of it so he did not. At their next session, she acted like she really believed him when he told her that he was innocent of the charges against him.

A couple of days later the trial began. Michael tried calling Kim one last time in an attempt to try to make some sense of this whole thing as he was truly in need of her love and support more than anything else right there. Michael really needed her in court so she could tell the truth as Kim had valuable information that could help prove his innocence.

Michael did not did not know exactly what she would say, but he knew she knew something because she was always aware of everything that was going on with him. Kim was always around and she had the uncanny ability to see right through the masks anybody wore, whether she knew them well or not. She would always tell Michael that he should not trust his friends and to especially watch out for Skin and Rob and the rest of the crew. She knew Michael inside and out and sometimes even better than he knew himself. Kim had already told Michael that she did not did not know whether she was going to be in court of not. Michael had given her the best years of his life and could not imagine how she could even think of not being there for him.

“You are a victim to yourself, so long as you are not willing to forgive others.” “Ultimate Justice comes only from the court of the Lord.” “Vengeance is mine sayeth the Lord.”

CHAPTER 36

THE TRIAL AND WRONGFUL CONVICTIONS

Michael found out through the media, while he was at the minimum-security prison camp, just weeks prior to being paroled.

Michael had the job of driving prisoners to their work release jobs. He had come back to the prison facility and read the newspaper as he routinely did, and that was when he found out that someone with his name was indicted federally. At first, Michael didn't think anything of it, but then it hit him. If he could have seen his face, it surely would have shown the fear; shock and concern like it smacked him upside the head.

One of the guys at the library, who was reading the same newspaper article, said, "You see this guy right here," pointing at the article, "He's in a lot of trouble." Michael could only reply, "Yes, he sure is." Michael grabbed the newspaper and took it with him, because he didn't want anyone to read the article and connect the dots. He called Kim as fast as he could get to a phone. He got no answer. Frustrated Michael decided to go for his evening jog. He was so lost in his thought that he couldn't remember if the article said he was facing a life sentence.

Michael completed his jog, showered, rereading the article. He realized the librarian possibly could put everything together so he went back to the library. He asked the librarian if he could keep quiet about the article. Michael went back to his unit to try Kim again. This time she answered, and the first thing she said was, "Are you okay baby?" Michael told her about what he had read in the newspaper article. "They got me, Skin, Rob and all the girls in the newspaper."

Kim said, "Yes, I know." He asked her "How did you find out?" "When I got home it was all over the news and several people called me to tell me to watch TV because you're going to be on it." Michael replied, "I had nothing to with anything they're alleging that I did." Michael said to his defense. "What you think I should do?" he asked her. "What do you mean what I think you should do, someone is suppose to be up there to see you soon." Kim said dryly. "I need to see you," Michael said. Kim responded, "Don't worry, I'll be there and I'll find out if I can buy some time to come see you." Michael asked, "How you going to do that?" "My cousin works for the sheriff department." Kim said.

When Michael called, back Kim told him "It's you they're looking for, and they'll be there to get you soon." Kim said.

Michael went back to library to talk to someone who is familiar with the law. He briefly asked a few question. The librarian told him that he needs to get an attorney right away. Michael made a few calls to different attorney's they all said the same thing "If they wanted you, they would have already been there to get you." The lawyers didn't want to talk to the authorities and couldn't do anything until they took custody of him. All Michael could do was wait.

Thankfully, Kim came to visit Michael that weekend. She came with a copy of the indictment, which was dated March 15, 2001. It was drawn up the same day the last government witness testified before the Grand Jury. One of the witnesses listed was Michael's ex-girlfriend Stacey Pete whom was one of the women Michael had cheated on Kim with.

Stacey's name appears to be there from the beginning to the end, but Michael's name didn't come up until at least halfway through it. While Michael read through the indictment, he could hardly believe what he was reading. "Conspiracy."

The indictment alleged that he conspired with two or more people to commit crimes. Michael knew for sure he had nothing to do with any robberies and he couldn't understand how it could be that by learning about the robberies after the fact that he could be charged with conspiracy let alone be convicted of conspiracy.

Convicted, Michael can only be viewed as a grave injustice. There was no evidence directly linking him to these crimes. The testimony that was relied upon was all lies. Which were bought and paid for with plea agreements that were solely based on lies and perjured testimony?

The trial began with jury selection. This in itself took pretty much an entire day, and it turned out worse than Michael could have imagined; his nightmare was coming true. There was not was not even one dark face present for selection. Michael told his attorney that he did not did not think it was a good idea to go through with it as things looked like those in his dreams, visions and nightmares. The lawyer told him not to worry.

Michael's fears were heightened even more when he learned that one of the jurors was from Jamesville, Beloit, home of the Ku-Klux-Klan. Michael was insistent that they stop the proceedings. Mr. Summers tried to calm Michael down, but during the next couple of days, he discontinued his medication.

Michael kept looking at the jury and he could imagine them with their white hoods completely covering their faces chanting "K.K.K.!"

He told his lawyer about it but was told not to pay attention to the jury and look straight ahead. He did his best, but when he looked at them for just a second, he could see their lips moving, saying, "Hang him, Hang him!" Michael thought the devil was playing tricks with him and it certainly did not did not help matters any when Michael was put in front with his co-defendants to the side. They put Rob to his right and Skin to his left. Michael was portrayed as the ringleader of the bunch as if he was the captain and Skin and Rob were his two lieutenants. Michael told his lawyer he did not like sitting there, but he paid no attention and did, as he wanted.

Michael finally felt a little more relaxed when he saw his parents and sisters and most importantly Kim. Michael had to point out to his attorney that she had been subpoenaed as a witness for both the prosecution and the defense.

Michael wanted her to testify for the government, because he wanted them to know that they were not were not messing with her, as Kim would have most assuredly been a hostile witness. That was probably why the prosecution did not did not want to call her as a witness.

Kim also acted like she knew Michael was innocent. He had already told his lawyer that he was not was not with Skin and Rob but had been home with her and the kids. He knew that they most certainly never planned any robberies with Michael, which was exactly what Kim had said more than once in her statements.

Michael told his lawyer that they needed to call Kim as a witness, but she never was. Mr. Summers did what he could to get Michael to calm down. Instead, he allowed the

Government to state that she was present, at which point, the defense was asked if they intended to call Kim as a witness and Mr. Summer said no. Kim stayed in the courtroom and listened to testimony until she heard Stacey testify. What Stacey said on the stand sent cold chills up Michael's spine and it seemed to also have the same effect on Kim. Especially knowing that when Stacey testified that she and Michael had been together for two years. Michael looked back at where Kim was sitting and saw the look of fury on her face. She left after Stacey's testimony and never returned.

There were still a few days left in the trial and Michael called Kim that night to thank her for coming to court and showing her support. "Why did not you tell me something was going on with you and Stacey for two years?" Kim blurted. All Michael could say was that he was sorry and then tried to explain that it was not was not for two years. "Did you really love her?" Kim asked. "I'm not sure, but I loved something," Michael admitted. "She testified that you told her that you loved her and she told you she loved you," said a hurt Kim. "Yeah, that's true," he admitted.

That is one of the few things that stood out in Michael's mind about the trial. Also, he knew one of the dudes on the jury from somewhere, but he could not place it. The guy was one of the youngest jury members and he always wore a black leather jacket and had stated during the selection that he had gone to college.

Michael's family did not stay around for the entire process as they dwindled away until the last days of the trial. Michael was glad they did not stay for the entire trial, because Rob and Skin spent more time talking to them and sending messages to them than Michael did. It seemed as if they appeared to be their family rather than Michael's perhaps because none of their family members were being too nice to them as they were the reason Michael was in this mess in the first place.

Another thing that Michael strongly objected to was the Government showed pictures of Michael smoking weed and looking all crazy. That was a part of his old life that he wanted to forget about.

He stood up the first time he saw that and said, "I object!" Michael was called to the bench and the judge agreed to cut the drugs and weed out of the pictures, just doing that calmed Michael down at least for a little while. He wondered what had happened to all of the pictures he had given his attorney. One of them was a good alibi and showed Michael too drunk to be the mastermind behind any robbery.

The Government started off by calling cops to the stand. First was Special Agent Steven Marshall, who was in charge of the investigation and did all of the questioning of everyone involved in the case. Then they called Detective Dan Durand and Detective Victor Hietzky, who was in charge of the robbery investigation before the Feds took the case.

All these guys really did was focus on harassing Michael all the time. Had they not wasted all their time constantly focusing on Michael, they might have already solved the case and caught the right people.

The prosecutors started calling witnesses who could not identify Michael or the co-defendants. Michael was not so concerned with them because he knew he was innocent and nobody would be pointing a finger at him.

Right after the victim witnesses, they called the first alleged conspirator witness, which was Stacey. She turned out to be the Government's star witness, although she was involved in almost every count in one way or another.

The last witness called was the biggest liar of them all. Victor Caldwell, and he was the only witness to say that Michael was directly involved with the planning of the robberies at Wendy's, Kohl's, and the Great Midwestern Bank. He said things that Michael did not think the devil himself would say. Victor could not even look Michael in the face. He looked to be the least convincing of all the witnesses. It was known that he was lying with his testimony as he kept looking down at his feet and twiddling his thumbs. He even stuttered and refused an answer question correctly. Mr. Summer did his best when questioning Victor, but it was still very different from proper representation.

When Victor came off the stand, he had to walk past Michael. Michael was not surprised that Victor did not even look at him. He took it as part of his little act for the jury's benefit. Victor was trained to make it seem like he was scared of Michael, which of course, he was not. Michael's feelings were hurt by all the things everyone said about him that were not true. It was just hard for Michael to believe that he actually once cared for all of these people testifying against him, and he would have even given them the shirt off his back.

First, there was Stacey who testified that she loved Michael, then the contrast of what Victor said. Michael always looked out for Victor like a brother for over twenty years. If anything, he got the best plea deal of all by trading his own life for Michael's. There was no reason for Michael to expect Victor to betray him as he had saved him from being killed more than once and even looked out for him after he had double-crossed some very serious people. Michael had given him his last dime and anything else he would ask for.

Next, there was Fossil. He really hurt Michael because he was a blood relation. Fossil had no dignity or heart or the principle stuff that most men are made of. Angie was next, one of his sisters. He was surprised that Angie was even involved in the first place. If Michael would have known Angie was involved when it was going on, he would have tried damn hard to talk her out of it. Here she was lying on the stand saying she heard words that she could not remember which made her believe that Michael was involved. Part of her deal was trading her life for Michael's

Next, it was Jim. Michael should have expected what was going to come from him. He was a straight up, sneaky dope fiend. Michael believes he was always jealous and wanted to get the better of him. The other guys were also jealous of Michael and most likely the girls as well.

Michael should have noticed something was wrong when Jim made an investment with him in the club. Jim smoked-up all the money he earned from a lawsuit and blamed it all on Michael. Jim's girlfriend Nicole loved Michael to death for who he was, Michael thought at one time that she may have wanted to be with him, but he was not down with messing with a brother's woman. However, he did treat her with the utmost respect simply because she was such a young girl. She had a one year old baby and Michael felt bad about that because she was just too young to be feeling trapped and with a child. Michael liked and cared for her as a daughter. It just was not fair that this poor girl was misguided by Jim, who was at least 14 years older than she was. Even though Michael treated her as a daughter, Nicole always tried to flirt with him. Of course, he would not respond to that as she was too young, plus she just was not worth risking anything that would get him in any kind of trouble.

When her boyfriend Jim spent all his money, Nicole blamed it on Michael he overheard her talking to Jim about it one day as if he was a child. Michael was much older than she was. He was the one that felt as if Jim was still wet behind the ears.

Even after all that mess, Michael still treated Nicole with nothing but respect. She used to baby-sit Michael's kids, and in turn, Kim would sometimes baby-sit Nicole's daughter so that she could go out with her girlfriends and have some young fun.

Jim and everyone else treated Nicole really good. Michael just could not understand why Nicole decided to give such false and damaging testimony against him regarding these robberies. She talked about a note used in their robbery. She said, Michael wrote it, knowing she was the one who actually wrote the note.

Rob's lawyer called only one witness to the stand and Michael would have to say it was a good one. It was Manny; he testified how he was involved in this whole robbery process. He testified that he saw Nicole write the note and Michael had nothing to do with it. He continued by saying that Michael was not even there when they planned to rob the Northwest Bank. He also said some stuff that no one knew until he took the stand. When Manny was done with his testimony, the D.A. was stunned and did not have any questions for him. All they could do was call back to the stand their number one and number two star witnesses, which were Mr. Caldwell and Ms. Stacey Pete.

The prosecutor was surprised because he thought they were done with everything. Now they were getting their obviously coached lies all mixed up. Michael's attorney, Mr. Summers finally woke up and began to notice what was going on.

Manny testified about how much Victor hated both him and Michael. He testified how Victor had robbed and tired to kill them both of them in the past. Unfortunately, the judge told the jury to disregard that comment, but it had already been said. Michael thought that Manny's testimony would affect the jury's decision in his favor. After Manny testified, Michael received a message from him. It said it was very important. One of the jurors was a friend of theirs who Manny had robbed once before. After recalling that they did not talk, anymore as they thought it could cause problems with the case.

Michael told his attorney right away, but he ignored him.

He acted as if he was paying attention to what was being said in the hearing, but it was obvious that he was not. Michael even tried it on a piece of note paper, and at first his attorney acted as if it was important, but then he wrote Michael back a note saying that it was not important and nothing could be done about it.

Michael later learned that his attorney could not have been more wrong. The story between Manny and the Juror was more serious than they had thought and it also involved Michael.

Before it was all over, Michael found out that Rob and Skin had a meeting with the D.A. and their lawyers during trial. They thought that they were going to lose the case and offered each of them a deal to testify against Michael which would get them out of prison in under twenty years, instead of a life sentence, or multiple life sentences.

They both refused and told their lawyers that they could not or would not lie against Michael. They both said that Michael had absolutely nothing to do with the robberies and Skin said it loud enough that Michael heard him say it. Both Rob and Skin told their attorneys that Michael's lawyer was doing one hell of a job and because of that; they thought they might get off and wanted to ride it out.

Michael was surprised, but not happy with his attorney as Rob and Skin seemed to be. Michael thought they would sell him out just as everyone else had.

Michael wrote his mother before the trial was over and told her what he thought about it. He told her that he thought Rob and Skin would tell the truth and at least try to help him get off.

The jury deliberated all day. Finally, they sent out a note, asking about conspiracies'. The judge again sent the jury instructions on conspiracy. For a long while, all they could do was wait. Michael had a good feeling and thought that he was going to be freed.

While the jury was in deliberation, all Michael could do was pray. During trial, he would meditate and read his Bible, as he fasted and prayed repeatedly. It was all he could do throughout the trial as so many things were running through his mind.

At one point, Mr. Summers did not want to bring Michael his Bible into the courtroom as he thought that it would send the wrong impression or that it may look as if Michael was faking something. Later, as time progressed during the trial, he told Michael that he knew he was not faking anything as he could tell what type of dedicated man he was. He ended up telling Michael a little story about another client he once had whom he had also told not to bring his Bible to the courtroom. Well, it turned out that this particular client brought his Bible anyway and luckily, he got off from his charges. That client of his at time was a black man who went before an all white jury.

To Michael's surprise, he finally got Rob and Skin to join him in praying for each other, but fasting was out of the question for them.

Before the jury came back, both Rob and Skin told Michael how sorry they were, and that they did not know how Michael ended up in court with them. They wished they had taken the stand to help him out, but unfortunately, they were not given the chance to do that. Knowing that made Michael feel a little better, but it did not help his situation very much.

Upon listening to Mr. Summers closely, Michael remembered him saying something similar while they were still in the courtroom. Before Michael left, he told him what the D.A. offered Skin and Rob. Unfortunately, it was not something that he wanted to hear and it upset him, so he requested a recess for a few moments.

After coming back from talking with Skin and Rob's lawyers Mr. Summers said, "I knew you were innocent, Michael." Michael said, "I told you that Joe." Michael asked, "Can we make their lawyers testify to what their clients told them?" He said he was not so sure about that. So Michael wrote a note to Skin and passed it in such a way that no one could see what he was doing. In the note he wrote, "Skin, please consider telling the truth for me, as you are probably the best and only one who can save me." Skin gave Michael his best "I'm sorry" look. He knew Skin was more than sorry.

A cop was making his way over and attempting to listen to the conversation they were having. That cop had never been in the courtroom before that. It was just the weirdest thing as he acted like he was checking the fire extinguisher and the speaker box, but it was obvious that he was actually eavesdropping. Finally, they came and announced that the jury was back with a verdict. They all stood with their lawyers and two D.A.'s. As they stood there, Michael could smell liquor around them. It was easy to tell that the prosecutors had been drinking and were acting a little inebriated.

. The Jury announced his name, "We the jury find the defendant, Michael L. Brown, guilty on count 1, conspiracy a class C felony, for the robbery of the Great Midwestern Bank on August 20, 1997; Guilty on count 10 Robbery Hobbs Act, a class c felony, for the robbery of Wendy's Restaurant on the night of July 31, 1997; guilty on count 14, robbery, Hobbs Act a class C felony, for the robbery of the Movie Gallery on December 28, 1997. All four counts are in violation of 18 U.S.C. § 1951 and 1952 Hobbs Act violations."

They continued, "Guilty on count 2, the use of a firearm in connection with a crime of violence, a class C felony for the Wendy's robbery; guilty of count 4, for the use of a firearm in connection with a crime of violence, a class C felony for the Kohl's robbery; count 17 use of a firearm in connection with a crime of violence a class C felony, in the robbery of the Great Midwest Bank with a firearm in violation of 18 U.S.C. § 924 (c) (1) and (2); guilty of count 16 Bank robbery by intimidation, a class C felony for the robbery of the Great Midwest Bank of August 20, 1997 and finally guilty on count 21 Bank robbery of the Northwest bank on January 24, 1998 as these two were in violation of 18 U.S.C. § 2113 (a).

Michael almost fell out. He couldn't believe what he was hearing. He knew he was innocent because he had nothing to do with these crimes. But he didn't understand what was being said a second time, let alone the first time.

It was later that Michael would realize the gun charges were separate from the robbery charges. Yet, there were never any guns presented at trial. Michael was in such a daze that he didn't hear anything after he was found guilty. His mind came back just as the judge was announcing "sentencing for this matter is set for two months from now, on March 6, 2002."

Michael was sick to his soul he looked at his attorney who did not even show any reaction to the jury's verdict. All Michael could say was "What did I do, my lord, why have they forsaken me?" Michael couldn't believe it when his co-defendants and God knows them ``had nothing to do with these robberies.

A couple of days later Michael was transported from the Dane County jail back to the state prison where he was serving time for the solicitation for prostitution, which he had accepted full responsibility for his roll. He was glad to leave the Count Jail because he would have some freedom of movement and he may find someone who could help him out and let him know there was something he could do to change his situation.

Right before Michael left for state prison. His attorney came to see him. This was certainly unusual since he didn't show his face before we began trial. His attorney told him, "I told you that this could happen and this was the worst we could have expected, but I did my best." Michael looked at the lawyer with such disdain as he examined his entire situation. "What happened?" Michael asked. His said attorney, "I don't think the jury listened to anything we had to say." Michael said, "You didn't say much for the jury to hear and you didn't even put on any type of defense, only one witness. Many you didn't even call any of my co-defendants. I almost had to fight with you to get you to do anything." The lawyer replied, "I told you that I made an agreement with your co-defendant's attorney not to call anybody that would help you by hurting them." Michael said, "I told you before I didn't agree to that, when they're the only ones who could prove I had nothing to do with these robberies." Michael paused for a minute then he said, "Listen man, it's not your fault, I'm just upset at the whole entire situation and my biggest fear was going in front of an all white jury." "I know that, but as I told you before, I have won my best cases with black defendants in front of all white juries," the lawyer said.

Michael said, "I bet none of them was as black as me and had a conviction for solicitation of prostitution." The prosecution wanted to send Michael up the river with the others. They had nothing on Michael and they knew it, but he knew they would try and connect him to the robberies. The lawyer said, "I've been thinking, I'll argue the appeal if you want me to and I think out best argument is the severance issue, but I'll tell you like I've told you before I'm a skeptic."

Before the attorney got up to leave he said, "It probably doesn't help much at this point, but I still believe your innocent Mr. Brown. Maybe after awhile when my caseload gets a little lighter, I can help you prove it. There's someone behind this who really wanted you to go down in a bad way, someone big who knows full well you're innocent. Whose is it that you pissed off and got on their bad side?" Michael answered, "I really don't know." The lawyer said, "I will have to go through the entire case file with a fine tooth comb, maybe I'll be able to find someone that I may have missed."

Michael was thinking that he should have done that before going to trial. The lawyer said, "One more thing Michael. I think the best and only way to prove you're innocent. We have to prove that your co-defendants and the witnesses lied, and to admit that they lied. Why they lied and who put them up to telling the lies. It's probably because they got great deals from the government. They'll probably think that if they change their testimonies they'll probably be charged with perjury. They may think that they'll get into trouble. Even though the statute of limitations had long since pasted."

After the court was called to order, they called, "Michael L. Brown, please stand." Michael stood and was feeling in a daze. He heard them read, "Guilty, guilty, guilty," Michael was found guilty on all nine counts charged against him.

Michael thought he was going to die right there on the spot. He stood there stunned and he could not gather clear thoughts in his head. All he heard over and over was, "GUILTY, GUILTY, GUILTY," echoing throughout the courtroom.

The next thing Michael remembers was back in his cell crying like a baby. Mr. Summers came to see him that night. Michael told him thanks for all his help and that he knew it was not his fault. After that, he sternly told him to get out of there, as he just was not up for company.

They were not due for sentencing for another 60 days and the court ordered a pre-sentence report from the Federal Probation Department. The lawyer advised Michael that it would not do any good to talk to them and Michael followed his advice.

Michael laid there in his cell pondering what had just happened in the courtroom. He was trying to figure what it all meant and thought about the case against him, which in truth was no case at all. Michael thought about how none of the victims of the crimes ever identified anybody. None of the supposed co-conspirators spoke against him. At least not until after they got their deals. They all denied that Michael was involved at all for years. At first, only Nicole Wampole said Michael was involved then later she admitted that she had lied.

First was the Wendy's robbery. Stacey Pete had testified that she conspired to do the robbery with Flemming but not Michael. There was no one else involved in the planning of the robbery.

Victor Caldwell testified that Michael planned and arranged for the female drivers. He also said that Michael had given both him and Flemming the weapons to use during the robbery. They both testified that Pete Cramer and Victor Caldwell stayed in the car while James Flemming went into Michael's apartment. At that point, James Flemming returned upset for some reason. James Flemming said, "I'm tired of giving Michael money for not doing anything." Victor Caldwell, on the other hand, stayed in the apartment. Victor testified that Alphonso Dean was involved by waiting outside the robbery. Once the robbery was done, Caldwell handed Dean the guns and the money. Dean denied any involvement, but everyone else said that Dean was involved.

Next was the Kohl's robbery. Stacey Pete testified that both she and Flemming thought that the place was too big and that they needed another person to help them complete this robbery. Stacey Pete testified that Michael's name never came up as the other person.

Victor Caldwell said that it was Michael's idea to rob Kohl's. He testified that both he and Michael once rode over to Kohl's to case the place and that Michael was at James Flemming's girlfriends house when they arrived after the robbery and that Flemming, Sutton, Caldwell and Michael split the money. Victor Caldwell said that he could not remember who the driver was and he thought that it was a man, but was not quite sure. Stacey, on the other hand, testified that she drove all three, Sutton, Flemming and Caldwell, during that particular robbery and that she had seen money and food stamps on the bed, but never saw anyone receive a split, and further testified that Michael had arrived about an hour later.

Next was the Great Midwestern Bank. Jill Phillips testified that she and James Flemming conspired together a couple of days prior to this robbery and that Michael's name came up in their conversation. She also testified that on the day of the robbery, she picked up both Robert Sutton and James Flemming at the Broadway Motel and went straight to the robbery.

They robbed the place and then drove to the downtown Milwaukee Mall. They went to a second mall where Michael showed up with his daughter, Key. James Flemming and the others were sent to Flemming's father's house to split the money even before going to that second mall. Jill never saw Michael get any money. Victor Caldwell says that Michael waited around the corner of the bank during the robbery. The Milwaukee Police Department report stated that James Flemming said that he had gone to Michael's apartment after picking up Sutton and that Kim and Michael were both there.

Sutton testified that James Flemming told Michael of his plan and asked him to go knowing he would not do it. He then took Robert Sutton and they both went to do the robbery. James testified that after they completed the robbery, they went to Milwaukee and called Michael to come and get some money for all the support and contacts he had supplied them with throughout the years.

Next was the Movie Gallery. Alphonso Dean testified that Michael asked him about security just days before the robbery. Dean continued to say that the first time Michael started asking questions about this was at his apartment in front of his girlfriend, Kim. He was not sure though if she had heard it. He also testified that the second time Brown asked was on the day of the robbery, while in his van with Victor Caldwell and James Maas. Brown asked the same question about security. James Maas denies ever being involved and that the planning happened over the phone with James Flemming and Alphonso Dean.

James Maas said that he split the robbery money with Michael at Stacey Pete's apartment. Alphonso Dean testified that he arrived later after work and Brown gave him his share of the money. Maas then had to admit that he lied and tried to pin his back robbery on James Flemming. Nicole Wampole tried to pin the Movie Gallery robbery on Michael and Victor Caldwell. She said that she took them to do it and then had to admit that she lied. She later testified that she and James Maas had robbed the Movie Gallery.

Next was the Great Northwest Bank robbery, Stacey Pete testified that Michael had helped plan and also asked her to drive. Stacey testified that she drove from the scene of the robbery to a get-a-way car, which was (per her testimony) Michael Ford van.

She testified that she parked about a block away and after the robbery, went back to the hotel where the money was divided up. She said Michael gave her $150 dollars. She admitted not saying all of this until after knowing about Vic's statement and his cooperation with the Feds. Victor Caldwell said that the plan was to go to another bank first, but instead they went with plan B. He testified that Michael gave him a disguise, which consisted of jacket, cup, glasses, a plastic bag and a robbery note.

Victor Caldwell testified that he and Stacey Pete drove around the corner from the bank, went in and robbed it with a note. They then drove around the corner to Michael's van. Victor got in the van and then they drove to the hotel while Stacey Pete followed them. Once back at the hotel, Michael split the money and kept most of it. He stated that Stacey or Michael wrote the note. Victor believed that Stacey wrote it because they were the only ones in the room when the note was written. He did not see who wrote it.

Stacey Pete testified that she did not write the note at first, but then she said she may have written it. She made it a point to remember all the way up to two weeks before the trial with that being her fifth story. She said that several notes were written and that she, Michael Caldwell were present.

Emmanuel Occassio said he saw Nicole Wampole writes the note and that only James Maas, Victor Caldwell and Nicole were present. Angie Cramer testified that she heard a conversation of robbery plans between Robert Sutton, James Flemming and Michael at his club. She could not remember exactly who said what, but she was asked whether they were talking about planning robberies or if any robberies had already been done. Although, her car was involved in many of the robberies, she testified that she only found out about them, minutes before they actually happened.

With all of this testimony, nothing matched. Every one of the witnesses had changed their statements after they had been given their deal from the government. They then changed their own involvement in their testimony at trial.

Michael went back to the State Prison to await his sentencing. He could barely talk to anyone, as he was just overwhelmed with all that had happened.

Before Michael left the county jail to head back to the State Prison, his sister Tammy came to see him and brought his kids. She was back in town for the Christmas season. Michael told Tammy that he did not know what to say or what to expect, but that he hoped for the best. He told his kids that he loved them all and that he was innocent of the crimes.

Tammy promised to always stay by her brother's side and to do whatever she could to help him get out, no matter what it took. Michael's mom and his other sister told him the same thing when they came to see him before he returned to the prison.

Sixty days later, it was time for sentencing. A couple of days prior to the sentencing the lawyer came to see Michael to inform him of the sentence he was going to get. It was a surprise visit and he started off with, "I think your family is a bunch of ingrates," Michael did not know what the word "ingrates," meant, but he did not like the sound of it.

Michael told the lawyer, "I do not know your mother and you sure do not know mine so do me a favor, since I do not disrespect your mother, do not disrespect mine. I do not know what my mother did to piss you off, but she is all I have in this world, and I advise you to stop now."

"Your mother has been calling around town looking for lawyers and bad mouthing me and the job I did for you," said Joe Summers. "She has a right to do that, and she has a right to her opinion," Michael said "I did not mean it like that," the lawyer said "Oh, you did not?" Michael said. "If you do not want me to represent you on the appeal then let me know," he said, "I did not say that," Michael told him. "I thank you for the job you did for me.," said Michael. "Good, then let us leave it at that and get to work on this sentencing and the appeal," he offered.

Michael went back to court on March 16, 2002, for sentencing. The judge really threw the book at him, but not before Michael told her, what he was thinking. He told her that the government built its conviction based on lies, by the actual perpetrators of the crimes. It was a gross miscarriage of justice. He also told her that the jury was not of his peers. They were all white folks with a built in hatred and fear of black men. Michael continued saying that he had told the truth from the very beginning. He continued by saying that he did the right thing and now he was being punished for it. He told the judge that the entire case was about racism and deception. He told her that God would prevail and so would the truth and that she, as well as the rest of them, would have to answer to him.

That was just a little of what he told the judge. The judge said that she believed all the witnesses and Michael stopped her and asked, "How could you? Why would you? You must know that they were lying?" Then the Marshall said, "Sit down Mr. Brown and do not interrupt. You've had your chance!"

Michael sat back down and refused to listen to anything else she had to say. He heard her pass sentencing and adding up the points. When she was finished, she said, "73.4 years in prison."

Michael told his lawyer to get him out of there, which he did. That same evening he came to see Michael and found that he had been drinking and may even have been drunk. He told Michael that he felt sorry for him and for what had happened.

Later that night, Michael was the headline news story. They showed his club and this criminal pyramid with Michael at the top. Michael asked the dudes in the cellblock to turn it off, which they did until Michael's story was over, as he did not want to hear the lies anymore.

"Go and sin no more. Repent and do not turn backwards. God said that when a man and a woman became one, they are one. So if you get with a male or female whore, you become one with them. It's best to choose a better half than yourself."

CHAPTER 37

THE BEGINNING OF THE END

Michael was returned to the State Prison a few days later. For they locked him up in the hole after for illegally reading his legal mail and finding out that he had a 73.4-year Federal sentence. They kept him in the hole at Oshkosh for about a month before transferring him to Waupun, which was a State maximum-security prison.

They labeled Michael a threat due to all the time he was facing. Michael's cousin Dino went to Waupun with him as he was transferred there on the crazy bus from Oshkosh. Dino had been in the hole the entire time Michael was at court. They asked Michael if he could talk to Dino about being non-violent towards the officers as he had a history of repeated violence towards them. Michael tried, but Dino just would not listen to anyone. Michael had so many other things to think about at the time, including dealing with his own problems that he was unwilling to put his energy towards someone who was not going to listen to anyone.

Dino was angry because he was still in prison when his sentence had been up for months. By the time he and Michael were put in Waupun together, Dino was within a few weeks of getting out, if he could only make them believe he was not crazy.

Michael advised Dino to be cool or he was not ever going to get out. He certainly did not want them to deem him crazy in a court, so he eventually calmed down and was finally released.

Around that time, Michael received a letter from the Feds stating they would be coming to get him in a couple of days as the State of Wisconsin had paroled him.

Michael notified all of his family and asked them to come and see him before the Feds took take him away to who-knows-where. Michael knew that in the Federal system he could end up just about anywhere in the U.S.A.

During that, time Michael's mother sent him addresses of top-notch appeals lawyers to write, looking for some help. He put together a cover letter detailing everything about his case and began mailing them out before leaving the State Prison. Michael mailed out about two-hundred letters in all and he received some responses. Most of them used the excuse that they were too busy, but they would keep his letter in their files.

Michael also wrote to the Innocence Project, headed by O.J.'s lawyer Barry Scheck. They were only taking D.N.A. cases, but said that they would also keep Michael's letter on file.

Before Michael was expecting to be transferred, he wanted his mother to visit him and pick up his things. She said that she would but he would just have to wait and see when she would be able to do that for him. One day unexpected Michael was called for a visit.

When he got to the visiting area, Michael was surprised to see someone that he thought he had forgotten all about. It was Kim, whom he had written and asked to bring the kids, as it would be some time before he would be able to see them again. Unfortunately, Kim did not have the kids with her and Michael could only ask her why she even came to see him. She said, "Because you asked me to." Michael said, "Yeah, to bring the kids." Kim asked, "Is that all you wanted me to come for?" Michael told her, "Well, I do have something that I wanted to tell you but not over the phone." "What is it Michael?" She asked. "I did not do this Kim," he told her. "I know that," she said. "I heard them planning and talking about doing those things, but you were not around," she told him. "What?" He asked surprised. "Yeah," she said. "I heard them talking about what they did after the fact. They would come over to buy some weed, but it was not my business." "It was not your business?" Michael asked. "Well yeah, when you were there," she said. "I also believe they came to the house the morning of the Great Midwestern Bank robbery," she admitted. "Why do you know that?" He asked her. "I just do." She said. Michael said, "The girl Jill testified that they did not come by that morning and I'm sure she had no reason to lie about what she said," said Michael. He continued, "I do not even know that girl and she already had her deal." "So where was I that morning?" he asked her. "I do not think you were there, but you may have been in the back sleeping," she told Michael. "I heard them talking about a bank robbery that they were going to do, but I could be mistaken."

Michael said, "So why did not you get on the stand and testify to all of that?" She told him, "I did not want to get in trouble, and there's more but I did not think it would help." "What? To help prove my innocence?" he asked. "Yes," said Kim. "You know what I know! That you do not want to help me," Michael said.

"Why did I come here then?" Kim asked. "You have to answer that yourself," he said and then asked her, "Why did you leave me in the first place Kim? Was it worth it?" She said, "I do not know Michael, Why did you cheat on me?" she accused. "It was a long time ago, and you have already forgiven me when I confessed it to you," Michael said "Besides, we did get back together after that and you knew how I was living."

"That's all an excuse Michael," she said. "No it's not," he said. Then he asked her, "Who told you not to testify? Was it your new boyfriend? Your mother?" She said, "I'm not going to answer those questions Michael." He told her he knew that it was one or even both of them who told her not to testify. "Why did you even come here then?" he asked. Then he asked her if she was in love with the new guy and if he treated her right. She first told him she did not know and they she told him "All men are dogs anyway, and it doesn't matter. It had nothing to do with us."

They sat there for a minute looking stupid, and then Michael said, "You can leave now if you want to. I have nothing more to say." "If that's what you want me to do, I will then," Kim offered. "Now you are asking what I want you to do!" Michael injected. "You should have known to get up there on that stand and tell them the truth, because that's what I really wanted you to do!" They sat there some more and did not say a word. Then Michael told Kim to take all of his things and split them between his mother and the kids. Kim told him that she was going to give it all to his mother. "She will be here tomorrow to see you anyway," Kim, informed him. Michael wanted to know why Kim gave Jazzman up. "You were all she had," Michael said. "I do not know," Kim said. "But I do not know why I should have to work so hard to take care of Jazzman while Angie, who is her real mother, does nothing but gets high." Michael said, "If you really loved her as I thought you did, all the other stuff shouldn't even matter. Jazzman had nothing or nowhere else to go and her mother may never get off dope," he said. "And what about Keya?" he asked. "You just gave up on her too? We were once a big happy family. How much of this is the influence of the dude you are living with? Whatever happened to 'for better or worse?' You always promised that if something ever happened to me you would still look out for the kids." Kim interrupted, "And I did."They sat in the uncomfortable silence until the end of the visit was announced. That was the end of it. They had nothing else to say to each other. To this day, Michael has not seen Kim again.

When he got back to the cellblock, the guys asked who he got a visit from. When he told them who it was, someone said, "And you did not kick her ass?" Michael told them no he had not. "She would not testify for you and she knew you were innocent?" someone asked. Michael said he did not want to talk about it. "Well, you ain't no pimp and you ain't no player," someone said. Michael only agreed and said, "You are right, and I do not want to be. I am a new man, a new creation in Christ and a Soldier for God. And He will help me prove my innocence."

Michael's mother and sisters came to visit him the next day. It was really nice to get to see people who loved him. After the visit, they took all of Michael's things with them. It was a really nice visit and the last time he ever saw them.

The next day was Michael's scheduled day to leave. He saw a story on Dateline and Nightline about some guys proving their innocence for crimes they had been convicted for. The story continued by saying that even though it took them years to do so they were still in the fight for their freedom. Michael then thought about what the lady shrink had told him after she asked him what he liked to do. He remembered her saying, "You can still make something of yourself in prison. You can still entertain and help people." Michael told her that all he wanted to do was prove his innocence.

Michael finally left and was taken to Dodge County Jail, which was a real crazy place. With the temptation of going crazy, Michael spent a lot of time staying in the law library and doing his thing. They had computers and Internet access along with legal sites. Michael stayed online as much as he could and learned a lot in just a couple of weeks. The Feds finally came and got him.

He was transferred to Chicago and then to Oklahoma City all in the same day. The Oklahoma Federal Transfer Center was a wild place, at least that's what Michael thought that the O.T.C. was, just too much of a wild place but little did he know that he had not seen anything yet.

He had not thought about it much, until after they told him where he was designated to. After the prison processes inmates in and escorts them to their unit, they call your name and number, and your designation.

"Michael L. Brown, #04909-090." The last three digits of a prison number represent your region and city of conviction. "You will be going to the United States Penitentiary in Florence, Colorado," the guard told him. Florence is the highest super Max prison in the United States. It has the tightest security in the world and is home to some of the most dangerous, smartest and insane criminals such as the World Trade Center Bombers, the Uni-bomber, the Shoe bomber, and abortion clinic bomber, The Aryan Brotherhood, the illegal mexicans in the mafia, gangster disciples, crips, D B, and many others. The list of notorious criminals is a long one, but you get the picture. U.S.P. Florence, Colorado is a real prison and very highly secured.

Michael saw news about U.S.P. Florence on Discovery and A&E's, "Crime and Punishment." It was the final destination for the world's highest profile criminals.

Michael went to his knees in prayer as he already heard stories that Federal prisons were either really good or really bad. He was soon going to find out for himself how it bad it was.

While at the Oklahoma Transfer Center, Michael ran into some good dudes who know a lot about the law. He told them about some of the facts surrounding his case and situation. Michael explained how the Feds had completely railroaded him. A couple of legal beagles believed Michael and told him that it is tough to get out of a Federal conviction, innocent or not. It was going to take everything Michael had to remain determined in his case, he was told. He was advised to stay away from traps, like MTV & BET, the gangs, sports, drugs, alcohol, gamboling, homosexuals and any other nonsense that he would meet up with in prison.

He was advised to study the law, and most importantly stay with God. Michael was told that he had to try everything that was positive and available. He was told to write every lawyer, politician and judge that he could, hope for the best and expect nothing. Basically, to be prepared to do it on his own and find all the support on the outside he could get.

I hope that someone would come along that will be able to help you. He was also told he would have to put together a team on the same wavelength as him.

One guy asked Michael about his designation. Michael told the guy he was going to U.S.P. Florence. "Try to find a dude there named Noah Iraon," he advised. Then he asked, "Do you know who he is?" Michael said, "The name sounds familiar." The guy said, "He is one of your homies from Chicago and he is the brother of Jesse Jackson." Then Michael knew who he was talking about.

Another brother told Michael that he had been in Atlanta with Noah. "He's my brother's Uncle and he's a really good dude. He had the biggest trial in American History. From the El Ruken gang trial. Noah was convicted of several murders and received several life sentences," he told Michael. Michael asked, "Will Noah still be in Florence when I get there?" he answered, "Yeah, he'll be there."

Michael left the O.T.C. on June 6, 2002 and arrived in Florence a little later that day via Con Air. Michael was seated on the plane within talking range of the female prisoners. Talking to the females was prohibited, but one girl was whispering to Michael from across the seats. "I know you," she said. "You were in Dana County Jail. I know they lied on you, but they had to for their deals." She continued, "I feel for you brother. If you ever need someone to testify for you, I will. I also heard some lies about some of your friends." Michael asked "Who?" She said, "Black! And I can't stand them lying on you."

She gave Michael her name and number and told him to remember if. "I wish you luck," she said. "I do not believe in luck, I believe in God," Michael said. "I know what you mean," and then she said, "Thank you, I will pray for you and your situation." Michael in turn said he would pray for her.

The check-in process is quite a trip when one gets to Florence. They already know all about you from your pre-sentence investigation and F.B.I. profile. They let you know immediately that the joint is a gang prison. It is full of organized crime members. So, if one had any enemies one can check-in now and be safe, before you are killed.

All that crazy talk just made Michael want to get out on the yard, as he just hated to be challenged. "I see you have a G tattoo," they told him. "Is that going to be a problem?" he was asked. Michael told them he was not scared of anyone and he rolled with God. "Alright then, you are going to the yard and you are on your own," they told him.

Michael went to his cellblock and met his new cellie "Shorty" from Detroit. Shorty introduced Michael to Noah Robinson. Noah was very friendly and took Michael in instantly. He took Michael out to the yard and introduced him to the shot caller of the G.D.'s, named Big Roy. Although Michael did not know it at the time. Big Roy took Michael under his wing with no expectations. Later on Michael would learn how much they really had in common.

Big Roy and Michael were both from the same hood in the South Side of Chicago, and they both caught their cases in Madison, Wisconsin. They knew many of the same people in both states. Michael later let Roy know where he stood, as he had done before with Noah and they became pretty close.

Michael was not really interested in getting involved with any groups or gangs. He explained that he was doing his own thing with God as well as the law study. He said he had to prove his innocence and the bogus conviction. Big Roy told Michael that he understood where he was coming from and that he was not asking Michael to come back into any type of gang-affiliated nonsense.

Michael was also introduced to a funny and cool dude named Homeboy Gun. He was a D.B. from the hood and was all about money. Michael quickly learned the ins and outs of doing Fed time from Roy, Gun and the others. Michael met the toughest, most organized dude who ran the wildest group on the yard. Michael's man, Peter Gun a.k.a. Dap, saved his ass more than once. Not on his own, but because of Noah. He was in charge of East Coast, New York and the Atlantic Islanders. He was probably the most influential man in the yard besides Noah as he was older and retired. He would always be on top of things and trying to be friends with almost everybody.

He was a real peacemaker and always tried to keep things cool. He was also a real businessman and a politician who would sometimes forget where he actually was. Living in the library, Michael met all the jailhouse lawyers and legal beagles. There was Sonny, Cookie, Jesse Mack, Jr. Andrea, Math and a few others. This would be all Michael would do when he first got there. He could not forget his homie though, Mr. Hoff, who was a cool white dude from Wisconsin. Their convictions were from the same judge and prosecutors. Like Dray, Mr. Hoff worked in the law library all the time. He and Michael spent many hours on their cases and collaborating on what they learned.

One good thing about where Michael was at was that there was a chapel and Michael's Christian brothers helped him to keep on the path. His brothers included Kevin, Booker T., Orlando Vince Jr., Kenny and Hiemmie. Michael had never before met so many grown men who loved the Lord so much. These brothers were willing to put their lives on the line for what they believed in. They were always studying the Word of God, spreading and preaching the Gospel. There were also some very dedicated pastors, especially Chaplin Browning, Chaplain Dave, Chaplain Huges, Chaplain Thacker and all the volunteers like Sister Rose of Colorado Springs Fellowship and Dick and Carol from Prison Fellowship Ministries. All of these people were a great help and inspiration.

With all that said, let us look deep into the darkness of the joint. U.S.P. Florence is filled with men who were completely and exceptionally depraved. They are the most dangerous men in America. Men that society is truly glad to have removed from their midst.

CHAPTER 38

THE REALITY OF PRISON, U.S.P. FLORENCE

For the most part, inmates are racist and filled with hate. Michael came to learn that as soon as he arrived at the Florence U.S.P. The facility is a disciplinary facility. It is a dumping ground for troublemakers, from the entire Federal Prison system.

Most of the guys there could not be housed anywhere else because no other prison, whether State or Federal, would accept them. They also housed State prisoners who could not be handled in some State systems.

The biggest, dirtiest mobs and gangs in the country are represented at Florence. Most of the men did not play well with others and they were always trying to make a name for themselves. If you are twenty years old with a life sentence and know that you are never going to get out, you tend to not care about much of anything. Unfortunately, with the sentencing laws there are a great deal of twenty-something's serving life sentences.

The place had the tendency to get very crazy with the yard filled with wild men. Florence has been quoted in National newspapers as "The Deadliest Prison in the United States." Michael knew that to be true, as he was there and saw it firsthand.

Around the yard, the prison gangs run the show and are in charge in everything from drug trafficking to murder. One had better believe that a place like that gets beyond description. Inmates at Florence spend more time on lock down status than any other prison because of the violence. It is a regular event to hear guns firing from the guard towers to break up fights and stabbings. In fact, it would sometimes sound like the hood with so many gunshots being fired.

The majority of incidents among the inmates in prison yards are stabbings, as it seems that everyone resorts to knives instead of fighting with their fists.

One of the stupidest things is how easily a person could get himself stabbed in the side of the neck. It is generally related to drug debts, gang-related disrespect or gambling debts. Florence had more murders per capita, the years it has been open than any other prison in the United States.

Michael was faced with a few narrow escapes himself. The gangs there claim anything that is not bolted down. They even claim certain cells as belonging to their gang. In one situation, they wanted Michael to move in with someone else so that they could reclaim his cell. It turned out to be no big thing, but it could have easily turned into a major conflict for someone else.

Michael stood his ground and proved nobody would be making any moves at him without him putting up a fight. There was an incident where some Crips cells were raided by the officers. Some shanks (knives) were found and the Crips all went into the SHU (hole). An officer gave Michael an option to move into one of the gang members now empty cells. Not realizing it was in actuality a trap, Michael went for it before realizing what was going down. The officer wanted Michael to have the cell because he realized that Michael was not a gang member and he was quiet. The staff knew it could have been a problem for any other guy, but they figured that Michael could handle and situation just fine. Fortunately, for the officers, they are at liberty to do that sort of thing just because they like to create problems for inmates they do not like. Dumb moves like this have caused riots over this sort of drama.

Michael did not think anything of the threat, as he just wanted to have a single cell, which is difficult to acquire in an overcrowded prison. The Crips wanted their cell back, and they came charging in to claim it but Michael defended himself. As it turned out, the Crips gave Michael respect for that as a man.

Michael's next conflict could have very easily been the deadliest. After his homie, Big Roy left Black set Michael up to be killed. He was helping Michael do some legal work and he read some paperwork that stated Michael talked to the cops about Skin. He did not consider that Skin had told Michael to tell the truth after he was charged or that Michael needed to tell the truth because he was facing a lot of time for something he did not do. Out of 11,000 pages of legal papers, Black only repeated that one thing to the big homies (Shot Callers).

Someone said it was the responsibility of all, as the most hated man on a prison yard is a snitch. There are millions of years of time being served in Federal prisons because of snitches.

Michael was certainly not a snitch and the trial he had to face was like fighting a war. Convicts have a way of screening everyone who comes into the prison, whether officers or inmates. They did not know Michael's situation, and the plan was to run him off the yard dead or alive.

At the time all, the big homies were having differences as they had recently lost both of their shot callers. Big Roy, from the G.D.'s, had been gone for a couple of months and the G.D.'s were beefing with each other and other gangs. The Vice Lords had just lost Black a few days before. Now V-dog was in charge of the Vice Lords and he wanted to squash the green light on Michael. Veno was in charge of the G.D.'s and he wanted to squash it as well. These guys were the shot callers, but some guys wanted to move on Michael anyway, more than likely to enhance their reputations. They mostly prey on the solo guy or the weak and if they thought Michael was soft or weak, they were about to get a surprise when they ran head on into Jesus Christ's brick wall.

As a Christian man, Michael thought he maybe should not be thinking like that, but God never said a man could not defend himself. Even Jesus Christ said, "He that hath no sword, let him sell his garment, and buy one."

He knew many gang members who did not like him simply because he had no intention of becoming one. Regardless of what was going on Michael would sit at their tables during chow time. Everything at Florence was segregated and inmates normally sit with their gang or the "car" they ride with.

Since Michael was from Chicago, and at the request of Noah & Big Roy, he usually sat with the Vice Lords. Other times he sat with the G.D.'s simply because of Roy. Some guys did not like it, as he was not with any one gang. That meant they were usually doing something with drugs, planning a hit or making booze, and if they had it in their books that you were a possible snitch, they did not want you hearing anything. It is easy to understand that they were bound to have enemies and they were always up to some type of crime. With information like that, it could cause someone in their gang to have more time added to their sentence. Not only that, it could possibly get the person that heard the information some time off his sentence, or even killed. Michael also believed some gang members had a problem with him simply because they knew he used to have money on the streets. Some of them even thought that he still had money, but that he was not contributing anything towards their cause. The truth was he did not have money and he did not believe in their causes. Michael had always made it clear that he was only passing through on his way home to where he could prove his innocence. All he wanted to do was serve God and fight his case and nothing else. Michael thought they may be planning to jump him anyway, so he thought he should get them first. It was a good thing that some of the other big guys on the yard stepped up and said, "Ain't nobody to be messing with Justice." a.k.a. Michael L. Brown.

There were some guys from New York who did not like G.D.'s or Chicago, which resulted in some pretty big beefs on the yard. It was a good thing that they liked Michael and had some respect for him, but that was only because of Noah. It was the BIG and New York guys that really had Michael's back and it even made them some enemies. Michael did not want to be the cause of a blood bath, so he asked them to let him handle it himself. Michael was mad when he learned that Noah knew the entire time but did not tell him. Michael could have been killed, but Noah had his own way of dealing with things. He was in the process of trying to straighten it out when it was in fact, Michael's responsibility. He just did not want the homies or anybody else thinking that he turned rivals against each other, nor did he want anyone thinking he had to run to Noah. Michael had looked up to Noah ever since he was a little kid, even though he had never met the man before coming to Florence. Noah and Jesse were always in the news in Chicago as the most prominent and wealthiest of black men. Of course, this was before Oprah came to town.

When Michael was a little boy in Chicago delivering newspapers, he saw Noah and his brother Jesse in the paper. The story said they were worth ten million dollars. Michael told himself, "I want to be like them."

Now he was furious with Noah because he was not sure if Noah agreed with the gangs. These gangs did not know about his case and they were not there to witness any of it. They just basically wanted to make a name for themselves at the expense of someone else.

The Big homies squashed any uproar for the day. The next day, however, Michael was feeling a bit strange about things, but he had a plan. He had found the instigators who were still pushing the issue, and he stepped up to one guy from each gang and said to each of them, "What's happening?" He caught them completely off guard. "Do you want to make something of this or what?" he asked him. They each said the same thing, "No, Michael." By the time he got to the third guy, one of Michael's homeboys came up and asked him, "What do you have your gloves on for Michael?" No sooner had he asked the question, when the sirens went off. Then Michael asked, "Is there something you have a problem with me about?" "No man," he answered. The sirens were sounding due to a multiple stabbing somewhere else on the yard, and as a result, the facility was locked down for about a month. When they finally came off lockdown a month later, the entire situation was squashed. Everything was cool and back to (AB) normal. Those gang members had their own problems with a racial riot between the Indians and the Blacks.

God had saved Michael again from doing something stupid by planning to unleash on those dudes. He may have even killed somebody in defending himself, but luckily, they had other things going on. Michael did not have a clue about the other things because it really was none of his business but sometimes he got the feeling that it was not entirely finished because they were mad that he stood up to them.

Since then, things between Michael and Noah were different. Michael still loved the man like a father and Noah treated him like a son, but Michael and his soul both belonged to God and it is in Him that Michael placed all his trust. Michael believes that everything happens for a reason. God gives us a choice and there is a reaction for every action we take. As God's word clearly states, "What you sow, so shall ye reap;"

As Michael told Noah, "Sometimes there are consequences." Noah said, "I love you like a son Michael. I was not going to let anything happen to you." Michael said, "I know that and I was not going to allow anything to happen to you either, but you know I have to be my own man." Noah was Michael's biggest supporter since his being locked up. Noah's wife, daughter, and family all support both Noah and Michael and if anything, Michael did not want to lose him as a friend or as someone who would help him on his case. Michael still thinks to this day that Noah was a blessing from God.

CHAPTER 39

MICHAELS TRANSFER TO U.S.P. VICTORVILLE

Michael was really glad to be transferred out of U.S.P. Florence. It was not his choice to go to Victorville, California but anywhere would have been better than Florence. The so-called homeboys, gangs, groups and the Mafia-type drama would not be missed very much, although the drama in U.S.P. Victorville would not be much different.

Upon his arrival, Michael had to spend his first night in the hole. Not that he did anything wrong, but the facility's procedure was to temporarily quarantine all incoming inmates until their file is reviewed, which is for their own good. So the next afternoon, Michael was released to the yard.

Michael was awakened early on his final morning at the Oklahoma City Transfer Center. Then fed breakfast consisting of two hard-boiled eggs, two pieces of bread, two granola bars an apple, and a bag of water in a brown paper sack. Then he and all the men who are being moved are herded into a bullpen where it is standing room only, and then the U.S. Marshals shackle and cuff everyone and march them to an airline terminal that is attached to the facility. The jet plane is an old commercial passenger jet that appears to be held together with duct tape. If a person was not afraid to fly to begin with, they most certainly would be after a journey on Con Air, the airline which caters expressly to federal prisoners operated by the U.S. Marshal Service.

The jet lands and takes off in Salt Lake City to drop off and pick up new inmates coming into the system. When the jet stopped on the tarmac in Salt Lake City, a person might think it was Air Force One, with so many Marshals encircling the plane armed with shotguns. A sobering sight indeed.

The second stop was in Las Vegas, Nevada. As the jet came in for a landing, Michael could see the resorts and casinos. The jet stopped on the tarmac and the Marshal's scrambled outside to flash their weaponry again. Some inmates are hustled off and the jet and others are brought on board. By 2 o'clock, that afternoon Con Air finally landed near Victorville, California. Michael and a bunch of others were transported from a military airstrip to the Prison complex. Some inmates were dropped at the lower level security prison called Federal Correctional Institute or F.C.I. and Michael and the remaining inmates were taken to the United States Penitentiary or U.S.P., which is high-level security. After four hours of intake, processing Michael was led to a cell in the (SHU). All the fasting he had been putting himself through made him get sick while he was being processed in. He had not eaten or drank anything in over twenty-four hours. Michael would sometime go for days without eating as he fasts regularly. But the sudden change of climate and altitude from flying across the country obviously had adverse affects on him.

Michael wrote to inform Kim and the kids about where he now was. He wanted to get closer to the kids and be sent to Wisconsin, but his security level was still too high for the Feds to move him to Oxford, Wisconsin. Due to the crimes he was convicted of involving the use of a gun, he had a pretty high security level, but that would drop after he served some time.

At that point, Michael had already served 4 years, including his county jail time. Oxford was a medium security level F.C.I. that held about a thousand inmates with a quarter of those inmates having life sentences.

Michael did not think he would have to be in U.S.P. Victorville long before being transferred again, because he had a very supportive unit team and a politician friend assured Michael that if he ever transferred to his district, he would do whatever he could to help Michael be moved closer to home. The politician friend had already been ringing some bells.

All Michael had to do now was what he normally did, which was keeping up on his law work, God's work and his peace and love work, plus stay out of the mix and he would soon get transferred back to Wisconsin.

Michael's brother's friend Katie Pam even began circulating a petition on the World Wide Web through www.iippi.org (Prison Program International) for Michael's transfer back home.

More than anything else, Michael knows he has Jesus, the one and only true God on his side. And He gives man the choice to do as he wants and there is a reaction for every action. God will see to it that Michael gets transferred back to Wisconsin.

Mentally, Michael was still studying the law through correspondence courses. He had already completed Introduction to Law, Civil Torts and now was working to complete Criminal Law.

Physically, Michael words out every day, except Sunday as it is God's day of rest. Monday, Wednesday, Friday was chest and arms days, the second hour on those days was back and shoulders. Tuesday, Thursday and Saturday are abdomen and back days. In total, Michael worked out at least two hours a day. Emotionally, Michael wrote and spoke what he felt.

Like U.S.P. Florence, U.S.P. Victorville was also a gang prison with mostly Crips and Bloods, Skin-heads and other racist White boys, but more than all the others is the EMME's which is the Mexican Mafia.

When a new inmate enters the doors, he is told the prison is controlled by the Mexican Mafia for the most part. However, the Warden and the U.S. Government are the real bosses and they prove it every now and then when they shoot to kill from gun towers or use concussion grenades and chemical bombs in the event of any violent conflicts. Plus, they have the key to the front door. The Blacks are indeed strong in U.S.P. Victorville, but they are still out numbered.

They are also too busy with their own internal conflicts, which are mainly over nonsense like colors.

Michael's brother Bruce's 19-year-old girlfriend Katie was the first person other than Michael's mother, who told him he had to write letters to everyone he could. Then Katie asked Michael to send a photo of him so that she could develop a webpage for those seeking justice on his behalf. Then one day, Vicky came upon the site while searching the web and thought that Michael's web page was not what it should or could be, so she offered to fix it up a little.

Vicky created Michael's second web page on www.BlackPlanet.com and it began getting inquiries almost instantly. Eventually, Vicky's Sister Michelle heard about Michael's situation and decided to write to Michael to help him out. Eventually, between the girls they created a page for him entitled justice2003@blackplanet.com where Michael's entire life and legal situation was summarized within seven pages and included a photo of him at Venice Beach in California.

The web site turned out to be much better than expected as people began e-mailing Michael and Vicky right away. Eventually, Michelle began responding back to e-mails to all those people who had contacted him attempting to get assistance. Many people expressed how Michael's story made them feel sad, mad or even excited to meet someone who had lived through what he had.

Michael began receiving advice, opinions, phone numbers and addresses to contact people who might help. There were also a lot of girls and older women who just wanted to talk to an incarcerated man who had been through hell, living in hell. For some reason the fact that he used to be a drug dealer, player, pimp, had worked in the sex industry and had worked with businesswomen who had done some work with him in the music industry, sparked their interest. They would always ask questions on topics ranging from him being a pimp to what guys did in prison about their sexual drive. Some would ask how to get into the music business, but many of them would ask if Michael was truly innocent and if he really believed he was going to be able to prove it, and of course, Michael would always write back and tell them "Yes. I'm innocent and with some help, I will prove it."

There were also plenty of people who donated their time, effort and money and Michael would send each of them a gift. At the time, Michael was waiting for a decision on his direct appeal and filing a Writ of Certiorari to the Supreme Court. He had been studying law everyday for almost 2 years already. Sometime Michael's studying would last to twenty hours a day.

Violence outside the prison's honors program increased, but within the honors program itself, it was somewhat less and he ended up staying in this program for almost a year and a half. Michael put in for a regular transfer about three different times while in the program and Administration submitted his transfer request each time.

But even though Michael's requests for transfers were approved by the prison administration, he seemingly was always turned down by the regional office. A couple of Wardens called in special favors to have Michael transferred, but someone higher up had cancelled the moves even after it had already been approved by the lower level. In turn, the Warden had to ask Michael who he had pissed off and Michael really did not have a clue.

The Regional office used the excuse that Michael had too much time to serve but not enough time served. Michael knew that excuse as a bunch of horse crap as there were guys with even more time than him as well as multiple life sentences who were serving time in F.C.I.

One thing for sure was that Florence U.S.P. was getting crazier and crazier. Something was happening within the honors program that had never happened before. The Administration had been carrying a list of all those who were considered rats, rapists and witness protection inmates and one unfortunate day, that list somehow was leaked on the yard and resulted in a great deal of butchering.

The Administration announced they had a reward out for the list and that reward would be revealed to anyone who would help to curb the violence within the system. Michael volunteered to help because he did not want to see anybody killed.

After Michael's direct appeal, he had to get to work on his certiorari. He helps back on the Internet business and his artwork so that he could buckle down and get to work with his legal stuff. He worked up to 20 hours a day doing legal reading, writing, and investigating, so much so, that his brain began to hurt. Not only was Michael doing his own legal stuff, but he began helping others with their legal needs. And not only did he help guys in prison, but there were many who asked for his help via the web. It was not long before Michael began acquiring a good reputation for his legal assistance, especially after Blakely v. Washington decision that made the 1984 Sentencing Enhancements illegal following that was the U.S. v Booker case that ruled the 1984 U.S. Sentencing Guidelines unconstitutional and no longer a mandatory sentencing scheme. The judges were actually illegally enhancing sentences with information presented by a pre-sentence report prepared by a U.S. Probation Officer, rather than actual Jury decisions based on the facts.

While Michael was in pursuit of some legal justice, his homies began talking about uniting the B.D.'s and the Vice Lords, but that certainly was not going to happen. Since Michael followed the Lord and was not interested, he left it alone.

It seem that when things were beginning to get better in Michael's case and soul, things at home get worse. Michael received a message one day from his sister Tammy. She wanted Michael to call his ex-wife Ingo to talk to her about her father who had just died. Michael and his father-in-law were very close. Even after Ingo and Michael split up her father told Michael, "You are still my son-in-law, no matter what." Michael really looked up to his father-in-law and idolized him a lot, as he had a great deal of good qualities in him. Like his father-in-law had done, Michael wanted to go from a nobody to a somebody that everybody loved.

Michael was able to call Ingo late that night because he was in the honors program, and he told her that he still loved her and her entire family, especially her dad. She told her she knew her father loved him and his other kids as well as his own grandkids, Marcus and Jazzman. Ingo cried the entire time they were on the phone. She mentioned to Michael about how the kids found her dad on the bathroom floor, the victim of a heart attack. He had had a previous heart condition and high blood pressure, which more than likely caused his death. Michael expressed to Ingo how sorry he was about her father passing and the fact that he could not be there for her in this time of need, but he assured her that his family would be there in his stead. Ingo told Michael she was tired and that she loved him so much. He responded by telling her that he was sorry again before he hung up.

The funeral was a few days later and it was very beautiful, many from Michael's family attended the funeral including Kim and the kids. Ingo and Kim had been mortal enemies for over ten years, but at the funeral, they finally buried the hatchet for the benefit of the children. They both realized they were not only mothers but also essentially sisters. It really hurt Michael to feel Ingo's pain, as well as the fact that he could not be there.

It was only a few days following his father-in-laws death that Michael's homeboys, the G.D.'s and the Vice Lords had a war on the yard. The war began over someone being called a homosexual or some other name, and was actually a beef that began in Chicago decades before.

The two groups had been trying to unite in prison because they were a minority not only in Florence, but in every Midwest prison as well. It seemed to be arranged so they always had something to prove to each other. And even though they were far out-numbered every time, they still challenged everyone, which made them look really stupid or crazy. Some thought that maybe they just wanted to seem that way so that no one would mess with them and leave them alone.

The altercation began in the recreation room. Six Vice Lords found themselves jumping on Gun who was one of Michael's homies. The Vice Lords got away until the G.D.'s ambushed four or five of them on the recreational yard. The whole ordeal went on all day going back and forth and almost to the point of the rivals killing each other. The Administration rounded-up everyone from the Chicago area, except Michael and his cellie, Michael a former G.D. from Chicago and his cellie, a former Vice Lord from Gary, Indiana, had decided not to get involved.

In the past couple of weeks Michael had been called to the Lieutenant's office, Captain's office, and Associate Warden's office for matters that he was not involved with and his cell was ransacked and searched three or four times within a couple of weeks.

First Michael was accused of leading some litigation against the Administration, and second he was accused of helping inmates gather information on prison administrators, judges and lawyers for prisoners to file claims against them. Lastly, he was accused of withholding information about a major prison drug and sex ring. The Administration asked Michael for some specific help but he refused finally Michael was told that his homies, the G.D.'s had made a threat on his life and a note indicating such had arrived in the mail.

Based on everything they said they had found out, they took Michael to SHU on February 10, 2005. He was called to the Lieutenant's office where he was told about the kite (note) that someone had mailed in. The gang was to put a hit on him over some phony paperwork stating that Michael testified against someone, but it was all lies, as Michael had never testified against anyone. He pleaded with the Captain, Lieutenant and Warden not to lock him down, but they said they could not take the risk. They even called the compound attorney on the phone that could not substantiate the rumor either, but stated they had better take proper precautions anyway.

From the hole, Michael had his first phone call during which he learned his mother had suffered a stroke on her way home from a casino. She was in the hospital but was thought to be okay. All Michael could do was pray for her constantly.

It would be a week before Michael could talk to his mother to as if she was okay, but he would have to wait until she was home from the hospital to wish her well. She promised him that she would be alright and Michael believed her.

He had a corner cell by himself in the very back in the SHU for most of the six months he was there. He was only permitted out of his cell for one hour 4 days a week for recreation.

Soon after that, Michael was taken to a television screen mental health visit with a psychologist from Leavenworth, Kansas. In their visit, he told them he was not crazy and that he was going to prove his innocence and go home. Following that visit, Michael along with several other prisoners, was moved via Con Air to the transfer center in Oklahoma City and help there for almost 9 months. He was very concerned for his family, especially his mother who he could not call because she had been back and forth from the hospital so often her phone had been disconnected.

He fasted and prayed a great deal on her behalf and he even took a job as a unit orderly to keep himself busy during his holdover at the transfer center, his job earned him $5.00 a week with which he could purchase candy, popcorn and tobacco. Smokes were $1.50 a pack and he could sell them for $100.00 a pack to other inmates because only a few unit orderlies were allowed to purchase tobacco. Not only that, but the entire federal prison system was soon to adopt a no-smoking policy in July 2005, which was just a few months away. In January 2006, the leftover tobacco was destroyed and from then on tobacco became an illegal black market item just like drugs.

On the morning when Michael had expected to be paid, God had been telling him to chill out and trust in him. Con Air was scheduled to pick him up for his transfer, but by the grace of God the plane broke down so Michael was taken back to the block and was able to get his payment transferred a couple of weeks later, Michael took two packs of cigarettes that a fellow had given him to help get some money together for his arrival in Victorville. He had to break up the smokes and stuff the tobacco in balloons that he swallowed. About two hours later Michael got sick from the nearly thirty-six balloons in his stomach that went straight into the toilet. Michael knew from experience that he would never do that again as it was definitely a lesson from God.

Michael thought of all the people he knew who had swallowed balloons filled with weed, cocaine and heroin and never got sick. All he swallowed was tobacco, which seemed odd as he personally knew that there had been people who died just from swallowing their own saliva, but were drunk off their behind. So off to Victorville he went.

"No matter where we go or what we do, we can rest assured that God is with us through it all. We are ever alone when we walk with God."

CHAPTER 40

MICHAELS MOTHERS DEATH

Arriving in Victorville, California, Michael was cleared out of the SHU and upon the advice of some Christian brothers there, he applied for the Code program, was accepted and he moved into unit 3B.

Michael moved into a cell with a boy named Richard Moore, a.k.a. Boss who used to be a big dope boy for the Bloods.

One day when Moore was in the chow hall in U.S.P. Lompoc California, some officers grabbed him and beat the crap out of him. He was shot up with some type of psychotropic drug, all out of retaliation before finding out that they had the wrong dude. They thought he had been involved with the crack riots. There were many other innocent bystanders who were also beat up, shot up and charged with assaulting officers.

Richard took Michael as a roommate at the request of Mr. Wells. Richard was also an ex-drug member turned Christian. Richie was a nice person, but his use of dope over the years, along with cops constantly beating him up, really messed him up. Not only that he had poor hygiene habits and all he did was sleep, eat and shit. Most of the time he would lay in the bed and talk to himself.

Michael was still grateful to be in the cell with Richie rather with a non-believer or a guy who smoked, drank booze, used drugs, broke the rules, had a negative attitude and did crime or otherwise lived in sin. Being in the cell with Richie Michael eventually got more settled and comfortable, but for the first couple of nights for some reason, he could not sleep. It was more than just being in a cell with a new Christian brother; Michael knew something was happening.

His approved phone list was finally activated into the phone system after almost a week and so he got up in the morning and called home. Michael learned that his mother was back in the hospital with complications from the stroke she had suffered five months prior which was the first week Michael was placed in the hole for reasons he still did not know. That was in February 2005, the same week his Certification of Appeal ability was due, and he still had received no answer.

He had been waiting on his property to arrive for over ten days now. He had already talked to all the staff about his property, and they all told him that he would get it as soon as it arrived or as soon as they could get it.

Finally, after lunch on July 21 2005, the unit officer told Michael to report to Receiving and Discharge (R&D) to get his property. Thank goodness, he was only forth in line as he happily took a laundry cart to roll his property to the unit, because it was too much to carry.

When Michael got back to the unit and as he was waiting for the officer to open the door, he suddenly got a strange warm feeling. Someone walked up and asked Michael "Is this your property?" "Yes," said Michael. "You sure have a lot of property," he said. "It's mostly legal work, transcripts and stuff, thanks to my mom," Michael admitted. For no apparent reason, tears welled up in Michael's eyes. He felt the presence of God and his mother there with him. Then he heard in his head, "It's alright son, it's alright!" As the officer came to the door he said, "Brown, as soon as you put your property up, you ate supposed to report to the chapel. They want you for something," he instructed. Michael unloaded the laundry cart and was in the process of returning the cart as he promised the R&D Officer he would, but someone else offered to return it for him.

Michael went straight to the chapel to await Chaplain Northway who was on the phone. He could hear the Chaplain's voice as he said, "Okay, Mrs. Brown." As he agreed with whoever was on the other end of the line. After he hung up the Chaplain asked, "Are you Michael?" "Yes," acknowledged Michael. He responded, "Please have a seat," and waved toward the chair, so Michael sat. "I'm sorry to have to tell you this, but I'm sure you know your mother had been in the hospital, but now she had taken a turn for the worse," he explained. "Where is she now, can I talk to her?" Michael asked. "Sure, they have taken her to a hospice unit at the hospital. I'll dial the number."

The Chaplain dialed the number and handed Michael the phone. His mother answered.

"Mom, are you okay?" Michael asked. "No baby, I'm not well," she told him. "Mom, I'm sorry for all the pain I caused you. I'm sorry I could not be there for you. Is there someone with you now?" he asked. "Tammy is here." She offered. "Everyone else left, but they will be back later." Michael asked his mother, "Have you been talking to God and saying your prayers?" She said, "Yes boy, I love you. Just be good and do what you have to get home." Michael said, "I will mom, I will." "Here, talk to your sister." She told him, and then Tammy got on the phone.

Michael could not do much else other than cry at that point. "Have you been praying for her?" Michael asked Tammy. "Have you been talking to her about God?" Tammy replied, "Of course boy, I've been reading her scriptures out of the Bible, and praying for her all the time!" Michael asked, "Tammy, how is she doing? Is she going to make it?" Tammy calmly told Michael, "It's doesn't look good big brother. She refuses any more chemo and says it's her time!" Michael cried, "God, no please!"

Michael's mothers younger brother Bruce, got on the phone and said, "Mike, it's her time. The illness she has us like putting a candy bar in a gas tank. It clogs up all her major organs, and they are almost gone." Michael told Bruce, "It's not over until God decides it is. I do not think it's her time." Uncle Bruce got real quiet, "Okay now, talk to you sisters and brothers," and then he gave the phone to Sasha. Michael talked to Sasha, Bruce and Matthew and finally by the time they got to Trisha, they just started crying.

Michael talked on the phone a good while and got to talk to everyone including his step dad, Charles. Then Chaplain Northway told Michael he would have to hang up. Michael needed to talk some more, but the inmate count was approaching.

He went back to the housing unit and several Christian brothers came to his cell, where Reese, Harry, Teke, Mr. Walls and a few other brothers prayed for his mother. Michael told them what happened with his mom and out of nowhere, they all began to cry. Michael himself began crying in the arms of these guys he met only a few days before. Michael was crying so much that the brothers comforted him until it was time for the inmate count.

The brothers prayed with Michael and told him his mother would be alright and that she would pull through.

Michael climbed up on the top bunk. His cellie was asleep on the lower bunk. Again, Michael got that strange warm feeling. He could feel someone or something talking to him from deep within his soul. He just knew that his mom would pull through and he was counting on it. The feeling said, “Everything was going to be alright, everything is going to be alright. I love you son, I have gone home.” It was just as clear to him as if someone said it aloud in the room. Michael felt like screaming out, “No, do not go!” But he felt something that made him know, “Let it go.”

An hour later after the count cleared, Michael ran over to the chapel. When he got there, he found the Chaplain on the phone again. He was saying, “Yes, Mrs. Brown, I’ll tell him!” After he hung up, he turned around and saw Michael. Michael spoke, “I know she did not make it, did she?” Chaplain Northway said, “No, she did not.”

Michael’s mother, Linda Brown passed away at the young age of 56. Chaplain Northway permitted Michael to call his family at the hospital and talk to everyone again for as long as he desired. He talked to Kim, Michael Jr. and Jazzman and all the other family members. Then he talked to Trisha last and they cried together over the phone.

When it was finally time to go, the Chaplain told Michael he would leave a note approving Michael to talk the next day as long as he needed. He left and returned to the unit, and he could not stop crying.

The funeral was a few days later. Tammy went to Western Union and sent some money to Michael’s account so he could continue calling from prison.

Both of Michael’s ex’s, his children’s mothers Ingo & Kim, did a lot to help the family deal with Linda Brown’s death. They helped plan the funeral, clean the house, and during it, all they got along well with each other. There was no fighting or arguing love was definitely in the air.

Michael, on the other hand, was feeling really bad that he could not be with his family at the service. Each of Linda’s grandkids and Michael’s three kids were giving something of their grandmother’s in her remembrance. Michael called and cried on both Ingo and Kim’s shoulders and they helped Michael to deal with his grief as best they could.

Michael’s mother loved both Ingo and Kim and she had done her best to show it in her own way. She loved each of them differently and for different reasons, but she mainly loved them because they loved her son.

CHAPTER 41

KIM COMES & GOES AFTER READING MICHAELS BOOK

Michael and Kim really got along well after the funeral. It has been a long time since Kim had told Michael she loved him without him asking. She also expressed some things to Michael that she never had before: She told him she wished he could be there for her and the family; She told him why she had left in 2001, when he was indicted, she said she was scared of the Feds and the entire situation; and she told him that if he were not in prison they would be together. Michael knew it without a doubt, despite all the girls. So, needless to say, hearing Kim say this really cheered him up.

Kim's feelings changed a few weeks later though after reading Michael's book. She never wanted to read the book before Tammy sent it to the publisher.

As a pimp, player and a hustler, Michael had been with over one hundred different girls and Kim really went off when she read about it in Michael's book. He reminded her, "You knew who I was and what I did as well as my business and how I played."

Kim knew some of the girls Michael had messed with, and there were some she did not know. She knew that Michael traveled and she thought that was because of the girls. Then there was Stacey who Kim disliked the most and who helped put Michael in prison.

Michael told Kim all those girls were now in the past. "They were why we were together. It's like you were living two different lives and as if you were a different person," she accused. "I am a different person now. I'm a God-fearing man," Michael pleaded with her. "I can't forget it Michael." Then she asked, "Do you have any other kids, I should know about?" "Now, you can forget it." Michael blurted at her.

Michael was distraught every day for about three weeks. He called Kim everyday expressing his deepest, most sincere apologies. "That book makes me look like a fool," she told him. "No it doesn't Kim. It actually makes you look like the sweetest person in the world as well as a wonderful mother and wife," Michael assured her.

"I wrote that book to help other not make the same mistakes I did so maybe they won't bring themselves into the same type of situation. I also wrote that book so that others may see the warning signs and come to the air of their loved ones as well as direct it to the guys and gals that are acting out, so that they may see the need for changing their behaviors." He went on to say, "This book can help others help themselves. Plus I wrote the book to introduce people to my own situation, that maybe I can get some help."

It hurt Michael that he wrote the book to help but it had only hurt Kim. She was so hurt that she told others a bunch of really bad stuff that was not even in the book. She told Michael that the book had far too much content dealing with drugs, sex and crime.

So in turn, Michael made some changes in it and cleaned it up as best as he could and explained the massage of each story in each chapter. After that, Kim and Michael's relationship was never the same again.

One day, Michael's daughter Keya whom he had not seen in a long time, came to visit him with her Aunt Laya, who is a beautiful and brilliant attorney in Phoenix Arizona, which is less than a day's drive from Victorville, California.

They came to visit Michael after his mother's burial just to be sure he was okay. This was certainly a surprise and it really did lift his spirits to see them. They laughed and they cried and they talked until they could not talk anymore, but before leaving the visit, they took a few photos for Michael to have.

Michael had been away for almost nine years and his little girl Keya was now 13-years-old and had really grown. In fact, she was almost as tall as her daddy. She's light skinned and is very pretty like her mother and her Aunt Laya. Michael was so glad to see his daughter, but also very sad when the visit was over and she had to go. It's really rough when a family member comes to visit and inmate, because one minute you are happy to see them but then it's so sad to see them go. Some inmates say that's why they do not like visits. Michael actually felt a little sick for a while after they left because he did not want them to leave, and to this day, he still misses Keya very badly.

However, he still says that Ingo was a really great mental help for Michael and the family. He talked to her all the time and cried on her shoulder over the telephone a few times. Michael loved both her and his mother Linda so very much. Linda loved Ingo mostly because Ingo loved her son. Come to find out, both Ingo and Linda were a lot alike, both being tough and stubborn black ladies, but good at heart for what they did and stood for.

"For God so loved the world that he gave his only begotten Son, that whosoever believeth in Him should not perish, but have everlasting life." John 3:16.

CHAPTER 42

CHINO AND BLACK BOB RULES TO THE DEATH

It took Michael a few days after his mother's passing to deal with his grieving and absorb the visit from Keya and Laya before he was able to function somewhat normally again. The normal routine of Michael's life was clouded with the thoughts of not having his mother around any longer. Granted, he had not been home in years, but at least he could get her on the phone every now and then or get a letter from her every so often. At the very least, she motivated Michael to keep up the strong fight to continue living.

For the moment, Michael had not realized that there was a war going on around him. Spiritually there was the Lord God in his life. There was also the physical evil of the devil battling hard on the yard during Michael's first months in Victorville.

This had been ignited primarily by two major shot callers who were requesting transfer to Victorville to put some order to the joint, specifically within the Latinos like Black Bob and Chino. These two men stirred-up the pot and got in where they fit in, which was at the top of the food chain, at least according to how they saw themselves anyway.

Black Bob and Chino together had more than 55 years of incarceration between them. Both of these men were in their early 50's. Bob is about 6'1", tall and slim with the face of a leader demon. He's not so much mean or rude, but firm and grim, especially if you had a problem with him or his people.

The Sereno's a.k.a. South Siders, the South Side of Los Angeles and are well known to be "hit men" for the Mexican Mafia. Not just some street gangs, but also for those that helped to control and distribute most of the drug that came into America from Mexico and to the west coast, and eventually reaches across the U.S.A.

Black Bob started out as a hit man in the streets, and then in the joint, or so his legend says. He became a shot caller and headman in all the Federal Bureau of Prisons and Chino had been Black Bob's homeboy since childhood. Chino is 5'7" stockier than Black Bob. He was definitely one in-shape Mexican who had the face and presence of a murderous general but the speech and thoughts of a Vice President who was able to take and delegate commands.

These guys were brought-in to clean-up and organize the different Spanish and Mexican factions. The biggest of which were the South Siders. Second to them in the prison system were the Texas Syndicate boys. Whose numbers are around a couple of hundred. There was also the Arizona Cowboys and a handful of no names and a few Colombians.

Victorville was the closest Black Bob and Chino had been to home in about twenty years. They were given a big homecoming and their people were giving them tobacco, drugs, booze and even some of the finest Spanish women officers. They were also the first only persons there to have conjugal visits; which were officially approved by the staff of the prison visiting room.

The staff itself was actually more fearful of these guys than they were of the inmates. In July of 2005 there were more Spanish inmates than any other race, outnumbering the Black by a couple of hundred. There were also more Hispanic staff members working as unit and compound officers than that of any other race.

Most staff members knew Black Bob, or at least their older friends and family knew of him from the streets. Like Bob, many staff were from South Central L.A., so needless to say, the staff knew to do as Bob asked or they may have to pay the consequences, which of course was something they never wanted to do.

He received special food, clothes, jewelry, alcohol, drugs, weapons, and money like a King's Ransom with no questions asked. This all began from the moment he stepped off the plane at the Victorville Airport. When Michael and the rest of the men were loaded into buses to be driven across the street to the prison complex, a few officers came aboard the bus where Black Bob and Chino were pointed-out to them. When it came time to be booked into the penitentiary, Bob and Chino were first to be called. Staff from off the street was brought in to process them in and they were immediately given a cell together right off the gate. This was something that just did not normally happen but staff obviously knew what these two men were able to accomplish physically against other people, so special considerations were made for them.

Black Bob and Chino were transferred to Victorville after some Mexicans had killed a white guy and tried to kill two more, which was causing a race war among the Mexicans and the Whites. Because of a drug deal gone badly, a white guy jumped a Mexican, so the Mexicans killed and flexed their muscles in process. This put all the other groups and races on the alert.

There were already the myths and rumors, some of which derived out of the fact that Black Bob supposedly got his name from killing Blacks and that Black Bob was a mad man. The Black in his name was supposed to have come from the black hand of made men. Not only was Bob supposedly killed one of his own people who tried to play him on a drug deal.

It was said that Bob killed him and cut open his stomach with a knife so that he could take the balloons of dope from the dead man's stomach.

Then there was Chino, also called the King of Chino. Chino is the name of a prison in California. He supposedly killed more than five men in every race: Whites, Blacks, and Mexican. Chino was said to have ordered the hits of more men than he could count on his fingers and toes. These two guys had reputations bigger than themselves, but they were usually pretty easy to talk to and they greeted and spoke to everyone, cordially, especially if they were spoken to first.

If someone had a problem with them or any of their men and it could be shown that they were in the wrong, they would straighten it up and make it right instantly. One would get an apology; sometimes witness the discipline that was meted-out usually consisting of a beating or a check-in of the person from their group who did the wrong.

These guys also controlled their groups in the streets from inside the prison system. The prison was like a training ground for learning to keep your mouth shut and carry out orders, such as drug trafficking or even murder. These men did not want anything to mess with their business. Prison would not hamper their "business as usual," but unfortunately, that was also hard to maintain. When they were in Victorville on yard, there were no major infractions until after they left.

After about 6 months on the prison yard, Black Bob died of stomach cancer. Some say it was from more than 25 years of prison drugs and alcohol abuse. When he died, the tension and grief was so thick one would've thought that the president himself had died.

The Mexicans were really grieving on the yard and Chino looked as if he had lost his better half, his mother or his wife. Some said he lost his edge or his command, but with losing, he did not really look like it. This man was in better shape at 50 than most of the younger men. Then one day without notice and reason, the Bureau of Prisons transferred Chino. No one knew who was going to take over command of the Mexicans or the drug trade and it was not as if their unity was divided or anything of that nature, it was just something that happened. The Black's numbers began dwindling and they needed to clean up their own back yard, especially with the Crips and the Blood who had been fighting for so long.

At Victorville it did not look like many people had money, but looks were always deceiving. There were a few dudes in prison who had more money and more power than it took to support a small country, and they had more drugs and drug addicts than anywhere in the nation.

Everyone either knew or felt that a race war could break out at any time. If it were to come to that, they would all take up their weapons. The swords would definitely come out and they would kill whoever they were at war with, whether it was the Blacks or Whites. It did not matter as it had happened before and it was certainly bound to happen again.

Riots, rapes and murder between the races were at high levels at institutions like Victorville. One thing for sure is that each man needed God in his life in a Penitentiary now more than ever.

The men in prison need to pray that it will not happen and they must know that if it does, God will protect His children.

"And we know that all things work together for good to them that love God, to them who are called according to His purpose." Romans 8:28.

CHAPTER 43

KIKO COMES AND RULES, WARDEN NORWOOD, TUCKIE DIES

It was not long after Michael's mom's death that the Blacks, particularly the Crips, had a true leader come to Victorville U.S.P...

Michael was outside talking to one of the guys from Chicago named G-Money when another fellow walked up. "What's up? Kiko!" said G-Money. Michael heard the name before but the face he remembered was of a female. G-Money introduced Michael as his Homeboy to Kiko. "When did you get here man?" G-Money asked Kiko. "Where are you coming from?"

Kiko said he had just arrived the day before from Coleman U.S.P. "I haven't seen you since being at Florence U.S.P. when they took you out of there on a sex scandal," G-Money said. "Yeah man, I was getting my money and getting my rocks off, until them suckers started running their mouths," Kiko said. "What happened to that broad? Was it the Assistant Warden, the head of the psychology and female officer?" "Yeah man, it was all three of them, but they got scared and started telling on each other. You know they wanted to be down, so I put them down with a real brother. So, what you got going on? Why are you here?" asked G-Money. "I came back home to be near my family. My sister, my daughter and my mom are in L.A. and I've been gone too long," explained Kiko. "Plus I came to get things in order around here with the homies. This is our stronghold and the esay's here have to share some, move over or move out of the way."

Then Michael said, "That's where I know you from man, Florence U.S.P. You were one leaving when I was arriving and the sec scandal was still hip talk on the yard there." Kiko said, "I just left Coleman U.S.P. Florida with one of yall's big homies. He was like a father to me. They call him Big Pop Noah Robinson, and they started calling me Robinson's Son." Michael interjected that Noah was also like a father to him. "He showed me the ropes here in the Feds and taught me the law. I was somewhat of his understudy!" Michael admitted. "Yeah, that dude is smart and he really knows the law. He's a rich and powerful man and he's really got it going on," Kiko boasted.

As G-Money, Michael and Kiko were standing there talking, about a hundred guys came walking up. At first, they did not know what they were up to so then Kiko began telling them what he had told Michael and G-Money about him being a writer. He said he had written a great book that he wanted us to check out. Michael told Kiko that he was also a writer and that he would read Kiko's book, if he were to check his out as well. Kiko agreed to read Michael's book. He them left them to meet with his homies who had been waiting to greet him and clue him in on taking charge of matters.

It was out of respect that Kiko took charge of the yard and the Brothers. He called together a big meeting on the yard and in an instant; all the Blacks were invited to attend, especially the Crips and Bloods. It was a meeting to instill uniformity and push peace, love, unity, and war, only if called for.

Kiko was about 6'3", brown skinned, slim and tall with a muscular build. He was about 45 years old and had an old school mind. He was well groomed and kept about eight braids in his hair. Needless to say, he was considered a five star General commander and chief, and was strictly business.

Kiko was a smooth disciplinarian and peaceful, but also loved to go to war. He would greet everyone with a handshake and a hug and was usually smiling but he also had a poker face so no one could tell what he was thinking. Michael knew the reputation Kiko had was as big as his demeanor. His cousin "Dog," who was about 5'10" and built like a tank, was always at his side. He never smiled and all he would ever say was "What's up."

Kiko was the highest-ranking shot caller for the Crips in the Bureau of Prison and surely had the biggest reputation for being the toughest, baddest, smartest and fairest shot caller they had. He had money, girls, and power and was a master at the art of war.

Kiko brought a lot of balance to the field for the brothers. He would speak out for what was right and he spoke against what was wrong for anyone, especially for the brothers. He expected no less than for the brothers to be at the top of their game, and if they were wrong, they were wrong whether they were White, Spanish, Officers or the Administration. Wrong was wrong.

Sometimes Kiko came on a little too strong. He was just a Commander and Chief who gave orders and was at the front lines of every confrontation and was several times over the couple of years that Michael was a Victorville U.S.P. with him. Kiko was the kind of person you would want as a friend and nothing more.

Michael and Kiko had become pretty good friends and remained that way for a long time. They kicked it in the law library every day studying their cases and law pertaining to other cases. They also discussed leisure books and authors. Both Kiko and Michael also talked about God often. Michael was the diehard Christian and Kiko was a believer whose mother was a preacher in L.A. so they got along just great.

The both networked all the time, however, there were times Michael was not into everything that Kiko was, especially gang banging. The most common things they shared and discussed were mainly God, the law, writing and physical fitness.

While sharing time there over a two-year period both the Crips and the Bloods had a couple of run-ins with each other. Kiko had been working on pushing the whole Black unity thing through and always found a reasonable way to squash any problems that arose. He would say things like, "We Blacks need to get money, make something of this life, get out and stay out and be ready for the others who call us the enemy."

The Crips and the Mexicans also had a couple of run-in's over the course of those couple of years as well. However, they did not really get out of control even though the Mexicans and Blacks had decades of killing on the streets, which was really surprising to see. You see, in prison they are pushed to live together, so they were not each other's enemies. "It's the system, the courts and the devil, not each other they would be fighting," as Kiko would day. Kiko even brought this to the attention of the Administration a couple of times.

Once when Michael and the brothers had been mistreated and roughed up badly by the officers, Kiko went to Warden Wood with about 100 others. They could have locked up the whole bunch for inciting a riot, but instead he took into account the real situation as he said he would, and an officer was disciplined instead.

Warden Wood was the same short size and shape as Elmer Fudd from Bugs bunny cartoons and even looked a lot like him. But Warden Wood was tough and he did not take any crap from anyone. He would lock someone down for absolutely nothing, but he was actually a pretty smart man and was accountable as well as easy to talk to. He would fix any problem as long as it was not frivolous.

Warden Wood had recently come to Victorville U.S.P. from Florence F.C.I. He used to assist the Wardens at Florence U.S.P., which was the most violent penitentiary in the nation.

The word on the compound was that Norwood got his start as an officer some 30 years prior when things were really hard-core. He received his first promotion while working the tier at Leavenworth U.S.P. in Kansas after a riot broke out. Several Officers had been taken hostage, one of which had happened to be Norwood, and a few other officers and inmates had been seriously beaten up and stabbed. The officers were pleading for their lives, but Norwood remained calm and tried to keep everyone else calm by telling the riotous convicts "You can make it through this safe and alive, just do not hurt anyone else." They say he was even cracking jokes by mimicking Elmer Fudd while he treated the injured inmates and officers who were pretty badly hurt.

Norwood was transferred to Victorville U.S.P. right after the Mexicans killed a White guy. Since he did not believe in total lock down or massive group punishment, they thought he would be the best man for the job.

There was a second incident that the Warden and Kiko had to deal with when one of the Mexican female officers allegedly called a brother a nigger and sided with the Mexican inmates in a racial dispute. Kiko and 100 other dudes went straight to the Warden with it, but not before scaring the woman half to death.

Kiko trusted that something would be done, preferably that the female officer would be fired. For any officer to take sides in a racial dispute could cause the ignition of an all-out war, despite the prejudice that could've gotten them all killed.

The Warden promised to look into it, which he did, but he never fired the officer who was at fault. He said that there was not enough proof, which was a typical response to be expected in regards to an inmate versus staff confrontation, even though there were over 100 witnesses.

The Officer ended up being transferred to a different housing unit and then eventually demoted after being involved in other similar situations.

It was one of the craziest incidents that Michael had witnessed with the Crips not being involved in a war, riot or racial dispute. It was certain that it could have turned into something serious had it been disputed.

Around this time the Crips founder and fearless leader, Tuckie was executed in California State Prison. The anger and potential violence was there as well as the tension being very crazy all over the yard, but all 300 Crips and Bloods as well as others went to the yard to pay their respects without a single incident.

Kiko himself led the ceremony. They had a moment of silence and prayed for a minute, which was probably the first time many of them had prayed in a long time. During the praying they were chanting, "Yes, Yes, Yes!" as Kiko was speaking about the injustice that had been done and how they were to seek justice for Tuckie by staying positive, learning, leaning on each other and staying together, getting out of jail and staying out, and making something positive of themselves. The whole meeting was pretty positive except for when they got into some talk about the White News system.

There was some debate and fighting to stop Tuckie's execution. Even the Reverend Jesse Jackson, Reverend Sharpton, Jamie Fox, Snoop Dog and others petitioned California Governor Arnold Schwarzenegger, who had been Tuckie's work out partner before he became an actor and then later the California Governor, to stop the execution, but no such luck. Jamie Fox himself even made a movie about Tuckie and about how people protested his innocence and that there was not enough evidence to prove his case. It showed how he was set up for his founding of the Crips and the death of some Asian business people in a robbery gone bad. It also showed how they only wanted to kill him in revenge for that as well as for not deliberately telling all the Crips' secrets. Tuckie's statement was, "I'm no snitch!"

In the end, the Crips gave him a peaceful celebration of his death as Tuckie requested in the death chamber just moments prior to his execution.

Tuckie was not a believer, but he did change by writing several Noble peace prize nominated children's books teaching kids not to join gangs and to get out of gangs if they were already in one. He taught them to go to school, go to work and make something of themselves.

Tuckie had also asked that the Crips and the Bloods get along, unite and do something positive for the community.

This was what Kiko preached to the men out there the day of Tuckie's memorial. The warden left them alone, regardless of the possibility of locking them up in the hole for group participation to incite a riot.

"A good man out of the good treasure of his heart bringeth forth that which is good." Luke 6:45.

CHAPTER 44

MICHAELS INVOLVEMENT IN PROGRAMS

Michael finally recovered and learned to deal with his mother's death in the summer of 2005. He realized that he needed to do what his mother would have wanted him to do. She told Michael, "Prove that you are an innocent man. The best thing you can do is become smarter than your attorney. There are some very smart attorney's in prison that one can learn from. Work hard, listen intently and then get yourself out of there and back home with your family and your kids."

That was what Michael had been working on during his entire experience in prison. He had not changed a lot of what he was already doing up to that point and he was doing it more often and better by cutting out the nonsense.

Michael began getting up at about 5:00am and preparing his work out with prayer. He would listen to the preachers on Christian Radio and meditate before officers even opened his door.

When the door was opened, he had already used the restroom, brushed his teeth, washed his face and was already stretching and preparing for his training. Michael would stretch for 15 to 30 minutes before going out to do a 3 to 5 mile run for 30 to 45 minutes. After running, he would walk the track and do push-ups at each lap and then do pull-ups off the soccer goal post, while doing dips in between the outside restrooms. He would do this for almost 30 to 40 minutes, 6 sets each with 25 repetitions before they would call the 10-minute movement at 8:00am.

At 8:00am, Michael would go to the law library to do legal reading and research until about 10:30. During that time, he was preparing his Writ of Certiorari, which was due in the Supreme Court on December 1, 2005. To date, he had been working on this for close to a year. Michael had read all the cases he could find pertaining to his appeal issues, and then read all the new cases that would come out in the criminal law reporter's logs. At times it would take him hours to complete, but sometimes he would just listen to the legal talk and give some legal wisdom that he just could not hold in, as he was getting a better grasp of the whole legal system and it's workings.

Michael at the time was also taking some legal correspondence courses. His brother Matthew had sent him some money to call home with, but he used the money to pay for his college books and lessons. The college, established in 1869, was one of the oldest legal colleges in the Nation. It had 2 year and 30 book lesson courses covering everything from introduction to law, the history of law, civil law, criminal law, wills and torts, and every aspect of law there was.

Emotionally, Michael continued learning how to deal with his feelings by asking himself what he was feeling and why he was choosing to feel that way. He wanted to understand why any given situation or experience would make him feel a particular way and how he could feel different about it.

On December 8, 2005, Michael was with the group of about 40 others who were moved into the program. The CODE unit is operated separate from the other housing units of the prison. The major reason a person would go to the CODE program is for positive change for those who are really serious about changing. Everyone in the program is supposed to be on similar roads to positive change. Some people in the program only played the part and really were not seriously seeking to change and they preyed on those that were, like the past drug dealers and rapists and hard cases.

CODE required mandatory meeting and participation in classes such as cognitive thinking, relapse prevention, communication skills, breaking barriers and after-care programs. They also offered some wellness classes. Classes always met Monday through Friday from 8:00 a.m. to 10:00 a.m., 12:00 p.m. to 1:00 p.m., and 2:00 p.m. to 3:00 p.m. three times a week minimum.

CODE gives a person the opportunity to get the tools they need to change and break free of a life of drugs and crime, and to stay free.

There is a lot of cocaine, methamphetamine and especially heroin use and that is why there is less violence in Victorville than you would expect in a high security prison. When things do happen, they will happen big and that is usually something to do with not being able to get their drugs.

The Blacks also have their issues with the chemicals. They want to control who is selling. It was said that allegedly the Crips and Bloods had made a pact after a few months so that no one else except their affiliates would get and sell any major weight. This was due to the fact that most of the dudes who were getting all the money were from out of town (not including L.A. or California).

They wanted to start their first and then take the business from the Mexicans. Not only did they have an issue among the Blacks who would be doing the selling, the also has issues with a few youngsters who were using cocaine, meth and mainly heroin. They cured them, at least temporarily, by giving the youngsters a beat down and running them up top. Meaning to the hole to check in but many of the other blacks were not any different based on the way they were smoking weed and drinking booze.

They were completely out of control, not alert and minding their P's and Q's about anything.

The CODE program kept accepting these predators into the program because they said they needed to meet a quota and had to fill the beds to get their budget money from the government. They also kept accepting the prey in the program even after they had several dirty urine analysis drug tests. Any other prison that was highly scrutinized with whom they accepted by three CODE specialists, drug & alcohol counselors, plus regular officers & had four officers opposed to the one that other units have.

They had more drugs and alcohol in the CODE unit than any other unit in the prison. There was a 128-person capacity allowed in the unit, but they were only supposed to be able to house 100 people, who was more conducive to a program atmosphere but they ended up staying over that.

About 65 of the people in there were addicts and the other 25 of so were known prison dealers. However, they usually had less violence because addicts had nothing but getting high on their minds. The five or six incidents they did have were over drugs and alcohol. It could have been real big and turned into a race riot and Michael could have been in it, were it not for God. Thanks to the Holy Spirit, Michael kept a level head. Michael and a few of the other Christian brothers, who were mostly Spanish, had a Bible study and prayer session in the unit. It began in Andrew Acosta's cell and at its peak there was about 20 brothers and bunches of other want to be believers attending.

"Being then made free from sin, ye become the servants of righteousness." Romans 6:18.

CHAPTER 45

FREEWAY, LIL' KURT

A few days a real scum bucket by the name of Freeway hit the yard with his homeboy, Robert Earl a.k.a. Lil Kurt. Eyes were open and watching. One day Robert Earl caught Michael in the yard after he had been at the Lt's office placing a request that Earl get to come to the yard. Michael knows the procedure all too well. When a guy first gets to Victorville, (or any other penitentiary) he is housed in the hole until they check him out and make certain it is safe to put him on the yard.

Earl told Michael that the word from Florence was that Michael was hot, but he was not going to say anything as long as Michael looked out for him. Michael told earl to get away from him and that it was all a lie and to do whatever he wanted about it.

A few days later, his cruddy homeboy Freeway came to Michael's unit requesting to talk to Michael. He stated that he knew Michael was hot and had been running a food and sandwich business. He also told him that Michael had better buy and sell food from him, or Michael would go down. Michael told him, "You do not know who you are messing with. What you are saying is a lie and I'm a child of God, but I'll have no problem taking you out."

It was not but a few days later that both Freeway and Robert Earl got into it with the Vice Lords in the kitchen and were stabbed several times, another reminder that God takes care of his children and God's children's enemies usually get each other. It never fails.

For some reason, over and over again this Captain Kurt character and Michael kept bumping heads. Michael's only wrong move with this guy was that he was confronting him with readiness for anything, but Michael was born this way and that was just the way he was.

After the Freeway incident, Captain Kurt went up to, Michael one day when he was drunk and said he needed to holler at him. He called Michael into his cell and showed him a knife he had in his pocket. "I think you have been watching and following me man," he accused Michael. "Why would I want to follow you? And if I were you, I would not show someone like me a knife unless you plan on using it," Michael told him. Again, he said, "The only one I follow and watch is Jesus." Michael told Kurt that he was all mixed up about him. Then for no apparent reason Kurt ran out of his own cell. Michael never really figured out why he did that but both he and Kurt managed to stay away from each other for a while after that.

A few weeks later, one of Kurt's boys names T.G. came to the yard. They hung out together almost every day for a couple of weeks until Kurt was able to get T.G. to move into his cell. The kid was about 28 years old, 6'3" 180 lbs and both skinny and blind as a bat.

They invested in the dope business and started starring Michael down every chance they got. Captain Kurt had obviously never been in prison before and was trying to monopolize the dope business in an effort to get power to be the head of the Crips, but they soon found out that he did not have what it took.

It was after they moved in that Michael was talking to Big Kent, an old school Christian brother Michael knew from Florence U.S.P., that Captain Kurt walked up all drunk and said he was going to get rid of Big Kent and Michael. Captain Kurt also mentioned he was going to have the Crips idolized. Big Kent was 6'6", 350 lbs, and assumed that he could crush just about anyone, but not that day as he just turned and walked away angry. Michael had never seen him do before.

Michael thought Captain Kurt was being stupid and drunk again, but earlier that morning Michael had been doing the floor job, when out of nowhere Kurt walked up to him and asked him if he was writing a book or something. Then his boy Bill came and grabbed him. During the next controlled move, Michael went to see Kiko, who was the head of the Crips as well as his friend. He explained how he had never come to him before, but that it was the third time this had happened.

He explained that Kurt had threatened him and pulled weapons on him. Michael told Kiko that something bad was going to happen to Kurt and that he mentioned to him that he only wanted to serve God and do his legal thing. Kiko told Michael not to trip and that he would handle it.

Lunchtime came and went and Michael could not be sure if Kiko had talked to Kurt or not. He had not thought so as he had not been anywhere and neither had Michael. He went back to the microwave area to warm up some lunch when, low and behold, along came Kurt. He said, "It's time for you to go," as he pulled out a weapon. Michael noticed that his boy T.G. came up right behind him so now Michael was blocked in.

Kurt had his weapon and Michael figured he had to get him first before taking out his boy who had no weapon. Michael told Kurt, "You are making a big mistake. I won't be able to control myself by myself after this goes down." They were in the middle of the unit where the officer could see what was happening, but he was not paying attention.

Then one of his boys pushed him aside and T.G. asked Michael to come in the room and talk to him, which he did. As soon as he did, he thought it was a major mistake as two other guys bordered the door with one standing in it. Michael told them, "I'm not going out like a sucker and I do not want to do nothing to him, but if he keeps coming at me like that for no reason, I'm not responsible for what happens."

Less than three days later, Captain Kurt was kicked out of the unit without explanation. Michael later heard it was because of his dope dealing. Less than a month after that, Captain Kurt was rushed to the hospital because his liver had failed and he almost died from all that drinking of prison wine. Michael, being the Christian man he is, felt sorry for him and even prayed for him. It is obvious that God doesn't like anyone messing with his children as Michael was safe and God says that revenge is His.

Thanks to some harsh criticism from Kim, Michael went back to editing his book and taking out a lot of the sex, and drugs and crime, Michael met a very smart kid from Arizona names Jason who helped him with editing. He was not an experienced writer or editor, but he was smart and really fast. Michael also had a new cellie named Chet to help him out and whom he convinced to come into the CODE program. This was fortunate, because the Administration was forcing CODE participants to accept cellie's and Michael did not want to get stuck with some negative guy.

Chet also needed some place to go because he kept getting in to it with some D.C. cats. It was obvious Chet had somewhat of a temper and Michael, did not want to see him kill anyone and surely did not want anyone to kill Chet. He wanted to see him get with God, because he knew Chet needed it, and he wanted to see Chet get his case overturned. Chet insisted he was innocent and Michael believed him.

Michael advised Chet that he should study law if he wanted to chance to get out, and encourage Chet to take the same law courses that Michael had. Michael was ever willing to sell Chet the books he already had to help him prove his innocence.

While Chet agreed it was a good idea, he also thought that he just was not ready yet. Michael tried understanding what he meant by that.

CHAPTER 46

LAW SCHOOL GRADUATION, NEWLY DISCOVERED EVIDENCE MOTION & MEETING JOE CORTEZ

In October 2006, Michael completed his schooling at Blackstone. Taking career Justice Correspondence Courses in Paralegal and Legal Assistant studies, averaging an 86.6% grade score. He completed a 2-year course in less than 18 months, and the only reason it took him that long was because of some financial troubles he experienced. However, he vowed that he would never again put himself in the position to have any more legal problems like he had been currently facing.

Michael was working on some big cases with some well-known attorneys and law firms on the West Coast. His clients were gifting an average of $100.00 per hour to Michael, and he had more work than he wanted. He soon realized that he needed to hire and assistant for himself, especially now that he was a Graduate Level Certified Paralegal Legal Assistant, which certainly gave him an extra boost in confidence and understanding.

Michael was not about to stop there, not until he was a law school graduate, and to this day he is still working toward that goal. There is nothing more important to Michael than God, his family, his case and his new craft as he had been utilizing it to help others free themselves. It made him feel good about working toward his own freedom as well as the freedom of others.

Michael's duties entailed working with legal research, investigating, legal writing administration, docket control, and filing briefs and motions, all of which he became very good at. Michael was very proud of himself when he received his Certificate of Completion of October 14, 2006. The staff in the Prison Education Department wanted Michael to be a participant in the first graduation ceremony at Victorville U.S.P. because he was the first inmate there to become a college graduate. Michael prayed to God to encourage others to do for themselves as he had done for himself.

Michael had been working on a few guy's cases over a period of about 6 months, doing most of that work for free or for some help to pay for his legal schooling. He was happy to see that there were so many more men who needed and wanted help just as much or more than Michael did, although they all had suffered some grave injustice.

Michael would try to answer anyone who had questions. He would give his opinion, advice and help look up cases, read cases, briefs and motions to the point where he was discouraged from going to the law library because he could not get his own work completed. Michael knew it was definitely time for him to get some limits and boundaries.

He did give out a great deal of free advice, opinions and interpretation of cases and case law and showed others how to legal research, writing and whatnot but boundaries were always a main concern. He would discuss anything with anyone except for officially taking their case.

One of the boundaries that Michael set was the fee for him to take a case was $1000.00 donation plus $1.00 per page to read transcripts. Michael still kept at least on pro bono case every day.

The fee that Michael set was not to just gain some funds for his case, but to discourage guys who were not serious. He wanted guys to get in there and learn it for themselves versus gangbanging, doping, drinking, watching M.T.V. and B.E.T. all day long. Every other non-important reprehensible thing, he would not encourage because he tried to motivate them into fighting for justice.

For whatever reason God had for each and every case, Michael had some success, but it would usually take a while and remove him from working on his own case as well as drain him mentally physically. However, Michael was not having the same success on his own case. He once believed in a myth that said lawyer and jailhouse lawyers can get others out, but not themselves.

So in October and November 2006 Michael filed Rule 33, which is a motion for a new trial for "Newly Discovered Evidence," on the grounds that he found that the Government had held some exculpatory evidence that could help prove Michael's innocence and was not turned over to the Defense. In this discovery, it is considered a serious violation of the U.S. Constitution.

The replying to Michael's Rule 33 Motion, the judge claimed it was premature and that until Michael received the documents himself, he had nothing to support his motion, although she did give Michael a tip. She told him what to do and how to get it refilled. This was very rare for a judge to do, however she knew the likelihood of Michael getting the documents without an order from the court was very slim. She also knew that the proper thing for her to do would be to order the Government to give up the information and then order a new trial.

So, Michael was beaten-up again, but he was not dead yet. All this did was make his fight harder and help more people than he already had. Now he knew better how to use that particular rules as well as use of evidence.

After all that was over with, graduation day soon came. The ceremony included a special guest Joe Cortez. He was a 5-time Golden Glove Boxing Champion Pro-Fighter, now retired and a pro referee and actor, Joe played a character in the new Rocky VI movie that came out Christmas Day 2006.

Joe was invited to the ceremony by his friend Tony Weeks, who is an officer and Recreation Specialist at the prison. He was also a pro boxer, pro referee and actor who also had a small role in Rocky VI.

Joe was a great speaker, a positive influence and a good man. He told some great stories and he was also a believer in God. He talked about overcoming adversities of his own and being born in Latin Spanish Harlem by a single mother in the 1950's.

Joe had accomplished some huge goals for being a poor little Spanish kid raised in Spanish Harlem around drugs, crime and street thugs. He went from being a boxing champion to a champion referee civil rights activist and embryonic research activist, helping in any way that he could.

Joe had been married to his wife for over 40 years and has raised three kids and covered every problem that arose with the help of God.

Joe was a huge inspiration for Michael and he stayed around after graduation to take photographs and sign autographs. Michael was one of the last inmates left, and he really enjoyed Joe's talk, but he did not want to get caught up in the praise of men.

As he was leaving Joe turned around and asked, "Michael, how much time do you have left?" Michael said, "I have a life sentence for a crime I did not commit." Joe said, "You are going to get out. You are going to prove your innocence. There is something about you, I can't explain it now, but it's something really good and I want you to make me a promise," Joe said with seriousness. Michael asked, "What is that?" "When you prove your innocence and you get out, stay out and help as many people as you can." Michael responded, "You got that!" Joe shook Michael's hand and grasped it with real compression.

He whispered, "One more thing Michael. I want you to come and see me in Vegas. I'm in the phone book and you'll probably get my people. Tell them about this day and they'll get me. I want to introduce you to some people, and I'll get you some Championship boxing tickets!" Joe promised. "I will man. I'll be giving you a call," Michael promised. "I'll see you then!"

CHAPTER 47

D.C.'S AND CRIPS WAR, MURDER NEW YEAR'S EVE 12/31/06

Michael called home for Christmas 2006. He almost did not want to call because he had been so miserably homesick and only had enough money and phone minutes to call home and tell each of his kids, "Merry Christmas. I love you and I am sorry I can't be there!"

He called his daughter Keya first as she was at her mother's house. The very first thing out of her mouth was, "Did you call your other kids first?" He gave her a truthful, "No," which did not do anything for the way he was already feeling. However, he did feel love because, after all, she was his daughter as well as a gift from God. Though she could at times be harsh, she said something that Michael had done around a month before Thanksgiving. He told her that he would be home one day and she replied, "Yeah right!" He told her then, as he told her on Christmas, "I love and miss you no matter what."

Michael then talked to Kim and his sister Tammy about all the negativity and they told him to try and understand his daughter, as she was hurt with the entire situation of not having a dad for the past nine years. They all agreed on that fact.

Both Kim and Tammy told Michael that he spoiled that girl rotten when he was out. . They also said, "She remembered that she was your princess." Michael said that he had never treated any of his kids different than the others.

Last Christmas they told Michael about her drinking at 13 years old and that now she was drinking and smoking. Both Kim and Tammy told Michael that she had a picture of her in a bra on www.myspace.com. Just hearing that really hurt his heart. He tried to think about everything positively. Michael's son always defended his sister and would say that it really was not that bad.

Kim stepped in to say, "Listen, this shrink I clean for thinks I should tell you not to tell the kids you are coming home because it can have a negative effect and cause them to act out like they are." Michael was beginning to get upset and said, "Yeah whatever."

Michael did not agree with Kim, but he did not feel like arguing either. He did not want to risk the chance of speaking hope from any of his kids, and so he left it at that. "Your oldest daughter Jazz is a straight A student, on the honor roll and received a scholarship at 17 years old. Michael Jr. earns all A's and they both mind me and act their age. Keya minds me too it's just when she leaves my house that she acts out."

Michael called back later that Christmas evening so that he could catch his son Michael Jr., as he had not spoken to him yet. He had been at his friend's house when Michael called the first time. Keya answered the phone. "Who is this?" Michael asked. "You do not even know my voice, that's a shame," she accused. "You surprised me I did not know you were going to be there. I thought you were going to see your brother and sisters, my other white family as you call them," said Michael. "Whatever dad," Keya said. "Did you get the presents I sent you?" he asked. She said she did, and then Michael told her, "Good," and tried to explain that he did not have much phone credits and then asked, "Can I talk to Michael and Jazzman?" "I told you Michael was not here, here's Jazzman," she sneered. Then Michael could hear her in the background "I'm glad he wants to talk to you and not to me," she said. Michael asked Jazz, "Let me talk to Keya again" "Okay, Merry Christmas Dad!" said Jazzman. Michael told her Merry Christmas and told her to tell her sister she never has to talk to him if she doesn't want to.

Michael knew Jazz did not pass along the message because she hated fighting and arguments. He apologized to his daughter as he did every year for not being able to be with her for Christmas, and then he would say, "Maybe next year baby!"

Michael spent the rest of Christmas in his cell in bed and upset and sicker than ever. They say that it gets easier and better as the years go by, but it most certainly doesn't for Michael as well as many others. It may have something to do with the love that Michael had for his family and his kids, and then being innocent and wrongly convicted.

Michael spent the next few days after Christmas 2006 clearing his calendar and finishing up all cases on his docket. He wanted to begin 2007 with a clean slate and focus especially on God, his case and his legal business. Needless to say, he got down to business.

On December 30, 2006 at 8:00am, the sirens and shooting went off on the yard. There was a war that broke out with about 100 Black people and it happened just as Michael was walking out the door to work at the Library he could see across the yard that people were punching and stabbing each other. Michael learned later that four guys had been life-flighted to the hospital where one was pronounced D.O.A. it was the D.C.'s and the Crips, and was just one more reminder that he was still in prison, a hell on earth, and that things never got any better, they only got worse.

When Michael arrived at Victorville U.S.P., the population was still only at partial capacity at about 1200 inmates. Soon it would become overcrowded and there would definitely be more violence, only due to the ignorance and violence that was bound to breed more ignorance and violence.

Michael wondered about his two good friends in each group that he was really cool with. He wondered if they were okay and if he had done enough to reach them.

Love was from D.C. and one of the best guys Michael had ever met, and from Washington D.C. no less. He had even recently made a contribution to sponsor Michael's book. Love was a big prison dope man who made his first million in the pen. He came to prison when he was only sixteen years old and he was now 36 and about to go home.

Michael could only wonder if Love was one of the men killed that day because he was supposed to receive some money from Love that very same day. Love helped save Michael's life after he had only been there six months and someone had wanted to jump him.

The D.C. East Coast car would tell them they were not dirty and were only getting money. In all certainty, they were getting more money than the Crips even thought it was the Crips yard.

Love was the first one to hit Michael with a care package when he first arrived on the compound. It included deodorant, soap, and hair grease. Michael and Love grew closer after about a year in the CODE program together. They always talked about God, the law, jealousy, haters and making something of themselves.

The person from the Crips was Kiko. Michael was actually cool with a few Crips. He would do a lot of legal work for the Crips and Love who was wrongfully convicted of murder 16 years ago at 16 years old, but to Kiko he was the best Crip friend. Kiko would listen when Michael talked even though he was years older. Michael had seen Kiko in action when he would tell others about being positive, using the word “Nigger,” God, and getting out and staying out.

Kiko would not stop “banging” and Michael never asked him why he stayed in at 45 years of age, but he did tell Michael a couple of times, “If I did not run this car then who would or could?” Kiko was right, because there was not anybody who could run it like he did.

Kiko had spent the last 16 years ruling and, like Michael, he usually ruled right as best as he could. Michael was supposed to be helping Kiko sponsor his book about guns, gang violence and stopping the nonsense, and Michael was indeed doing so. What Kiko did not know was that part of the money to sponsor Kiko’s book was coming from Love and the D.C. car, which was Michael’s back-up plan.

Michael spent from December 29, 2006 to New Years Eve 2007, twenty seven hours fasting and praying for everyone-family, friends, from the unsaved and lost souls to the saved so that we all could have a better relationship with God.

“It isn’t how many times we fail; it’s how many times we get back up.”

CHAPTER 48

TRANSFERRING FROM VICTORVILLE TO TUCSON

Six weeks off lockdown after the melee between the Crips and DC Blacks. A Crip named Fish was dead and three DC Blacks were paralyzed. Tragic Black-on-Black violent nonsense. Some good guys were gone and Michael had lost a good friend. Michael was working on Fish's case and making some progress.

It was said that Fish caused the whole melee by attempting to get one of the DC guys to pay for the drugs he sold him. Fish was normally a humble dude, at least within but when a man in prison even thinks that he's being played for a fool or jerked around, he feels this is something he has to do before his image is ruined. This is especially true for a member of one of the biggest gangs in the country when a member of a rival gang notorious for scandal on your home turf.

Victorville is an hour or two from L.A. and has about three hundred Crips and Blood many of whom were broke and staying out of the way. The DC Blacks were willing to do whatever it took to stay in business and were making more money selling drugs and tobacco than any other group on the yard, even if they were only about fifty strong and greatly outnumbered.

The DC guy who owed Fish money was well known throughout the system, not for his scandalous or toughness or even homosexuality as many DC known for, but for his money. The DC guy had won about one million dollars in a lawsuit against the Federal Bureau of Prison (FBOP) after staff calmly watched him nearly burn to death in a prison back east the staff had claimed that they could not get to him because of a door, being locked.

This guy received thousands of dollars monthly, but unfortunately, had spent most of it on drugs and other bad prison habits. He owed a lot of money to dope dealers on the yard, but he always paid and looked out for his homeboys first, which unfortunately got Fish mad and ultimately led to him being killed. Several others were left handicapped or severely injured. The DC Blacks are now rarely allowed in West Coast federal prisons and California prisons.

Six weeks later, lockdown was over and Michael was ready to go. He had work to do and, more importantly, was up for transfer. Federal prisoner are eligible for transfer after spending eighteen months at an institution. Every six months, the Unit Teams (consisting of a Counselor, Case Manager and Unit Manager) conduct a meeting with each prisoner where they can request a transfer after eighteen months at an institution. The FBOP can transfer a prisoner whenever it wanted and it's done quite a lot, especially with troublemakers. The FBOP frequently does this to get rid of trouble causing prisoners; simply keeping them in the Special Housing Unit (SHU) isn't good for the prison, or for the prisoner. If there happens to be a new penitentiary opening somewhere and if they are in need of prisoners who are not troublemakers, they can operate without many incidents.

During the spring of 2007, Michael was a couple of months beyond the eighteen months required for transfer eligibility. Things were getting bad, with the drug infested danger and violence that was always in the air. Especially after the local guys had taken a hit like they did, things were bound to get worse and Michael did not want to get caught in it, or anything that would cause him to be unable go to the law library.

As soon as the lockdown was over, Michael went to the Unit Team and requested that he be put in for a transfer to Federal Correctional Institution (FOCI) Oxford, a medium much closer to his family.

Most guys with thirty or more year sentences are required to do at least ten years at a maximum-security prison, before being eligible to have their security level reduced. unfortunately, that is another one of the policy's the FBOP changes whenever it fits their interest, as guys with multiple life sentences have been known to come straight from court to medium (or lower) security prison, especially prior to 2001. Certain prisoners are still sent to low security prison for (cooperation) or because there unable to hang in a maximum or high security prison.

CHAPTER 49

DRUGS, BUT NO TRANSFER AT VICTORVILLE

In that, Victorville was an hour plus drive from Los Angeles. The land of gangs, drugs, power and money, the addicts and drugs spread from there like leaves falling from a tree.

All of these vices and people crossed over into the prison system. Some of the people who controlled these markets were the very same ones in prison. Michael knew several guys who had found large quantities of heroin, cocaine or marijuana by just walking around the yard. A couple of them were off and running after that, having "come up" from the found drugs.

Michael would not have believed it, if he had not seen it with his own eyes; but a couple of them, including Colombians, were attacked in their cells and robbed of everything they owned. Some had to ask their people outside to wire tens of thousands of dollars to their attackers.

This was not just happening at the U.S.P., but also at the lower security FCI next door. Some say that began next door because that prison had opened one year before the U.S.P. and there were more gang-bangers and Mexican rivalry. Most of the guys were straight off the streets of L.A. and did not know how to act. Having never been in the Federal prison system, and surrounded by convicts from all over the world.

Michael was still waiting for a response from his Unit Team about his transfer to FCI Oxford, when he received a message from the Unit Case Manager, to come talk to her. She told him that the Unit Manager was going to turn down his transfer.

Later that same day, Michael went to have a talk with the Unit Manager, a six foot six black man who said, "I do not know you, I'm not willing to take the risk on you."

Michael told to himself "I've done everything asked or required of me and I know that currently and in the past, staff have taken risks on other guys who had less time in than me Michael told the Unit Manager that there were letters in his file on from past Wardens, and a former Regional Director, who had recommended Michael for a transfer, so why would not this Unit Manager do the same? He said, "That's them, I'm me, and it has to get through me before it gets to them."

Michael's next thought was "Who is this guy and what did I do to him?" Michael said, "Look sir, my daughter is sick, she has been in and out of the hospital and has a rare illness. Oxford is less than one hour from her and I'm just trying to get there."

"Well, it's not going to be happening right now, you'll have to give me more time, to get to know you" the Unit Manager replied. Michael then said that he heard Tucson is looking for model inmates to open up that prison. The unit manager responded, "yes they are". "Sign me up," as he knew he was not getting anywhere with this Unit Manager. Michael went to with other unit team members and the CODE program staff. They told Michael not to worry, as this Unit Manager was a jerk and they would do whatever they could to help him out. A couple of days later, as Michael was returning from lunch, he heard the sirens go off and shooting. As he looked around to see where it was coming from, he saw staff running out of the door saying "race riot next door at the FCI".

The SUP was locked down, so staff could assist at the FOCI. It was not until the following day that Michael found out what had happened. There was a race riot next door between the Blacks and the Mexicans. At least one of each ended up in the Intensive Care Unit (I.C.U.) and several others had been stabbed or beaten.

The very next day, the CODE program Coordinator called Michael in and said, “I know you are trying to get a lower security transfer to Oxford, unfortunately I’m unable to get you to Oxford right now, but what I can do is get you a lower security transfer to next door, as they are looking for some older and more mature Black and Mexican inmates to help defuse the situation over there. After completing six months to a year over there, you will be eligible to transfer to Oxford as you’ll have a lower security level there.”

Michael sat and thought for a minute, then said, “Thanks but no thanks, I’m sure it could be good but odds are more than likely, it would turn out bad.” Michael figured that he would do better at U.S.P. Tucson as it was a new prison and he could work his way from there.

CHAPTER 50

ARRIVING AT TUCSON, THE G.D.'S AND RUFF

On May 1, 2007 at 4:00 a.m., staff came to Michael's cell and said, "You have ten minutes to pack all your stuff, you are being transferred."

Michael kept most of his property packed at all times because he never knew when something like this was going to happen. It took him an hour to get completely ready.

U.S.P. Tucson only had two housing units open, Units A and F. On the yard, there were only about two-hundred prisoners in a prison built for 1400-1500. Luckily, for Michael, he was taken to a unit, which had many open cells. Unfortunately, he was only in the cell for a moment before he was assigned a cellie (aka Cellmate). It was one of the guys from Victorville, who was on the bus with Michael. Within five minutes of being in their new cell, two Crips from L.A. Appeared at the cell door. The first thing they wanted to know was "Where're you from? Who do you ride with?" Jeff said he was from L.A. and rides by himself. Michael responded that he was from Madison Wisconsin. The Crips did not know where that was. They knew Green Bay, from the Packers football team, Milwaukee, from the TV show Happy Days. The two Crips left.

Later that same night, a guy named "Ruff" came up to Michael and asked "Remember me?" ah, you are Ruff from Florence, right?" Michael responded.

Ruff said "Yeah man," acting all tough. "Where and how have you been?" Ruff was one of the G.D. guys that had been kicked off the compound at Florence.

Ruff said, "I've been on the East Coast since Florence," with an attitude as if he were the big boss or something. The following day, Michael found out why there were only 10 G.D.'s on the yard. Being that Ruff was their "Shot Caller," all 160 lbs of him, the rest of the guys looked as if they were in the Sugar Hill Gang rather than G.D.'s. Some of the G.D.'s carefully approached Michael to introduce themselves, and the others just looked like they wanted to play tough simply because they had been in a gang from Chicago. Michael did not have time to pay them any mind and went about his own business.

The next morning Michael made a trip to the commissary and spent the monthly spending limit of two-hundred and ninety dollars. Rarely did Michael ever do that, but he had made up his mind before arriving at Tucson that he was going to pick up the pace in all aspects of his life, He bought all the healthiest food that the commissary had and told himself that he would only eat health foods, even if he had to buy it himself. He also decided to double his workouts, which he started on day one. He made it a point to do that at least three to five hours a day in the hot Tucson sun. He bought two pair of shoes to last him until he received his property. Michael also bought Jeff what he needed while he was there, which was not much more than a little food and some basic hygiene items. Michael did the same for a friend of his named Danny, who was to be a former Hells Angel from L.A.

About a week later, Michael was told to go to R&D for his property. He planned to see Ruff that same day, before Ruff came to see him, as he wanted to show his PSI and court paperwork and to establish that he was not a rat. He did not want to be asked or bothered by Ruff or any of the other guys in his crew.

Michael handed his PSI to Ruff and asked him to take his time reading it, so as to clear up any rumors. Michael mentioned to Ruff that after they were done with it, to please not ask for it anymore. Ruff had not come back and twenty-four hours had elapsed. That's when he saw him reading the PSI with his crew on the yard playing around with it, Michael walked up to him and asked for his paperwork back. Ruff asked, "What was up with the rumors?" as he did not see anything in Michael's paperwork.

Michael knew that a story of a bad rumor was a move to try to get him back in the group, but Michael was completely done with that part of his life.

Ruff then said that he really had not even read it yet and would not be done for a while As Michael started to leave, Ruff asked one more thing, "Do you still run that Internet business?" Michael replied, "Yes, I do." Ruff wanted Michael to "hook him up" so that Ruff could try and catch a girl on the net. Michael told Ruff to get him a picture and he'd see what he could do. As suggested, Ruff did the very next day.

CHAPTER 51

MONEY, KIM AND IRA ROBBINS

Before leaving U.S.P. Victorville, Michael had done fairly well with his legal practice, considering the circumstances. He had saved enough money to self-publish his books. Michael was just waiting on his sister Tammy to finish scanning his latest manuscript and check it for grammar, punctuation, and spelling before sending it to the publishing company. Tammy had the book for a couple of months, before Michael even left Victorville. Michael made contacts with the publishing company so he knew they were waiting. Tammy held half of the money, one thousand dollars, and Kim held the other half.

Michael had a total of three-book ready, as well as the money. Unfortunately, he found out that Kim had spent the money she promised to save for his book project. Needless to say, Michael was upset, as he had been working so hard to make money from the sale of his books to use in fighting his wrongful conviction. It just about killed him when he found out that Kim spent the money for gifts and feel good items. He had every right to feel that his freedom was more important than ridiculous unnecessary gifts. Michael felt as if Kim did not care whether he got out or not, and with her doing this, it was telling him that she did not believe in him nor would he ever be getting out.

Thinking back a few weeks before this happened Michael had found something else out. He did not want to know or think about it, although he had seen it coming. Kim had been seeing some other guy, a bum with a lot of kids, no job, a criminal record, and a drug habit. When Michael first mentioned it to her, she denied everything. Michael knew that these types of things happen to the vast majority of prisoners. Their loved ones abandon them or leave them for someone else that is worse. He knew that everyone eventually gets hurt, but he thought could not and would not even happen to him. Still, he was more concerned for Kim and wished that she had just told him the truth, from the beginning.

Michael went to Tucson with a different attitude. Inside, he felt as though he had to forgive simply because she asked him to, but he was not to know all that happened.
The other half of the money which Michael sister had been holding was not being used for him to get established in Tucson, as starting at a new prison takes funds and there were not many guys to do legal work for yet, the guys that had agreement with at Victorville were no longer paying, now that he was no longer.

Michael knew he had to get a prison job. He was hired to work the main corridor of to the Administrative office.

Michael came to Tucson with a positive attitude. However, not long after Michael arrived his money began to run out.

The next traumatic event in involved the newest member of his legal team, Ira, of Ira and Associates. Ira was a former Milwaukee police officer, private investigator, and a legal consultant, who now called himself an “Investigative Consultant”. Ira stopped answering Michael’s letters and phone calls. He was also not answering calls from Michael’s family.

Michael called and wrote many times, to no avail. Ira just decided one day to not respond and Michael could not understand why. The last couple of letters that Michael had sent were sent certified mail, and sure enough, the delivery confirmation slip was signed, so he knew he was still alive. Ira was still doing business and certainly knew Michael wanted to talk to him.

In the last letter, he asked Ira to return of all the transcripts, no response came. Then, after a month's time Ira wrote to Michael say the transcripts had been sent but the prison had returned them.

Michael sent Ira another letter asking him to send the transcripts again, but this time to mark them as "Legal Mail," and to enclose a package authorization. More than month went by without a response.

Needless to say, Michael was disappointed, hurt and angry. It had been more than two years since Ira had first come into Michael and his families' lives. Michael's family had paid Robin thousands of dollars Ira had promised Michael that he would do whatever he could to help him out but then did nothing. Michael felt like he had been robbed and left for dead.

Michael filed complaints, which including a civil case, due to Ira taking all Michael's money, with no work performed or transcripts for nothing. Michael called his sister Tammy; she had just sent Ira another check. Michael told her to get it out of the mailbox or call the bank and stop payment, which she did. She told Michael that was the last money she had, due to the struggling real estate market and her declining financial situation, but she wanted to make sure that Ira had some money to work with.

Michael had received a letter from the Wisconsin State Attorney; before leaving Victorville, telling him, that Ira was under investigation for practicing without a license and wire fraud, and that they wanted Michael to participate in helping them prosecute him. Michael was against all that and did not trust the Government, so he declined. Later Michael wrote them back and asked what they wanted him to do to help, because he did not want to see Ira ripping off other people and wanted to get his transcripts and money back. They agreed to do what they could to help.

CHAPTER 52

AUNT IDA'S DEATH

One of Michael's most loved ladies was Ida Caldwell. Unfortunately, she had passed away. Michael first heard of this from his sister Tammy. It was a shock, and he could not believe his ears. He was shaken and shocked by the sad news.

Tammy told Michael the details of her passing. It was not like she was a spring chicken anymore, but thoughts of her, remained in his heart., She was in her thirties or forties, and took Michael and his siblings in when they were young, as their mother was serving time in prison.

Ida took good care of Michael and his brothers and sisters, and taught them how to take care of themselves. Michael was only fifteen when they went to live with Ida. She always used to say that he was a grown man. Tuttie was fourteen, Tammy was ten, and Duce was only five or six. Ida was a cousin of Michael's grandmother. Everyone always called her "Aunt Ida," because that was how they thought of her-as a member of their immediate family.

After Ida's mother died when she was young, Michael's grandmother took care of her.

This was what "true black" families did for each other back then. Aunt Ida was one person that Michael could not wait to show his gratitude. Show her that he was making something of his life, and just hang out with her. He admired and appreciated her so much. She worked for the University of Wisconsin, as a laboratory tech for more than twenty years. She was someone Michael could really talk to about any and everything. If she thought something was going on with Michael, she would show concern and find out what it was, and help him with it. Aunt Ida never did drug a day in her life; she only drank a little on her birthday.

Aunt Ida had eight children of her own, Reesa, Como, DB, Mary, Al, Herm, Lolita (a.k.a. LaLa) and Kerm, all by her husband Sunny. As a couple, they fought like cats and dogs. Ida knew a lot about relationships, both the good and the bad. It was just fortunate she could hold her own. She loved teasing Michael in front of girls showing his baby pictures. She'd embarrass him by saying his "member" was small and crocked as a young boy.

After her husband's death, Ida always dated men that were about half her age, and was not ever afraid to tell anyone that it was just all about sex. Ida also taught Michael how to shoot dice. She was a woman who had a story was born and raised in the south, on the border of Tennessee and Arkansas. She moved to Chicago in her later teens, with the big black migration throughout the 30's or 40's, for the job market.

After hearing the news from Tammy, Michael called Kim who told him it was true. She was rather nonchalant about it. Supposedly, LaLa had gotten into an argument with Ida and cursed her. The last thing she said was "I hope you die". Later on that night, Ida died of a heart attack.

Lolita was supposedly arguing with Ida over her not wanting to give her money for drugs. When LaLa found out what had happened to her mother, she went into a nut house that day.

Michael called Como. Michael always wanted to believed Como, as did most people who knew him. He was a man of honor and respect. A twenty-year Navy man who retired to become some kind of scientist. Ida was always so proud of him and so was everyone else who knew him. Michael called on the day of the funeral he was happy to hear from Michael and that Ida would have been, too. Michael said he was sorry and expressed his condolences for Como's loss. Como was his usual happy-go-lucky self at first but could tell he was becoming sad. Como began to tell Michael the story of the last day with LaLa. Michael told Como that Ida was in a better place he did not know what else to say. With all the talking going on Michael was beginning to get choked up, he was wondering if his lying-ass cousin Victor Caldwell was there. He met Victor when he was staying with Aunt Ida while going down to Vic's mom's house with his cousin Kermit back in the 80's on summer vacation.

Michael finished his call to Como without asking about Victor, Later that day; Michael called Tammy and Mathew, who had attended the funeral. In speaking to them, he found out that Victor had not shown up. Had Victor shown everyone would have had the opportunity to talk to him and ask if he would come forward and tell the truth so Michael would not have to die in prison, for crimes he did not commit. Victor had mentioned to some people that he was willing to come clean with the truth, and mentioned that Michael had nothing to do with the robberies and never gave a gun to anyone. To this day Michael lives on the hope that Victor would understand that he should stand up and do the right thing.

CHAPTER 53

DANNY FABRICANT

Most Pens/Prisons have a few guys who make $ by doing substandard legal work. Once they get a bunch of clients (who they make pay up front) they start the legal work & then Check-In, leaving all of them hunting for someone else to take over the mess that's been made of their court filings. Or, if the guy hasn't checked in, yet, when the stuff gets Denied, his Clients make him give the $ back, plus more & usually beat him up or stab him.

While in Victorville, I met, and became friends with Danny, who is the best Jail Litigator I've ever seen, or even heard of. He was one of the four Hells Angels that were at Victorville. I later found out that he was not a Hells Angel anymore, but the four of them always hung out together. He looks like a short, muscular Santa Clause, with long white/grey hair in a ponytail and a full white beard.

He was very well known in Victorville both for his legal knowledge and the huge number of Administrative Appeals he regularly filed—usually two each week. He filed so many over the Education Dept. (Where the Law Library was) that the Head of that Dept. had him assigned there, secretly.

She called him into her office and asked him "Where do you work?" He told her that he did not have a job and that was why he was there all the time. She told him, "Well, I had you assigned here. You work for me now." He asked her, "What is it you expect me to do?" She told him "You are in charge of everything here that any prisoner had anything to do with."

Danny was very selective about who he would help or give legal advice to. Anytime he was asked for help, he would ask the person "Does you case have anything to do with a Sex Crime, and did you tell on anyone?" He never asked me that.

He was in his late 50's when I met him. He was doing Life sentences for a few small meth sales. The Hells Angel he was supposed to have sold the meth to, Michael Kramer, had become an ATF Informant after assaulting, kidnapping, murdering and trying to cut the head off of Cynthia Garcia who "...disrespected him," less than an hour after he met her, in Arizona, in late 2001. **[You can Google the two names & read the story in detail, as it was the topic of several AZ newspaper articles and has been mentioned in several books about the Hells Angels]**

Kramer contacted an AZ cop he used to be a Rat for [obviously, this was not known by the other Hells Angels] and that cop put him in touch with an ATF Agent (Ciccone) in Los Angeles, who signed him up, started paying him and had him move to Los Angeles, to transfer into Danny's Hells Angels Charter, to get Danny. Apparently, Danny was as popular with the ATF as he is with Prison higher-ups.

In October 2003, as a reward for framing Danny, Kramer pled Guilty in AZ Federal Court to VICAR Murder and in AZ State court, to Manslaughter. The plea agreements guarantee that his punishments will be five years, of probation, when is eventually sentenced—maybe in 2012?

Danny, and his wife, were arrested in Dec. 2003, as part of the Five-State, 'Photo-Op' mass arrests of 40+ Hells Angels over the 2002 shootout at a Laughlin, Nevada casino, 16

Hells Angels in AZ, who were all charged with the Kramer's Murder/Beheading of the woman, under Federal VICAR [Violent Crime in Aid of Racketeering] laws and 20+ assorted Hells Angels in CA, who were never charged with anything.

Danny, and his wife Rachel (who is 31 years younger than he is, and gorgeous [I saw a wedding picture]), were convicted of three small meth sales, to Kramer, in a mid-2004 trail. Danny received Life sentences (because of prior drug convictions) and his wife (who'd never been arrested before) got a 97-month sentence, because she would not 'cooperate.'

In March 2006, the AZ Federal case against the 16 Hells Angels charged with Kramer's murder was dismissed. In October 2006 the 44 Defendant prosecutions over the Casino shoot-out, in which three people died, fell apart. The ATF Agent (Ciccone) had withheld documents that were supposed to be turned over to the defense, in both cases.

In the Casino case, three+ weeks into the trial for the first group of 11, six entered Guilty pleas, to a minor charge, for no more than 30-month sentences & all State and Federal charges against the other 38 were dismissed. ** [This story is also available, on-line.]**

Danny helped me prepare my court filings. He never asked me for a dime. He never asked anyone he helped for anything—if someone insisted on paying him something, he would have them bring him a pint of Ice Cream from the store. Cheapest and best Lawyer I've ever seen.

In early 2007, the Tucson Penitentiary opened up. In Victorville, they put up notices advising anyone who wanted to go there, to submit a request. In true Bureau of Prisons fashion, they decided to pick guys who had not had a write up in the last year or two, and, once a week for about 6 weeks, without warning, they were told (at 3:00 am) "Pack up your stuff. You are going to Tucson." A 'reward' for not breaking any rules. Danny & I were among the second busload.

At Tucson, Danny and I spent our time in the Law Library. Danny started filing four or five appeals a week, on everything at Tucson. A few 'Control Freaks' in the upper staff had everything backwards and there were a lot of things that were required, that were not here. Danny's counselor said that he'd Filed 100 appeals—37 of which were Granted and all kinds of things were changed, for the better. After the first couple of months, a really reasonable Assoc. Warden was assigned to handle all of his appeals.

Danny & I used to work out at the same time every morning, on the playground. It turned out that we would jog on opposite days. Whenever we would pass each other, we'd insult each other.

Before Danny's 2004 trial, his Judge, one of the two worst & most often reversed, in the Los Angeles Federal Court system, made a ruling that he could not tell the jury anything about Informant Kramer killing & beheading the woman.

In Sept. 2007, the 9th Circuit reversed Danny's conviction, because of that ruling. The upper staffs at Tucson were happier than Danny was about his reversal, because it meant that he would be going back to Los Angeles, and they'd be rid of him.

In Mid December '07, he was picked up by three U.S. Marshals and flown straight back to Los Angeles. I thought I'd never see him again…

CHAPTER 54

DOPE TRADE, BIG BUST

Other than the few officers and Crips that got busted or quit, there was still not a tight hold on the drug trade on the yard. The Arizona Mexican car was building and making plans to come up, but a lot of guys were fearful of getting busted and transferred away from home. Most of the guys in the business did not have anyone local on the streets to bring drugs in.

Through the efforts of whites, mexicans, and blacks working together, they were off and running, using the visiting room as a conveyer belt for bringing drugs in. They went from one or two visitors to using three or four visitors at a time every weekend. But, just like everything else, everybody began noticing and the busts started happening.

It had a good run for a few months, not only using the visiting room, but also bribing staff members to bring things in. Some female staff would bring in packages not for money but for their relationships and "love". They had "mules" of every race going to the visiting room and swallowing ten to thirty double-wrapped balloons containing heroin, cocaine, marijuana, and at time tobacco.   The female visitors would enter the prison facility with drugs in their vaginas to sneak them through the drug detector device that has the ability to detect certain chemicals. Next, they go through a metal detector before finally entering the visiting room. The visitors check out the scene in the visiting room, looking for telltale signs, such as extra staff, officers watching or being seated close to the staff desk where there are more cameras and staff. The visitors would not want to show signs that something may be wrong. If all looks good, the female visitor will go to the visitors bathroom and take the drugs out of her vagina, rinse them off, and then put them their mouth to be exchanged on the initial kiss that the visitors are allowed to give a prisoner at the start and end of each visit. Or, place it in the food the visitor buys out of the vending machine.

If visitor happened to alert the drug detector while going through it, officers would ask for permission to search the visitor. There is no law that allows prison officers to forcibly search any visitor. If a search request is denied the visitor can be asked to leave. If the visitor refuses consent for a search, they will be denied visiting for at least twenty-four hours.

The mules the dealers were using had been warned several times

To refuse to be searched and simply leave. That is what one of mules did not do and that is why she got caught. This same visitor had come before with two or three other women on previous occasions. The women accompanying her were also mules and some say this was why the big bust happened the following weekend. When the mules came, the investigators stopped the women's car in the parking lot, and told them to give their drugs up. They gave up the drugs. One lady who had been holding the drugs was in her late fifties and should have known better. All three women were released that day and later in the evening the guys in prison were taken to the lock up unit know as (SHU) Special Housing Unit.

All of this started a domino effect. The house where the women were staying in Tucson was later that evening in the next few months several people were busted in Tucson, and

Phoenix. After that the well dried up for the dealers and users, but not for the snitches who kept telling

CHAPTER 55

THE G.D.'S TAKEN OFF THE YARD.

It had been several months that the G.D.'s were on the yard at Tucson without an incident involving them, which was unusual for them. The G.D.'s always seemed to have something to prove or they did something that causes problems for themselves and others it was a basketball game in the gym on the evening, in the spring of 2008. People started running everywhere, most of them just trying to get out of the way. Michael was in the unit when something is happening on the yard everyone goes to the window to see what is happening. Michael saw guys running and more guys running behind them with baseball bats in their hands.

Michael went to the unit ice machine to fill his jugs with ice, because he figured the institution may be on lockdown for a while He returned to the window to see what else was happening. He saw a guy covered in blood being escorted to medical thought the guy was a G.D., but he could not be sure. Officers came into the unit yelling, "lockdown, everyone return to your cell!"

About an hour later, when some guys were brought back to the unit, Michael heard the G.D.'s had moved on the Muslims or DC Blacks. Many of the DC Blacks are Muslims. Michael thought, "Man, not again." they're crazy Michael's cellie '87' came back in the cell and told him the entire story. One of the G.D. guys had been stabbed by one of the DC Muslims in a dispute over a chair. The G.D. guy did not retaliate, so some of his homies did after learning what happened.

One of the G.D.'s was so upset that he went to get a baseball bat he ended up getting bats for all the G.D.'s who then went after the DC Muslims, chasing them around the gym area. Some of them had seen it coming and ran out of the gym door but could not get out of the second door. They barricaded themselves against the gym doors so the G.D.'s could not get through or so they thought, until one of the G.D.'s broke the large window on the door with a baseball bat. The broken glass made the footing but the DC, were still holding that door for dear life. One of the DC Muslims got hold of a bat and chased some G.D.'s out to the yard, which was what Michael had seen. Some G.D.'s saw a DC Muslim in the adjoining barbershop, so the G.D.'s went in there and beat the guy to a pulp with the bats. The word is he is still on a ventilator and barely surviving.

The officers finally arrived with mace and tear-gas guns, and made everyone get on the ground. Those not beaten or bloody were returned to the units and the prison was on another lock down. '87' told Michael that he had saved a bunch of them from being killed by jumping in front of some DC Muslims and telling the G.D.'s "It's over."

It took about a week before staff came to the unit and started taking guys away. Michael prayed they would not include him, and he prayed for his cellie as they took him away. They took all the G.D.'s off the yard and then all gang members from the Chicago area, including the El Rukins and Vice Lords. For months afterwards guys were asking Michael to tell his cellie "Thank you" for saving their lives.

Michael had a long talk with '87' before he left and they even read some scriptures together and Michael pleaded with him to get out. '87' was a couple of years older than Michael but had only been in prison for a few years. While he seemed to be wanting to change, it just was not happening.

CHAPTER 56

COMING' OFF LOCKDOWN

Just before Michael's birthday, the prison finally came off lockdown. He continued pressing his unit team for a transfer to a lower security prison as he had been doing for years. Michael was ready to get away from all the nonsense that is pervasive in Maximum Security UPS'S. Only one day after coming off lockdown, the Sereno's were trying to kill each other for some unknown reason, but Michael knew it had something to do with money, drugs and power. Rumor had it that a shot caller in the SHU was sending out hit lists on guys who were drinking or using drugs while the shot caller sat in the SHU. Officers were running into one unit where an alarm had sounded as another alarm went off in a different unit. They could not respond to all the alarms at once. The officers did not know which way to go. Michael looked out the window and saw that Sereno's were going at it on the yard, as well.

Michael went to fill his jugs with ice, as he knew there was going to be another lockdown. After getting ice and something to eat, Michael tried calling his family, but nobody was home. He finally made contact with his younger brother Bruce, whose first question was whether he had talked to Kim or his kids. Michael said, "No, not in awhile."

Bruce suggested that he should call them, as Kim and Angie had gotten into it. Angie threatened Kim about Jazz not being able to attend a funeral in Texas. Michael decided he had better call.

An hour after the alarms went off and after talking to his brother Bruce, prisoners still were not locked in their cells, yet. To make use of his time he called Kim's house and Jazzman picked up the phone. Michael talked to her and she told him she was broke up about her grandmother's death, but not as much as he had thought. He asked her what was wrong and she told him that her real mother Angie was mad at her because she had told Angie she did not think she would attend the funeral.

Michael asked Jazz if she was okay with that and she said, "Yes, Dad, but sometimes I wish people would let me think and speak for myself. I know Kim can't afford to send me, plus I just started a new job, and graduation is in a couple of weeks." Then she said, "Dad, I just wish sometimes that someone would let me think and speak for myself, maybe you could talk to someone for me?"

"I will, Jazz, I will. I'm sorry that I'm not there for you in times like these. I know they all love you and mean well, I just do not want you to make the same mistakes we all made," Michael answered.

Jazz said, "Daddy, it's just my mom and Kim." Michael let her know he understood and, he would do the best he could, and he told her he loved her.

Michael later called Kim's cell phone. He always began the conversation with a warm hello and asked, "How are you and the kids doing?" Kim said, "They are all fine." Then, Michael asked, "What is this I hear about you and Angie fighting?"

"I'm sure you heard that Jazz's great grandmother died, right? Well, Angie called here and did not ask, but demanded that Jazz be there, and she did not explain how that was going to happen. I was upset, after that call. Then she called back again telling me that her cousin Genies or her nephews would be picking Jazz up and taking her down there, but she was rude and demanding about it." Kim said.

Michael told her that grief is a strange thing and people handle it in different ways. She said, "No, Angie was mean and rude on purpose." She continued telling Michael they were wanting to send Jazz down there with Genies and Kim was cool with that if Genies was going, because she was about Kim's age, and mature and responsible.

However, Genies decided at the last minute that she was not going. Then Kim said Angie called and told her that Angie's nephews and nieces, Courtney, Carl, Shimika and Terse would be coming to get her, but they were all in their early twenties, smoked and drank, and may not even have had driver's licenses or car insurance, and Kim was not having it. Even more importantly, Jazz just started a new job and it took a little while to get her back on the right track. Plus she was graduating in a couple of weeks and Kim was concerned that if Jazz went down there with someone irresponsible, like her mother, they might convince her to stay, or she might get introduced to someone that could get her into smoking, drinking or some other trouble. She told Jazz that she just did not want her going.

Michael asked Kim a question: "You told her you did not WANT her to go or that she COULD NOT go?" Kim just paused for a minute and then they agreed that they both did not want her to go. Michael said, "Good! Okay."

Michael finally had a chance to say something that he had wanted to say concerning his love and appreciation. He said, "Kim, you know I love you and appreciate what you are doing for my kids. From everything, you tell me, I think you are right, and I totally agree. I know Jazz is as much or more your daughter as she is Angie's because love is thicker than blood and you raised the girl with your blood, sweat and tears. And when I went to prison and no one else wanted to do it. But there's just one thing I want to ask you. Do you think you could let Jazz think and feel for herself sometimes?"

Kim said, "What?" and Michael repeated, "Do you think you could let Jazz think for herself? Jazz said that she totally agreed with you on the situation, even though she wanted to go. She wanted to be able to tell you and Angie what she thought and felt." Kim said, "Where the hell did all that shits come from?" Michael started to say "Jazzman: but he stopped right there so as not to break confidence with Jazz.

Kim went off, acting like some thug, hood or nappy haired girl with no sense, saying, and "I raised this girl when you went to prison and no one else did anything about it. If I let this girl think and speak for herself, she would be in prison like you. Or be a teenage mother just like her mother was. A high school dropout or strung out on drugs and alcohol. You just do not know what I go through with this girl every day."

Michael slipped and said, "I know, Baby it's hard, but Jazz asked me to talk to you and Angie, so I am. Am I wrong for that? It's bad enough that I can't be there for her physically, but at least I can do something she asks of me."

Kim started yelling "JAZZMAN", and Michael said, "Please do not say anything or she will not tell me anything ever again. Am I wrong for asking you to let her speak and think?"

Kim said, "You know what, Michael? F@** you!" and hung up the phone. Michael was so mad that he did not think he would ever again tell anyone what he was thinking or feeling. One of his biggest hopes was to be a part of his kid's lives and have them come to him for advice or help whenever they needed to. His thoughts were "To HELL with Kim! I'm done with her"

Michael went to bed that night so angry, upset and disappointed that he could not sleep. He told himself, "If I'm not invited, I'll never be involved in their lives ever again, as no one cares what I have to say, especially Kim and my kids." never call Kim ever again.

Angie, jazzman's mother, came back into Michael's life for a short time. One day she contacted him through the unit staff, claiming it was an emergency. When Michael first called her, she talked to him about her battle with cancer and remission. It was good to talk to her. They talked about everything, life, love, God being black, coming from a single parent home, and especially their daughter.

Eventually, Angie let Michael know she just wanted to talk to him, tell him she loved him, always had and always would. It had been a long time as they had gone through so many battles, including her drug addiction and grief from family deaths. They talked weekly for a couple of months. Angie had a job, and a place to live, but one day she fell off and disappointed him. He did not hear from her again. He, at times, heard that she was on drugs again, had financial problems and found a new man.

Let Go of Emotional Wounds And Reclaim Love.

CHAPTER 57

PAISA'S AND SERENO'S, ASSORTED VIOLENCE

A Major riot happened into the chow hall one day. As a bunch of Sereno's got to the chow hall, they made a move on the Paisa's, attempting to stab one of them. All of the Sereno's had knives in their hands, while the Paisa's had hard plastic food trays and cups, which they began to throw in the direction of the Sereno's. Though they were flying and bouncing around the entire chow hall, it did not matter to them. The blacks and whites just sat there and watched, as they ate. The officers could not stop it, as there were at least forty prisoners going at it and only a handful of officers in the room. The Sereno's decided to back up against the wall because they were out numbered about four to one by the Paisa's. The officers finally got control of the situation and unfortunately, it was back to the cell.

After three or four weeks of lockdown, they finally let the prison return to normal operation. They allowed trips to the chow hall for meals a couple of units at a time, and then later to the yard. Tension and friction was obvious and still in the air. It was found out that during the lockdown, there had been a race riot at Florence. The skinheads had a party on Hitler's birthday. They celebrated by drinking homemade liquor and hollering racial remarks and using the "N" word. A brother did not agree with what they were saying and said something and before long, a fight broke out. Rumor had it a tower officer had fired a shot at a Skinhead, but instead hit and killed a black man, which led to the blacks trying to kill a white in retaliation. That incident itself sent shockwaves throughout the system, including Tucson.

Here, the whites and blacks in B-1 had been drinking (homemade brew.) A black man told a white guy to stay out of his business and pushed the guy away, kicking off a racial fight inside B-1 involving knives and weapons. Guys were stabbed, beaten, and then maced by officers. That day the incident was squashed as being caused by alcohol rather than race.

With the news from Florence that there were bodies, (meaning dead guys) due to race, some people at Tucson thought maybe the whites would try to make a move here, even though they were heavily outnumbered. Some whites were warned that perhaps the blacks would try and retaliate at Tucson because of the situation at Florence. Shortly thereafter the Southern Whites and Dirty White Boy cars joined together to make a hit on two white boys from Nebraska who they heard were allegedly working for SIS (prison investigation staff). The two whites who were to be hit were, brothers living in the same unit.

They saw the hitters coming from both directions on the second floor tier. They quickly jumped over the railing down to the first floor and made a run for the exit. One tripped and fell at the door, while the other one began knife fighting with one of the hitters in the doorway. The staff had heard this was going to happen beforehand, so they were prepared and began firing rubber bullets at the guys. The two white boys made a run for the main corridor door. An officer locked it and stopped the hitters from being able to get at them. Michael knew a lockdown was coming again.

Can't We All Just Get Along?

CHAPTER 58

CHANGING TUCSON TO A SEX OFFENDER YARD

Rumor floating around when the lockdown ended was that a bus full of sex offenders and child molesters were brought to Unit C2, along with all the ones who had been the SHU. This made about 60. It definitely sent shockwaves throughout the prison. There were already rumors that the entire prison was now labeled a sex offender prison and the normal replaced with sex offender, child molesters, and other social outsiders.

Of course, the prisoners on the yard were furious, many having children themselves and everyone hated child molesters. There's an unwritten code for prisoners, that they are to stab or assault child molesters whenever they have an opportunity to get to one.

Earlier the Administration attempted to slide some child molesters onto the yard, undercover. It was discovered who they were and they were all assaulted and stabbed. Some prisoners wanted them to come to the yard so they could extort, stab, beat, rape and prey on them This obviously would be difficult for staff and would have to be done carefully, as every time a molester was discovered on the yard he would be beaten, stabbed, and or checked in to protective custody, ("PC" of "Punk City").

No matter what the Administration planned on, most of the prisoners always seemed to be talking about it and the majority of them were extremely upset. Some even talked of filing lawsuits, and others mentioned they would be more than happy to transfer away from "Cho Mo" prison.

Unit C2 was soon completely, filled with sex offenders. For many months, they did not come into contact with the rest of the yard. While the sex offenders were being brought here, the "normal" prisoners were being moved to other penitentiary.

CHAPTER 59

NEW WARDEN & NEW POLITICS ON THE YARD

The old Warden, Chavez, a short, comedic, George Lopez look-alike, was out. The new Warden, a tall, middle-aged white guy, NBA Chuck Berry look-alike, was in. He came from FCI Phoenix, though he looked like he came from Saturn. He came here to lay down the law. No one, not even staff, was willing to challenge him. Guys that knew him from the old days at Lewisburg or Phoenix said he was no nonsense.

The new Warden seemed to know what he was doing more than Chavez had, and he treated guys with respect and dignity, along with enforcing the rules and policies with a big stick. He was firm but fair. The Wardens in the old days had to be tough, but Michael at least, it seemed that the new Warden needed more politics and smarts than muscle, as the saying goes, "brains over brawn."

It certainly is a position of politics, as most Wardens are appointed to the position by the Presidential Cabinet or political appointees that operate the Department of Michael. There was no more focus on rehabilitation; only punishment. Prisoners had to rehabilitate themselves if they wanted to change. Some actually did it. The BOP also no longer paid for college courses. Prisoners would have to pay for those themselves, which most could not afford. There were also no more prisoners' benefits for education, as the parole board was abolished. The only incentive was a transfer, closer to home.

One thing Michael noticed that made a good Warden was one who disciplined staff as well as prisoners. The new Warden promised changes, such as more safety officers, more programs, more TV's and tables in the units, transfers for inmates who had at least twelve months at Tucson as well as those who wanted to leave or be within five hundred miles of their homes. Anyone that was eligible for a lower security facility would get transferred. There were guys who had been designated for months but had not left yet. With this new Warden, inmates began to leave a few weeks after the Warden's arrival. He was definitely making things happen.

The Warden opened unit C1 for the check-ins, and snitches, who were flooding the SHU. That move made a lot of prisoners mad. There was really nothing they could do about it, because if they talked about doing something. The new Warden would have them locked up and transferred in a heartbeat. After a few weeks at Tucson, the new Warden out a memo saying the Tucson was going to become sex offenders' prison as well as Care Level Three Medical, which meant wheel chairs, handicapped, and those dying, with deadly diseases. This now meant that another 350 prisoners would be re-designated within weeks to. Anyone who did not want to leave could submit a request to stay, but they would have to pass a Security clearance and agree not to assault the sex offenders. This was the first time anything like this had ever happened – especially with all those hardcore criminals in the BOP.

CHAPTER 60

JAZZMAN'S GRADUATION

Michael's eldest daughter Jazzman was graduating high school. It was one of the happiest yet saddest days, of he's life. He could not have been happier she was graduating, but he was sad he could not be there to share it with her. He received an invitation from Jazz. It was and the only thing she had sent him in years. Michael called her as soon as he received it, several days before graduation. His baby was all grown up.

Kim and her parents attended the graduation. It was Michael's baby girl's special day, no matter what else was happening.

Michael called Jazzman the morning of the big event and told her he loved her and missed her. She said, "I know, Dad." Michael also said he was sorry for not being there and hated that he could not attend the big event. She said, "That's okay, Dad." He also let her know he was so proud of her, and again she said, "I know, Dad."

Later on that night, Michael called Jazzman again. She was getting ready to go out with her friends, which had her in a good, happy mood. Michael repeated what he said earlier that day. That he loved and missed her.

CHAPTER 61

PAISA'S SHOT CALLER HIT, LOCKDOWN

A short lockdown was over for a day or two, when violence struck again. Michael was on the yard when all of a sudden some Paisa's attacked their shot caller. There were ten against one and no one else did anything to stop the attack. The Paisa's had hit their own shot caller the same shot caller who had called a meeting in the yard just a couple of months earlier, for unity. One thing about being a shot caller, someone else is always bucking for the position. Some men just think about it, but some actually plan to get it by a hostile takeover. The Paisa's hit the shot caller until he fell, then stomped, kicked, and stabbed him for at least two minutes in the middle of the yard and right in front of the gun tower before any staff even noticed. The officer in the tower never saw it.

When the officers finally arrived, the Paisa's shot caller lay motionless on the ground covered in blood. This was a man who never walked anywhere alone, usually having four or five guys with him. Everyone thought the shot caller was done for, but when the medical golf cart pulled up, he began to move a little. If they thought they had killed him, they were wrong and in for some revenge. The prison went on lockdown, but to everyone's surprise, they unlocked the doors the very next morning. He could feel the tension in the air.

Anyone with any common sense knew something was about to happen. About one hundred Paisa's were talking in the chow hall, and about twenty went to talk with the Warden, Captain, SIA, SIS and Assistant Wardens. The Paisa's then headed for the yard and the SIA Officer called over the radio for the yard to open. He knew what he was doing. Once he opened the yard, a big rowdy fight was going to begin. As soon as they made it to the yard, the melee kicked off. They went at it for at least ten minutes, using their, fists, feet, knives and whatever they could and then the gun tower started shooting. The sirens were going off, most guys just ran for the units. The officers in the units were hollering "Lockdown! Lockdown! Lockdown…! Michael knew it was going to last a while…

CHAPTER 62

THE YARD IS SPLIT

The yard was split into two parts, north and south in late October of 2008. The four open units on south side were mostly normal guys left over Supposedly, guys were on the south side due to them not having sex offenses, who were not rats and care not Care Level III (sick and dying) or HTP (Hard to Place) inmates.

Not everyone who was HTP was rats or snitches. Some of them were hard to place due to fighting all the time or being homosexuals. Many of the north side guys were "check-ins" for a variety of reasons. They checked-in at every prison they went to. Many of these inmates had current enemies on the north side.

Some were dropouts from prison gangs/groups. Some went into debt at every prison they been to, and ran out of prisons. Some were guys who did not want to follow orders from or pay for protection to gangs/groups in power at other prisons. These guys were sometimes beat up and ran off the yard! Federal prison is not nice places.

The inmates from unit B-1 were the last general population guys to be moved around. I was asked by the staff to stay on the north side. In return, they would keep putting me in for a lower security transfer. They also wanted me to stick around through the yard separation and reintegration to help keep peace on the yard, I agreed because I did not want to move several hundred pounds of legal work and law.

I stayed on the north side despite they gossip or rumors that would start about me and anyone else that stayed. I later asked about going to the south side. As soon as I did, staff told me to "stick with us," and said they would not put anyone in my cell unless they absolutely had to. So once again, I agreed to stay.

CHAPTER 63

MICHAEL VS DEPARTMENT OF JUSTICE

Brown vs. U.S. Department of Justice (my civil lawsuit) seemed to be at a standstill. The Government kept spinning its wheels and delaying as they usually do.

While they were doing all this stalling, manipulating and destroying evidence, things.

We're starting to happen. Witnesses were coming forward and evidence was starting to develop from people who had never spoken up before. Some of those were people who I thought would not speak up because they had lied, before, but now wanted to tell the truth. Some had underlying motives from the beginning.

I can now see things a lot more clearly as my innocence is beginning to be proven, even with all the Government's stalling and delaying.

CHAPTER 64

FALSELY ACCUSED OF HELPING TO FILE A LAWSUIT & OF BEING A RAT

In order to help keep the peace on the yard, Michael had to come out of his shell, and deal with people he would not normally deal with. The money HE was making from legal work, (which he called donations), was decent, but it was not enough.

Michael decided to open a prison store. Buying food from the commissary and selling it for a fifty percent mark up to those who could not go to the commissary on commissary day. The running of prison stores in Tucson is greatly helped by the practice of the upper staff, in restricting/suspending the access to the prison commissary. As punishment, any time any prisoner gets any sort of write up. If Tucson did not do this, most of the stores would not be in operation.

In opening a store, along with making money comes conflict, jealousy, envy, and problems. Michael needed the money for litigation. Even if he may have been violating minor prison rules, this was his justification. Michael used his intelligent creativity, and stature to help keep a relative amount of peace on the yard. Without peace, Michael could not litigate his case or make money.

Michael also had a job as the "number one orderly or head orderly", which is a fancy name for janitor. Michael's job as head orderly was cleaning officers for the Captains and Lieutenant's. Michael also spent a fair amount of time working diplomatic duties for other inmates. In the years Michael had the job he was accused several of being when this happened, he dealt with it swiftly.

No one had ever actually called Michael a snitch to his face, but the statements would later get back to him and he would go and address that person. On several different occasions, he had to go see several inmates who were part of a gang, geographical crew or click when confronted with the allegations; they all claimed not to have made such an accusation. Not only did Michael have inmates coming after him, but so was the Investigative staff, who was accusing Michael of lawsuits against the Institution. An officer asked Michael if he knew who had filed the lawsuit against him and the Administration, Michael responded "No." He then asked if Michael could find out who had filed the actual suit against him and the Administration, Michael responded, "I could if I really wanted to." The officer told him. He would return a favor for a favor Michael walked away with no intention of assisting the prison.

One reason Michael did not want to help this particular officer was he had been involved in shipping Michael to Victorville, after he had been sitting in the SHU for six months at Florence.

This had happened over some false rumors by prison staff and inmates.

This lawsuit seemed to have the Administration really concern or they would not be questioning inmates who were known for filing meritorious claims against prison officials it would not shock me if the prison Administration allowed or caused something to go down just to justify their actions that were the basis of the lawsuit.

A few days later Michael was approached by staff. The staff member told Michael that he knew who had filed the lawsuit against him and other prison Administrative staff. When Michael asked him, "who?" he was told "It was you." Michael asked him, "Are you serious?" The reply was, "Yes, I know it was you." Michael asked, "What would I have to gain from filing against the prison Administration?" He responded "I looked at some of your previous lawsuits and one word stuck out to me." That word being "Latino," which matched language used in the pending lawsuit.

Michael told him, "First of all, those suits are ten years old and I certainly do not use the same language in suits from ten years ago and in fact, I haven't filed anything of that nature for almost ten years." Michael offered "Maybe there was someone from the same geographical area that used the same terms I used." He stated, "That could be one possibility," but he assured Michael that when he found out who had actually filed this suit he was going to "make their life hell."

Michael was well aware of how staff could make someone's life a living hell by having inmates setup to be robbed, receiving new Federal charges or killed. Those reasons alone were why Michael would never do anything to cross him, especially not on behalf of some lying scared cowards. The next day, several Hispanic prisoners came to Michael and told him staff had called them up to the office and questioned them concerning Michael's involvement in filing the lawsuit. They said, they told the staff, "He had nothing to do with filing that suit." Michael in turn told them, "You all will need to keep my name out of all this crap," It's funny how things happen Michael later learned that some of these inmates were asked whether they were interested in helping staff set up Michael. They were told they would paid for it.

About a week later, the staff who had threatened Michael came to him and apologized for falsely accusing him of being involved in the filing of the suit. Michael could not believe the words that were coming out of his mouth because in all the years he had known the him, he had never heard any inmate ever receiving an apology from him.

CHAPTER 65

MICHAEL'S FBI & FIOA BATTLE CONTINUES

On October 7, 2009, the United States Department of Justice admitted that they had located 1754 pages of documents responsive to Michael's Freedom of Information Act request. They agreed to release 920 pages.

Civil Action Number 10-247 (ESH), the second lawsuit the defendants the United States Department of Justice, verses Michael L. Brown the Plaintiff, moved for summary judgment after over a year of the plaintiff fighting and waiting for the files of the government's star witness VAC. Plaintiff after thirteen years of trying to obtain the truth he and his legal team managed to obtain a Privacy Waiver Certificate of Identity and Affidavit. VAC tells the truth the whole truth and nothing but the truth, has it documented, and authorizes the releases of the files proving it. It was not something that took one try at it nor was it something that was expected. After working, hoping, praying, and every logical legal effort plaintiff and his legal team obtains what they believe to be the DNA needed and of course not to be unexpected once the government became aware of it sent their agents on a mission to discourage, intimidate, and manipulate their former star witness. Plaintiff was not done yet both his life was at stake that was all and everything he had. Plaintiff brought legal action against the defendants for their illegal, misconduct, destructive and dishonorable tactics of threatening, intimidating a witness. The lawsuit was filed by plaintiff and the government fought him tooth and nail. The defendants filed a motion for summary judgment to have the case dismissed. They claimed that VAC changed his mind on his own and withdraw his privacy waiver and certificate of identity. This did not happen until after the FBI had agreed to release the files.

They took a year and plaintiff went to FBI headquarters and they ordered the field offices to release the files to the defendant. The defendants disobeyed their superiors at the FBI FIOA Office fought it any way. The courts did not honor the defendant's summary judgment and set a briefing schedule, in which everyone briefed and ended in June 2010 and plaintiff is awaiting a decision from the courts.

CHAPTER 66

MICHAEL'S CHILDREN BECOME ADULTS

Summer of 2010. Michael started calling Jazzman, T'keyah, and Michael more often. Michael never missed any holidays or birthdays with phone calls, letters, cards, gifts, money or whatever he could come up with. It was amazing how much the kids had grown. Jazzman was 20, a young lady working two jobs and going to school.

T'keyah 17, (going on 27) driving the car her mother bought, her talking about hanging out, boys and college. She was a senior in high school. Michael Jr. about to start high school wanted to play football and even said "school isn't bad dad". He was real passionate about it. Michael Jr. was disappointed that he had received his first B in years. He was usually a straight A student and he was upset at himself. Michael told him "It will be ok son, just always do your best." Michael. Heard that his stepson Marcus was doing well working as a cook and going to school to be a chef. This made Michael proud and made him fight even harder to get out of prison.

When Michael started talking to his children almost every day, it was inevitable that he would have to talk to their mothers. Michael was trying to avoid them, for several reasons. Kim had let Michael know she could use some financial help with the kids and thought he was wasting money on people who were not going to help him. Michael reminded her that she had said "do not worry about nothing, you do whatever you have to prove your innocence and get out of prison and I'll take care of the kids as much as I can." Michael told her I do not waste anything inside. Everyone I send money to besides my kids, is for legal assistance and they all have been some help Michael felt bad not being able to do more for his kids. He said to Kim "One day soon you'll have all the help you need, I'll be there."

Michael also had the chance to talk to Ingo (Keya and Marcus's mother). One time Ingo picked up Kenya's phone and said "How are you doing stranger? You can't call me no more." Michael said "I've been really busy working on my case, the book and when I'm not doing that I'm doing what I can from here for the kids." Ingo said, "Well you can still call me. Your daughter is doing well she's growing up real fast. She's going into her senior year in a couple days

Michael also spoke to his youngest sister, Sasha who graduated with honors from college, and was preparing to go to grad school. Sasha wanted to work in the legal profession with the hope of helping him. Michael told her "Congratulations sweetheart, I'm so proud of you and I know mom would be too." Sasha could not stop crying, Sasha replied "Thank you big brother I love you and miss you more than I can say, I wish you were here." "Just take care of yourself and come home" Michael said "I will."

CHAPTER 67

UNEXPECTED ANGEL IN DISGUISE

Michael met Chantage Romero his Angel in disguise. Chantage was willing to find and interview witnesses who were spread all over the country. She was warned that she would possibly be threatened, harassed or jailed. Chantage had no specific experience. She was doing this to obtain Michael for herself, as much as for Michael.

Chantage attacked the case as if it was her own freedom at stake she located, called and talked to all the governments' star witnesses. At first, she came up empty handed, but she was relentless.

It started off strictly business between Chantage and Michael and then she started having personal issues. And have things stopped for months. Michael's mission never changed. HE was in search of freedom; .He now had to change strategies now that Chantage was not around. Angie begged to help but did absolutely nothing but spent the money Michael sent her for travel and expenses, feeding her habits. Michael's Sister Tricia and a friend "E" put forth a good effort but came out of it with little results. By the time, he was done with these three he was out several thousand dollars, and had not gotten much accomplished.

Michael contacted Chantage again. Chantage responded, "I hate to start something and do not finish, so let's do this!" Michael and CHANTAGE put their heads together. Then she started calling witnesses again. Michael and Chantage started strategizing everyday reading his book and transcripts over the phone, even discussing ideas from television programs and movies. Nothing was out of the question. Chantage and Michael eventually decided to sit down and talk.

Michael paid for Chantage's round trip ticket from Chicago to Tucson, right before New Year's 2010. It was a very constructive meeting. They spent their two days of prison visiting going over the case from the beginning to the present.

Michael found out this woman was smart, courageous, tenacious, resilient and good to. Born in California, and moved all over the southwest. Later moving to Chicago in 2000. Like Michael Chantage was born to a Military father, and a rebellious mother. Chant age was an attractive woman who had been through a lot, like Michael. By the time they were done visiting each other they had agreed on many things and they were both ready to work. Michael thought this was the one to help prove his innocence and release.

Once Chant age arrived back home safely she put in some good work. Chant age obtained some documented evidence she believed was helpful in proving Michael's innocence, however both Chant age and Michael felt they still needed more. Chantage meet with several of the people who gave false testimony at Michael's trail. She recorded the conversations, with the consent of each person. Each person admitted that they had lied. Each person explained why they had lied, mostly at the urging of the agents and prosecutors. Each person stated that they were now willing to tell the truth in court. Chantage prepared declaration for each person to sign, based on their admissions. Almost a year later Michael paid for another round trip flight to the southwest, for Chantage to visit her father and other family members she had not seen in twenty years. After that, Michael never heard from Chantage ever again.

CHAPTER 68

DANNY'S RETURN

In mid-January, 2010 Danny came back from about 25 months in "...the lovely & exciting Metro Detention Center L.A." (His words) He, again, had Life sentences, after another trial in which "...Justice did not prevail."

As was to be expected with Danny, he had several 'adventures' during the 25 months he was gone, starting the day he left.

When Federal Marshals fly a prisoner somewhere, on a commercial airplane, there are usually two of them. However, because Danny, on the day he received the Life sentences in his case (after Trial I), ruined one eye of an Idiot (who was sending his wife Love letters, in the MDC-LA Women's section) in the Court holding tank, they sent three Marshals.

The four of them, with Danny wearing a plain white t-shirt, tan elastic-waistband pants 6" too long and blue canvas shoes, chained up with a (fake) 'Black box" around the waist chain/handcuffs and his hair all over the place (they took his hair ties), took a U.S. Air flight from Tucson to Phoenix. The first flight was uneventful.

The second plane was late—it turned out to be about three hours late. Danny, and the three Marshals positioned around him, was soon joined by about by about a half-dozen Airport Cops (with their Cannondale Bicycles) in the Boarding area. It seems that when the first Airport Cop rode up, one of the Marshals said the 'magic words' to him – Hells Angel.

The half dozen Airport Cops in short pants groovy helmets and bat utility belt, were helping to protect the passengers from the chained up, 5'7", 180 pound, 60-year-old Danny.

This was about 10 days before Christmas, '07. A month or so before that, it had been National news that a Phoenix Airport Cop had Tazered a pregnant woman, killing her. There were 75 or so passengers standing and sitting around, impatiently waiting for the plane to arrive. There isn't much of interest to look at in Airport Boarding Areas, so everyone is watching Danny, surrounded by almost 10 cops (including the three plainclothes marshals), while talking on cell phones.

A woman starts taking pictures of Danny, with her phone/camera. One of the Airport Cops tells her, in a loud voice. "Hey, you can't take his picture." That was Danny's cue to stand up for the poor woman's right to take pictures of any damn thing she wanted to.

Danny tells the cop in a voice even louder than the cop used on the woman: "Hey stupid, this is America. Who do you think you are? You can't tell these people what they can and can't do. These people can take pictures of anything they want to. What are you going to do—tazor this woman too!"

All of a sudden, everyone in the Boarding Area is standing up, with camera phones in hand, taking pictures and filming Danny and the cops. The one loudmouth cop, who had not learned his lesson, starts yelling at all the people to stop taking pictures, which gets several of the passengers (there always seems to be Lawyer flying somewhere) arguing with the cops, that they have every right to take pictures. Danny starts yelling at the loudmouth cop (who did not even appear to have a tazor) to "Put that Tazor down."

The cops call for reinforcements. The Marshals are trying to get Danny to walk away, but he sits down and tells them "I'm not going anywhere, let's see how this ends."

It takes the Supervising Airport Cops about ten minutes to make the first batch of cops leave and to apologize to, and calm down the angry, picture-taking crowd

An announcement is then made that there's another U.S. Air flight, with available seats, to LAX, leaving in 20 minutes. The whole mob rapidly heads to the other Terminal. Danny and the Marshals too. A woman from the Airline intercepts them and tells them that several passengers had said that they did not want 'Him' on the plane with them so had to go back and wait for the original plane. Another half-empty plane took the rest of the passengers, an hour and half after that. Danny and the Marshall's finally flew to LA on a plane with just them, the crew and two young guys in Air Force uniforms, who got free upgrades to First Class.

The Government made a verbal plea offer to Danny, Plead Guilty, to whatever, for a Ten Year sentence. Danny said that any plea agreement would have to include allowing his wife, Rachel, whose conviction had not yet been reversed, to plead guilty to only a misdemeanor. The Government said No to that, so that was the end of the discussion.

A few days later, when Danny made his first Court appearance (again representing himself), a young Attorney walked up in the middle of Danny and the Judge talking and asked the Judge if he could be appointed as advisory council.

The Judge asked him, "You, or your office?" The Attorney told the Judge "Me personally." The Judge asked Danny if he had any objection. "No." The Judge declared the Attorney to be Advisory Counsel and set a date to hear the dozen or so Motions Danny had filed before he left Tucson.

Danny and the Attorney then sat down and Danny asked him "Who are you?" Sean Kennedy, THE Federal Public Defender for the L.A. Federal Courts.

Hundreds of hours were spent preparing for Trail II.

Hundreds of hours were spent locating and interviewing potential witnesses about Kramer's past, and crimes he committed while working as an Informant, in several States.

Kramer had identified several people as his 'playmates' in the AZ murder. Less than two months after recording a conversation with one of them, Kramer ran the guy and his motorcycle over, with his pick-up truck, killing him. The ATF never made a report of that – apparently it was not important enough.

In September 2011, an AZ Hells Angelis supposed to start trial for the woman's murder. He is facing the Death Penalty, in AZ State Court. It will be the only other case Kramer will have testified in, besides Danny's two trials.

There were dozens more Motions filed and heard. 90% of the Motions filed by the Government were granted. 90% of the Motions filed by Danny and his (now) co-counsel were denied, including all of the Motions asking for approval for subpoenas for numerous witnesses from outside the area of the L.A. Federal Court(,many of whom had bought meth FROM Kramer, while he was working as an informant), and Motions to bring two witnesses from CA prisons.

The Government admitted that Kramer, as of July 2008, had received over $417,000 from the ATF and Witness Protection Program (WITSEC), but they would not provide a breakdown of what the $ was for, and the Judge (of course) refused to Order them to provide a breakdown.

During Trial II, Kramer admitted that he had not reported that income to the IRS. [Does anyone think he'll be made to pay anything? Or be prosecuted?] Kramer, and his family, will remain in WITSEC for the rest of their lives -- your Federal Tax Dollars at work.

A surprising admission came out during Trail II. ATF Ciccone testified that Kramer, who had previously been convicted of robbery, and had served AZ prison sentences, was given permission, by the ATF and the U.S. Attorney's Office in L.A. to carry a gun, while running around drunk and wired on methamphetamine every day.

The Judge also refused to let Danny testify at his own trial. You get the picture. Danny was again convicted.

Some good that came out of the reversals. The Government did not want Danny's wife in Trial II, as she was found Not Guilty of two things in Trial I, and the new jurors would certainly feel sorry for her, again. She pled Guilty to one Felony Count and was sentenced to Time Served, after her conviction was finally reversed. She got out in July 2008, after serving over 4 ½ years.

Danny's trial court file has over 900 documents in it, as of Aug 2011. Several hundred of those documents are motions filed by Danny, and denied. The Court of Appeals only has to decide that the Judge was wrong on one of them. His co-counsel has 160+ attorneys under him – the L.A. Federal Public Defender's Office is the largest in the country. The top people in his Appellate Dept. are working with Danny on the appeal. Danny will be going back for Trial III, earlier year. Danny says "We're going to keep having trials till we get it right!"

When Danny got back to Tucson, he already knew that it would not be anything like the 'normal' Penitentiary he'd left, 25 months before. The SIS people (who show up, en mass, to interview all new arrivals) were very happy to see him, as there were maybe 30 normal 'Guests' (Danny's deposition) left over from 2007. [Pretty much the only 'normal' Guests who've arrived here in the last three years have been the Medical Care Level III guys.]

The SIS people put Danny in the housing unit with the highest percentage of Sex Offenders, 'Chicken 2,' so they could use him as the 'Good example' of why it's OK to be put in that Unit. Danny says there are maybe five guys in the whole unit he talks to.

Danny had an annoying habit of calling me 'crack head.' I've never smoked Crack in my life. I call him lots of stuff, but nothing has any affect on him. I try to out-insult him, but he always wins. He says my idea of an insult is calling somebody "Poo-Poo Head."

He has a very dry and clinical way of describing the disgusting things that happen in this Prison full of Perverts, on an almost daily basis. When people stare at him, open-mouthed, after he describing really sick things I can't put in this book, he'll say "HOW could I make this up?"

Even though he's over 60, he's one of the strongest guys in this place. There aren't a lot of guys, anywhere, who can do 10 sets of 50 dips, in less than two hours, with sets of 50 of other exercises in between.

Danny's the only 'Motorcycle Enthusiast' (he dislikes the term 'Biker') I've ever seen who has no tattoos. Whenever anyone asks him, "Why do not you have any tattoos?" he tells them, with a straight face, "My mom won't let me."

He likes to make up fake flyers, for other 'Guests' to sign up for things; 'Grand Canyon Field Trip,' 'Gay Prison Gang wants you.' 'JOIN NAMBLA [North American Man-Boy Love Association] NOW!' He has people hang them up in the housing units, and people actually sign up, thinking the sheets are real! Only in Tucson…

He even made up a Rap Song, for the Perverts;

"I'm a Child Molester; I think I'm real cool,

Every Day I hang out by the Elementary School;

I'm a Child Molester, Do not know why all the fuss,

Just tried to get my old job back, driving the school bus;

I'm a Child Molester, I think life's just dandy,

Look, here comes a little girl, now where'd I put that candy;

I'm a Child Molester, in mud puddles I go stamping,

Can't wait till next summer when I take the Cub Scouts camping;

I'm a Child Molester; some folks think I'm sick,

Cause when I see a little boy, I want to suck his d**k;

I'm a child Molester now; I'm a big tough con;

Skipping down the hallways, at U.S.P. Tucson."

[Used with permission, ©Danny Fabricant, 2011]

The case Danny is serving time on is the third Federal case that he's had. He won the first two. His first Federal case was filed in 1976, over him ordering merchandise, in the early 70's, under made up names. He was charged with defrauding several Book-of –the-Month and Record clubs (back in the 70's they did not have CD's, or even 4 or 8 track tapes), as well as Spiegel's and other mail-order companies. There was no name so stupid that the companies would not send the merchandise to it.

He won that case, representing himself, over "Pre-Indictment Delay,' a loophole almost never successfully used.

In 1986, he and the Hells Angels President who ran a leg of the Olympic Torch (in 1984) were charged with a Federal Murder Conspiracy. He again represented himself. After a seven-week trial, they were found Not Guilty.

Danny usually spices up his Court filings with sarcasm and humor. When I write up Pleading and Motions, he'll take the little Word Processor & edit what I've written, often with sarcasm. It doesn't seem to have hurt, as I seem to win a higher percentage of Motions after he'd edited what I've written. He says that Judges get bored with 'normal' cases and paperwork.

Danny always brings me back to reality. All the time, I try to tell him my vision of things and I guess I complain about the things that have happened to me. He will patiently listen to me and then remind me that "You are Black," or "You are a Black, Drug Dealing, Pimp," or "Who do you think you are, Obama?"

Danny doesn't often use the term 'Drug Dealer," except when insulting me. He says it has a 'negative connotation.' He prefers 'Wholesaler of Recreational Substances.'

I personally prefer 'Business Manager' to Pimp, which also has a 'negative connotation.'

CHAPTER 69

FEDERAL PRISONS & U.S.P. TUCSON, MID-2011

The 140+ Federal Prisons (including private prisons) presently hold about 220,000 Guests. Their fiscal 2011 budget was $6,800,000,000+. U.S.P. Tucson has about 1,600, including a steady population of about 170 in the SHU. Among the 140+, prisons are 20 Penitentiaries (Pens)

in the other 19 'normal 'Pens, various groups of the Guests are headed by 1 or 2 guys who are 'Shot Callers. There can be 15 or 20 different groups in a Pen. A large percentage of the Shot Callers are psychopaths and/or heroin addicts. These Shot Callers often make life & death decisions affecting the guys [unlucky enough] to be in their group. Shot callers set (and regularly increase) the monthly (or weekly) protection payments of those in their group who can be squeezed to pay. Much of this money pays for the drugs consumed by each group's Shot Caller(s). They also decide that certain guys will have their families/friends regularly bring drugs in, through the visiting room. Some guys are tasked with making, and hiding, multi gallons of wine, in their cells. Some are ordered to keep piles of Shanks in their cells. Other guys in the group are sent on 'missions, 'to assault, stab or even kill guys who have displeased the Shot Caller. If anyone refuses, he then becomes a target.

When a guy in one group 'disrespects, cheats, steals from or runs up a drug/alcohol/gambling/etc. debt with someone from another group, the groups' Shot Callers get together and decide what should happen to the offending party. Much of the assaulting is because of these kinds of things. The Shot Callers have the offending party (at least) beaten up, in-house. Or, one group's Shot Caller will tell the other group's Shot Caller to 'Go F**k Yourself, ' and then there's another War, usually over something really stupid.

When someone is transferred between Pens, the group's Shot Caller in the new Pen will make contact with the Shot Caller at the last Pen (if he hasn't already been contacted about the guy) to find out if there was a negative reason for the guy being transferred. There is no 'hiding.' If a guy checked in, or was forcibly Checked In, the same thing will happen at the new Pen--often with a beating/stabbing. If nothing is known about the guy, he will first be told to produce his Court documents. The prison's Electronic Law Library will be checked for any appeal ruling, or the guy's name showing up as testifying against someone. The Internet will be checked for any news stories about the guy. His Court Docket will also be checked, on line, to see if he 'cooperated' with law enforcement. Within a couple of days of the new guys' arrival, if there is anything bad about a new guy, it will be known. If anything bad is found, he will be beaten off the yard. Hundreds of guys this happened to are now at Tucson.

Once a week, Tucson holds an Orientation for new arrivals. Welcome to Pervert Land! Some videos are shown, the Warden & numerous other upper staff give little speeches & everyone gets a lovely 'Welcome to U.S.P. Tucson' booklet. Among the staff who give the little speeches is a woman from the Psych Dept. She tells everyone the current percentage of the Guests here who are Sex Offenders. As of August 2011, it was 68%. For a person to be designated (by the BOP) as a Sex Offender, that person must be currently serving a sentence after being convicted of a Sex Crime(s). Those range from possessing Kiddy Porn, to taking a minor across State Lines for Sex, to Rape/Murder on federal property/land. For a Sex Offender be in one of the 20 Federal Pens, he had to have received a long sentence, as there are tens of thousands of Sex Offenders in the 100+ FCI

with sentences of (usually) 25 years or less.
Another 15-20% of the Guests here fall under the 'Walsh Act. 'That means they have previously been convicted of a Sex Crime(s) and must register as Sex Offenders, if they are ever released.
There are 50-75 'normal' Guests here. This includes 25-30 of the 100+ 'Medical Care Level III' guys, in Unit A-l, and maybe 5 in each of the other 11 (128 bed) Units.
Nearly all the rest of the Guests are here because they can't be in any of the other 19 Federal Pens, for a variety of reasons, such as;
* They 'assisted' law enforcement and/or testified against their (former) friends or even family, but still got huge sentences.
* They are 'in-prison Rats.' When these guys are caught 'telling' in other Pens, they are, no later than that day, attacked & stabbed, numerous times, by a 'team' from their 'group.' Nearly half of the Guests here now are active 'in prison Rats.' They tell on everything-often other Rats. Nearly all federal prisons have E-mail. This makes telling quick and easy. The Rats just log onto the system and send a 'Staff Message, 'addressed to the Warden. Warden messages are read within minutes, in the Lieutenant's (LT's) Office & quickly acted on. No need to write out & drop notes in the Unit Mailbox, like in the old days.
Some of the Rats like to tell in person. Who knows why. There are often lines of them, outside the LT's of f ice. When one of the LTs finally starts listening to one of them, they get so disgusted they end up throwing them out of the office, because they just will not shut up. It is like opening a faucet & the handle falling off. The Rats will also tell (usually untruthfully) on staff members, for giving/selling drugs or tobacco to other prisoners, or a Unit cop, for not searching the required 5 cells per shift; speeding around in one of the electric Golf Carts; eating prisoner food in the Chow Hall, or other nonsense. The cops are usually told which scumbag told on them and for what. Most of the Rats are not very bright. The Rats' cells are later searched by the same cop(s) they told on, such as for not searching enough cells. Amazingly, shanks are often found during these searches. This causes the Rat(s) to get a Major write-up, sit in the SI-lU for many months, lose several months of their 47 days a year of accrued credits [as of 08/01/2011, also get fined, up to $500.00] & if it's their 2nd time, they're shipped to one of the other 19 Pens. What a shame.

* They joined, and then 'left, 'one of the many prison gangs, or outside street gangs. One does not simply 'retire' from groups like these. In order to be sent here, they have to 'Debrief.' Most of these 'Drop-Outs' have standing 'Hit' Orders out on them.

* They ran up huge debts (gambling, drugs, alcohol and/or serial borrowing) and 'Checked-In, 'to avoid having to pay, in other Pens.
*They are 'Cell thieves, 'who, when caught, were assaulted/stabbed, in other Pens.
* They are one of the 100+ flamboyant or 'out-front, Man- Eating' Homosexuals, who were run off (made to Check In) from other Pens, by their group or (former) gang.
* They have SERIOUS Mental Health issues--at least 5% of the Guests are visibly 'mentally challenged' [to be politically correct]. For whatever reason(s) they cannot be in a 'normal 'Pen, but they are not so bad that they have to be in a Psychiatric Hospital-prison (Like where the Tucson Congresswoman shooter is)
* Many have several, or all, of the above wonderful qualities.
Having so many Sex Offenders causes the Library Staff to remove the Department Store

ads from the Sunday papers. The Unit cops kept finding Wal-Mart, Target & K-Mart ads, with children modeling underwear or bathing suits, cut out and taped up inside lockers or above the lower bunks.

Maybe 5 % of the Sex Offenders are also 'Gunners. 'Those are guys who stalk and then masturbate, while staring at female employees. These guys will often hide in closets left unlocked or behind trash collection carts. Some wear oversize baggy clothes with one of the pockets removed from their pants and will strike up conversations with female staff, while masturbating right in front of them. When there are female staff working the Units, these perverts will all be at their windows, masturbating while watching them doing the Counts...

The cell thieves and serial borrowers here, when caught or confronted, usually tell the guy(s) "If you hit me, I'll tell on you." The guys they're caught stealing from, or who they owe, usually won't beat them up, as they're afraid of being sent back to a 'real' Pen, so they either do nothing, or they'll get a 'shank, ' hide it in the guy's cell & then tell on him.

Tucson averages about one Check-In, every day. In mid-2010, when the SHU filled up with Check-Ins, Staff started ordering them to go back to the Yard. When they refuse, they are given a write-up, for Refusing to 'Program.'

They are then found guilty, in a Kangaroo Court-type Hearing. As punishment, several weeks of the 47 days a year prisoners earn against their sentences, are taken away. This is done bi-monthly. If they keep refusing, they keep losing earned credits. That means it will be months (or years) longer until these scumbags get out and molest more kids, or hurt more people who do not have it coming. What a tragedy...

Another group worth describing are the Rx Pill guys. This group (200+) was created, mostly, by the Psychology Dept. all Sex Offenders have to see at least quarterly] freely prescribing various Psych medicines and sleeping pills to everyone who asks for them. The Medical Dept. Doctors (who usually last less than a year, before quitting in disgust) likewise prescribe piles of pain pills to anyone with a seemingly valid complaint/ailment. It does not take much imagination to picture the Guests here explaining to each other the symptoms to describe to the Psyche, or overworked Doctors, to get Rxs for 'the good stuff.

Every morning and evening, there are long lines of guys being doled out their daily 'Controlled Meds.' At least the Pharmacy is not stupid enough to give these guys a month's supply of 'the good stuff, 'once a month. Some of the guys happily take their pills, as they are handed to them.

Others, who have made a business of selling the pills, have learned how to not actually take/swallow them. Even with Officers standing there watching them take the pills, and looking in their mouths with a flashlight immediately afterwards, these guys get away without actually swallowing them. Either the pills are then saved up and 5-10 are taken at a time, or they are sold to the dope fiends. The $ for the daily doses of pills is often used to buy more conventional drugs, like Heroin, Coke, Methamphetamine or Marijuana--all regularly available here.

All of this causes it own problems, such as; Dope fiends (with no $) buying pills on credit, large mental defectives eating handfuls of psych medicines (often washed down with a homemade wine) and wandering around in a stupor-often committing random violence, against other Guests, or Staff. Or fatal overdoses (what a shame)

If there were not 100+ (out-front, Man-Eating/effeminate)

Homos here, some of the dope fiends might be able to sell Oral

Sex for more than the going rate of (up to) $5.oo. But, money rarely changes hand for Sex here. One of the Units, Baby Love) I, has so many out-front Homos, it's called West

Hollywood.

Some of the weaker Guests are forced to get Rxs and give the pills to others. Sometimes the old, ugly Homos will use the pills to pay younger guys to have sex with them. Just like outside. [Then there is the prisoners. .1

As far as the Guests of Tucson go 90+ percentages of them should never be let out.

CHAPTER 70

THE STATE OF PRISON TODAY, U.S.P. TUCSON

There's less programs and schooling, more youngsters, more addicts, more people who are illiterate, ignorant or both, it's a shame. We need to stop Arguing, Gossiping, and Spreading Rumors about any and everything. Usually it's about another poor person with nothing. This can get us indicted or killed. Or, about some celebrity who's not concerned about us and has everything. We should go back to preschool remember stick and stones, people can and will say anything as long as they are not putting their hands on you. Leave it alone, usually if you ignore it, it will go away.

FIGHTING, STABBING, SHOOTING, AND KILLING, Violence about nothing usually what someone said, how someone feels disrespected when we really were not or shouldn't care anyway. If you're not willing to kill for it or die for it, then leave it alone or resolve it peacefully.

ORAL AND ANAL SEX, MASTURBATING, FELCHING, VOYEURISM, STALKING, GUNNING, ADULT & KIDDY PORN.

Personally, I do not like to tease or taunt myself, or anyone else for that matter, especially in prison. I will not put something or someone else in control of me. It's about self-control. It's either the real thing or nothing at all with me. We should wait for the real thing, a mature adult. Lusting after something, or someone else I can't have right now, is a big waste of time. It redirects energy and focus for something or someone that is just not right. There are guys that will drop everything they are doing to watch a woman walk, intensely. Or, they will go and get a book, magazine, little boy or girl underwear ads out of the Sunday newspaper, or other people's family pictures. Chantage if you ask me. Then there are the guys that pull their penises out and masturbate in front of women; scaring these ladies badly. Some of these guys actually believe that women like them and enjoy this being done, in their honor. This bi lack of self-control only increases and becomes more out of control. More positive productive things can be done to better ones self and prepare you for adult mature women.

HOMOSEXUALITY: I'm not a homosexual and I have nothing against any homosexuality. But, I know that a lot of these guys do this, again, out of a lack of self-control. They feel like they cannot wait when they really do not want to wait so they go to what they think is the next best thing. But it's not for me. And, a lot of what goes on in prison is rape or borderline rape. These guys are influenced, pressured, bought or sold into it because they believe they have nobody or nothing to care for.

So they turn to people and things that they think will care or make them not care and help the situation but it usually doesn't work. I'm a man of faith, businessman, a litigator, so I believe in respecting they neighbors even if I do not agree with what they do, it's their business, not mine. I'm a businessman so my clients or customers come in all sizes, shapes and sorts. I'm a litigator so I'm all about fighting for people rights per law I abide by the law and fight for people's rights.

SNITCHING, TELLING, on people I'm strongly starting to believe that these guys nowadays are telling just to be telling because they are not getting anything out of it. A lot of them do not have any friends inside nor outside of prison so they strike up a conversation with anyone that will listen, telling everything about everybody most of which is usually untrue. They tell what someone else tells them without ever confirming the source of information or how or who it hurts. Some people have legitimate issues other talk too much. Nowadays here in U.S.P. Tucson these guys line up to tell anything in front of any and everybody. They would get hurt or killed anywhere else and still could here at the wrong time with the wrong person. The other side of it is these guys who tell for money or tell attempting to get release from jail or prison they make up things, lie on people or tell half the story. The truth doesn't matter to them. They tell just enough to look truthful they're real dangerous.

SPENDING TOO MUCH TIME WORRYING ABOUT SOMEONE OR SOMETHING ELSE. I never understand how people can do this. We are in such a bad situation already personally today. Too many people worry about what other people are doing, they are really not concerned at all. That is the way to misdirect people attention off them or their attention off themselves. To have a healthy general concern is good. Go talk to that person not talk about the person. And start off saying I think and feel this way because this is what I see or hear.

DEPENDING ON OTHERS in society or in prison to help them when the only person you can really count on is yourself. Especially hoping and depending on lawyers, friends and family in here or in society. Out of sight out of mind, that is how most people think. As time goes on it gets even worse. Unexpected things happen, and people get busy even if they care. Anybody can lie and really do not care when they can they do. That is the worst. Some people are glad some of us are locked up and they do not have to worry no more and they know where we're at. Those who wait, depend and rely on God to much God gave you hands, feet, eyes, ears and a brain for a reason, so use it.

NEGATIVITIES LIKE, RUMORS, GOSSIP AND BACK BITING can be hurtful or kill. If people feel so strongly about, something or someone stay away or confront it. We can be who you want to be. We do not have to stay who you were. Actions speak louder than words. Facts speak for themselves. Having nothing to prove, means you know yourself. Real men and women do not gossip and spread rumors. People should repeat only positive truths. People should only say things to people directly. People should do things to get out of a prison mind set. Negativity hurts kills and keeps us imprisoned.

We should be and do everything to better ourselves body, mind and soul and those around us. Non-positive, non-productive thoughts, actions and words are a waste of time, energy & resources, and only makes things worse.

EVERYDAY WE SHOULD

MENTALLY- read, write, listen, learn, watch, question, investigate and only depend on reliable sources.

PHYSICALLY- walk, jog, run, exercise, and eat right, low fats, sugars, grease and white foods, lots of water & vitamins.

EMOTIONALLY- identify what you feel and why & express it properly. (Feeling words)

SPIRITUALLY- Pray = talk to God or your higher power, read, listen. Meditate = concentrate on one thing or nothing.

Be positive, productive, love not hate. Hate breeds more hate. Violence breeds more violence and people get hurt or killed. We are a part of the problem or a part of the solution. Say what you mean, do what you say. Be somebody good or great. Being bad gets us nowhere. Be yourself & a leader.

CHAPTER 71

NOT SPENDING ENOUGH TIME WORKING ON SELF.

NOVEMBER 2010 INCIDENTS

On November 9, 2010, U.S.P.-Tucson had its first full lockdown in more than two years.

There are 300+ Paisa's (Mexico Mexicans) here. A few of them got into an argument with some of the 10 or so Latin Kings. The leader of the Latin Kings told the leader of the Paisa's that they'd all have to get off the Yard. The Paisa's Leader said, "No, YOU get off the Yard."

The next morning, five of the Latin Kings were attacked so badly they had to be taken to outside hospitals. A week or so later, two were still there. The rest the Latin Kings were removed from the yard & 20+ Paisa's who were identified from the security camera tapes were bused to Victorville.

In other prison, Lockdowns include all of the Guests. In Tucson, it doesn't include the kitchen workers. Other prisons keep thousands of frozen sack meals, for their many Lockdowns. Here, the kitchen still makes up the regular meals, which are put in Styrofoam containers & distributed to the cells. Very civilized.

The place was on full lockdown for only two days. The next two days, everyone went to the Chow Hall & we were allowed out to the playground, by sides. By Friday, everything was back to normal.

On Nov. 15th, the first Murder occurred here. But, inasmuch as it happened in 'The Hole' (Special Housing Unit), there was no lockdown, or even any disruption of anything.

A whacked out white guy apparently suffocated or strangled his cellmate, a Native American, in The Hole.

By coincidence, a large group from Regional Headquarters was here that day, on an inspection tour. Quite a cluster****. Add in a bunch of FBI Agents (who investigate all crimes committed in Federal Prisons), who had to interview all of the disrupted & uncooperative Guests in the hole, who were anywhere in the vicinity of the cell the murder happened in.

If this was a 'normal' Penitentiary, the Natives would kill some White Guy, to retaliate. It is doubtful that there will be any retaliation, but the general consensus among the few 'normal' [not Sex Offenders, Check Ins or Rats] Guests here is "I hope they take out one of the Sex Offenders."

A growing problem here is caused by the Psych department. (Who all the Sex Offenders have to regularly see) freely prescribing Psych medicines and or sleeping pills to anyone who asks for them. The Medical Department Doctors, who usually last less than a year before quitting, in disgust, end up prescribing pain medication to just about anyone with a seemingly valid complaint. It doesn't take a lot of imagination to visualize the Guests explaining to each other what symptoms to tell the Psych's, or overworked Doctors, they have.

Most of the hard meds are taken for mental health issues and pain relief. These guys say and do any and everything to get on the drugs they use and abuse them and they get broke barter trade and sell them. These guys are just like the dope fiends on the streets. They will steal, kill and suck ****, for it and there's a lot of this happening more and more everyday especially the latter (sucking ****). Sometimes some of these guys trade their scripts for dope, which go for 4 books of stamps each. A book of stamps is valued at $5.00 each, they trade them for real dope, Mexican black tar heroin that has a long, harder lasting affect and doesn't clog up a needle, like the oxycontin does at times. The Paisa's have the illegal drug market on lock and they get/buy/trade all the scripts they can to keep them on lock also.

Several hundred of the Guests go to the 'Pill Call Lines' once or twice a day, to pick up their individual doses of the various Psych, pain and/or sleeping pills. At least prison do not just hand these guys a week's or month's supply, but even with officers supervising the taking of the individual doses & looking in the guys' mouths afterwards, many of the Guests manage to not actually swallow the pills.

The Guests either save them up and then take many days' worth at once or sell them. The taking of large amounts sometimes causes them to wander around in drunken stupors, or commit random violent acts.

Some of the weaker Guests are forced to get Rxs and just give the pills to guys who will either take piles of them or sell them. It also causes more check-ins, by dope fiends who buy pills, on credit, & then check-in when their bills get higher than they can personally pay.

It's not like they can sell sex here. There are so many Homosexuals here that the ugly ones have to pay guys to have sex with them – just like outside!! [Then there are the prisoners…….]

CHAPTER 72

U.S.P. TUCSON STAFF-INMATE RELATIONS

This portion of the book is intended to paint a more human picture of those whom I deal with on a day-to-day basis – to put a face on the person. This is my place to describe some of the staff members who either make my life and the lives of hundreds of other men tolerable or a living hell. A good staff is required in order to operate a prison efficiently, safely and productively, meaning it attains its goal of containment and warehousing of prisoners while at the same time providing for the many and varied daily needs of inmates. U.S.P. Tucson is largely, staffed by individuals who qualify as efficient and humane, and who really care about the quality of the job functions they perform. They should, because many people—both inside and outside the prison walls—depend on the. Staff is recognized as being professional, fair, and honest, or not. Could you imagine a hospital being staffed by individuals who do not care about the level and quality of care they provide to people in their facility? Those in the BOP who genuinely do care about the level of service they deliver are worth mentioning. At the same time, not anyone who is not concerned about their reputation in front of the inmates should mind being accurately described within these pages. The public has every right to be aware of the types of person they are paying to run prisons. The cost of operating America's prisons is staggering and a large portion of that expense is payroll.

WARDENS

Among the administrative staff, none is more visible or frequently put on the spot than the warden, nor is anyone else held more accountable. U.S.P. Tucson is part of a Federal Correction Complex, or FCC, of which Craig Apker is the Complex Warden. Apker, being the top dog, has responsibility for three prisons: the maximum-security U.S.P., a medium-security FCI and a minimum-security camp.

Apker is a seasoned veteran warden, who transferred from the Phoenix FCI to guide Tucson through its transition into a sex offender prison. He is a no-nonsense man of his word who commands respect and enforces the chain of command concept. He often steps in when it breaks down. Predictably, he can be heard to say, "I am a strict enforcer of the chain of command." He is visible to inmates and is seen frequently walking the compound and making himself available to inmates at lunch. More important is his willingness to actually listen to inmates and respond to their needs. Apker was indeed the right pick for this institution.

His relatively calm environment at U.S.P. Tucson is proof of his abilities to command a large staff—some of whom are green to BOP operations – and an ever-changing inmate population.

At this institution, there are several Associate Wardens (AWs), much like vice-presidents in large corporations, each overseeing specific areas such as custody and security, inmate trust fund and commissary services, institution maintenance, food services, health services, and so on. These are AW's Sanchez, Beckwith, McClintock, and Hollenbeck.

One of wardens is one who stands out in my mind because of on my experience working around him. No one really thinks of how important trust between staff and inmates is at a federal institution, perhaps because they assume there isn't – shouldn't be any such thing, but Warden Louis Winn gave me the first opportunity to show that I could be trusted by the administrative staff.

Complex Warden Craig Apker, Warden Louis Winn. Associates Wardens: Beckwith, Hollenbeck, Lamb, McClontock, Nicklin.Captain-Barnheart, Dep. Capt. Swepson

LIEUTENANTS

Lieutenants form the hierarchy or custody staff at a U.S.P., and there are several here at Tucson. A lieutenant is always on-duty at the institution, 24 hours a day. They are as varied as any other individual is, but most have worked their way into their current position after serving for some length of time as correctional officers, at other institutions. They range from highly trained and well-seasoned professionals to those that are just plain lazy and who seem not to care about the job.

I offer the example of the institution's Senior Lieutenants. Senior Lieutenants are the acting warden, sheriff, mayor, and governor of the prison when no senior administrative staff is on hand, particularly on weekends and holidays. They handle everything ranging from inmate and staff movement to fights and riot, making the call on the smallest to biggest details, supervising staff and officers, inmate and staff job assignments and are generally responsible for who does what, when, where and how.

Lt. Munoz, one of the institutions is Senior Lieutenants, is a big guy and makes a big impression. Munoz has over twenty years experience in corrections, mainly at UPS's and has experience virtually every type of prison situation imaginable. At one time, he was on the special security detail for Timothy McVeigh, who was eventually executed for his role in the bombing of the Federal Building in Oklahoma City. As part of his duties, Munoz assisted in transporting McVeigh back and forth to court appearances. I asked Munoz if McVeigh ever discussed his innocence or guilt with his escorts, but Munoz replied, "No, he never did "But he did tell the offices a joke every day, and the officers told him a joke in return." When I asked Munoz if he had any hard feelings against a man who hated the government, he reflected, "At first I did some, but I knew what was going to happen to him and so did he. He had to answer to God, not to me, so there was no need for me to treat him bad or punish him. I just wanted to do my job correctly and for him to do as he was supposed to and obey the orders he was given." Based partly on his knowledge of with this situation, Munoz believers that some lawyers are greedy and lousy. This was reinforced by observing that when McVeigh's attorney came to visit him just minutes before his scheduled execution, he brought an armload of magazines for McVeigh to autograph, and later sold them for a 1,000.00 apiece.

I respect Lt. Munoz, not only is he committed to his job, but he is also a dedicated father, husband, die-hard Steelers fan, and who is by-the-book but not beyond being human. I witnessed an example of this on the day president-elect Barrack Obama was sworn to office. Instead of listening to music on the radio as he normally does, Munoz was listening to the inauguration. I was cleaning nearby and when he looked at me, I could see he was very involved in listening to the event, as he had a very emotional look in his eyes. He asked me, "What do you think about all this?" but I could not even talk at the moment, being affected me by what I was hearing from the Capitol steps in Washington. After clearing my throat, all I could manage was "Amazing" to which Munoz responded, "Me too." In that brief exchange I recognized a proud man who was emotionally stumped by what the ceremony represented – a mixed minority being sworn-in as the most powerful and influential leader in the free world.

Lt. Pea is another Senior Lieutenant at U.S.P. Tucson, and I will never forget when I heard it was announced to staff that he was coming from the FCI to work here. Staff and inmates alike already seemed to know Pea, which made him a sort of legend in my mind. Most of Lt. Pea's history came out of Atlanta U.S.P. where he had spent much of his twenty-plus years in the federal system. The biggest talk about Pea was that he is tough, mean, aggressive and even crazy. Others said, "He does not take any shit," but it was also said he did not discriminate based on race or gender. I would later learn that all this was true – except the part about Pea being crazy – but I would also come to recognize his finer qualities, which had not been mentioned. Pea came over to the U.S.P. just months after it opened and became Operations Lieutenant during day shift, and things were just getting started. The U.S.P. needed someone to walk tall and carry a big stick, and this task fell on Lt. Pea. He was not afraid of confrontation and want not afraid to fight. He was willing to let little stuff slide, but he was not about to ignore the big stuff – not at his institution and definitely no t on his watch. When it came to drugs, crime, and violence – particularly black-on-black violence or violence against his officers – Pea's motto was "give-in and give up or be shut-down, rolled over, and stomped on." The talk about his bigger-than-life persona proved to be true, but I was also slowly being exposed to his finer qualities. I was learning that an inmate could properly address his concerns to LT Pea, he would help him in any way he could, especially when his involvement would prevent further problems for the inmate, his staff, or the institution. Pea was big on protecting people and their rights, if you had it coming, Pea would see that you got it, good, bad, or otherwise. This meant that inmates got needed health care; or perhaps evens an apology from staff, I quickly learned that if someone on Pea's staff messed up, they were chewed out, forced to apologize, written up, and possibly sent home or even fired, if warranted. Likewise, if an inmate messed up, he would be chewed out, forced to apologize, written up and possibly sent to the SHU, if warranted. It is said that, if a staff member or inmate did not respect Pea's decisions, he could tell him to his face, write him up, and if that did not make it better, then they were free to go into a room with him and "fight like men."

Rumor also has it that Pea was brought to the U.S.P. to help clean up problems in the SHU, where things had definitely gotten out of hand. Inmates were throwing feces on each other and on the guards, cuffed inmates were jumping staff while in route to the rec cage, and inmates were routinely setting off fire sprinklers and flooding their cells. After several months of Pea working in the SHU, things began to be straightened out. It took his thoughtful, direct, visible approach to accomplish this. Inmates who wanted to see a chaplain got to see one, inmates who needed medical care had their needs taken care of , those who deserved a break received one.

One afternoon an older white inmate complained of chest pain and believed he was having a heart attack. Lt. Pea authorized contacting the local Tucson fire department and EMT squad, but when the emergency crews arrived at the prison gate, they refused to enter. "I do not want to go in and help those animals, they are criminals and animals!" said the fire chief. Lt. Pea's immediate response was, "What did you say?" giving the man an opportunity to change his tune, but the man simply repeated his statement and once again refused to enter the institution. Pea told him, "Listen man, there are unarmed women who work in this prison and you are a big, old man. What are you scared of?

These guys are human beings just like you. They made some bad choices and are paying their debt to society, and I know if you needed help some of them would help you and so would I, so what is your problem? You do not want any problems with me so get in here and do your job!" The emergency crew did not budge and the exchange was repeated once more, but Pea added, these guys are locked-down and away from you so come one, this man may be dying." By this point, the men were probably more intimidated by Lt. Pea than they were of any federal prisoners, so they relented and entered the institution to help them.

Lt. Palomeres – Feisty Spanish LT who was attacked in the middle of a black and white race riot. After that, she excelled.

Lt. Hunt – Big Hunt, not Little Hunt. Mr. "You betcha" (what he always says when greeted). I respect everybody or almost everybody; I do not respect everything. I believe I have already talked about Big Hunt and Little Hunt, before, but some people and some things are worth repeating. They do not call him Big Hunt for no reason – he's only about six feet tall, but he is as wide as the average door; no fat all on his legs, shoulders, chest, and arms, yet he moves really well. You would think his attitude would be of a read big and bag tough guy, but it is not – he just gives people straight, direct, and honest answers. I have a lot of respect for Big Hunt. He is one of the calmest, cool, and collected people I have ever seen. I am not saying that because I believe he is from the areas where I was born and where I moved to and grew up – Chicago & Marion Illinois, Madison and Oxford Wisconsin – but he is similar to Korean and probably more. Big Hunt and I have had some serious conversations about almost everything and some intense ones about the things that really matter in life. In addition, some of the responses he has given me one would not think a correctional officer, especially a supervisor, would answer an inmate like that. Nothing immoral, illegal, or unethical was said – just straight-up questions, answers, and conversations were held. The day before this book was last written; he showed me something, again. They say you can never tell how a person really is until you see them under pressure or in an intense situation. I have seen him react to violent physical situations – none as violent as where he previously worked, I am sure (U.S.P. Marion Super Max, U.S.P. Leavenworth) – and let us just say he handled his business. A crazy, big, old, black DC guy tried to kill himself several-times. He was yelling and screaming saying what he's going to do to himself and everybody else, and Big Hunt just sat there and listened, the four of his officers surrounded the guy and were more than ready to throw him to the ground and beat the crap out of him, but Big Hunt just listened and, in between the guy's rants, he tried to talk to the guy. When the guy finally ran out of breath, he talked him down in a real calm and collected voice. And, instead of locking the guy up, he let him go back to the unit. A half hour later, they guy came and ate chow. That very same day, an older black guy in a wheelchair came to him with some sort of medical problem. Again, I could not and was not trying to hear the entire conversation, but right away, I saw Big Hunt help the guy with his medical problem; afterwards, they seemed like they knew each other from somewhere, before. Big Hunt had been around for a little while – about the same amount of time I have been in, thirteen years. I have also seen him give a few guys a break, most of which never did whatever it was they did, again. They came by, thanked him for it, and said it would never happen, again. More than anything, we talk about working out, but we do not shy away from race, religion, and politics.

Lt. Lamb – I remember when he was here at U.S.P. Tucson, before, and then he left to go to U.S.P. Beaumont, Texas. He is very dark skinned, too. I am not sure if he is part Mexican, part black, or part Middle-Eastern, but he talks pure proper English like a straight-up white guy. I have only worked for him three or four times before, he left and since he has been back. And, the second-to-last time, he snapped at me for no reason, hollering, cussing, screaming as I knocked and walked into his office to clean it, so I left and did not come back for a while. In addition, when I did, he was still in that mood and took three inmates to the SHU that day, himself – he did not have to, he is a supervisor that is not his job. However, one day, the time after that, I was cleaning in his office, he was in with another LT, and out of nowhere, he said to me, "Brown, you have a lot of time, do not you?" And, I said yes; he said, "Well, keep your nose clean and keep doing what you've been doing and maybe something will happen." I told him I will do everything I can – I study and fight the law all day every day. That is for my case and well-being and my mind. I work out every day for my body and my mind and I pray to my God all the time. I have too much time for crimes I did not commit and I will do anything but sell my soul to prove it and win this. He said keep doing it.

Lt. Selby – short, middle-aged white guy, looks like a "Regular Joe," farmer/carpenter-type. When you talk to the guy, he is amazingly smart and well traveled. These Federal jobs take these guys all over and far, but it is still what's inside that counts.

Lt. Bassett – short, stocky, black, light complexion. He is new, so not well known. Some people say he suffers from a "short-man complex." I do not see him that way. He is professional, respectful; he can be worked with, but he can also be a hard-a**.

Lt. Hansen, probably one of the most "By the Book" guys here. Quiet, mellow. He acts much differently than he looks. He could do a biker-gang commercial, with a mean, bulldog look, like "Do not ask me nothing; do not tell me nothing, handle it or I will." I have never known him to go out of his way to make a problem for anyone, staff or inmate. In over a year working for him, he only has to ask me to do something once.

Of notable mention, is Lt. Jones, someone I can relate to in many respects. On numerous occasions, he had said that he is a human being first and his job is not going to change that fact. One day, Lt. Jones asked me, "Why do you make the coffee only on certain days?" I answered, "Certain officers do not like inmates to make the coffee," He said, "Officers need to trust some inmates to a certain extent." From that, I realized Lt. Jones was one of the good guys.

Another down-to-earth person is Lt. Rivera. He likes to tell jokes and talk trash, but even though he is a joker, he is hip to what is going on in the hip-hop culture and his own generation. This provides a great balance between the two worlds and makes for fast and funny verbal games between us.

Another lieutenant who is willing to lead and pass along the knowledge he has gained during his life is Lt. Lillard. He is a proud Christian man who loves his rock 'n' roll. I remember a story he once told me concerning the song "I Can Feel It in the Air Tonight" by Phil Collins. The song is about a man who committed a serious crime and kept it a secret. One day, after hearing the song, the man decided to confess to his wrongdoing. I believe what Lt. Lillard was meaning to relate to me was that we all have to face our own sins and death, and to not hold onto anything that will keep us bound. It was a well-received lesson, which I try to incorporate into my daily life.

Before mentioning the next lieutenant, I want to emphasize the fact that we tend to categorize people by the way, they look, without waiting to determine their true character. I am guilty of that same false characterization based on my first impression of Lt. Rainey. Well, what can I say? At first glance, you would think he is something he is not, but the truth is that if you come to him with a bonafide issue, he will help you if it is within his power to do so. He does not like whiners, or people who say one thing but do the exact opposite, but applies this standard to both inmates and staff alike and holds them equally accountable.

Then there is Lt. Santiago, who I met nearly ten years ago. At first, he seemed timid, but now he is quick to initiate a conversation or confrontation and to address issues. He is fair and honest – two attributes that I highly respect.

Lt. Godwin, AKA "The Reverend," holds his Christian faith in high regard and makes solid decisions based on that viewpoint. Personally, I have never heard anything derogatory about him, which speaks volumes about his character. I respect what God is doing in his life and it reflects in his actions. What better endorsement of a man can there be in this life?

What would you visualize about a man who is nicknamed "Corn-fed?" Based on his looks and size, I would not want to meet him mad in a dark alley, but Lt. Hendrix is really a good guy. From what I have seen, he is tough but fair, and funny to boot. He isn't afraid of anything and likes to get his laugh on; using those attributes to deal with inmates accordingly.

My first conversation with Lt. McElroy included him telling me, "I've never seen a black person until I went into the military," and we both laughed. What an icebreaker. The amazing thing to me is that he apparently gets along better with minority inmates than he does with those of his own race, but that does not stop him from being himself. Everyday Lt. McElroy works, he puts on the rock 'n' roll and proceeds to play air guitar. When he asked me if I want to play too, and I decline, he says, "What, you think your friends would not think you were cool?" causing us both to laugh.

Immediately after arriving for work one day, Lt. Stronick shouted, "You are fired!" When I inquired why, he said, "Because I've asked you for three days in a row to clean the cells down in the SHU." When I replied that I did not have any keys to accomplish this, he just laughed until he could not laugh anymore. When I asked him what was so funny, he replied, "Something I forgot, that you are an inmate and not one of my officers." While Stronick can be a tough guy, he is also fair and always concerned. I remember meeting Stronick back when I first came to prison at another institution, and he observed that I did not speak with anyone. He asked me one day, "Why do you seem mad at the world?" and I replied, "I got a lot of time for something I did not do and it seems as if there is no hope. And a part of me feels like I am dying." While I do not remember exactly what he said to me at that time, I do remember thinking to myself, "He doesn't care. Why is he all in my business?" However, seven or eight years later, Stronick transferred here to Tucson, and when he saw me here he said, "I know you!" and I reminded him, "Yeah, I was at another institution with you about eight years ago." Then it seemed to hit him, and he stated, "Back then, you seemed to be mad at the world. Now you walk around with a smile on your face. I guess God is good!" I said, "Not only is God good, but he's been working in my life. I have gone to school, got a few degrees, and learned a lot about my criminal case. And, if God is willing, I might be getting out of here, soon." It seems to me – now that I think about it – many people do care. And Stronick's question to me nearly eight years ago still rings in my mind.

Speaking of tough reminds me of Lt. Palomeres. For a tough street-smart female, she is actually hip. I find her handling of prison operations to be to be authoritative, both giving and demanding respect. One time she said to me, "You think you are 'Super Orderly' but you can be replaced!" but I shot back, "You may be able to replace 'Super Orderly' but can you replace 'Superman'?" causing us both to break-out in laughter.

Another female lieutenant is Lt. Philips, who strikes me as someone who can really relate to many varied situations. She is the "Queen Bee" in the full sense of the term, and would easily fit the role of judge or executioner. But I have known her to deftly resolve issue that other officers seemingly could not, making me wonder if she sees her job as a fish sees water – a natural combination.

They say that where there is smoke, there is fire, and this could not be truer of Lieutenants Birmingham and McElroy. They always seem to be together, but in fact, they are very different people from one another. Birmingham's jokes are dry but funny, while McElroy is known as "the hick from the sticks." What they share in common is a distrust of politics and mistrust of politicians and they hate anyone who lies, cheats, or steals. They are more concerned with the safety of staff, inmates and the public and want everyone to have fun regardless of their situations.

Some lieutenants diffuse tense situations with prowess, tact, and sometimes-even humor. That is Lt. Bebe. He does not seem to care what come out of his mouth. Bebe seems to take everything in stride, and will even talk trash to a guy three times his size, although it is often difficult to determine if he is serious or just being funny.

Among the wisest in my opinion are Lieutenants Silva and Alvarez. Lt. Silva is an understanding person who came from the streets, so he is not afraid to fight but likewise is willing to evaluate a situation and proceed based on what he believes to be the best course of action. The trade-off is he thinks he is a comedian, even though the jokes are as stale as week-old bread! Lt. Alvarez, another lieutenant I see as being wise – even wiser than most lieutenants or officers – is a stickler for BOP policies, but does use his common sense to make the necessary decisions.

Bassette, Bebe, Birmingham, Chopko, Goodwin, Hansen, Hendrix, Hunt, Rivera, Jones, Lillard, Lambert, Koran, Mcelroy, Munoz, Pea, Rainey, Reed, Santiago, Selby, Silvia, Stronick, Turner, IJring.

SIS LIEUTENANTS

The "Three Amigos" at U.S.P. Tucson are the SIS and SIA Lieutenants. Although they do not like that nickname, Lieutenants Ontravious, Fortes and Mendez form the investigative body of the institution who look into all incidents of inmate-vs.-inmate (SIS) and inmate-vs.-staff (SIA) and ultimately make the determination of who is at fault and who will be punished. An institution of this size, especially a U.S.P., is a small city in itself and requires its own police force. In my opinion, these are decent guys with a tough job to do, and they do it well. SIS and SIA are always somewhat unpopular among the prison population, but their job is to protect inmates and staff and, whenever possible, stop harmful activities before they start. This means keeping their ear to the ground and being aware of all potential issues – not an easy task and ever much unappreciated, to say the least. Among the three, the most calm, cool and collected is Lt. Fortes, although I have seen him explode. The saying is true – dynamite comes in small packages, but overall he is an understanding individual who is mostly concerned with the bigger problems facing the institution and does not get tangled-up in petty non-issues. I call Lt. Ontavious the "vice president of investigations," although at times he acts as if he has been promoted to 'president". The only situation I ever had with him was resolved peaceably after we took the time to understand each other's point of view and came to a mutual understanding. In my opinion, Lt. Ontavious solves problems by being levelheaded and fair-minded. Although Lt. Mendez's actual title is "SIA/Special Investigative Agent" I call him "HHIC/Head Hispanic in Charge". Sometime I even refer to him as the devil, perhaps only because he is such a devil for details. The way he sees it, everyone is guilty before they are even charged with a crime or infraction of the rules. He had expressed his interest in becoming the Inspector General, and my money says he will get his wish. He is a good addition to the prison because he really believes in what he does. His job includes supervising the many S.I.S. Lieutenants's

SIS Barker (aka Captain Kangaroo)

SIS Lt. Cooper, the Inspector Clouseau of U.S.P.-Tucson

SIS Lt. Jones, the short Refrigerator Perry.

Because there is no other Federal Penitentiary like this one, all of the training and experience of the various SIS staff has completely gone to waste. Nothing happens here as it does in a 'normal' Pen. The more the SIS people try to respond to things as they would in a 'normal' Pen, the sillier the results come out.

Reed – Congratulations to you Hillbilly Redneck .Case Manager Baldy – A good officer, with a good personality, when I worked for him. I am sure you will make a good case manager. Never gets too excited about anything and does a fine job.

Counselor Olivarez – you went from the mailroom and R&D to counselor, from doing next to nothing to a little something. You have to be a better "hider", now. Rumor is that you do as good as a job as any counselor in the BOP – once they find you. (You are too big to hide) Good officer and good counselor.

Lt. Uring – Country Redneck Hillbilly, with the brute strength of a professional wrestler.

Lt. Koran – Toughest short big man, with a higher intelligence level than most .Sometimes seems a little smart-alecky. When it comes to his knowledge, he is nicknamed by me "Alex Trebek," because he shouts questions at people all the time. Most do not know any answers. I surprise him more than once by my answers to his questions on history, science, math and geography. Smart, tough, funny, military, and witty.

Lt. Birmingham – "Good Dude" really describes him. I do not know anyone who has anything bad to say about him, except he's got to be crazy, because since I've known him, three prisons (he's been where I've been), he stays in the hole (SHU) –. Ninety-nine percent of the time, if he tells you he is going to do something, he does it. He will speak and hold a short conversation with anyone. He has been known to spin a person or two, never me, but I have seen him in action with the big smile and the hand motions. I told him before, he should run for office.

SIA Mendez: SIS-Baker, Cooper, Fortez, Jones, Ontraverious, Palamores, Rivera.

Case Manager Moreno – A good guy that will help you when you can, but sometimes he seems to have this "I do not want to deal with you unless I have to" attitude. I have seen him be promoted, I think, twice since I have been here. I think he has a difficult time with difficult inmates. Perhaps Moreno's biggest issue is that he is a St. Louis Rams fan.

OFFICERS

Officer Adleman – He is all right; he has been my supervisor at least twice, and worked my unit for months. He has several nicknames, including Robo Cop, and Walk-A-Lot. He kind of looks like and can remind you of the cop on Night Court – Bull – although; he could be somewhat more aggressive, and funny.

Officer Arandulas is a cool Mexican dude, complete with dark shades and tattoos. He has got the physique of a boxer, and thinks he is a playboy.

Officer Ashworth is a playboy who always has something slick to say, but with words of wisdom tucked inside.

Ms. A______, a tall, blond, lady who walks around with a real tough-girl attitude. She sounds like a cross between Fran Drescher and Lady Gaga and acts like a gangster. One day, I asked her, "How do you pronounce your name?" She said, "Just call me Ms. A" with a Brooklyn accent, and attitude. She is also a pro tennis player I heard her telling some young guys, "I'm tough, I'm ghetto, I'm a Hood Rat from Brooklyn." I do not think she really knows what a Hood Rat is. She looks like a cross between Lady Gaga and Olive Oil. [For those of you born after 1970, Olive Oil was Popeye's girlfriend. Popeye was… Oh, never mind…] she is about 5'9" and maybe 100 lbs with the uniform, boots, handcuffs, radio, sap gloves, baton, and mace. However, I would not underestimate her – I do not underestimate anyone.

Officer Barron, Old School Hack, will advise you.

Officer Beardsley – who is always sticking his chest out as if he is the biggest guy with the biggest Pecs in the world. Good guy, not a hard-ass, but not a softie. He knows his stuff, though, on how to survive in prison and deal with all sorts of inmates. Having been at FFC Victorville for a few years, he knows how to deal with West Coast Boys. Victorville's no joke – not bad for a blond-haired, blue-eyed devil.

Officer Branch is a younger officer. This can be a blessing or a curse because younger officers tend to be edgy when they do not connect well with younger inmates, although Branch listens to the same hip-hop music, which gives him something in common with them. He takes job responsibilities seriously, but always finds room to pass alone a little bit of wisdom.

Officer Boncore has a history prior to joining the BOP including ultimate fighter, street fighter, Military Special Forces, and playboy. Originally, from New York, but lacking any accent, Boncore is actually quiet, that is until someone pisses him off and then he is all business. I have personally seen him run down and body slam numerous trouble-making inmates. He is a no-nonsense individual and generally a mellow guy, underneath an exterior that is probably tattooed head-to-toe. He could be accurately described as a gentleman who gets along with everyone. You have to be a real jerk for Boncore not to at least talk civilly to you. Whether discussing girls, cars, sports, healthy eating, or working out, Boncore is always good for an intelligent conversation. He is usually the first to spot danger and the first on the scene to stop it.

Officer Borunda – a Mexican Dom DeLuise/Martha Stewart. He is always trying to ride me about not working enough and the floors, windows, doors, etc always being dirty.

Officer Broomfield –Our first dealings were not cordial. I thought she had accused me of being gay, I said, "I'm not gay." She said, "That's not what I said; I said people are regularly coming to talk to you and you stay in your cell alone. Months later, I discovered she is very cool and gets along with everyone. Once she said, "There's this place with good, inexpensive college correspondence courses. She hates "gunners." When she encounters one, she royally cusses them out.

While some officers are known to be a bit lazy, only one is nicknamed "Sleepy," and that is Officer Caldwell, because whether he is standing, sitting, or just leaning on the wall, he is often asleep. He is mostly concerned with doing his eight hours and getting home in one piece, but at least the man had his priorities in order!

Officer Castro – AKA Fidel's Little Brother. Hair black and curly – you know, he is a Cuban. Quiet, mild-mannered dude. Usually, he will get loud if you hinder him from doing his job, but that is about it. He takes nothing personally, not in a negative way. "Eight and to the gate" is what he says and does. You can see it in him that he had bigger, better, or just different ambitions.

Officer Chi – cool, relaxed, Chicago-style swagger, short, Irish or Italian, white, knowledgeable; knows what is happening in the world, on the streets, and in prison. From the north side of Chicago, where the neighborhoods can be separate, but the people are who they are and do what they can to help each other.

Officer Chornigrapher – good dude, quiet. I know I surprised him one day and I almost surprised myself. He dropped some money one day – a big wad of rolled-up bills. It was on morning shift. They were coming in about 7:45 a.m. He was walking down the hall and dropped the wad of bills. I chased him down and gave it to him, and his mouth about dropped as if no one ever gave him something he had lost – especially not by a black inmate. I politely asked him, "Did you lose something?" He would not answer, so I said, "I think this is yours." And he said, "Thanks man thanks."

Officer Colburn – short, chubby, white. I mean Johannes' son – that is what I call him. Johannes is the good counselor who looks like he came off the special Ed bus, but is a good guy and not dumb at all. Is always laughing and saying something funny. Colburn is a quieter version who will sneak up on you. He is about his business and does his job, but will say something that will make you say, "Not you, too" and "where did that come from?"

Officer Conrad – "AKA Conrizzle" he told me to call him one day. This guy deserves his own show in Vegas – three of them, actually: one for his Skinny Elvis look-alike sessions, two for his Elvis impressions, and three for his rapper impersonations. He is a Jack-of-all-trades, but I do not think he has mastered any. Of course, in doing all this, he is really. Stand-up comedian really should have been his choice profession, Conrad makes it known, when he works the unit, "Do not **** with me and I will not **** with you." He was serious about that one thing. If no one ever took him seriously about anything, they did, because nothing bad ever happens in his units.

Officer Crow: Good officer, good dude; pretty quiet and mellow. Crow does not bother anyone and he does not let anyone bother him or his fellow officers. It is the quiet ones you have to watch out for. Big, black, bald-headed, about 6'6" 250 lbs, no fat at all. I have heard people call him the Black Gomer Pyle. I tell them to watch out.

Officer Davis – he is a cross between a shamrock and TNT: powerful, short, happy-go-lucky all the time. He is usually very friendly and professional, but sometimes deep in thought, and always with a smile on his face Davis is proud of his Irish roots – you can see the tattoo of his four-leaf clover in colored ink on his forearm. If you listen to some of the COs around here, mainly Officer Padia, they will tell you Davis is Irish and Mexican, especially when he gets mad – so, watch out! Davis is usually pretty calm. One day, Davis exploded worse than any drunken Irish man did. One day Michael was mopping the floor. Davis came out of the Lt's office screaming, "RRRRRR," and kicked the 'wet-floor' signs about 50 feet down the corridor. Michael leaned back against the wall with his dust mop just as that was happening. Davis than kicked the dust mop 50 feet down the hall, just missing Michael's face by an inch and breaking the mop in half. The next time Davis saw Michael after that, Davis apologized, "My fault, Brown – it had nothing to do with you. I was pretty mad, huh?" Michael and he laughed.

At first glance, there is nothing special or especially notable about Officer Detrick. He is quiet and usually does not have much to say, but an inmate who deals with him will quickly find that Detrick will assist with anything that falls within his authority. That is one reason why he stands out in my mind as a good officer. One day, he walked past me and said hello, but I did not respond, and the next day I felt bad for it so I went to him and apologized for being rude. He told me, "We all have bad days, but if you had not come and spoken with me today, I would have thought something was up with you, but because you did, I think you are alright."

Officer Darre I attempted to have a conversation with him one time, I heard him talking about cars with a couple of COs and of inmates. Much of what he had said was incorrect. I went up to him, introduced myself (which I am sure he already knew), and told him that I was ASE-certified mechanic, and that one of my passions is automobiles of all periods. I pulled out my degrees and certificates that I happened to have in my bag. The officer backed me out of his office and seemed as if he was spooked and did not want to listen, unless someone else was around, as if I had a bad contagious illness or something. He finally told me, once I asked him real serious-like, "What is wrong?" he said, "There are just too many shady people around here, too much lying and telling and setting people up, so if you do not mind, let us talk out here in front of the cameras." I said, "Do not worry about it," and walked away, but not before saying, "Everybody in here is not a snitch, sex offender, or bad guy and. As a matter of fact, some of us are innocent." And I said, "If and when you get a chance, you should read one of my book – they are floating around here with staff and will be on the net real soon," As I walked away. "I just wanted to share with you some correct knowledge and up-to-date information that I believe would be helpful with your car ventures." A month or so after that, he kept trying to talk to me. By then, I was busy and I told him that no apology is needed and I knew no disrespect was intended. He makes sure to speak to me all the time, now, especially after he sees many of his officers holding conversations with me about some real serious stuff, sometimes about much of nothing – just making jokes and laughing. I make sure to speak back.

Diaz work in Medical, is hip and handles his business. He takes care of the prisoners with a cool Mexican demeanor.

The other Officer Diaz, I had a few conversations with him – mainly about how he's glad he never ended up in prison, how he had a few dealings with the law, and how it very well could've happened. But he changed his life and got married a beautiful wife who also works here and he went through different businesses, jobs until he ended up working here.

Officer Diego, This is one cool dude – Mexican for real – he does not fake it. His nickname around here is "Diablo" (Devil). I am not sure why they call him that. He is about 5'10" and 250 pounds with his East L.A. walk. I am sure that that is where he is from. Diego does not bother anyone, but he will not let you disrespect him or his fellow staff. Diego is always wearing these cool, expensive sunglasses and is tattooed from neck to toe. When he talks to me it's "What's up, Big Brown?" And, I always say, "What's up Diego. Are you ready?" Diego says "Let us do it, I'm ready to go!" had I not been to southern California (South Central), I would not know what the hell he was talking about, but now I do and I believe he is "ready to go".

Officer Dooner – "Mr. I do not want to do nothing if I do not have to." Great work ethic for a good dude. Burly, bearded, white guy who looks like a bad biker, but has the attitude of Al Bundy. He is all right.

Officer Eban – African, short, extra dark, extremely laid-back, with an African-New York swagger, really deep accent, approachable, he will listen and talk to those who want to talk or need his help… Has experience and knowledge.

Officer Ferguson – Quiet, mild-mannered, always good for a laugh; wants to see people prosper and does not mind helping them to do so; hardly ever offended.

Officer Folghum – Mexican, AKA Cake Boy, I mean Dough Boy. My work partner and I gave him that name. Every time we see him, he is eating some cake and hanging out with Officer Pedia. I always see him smiling and laughing and have never seen him get mad, but one time he almost yanked a dude up for being out of bounds way after the hourly move had ended. I wonder, were do these guys get all these cool fake shades, but his are not fake – he is actually wearing designer sunglasses that are Transitions. And, he is just like his glasses when he is out – he can get in with the inmates and their wanna-be-convict mentalities. The look, the feel, the talk, and attitude makes you want to say, "This is a real and tough dude." He is about 5'8" and 230 lbs. a little big boy, he makes a dude move out of his way. But when he comes in the building and it is just you and him, he can hold a conversation on just about anything, or at least he listens and tries to do the right thing. A jokester, even though many of his jokes are old and stale – the way he looks when he is telling them. And, half the time, when he is not eating some sort of Mexican food, he is always eating some cookies or cake. That is why my co-worker and I gave him the nickname Cake Boy. When people started calling him that, he did not laugh he did not get mad. One day he asked and I admitted that nicknamed him that. He said, "If you are going to call me anything, call me Dough Boy, because I am getting this money, and taking a bite of that cake."

"Flores Times Five." Two females and three guys. Of the five officers named Flores, one is a realist who encouraged me to pursue my interests and to stay out of prison once I am released. She told me on numerous occasions that I can make a real difference.

Considering what I have been through in my life, those words are very encouraging to me. They helped me persevere when I wanted to give up on writing this book. I believe she genuinely meant every word of what she said.

Sis Officer Flores once told me "Everyone deserves a second chance in life, relationships, their job, and especially with God. You give it and you get it." She often motivates me with her words.

Then we have Flores who mainly works the mailroom, Flores who works SHU, and Flores who works compound. I would not be surprised to learn that all are related to each other because all are very good guys and always have encouraging words to share. I have never heard any of them say anything bad, wrong, or rude to anyone.

Franco is one of the most laid-back guys at U.S.P. Tucson. If you did not know better, you might think he is a bit goofy or a little silly, but he is just straight up funny. Franco is a decent person and will not mess with anybody unless they deserve it. I have seen him get angry only a couple of times, and then if I had not seen it with my own eyes, I would not have believed it. Since the day he heard I was writing a book, he started calling me "Rich Dude," When Franco tells me, "You better not end up back in here" and I retort, "I have to get out of here first," he replies, "I have no doubt you will."

Officer Graham – AKA Golden Graham/Mini-Wheat's/Big-Killer Graham. He is about 5'1" short, wide, and will kill you with his looks and seriousness, if you let him. He does his job almost too well with his own personality of TNT and he can talk trash with the best of them. He will make you laugh without even trying.

Officer Gilke-White – a dark skinned skinny. Seems to have a knack for this type of work.

Officer Graves is a cool, quiet, black officer who stays to himself. He is a biker and does not talk to many people, but to those he does speak to he will likely say something serious.

I knew Officer Grisby's father at another institution, and they are very much alike. His dad was a unit counselor at the time, and we got along well. In fact, when I met the younger Grisby at Tucson, I felt as if I were talking to the elder Grisby because both men had a similar demeanor and temperament: they are caring, kind and helpful, even though they are in positions of authority. They are men who would give you the shirt off their backs. The apple does not fall far from the tree.

Some officers who have worked at hard-core BOP institutions tend to be very guarded when they first arrive at Tucson. This applies to Officer Grotifend, but underneath the guarded exterior is a good guy. My reason for thinking this is I was running the track when I was having a particularly tough day. Grotifend must have sensed this and let me to be the last inmate to leave the yard at recall. When I walked past him he said, "I hope you got that out of your system." I just nodded my head, and the next day, he never mentioned anything, like it had never happened.

Officer Guzman is one of the calmest and most collected officers I have ever met. He does his job well. He does not even let being screamed at affect him. He is one of the few people I fully respect. Once he said to me, “Brown, just because you have to work with these people doesn’t mean you have to drink with them.” Another time, he shared these words of truth: “You can't please everybody. No matter how great you do your job or how great of a person you are, someone will always hate you.” When I heard him say that, my jaw almost hit the floor because it was so contrary to his normal attitude.

Officer Hellman – one of those cock-strong and cocky white boys. He calls Michael the “Black Matlock.” He had always been cool with me, but let some guys tell it– especially some of the white guys – he is everything but cool. We had not had many conversations until recently He, like many other cool staff here, got snitched on and lied about by one or more rat inmate. That drew my attention and compassion. Cop or crook, it is not cool to be lied about. The crazy part it is it is usually your own people who do it to you – friends, family, co-workers, or people of your same race. He told me what I already knew: several snitch notes were dropped, including one with who is doing what in the unit and institution, including some lies about me to Hellman. I told him, “Welcome to the club.” He told me, “I’m going by the book from now on, no more breaks.” I said, “Do not let nothing or no one change you into someone that you are not.” A couple of days later, he was back on the unit – his usual self and better. This guy’s usually tough and quiet, but sometimes you could hear him singing everything from rock, country, R&B, and especially hip-hop songs. One time, I told him, “You need to be on America’s Got Talent as the tough-man singer.”

I am especially thankful to know young Mr. Hernandez, who works in Tower 7, in the middle of the playground. I say this because he lets me to be the first inmate on the yard and the last to leave the yard, in the morning. I also appreciate the head nod (a form of acknowledgement and recognition; kind of a “hello”) which really speaks volumes about the man.

Inmates who had worked for Officer Herrera told me he was a hard man and totally, by the book, so at first he and I did not really speak to each other. But, that all changed the day we sat down together and talked about everything from politics to R&B. Since then, we have had numerous bouts of mental sparring, which have been good for me and probably enlightening for him, as well.

Another staff member that is really into his job is Officer Haliberton. One time he said to me, “I do not want to see it and I do not want to hear it, because that’s how people get conspiracies.” Overall, I think he is all about doing his job well.

Officer House – big, burly, white guy, 6’ 250 lbs., of nearly all muscle. He thinks he is king of the world, if you ask him, and certainly, he thinks he has all the ladies. I am not sure how, with the big head of his, and I do not just mean physical. In his mind, he is the super sh**; professionally, he is fair. As an officer, he will apply the rules; as a person, he will give a guy a break. If you cross him, he will get you he is going to save face. Overall, he is a good dude and does not mess with anybody. About him being this good-looking, muscle-bound playboy, which is not for me to say. Some describe him as looking like Tweedle Dee and Tweedle Dum or “Alice in Wonderland” – all he needs is a cap with a propeller.

At the top of the list is Big John, head of food services. He runs the chow hall like a soul-food restaurant – he just puts in another bone for each new arrival and makes sure everyone is fed for minimal cost. A businessperson and family man, he’s ex-military and expects much from young urban black inmates at the institution, hoping they will find their way just as he found his. I appreciate the wise advice he has given me on numerous occasions, but I am concerned that he is a cheese head (Green Bay Packers fan).

It is also worth mentioning that a talented kitchen crew consisting of Ramirez, Seymour, Bunyan, Brown and others, ably assists Big John in operating food services. Officer Brown, in particular, is really into working out and bodybuilding, and takes care of himself and his family. He also tries to bestow knowledge on the younger inmates he encounters, which I find very admirable. Overall, Mr. John could not do as good of a job as he does with food service without the officers who assist him.

Officer Katsher is a young, white guy who always seems to enjoy his job. One evening after dark, a group of 20 or so Mexicans had gathered at the bleachers on the yard during rec time, and the spotlight converged on the yard. Katscher was the first officer on the yard and he immediately ran up into the bleachers and sat down in the midst of the group and asked, “So what are we talking about guys?” It turned out that the group was not discussing anything hostile, and the group was allowed to remain gathered, but it showed that Katscher could use his easy-going attitude to disarm a potentially-volatile situation.

Officer Kelly is big and bad but also cool, until someone gets him mad. He always says to me, “Brown, you do not look like an intellectual nor do you look forty years old” to which I reply, “I'm not. I'm Me, Then I'll tell him he doesn't look like no killer or player. One day I called him Teddy. “Teddy?” he asked, “Like Teddy Roosevelt?” “No,” I said, “like teddy bear!” and I have called him teddy from then on.

Among the other black officer are six who have the last name of Lewis, although none is related to each other. The oldest is a short, quiet man, with a full white beard who reminds me of a great uncle of mine. Although this Officer Lewis does not talk much, when he does speak he bestows a great amount of wisdom.

Officer Lollies – Old Timer CO – and old-school hack, they used to call them. You can tell by the look in his eye he has been through a lot. Lollies does not look to hate anyone, though, or hold anything against anyone for any faults. Lollies is always laughing and smiling, especially if he knows you. And, he is good to tell and instigate a joke. He is rough and ready to go at any time, but glad he does not have to and does not want anything to kick off. He looks, sounds, and acts like and reminds most COs of Oscar the Grouch.

The Four Lopez's: of the four officers Tucson who bear the Surname of Lopez, one is a drill instructor who is always pushy and bossing around inmates and junior officers. But, he does take his job seriously and can be depended on to be funny or at least he tries to be. An example of this is his knack for giving everyone around him a nickname, like calling one inmate “catfish” because he is always digging in the trash.

The youngest Lopez is also one of the newer employees of the BOP and is the real quiet type. I have seen this before, though, and it is only a matter of time before he has learned the ropes and comes out of his shell. My guess is he will make an exemplary officer some day.

Then there's “Playboy Lopez,” who always refers to himself in the third-person, but does not seem to notice himself doing so. He is laid-back when dealing with inmates, unless he feels someone is trying to run a game on him, then he's all over them like a girl he bought a drink for at the bar.

Not to be confused with "Lazy-Boy Lopez," so named because, if there is a chair nearby, you can be sure he's sitting in it, and if there isn't a chair nearby, you can be believe he'll find one. Rumor has it that he had a Lazy boy® recliner in every room of his house, including the bathroom. But to be fair, I have to admit that he does his job well, and he could easily pass for George Lopez, the comedian, in both looks and his ability to entertain and be funny.

Officer Marlo knows when to hold 'em, knows when to fold 'em, knows when to fight and knows when to run. This guy thinks he is a player and is not afraid of anything, but to his credit – unlike some of his fellow officers – he will talk to anyone and help him or her if he can. He really is not concerned with a man's race, weight, height, where he is from, or how much money he once had. He has a fondness for dogs and that is a positive attribute for a man, as far as I am concerned. But, he is the first to tell you he does not want to be here, likely because of the whispering among the staff and inmates about some incidents concerning him. Some might even consider him just plain lazy, but he has dealt with his issues and lived to fight another day.

Officer McHaney often works my housing unit, so I get to witness firsthand how he handles himself and the inmates for whom he bears responsibility. McHaney is an example of all that is right and good within the BOP, handling his responsibilities professionally and maturely, showing the right mix of compassion and humanity combined with authority and oversight.

Another very smooth, quiet, black officer is McMillan. He does not mess with anyone and he pretty much leaves inmates to take care of themselves. If you are not watching though, he will come at you out of nowhere like a little linebacker.

Christopher Mohammad, Charles Roberts – these two guys are related to my pops and me. They work in Corrections; one is a Black Muslim, the other is a retired white guy. A brother and stepfather who have hearts, who did and still do their jobs well, do not judge people, and help whomever they can.

Officer Murillo – Mexican. Another would-have-been street dude, tough-guy, troublemaker, or a hell of a businessperson. Every time I see him, he is always taking care of some business – more stuff than just regular officer work. Short, suave, husband and father, who's choices to be a father and husband kept him from, being in here with us. He is always asking me, "Brown, what is up with your case?" Good-spirited dude, he is always telling me he is glad he made the choices he did. Some of us have made the choices we did and hope we have learned and changed. "Especially you, Brown. You are too smart and too good of a dude to be stuck up in here, and you are family needs you." And I say, "I know."

Officer O'Broctor – she looks and acts like Jenna on "Sons of Anarchy." But, she is taller, bigger, not fat, meaner, with longer hair and a worse attitude, most times, and a walk that says, "I'm not to be *ucked with." She is petty, at times. She has more tattoos than most men and more testosterone. With those shades, she could also be Terminator's wife. There are many of these women on TV, kicking men's butts. She needs her own show –

"Terminator Biker Chick." She has a job to do and she does it, sometimes over aggressively – I respect that.

Officer Olivarez – 5'9" 235 lbs, short hair, all-black Blues Brothers shades (AKA Locs) on all the time. Good dude, Rough and Ready Mexican – at least, that is how he comes off most of the time. I found out later that this is the second prison we were at together. One of our first encounters was during the time of the Mexican riots in Tucson, when we were coming off lockdown and into phase in programs, (where we only are out of our cells at limited supervised times after a major lockdown). I was rushing to the Laundry room to get my clothes .As soon as I arrived at the door; he slammed it in my face, hollering, "Too late, the move is over." I said, "No, it's not." And, as I was talking to him, they announced it over the intercom system – it must have just ended on the radio. I walked away angry, and he could tell. I believe he liked it.

The next time we encountered each other, he was an acting Lt. When I was his orderly, we got to know each other a little. I never made mention of the previous incident we had and I made it a point of going out of my way to do my job. Ever since then, we usually greet and speak to each other about manly-man stuff like girls, cars, sports, gangs, streets, hood, and South Central L.A., where he's from.

Officer Pasillas – Real good dude and a real good CO. he lets nothing and no one bother him. He will try to help everyone he can while still staying professional. But, when it comes to a good practical joke, I have never seen him pass up on one while still keeping everything by the book, or sometimes a little off the book. His new nickname from me is Munedo or Mededa, depending on which angle he comes from with me. Nothing seems to ever bother him. I have seen him check some dudes real good, but seconds later, he is smiling and laughing like it was nothing. He's about 6'3" with short-cut hair slicked back, very debonair, classy, kind of a 40-something Ricky Martin – a straight one, of course – cool and smooth for a crazy Mexican. This dude can be talked to about anything relevant and he can have some unbelievable insight that can make you ask, "Where the hell did that came from?" If you have real issues, he will go to bat for and with you, but when it comes time to lay down the law, watch out or get ready for him to give you some. I mess with him all the time and he messes with me. And, if you walk past him without speaking, he will call you on it and ask what is your problem.

Officer Pantoja (from New Mexico) – Good tough lady officer, which she showed in the summer of 2010. She came back after being physically attacked by an inmate who jumped over her desk and started choking her before other inmates stopped the attacker. After being out for a few days, staff and inmates alike were glad to see her return.

Officer Parker comes off like an army general one minute, but the next minute he is an intellectual with a PhD. When he speaks, it is almost as if he was saying, "Listen to me because I know what I'm talking about."

Officer Polk is very much laid-back and it seems his only concern is getting his job done. He does his eight hours and lets me do mine.

Officer Pool – always happy, always smiling, always speaking to everyone. I do not think there is one time in over a year that I have seen him when he did not seem to be in a good mood, even when he was sick, and when dudes were lying and telling on him, too. He is always telling me, "Brown, you are always gone, quiet or you are never in the unit." I told him as I have told many others: "If it's not about me proving my innocence, getting out of prison, or if it's not going to get me a date with Janet Jackson or a million dollars, legally, then I'm not doing it." The thing that I remember most about Pool, and tells me a lot about him, was the story he told me about being a bone-marrow donor a short while after returning from a tour in the military and how much he really likes knowing he helped someone and how painful it was then. And how they came out with a newer, much less painful method, soon afterwards.

SOS Reno's normal greeting is "Search that inmate!" He is a genuinely funny guy and I find myself either laughing at him, or with him. I've noticed that one-day he'll be listening to hip-hop, and the next he's wearing cowboy boots. I guess you could say he is well rounded and strong-minded.

Officer Reyes – "Cheech and Chong's little brother," is the first thing that comes to mind when describing Reyes. I can see him singing that song, "Born in East L.A." I am not sure where he is from, but that is what he acts like, just a little stranger than normal. He is not built like them though – he is shorter, thinner, and bald with glasses. But he eats, farts, and drinks soda like he is dying of thirst. I can only imagine how he drinks in the bar. One thing I can say, he doesn't bother anyone unless you bother him – then he can act like a young, wild, crazy, cussing gang-banger until he cools off. Some officers swear to his face that he's black, but he insists he's Mexican.

Officer Rios always has a smile on his face, always has jokes and a funny word of wisdom to impart to others. In my opinion, he is always pushing hope, and I do not think he has a bad word to say about anyone. I'm pretty sure he has a reverse Napoleon complex and when he gets mad, he cusses like a drunken sailor with one heck of a mean streak.

Officer Rivera – Cuban, Dominican. Not that dark, and certainly not that handsome. A modern-day Ricky Ricardo, he is about six feet tall, two hundred pounds, not fat, but not built, and has nerve. He loves to talk and make fun of people – particularly me. He is a funny dude who thinks he is a straight-up ladies man. He had one of those crazy big Spanish boy laughs. You can tell he has been around, but not too much; he is culturally diverse in dealing with people; direct and funny and good to laugh with.

When I first encountered Officer Robles, he reminded me of an old Clint Eastwood cowboy movie because he is as cool as a cactus and crazier than a road lizard. Robles is a true Mexican and a true soldier. I question if the reason he never removes his dark sunglasses is that he has bloodshot eyes from drinking too much tequila the night before and maybe even ate the worm. Or perhaps he is hiding something? Makes me wonder.

Officer Rodriguez – Confident, thorough, solid, Hispanic, from the Chicago-Humboldt Park area. Smart, can be loud and aggressive. Really intelligent, especially for his age; strong Chicago style; political; hates no one, but loves his culture, era, city, neighborhood, and race.

Officer Rosalos thinks he is a player, but is always saying something meaningful and really means well.

Officer Russina – "White Russian," hard-ass, short, stocky, with some East Coast influences. At one time, he seemed hotheaded; now, he is more collected.

Officer Salazar – I am going to pray for him. I know he is smart enough to handle his own. I have seen him deal with a few tough situations when the yard was open – from serious threats to fights to stabbings to dude throwing rocks and dirt, and he kept going. The reason he needs praying for if the same reason the two Captains do – they are die-hard Raiders fans. The trouble with the Raiders is that they have been nowhere for years. They are so bad that the Christians are always praying for them. These people actually pay for tickets to go see the games.

Officer Sanchez – nice, quiet lady, very professional, tough, does her job well, but has a big heart – the way she deals with people, you can just tell.

One of the officers who tends to stay off the radar at Tucson is the other Officer Sanchez. He is a decent, polite, respectful person and all-around good guy. I am sure that is it were left up to him, no one would ever get hurt on his watch. He is easy to talk with and for some reason always seems to be grinning.

Ms. Shelby is a compound officer who reminds me of one of the MVP WNBA girls from the hood, because she is not scared of anything and knows what to do to take control. She speaks positively to me not only from an office's perspective, but almost like a sister, seeing things as they are and also how they should be.

One of the coolest young white officers is Stangl, AKA "Kid Rock" or "M&M". True to these monikers, he can at times just talk plain crazy, causing him trouble when it is though he talks too much or is too friendly with some inmates. Once he even took off his uniform shirt to play ball with inmates and actually slammed on the guy, but there were no injuries, either physical or otherwise. He readily admits that the only reason he did not end up on my side of the wire was two tours in the military, serving in both Iraq and Afghanistan.

I always hear Officer Stewart rapping some up-to-date hip-hop, and he does not hide the fact that he is young and hip. His only concern is that he performs his duties diligently.

Officer Taylor lets inmates do their time if they let him do his.

One officer who always greets me and speaks with me if Officer Tamajio. He is not afraid to speak him mind or to get you to speak yours.I once was asked, "What's the difference between a hillbilly and a redneck?" when I replied that I did not know, I was told, "The Mason-Dixon Line!" Officer Uring is a hillbilly, while his best friend, Officer Reed, is a redneck. Aside from originating on different sides of the Mason-Dixon Line, they are very similar: both love partying, gambling, golfing, running, softball, and working out. I think they take care of themselves so they can drink more. They are true examples of a modern-day hillbilly and a redneck, and their actions and conversations are sufficient cause to believe "what happens in the sticks stays in the sticks." They each are one heck of an officer, at that.

Then there is Officer Weatherwax: a well-trained and highly seasoned tower guard who is also a training officer with many years of experience. Weatherwax talks to inmates man-to-man, and has said, "You guys are not scumbag. To me, you are men."

Officer Gamboza – he is short and his personality is short and straight to the point.

Officer Bountski – John Belushi jailhouse mentality; funny, good; "I do not mess with you; you do not mess with me."

Officer Rodriguez – he is an all right CO, but wants to be a Lt., Capt., or AW, badly.

Unnamed Officer in A Unit who is always talking about, "You did not write a book? I better not be in it!" in front of people. When people aren't around, he says, "You got me in your book, do not you?" Guess what… you now have your fifteen seconds of fame.

Officer Nink – this good officer sometimes seems lost. Every time I see him he is always walking around and around or back and forth. He does not give anyone a hard time, except me, with his bad jokes. Attempting to get a conversation out of him would be like trying to talk to someone who is a cross between a hippie stoner and a preacher. "Well, you know…" he starts all his sentences, but when he finally comes out with it, he is usually pretty funny. Boncore's miniature brother, the evil one. He has body slammed a couple of guys, mostly drunk troublemakers who deserved it. Like many inmates, he has been in the "hole" (SHU) ever since he started working here two years ago. The difference is that he gets to leave after his shift.

Officer Klutter – by-the-book attitude, appearance and look, a good CO.

Officer Koontz – cool as can be; usually thinks he's cooler than ice. Levelheaded CO who does not mess with…

Officer Blood, an Officer and a Gentleman.

Officer Parks – hard-core appearance; bigger; smarter; better-than-all-other-brothers attitude; straight up CO.

Officer Hernandez, Mohawk Biker Boy, by the book.

Officer Benitez – milk-mannered, good CO. some people call him "Sun Glasses."

Officer Soto – cool, calm and collected most of the time; will get nasty if she needs to, but never with me.

Officer Schwartzer – cool CO; does not bother anyone but he watches, listens and wants to know everything.

Officer Ryan – he is a modern-day Benny Hill, old, white, loud, crazy, and always good for a laugh. He is not a dummy, though – he is smart and sarcastic and he does not mind cussing an inmate out if he cusses at him or if he deserves it. Some people around here call him Pea's twin white brother, although Ryan is louder and crazier. Ryan and Pea, those two love each other; they act like brothers. They both can go into the CO's museum – they are dinosaurs. When it is time to get down to business, Ryan does not have a problem of "going hard," as they say around here.

Officer Morales – "The Hound Dog," SIS used to call him. When he was SIS, they used to say he could find anything anywhere. He is built and acts more like a Mexican pit bull – short, stocky, powerful, with an amazing bite. He once was on the trail of an associate of mine who was hiding and using a cell phone. He chased the inmate Stacks and attempted to snag the cell out of his hand. Punches were thrown, which gave Stacks, the opportunity to break away and flush the phone down the toilet. But, Pit Bull got it out, somehow, and took Stacks down. Pit Bull came to work a day or so later with a black eye, but a smile on his face that said, "mission accomplished". Stacks later sent word out to watch out for this guy and apologized to Pit Bill. Pit Bull later retired from SIS and went to Recreation.

Officer Ramirez (from Rec.) – pretty mean-looking black lady that kind of reminds me of the actress/comedian Tosha Smith from "How Did I Get Married?" She is always loud, aggressive, and cusses out people quickly. One might say she's hood, ghetto-born, and raised in one of those areas. She is referred to as Tosha Smith's Big Sister. If you stand around long enough and let her cool off, she will do her job and help you out, but do not say anything to set her off, because she will never stop until she gets her point across.

Officer Nava – He is one of the guys who wants to be a very hard-a** all the time. I've never done anything to him and he's never done anything to me, but he is one of those who's talked about all the time – for taking any and everything from an inmate, contraband or not, searching inmates all the time, sticking his chest out, and giving smart-a** answers to questions. He is the kind of guy you have to learn to ignore and pay him no mind. He has not been around the BOP that long. He sure doesn't act like it – he's one of those officers who does things here he would not do anywhere else and says he wants to be captain, then warden, but has no idea of how things really go, it now seems as though he's trying and slacking off a little on the things that do not really matter or make a difference. He reminds me of that cartoon character "Stumpy." Generally, though, he is about his job and, I hate to say it, but like anything else, there is a need for him, somewhere.

Officer John, quiet, pleasant mannered, likeable.

Officer Williams – a Razorback with a Razorback mentality; a good CO; straight-up until you piss him off. Then he wants to search you, shake down your cell, he will clean you out & will call you out. While laughing aloud.

Officer Jerazano is a younger cool Mexican dude who is quiet and smart. He can generally be found working compound. I have known Jerazano for the entire four plus years I have been at U.S.P. Tucson and he is always asking questions and talking about the law, sports, cars, girls, and especially this book I am writing (perhaps he wants to know what I said about him?)

Bran is a real quiet officer. He is short and shy. In fact, his looks match his personality, in that he is unobtrusive and seems to want to be that way.

Officer Alvarez is one hell of a man who never seems to let anything get him down. He is a good person and funny too, and actually reminds me of one of the Three Stooges – the fat one. The truth is that Alvarez used to be fat but he has lost a lot of that excess weight. Now he reminds me of the entertainer Cedric (the only difference being that Alvarez is not black) but he thinks he is Wilt Chamberlain, the player of the decade who claimed to have slept with ten-thousand women.

At Tucson there is a big polar bear named Bryant. Officer Bryant is a former lieutenant, now counselor, and has one of the most positive attitudes I have seen in anyone who works in prison. This dude is a great guy who honestly admits that if it were not for his wife and family he would be on my side of the razor wire. In fact, he used to spend his time sitting in a bar drinking his life away, fighting and sleeping around, but then he grew-up and got a job in corrections.

Jackson AKA Ears hears everything with his big ears, Kool CO.

Ms. Smith, short, smart, strong and fearless. Bothers no one. Does her job well, but takes no BS. Observes everything behind those shades she always wears.

Mr. Kwon is combative, confrontational, Asian man who works in the institution kitchen and gives everyone around him a hard time. They say that about his and it seems that ways at times. He just has his pet peeves like everyone one else. He hates people who lie, steal, and are fakes, and he loves to catch them, when he can. Kwon tries to bring out the best work performances out of everyone who works in the kitchen, if you do that he will give you as extra food as he can. Michael has seen him do this to other inmates and he use to try to do it to Michael. Sometimes Kwon can be a very hard-a**. I have heard of Kwon being a jerk to a handicapped guy in a wheelchair. Kwon threaten to fire the guys for not rolling the napkins around the sporks right because the inmate was not putting forth any effort. Sometimes it seems he does it to get a rise out of some people. The best thing to do is ignore Kwon. Eat and leave is how he should be dealt with. Kwon however can be very creative when it comes to his "culinary experiments". Some people like to joke he cooks with cats and dogs, which is custom where he comes from, most people do not complain about what he cooks because it is usually very good. Kwon and his tactics will only bother you if you let it. Kwon's favorite sayings are "It is what it is" and "that is not a threat it's a promise."

Kwon's co-workers Kolosmo self-described As*****.

Alexander self describes himself as Dedicated Family Man.

Lucinaro described as Real.

Dunkan Edwards-Kool.

EPPO Melcher – Emergency Preparedness Personnel Officer. Quiet, strictly business, if you see or hear of him coming it is all-bad.

Officer Moore – Funny, good spirited, good guy, always with something positive to say.

DIFFICULT OFFICERS

While some officers operate strictly by the book, some take it to an extreme, excusing their thinly disguised power trip attitudes as "only doing their job." All inmates know who these officers are, whether they have had dealings with them directly or not, because they make their presence known; they are more than extroverted – they demand attention.

The first officers in this category who come to mind are Sylvia, Nava and Bowersox. They always seem to be in a confrontation with inmates and are constantly shaking down inmates, searching cells. For their efforts, they uncover contraband, hooch, tobacco and drugs. I guess there is a need for guys like this. I know that if I stay out of their way and do what I am supposed to, I will not have any problems with them.

I stayed away from one officer because he had a flare-up with another inmate that I did not want to boil over onto me. Officer Mariago, who is very arrogant with a cocky attitude, claims to hate everyone equally. He had a run-in with an inmate known as "Catfish", and neither of them would back down/. It was totally a testosterone thing. When I would not speak to him or go near him, he eventually asked what the problem was, so I told him. He acknowledged that it had nothing to do with me and that he was only trying to get "Catfish." He admitted he was wrong and said he wanted me to come back to work.

Officer Carlisle -- white, tall, slim, muscular, military, well groomed. Top cop some of his fellow officers call him. Bi-polar is what some of the inmates call him. Talks to himself, and nobody else, than the next minute talks to everybody. Usually real quiet otherwise. Too thorough with his job some say, looks for and watches everything. Over all he is a good CO who does not mess with nobody.

Officer Yamas – AKA Mini Mouse. Spanish, Indian, Middle-Eastern? About 5' 100 lbs soaking wet. Good personality until you piss her off. Then she is big, bad and starts yelling in many languages. Move out of the way, and do not mess with her. Does not bother or talk to anyone.

Officer Hookland. Hilarious, short, skinny, light skinned black lady officer. Usually quiet & professional, will talk crazy & cuss you out.

Macias family. Talk about keeping it in the family, obviously there is a lot of that around here in the BOP.

The opportunity cannot be passed up, to show appreciation for the Macias family. The two older guys work in CMS, keeping the place maintained & up & running. A wife and kid (s) work all around the Complex. Good and funny people. They are sometimes regular COs or acting administrators. Often they have to do regular CO duties. From serving and protecting, to correcting and rehabilitating. They are one heck of a team. The oldest looking and biggest of them could pass for Pancho Villa's brother, with a huge handlebar mustache, he looks like a guitar playing killer. The other one could pass for an original Mariachi band member. All he needs is the big hat, a rhinestone embroidered suit and an accordion. He would not even have to sing. The two younger ones are modern-day versions of their elders, more of a popular Latino band version. One of them I know is a son of the elder one the other is he is not a son he could pass for one he must be a cousin or something. And the Mrs. could pass for one of them mean blond Mexican women. I am not even sure if she is Mexican. She is usually pretty nice and helpful but she can be REALLY mean when somebody acts stupid with her. Their in-laws Mr. and Mrs. Shannon are quiet, reserved, good helpful, people. People you would not even know they are related if you did not know already.

*Correction! The youngest Macias is the son of the younger Macias's brother. No wonder. Even in his CO's uniform, he looks as as if he wants to break out the Mariachi Accordion & Tequila.

CUSTODIAL MAINTENANCE SERVICES

The daunting task of maintaining the institution depends on the staff and inmates who work in Custodial Maintenance Services, referred to simply as CMS. CMS handles all plumbing, electrical, welding, HVAC, painting and building maintenance needs. Officers Wands, Ferjado, Taramijo, Dittiger, Parker, Bundi, Shannon, Montoya, Kunes and the Macias brothers provide inmates with on-the-job vocational training in their respective positions. This is the only area within the institution where inmates handle as tools, ladders, and heavy pushcarts. It never seems to fail that after I expertly waxed the main corridor floor they lug their heavy equipment through there and mess it up!

Unit Manager Pendleton – Good dude who is previously mentioned in this book. He deserves a promotion, and he probably needs a vacation. He is white, superbly cool and dresses very sharp, but sometimes he can seem stressed out.

Unit Manager Pennington – I do not know a lot about him, even though I used to work for him when he was a Lt.

Unit Manager Miller – Happy Retirement! He was a good dude and always tried to help me, even though it did not work, he tried or maybe he fooled me. He seemed to be a spin artist at times. After spending 20 plus years in government work, you learn how to be a spin master, and he was the greatest I have ever seen. He'd be quick to tell you, "I'll take care of it" or "I'll be right there," and then come up with some sort of emergency he could hide behind, yet he was "still working on the issues,"

AW Lamb when this place first opened, he was a Lt. He seems to have been promoted two levels, very quickly. He came in and took over Medical, he deserves it. Before, there seemed to be more of a backlog and they were riding in slow motion. There were many problems with the place, mainly because of the many people who went to Medical with little to no problems – some just to see the women PA's. Others because they think they are dying of the common cold. However, there are people with legitimate problems that were having difficulty being taken care of – that has seemed to get a lot better with Lamb in charge.

HEALTH SERVICES

Dr. Drennan is the Health Service Administrator (HSA). I know that the Medical Department is often overwhelmed and struggles to keep up, but I believe they all do their best to help the inmates who rely on them.

One recent yet seasoned addition to the Health Services staff is Commander Walker. I was familiar with PA Walker from other institutions, and although he is slightly older, he is very hip. He is also a strong Christian man and a very caring person who really enjoys his job and helping others, and it shows in how he handles both inmates and staff.

PA Dunigan is also in Health Services. He is thorough in his job performance, which shows he really cares.

Ms. England and Ms. Madrid, they are like close partners or sister always together one white and one Spanish one is real nice and quiet and ones real mean and gets loud, but they are real helpful when it comes to medical issues.

PA Meyers Helpful, sometimes mean, & aggressive. Five foot tall and covered with tattoos. She will back down inmates twice her size.

Inmates find Nurse Criswell is very approachable when they have medical concerns. Even though she is limited in what she can do, she tries her best to resolve medical complaints that are brought to her attention. Her passion for practicing medicine is clearly evident and she is a definite asset to Health Services.

Doctor Hagerty, PA Lawrance and Nurse/Pharmacist Calvin. These people do it all. They do not turn down anybody, love their jobs and enjoy helping people who need help. Ms. Calvin is the fastest worker I have ever seen. Ms. Hagerty was allegedly yelled at for paying too much attention to inmates. Ms. Lawrance will give you what you need. They really do their jobs. They all have always helped me. Ms. Englan and Ms. Madrid, they Are like like close partners or sister always together. One white and one Hispanic, one is real nice and quiet and one is real mean. They are both very helpful when it comes to medical issues.

Calvin, Criswell, Drennan, Dunnigan, England, Hagerty, Heard, Lawrence, Meyers, Walker.

PSYCHOLOGY

We all know that society has given up on mental-health treatment, and instead our prisons are filled with inmates who have mental disorders. The focus of the Psychology Department is to treat these inmates so they can function within a prison setting. They also provide counseling programs and classes such as anger management, rational thinking, and treat inmates who do not have extreme psychological problems.

Dr. Hayden: When asked on 10/5/10, Dr. Hayden, the head of Psychology, said he thought the Psychology Department was excellent.
Fiero, Green, Griffin, Israel, Jaquez, Mitstiffer, Ontario, Pujo, Sage, Stein.

EDUCATION DEPARTMENT

The Education Department Staff at the institution provide many essential functions, including (but not limited to) GED instruction & testing, ESC, Adult Continuing Education, Computer 101, typing, College Prep and Parenting. They also operate a regular library, an Electronic Law Library, A CD-ROM Video Library, and provide access to electronic hardware such as mini word processors & printers, photocopier and typewriters. Their function is to assist with educational and rehabilitation programs and needs.

The Staff:

Mr. Amico: Supervisor of Education: Exremly competent.

Mr. Clark: Assistant Supervisor of Education: Well-meaning.

Ms. Corona: Always Happy, very bubbly personality

Mr. Broken shire: Impersonal, chilly, no sense of humor.

Mr. Dugout: Competent and helpful.

Ms. Farjardo: Down-to-earth, goal-oriented leader.

Ms. Garcia: Helpful and Professional.

Ms. Haiger: Warm, easy-going, very personable & friendly.

Mr. McLaughlin: Communicative and informative.

Ms. Rabius: Self-confident, sensible and friendly.

Ms. Smith: Very helpful & friendly.

RELIGIOUS SERVICES

It is a blessing to have Religious Services staff such as Chaplains Barnett, Elliott, and Father Bui. They are shouldered with the difficult task of ensuring each faith group is provided their individual faiths, and they also have the un-envious task or informing inmates when a loved one is ill or passes away. Chaplin Neapu-Pretty good Chaplain older and quiet. Chaplian Assistant- Haror, younger and can get excited, but always helpful and faithful especially with grief issues. Chaplin Neau-Pretty good Chaplin older and quiet. Chaplain Assistant-Haror younger and gets excited but are always helpful and faithful especially with grief issues.

Elliott, Niamtu.

COMMISSARY & LAUNDRY CLOTHING ROOM

Officers Mabry, Kurt, Moreno, Allison, Kurtz, and County rotate between working in the institution laundry, clothing room and commissary, which puts them in control of what inmates wear and purchase. In short, their job is to keep inmates fed and clothed. I have noticed some form of inter-department competition between commissary and laundry: apparently a long-running joke over who can find the funniest looking inmate or staff member. They have even gone so far as wearing fake goofy teeth and costumes.

TRUST FUND GARCIA & LOPEZ

The bean counters of USP Tucson. These are the guys over commissary and laundry among other things. Their dedication & skills are wasted by their working for the Government. They treat every dollar they have to spend as if it was coming out of their paychecks. Garcia has to listen to all the many complaints and suggestions of the 1,600 guest here, about laundry and commissary.

RECREATION

The recreation department at any institution is important for many reasons, perhaps none more important than that it gives inmates something to do to occupy their minds and bodies. Without adequate recreational opportunities, inmates would go crazy. The recreation at Tucson, overseen by Department Head Mr. Anderson and staffed by Tolin, Ramirez, and others, provides work-out equipment, sports TV, ping-pong, cardio-vascular machines, a gym, even a barber shop. They also offer hobby craft, a form of "arts and crafts" in which inmates can learn a creative skill or craft and make items, which can be mailed home to love ones. Recreation also has responsibility for selecting, and showing the institution movies each week.

Anderson, Ferguson, Golloolie, Ramirez, Morales, Frogperson, Tolin.

SAFETY

The mission the Safety Department is to provide a safe, hazard-free environment for inmates and staff to live and work. Mr. Leroy Smith is Safety Manager. Smith is easy to spot, impeccably dressed in suit and tie and sporting a watch as large as Big Ben and looking like it cost a million bucks. Smith is well known within the BOP as one who has stood-up for inmates rights, even blowing the whistle on a UNICOR computer recycling operation, which posed health hazards to inmates. This resulted in him being labeled within the ranks of the BOP as a troublemaker, but set him apart as one who cares about inmates as humans. Smith is ably assisted by Officers Morietti and Andrews, who have the responsibility for checking all safety systems within the institution, including fire alarms and sprinklers, fire extinguishers, PPE (Personal Protection Equipment), and lifesaving equipment, and ensuring that everything that relates to safety is working properly and operating within the prescribed parameters. The catchphrase of the Safety Department is "Safety Is No Accident" and Smith's favorite quote is, "Safety is the bottom line" but anyone who works in Safety will tell you that BOP stands for "Based On Panic" or "Backwards on Purpose".

Andrews, Murrieta, Smith.

UNIT TEAMS

Unit Managers Miller, now Pennington, along with Case Managers County, Shehey, Mixon and Moreno, and Counselors Johannes and Brown, along with their administrative assistants, make up the North side Unit Teams. These are the advocates for the inmate population who handle inmate requests, and concerns dealing with housing, legal needs, discipline, telephone, finance and more. Their jobs require more regular interaction with inmates than other staff. They do a good job and often go beyond what is required.

Johannes, (AKA "Don Rickles") for example, is one of the funniest, craziest, most special guys here. While he may SEEM to have ridden the "Special Bus", he knows what is happening. He stays on top of his job, and is responsive to legitimate needs. He's often heard shouting "Holler!" which is slang for "Hello", "Hi" and even "Yes", "No", "Maybe", "So?", and "I do not know". It is an affirmative defense. Personally, I appreciate having Johannes as my Unit Team Counselor.

Case Manager Mixon, Strong-willed black woman. Quiet, very helpful, always thinking or smiling. Independent thinker. Smart, loves her work, and does not miss a thing.

Counselor Mrs. Brown, strong black woman with attitude. She does her job. She can be mean and rude. She can and will let you have it, only if she has to. With some guys, she has to; with other, she does not, never with me. She will help anybody.

Mr. Brown, Mrs. Brown's husband, they make a good team. He is one cool dude. Athletic, mellow, quiet. Both of them have that East Coast Urban swagger. He is a diehard Die-hard Stealers fans.

My first impression of Unit Manager Pendleton when he was at U.S.P. Victorville was that of a sharp-talking, slick-dressing, cool white guy who really enjoyed his job. I remember one incident at another institution when Pendleton single-handedly prevented an inmate from being killed by an angry mob who had already killed another inmate. That even changed my view of him and now I see him as a man of honor. But I have also seen him lose his cool a couple of times to the point that I did not know what he was going to do. One time after he cooled down after getting very crazy I said to him, "That's a small thing to a giant." Then one time when I had lost my cool he repeated my words back to me." Since his arrival at Tucson, he had been a Case Manager, acting Unit Manager, and now Unit Manager. I appreciate the fact that if I have a problem I can bring it to him and I now that he will help me if he can. It is my belief that he generally 8 cares about everyone. I think more people like him need to be hired to work in the federal prisons – people who derive great personal satisfaction by helping those who deserve to be helped.

From the Warden's office to the housing units, the secretaries and administrative assistants are the glue that holds the institution together. These women handle everything from transfer paperwork and inmate releases to visitation requests, grievances, and more. Although rarely seen by inmates, they keep the institution running smoothly, and they deserve to be treated as the professionals that they are. I personally find that by treating them with respect I get the same in return, and when I speak to them, they listen I know that if I bring an issue to them that is within their realm of control they will help me resolve it.

Baldy, Brown, Bryant, County, Flores, Johannes, Miller, Mixon, Moreno, Olivarez, Pendleton, Pennington, Ruiz, Shehey, Snodyrass.

R&D AND MAIL ROOM

The Receiving and Discharge (R&D) and Mail Room departments are staffed by Officers Rodriguez, Olivarez, McElroy, Flores, Ortega, and Kunez, but the real boss is Ms. Serrato and she bossed all the men around. These departments have come a long ways in resolving the handling of inmate mail, which includes legal mail, and inmate personal property. You see, when an inmate is transferred between institutions, their property will travel with them or it may arrive days, weeks, or even months later, if ever. When property does not arrive with the inmate, it often gets lost or sometimes even destroyed. An inmate does not have anything to really survive on until their property arrives. They depend on fast, efficient handling of their personal belongings. Imagine moving to a new neighborhood, only to find that the moving company has lost all of your possessions! And inmate mail, especially legal mail, is a major sensitive issue with all inmates. Mail is an inmate's primary vehicle for corresponding with family, friends, and loved ones. Legal mail, which is handled differently than regular mail due to it sensitive nature, is an inmate's link to their attorney and the courts concerning their cases and prison sentences. Inmates rely heavily on the efficient handling of their mail in general these officers take their responsibilities seriously and have gotten a handle on resolving situations involving inmate property and mail. Now, if property is lost, a trace is put on it, and most mail is delivered promptly. Overall, the staff in R&D and Mail Room confronts many issues every day, but they are always good for a laugh. Personally, I like to tease them about how they had to come to prison to get a post office job! Blake, Flores, Grisby, McElroy, Miranda, Molinar, Ortega, Olivarez, Rodriguez, Seratto, Southern

Others in Alphabetical

A

Acola- AKA Cola 5'+, 125. Bald headed. Always with a mean, tough guy look on his face. He does not say much and is always searching everything.

Acosta- "Redo Boy", 6', 250 lb Mexican White cowboy. He is the whitest looking and acting Mexican I have ever seen. He can get a little dark at night. He looks like he belongs in a pair of overalls, instead of a prison uniform. He is not afraid to wrestle an inmate down and hog-tie him. Overall, he is a good CO, who will help you if he can.

B

Bias- Hard to describe. I do not know if he is black, white or Hispanic. Maybe all of the above. He is about 6', 240 lbs. very quiet, laid back dude, who loves his motorcycles.

Blake- Good person but a terrible (former) Mailroom Supervisor. Like a pit bull in a skirt.

Captain Barnhart- He is an extremely smart, people person, a politician and security conscious. He has a military background. I have worked for him off and on throughout my entire incarceration. He looks, acts, and dresses super cool and fly. He can be a Hell of a people person, knows all the languages and slang terms. He is probably one of the most diverse people I have met in prison. He is kind of a jack-of-all-trades, but I am not sure if he has mastered any. He is aright for "a white guy who barely has his CEO." (Those are his words.)

Boone- He's alright, Big, Black, Country looking dude 6'S" 300 lbs, with a baseball cap. He does not bother anybody. He will talk trash with the best of them and always seems to be looking for some action.

Bororquez- The biggest dam Spaniard I have ever seen. Youngster. Pretty laid back and cool. Pretty hip too. He knows what is happening and knows what to do.

Boston- AKA "Boston Chicken". Some call him that because he looks like he eats 24/7. He kind of looks and acts like Cederic the Entertainer. He talks, laughs, and smiles a lot and always has something funny to say.

New L.T. Brown- 510" 225. Farmers build. Short hair, wire rim glasses. Rough around the edges but a Good Dude. I have known him since Tucson opened. He first worked Education. He was good at that too. He always says, "I know what you are up to Brown, I'm watching you". Most of the time I ignored him. A couple of times I would say, "I'm not up to nothing you are wasting your time watching." He was one of the best staff in Education. He would do his job and help if you asked.

Bryant- AKA "Granpubba".That is what they called him when he worked in the SHU. Polar Bear is what they call him on the yard, after I called him a Big Teddy Bear in my book. He said, "I can't be a Teddy Bear, they're brown or black. I'm white, so I can only be a Polar Bear". Before he was a counselor, he was a LT. I asked him "why'd you quit being a LT?" He said "I only want to be responsible for my own mess not everyone else's.

Byler- Tall slim white guy, tries to act real mean, but is really fly and cool. Sometimes he looks like he does not know what the hell he is doing. The next time he thinks he knows everything, but is about to stumble over his own feet.

Barnheart (2)-O Captain Capt. & Secretaries (Sec.)
Benitez-O
Blood-O
Bran-O
Brown (3) l-LT, 1-PS, 1-Unit Team (UT),
Bountski-O
Bowersox-O

C

Mrs. C. - SIS. Reluctant, suspicious, with a very serious demeanor. Hates all inmates and is not afraid to say so. Especially hates child molesters, gunners and snitches. Certainly cannot fault her for that.

Cesena- Lil Cock Diesel. He is short, stocky and cocky. He does not sweat the small stuff big stuff he will.

Lt. Chopko- "The youngster" of the other Lt. 's. He looks like he is not even old enough to drink. He has an evil half smirk smile.

Contreras- I have been kind of not wanting to write about SIS. These guys have a lot of power. They are like the FBI of the institution and can be dangerous, right or wrong. But 515 Contreras is one guy who has always treated me, my coworkers, and all other inmates with complete respect.

Cordova- Big dude. At first glance, you would think he is a Samoan. He is about 5'9" 300 lbs. Built like a tank. He is a relaxed guy until you cross him and then he is all over you like a sumo wrestler.

Cota- Good dude, mellow 61311, 170 lbs Mexican American who love his heritage. Cota is deep into American moguls and Mustangs (the car)

Crow- 6151, light skinned, bald headed, well-built black guy. Always smiling, kind of goofy looking! Good man with a big heart.

C.-O-Special Investigative Services (919)
Carlisle-O
Contreras -o
Corona -0
Criswell-Health Services (I-IS)
Crow-0

D

Delgotto- Pretty sure he is of Middle Eastern descent. He has the North Chicago swagger. Amn dedicated to his family, his job and taking advantage of the opportunities in life.

Drennan-HS
Dunigan-HS

E

Edwards S. - Short, Stocky, and Mexican with a white guy name. Really good guy. Efficient and patient. Does his job well.

Ego" is some of s many nick names. He loves to start crap
and play. Games' told all the time it is a dangerous game. Another of •s nicknames is "Mr. Duces" because he loves to hit his body a arm for any little thing. He has other officers coming to s aid every time he starts some crap he
cannot finish. He t inks he knows everything because he worked in the state prison system.

Mrs. England- Very devoted to her job, helpful, and reliable. She is one of the best medical staff.

Escobar- Short, spunky, in-shape lady. Fairly new to the job. Looking to stand the test of time.
Edwards -0
England-HS

F

S. Fierro- Loyal to her desire to help people change. Very funny and good with people.
Flores-O' S
Fitzgerald-C
Franco-O

G

Gergivich- AKA Big G." 6' 300 lbs. Red hair and bearded. Early 30's. A younger, friendlier, happier version of Grizzly Adams. He is not to happy, friendly, or afraid to do his job. He will fight at the drop of a hat if need be, as he loves a good brawl. When I went to the SHU he, Diego, and two other officers made sure all my stuff was sate. "Brown, I did what I could to secure your property especially those books you wrote. They sure make some good and interesting reading."

Gonzales- AKA "Gonzo" 63', 250. Big and well built. Always hacking and coughing or maybe just trying to scare people. He is usually pretty mellow and laid back, but he will go Gonzo on someone in a minute,

Gonzales- Gonzales II. There are about five Gonzaleses that work here. No. II is middle aged, average height and weight. He walks around making the craziest faces.

C. Green - Faithful to the concept of change. Believes that everyone should journalize.

Griffen- Attitude. Outspoken she, will say what is on her mind.

D. Griffin- Wants to help people change. She is good with everybody.

Gulretezze- Quiet laid back, cool dude. Sometimes he look likes a natural born killer, who never smiles, or talks. He always gives me that look to say "What up Brown".
Gamboza-0
Garcia (4)-C
Graham-C
Graves - P
Griffin-PG
Gilke-C
Gonzales-C
Griffin-PG
Grisby- R&D Mail Room (R&D & MR)
Guzman-O

H
Haden- Mr. Man in Charge. Does not talk to many people, or maybe it is just me.

Hammond- Freaking crazy. You never know what he is going to say or do. What he hears often is "Dam, what the hell are you doing?" I would always tell him going to make a good character in my book and the movie.

Heard- Head lady at medical. She patiently listens when people come to her about medical issues. Then she tells everyone to 'Go to Sick call tomorrow.

Henson- Big "H', "The Culligan **man, Big** Cool as a Fan", is just some of his nick names. Really big, dude, 6'9", 350, light-skinned Black guy. Former College football player, who played some pro ball before getting hurt. They call him the Culligan man because he delivers! And, because the only job I ever seen him do was Water Treatment here at the prison. Except for the few times, I saw him take a few guys down to stop a problem; he is too cool to bother anyone. Who is not a problem.

Hoops- Short white guy with Terminator glasses. He searches everything and everybody. He is always looking for something. He will take you through some hoops.
Hagar-Education (EDU)
Hagarty- HS
Hansen-LT
Hayden- PSY
Hellman-O
Henson-O-Custodial Maintenance Service (CMS)
Hernandez-O
Herrera-O
Haliburton-O
Hookland-O

Houltz-C

I

Ivlorales_ that runs laundry does not rotate with commissary though commissary fills in for him sometimes. He treats laundry like a Mexican Korean dry cleaning service / designer clothing store. He is a decent guys clothing is his work. He tries to save money at every corner.

Israel- She can give you a look that helps. And when she gets to doing her thing, she is pushy, but amazing. She can also give you the Look of Death, if you're not getting it or doing something you're not supposed to.
Jiff-0
IJring-LT

J

Jaquez- 6'2", 250. Fair skinned Mexican with an average build. Funny guy most of the time. Sometimes his jokes are out there and we do not know what he's talking about. Helpful. Serious about his job, and knowledgeable about a little of everything.

CO John- AKA "Lil John". He is just the opposite of Lil John the rapper/actor, who is loud, obnoxious, crazy, and. This Lil John is pretty soft spoken, shy and quiet, but he is a pretty good dude who messes with no one. Johnson- 5'+ muscular white guy. No hair no cap and always with Urff. One day Johnson and Urff came up to me and spoke at the same time. "What do I have to do to get in your book Brown? Give you a hard time and send you to the SHU?" That is exactly what happened. Now you are in the book. Happy?

Jury- She was very gung ho on all inmates when she first started. Extra hard on child molesters, perverts, gunners, stalkers and game players. For those who play hardball, she plays it right back. If you are not one of the above, and you stay out of her way, she will stay out of yours.
Jackson-C
Jaramillo-CMS
Jerazona-O
J. Michaels-O
John (2)-FS, C
Johnson-C

K

Killman- The physical therapist. A buf fed short lady. She has a good personality and is about as nice and helpful as they get around here, especially if you are on her patient list.

Kunez- A pretty good R&D & Mail room officer. Helpful. She hardly talks to inmates, except to me. She would say strongly, "What do you want Brown?" I am not sure how she is as a Case Manager yet. I will find out soon. I will be requesting to be transferred to FCI Oxford soon. I have not heard anyone say anything bad about her. She is serious about her business. Her husband, CMS Kunez, is a good guy who is serious about his business also.
Katcher-C
Kelly-C
Klutter—C

Koontz-Q
Kwon- F'S

L

Lambart- Smallest lady on the yard, with the biggest heart. You couldn't tell it by her mean looks but her Case Manager work speaks for itself. If you have something coming she'll get it for you.
Mr. Lewis- AKA "Papa Smurf". He is about 5'+, 155, Baldhead full grey/white beard and real dark. He can be a real hard *ass* but most of the time he is a 'gentleman and a scholar'. He always has a story to tell about how rough it was back in the day, chopping cotton, walking 40 miles to school and the good parties. He supplies lots of words of wisdom to the guys but he can also tell some wild ones. He has a son that works here; we call him "Lil **Lewis".**
Lewis Jr. - AKA "Lil Lewis" 30's **5'+,** 135 Lil Lewis is almost the polar opposite of his dad. He looks like he could be one of those well groomed, slim, toned, dark models, but shorter. Lil Lewis is very quiet. He is a good CO who does not bother anyone, unless you bother him, then watch out.
Last name unknown- Short, average build, with short hair Mexican originally from East L.A, who worked as a tech in the Administrative Of f ice. We used to always talk and he'd always ask "When are you going to finish that book and go home Brown"
Last name unknown- Short, average build, going gray, Mexican C.O. who's now part of 515. To always spoke to me with respect and treated me like a human being.

Ludwich- AKA "The Big Lug" because that is what he is. He is a cross between Frankenstein's Monster and Randy Savage. He is a straight up muscle head. He is about 69" 350. Tatted up from neck to toe. He's fun to watch and talk about.

Lujan- 59", 300 pound. Chubby Mexican guy. Looks like the guy who hosts the Mexican talk show with the pretty lady and is always dancing and cooking. He is funny and real cool sometimes. Other times, he's extremely by the book.
Lamb-Associate Warden (AW)
Lewis Sr.-C
Lollies-C
Lopez (4)-C
LNU (2)-C

M

Madalozzo- "Mad Dog" is what he asks to be called by staff and inmates. Some call him Puppy Dog. You cannot say that based on his looks. He is 6'+, 280 lbs. Big, ugly looking, mean and bald, but he is really a good dude overall.
Mrs. Madrids- 518. Mean, Candid and non-tolerant, with the faces she makes. Her AKA is "Pocahontas". Her attitude is just the opposite. She hates child molesters, gunners and the many snitches 815 use for information. (So do I)
Martinez- 815. One of the tallest mexican guys I ever met. Hard core. We've had two run-ins in the past. Now he calls me "Going down Brown," due to writing about staff in this book.
Marriata- mature, experienced, sassy Hispanic woman. Quiet till you get on. her nerves and then watch out. A pleasant person.

Mayarga- Usually works Main Corridor and SHU. When he does, he can be a real hard ass. He's 510" with an "5" on his chest. He's a former marine and lets you know it. He can have a serious attitude. He's like Halliburton. Believes inmates don't deserve anything despite, the Constitution.
McElroy- R&D AKA Dr. Spock. That's exactly who he looks like even though he's Mexican. Always tells me "Brown I'll give you your Janet Jackson poster back when you get out. Until then, it's in my office."
Magee- AKA Cheese Burgler, and/or Ronald McDonald. That's who he looks like. He's alright, not a stickler for the little rules, even though he took my Cheese Burgers one day.
Metcalf- Die hard Arizona Republican. Well educated. Big Governor Jan Brewer fan and a really big dude. About 56", 300 lbs without much fat.
Michael's- Real down to earth modern day Arizona white guy, who speaks Spanish better than most Hispanics. Reminds me of some brothers I know, mixed with some crazy Mexican blood.
Mitstiffer- Fair, equal opportunity psych lady. *She's* conservative but willing to help anyone who's serious about helping themselves.
Miranda- (R&D) He's real smart, helpful and respectful unless you piss him off. But over all, he's a good dude and he'll keep you on your toes.
Molinar (R&D) where do I start? She can be the best of both worlds when it comes to her job and personality. She's this little beautiful spanish lady who doesn't mess with anyone. She's barely five feet tall and maybe 100 pounds. I've seen her get in the face of guys three times her size, with no fear. I've also seen her be helpful to inmates, by getting them good time credits, old warrants squashed, etc. I've seen her have talks with other inmates and me about changing our lives, staying out of prison and doing something different for ourselves our families. She's another one that could be a Mexican comedian, lawyer, or gangster. The world is probably safer with her working here.
Moore- 6'2" skinny, care free helpful. A guy who loves his piercings. At a party, he'd can be one wild and crazy guy.
Moraga- Short chunky Mexican. Cool with most people, especially his people. He can be an a**hole if you make him be. Mr. Pringles some call him as he looks like the man on the Pringles can.
Morales- Always cool. Walks and talks real slow. When he talks, he always has something positive and constructive to say.
Morales- No.11, from Commissary. He looks like a 35-year-old G. Gordon Liddy.
Morales- That runs laundry does not rotate with commissary though commissary fills in for him sometimes. He treats laundry like a Mexican Korean dry cleaning service / designer clothing store. He's a decent guys clothing is his work. He tries to save money at every corner.
Morales- No.11 from Commissary. He looks like a 35 year old. G. Gordon Litty.
Morales- Laundry/Clothing Room. He runs the laundry like a Mexican Korean dry cleaning service. He's a decent guy, dedicated to his work. He tries to save the BOP money.
Marcia's (4)- 2-CMS, 1-C,1-UT
Mariago-C
Mario- C,LT
Maybry- C
Mayora-C

McElroy (2) LT.,RD
McHanney-C
McMillan-O
Melcher- Emergence Officer (EPPO)
Mendez- Special Investigative Agent (SIA)
Meyers -HS
Miller-UT
Mixon-UT
Mohammed-C
MayargaO
Morales (3) 2-0, 1- Recreation (Rec.)
Murillo-O

N
Nemsick- I thought he and Elliot were brothers and even got them confused before. He still thinks he's back in Iraq or Afghanistan. I've never seen him physically abuse anyone but he screams and yells at people like he's a Boot Camp Drill Instructor. He has the biggest feet I've ever seen. He's not really big just about 64" 250. Slim balding white guy who always wearing his Oakleys. He treats me alright though.
Nava-0
Nielsen-Sec
Nink-O

O
Ochoa- Short, skinny Mexican. Always smiling. Sometimes he has the look of a confused rookie.
Q'Donnel- Good white dude about 6', 230 balding. Not very excitable, quiet.
Olivas- Acting LT. I've known him for a while. He's been at Tucson since it opened. We had words one time, the first year. This was the time of Sereno's and Paisa's war. We were on and off of lock down and there was a lot of tension. He was working the Work Corridor and I was a few seconds late coming
in. He slammed the door in my face and locked it. He looks like a cross between a Sereno's and Erik Estrada, except he's always looking hard.
Ontario- Down to earth. She will talk to you and listen as well. She will help you if need be.
Ortiz- Tall skinny Mexican, always wearing a baseball cap and shades. His sun is always shinning.
Owens- He's the tallest, blackest, guy I ever seen working at a prison, with long dreads. He came to Tucson from USP Beaumont. Nobody knows what to expect out of him yet. He seems cool and tells us he's not sweating the small stuff. He thinks he's Wilt CharTherlin with the same mission most of the time (lO, 000 women).
C' Broctor-O
Olivarez-UT

P
Phillips- 6', 250. Funny looking white guy who always wears a baseball cap. His always a straight up dude, his yeses are yes and his no's are no.

Pujo- ATCA "Smily Face," because she's always smiling. Even if you catch her when she's doing something or deep in thought as soon as she notices you, she smiles as wide as the sea. She's a good Psychologist aide good teacher. I've learned a lot in her classes.

Pullen-(CMC) Case Manager Coordinator, Good dude I've known him since the early 2000's when I first came into the system, back in U.S.P. Florence. I watched this guy talk, walk crawl, run, and work his way up the ladder, with more to come. Not bad for an average looking white guy. Mrs. Pullen works here too and is a good person, but she likes to wear the pants, that she picked out for him and her.
Padilla-0 515
Pantoj a-0
Parks-C
Parkers-CMS
Pendleton-UT
Pennington-UT
PC 1k-C
Pool -0

R
Reed-SHU's number one officer, Mr. White Shirt. Some people say he will be the next LT. And then the next warden. He's about 5'9" 125 lbs. Reminds you of a grasshopper. He tries to act real serious but when he smiles, he looks like the Joker, from the Batman Movie.

Renteria- Smooth, Cool, Crazy Mexican with a soul!. Runs the kitchen like a Mexican soul food joint. He's got Salsa and Soul in his blood.
J. Rodriguez- Tall, slim, young, athletic, piercings, ball cap. Quiet, he knows what's up.

A. Rodriguez- I've known him since early 2000, from U.S.P. Florence, before the mustache and beard, which is bigger than he is. He can be a stickler for some rules. He wants to be a Captain.

Ross- Cool, white dude in a cool white dude way. About 6' 230, stocky, early 40's with a Marine flat top and a bulldog look. Rarely smiles and doesn't like many people. He is pretty hip to the ways of the world and prison. He has been around the world in the military and around a few prisons.
Ruiz- about 5'9", 175 lbs, Rico Swave mentality. He has other staff refer to him as Daddy Reese. I once heard a 515 lady say, "with those glasses on he looks like a Mexican porn star". I don't think she meant it in a good way.
Ramirez (2)-Rec, FS
Reno AKA Peno-C
Reyes-0
Rios-0
Rivera- (2) 0, LT
Robles -0
Rodriguez (4)-C
Rosalos-0
Russian -0

Ryan-C

S

Sage- Very sociable maybe she has to be or it is just in her to talk to and help people. She's always trying to read someone's mind.

Salazar- All around average Mexican guy. Always by the book and can be a real hard ass. He's always been fair with me although I do my best to stay out of his hair.

Sanchez- Down to earth, elegant, intriguing. Speaks her mind. One minute she's quiet the next minute she looks like a lady Gansta chick.

Sanchez- There is about three or four Sanchez's who work around here. Sanchez No. I looks and acts like the boxer Roberto Duran.

R. Sanchez- Committed to helping people change, down to earth.
Santa Cruz- Good little dude, about 56", 150. Light skinned Mexican. Funny dude. Part time comedian, part time singer, dancer and bullfighter who is always talking trash.

Secretaries- They are the people who keep the prison running. If they do something wrong you are done, if they do it right you will probably get the blessings you've been looking for. The ones here I know are all really good people and seem to care: Mrs. Andrews, Mrs. Barnhart, Mrs. Bassette, Mrs. Diaz, Mrs. Dumass, Mr.Harbor, Mrs. Lara, Mrs. Louis, Mrs. Nielsen, Mrs. Shannon, Mrs. Smith, Mrs. Stangl.

Serray- Cool white dude about 59", 165 lbs. Not very athletic looking. Always with his shades on. He thinks he's cooler, bigger and badder than what he is and says he ain't afraid of nothing.

Ms. Seymore-Kitchen staff, She's about 5'+, 100 lbs with long red hair. Always sunburned. Urban, crazy, sexy and cool but will go ghetto on you and act a damm fool in a minute. She can be talkative, fast paced, energetic, hip, relaxed and down to earth. She's very soulful with a lot of pep.

Southers- 57" 165, medium build short hair. Has a squeaky, funny voice, he looks and acts pretty normal. He always reminds me that he is not the Southern who runs the nail room, so that I don't go postal on him. He goes back and forth from the U.S.P. to the FCI mailrooms.

Stein- Really nice, really helpful, with a strong look and personality.

Swansinger- Tall for a lady. Brunet, slim, walks real fast, talks real fast, and a mild mannered person. Usually real quiet, cool and collected. She reminds me of a swan.
Santiago-LT
Schead-AKA 011-C
Schwartzer-O
Shannon's (3)- 2-045, 1-SEC
Shelby -0

Smith- (3) Safety (SFT) , Sec, 0
Soto-0
Stangi -o
Stewart -o
Swepson-Gufstaff son- Deputy (Dep.) Capt.
Silvia-LT
Sylvia-LT

T

LT. Turner- Real big, but not real tall, maybe 5'+ real black, bald headed dude. "Mister by the Book". You will hardly ever see him laugh; he wears the super serious suit. Muscular, with a tough guy, I know everything, Chicago Swagger.
) Tamaj io-O
Taylor- (2) 0
Tinkler-Sec.

U

Urff- 6'9", Goofy looking, slim but buf fed. White guy. Always wearing a baseball cap and always with his partner Johnson. They do everything together.

V

Vandervan- Tall skinny red haired guy, Irish or Scottish descent. Mr. Perfectionist, who can't stand to see someone doing their job without putting in his two cents worth, He's an OK dude.

W

Watkins- Big young, cool, white guy 6'S" 250. Walks around mumbling to himself, looking tired. He's always looking for something. Not dumb at all and never misses a day at the gym.
Yorty- He's about 6', 200. Going bald. Always looking like he's got some dip in his mouth. A CO who loves his job and love his country. I don't have any issues with him. Almost every time I see him, I can imagine him singing or whistling the National Anthem.
Walker- IIS
Weatherwax—0
Williams-0 Watkins- Big, young, cool, White guy. 65" 250. Walks around mumbling to himself, looking tired. He's always looking for something. Not dumb at all and never misses a day at the gym.

Y

Yamas -0
Yorty-0

Others

The Five openly Gay Officers. Y'all know who you are. Congratulations on the New York marriages & ending Don't Ask, Don't Tell things. Keep up the battle.

Captain. Dep. Capt- Swepson-Cufstaffson. Very smart and very strong willed, Strong Minded, Mentally, Physically and emotionally strong African American woman, who isn't afraid of anything, especially of speaking her mind.

Epilogue 1

Sometimes, people look at those who work in a prison setting as if they look at the prisoners themselves. Realistically, who grows up thinking they want to work in a prison? The prison population at large needs to be kept safe from violent inmates who would cause trouble without regard for the safety of others. I have met dudes in prison who I would not want as my neighbor in the free community. In addition, prison needs to offer inmates opportunities to learn skills and trades to occupy themselves during their term of incarceration, and to support themselves if and when they are released. Prisoners need opportunities for rehabilitation, and they cannot do it all by themselves. They need to learn how to get out and stay out of prison, and that ominous task ultimately falls on prison staff. Joe Public must remember that the vast majority of prisoner will one day be set loose. Avenues need to be explored by which fewer inmates return to prison. Technically, everyone who works in a prison is a Corrections Officer. Most inmates have been taught to hate and rebel against authority, so prison employees must work all the harder to establish respect for themselves and a rapport with the inmate population, whereby they live and work together in harmony instead of fear and violence.

In most prisons, if a prisoner is seen talking to staff member – especially upper staff – the inmates would think they are snitching. People have been stabbed and killed for that. If they see me or a couple of my friends, like Danny, talking to staff, they know we are letting them have it, or we are trying to learn or fix something.

You cannot blame prison staff for you being in prison. We must look at ourselves and realize these prison staff members did not put us here. It's not one man's fault, it is not the white man, the government, the judge, jury, prosecutor, the warden, the prison administration, or the correctional officers' fault that we are here. *It is* usually the cops and people on the streets caused the problem. Guilty or innocent, we should learn from this .We can only read so many books before we have to have some first-hand knowledge, and sometimes the best sort of information and knowledge is word of mouth. Man is a creature that was not built to be alone, talk to himself, nor talk about the same old things all the time and expect a different result (that is called insanity) and for not reading, writing, and communicating.

There is good reason to talk to and get along with staff members in prison – they can make your time easier or worse. For this same reason, if you truly want to learn, you need to read all the newspapers, magazines and books you can get your hands on. To learn and enhance your thinking and not have a one-track mind. How many times can one talk about what goes on inside of prison? Nothing really changes – it's the same old things: rumors, gossip, back-biting, drugs, sex, crime, lies, who's gay, who is straight, who is having sex with whom, what this certain female staff member's body looks like, what staff member is sleeping with whom, what inmate's girlfriend or wife left them, who's got the hooch (wine), who's got the dope (who's hot (hot=snitch), who's not, who's got money, who's broke, who's a piece of crap, who was doing what. More than half of that gossip is a lie.

We must read, write, learn, and eventually talk about what bothers and interests us with people who or want to know as much as you.

I am not sure how it started, or why, but I have able to obtain information from people by just asking. Of course, he knows which lines not to cross. Normally, I ask questions to get answers. What I could not get out of a book or those that just were not clear enough.

"Why do these people talk to me?" Maybe because I asked legitimate straightforward non-crossing-the-line questions. Some officers try too hard to fit in with a few guys they think are intelligent, hard, or cool. Certain inmates try too hard to fit in with staff.

There are a lot more negative inmates than there are positive inmates. I would say the ratio is about 80% bad acting and negative thinking to about 20% positive acting and thinking. Some people try too hard to impress other people by being hard, mean, aggressive, and negative. Just be yourself. It is not just inmates who have skeletons in their closets – so do the prison staff. Some officers and some inmates are alike. We have more in common then we have differences. Most of us have the same needs: food, clothes, shelter, life liberty, and the pursuit of happiness. Most of the prisoners have just made some bad decisions and some mistakes. As several officers have told me in different ways, "We've all thought about it, most of us have done it. You guys got caught, we did not, and none of us should forget that."

U.S.P. Tucson is the safest maximum-security prison in America, but this could change at any time. It is still a maximum-security prison filled with guys who have committed some of the most heinous, and sickest, crimes you do not want to know the details of.

If we want the prison staff and the world to change their minds about us, we have to change first. Then we have to walk the walk, talk the talk, and be productive and positive. We are part of the problem or part of the solution.

I start to remember some of the profound things people have said. Family, friends and most recently staff members I see every day

Capt. Barnheart: "Apply your smarts. Look at me, I barely have a GED."

Lt, Uring: "Train yourself; you have to work hard every day,"

Lt. Coran: "You have to work smart; you are smarter than the average inmate."

Lt. Reed: "You have to keep fighting until you think you can't, and fight more."

Officer Boncore: "Keep the faith; if God brought you to it, God will bring you through it." (It is tattooed on his forearm)

Lt. Pea: "You already know what to do, just do it!"

EPILOGUE 2

Prison, especially ones like the United States Penitentiary at Victorville, California, the United States Penitentiary at Florence, Colorado, and the United States Penitentiary in Tucson. They're vipers' nests for gangs and retaliation. These places are filled with anger, hate, animosity and spite. The Blacks have the Crips and Bloods as well as the Muslims. The Latinos have the Pisa's, the Surenou and the Mexican Mafia, Los Emmis.

The Whites have the Skin Heads, The Dirty White Boys, The Nazi Low Riders and the Arian Brotherhood. Many of whom would just as soon cut a brother open just to see what he ate for dinner.

These places have reputations for beatings, rapes, murder and the motto "Snitch, Parole or Die." Since there isn't Parole any longer, it's now all about dying slow or dying fast.

INJUSTICE

(A POEM BY MICHAEL L. BROWN)

It is a cold, cold world outside,
Just look at the deception and genocide.
Lost souls searching for a way out.
Hurt, unfocused, uninformed of what it's all about.
Sell out lawyers, racist prosecutors and a devil for a judge
Now tell me how can we win?
For all of them about cry a grudge.
Once we lose the case, it gets worse.
Our only hope is to continue to fight and pray,
Then we can get the case reversed.
Supreme Court, what a beautiful hideout for the real gangsters.
Every time we try to get our case heard,
We're laughed at and called wanksters
Federal Penitentiary, what a joke.
After they sentence us, we are sent here to be smoked.
Oh, that's neat, they have this maximum spot
Called ADX 23/0ne.
How in the hell can that be fun?
Michael yeah! Just us.

Michael Lynn Brown, a.k.a. Justice, wrote this poem, his books and everything else:

1. To help others not to fall into these situations and how to get out of them, if you have.
2. For his children and loved ones to get to know him for it and for them. It's all he has.
3. To hopefully get attention and get some help, support, and assistance in his battle against injustice. To get together some funds for top-notch assistance from the wealthy, prominent powers that be.

Peace & love,

"Michael"

A SPECIAL FAMILY TRIBUTE

I would like to make a Special Tribute to one of my favorite cousins Lolita Caldwell Wascow, who recently passed away, on 08/02/2010. She was always about asking me and telling people how much she loved me.

We lost her mother, Ida Caldwell, on 07/23/2008. I called her My Favorite Aunt Ida. She could not keep me from running the streets, but she reminded me to be myself. Before she died, she lost her daughter Teresa Caldwell and her son Herman Caldwell in 2008.

Herman never turned me down or ever told me no. His only 'fault' was introducing me to Kim. I owe you one.

They helped raise my siblings and me when my mother was in Federal Prison. They treated us like one of their own. Ida treated us better than her own grown children did. I love that woman.

Pro Boxer, Referee, Joe Cortez, and Michael 2006

Michael

Butter and Melissa

Aunt Ruth and Doris's Mother

Suzie 2/16/2009

Kari and Her Son

Step Son Marcus Daughter Keya

Lil Sis Trzeza and Shalanda

Tiffany Summer Niece 2004

Michael Brown

Michael Brown, Noah Robinson, My Mentor

Sisters Linda T.D. Brown and Sash A.Brown

My Son Michael JR 2008

Michael Jr 1998

Kim and Michael Jr

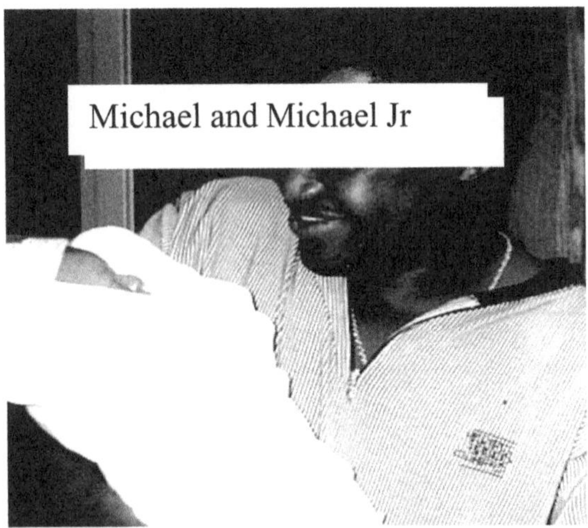
Michael and Michael Jr

New Years Eve 2001

Thanksgiving 2000

Michael and Stacy

Christmas 2000

Brother Bruce, Mother in law, brother in law

Lil Brother Bruce, Sister Tammy, Uncle Bruce, Cousin Loita

Leo, Bro, Sister, Uncle Daughter

Cousins Ray, Courtney

Nicki and Tracy, Lizzie

Cousins Jason, Lolita

ROBERT D. SUTTON

JAMES HARVEY FLEMMING

DEAN, ALPHONSO LASHAWN

CALDWELL, VICTOR ANTHONY

MAASS, JAMES WARREN

WAMPOLE, NICOLE CATHERINE

Pall Bearers

Matthew Brown

Bruce Brown

Larry Brown

Bruce Moore

Charles Roberts

Aaron Black

In Loving Memory
Of
Linda "Patty" Brown

Mama, we

N

I'm Free

Be not burdened with times of sorrow,
I wish you the sunshine of tomorrow.
My life's been full, I savored much,
Good friends, good times, a loved one's touch.
Perhaps my time seemed all too brief,
Don't lengthen it now with undue grief.
Lift up your heart and share with me,
God wanted me now, He set me free!

IN LOVING MEMORY

Thirl Reynolds

DATE OF BIRTH
August 4, 1939
Prescott, Arkansas

DATE OF DEATH
January 8, 2005
Sun Prairie, Wisconsin

SERVICE
Saturday, January 15, 2005 at 12:00 PM
Gunderson East Funeral Home
Madison, Wisconsin

PRESIDING
Reverend D. Steven Moss

INTERMENT
Roselawn Memorial Park
Monona, Wisconsin

FALLBEARERS

Hilton Weathers   Harry Williams
[illegible]   [illegible]
Rick Hugo   Dean Sonneberg
Julian Tijerina   Greg Gossett

Gunderson East Funeral Home, Madison WI

Moms Family

Mom Mrs. Brown

Moms Funeral

Brother Bruce and Aaron, Cousin Larry

2005 Sasha's Graduation Michael 1987
Sasha, Moms and Pops

Obituary
Linda "Patty" Brown

Pat was born on March 30, 1949, to Rufus and Mary Moore. She graduated from Thornton Township high school in Harvey, Illinois.

Patty received and accepted Christ into her life at an early age.

1992 Linda's graduation Mom Sasha &Tricia 1998

Pat was preceded in death by her beloved parents Rufus and Mary Moore and her cousin, Samuel Massey.

When God so gently whispered Patty's name on July 22, 2005, after laughing, talking and doing her bam/bam dance one last time with her children,
she answered his call, ready and willing. She leaves behind, six children, Mike, Matthew (Tootie), Tammy, Bruce, Tricia and Sasha. Special friend, Charles Roberts (Dad). Two brothers, Darnell Orr and Bruce Moore. Her grandchildren, Jasmine, Tiffany, Ty'keyah, Michael, Marcus and Donelle. And a host of nieces, nephews, cousins and friends.

Mom and Sasha Mom and daughter
Linda E. and Linda Tammy

Sasha, Bruce, Tricia , Michael, Tiffany,
Mom Linda E. Moore Brown 1998
Tammy

Charles Roberts 2000 — Grandma Mary Moore and her Siblings 1970

Mathew & Daughter 2002 — Mom, Michael & Sasha 2008 Waupun State Prison

Mom Linda and Pops Charles Uncle Bruce

Acknowledgement

The Brown family, wish to acknowledge, with our deepest appreciation, the many comforting messages, floral tributes, prayers, and the many other expressions of kindness and concern evidenced at this time in thought and deed. May God bless and sustain each and every one of you.

When I Must Leave You Now

When I must leave you for a little while
Please do not grieve and shed wild tears
And hug your sorrow to you through the years
But start out bravely with a gallant smile
And for my sake and in my name
Live on and do all things the same
Feed not your loneliness on empty days
But fill each waking hour in useful ways
Reach out your hand in comfort and in cheer
And I in turn will comfort you and hold you near
And never, never be afraid to die
For I am waiting for you in the sky

Left and Right
Uncle Willie Pierce, Cousin Compose Caldwell, Uncle Darnell Orr, Brother Bruce Brown and Michael L Brown

CPSIA information can be obtained at www.ICGtesting.com
Printed in the USA
BVOW10s0105060415

394844BV00014B/88/P

9 781456 320638